Er. D.C. Gupta

# Electrostatics

## for JEE Main & Advanced (Study Package for Physics)

Fully Solved

Includes Past JEE & KVPY Questions

Useful for Class 12, KVPY & Olympiads

- **Head Office :** B-32, Shivalik Main Road, Malviya Nagar, New Delhi-110017
- **Sales Office :** B-48, Shivalik Main Road, Malviya Nagar, New Delhi-110017
  **Tel. :** 011-26691021 / 26691713

**Page Layout : Prakash Chandra Sahoo**

Typeset by Disha DTP Team

*Printed at*: **Repro Knowledgecast Limited, Thane**

---

**For further information about the books from DISHA,**

Log on to www.dishapublication.com or email to info@dishapublication.com

| STUDY PACKAGE IN PHYSICS FOR JEE MAIN & ADVANCED | | | |
|---|---|---|---|
| **Booklet No.** | **Title** | **Chapter Nos.** | **Page Nos.** |
| 1 | Units, Measurements & Motion | Ch 0. Mathematics Used in Physics<br>Ch 1. Units and Measurements<br>Ch 2. Vectors<br>Ch 3. Motion in a Straight Line<br>Ch 4. Motion in a Plane | 1-202 |
| 2 | Laws of Motion and Circular Motion | Ch 5. Laws of Motion and Equilibrium<br>Ch 6. Circular Motion | 203-318 |
| 3 | Work Energy, Power & Gravitation | Ch 7. Work, Energy and Power<br>Ch 8. Collisions and Centre of Mass<br>Ch 9. Gravitation | 319-480 |
| 4 | Rotational Motion | Ch 1. Rotational Mechanics | 1-120 |
| 5 | Properties of Matter & SHM | Ch 2. Properties of Matter<br>Ch 3. Fluid Mechanics<br>Ch 4. Simple Harmonic Motion | 121-364 |
| 6 | Heat & Thermodynamics | Ch 5. Thermometry, Expansion & Calorimetry<br>Ch 6. Kinetic Theory of Gases<br>Ch 7. Laws of Thermodynamics<br>Ch 8. Heat Transfer | 365-570 |
| 7 | Waves | Ch 9. Wave – I<br>Ch 10. Wave –II | 571-698 |
| 8 | Electrostatics | Ch 0. Mathematics Used in Physics<br>Ch 1. Electrostatics<br>Ch 2. Capacitance & Capacitors | 1-216 |
| 9 | Current Electricity | Ch 3. DC and DC circuits<br>Ch 4. Thermal and Chemical effects of Current" | 217-338 |
| 10 | Magnetism, EMI & AC | Ch 5. Magnetic Force on Moving Charges & Conductor<br>Ch 6. Magnetic Effects of Current<br>Ch 7. Permanent Magnet & Magnetic Properties of Substance<br>Ch 8. Electromagnetic Induction<br>Ch 9. AC and EM Waves | 339-618 |
| 11 | Ray & Wave Optics | Ch 1. Reflection of Light<br>Ch 2. Refraction and Dispersion<br>Ch 3. Refraction at Spherical Surface, Lenses and Photometry<br>Ch 4. Wave optics | 1-244 |
| 12 | Modern Physics | Ch 5. Electron, Photon, Atoms, Photoelectric Effect and X-rays<br>Ch 6. Nuclear Physics<br>Ch 7. Electronics & Communication | 245-384 |

# Contents

## Study Package Booklet 8 - Electrostatics

# CHAPTER

# Mathematics Used in Physics (I - VI)

$$\frac{\partial(xy)}{\partial x} = y, \quad \frac{\partial(xy)}{\partial y} = x$$

$\varepsilon = v_R + v_L$ $\quad i = I\sin(\omega t)$ $\quad \frac{di}{dt} = \omega I\cos(\omega t)$

$L = 4.22$ mH

$\varepsilon = \varepsilon_m \sin \omega t$

$\omega = 2\pi f$

$f = 100$ Hz

$v_L = L\frac{di}{dt} = L\omega I\cos(\omega t)$

$v_L = L\omega I\cos(\omega t)$

$V_R = RI \qquad V_L = X_L I_L = (L\omega)$ since $I = I_L$

- PARTIAL DIFFERENTIATION
- USES OF DIFFERENTIATION AND INTEGRATION
- AREA BOUNDED BY THE CURVE
- SOLID ANGLE
- COMPLEX NUMBER AND PHASOR

## PARTIAL DIFFERENTIATION

In physics, we often come across quantities which depend on two or more variables. For example electric potential $V$ depends on $x$, $y$ coordinates as : $V = xy$. For given pair of value of $x$ and $y$, $V$ has a definite value. If we differentiate quantity $V$ w.r.t. $x$ keeping y constant, then it is known as partial differentiation and represented by $\frac{\partial V}{\partial x}$. Similarly differentiation of $V$ w.r.t. $y$ keeping $x$ is constant is represented by $\frac{\partial V}{\partial y}$.

Thus $$\frac{\partial V}{\partial x} = \frac{\partial (xy)}{\partial x} = y$$

and $$\frac{\partial V}{\partial y} = \frac{\partial (xy)}{\partial y} = x$$

In general if $f$ is a function of $n$ variables $x_1, x_2, \ldots\ldots x_n$, then partial differential coefficient of $f$ with respect to $x_1$, keeping all the variables except $x_1$ as constant can be written as $\frac{\partial f}{\partial x_1}$.

**Ex. 1** **Given $\phi = a(x^2 + y^2) + bz^2$, where $a$ and $b$ are constants. Find partial differentiation of $\phi$ w.r.t. $x$, $y$ and $z$.**

**Sol.**

$$\frac{\partial \phi}{\partial x} = \frac{\partial}{\partial x}\left[a(x^2 + y^2) + bz^2\right]$$

$$= a \times 2x = 2ax,$$

$$\frac{\partial \phi}{\partial y} = \frac{\partial}{\partial y}\left[a(x^2 + y^2) + bz^2\right]$$

$$= a \times 2y = 2ay,$$

and $$\frac{\partial \phi}{\partial z} = \frac{\partial}{\partial z}\left[a(x^2 + y^2) + bz^2\right]$$

$$= b \times 2z = 2bz$$

## INTEGRATION BY SUBSTITUTION

**Ex. 2** **Evaluate $\int_0^t A\sin 2\omega t \, dt$, where $A$ and $\omega$ are constants.**

**Sol.** Substituting

$$2\omega t = z.$$

On differentiating, we have

$$\frac{d(2\omega t)}{dt} = \frac{dz}{dt}$$

or $$2\omega = \frac{dz}{dt}$$

$$\therefore \quad dt = \frac{dz}{2\omega}$$

Thus $$\int_0^t A\sin 2\omega t \, dt = \frac{A}{2\omega}\int_0^t \sin z \, dz$$

$$= \frac{A}{2\omega}\left|-\cos z\right|_0^t$$

$$= \frac{A}{2\omega}\left|-\cos 2\omega t\right|_0^t$$

$$= \frac{A}{2\omega}(1 - \cos 2\omega t)$$ ***Ans.***

**Ex. 3** **Evaluate $\int_0^T \sin^2\omega t \, dt$, where $\omega = \frac{2\pi}{T}$**

**Sol.** We know that

$$\sin^2\theta = \frac{1 - \cos 2\theta}{2}$$

$$\therefore \quad \int_0^T \sin^2 \omega t \, dt = \int_0^T \left[\frac{1 - \cos 2\omega t}{2}\right] dt$$

$$= \frac{1}{2}\left|t - \frac{\sin 2\omega t}{2\omega}\right|_0^T$$

$$= \frac{1}{2}\left[\left\{T - \frac{\sin 2\left(\frac{2\pi}{T}\right)T}{2\omega}\right\} - \{0-0\}\right]$$

$$= \frac{1}{2}[T-0]$$

$$= \frac{T}{2} \qquad \textit{Ans.}$$

**Ex. 4** **Evaluate** $\int(xdy + ydx)$

**Sol.** We know that

$$d(xy) = xdy + ydx$$

$$\therefore \quad \int(xdy + ydx) = \int d(xy)$$

$$= xy + C \qquad \textit{Ans.}$$

**Ex. 5** **Evaluate** $\int\left(x^2dy + 2xydx\right)$

**Sol.** We know that

$$\frac{d}{dx}\left(x^2y\right) = x^2\frac{dy}{dx} + y \times 2x$$

or
$$d\left(x^2y\right) = x^2dy + 2xydx$$

Thus we can write

$$\int\left(x^2dy + 2xy\,dx\right) = \int d\left(x^2y\right) = x^2y + C \qquad \textit{Ans.}$$

**Ex. 6** **Evaluate** $\int \sin^3\theta\, d\theta$

**Sol.**

$$\int \sin^3\theta\, d\theta = \int \sin^2\theta \sin\theta\, d\theta$$

$$= \int\left(1-\cos^2\theta\right)d\cos\theta$$

$$= \left(\cos\theta - \frac{\cos^3\theta}{3} + C\right)$$

## USES OF DIFFERENTIATION AND INTEGRATION

### Finding maxima and minima :

Suppose a quantity is defined by a function of $x$ as : $y = f(x)$.

For maximum and minimum value of $y$, put $\frac{dy}{dx} = 0$. On doing this the values of $x$ can be obtained; some of them may corresponds to maxima and some of them corresponds to minima (if $x$ has many values). If $\frac{d^2y}{dx^2} < 0$, then $y$ is maximum for a certain value of $x$ and if $\frac{d^2y}{dx^2}$ is $> 0$, then y will be minimum for other value of $x$.

**Ex. 7** **Divide 10 into two such parts, so that their product is maximum.**

**Sol.** Let $x$ is one of the parts of 10, then second will be $10 - x$. If $y$ is their product, then

$$y = x(10-x)$$

$$= 10x - x^2.$$

For maximum value of $y$, $\frac{dy}{dx} = 0$,

or
$$\frac{d}{dx}\left(10x - x^2\right) = 0$$

or
$$10 - 2x = 0$$

or
$$x = 5$$

Thus 5 and 5 are the two required parts. Their product is 25.

### Area bounded by the curve

Suppose a curve which is defined by a function of x as; $y = f(x)$. The plot of the curve is shown in figure. Take a small element of curve of width $dx$. The corresponding average value on $y$-axis is $y$. The area of the shaded strip (assuming rectangle)

$$dA = y\,dx$$

The area bounded between $x_1$ and $x_2$ is given by

$$A = \int_{x_1}^{x_2} y\,dx = \int_{x_1}^{x_2} f(x)dx$$

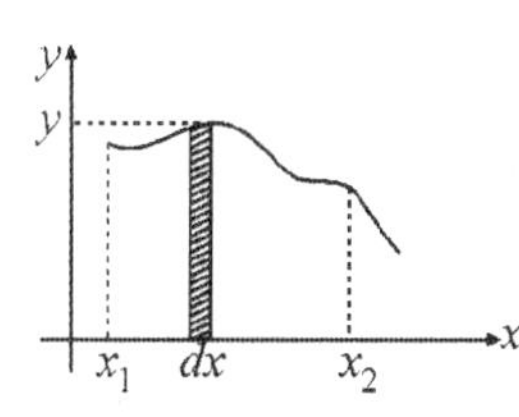

*Fig. 0.1*

**Ex. 8** **Figure shows the parabolic curve $y = 2x^2$. Find the area bounded by the curve between 0 and 5.**

**Sol.** The area bounded by the curve is given by

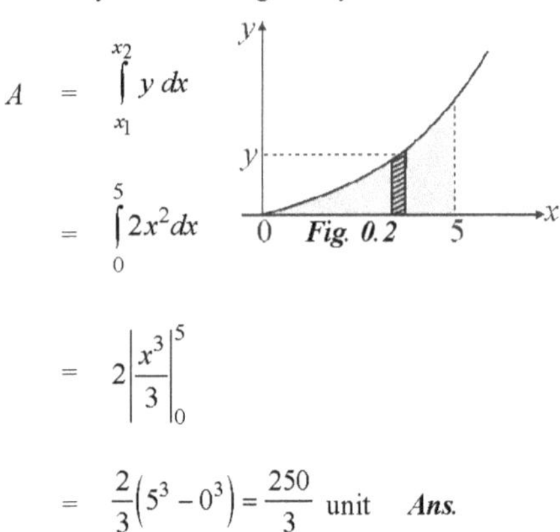


$$A = \int_{x_1}^{x_2} y\,dx$$

$$= \int_0^5 2x^2 dx$$

$$= 2\left|\frac{x^3}{3}\right|_0^5$$

$$= \frac{2}{3}\left(5^3 - 0^3\right) = \frac{250}{3} \text{ unit} \quad \textit{Ans.}$$

**Ex. 9** **Find the area bounded by the curve $y = e^{-x}$, the $x$-axis and the $y$-axis.**

**Sol.** The given function decreases with increase in value of $x$. For $y$ to be zero,

$$e^{-x} = 0$$

which gives $\quad x = \infty$

At $\quad x = 0,\ y = e^{-0} = 1$

The area bounded by the curve is given by

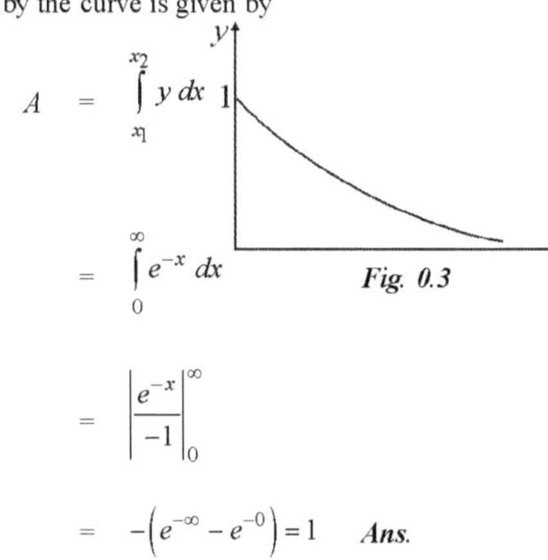


$$A = \int_{x_1}^{x_2} y\,dx$$

$$= \int_0^{\infty} e^{-x}\,dx$$

$$= \left|\frac{e^{-x}}{-1}\right|_0^{\infty}$$

$$= -\left(e^{-\infty} - e^{-0}\right) = 1 \quad \textit{Ans.}$$

### Finding the average value :

Suppose a quantity $y$ is the function of $x$. We have to find its average value between $x$ values from $x_1$ to $x_2$. The average value of $y$ can be obtained as :

$$y_{\text{average}} = \bar{y} = \frac{\int_{x_1}^{x_2} y\,dx}{(x_2 - x_1)}$$

**Ex. 10** **Find average value of sinθ in one complete cycle from 0 to 2π radian.**

**Sol.** The average value sinθ is given by

$$[\sin\theta]_{average}^{0\ to\ 2\pi} = \frac{\int_0^{2\pi} \sin\theta\, d\theta}{(2\pi - 0)}$$

$$= \frac{\left|-\cos\theta\right|_0^{2\pi}}{2\pi}$$

$$= \left[-\cos 2\pi - (-\cos 0)\right]$$

$$= -1 + 1 = 0 \quad \textit{Ans.}$$

## SOLID ANGLE

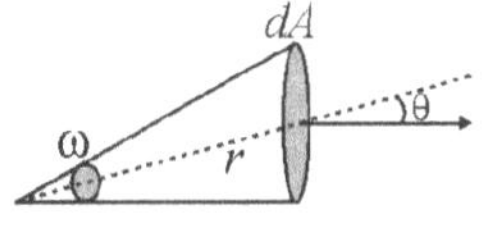


Fig. 0.4

Solid angle is the analogue in three dimensions of the usual angle in two dimensions. The solid angle subtended by any surface $dA$ at a point $O$ at a distance $r$ away is given by

$$d\omega = \frac{dA\cos\theta}{r^2}.$$

The total solid angle is given by

$$\omega = \int \frac{dA\cos\theta}{r^2}$$

The SI unit of solid angle is steradian. The solid angle will be $4\pi$. It does not depend on the shape of the surface enclosed. In the following cases the total solid angle subtended is $4\pi$.

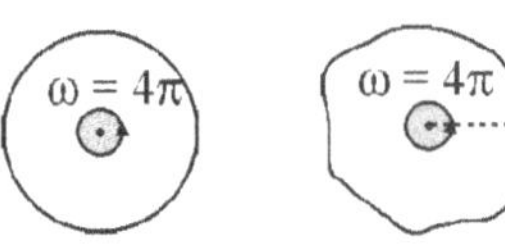


Fig. 0.5 Fig. 0.6

**Ex. 11** **Find solid angle subtended at the centre $O$ by the shaded surface shown in figure.**

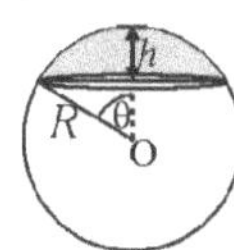


*Fig. 0.7*

**Sol.** Suppose $R$ is the radius of the spherical surface. The surface area of $h$ height of the spherical cap is given by

$$A = 2\pi Rh,$$

where

$$h = R(1-\cos\theta)$$

$$\therefore \quad A = 2\pi R^2(1-\cos\theta)$$

The solid angle subtended is given by

$$\omega = \frac{A\cos 0^\circ}{R^2}$$

Substituting value of $A$, we have

$$\omega = \frac{2\pi R^2(1-\cos\theta)}{R^2}$$

$$= 2\pi(1-\cos\theta) \qquad \textit{Ans.}$$

### Sagitta theorem

In a circle of radius $R$ and a cord of length $d$

$$(2R-h)\times h = \frac{d}{2}\times\frac{d}{2}$$

or

$$2Rh-h^2 = \frac{d^2}{4}$$

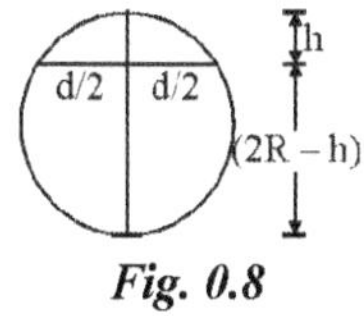


*Fig. 0.8*

**Ex. 12** **The diameter of aperture of a plano-convex lens is $d$ and its maximum thickness is $t$. Calculate radius of curvature of the lens.**

**Sol.** If $R$ is the radius of curvature of the lens, then

$$(2R-t)t = \frac{d}{2}\times\frac{d}{2}$$

$$2Rt-t^2 = \frac{d^2}{4}$$

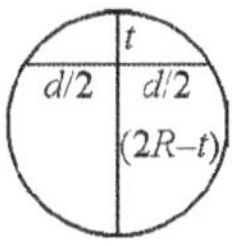

*Fig. 0.9*

In a case, $t << R$, $t^2$ can be neglected and

$$2Rt = \frac{d^2}{4}$$

and

$$R = \frac{d^2}{8t}. \qquad \textit{Ans.}$$

## Complex number and phasor

A number (quantity), which is made of two parts; real and imaginary parts is called complex number. If $j=\sqrt{-1}$ is an number (operator), then a phasor A in cartesian form can be written as :

$$A = a+jb,$$

where $a$ is the $x$-component and $b$ is the $y$-component of phasor $A$.

The magnitude of $A$

$$A = \sqrt{a^2+b^2}.$$

If $\theta$ is the angle made by phasor $A$ with the positive $x$-axis, then

$$\tan\theta = \frac{b}{a}$$

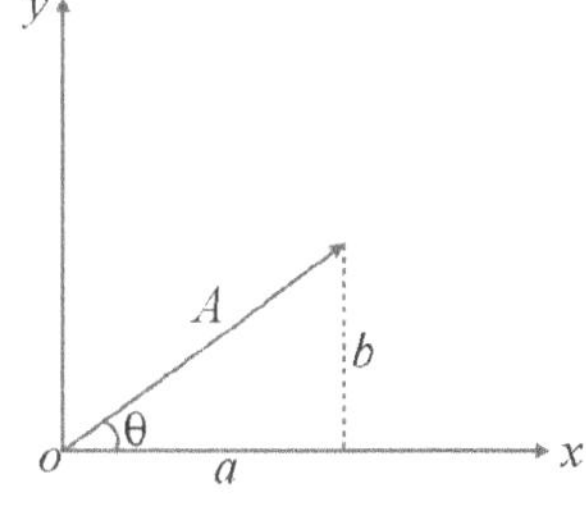


*Fig. 0.10*

Also $j^2=-1;\ j^3=-j;\ j^4=+1$.

In polar form the phasor A can be written as;

$$A = A\cos\theta + jA\sin\theta.$$

## Average value :

(i) If x is the function of t, then its average value between $t_1$ and $t_2$ :

$$x_{av} = \frac{\int_{t_1}^{t_2} x\,dt}{(t_2 - t_1)}.$$

(ii) Average value of $\sin\theta$ or $\cos\theta$ over one complete cycle :

$$\frac{1}{T}\int_0^T \sin\omega t\,dt = 0, \qquad \left[\omega = \frac{2\pi}{T}\right]$$

and

$$\frac{1}{T}\int_0^T \cos\omega t\,dt = 0.$$

(iii) RMS value of $i = i_0 \sin\omega t$ over the cycle :

$$i_{rms} = \sqrt{\frac{1}{T}\int_0^T i^2\,dt}$$

$$= \sqrt{\frac{1}{T}\int_0^T i_0^2 \sin^2 \omega t\,dt}$$

$$= \frac{i_0}{\sqrt{2}}.$$

CHAPTER

# Electrostatics

(1-130)

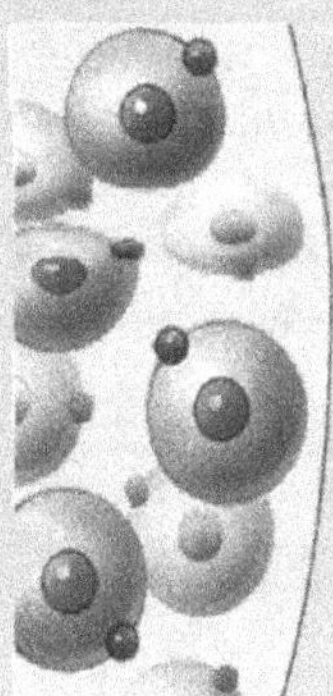

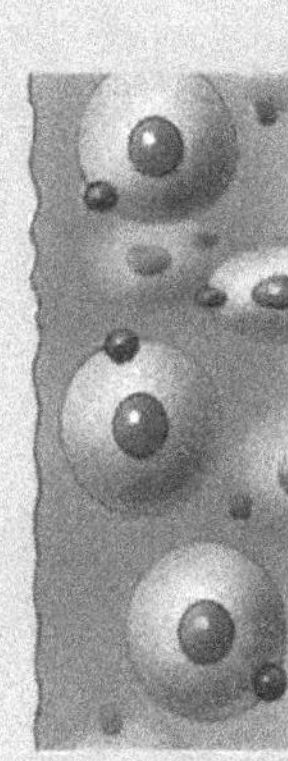

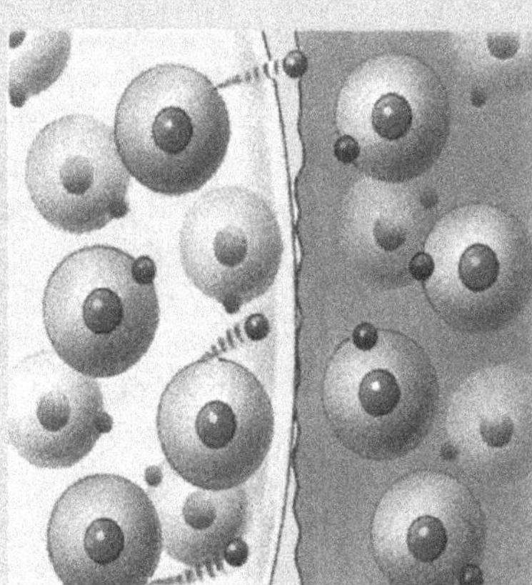

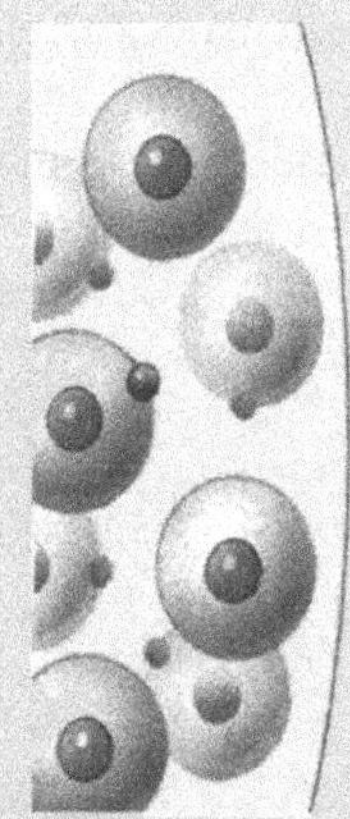

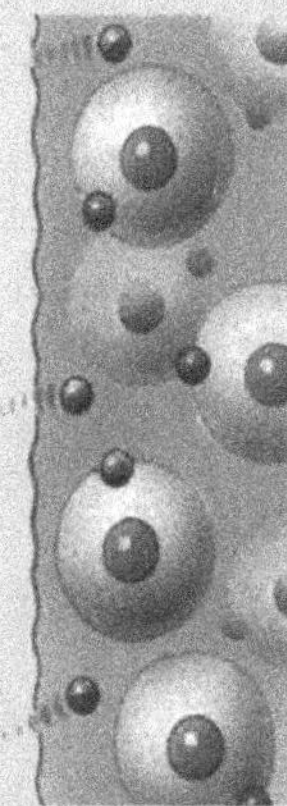

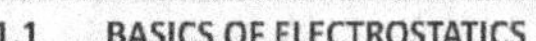



Electrostatics

## 1.1 BASICS OF ELECTROSTATICS

### Electric charge

The word electric charge was derived from Greek word elektron, meaning amber. It was known to the ancient Greeks as long ago as 600 B.C. that amber rubbed with wool, acquires property of attracting light objects. It has now concluded that there are two kinds of electric charges; positive charge and negative charge. The experiments lead to the fundamental results that (1) like charges repel, (2) unlike charges attract.

### Where does charge come from?

The process of acquiring charge consists of transferring something from one body to another, so that one body has an excess and the other a deficiency of that something. It was not until the end of nineteenth century that this "something" was found to consist of very small, negatively charged particles, known today as **electron** discovered by Sir J.J. Thomson.

To give a body an excess negative charge, we may add a number of electrons. And to give excess of positive charge, we may remove the electrons from the body.

**Note:** The "Charge" of a body refers to its excess charge only. The excess charge is always a very small fraction of the total positive or negative charge in the body.

### Conductors and insulators

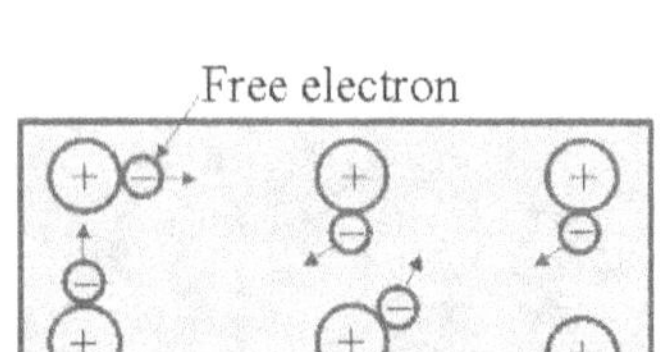


*Fig. 1.1*

Conductors permit the passage of charge through them, while insulators do not. Metals in general are good conductors, while most of non metals are insulators. Within a metallic conductor, a few outer electrons become detached from each atom and can move freely throughout the metal in the same way that the molecule of a gas can move through the spaces between grains of sand in sand-filled container. In fact, these **free electrons** are often referred to an electron gas. The positive nucleus and the remainder of the electrons remain fixed in position. On the other hand, there are no or at most very few free electrons within an insulator,.

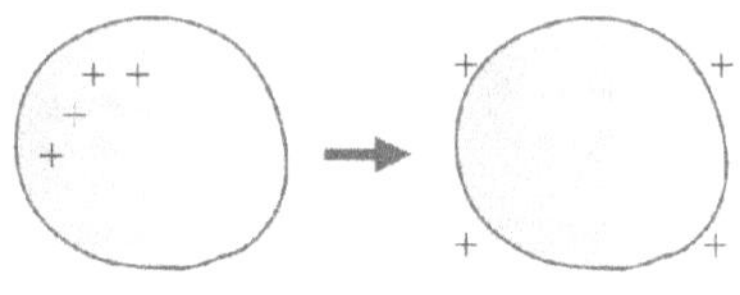

Conductor on charging

*Fig. 1.2*

Charge given to conducting body spreads over its surface, because of repulsion between the like charges. It happens because of high mobility of charge carriers in metals. When some charge is put any where on or in the conducting body, it ultimately will speed over its surface.

When charge is given to insulator, it remains at its position. Because there are no or very few charge carriers in an insulator.

### Impact on body after charging

1. When body is charged positively, it means removal of electrons from the body, resulting decrease of mass of the body.
2. When body is charged negatively, it means addition of electrons on the body, resulting increase of mass of the body.
3. Body either positively charged or negatively charged, it will increase in size because of repulsion between the like charges.

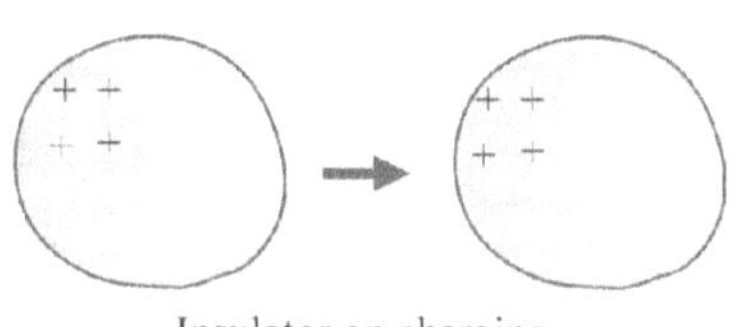

Insulator on charging

*Fig. 1.3*

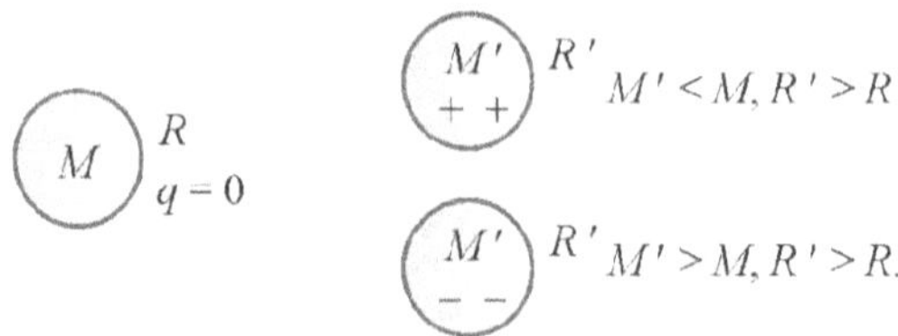


*Fig. 1.4*

## Test of charging of body

Let us consider a charged body brings near an uncharged body. It is clear from the figure, that there will be attraction between them.

The repulsion can be possible when both the bodies are charged. Therefore we can conclude that repulsion is the sure test of charging.

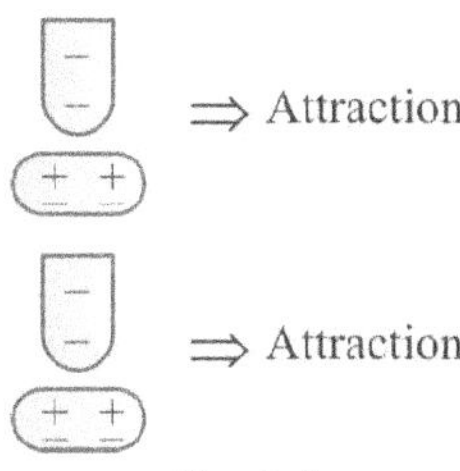


*Fig. 1.5*

## Methods of charging

1. **By rubbing:** Static electricity builds when two different non-metal materials rub together. Rubbing or friction makes electrons move. This gives one material a positive charge and the other a negative charge. The charges stay, or remain static, on the surfaces of the materials, until they have a pathway along which they can flow suddenly, or discharge.

   The energy of rubbing or friction gives extra energy to electrons. This allows some of them to break free from their nuclei and wander off on their own. It is known as "separating charge". Some electrons pass or transfer from one material to the other.

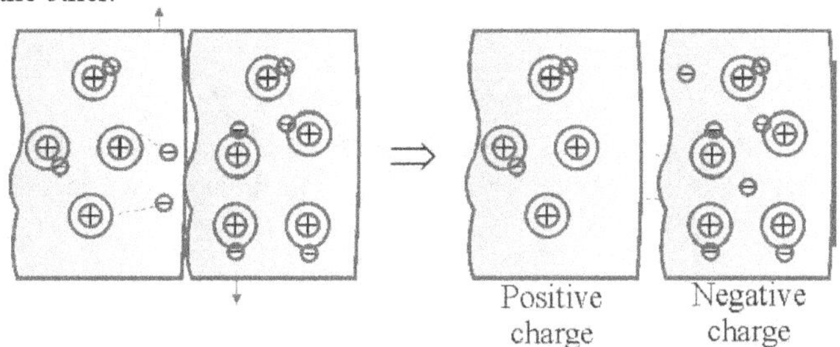


*Fig. 1.6*

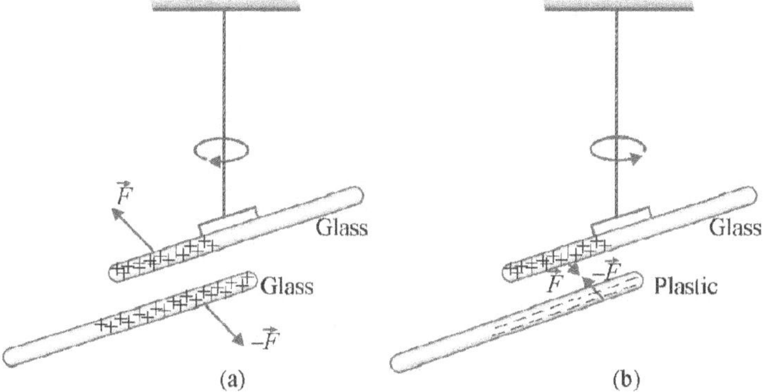


Fig. (a) Two charged rods of the same signs repel each other.
(b) Two charged rods of opposite signs attract each other.

*Fig. 1.7*

   When glass rod is rubbed with silk, it aquires positive charge and by convention silk will aquires some amount of negative charge. Similarly when a plastic rod rubbed with fur it acquires negative charge, and the fur itself is found to acquire a positive charge. Moreover, if the rod and fur are brought into contact with one another, the charge is found to disappear from both. Similar observations are true for the glass rod and silk cloth.

2. **By conduction (by touch without rubbing):**

   Because of having excess free electrons in metals they can be charged by conduction. When two conductors, one charged and other uncharged bring in contact, the same type of charge will appear on both the conductors. Charge on any conductor is proportional to its size.

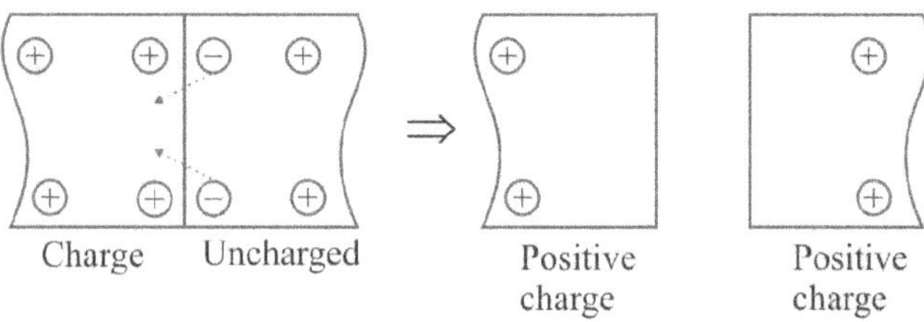


*Fig. 1.8*

3. **By induction (without touch):** If a charged body is brought near an uncharged body, then neutral body becomes oppositely charged. By induction method, we can charge any type of material body. From the figure one can understand the steps follow in the charging of the body by induction.

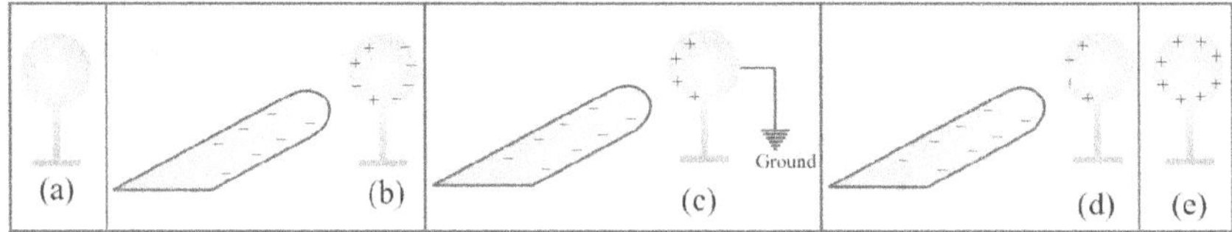


*Fig. 1.9. Charging by induction*

The magnitude of induced charge depends on the material of the body being charged. If $q$ is the inducing charge and $q'$ is the induced charge, then

$$|q'| = q\left(1 - \frac{1}{k}\right)$$

For metals $k = \infty$, $q' = q$, and for non-metals $k < \infty$, $\therefore\ q' < q$

## 1.2 EARTHING OR GROUNDING

We know that sea is the very large reservoir of water; from which if few buckets of water is taken out, the level of water in sea will remain almost same, practically same. On the same way earth can be regarded as a large reservoir of oppositely charged particles; electrons and protons, on a whole, is electrically neutral. By any means, if we take out or add some electrons to the earth, its charge will remain almost zero, practically zero. Thus the earth is regarded as a large capacitor with zero potential under all practical situations. Any body connected to earth becomes its part and hence of zero potential.

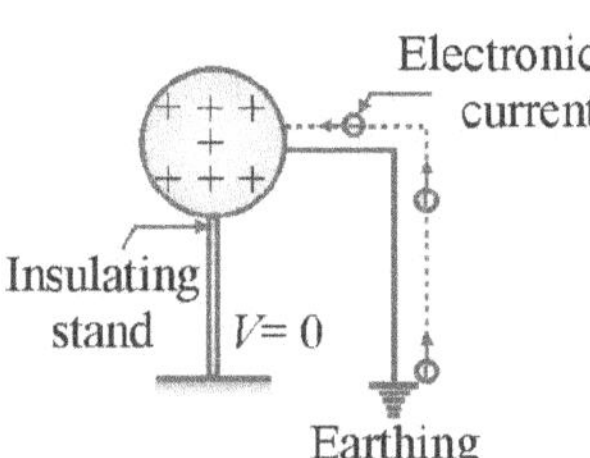


*Fig. 1.10*

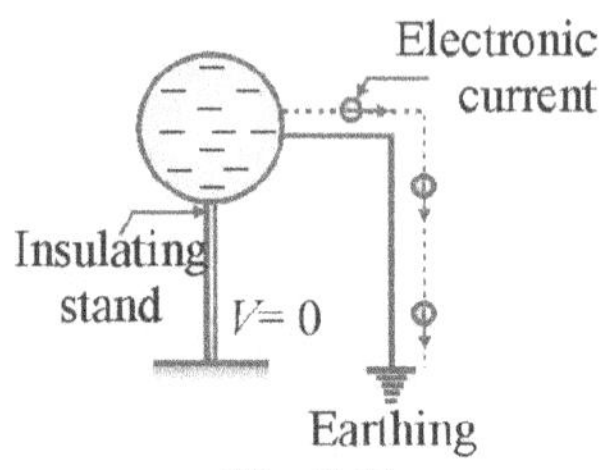


*Fig. 1.11*

(i) When a positively charged body is connected to the earth, the electrons start flowing from the earth till the positive charge of the body becomes zero, and hence potential of the body $V$ becomes zero.

(ii) When a negatively charged body is connected to earth, the electrons from the body start flowing to the earth, till the body becomes neutral and hence its potential becomes zero.

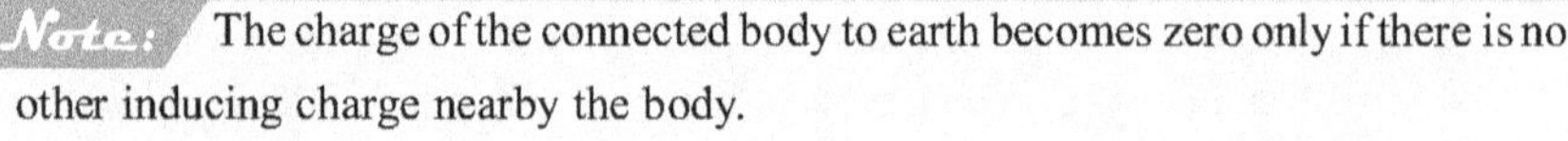

**Note:** The charge of the connected body to earth becomes zero only if there is no other inducing charge nearby the body.

## 1.3 GOLD LEAF ELECTROSCOPE

It is used to detect the charge on the body. It consists of a gold leaf attached to the brass strip which is suspended with the help of a brass rod in a glass jar (see figure).

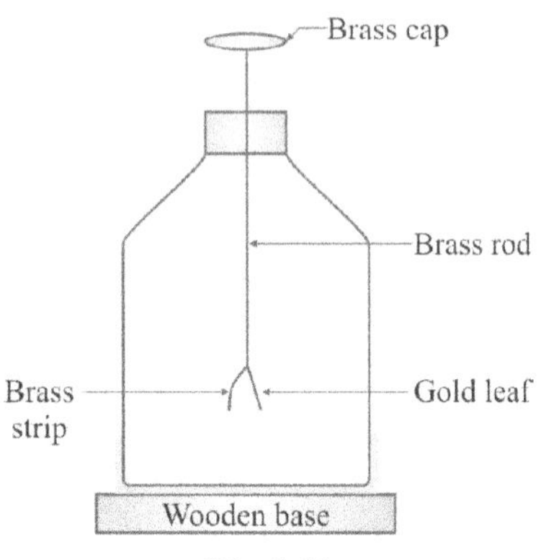


*Fig. 1.12*

### Uses of gold leaf electroscope

1. **To detect the charge :** Bring the body near the brass cap of the electroscope. If the gold leaf diverges outward, the body is electrically charged. However if no divergence takes place, then body has no charge.

2. **Identification of charge :**

(a) **By conduction :** First of all, charge the electroscope positively. Then touch the body under consideration to the brass cap of the electroscope. If the divergence of the gold leaf increases then the body is positively charged. However if divergence of gold leaf decreases then body will be negatively charged.

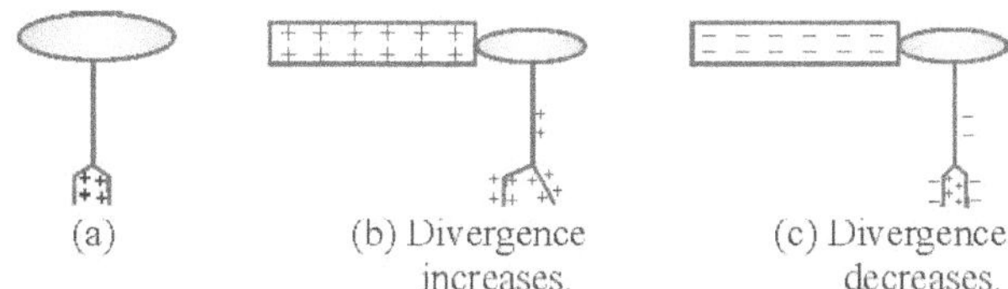


*Fig. 1.13*

When positively charged body touches the brass cap of the electroscope, the positive charge on the leaf will increase and hence divergence of it increases. But when negatively charged body touches the brass cap of the electroscope, the positive charge on the leaf will decrease and hence divergence of it decreases.

(b) **By induction** : First charge the electroscope positively. Then bring the body under consideration near the brass cap of the electroscope.

If the divergence of the gold leaf increases, then the object is positively charged. However if divergence of the gold leaf decreases then the object is negatively charged.

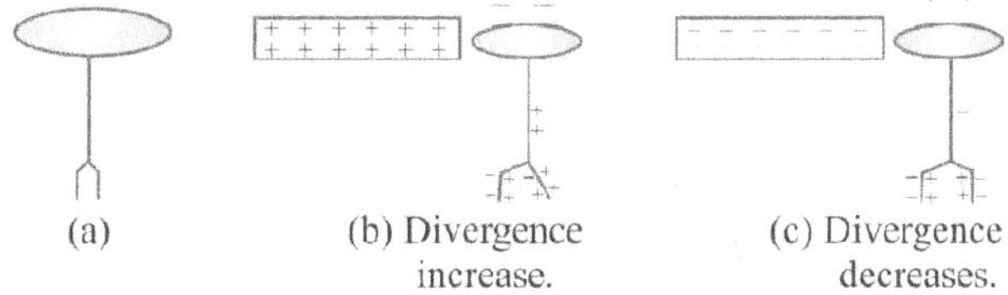


*Fig. 1.14*

When positively charged body brings near the brass cap of the electroscope, the negative charge induces on the brass cap and positive charge on the gold leaf and hence divergence of the leaf will increase. However when negatively charged body brings near the brass cap, the positive charge induces on the brass cap and negative charge on gold leaf and hence divergence of the leaf will decrease.

## 1.4 LIGHTNING AND LIGHTNING CONDUCTOR

The occurance of lightning depends on the atmospheric conditions. It needs a weather in which moisture-laden warm air near the earth rises rapidly. As the moist air rises, it collides with the other drops of moisture and air molecules and so lose or gain electric charges by friction. Usually, the moisture drops become positive and the air molecules negative. When moist air becomes cold enough, it condenses to form a cloud. The lower part of the cloud usually becomes negative and upper most part of the cloud becomes positive. The sudden movements in the cloud cause this charge to discharge in a flash of lightening to another cloud or the earth. When such a charged cloud moves over a tall building, the positive charge will induce over it. Since this induce charge is of very high order, so the building experiences a bursting force and hence cracks will develope in it. The building can be saved from destruction by using lightning conductor.

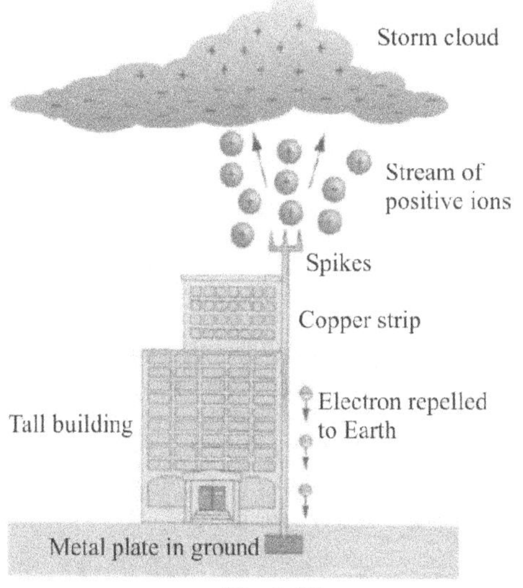


*Fig. 1.15*

A lightning conductor is made of copper and has sharp pointed edges. It is connected to the earth by the metal conductor running down the building and terminating in a buried metal plate. In the presence of lightning conductor, most of the charge will induce on it, which soonly move to the earth without harming the building.

**Ex. 1** *Fig. 1.16* **shows an uncharged, insulated conductor** $AB$**, which is in contact with gold leaf electroscope** $C$**. A positively charged rod is brought near the end** $A$**. Answer the following questions.**

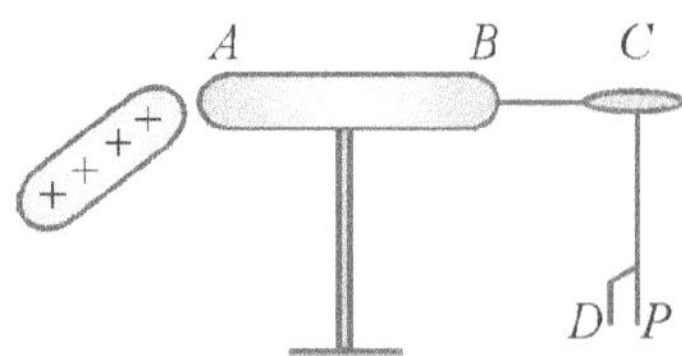


*Fig. 1.16*

**(i) What charge is developed at** $A$ **and why?**

**(ii) What charge is present at** $B$**,** $C$ **and** $D$**, and why?**

**(iii) How is gold leaf affected?**

**(iv) If positively charged rod is taken away, give your observations.**

**Sol.**

(i) The electrons of the atoms of the rod are attracted and so end $A$ of the rod becomes negative and end $B$ thus have deficiency of electrons and so becomes positive if the cap $C$ was not connected. As cap $C$ is connected to the end $B$ of the rod, so deficiency of electrons is created at $C$ which will carry on to $D$. So end $D$ becomes positively charged.

(ii) The end $B$ and $C$ will not have any charge, where as end $D$ has positive charge.

(iii) The gold leaf will diverge, because positive charge on gold leaf repels positive charge on the plate $P$.

(iv) When positively charged rod is taken away, the leaves collapse because the electron from end $A$ flow back to the end $D$ and hence no deficiency of electrons remain at the end.

**Ex. 2** **A glass rod rubbed with silk is brought close to two uncharged metallic spheres in contact with each other, inducing charges on them as shown in** *fig. 1.17***. Describe what happens when**

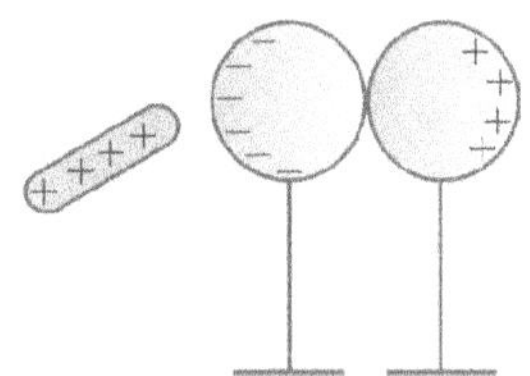

*Fig. 1.17*

**(i) the spheres are slightly separated, and**

**(ii) the glass rod is subsequently removed, and finally**

**(iii) the sphere are separated far apart.**

**Sol.**

(i) Little change in the distribution of charges.

(ii) The charges on the sphere are redistributed; positive and negative charges will face each other.

(iii) Charge on each sphere will be uniformly distributed.

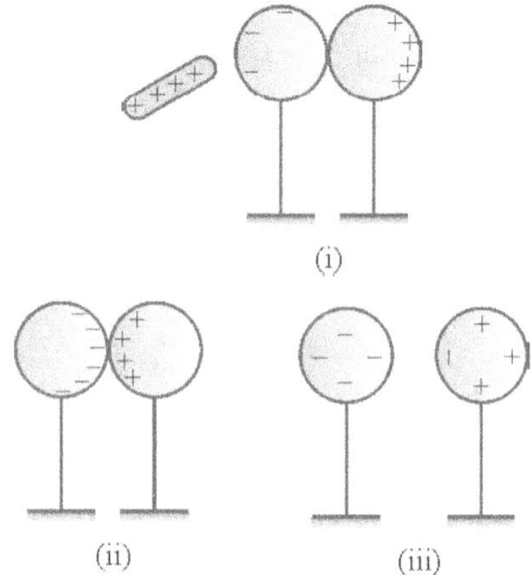


*Fig. 1.18*

**Ex. 3** **A metal sphere, a cylindrical conductor and a conical conductor are mounted on insulated stands such that they are in electrical contact. A highly charged ebonite rod is brought near sphere** $X$**. Answer the following questions :**

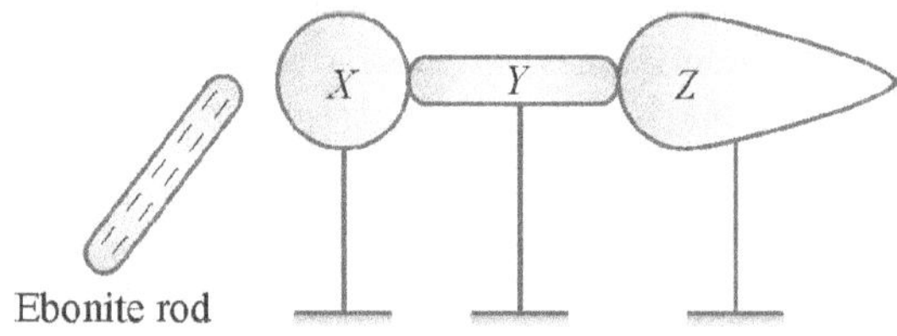


*Fig. 1.19*

**(i) What will be the charges on** $X$**,** $Y$ **and** $Z$**?**

**(ii) If conductor** $Z$ **is earthed for a moment and the ebonite rod is removed, state the charges on** $X$**,** $Y$**,** $Z$**.**

**(iii) In the presence of ebonite rod, conductors** $Y$ **and** $Z$ **are removed. What is the charge on each of them ?**

**(iv) What will you observe if a lighted candle is placed near the pointed end of** $Z$ **?**

**(v) The ebonite rod is made to touch** $X$**. What charges are on** $X$**,** $Y$ **and** $Z$**.**

**Sol.**

(i) The negatively charged ebonite rod repels the electrons and so electrons from $X$ move to the $Z$. Therefore $X$ becomes positively charged and $Z$ becomes negatively charged, while Y will have no charge.

(ii) When conductor $Z$ is earthed, its negative charge flows to the earth. After removal of the ebonite rod, all the three become positively charged (the charge of $X$ now spread to all the three).

(iii) When $Z$ is removed in the presence of ebonite rod, it will have negative charge. As soon as $Z$ is removed more electrons from $X$ will flow into $Y$. Thus now $Y$ becomes negatively charged. So when $Y$ is now removed, it will have negative charge.

(iv) Because of the excessive charge density at the pointed end of conductor $Z$, it ionise the surrounding air and so charges leak from it and set up an electric wind. Thus the candle flame will bend away from $Z$.

(v) When ebonite rod is touched with $X$, the negative charge will conduct in all the three.

**Ex. 4** **The diagram shows a gold coated pith-ball suspended between two plates and closer to the plate *A*.**

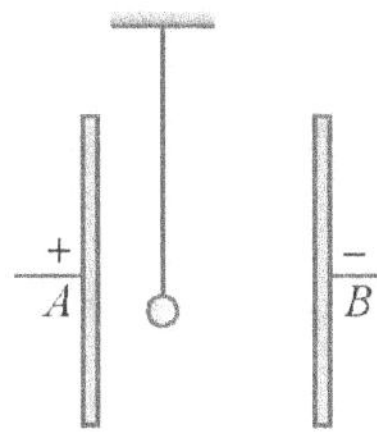


*Fig. 1.20*

**(i)** **Plates *A* and *B* are connected to the positive and negative poles of a high tension battery. What happens to the pith-ball ? Give reason.**

**(ii)** **What would happen if *B* is earthed ? Give reasons.**

**Sol.**

(i) The opposite charges are induced on both sides of the ball. On being close to plate *A*, the ball experiences a net force towards this plate, and so string becomes slent from the vertical.

(ii) When plate *B* is earthed, it becomes neutral. The opposite charges are induced on the both sides of the ball. Now plate *A* exerts net attractive force on the ball. The ball will touch the plate *A* and becomes positively charged due to conduction. Now plate *A* repels the ball. The ball moves to mean position, but due to inertia, it crosses the mean position and then touches the plate *B*. There it becomes neutral. The ball swing back and repeats its motion till entire charge of plate *A* flows into the earth.

## Properties of charge

1. Charge always be associated with mass.
2. It can be transferred from one body to another.
3. Charge is conserved. It can neither be created nor be destroyed.
4. Charge is quantised. That is, any body can have charge in integral multiple of smallest charge called electronic charge

   or $q = \pm ne$, where $n = 1, 2, 3, .......$, $e = 1.6 \times 10^{-19}$ C.
5. Charge is relativistically invariant. That is, $q_{rest} = q_{motion}$.
6. Moving charge produces magnetic field in addition to electric field.
7. Accelerated charge radiates energy.

## Types of charge densities

1. **Point charge :** When linear size of charged body is much smaller than the distance under consideration, the size may be ignored and the charge body is called **point charge**.
2. **Linear charge density:** Charge per unit length of the object is called linear charge density. It is defined as;

$$\lambda = \frac{dq}{d\ell}$$

$$= \frac{q}{\ell} \text{ (simply)}$$

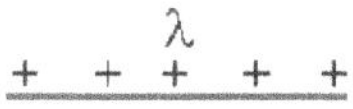

*Fig. 1.21*

SI unit of λ is C/m.

3. **Surface charge density:** The charge per unit surface of the body is called surface charge density. It is defined as ;

$$\sigma = \frac{dq}{dA}$$

$$= \frac{q}{A} \text{ (simply)}$$

SI unit of σ is C/m$^2$.

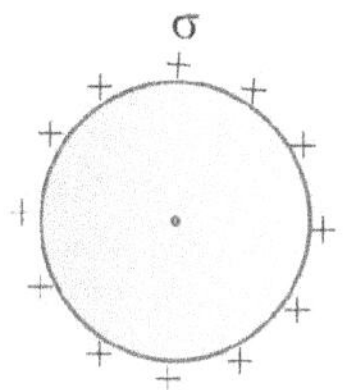

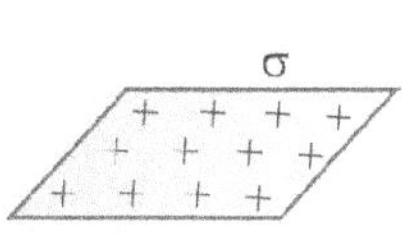

*Fig. 1.22*

4. **Volume charge density:** The charge per unit volume of the body is called volume charge density. It is defined as ;

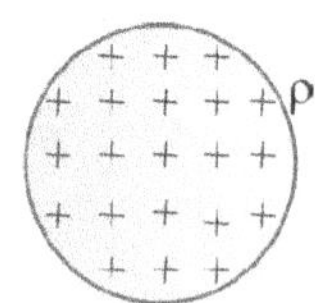

*Fig. 1.23*

$$\rho = \frac{dq}{dV}$$

$$= \frac{q}{V} \text{ (simply)}$$

SI unit of ρ is $C/m^3$.

### Charge versus mass

| | Charge | | Mass |
|---|---|---|---|
| **1.** | Electric charge can be positive or negative. | **1.** | Mass of body is always positive. |
| **2.** | Charge is conserved. | **2.** | Mass is not conserved as it can be converted into energy and vice versa by $E = mc^2$. |
| **3.** | Charge is quantized. | **3.** | Quantization of mass is yet to be established. |
| **4.** | Charge is relativistically invariant, i.e., $q_{rest} = q_{motion}$. | **4.** | Mass is relativistically variant. Mass in motion $m = \frac{m_0}{\sqrt{1-v^2/c^2}}$, where $m_0$ is rest mass object. |
| **5.** | Force between charges may be attractive or repulsive. | **5.** | Force between masses always be attractive. |

## 1.5 COULOMB'S LAW

The force between two point charges at rest is directly proportional to the product of the charges and inversely proportional to the square of the distance between them. Thus, if two point charges $q_1$, $q_2$ are separated by a distance $r$ in free space, the magnitude of the force ($F$) between them is given by

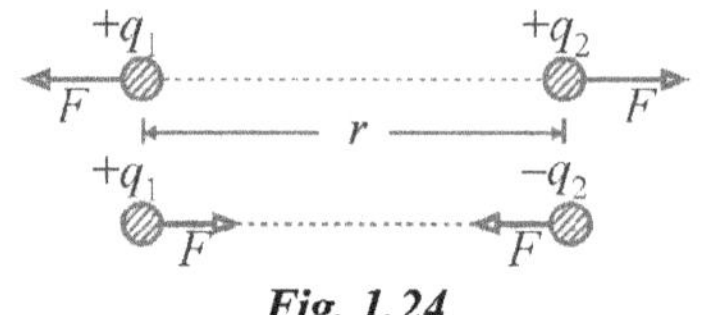

*Fig. 1.24*

$$F = k\frac{q_1 q_2}{r^2},$$

where $k$ is a constant. For historical reason and so simplifies many other formulas in electricity and magnetism, the constant $k$ is usually written $\frac{1}{4\pi \epsilon_0}$. Thus Coulomb's law can be written as

$$F = \frac{1}{4\pi \epsilon_0}\frac{|q_1||q_2|}{r^2} \quad \dots(1)$$

If the particles repel each other, the force on each particle is directed away from the other particle. If the particles attract each other, the force on each particle is directed toward the other particle.

Coulomb's law has proved its validity by experimental tests; no exceptions to it have ever been found. It holds even within the atom, correctly describing the force between the positively charged nucleus and each of the negatively charged electrons. This law also correctly accounts for the forces that bind atoms together to form molecules, and for the forces that bind atoms and molecules together to form solids and liquids.

**Note:**

1. In using Coulomb's law in scalar form, one should not put charges with signs; only place their numerical values.
2. Signs of charges are put in the vector form of Coulomb's law.

### More about Coulomb's law

1. The force between any two charges is independent of the presence of other charges.
2. Coulomb's law holds for point charges (whose dimensions) are small compared to their separation.
3. Coulomb's law holds for charges at rest or nearly at rest.
4. Coulomb's law holds over wide range from atomic distances ($10^{-15}$ m) to many kilometers.
5. In the CGS system the constant $k$ = 1, without unit. The unit of charge is stat coulomb or the esu (electro static unit). The conversion factor $1C = 3 \times 10^9$ esu. Thus

$$\therefore \quad F = \frac{q_1 q_2}{r^2}. \quad \text{(in CGS system of units)}$$

6. **In SI system of unit:** In SI system $k = \frac{1}{4\pi \in_0}$, where $\in_0$ is called permittivity of free space. The introduction of $\left(\frac{1}{4\pi \in_0}\right)$ will simplify some formulas to be encountered later. Thus coulomb's law is usually written as

$$F = \frac{1}{4\pi \in_0} \frac{q_1 q_2}{r^2}$$

with $$\frac{1}{4\pi \in_0} = 9 \times 10^9 \ \text{N.m}^2/\text{C}^2,$$

and $$\in_0 = 8.854 \times 10^{-12} \frac{\text{C}^2}{\text{N-m}^2}.$$

**Note:** In electrostatics problems, charges as large as one coulomb are unusual; the microcoulomb is often used.

7. When a dielectric medium is completely filled in between the charges, the force between the same charges decreases by a factor $k$ (dielectric constant). Thus

$$F_{\text{med}} = \frac{1}{4\pi \in_0 k} \frac{q_1 q_2}{r^2}$$

$$= \frac{F_{\text{free space}}}{k}$$

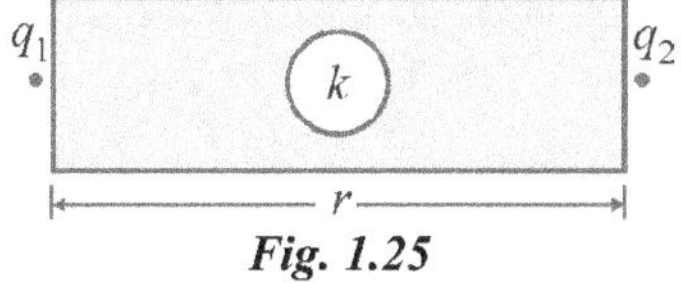

*Fig. 1.25*

As $$F_{\text{free space}} \simeq F_{\text{air}},$$

or $$F_{\text{med}} \simeq \frac{F_{\text{air}}}{k}$$

Above equation can also be written as

$$F = \frac{1}{4\pi \in} \frac{q_1 q_2}{r^2}$$

where, $\in = k\in_0 = \in_r \in_0$, is called permittivity of the medium, and $\in_r$ is the relative permittivity of the medium.

**Dielectric constant k:**

| Medium | $k$ |
|---|---|
| Vacuum (free space) | 1 |
| Air (one atmosphere) | $1.00546 \simeq 1$ |
| Water | 80 |
| Metals | $\infty$ |

8. If dielectric is inserted in some part of the space between the charges, then force between them can be calculated as follows:

When dielectric is filled completely between the charges, the force between them for a separation r is given by

$$F = \frac{1}{4\pi \epsilon_0 k} \frac{q_1 q_2}{r^2}.$$

This force is decreased by a factor $\frac{1}{k}$ in comparison to the force between them in free space. This effect of decrease of force can be achieved, if we remove the dielectric and increases the separation between the charges. Let required separation is $r'$. Thus we can write

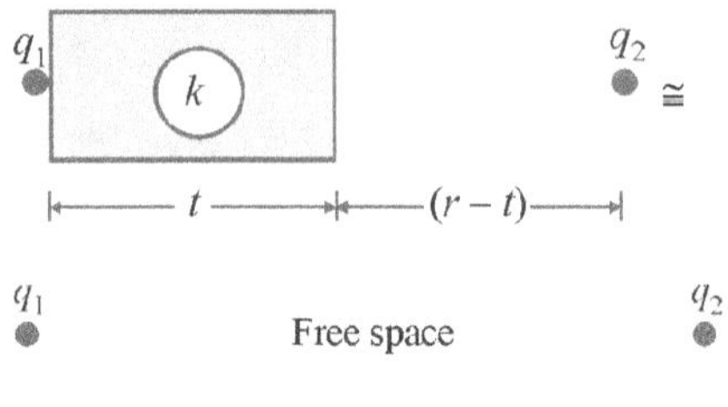


Fig. 1.26

$$\frac{1}{4\pi \epsilon_0 k} \frac{q_1 q_2}{r^2} = \frac{1}{4\pi \epsilon_0} \frac{q_1 q_2}{r'^2}$$

which gives $\quad r' = \sqrt{k}\, r$

Now move to the situation in which dielectric $k$ is occupied a length $t$. In this case we can remove the dielectric and effectively increase the distant by $\sqrt{k}\, r$ . Thus

The force between the charges now

$$F = \frac{1}{4\pi \epsilon_0} \frac{q_1 q_2}{[(r-t)+\sqrt{k}t]^2}$$

9. 1 coulomb of charge $= \frac{1}{1.6\times 10^{-19}}$

$= 6.25 \times 10^{18}$ electrons

## Vector form of Coulomb's law

(a) **In terms of unit vector :** If $\hat{r}$ is the unit vector of $r$ from 1 towards 2, and charges are placed at separation $r$, then force on charge $q_2$ due to charge $q_1$

$$\vec{F}_{21} = \left(\frac{1}{4\pi \epsilon_0}\right) \frac{q_1 q_2}{r^2} \hat{r} \qquad \ldots(2)$$

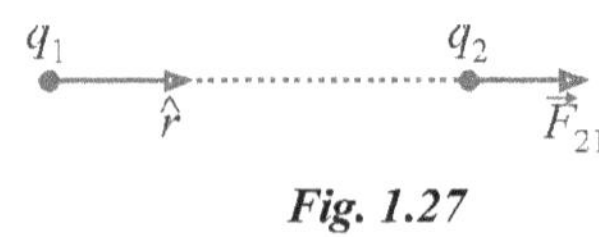


Fig. 1.27

(b) **In terms of position vector :** Consider a system of two charges $q_1$ and $q_2$ placed at position $\vec{r}_1$ and $\vec{r}_2$ with respect to the origin of the coordinate system . The force on one charge by the other can be obtained as

$$\vec{r}_1 + \vec{r}_{21} = \vec{r}_2$$

or $$\vec{r}_{21} = \vec{r}_2 - \vec{r}_1$$

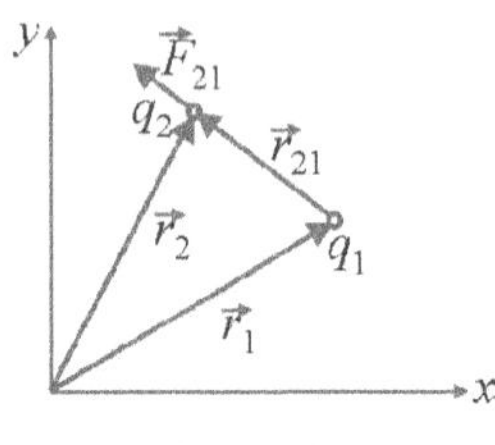


Fig. 1.28

$\therefore$ $$\vec{F}_{21} = \left(\frac{1}{4\pi \epsilon_0}\right) \frac{q_1 q_2 \vec{r}_{12}}{r_{12}^{3}}$$

or $$\vec{F}_{21} = \frac{1}{4\pi \epsilon_0} \frac{q_1 q_2 (\vec{r}_2 - \vec{r}_1)}{|\vec{r}_2 - \vec{r}_1|^3} \qquad \ldots(3)$$

If more than two charges are present, then the force exerted on any one say $q_1$, by all others $q_2, q_3$, .... etc., can be obtained by adding vectorially all the forces. i.e.,

$$\vec{F}_1 = \vec{F}_{12} + \vec{F}_{13} + \ldots + \ldots$$

$$= \frac{1}{4\pi \epsilon_0}\left[\frac{q_1 q_2}{r_{21}^2}\hat{r}_{12} + \frac{q_1 q_3}{r_{31}^2}\hat{r}_{13} + \ldots\right]$$

Let us consider situations where the charge is spread over a region instead of being concentrated at particular point, then

$$\vec{F}_1 = \frac{1}{4\pi \epsilon_0}\int \frac{q_1 dq}{r^2}\hat{r} \quad \ldots(4)$$

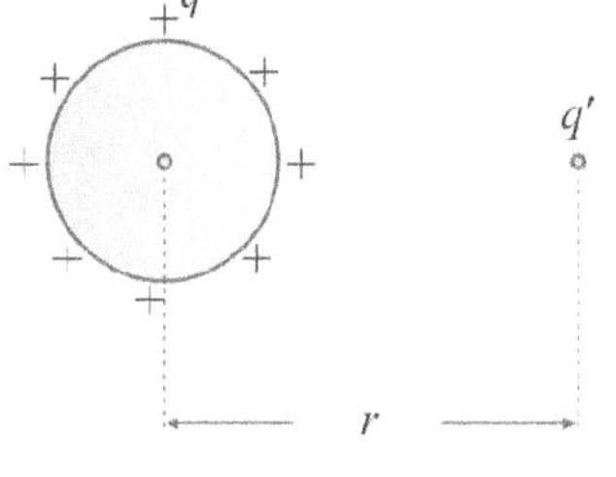


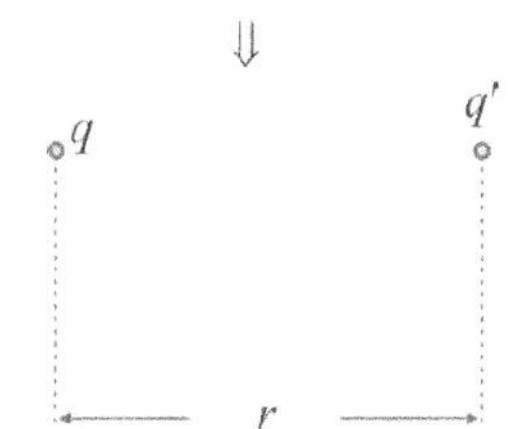


Fig. 1.29

## Two shell theorems

**Theorem 1 :** A shell of uniform charge attracts or repels a charged particle that is outside the shell as if all the shell's charge were concentrated at its centre. Thus

**Theorem 2 :** A shell of uniform charge exerts no electrostatic force on a charged particle that is located inside it.

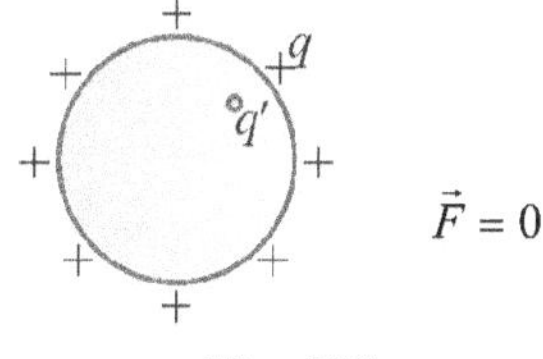


Fig. 130

***Note:***

1. When two identical spheres with charges $q_1$ and $q_2$ touch together and separated, the charge on each sphere will be $\frac{q_1 + q_2}{2}$. If $q_2$ is negative, then each one has a charge $\frac{(q_1 - q_2)}{2}$.
2. If one sphere has charge q and other identical sphere has no charge, then each sphere will have a charge $q/2$.
3. If sphere 1 with a charge $q$ touches to the uncharged sphere 2, of half the radius of 1, then charge on them are : $q_1 + q_2 = q \quad \ldots$(i)

   $q_1 = 2q_2 \quad \ldots$(ii)

   On solving both the equations, we get $q_1 = \frac{2q}{3}$, $q_2 = \frac{q}{3}$.

**Ex. 5** **A charge $Q$ is to be divided into two such parts, so that force between them when placed at some separation is maximum. Find their values.**

**Sol.**

Let one of the part is $q$, the other will be $(Q - q)$. The force between them for separation $r$ is

$$F = \left(\frac{1}{4\pi \epsilon_0}\right)\frac{q(Q-q)}{r^2} = \frac{1}{4\pi \epsilon_0}\left(Qq - q^2\right)$$

For, $F$ to be maximum, $\frac{dF}{dq} = 0$

or $\frac{d\left(Qq - q^2\right)}{dq} = 0$

or $Q - 2q = 0$

or $q = \frac{Q}{2}$

Therefore the charges are $\frac{Q}{2}$ and $\frac{Q}{2}$. *Ans.*

**Ex. 6** **Consider a fixed charge $Q$ and another charge $q$ is placed at a distance $x_0$ from $Q$ on a smooth plane surface. Find the velocity of charge $q$ as a function of $x$.**

**Sol.**

Let at any instant the separation between them is $x$. The force between them is

Fig. 1.31

$$F = \frac{1}{4\pi \epsilon_0}\frac{Qq}{x^2}$$

and acceleration $a = \frac{1}{4\pi \epsilon_0 m}\frac{Qq}{x^2}$

or $$\frac{v\,dv}{dx} = \frac{1}{4\pi \in_0 m} Qqx^{-2}$$

or $$\int_0^v v\,dv = \frac{1}{4\pi \in_0 m} Qq \int_{x_0}^{x} x^{-2}dx$$

or $$\frac{v^2}{2} = \frac{1}{4\pi \in_0 m} Qq \left|\frac{1}{-x}\right|_{x_0}^{x}$$

or $$v = \left[\frac{Qq}{2\pi \in_0 m}\left\{\frac{1}{x_0} - \frac{1}{x}\right\}\right]^{1/2} \quad \textit{. Ans.}$$

**Ex. 7** **Two equally charged identical metal spheres *A* and *B* repel each other with a force 2.0 × 10$^{-5}$N. Another identical uncharged sphere C is touched to A and then placed at the mid point between *A* and *B*. What is the net electric force on C?**

## Sol.

Suppose charge of each sphere is $q$, the force between spheres $A$ and $B$ for separation $r$,

$$F = 2.0 \times 10^{-5} = \frac{1}{4\pi \in_0}\frac{q^2}{r^2} \quad ...(i)$$

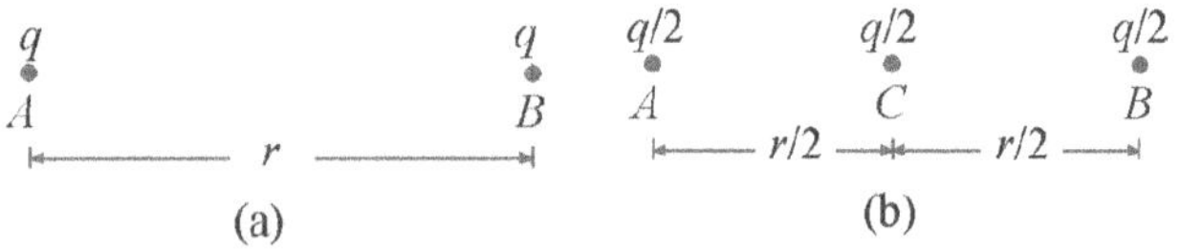

q A —— r —— q B (a)  q/2 A —— r/2 —— q/2 C —— r/2 —— q/2 B (b)

*Fig. 1.32*

When uncharged sphere $C$ is touched to the sphere $A$, the charge on each one becomes $q/2$. Thus force between $A$ and $C$

$$F_{AC} = \frac{1}{4\pi \in_0}\frac{(q/2)(q/2)}{(r/2)^2} = F,$$

and force between $B$ and $C$,

$$F_{BC} = \frac{1}{4\pi \in_0}\frac{\left(\frac{q}{2}\right)q}{\left(\frac{r}{2}\right)^2} = 2F.$$

Thus the net force on the sphere $C$

$$= 2F - F = F$$
$$= 2.0 \times 10^{-5}\text{ N from } C \text{ to } A. \quad \textit{Ans.}$$

**Ex. 8** **The force between two point charges placed at a separation *r* is *F*. Find the force between the same charges, if half the space between them is filled with a dielectric of dielectric constant 4.**

## Sol.

Given force between two point charges

$$F = \frac{1}{4\pi \in_0}\frac{q^2}{r^2}$$

When half the space is filled with a dielectric $k$, the force between them becomes

$$F' = \frac{1}{4\pi \in_0}\frac{q^2}{\left[\frac{r}{2}+\frac{r}{2}\sqrt{k}\right]^2}$$

$$= \frac{1}{4\pi \in_0}\frac{q^2}{\left[\frac{r}{2}+\frac{r}{2}\sqrt{4}\right]^2}$$

$$= \frac{4}{9}\frac{1}{4\pi \in_0}\frac{q^2}{r^2}$$

$$= \frac{4}{9}F. \quad \textit{Ans.}$$

**Ex. 9** **Let us consider two, small balls of masses $m_1$ and $m_2$ and having charges $q_1$ and $q_2$ respectively are suspended with the help of two strings with the same point. Discuss about the equilibrium of the balls.**

**Sol.** Consider the equilibrium of first ball, we have

$$T_1 \sin\theta_1 = F_e \quad ....(i)$$

and $$T_1 \cos\theta_1 = m_1 g \quad ...(ii)$$

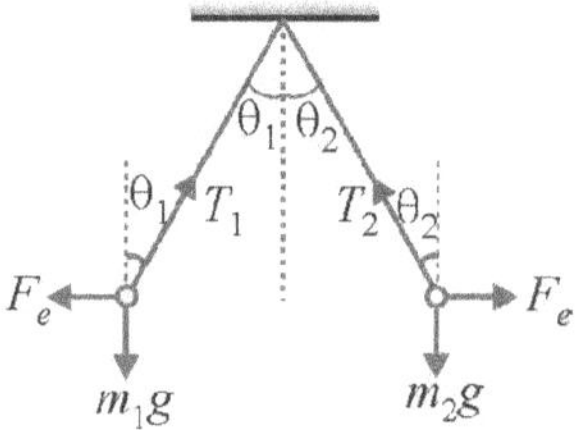


*Fig. 1.33*

From (i) and (ii), $$\tan\theta_1 = \frac{F_e}{m_1 g} \quad ...(iii)$$

Similarly $$\tan\theta_2 = \frac{F_e}{m_2 g} \quad ...(iv)$$

(i) If $m_1 = m_2$, then $\theta_1 = \theta_2$.

(ii) If $m_1 < m_2$, $\theta_1 > \theta_2$.

(iii) If $m_1 > m_2$ then $\theta_1 < \theta_2$.

**Ex. 10** **Two small equally charged spheres, each of mass *m*, are suspended from the same point by silk threads of length *ℓ*. The distance between the spheres $x << \ell$. Find the rate $\frac{dq}{dt}$ with which the charge leaks off each sphere if their approach velocity as $v = \frac{a}{\sqrt{x}}$, where a is a constant.**

**Sol.**

Considering equilibrium of either ball, we have

$$\tan\theta = \frac{F_e}{mg}$$

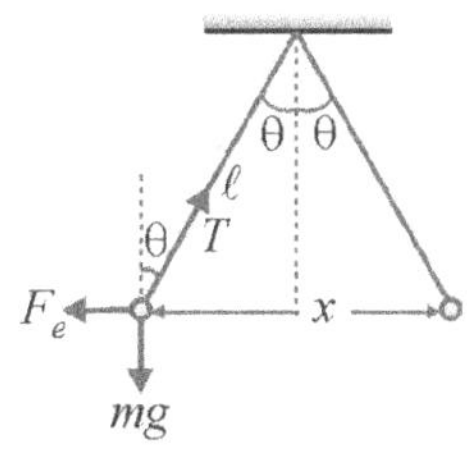


*Fig. 1.34*

For small $x$, $\tan\theta \simeq \sin\theta = \frac{x/2}{\ell}$

$$\therefore \quad \frac{x}{2\ell} = \frac{\left(\frac{1}{4\pi\epsilon_0}\right)\frac{q^2}{x^2}}{mg}$$

or $$x^3 = \frac{q^2\ell}{2\pi\epsilon_0 mg} \quad \ldots(i)$$

Differentiating above equation w.r.t. time, we have

$$\frac{dx^3}{dt} = \frac{\ell}{2\pi\epsilon_0 mg}\frac{dq^2}{dt}$$

or $$3x^2\frac{dx}{dt} = \frac{1}{2\pi\epsilon_0 mg}\times 2q\frac{dq}{dt}$$

or $$\frac{dq}{dt} = \frac{3x^2 v\times 2\pi\epsilon_0 mg}{q}$$

$$= \frac{3x^2\left(\frac{a}{\sqrt{x}}\right)\times 2\pi\epsilon_0 mg}{q}$$

$$= (2\pi\epsilon_0 mga)\left(\frac{3x^{3/2}}{q}\right) \quad \ldots(ii)$$

Now from equations (i) and (ii), we have

$$\frac{dq}{dt} = \frac{3}{2}a\sqrt{2\pi\epsilon_0\frac{mg}{\ell}}. \quad \textit{Ans.}$$

**Ex. 11** **A thin wire ring of radius $r$ has an electric charge $q$. What will be the increment of the force strengthening the wire if a point charge $q_0$ is placed at the ring's centre?**

**Sol.**

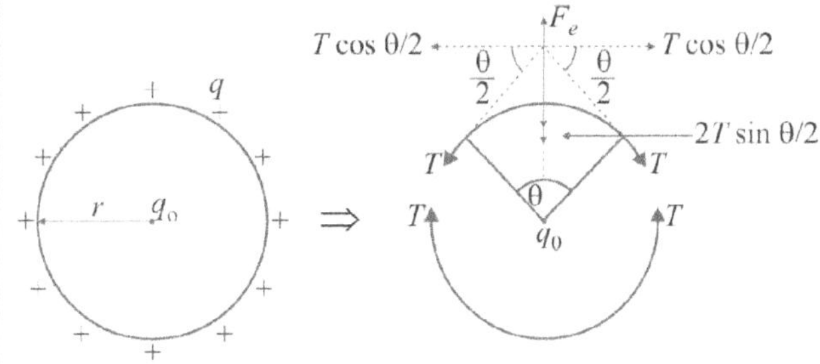


*Fig. 1.35*

Choose a small element of ring of charge $dq$.

The force stretching the each element of wire is

$$F_e = \frac{1}{4\pi\epsilon_0}\frac{(dq)q_0}{r^2}.$$

Since entire loop is in equilibrium, so its small element must be in equilibrium. Let us consider small element of the loop as shown in *fig. 1.35*, for the equilibrium, we have

$$2T\sin\frac{\theta}{2} = F_e = \frac{1}{4\pi\epsilon_0}\frac{(dq)q_0}{r^2}$$

For small $\theta$, $\sin\frac{\theta}{2} \simeq \frac{\theta}{2}$

$$2T\times\frac{\theta}{2} = \frac{1}{4\pi\epsilon_0}\frac{(dq)q_0}{r^2}$$

or $$T\theta = \frac{1}{4\pi\epsilon_0}\frac{\left[\left(\frac{q}{2\pi}\right)\theta\right]q_0}{r^2}$$

or $$T = \frac{qq_0}{8\pi^2\epsilon_0 r^2}$$

$$T = \frac{qq_0}{8\pi^2\epsilon_0 r^2}. \quad \textit{Ans.}$$

**Ex. 12** **Two identical charged spheres are suspended by strings of equal length. The strings make an angle 30° with each other. When suspended in a liquid of density 800 kg/m$^3$, the angle remains the same. What is the dielectric constant of the liquid? The density of material of sphere is 1600 kg/m$^3$.**

**Sol.**

Considering the equilibrium of either sphere we have,

$$T\sin\theta = F_e \text{ and } T\cos\theta = mg$$

$$\therefore \quad \tan\theta = \frac{F_e}{mg} \quad \ldots(i)$$

When the system is placed in liquid

$$\tan\theta = \frac{(F_e/k)}{mg - V\rho_\ell g}$$

$$= \frac{F_e/k}{\left(mg - \frac{mg}{1600}\times 800g\right)}$$

$$= \frac{F_e/k}{(mg/2)} \quad \ldots(ii)$$

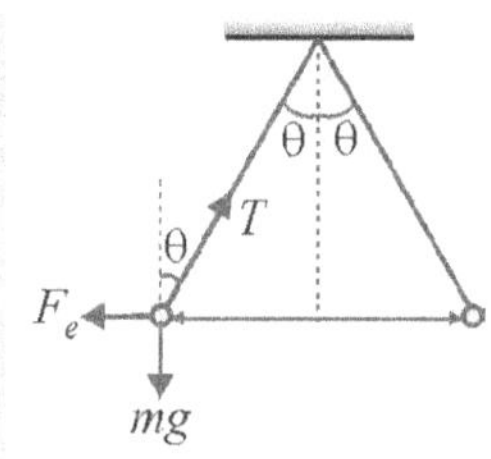


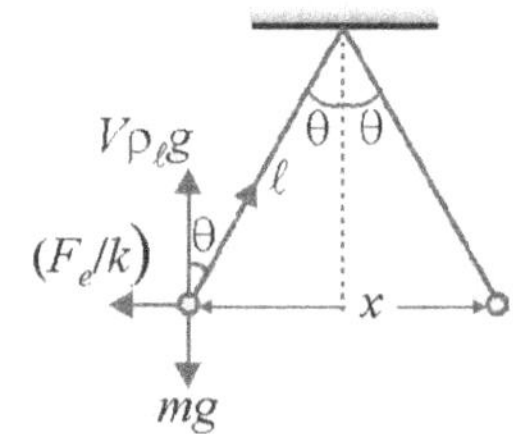


*Fig. 1.36*

From equations (i) & (ii), we get

$$\frac{F_e}{mg} = \frac{F_e/k}{(mg/2)} \Rightarrow k = 2$$

**Test charge $q_0$ :** It is proposed charge which is used to define $\vec{E}$ and $V$ etc. It is too small that its effect at the point under consideration is zero.

## 1.6 ELECTRIC FIELD

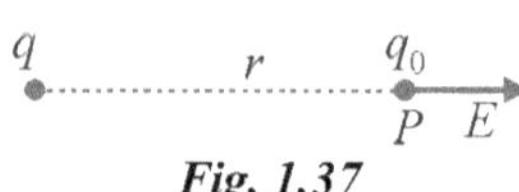


*Fig. 1.37*

The charge and its influence can only be seen when we bring another charge (test charge) in the vicinity of the first charge. It means there is something but not visible around every charge, in which other charges experience force. This something is known as electric field. Electric field is a vector field. The electric field strength, is usually called electric field at any point is the force experiences by unit test charge at that point. If $\vec{F}$ is the force acts on test charge $q_0$, then the electric field

$$\vec{E} = \frac{\vec{F}}{q_0}.$$

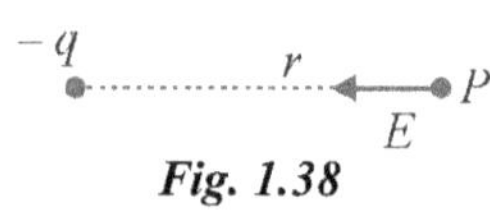


*Fig. 1.38*

The direction of field $\vec{E}$ is that of the force $\vec{F}$ acts on the positive test charge.The SI unit of electric field is newton per coulomb (N/C). Also $1\ \text{N/C} = 1\ \text{V/m}$

The field due to negative charge is towards it.

**Electric field due to a point charge :** The force $\vec{F}$ between charge q and test charge $q_0$ is $\vec{F} = \frac{1}{4\pi\epsilon_0}\frac{qq_0}{r^2}$. Thus electric field at a distance r from q

$$\vec{E} = \frac{\vec{F}}{q_0} = \left(\frac{1}{4\pi\epsilon_0}\frac{|q|q_0}{r^2}\right)/q_0$$

or

$$E = \frac{1}{4\pi\epsilon_0}\frac{|q|}{r^2}.$$

Electric field due to many charges can be obtained by the principle of superposition. Thus if $\vec{E}_1, \vec{E}_2, \ldots\ldots, \vec{E}_n$ are the electric fields produced by the charges $q_1, q_2, \ldots\ldots, q_n$ at any point, then resultant field at that point

$$\vec{E} = \vec{E}_1 + \vec{E}_2 + \ldots\ldots + \vec{E}_n.$$

**Concept plus**

The force between charged particles was originally thought of as direct and instantaneous interaction between the charges. That is;

$$\text{Charge } q_1 \longleftrightarrow \text{Charge } q_2$$

or

$$F = \frac{1}{4\pi\epsilon_0}\frac{q_1q_2}{r^2}.$$

Today, we think of the electric field in the interaction between charged objects. Thus have two tasks : (1) Calculating the electric field produced by a given charge, and (2) calculating the force that a given field exerts on a charge placed in it.

$$\text{Charge } q_1 \longleftrightarrow \text{field } \vec{E} \longleftrightarrow \text{Charge } q_2$$

That is $\quad \vec{F}_{21} = \vec{E}_1 q_2$

and $\quad \vec{F}_{12} = \vec{E}_2 q_1.$

## 1.7 ELECTRIC FIELD LINES (EFL)

A very nice way to visualise electric field, is the lines of force, now usually called **electric field lines**. The idea of lines of force was introduced by Micheal Faraday. These are the imaginary lines, but can be visualised by the motion of the test charge.

### Properties of electric lines of field

1. Every line of field is a continuous and smooth curve originating from a positive charge and ending on a negative charge.
2. The tangent to a line of field to any point gives the direction of $\vec{E}$ at that point.
3. They do not path but leave or end on a charged conductor normally when the charges on the conductor are in equilibrium.
4. Lines of fields are never intersect. If it happens then we say that at the point of intersection the electric intensity is zero, otherwise it would have to be tangential to two different curves at the same instant which is not possible.
5. The number per unit area crossing a surface at right angle to the field direction at every point is proportional to the electric intensity. Hence lines of field are closely spaced where the intensity is large and are widely separated where the intensity is small.

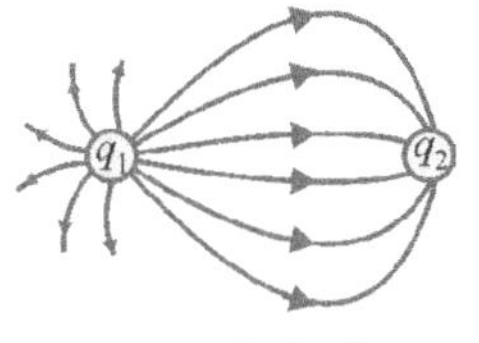

$|q_1| = 2q_2$

(a)

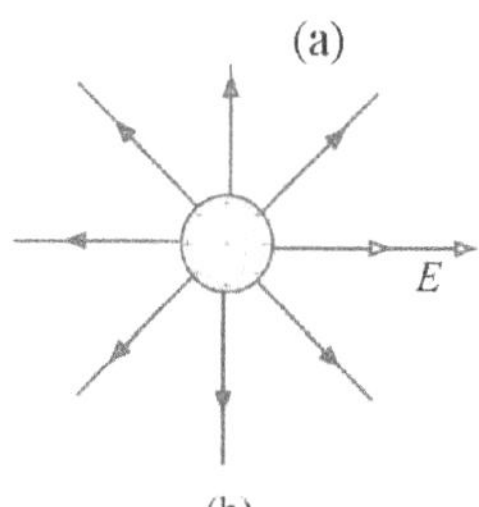

(b)

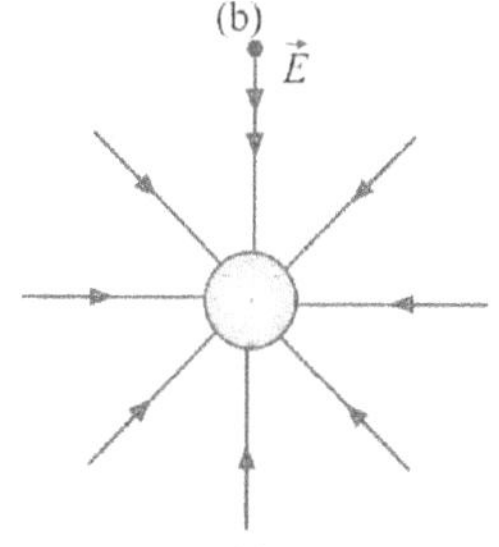

(c)

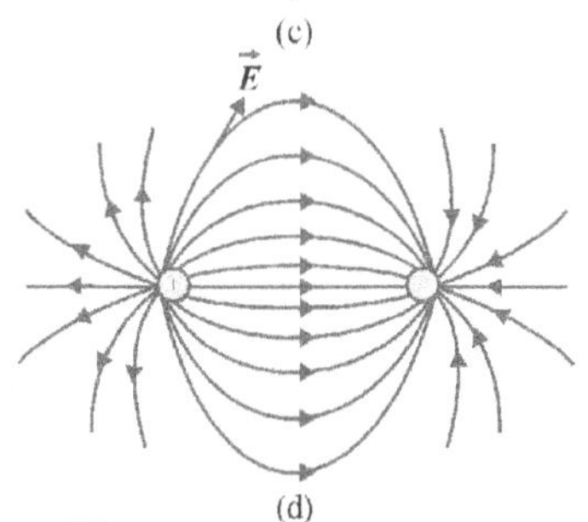

(d)

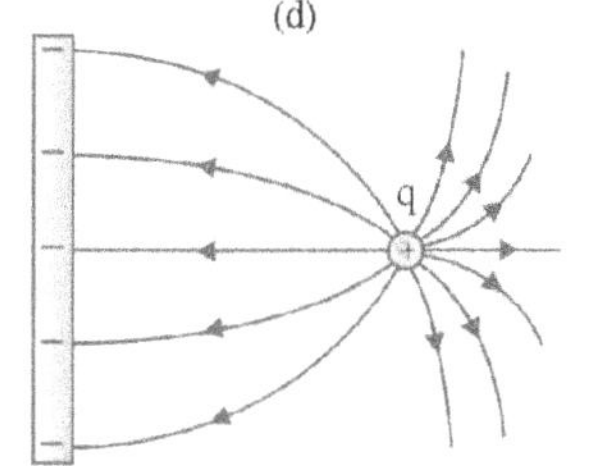

(e)

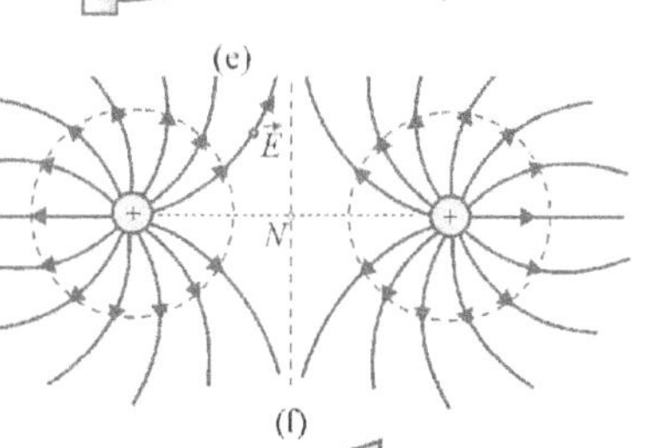

(f)

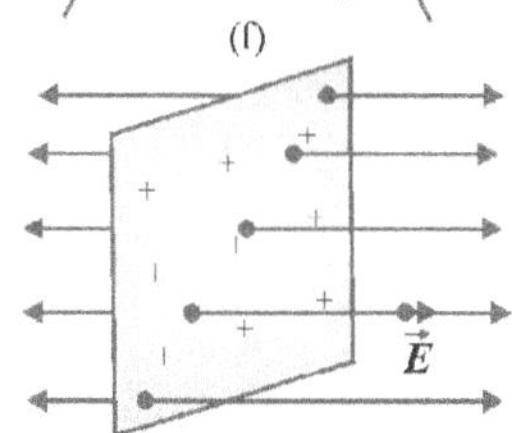

*Fig. 1.39*

We define unit field (1 N/C) arbitrarily as corresponding to unit density of lines of force (one line/m$^2$) To determine the number of lines per unit charge let us draw a spherical surface of radius r around the charge $q$, at its centre. The electric field $E$ at the surface is given by $E = \frac{1}{4\pi \epsilon_0}\frac{q}{r^2}$. As the density of lines of force is $E$, the total numbers of lines of force originating at $q$ and crossing the spherical surface will be $4\pi r^2 E = \frac{q}{\epsilon_0}$. Hence the number of lines originating from a unit charge is $(1/\epsilon_0)$.

**Neutral point :** It means the net electric field, at the point due to all the charges is zero.

(a) Let us consider two charges of same sign are placed at some separation $r$. Let the neutral point is at a distance $x$ from $q_1$. For neutral point,

$$\vec{E}_{net} = 0$$

or $$\vec{E}_1 + \vec{E}_2 = 0$$

or $$\vec{E}_1 = -\vec{E}_2$$

*Fig. 1.40*

That is intensity of fields at the point are equal in magnitude and opposite in directions.

$$\therefore \quad \frac{1}{4\pi \epsilon_0}\frac{q_1}{x^2} = \frac{1}{4\pi \epsilon_0}\frac{q_2}{(r-x)^2}$$

or $$\frac{x^2}{(r-x)^2} = \frac{q_1}{q_2}$$

After solving for $x$, we will get the position of neutral point.

**Note:** When charges are of same sign, the neutral point must be in between the charges.

(b) Consider now two charges of opposite signs, let $q_1 = 8q$ and $q_2 = -2q$ are placed at some separation. In this case neutral point will not be in between the charges. It will be away from charges and close to charge of smaller magnitude. For neutral point

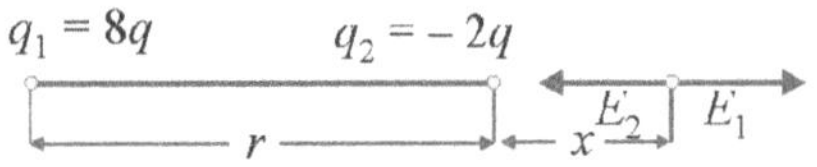

$q_1 = 8q$ $q_2 = -2q$ $r$ $x$ $E_2$ $E_1$

Fig. 1.41

$$E_1 = E_2$$

or
$$\frac{1}{4\pi \epsilon_0}\frac{8q}{(r+x)^2} = \left(\frac{1}{4\pi \epsilon_0}\right)\frac{2q}{x^2}$$

or
$$\left(\frac{x}{r+x}\right)^2 = \frac{1}{4}$$

or
$$\frac{x}{r+x} = \frac{1}{2}$$

or
$$x = r$$

Thus the neutral point is at a distance $r$ from $q_2$.

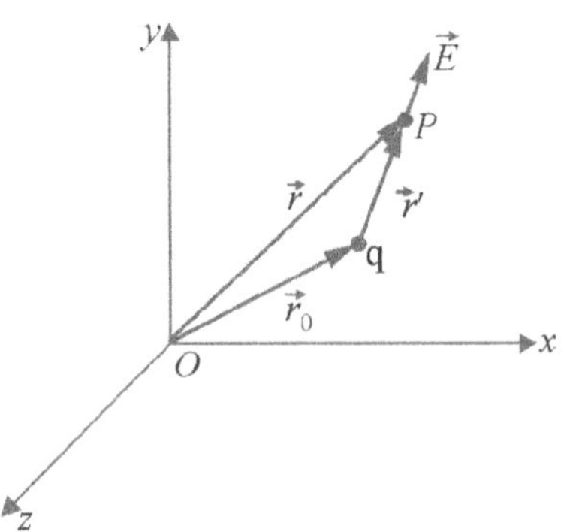


Fig. 1.42

### $\vec{E}$ in terms of $\vec{r}$ :

Consider a charge $q$ is placed at position $\vec{r}_0$ with respect to the origin of the coordinate system. To get the electric field at a point $P$, we have

$$\vec{r}_0 + \vec{r}\,' = \vec{r}$$

or
$$\vec{r}\,' = \vec{r} - \vec{r}_0$$

Electric field
$$\vec{E} = \frac{1}{4\pi \epsilon_0}\frac{q\vec{r}\,'}{r'^3}$$

or
$$\vec{E} = \frac{1}{4\pi \epsilon_0}\frac{q(\vec{r}-\vec{r}_0)}{|\vec{r}-\vec{r}_0|^3}.$$

## Equilibrium of system of charges

The equilibrium of any object of the system means, net force and net torque on it must be zero.

On being point charges, it requires only $\vec{F}_{net} = 0$ for translational equilibrium. For system of charges to be in equilibrium, the net force on each charge of the system must be zero.

## Stable / unstable equilibrium

After displacing charged particle from its equilibrium position, if it return back to its mean position then it is said to be in stable equilibrium otherwise unstable equilibrium. The potential energy $U$ of stable equilibrium is minimum while that of unstable it is maximum.

**Ex. 13** **A positive point charge 50μC is located in the plane *xy* at the point vector $r_0 = 2\hat{i} + 3\hat{j}$, where $\hat{i}$ and $\hat{j}$ are the unit vectors of the x and y axis. Find the vector of the electric field strength $\vec{E}$ and its magnitude at the point with radius vector $\vec{r} = 8\hat{i} - 5\hat{j}$. Here $\vec{r}_0$ and $\vec{r}$ are expressed in meter.**

**Sol.**

Given $\quad q = 50\mu C = 50 \times 10^{-6} C.$

We know that
$$\vec{E} = \frac{1}{4\pi \epsilon_0} \frac{q(\vec{r} - \vec{r}_0)}{|\vec{r} - \vec{r}_0|^3}$$

$$= 9 \times 10^9 \times (50 \times 10^{-6}) \frac{[(8\hat{i} - 5\hat{j}) - (2\hat{i} + 3\hat{j})]}{|(8\hat{i} - 5\hat{j}) - (2\hat{i} + 3\hat{j})|^3}$$

$$= 9 \times 10^9 \times 50 \times 10^{-6} \frac{(6\hat{i} - 8\hat{j})}{|(6\hat{i} - 8\hat{j})|^3}$$

$$= 4.5 \times 10^5 \frac{(6\hat{i} - 8\hat{j})}{10^3}$$

$$= 4.5 \times 10^2 (6\hat{i} - 8\hat{j})$$

$$= 2.7\hat{i} - 3.6\hat{j}\ kV/m$$

$$= 4.5\ kV/m. \qquad \textit{Ans.}$$

**Ex. 14** **A charge particle $q_0$ is placed between two identical charge particles each of $q_0$. Discuss the equilibrium of charge $q_0$.**

**Sol.**

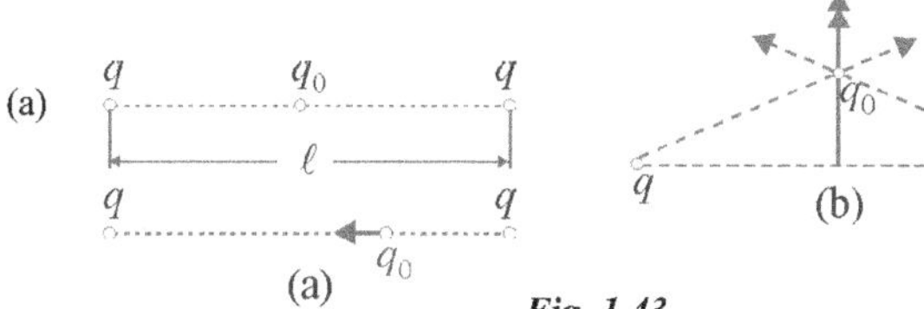


*Fig. 1.43*

Displace charge $q_0$ slightly along line joining $q$ and $q$ and left free. The charge $q_0$ will return to its initial position, so it indicates stable equilibrium along the axis. If the charge $q_0$ is displaced slightly perpendicular to axis of charges $q$ and $q$, it will not return to initial position. It indicates unstable equilibrium along equator.

(b) $-q \quad q_0 \quad -q$ Or $q \quad -q_0 \quad q$

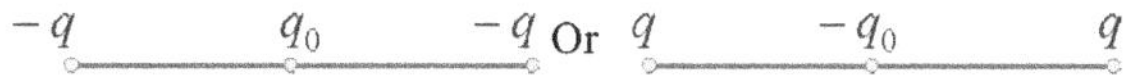

*Fig. 1.44*

Unstable equilibrium along axis, and stable equilibrium along equator.

**Ex. 15** **A charge $q$ is placed at the centre of the line joining two charges $Q$. The system of three charges to be in equilibrium, what should be the value of $q$.**

**Sol.**

The charge $q$ is in equilibrium, because it is at the centre of two identical charges.

For equilibrium of charge $Q$,

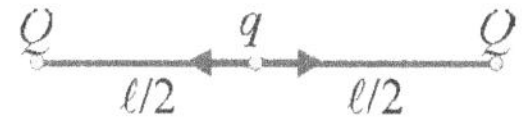

$Q \quad q \quad Q$
$\ell/2 \quad \ell/2$

*Fig. 1.45*

$$\vec{F} = 0$$

or
$$\frac{Qq}{(\ell/2)^2} + \frac{QQ}{\ell^2} = 0,$$

which gives
$$q = \frac{-Q}{4}. \qquad \textit{Ans.}$$

**Ex. 16** **Two positive charges $q_1$ and $q_2$ are located at the points with radius vectors $\vec{r}$ and $\vec{r}$. Find a negative charge $q_3$ and a radius vector $\vec{r}$ of the point at which it has to be placed for the force acting on each the three charges to be equal to zero.**

**Sol.**

The position of the charges are shown in the figure

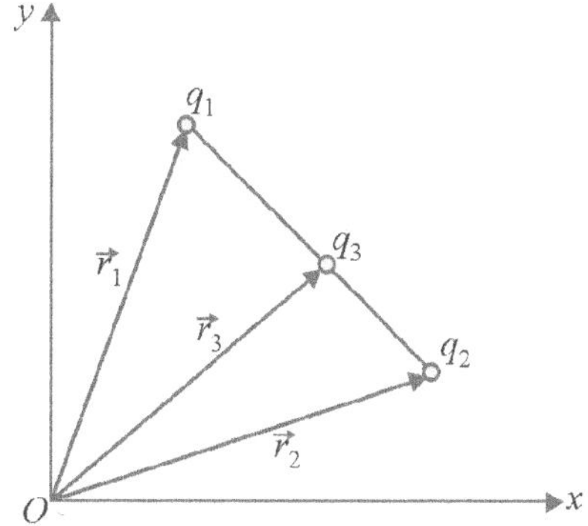


*Fig. 1.46*

For the equilibrium of $q_1$,

$$\vec{F}_{12} + \vec{F}_{13} = 0$$

or
$$\frac{kq_1q_2(\vec{r}_1 - \vec{r}_2)}{|\vec{r}_1 - \vec{r}_2|^3} + k\frac{q_1q_3(\vec{r}_1 - \vec{r}_3)}{|\vec{r}_1 - \vec{r}_3|^3} = 0 \qquad \text{...(i)}$$

Since
$$\frac{(\vec{r}_2 - \vec{r}_1)}{|\vec{r}_2 - \vec{r}_1|} = -\frac{(\vec{r}_1 - \vec{r}_3)}{|\vec{r}_1 - \vec{r}_3|}$$

∴ Equilibrium (i) reduces to

$$\frac{q_2}{|\vec{r}_2 - \vec{r}_1|^2} = \frac{q_3}{|\vec{r}_1 - \vec{r}_3|^2}$$

or
$$\sqrt{q_2}(\vec{r}_1 - \vec{r}_3) + \sqrt{q_3}(\vec{r}_2 - \vec{r}_1) = 0 \qquad \text{...(ii)}$$

Now for the equilibrium of $q_3$,

$$\vec{F}_{31} + \vec{F}_{32} = 0$$

or
$$\frac{kq_1q_3(\vec{r}_1 - \vec{r}_3)}{|\vec{r}_1 - \vec{r}_3|^3} + \frac{kq_2q_3(\vec{r}_2 - \vec{r}_3)}{|\vec{r}_2 - \vec{r}_3|^3} = 0 \quad \text{... (iii)}$$

Since
$$\frac{(\vec{r}_1 - \vec{r}_3)}{|\vec{r}_1 - \vec{r}_3|} = -\frac{(\vec{r}_2 - \vec{r}_3)}{|\vec{r}_2 - \vec{r}_3|}$$

∴ Equation (iii) can be written as

$$\sqrt{q_1}(\vec{r}_2 - \vec{r}_3) + \sqrt{q_2}(\vec{r}_1 - \vec{r}_3) = 0$$

or
$$\vec{r} = \frac{\sqrt{q_1}\vec{r}_2 + \sqrt{q_2}\vec{r}_1}{\sqrt{q_1} + \sqrt{q_2}} \quad \text{... (iv)}$$

From equations (ii) and (iv), we get

$$q = \frac{q_1q_2}{(\sqrt{q_1} + \sqrt{q_2})^2}. \quad \textit{Ans.}$$

## 1.8 ELECTRIC POTENTIAL ENERGY (EPE)

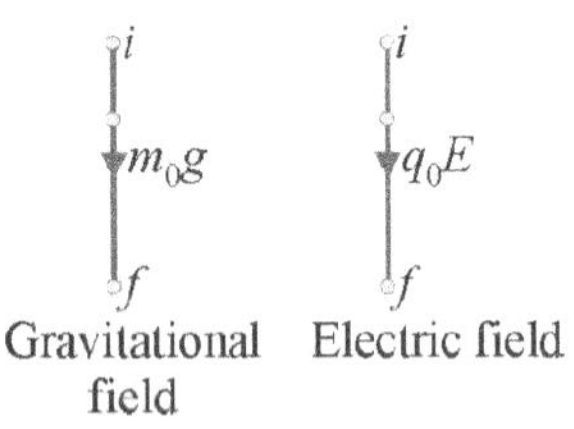


*Fig. 1.47*

We have defined the difference in gravitational potential energy

$$\Delta U = U_f - U_i$$

$$= -\left[W_{if}\right]_{\text{gravitional force}}.$$

Similarly we can define change in electric potential energy as

$$\Delta U = U_f - U_i$$

$$= -\left[W_{if}\right]_{\text{electric force}}. \quad .....(1)$$

If $W_{\text{agent}}$ is the work done by agent to move the charge slowly without change in K.E., then we can write

$$W_{\text{electric force}} + W_{\text{agent}} = \Delta\text{K.E.} = 0$$

$$\therefore \quad W_{\text{agent}} = -W_{\text{electric force}} \quad [F_{\text{electric}} = F_{\text{agent}}]$$

Thus from equation (1),
$$\Delta U = U_f - U_i = \left[W_{if}\right]_{\text{agent}} \quad ...(2)$$

If our reference position is of zero potential energy, i.e.,

$$U_i = 0, \ r_i = \infty, \text{ then}$$

$$U_f = U = \left[W_\infty^f\right]_{\text{agent}} \quad ...(3)$$

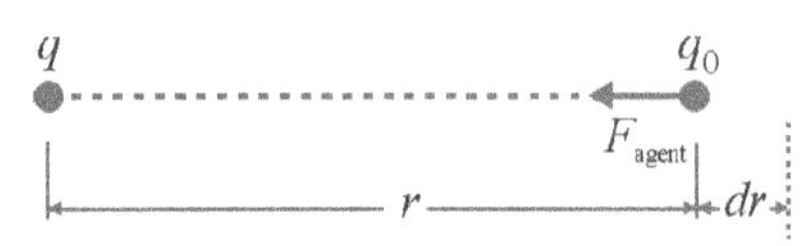


*Fig. 1.48*

Now let us consider two charged system, in which one charge $q$ is fixed and other charge $q_0$ brings from infinity to a separation $r$ from $q$, then

$$\left[W_\infty^f\right]_{\text{agent}} = \int_\infty^r F.\,d\vec{r}$$

$$= \int_\infty^r F_{agent}\,dr\cos 180°$$

$$= \frac{-1}{4\pi\epsilon_0}\int_\infty^r \frac{q\,q_0}{r^2}\,dr$$

$$\left[W_\infty^f\right]_{\text{agent}} = \frac{1}{4\pi\epsilon_0}\frac{qq_0}{r}$$

$$\therefore \quad U = \left[W_\infty^f\right]_{\text{agent}} = \frac{1}{4\pi\epsilon_0}\frac{qq_0}{r}.$$

**Note:**

We have derived above equation by keeping $q$ fixed and moving $q_0$. The same result will be obtained if both the charges move and placed at a separation $r$. For charges $q_1$ and $q_2$, we have

$$U = \frac{1}{4\pi \in_0} \frac{q_1 q_2}{r}.$$

The potential energy of system of charges shown in *fig. 1.49* is

$$U = \frac{1}{4\pi \in_0}\left[\frac{q_1 q_2}{r_{12}} + \frac{q_1 q_3}{r_{13}} + \frac{q_2 q_3}{r_{23}}\right].$$

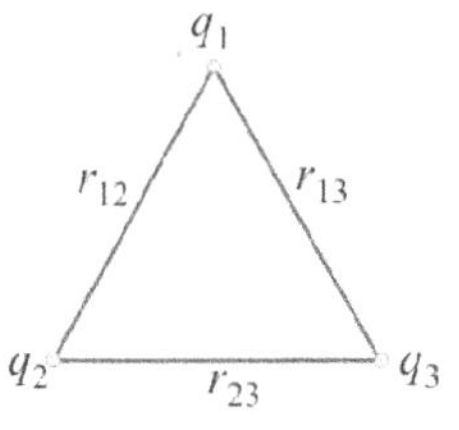


*Fig. 1.49*

## 1.9 POTENTIAL DIFFERENCE

In a pipe line carrying water under gravity, the direction of flow of water depends on the difference of levels of two ends of the pipes. On the same way the potential difference gives the idea of the direction of the electric field. The electric field always runs from higher potential to lower potential.

The potential difference $\Delta V$ between any two points f and i in an electric field is equal to the difference in potential energy per unit charge between the two points. Thus potential difference

$V_f$ $V_i$ $E$

*Fig. 1.50*

$$\Delta V = V_f - V_i = \frac{\Delta U}{q_0}$$

Since $\quad \Delta U = -\left[W_i^f\right]_{\text{electric force}} = \left[W_i^f\right]_{\text{agent}}$

$\therefore \quad \Delta V = V_f - V_i = \left[\frac{W_i^f}{q_0}\right]_{\text{agent}} \quad \ldots(1)$

or $\quad W_i^f = (V_f - V_i)\,q_0 = \Delta V q_0 \quad \ldots(2)$

If we define potential energy to be zero at infinity, then potential must also be zero at infinity. We can then define the potential at any point in an electric field as

$$V_f - V_\infty = \frac{[W_\infty^f]_{\text{agent}}}{q_0}$$

or $\quad V_f = V = \dfrac{\left[W_\infty^f\right]_{\text{agent}}}{q_0}.$

### Potential due to a point charge

The potential at any point in the electric field of a point charge is the work done in bringing a unit test charge from infinity to that point. The work done on charge $q_0$ in bringing from infinity to a point $P$ at a distance $r$ from the charge $q$

$$\left[W_\infty^P\right]_{agent} = \frac{1}{4\pi \in_0} \frac{q q_0}{r}.$$

Thus potential at $P$

$$V = \frac{\left[W_{\infty}^{P}\right]_{\text{agent}}}{q_0}$$

$$= \frac{\left[\frac{1}{4\pi \epsilon_0}\frac{qq_0}{r}\right]}{q_0}$$

or $$V = \frac{1}{4\pi \epsilon_0}\frac{q}{r}.$$

It is scalar quantity. Its SI unit is J/C or V.

### Potential due to many charges

We can define the net potential at a point due to a system of many charges with the help of the superposition principle. We calculate the potential due to each charge at the given point separately including the sign of charges. Then we sum the potentials. For n charges, the net potential

$$V = \sum_{i=1}^{n} V_i = \frac{1}{4\pi \epsilon_0}\sum_{i=1}^{n}\frac{q_i}{r_i}.$$

Here $q_i$ is the value of $i^{\text{th}}$ charge, and $r_i$ is the radial distance of the given point from the charge.

**Note:** In using the formula of potential and potential energy, the sign of the charges should be included.

### Potential from field

Let us consider a charge $q_0$ is left to move in an electric field. The electric field exerts force on the charge

$$\vec{F}_e = \vec{E}q_0$$

For small displacement, work done by the electric field

$$[dW]_{\text{electric force}} = \vec{F}_e.d\vec{r} \qquad \ldots(1)$$

The change in potential $dV$ is given

$$dV = \frac{-[dW]_{\text{electric force}}}{q_0}$$

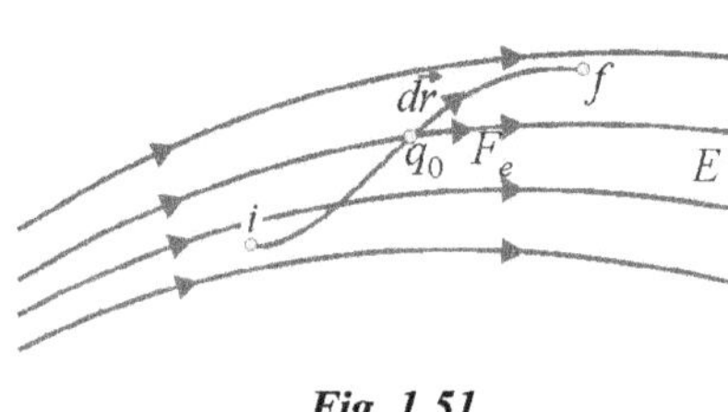


*Fig. 1.51*

From equation (1), $$dV = -\frac{\vec{F}_e.d\vec{r}}{q_0} = -\vec{E}.d\vec{r} \qquad \left[\text{as } \frac{\vec{F}_e}{q} = \vec{E}\right]$$

and $$V = V_f - V_i = -\int_i^f \vec{E}.d\vec{r} \qquad \ldots(2)$$

Differentiating both sides of above equation, we get

$$E = \frac{-dV}{dr} \qquad \ldots..(3)$$

**Conclusion :**

1. In the book potential difference between $A$ and $B$ means $V_A - V_B$.

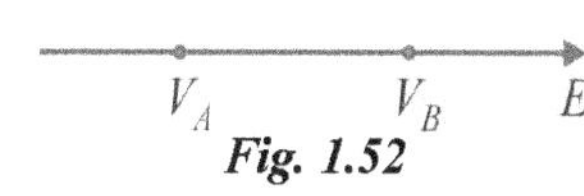

*Fig. 1.52*

2. $$V_B - V_A = -\int_A^B \vec{E}\cdot d\vec{r}$$

or $$V_A - V_B = \int_A^B \vec{E}\cdot d\vec{r}$$

**For 3D field :** If $E_x$, $E_y$ and $E_z$ are the components of field along $x$, $y$ and $z$-axes respectively, then we can write

$$E_x = -\frac{\partial V}{\partial x},\ E_y = -\frac{\partial V}{\partial y},\ E_z = -\frac{\partial V}{\partial z},$$

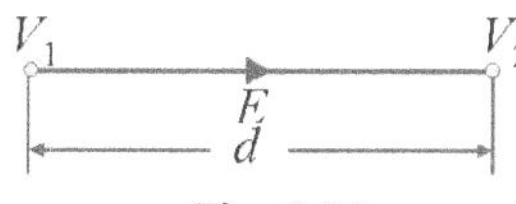

*Fig. 1.53*

and resultant field $$\vec{E} = E_x\hat{i} + E_y\hat{j} + E_z\hat{k}$$

For uniform field, we can write

$$E = -\frac{\Delta V}{\Delta r} = \frac{-(V_2 - V_1)}{d}$$

$$= \frac{V_1 - V_2}{d}$$

or $$V_1 - V_2 = Ed.$$

**Ex. 17** **There is an infinite straight chain of alternating charges $q$ and $-q$. The distance between neighbouring charges is equal to $a$. Find the interaction energy of each charge with all the others.**

**Sol.**

$$\begin{matrix} -q & q & -q & q & -q & q & -q \\ -3a & -2a & -a & 0 & a & 2a & 3a \end{matrix}$$

The interaction energy of charge at 0 due to charges on right of 0:

$$U = \frac{1}{4\pi \in_0}\left[\frac{q(-q)}{a} + \frac{qq}{2a} + \frac{q(-q)}{3a} + \frac{qq}{4a} + \ldots\infty\right]$$

$$= \frac{q^2}{4\pi \in_0 a}\left[-1 + \frac{1}{2} - \frac{1}{3} + \frac{1}{4}\ldots\right] = -\frac{q^2}{4\pi \in_0 a}\ell n2$$

The same interaction energy due to charges on left of 0, so

$$\therefore \quad U_{\text{Total}} = 2U$$

$$= \frac{-2q^2}{4\pi \in_0 a}\ell n2.$$

**Ex. 18** **Determine the electric field strength vector if the potential of this field depends on $x$, $y$ co-ordinates as $V = a(x^2 - y^2)$.**

**Sol.**

We know that, $$E_x = -\frac{\partial V}{\partial x} = -2ax,$$

and $$E_y = -\frac{\partial V}{\partial y} = 2ay$$

$$\therefore \quad \vec{E} = E_x\hat{i} + E_y\hat{j}$$

$$= 2a(-x\hat{i} + y\hat{j}).$$ **Ans.**

**Ex. 19** **An electric field $\vec{E} = \vec{i}Ax$ exist in the space, where $A = 10\ V/m^2$. Take the potential at (10m, 20m) to be zero. Find the potential at the origin.**

**Sol.**

Line $BC$ is the equipotential line, so

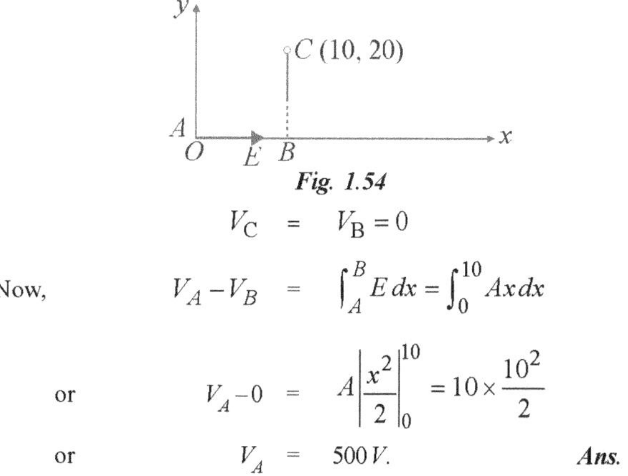

*Fig. 1.54*

$$V_C = V_B = 0$$

Now, $$V_A - V_B = \int_A^B E\,dx = \int_0^{10} Ax\,dx$$

or $$V_A - 0 = A\left|\frac{x^2}{2}\right|_0^{10} = 10 \times \frac{10^2}{2}$$

or $$V_A = 500\,V.$$ **Ans.**

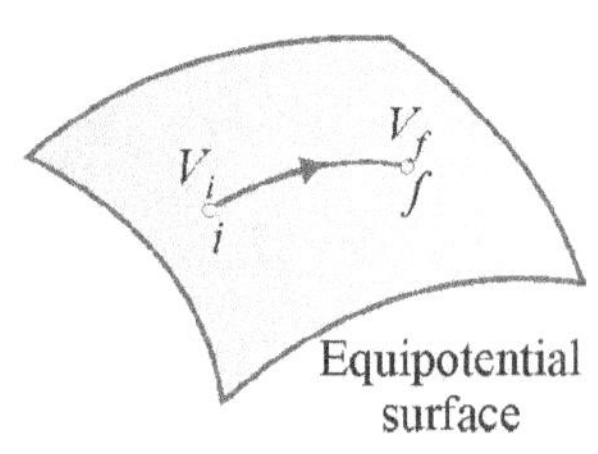

*Fig. 1.55*

## 1.10 EQUIPOTENTIAL SURFACE

A locus of points in space that all have the same potential is called equipotential surface. On the equipotential:

1. No net work done on a charge by an electric field as the charge moves between two points on the same equipotential surface. As $V_f = V_i$ and so $\Delta V = 0$

$$\therefore \quad W_i^f = \Delta V q_0 = 0.$$

2. Equipotential surface is perpendicular to electric lines of field.
3. It may be of any shape.
4. The equipotential surfaces are a family of concentric spheres for a sphere of charge or a point charge and are a family of concentric cylinders for a line charge or cylinder of charge.

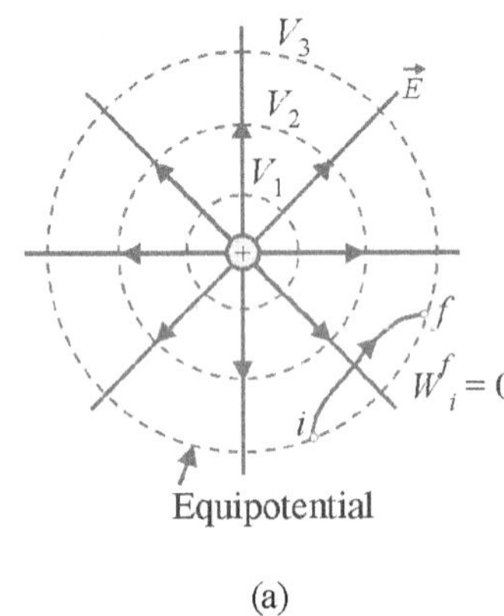

(a)

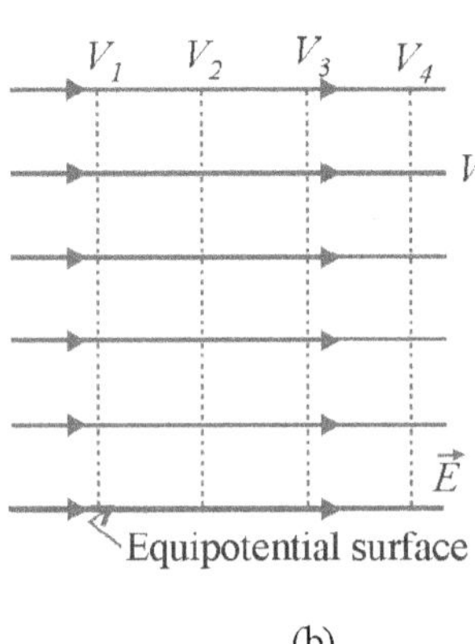

(b)

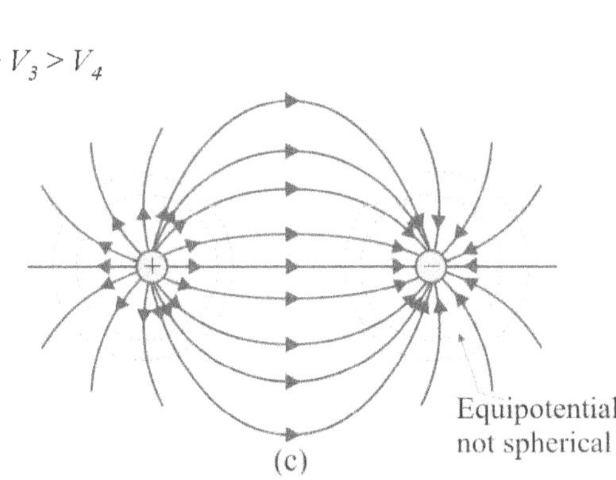

(c)

*Fig. 1.56*

**Ex. 20** **Some equipotential surfaces are shown in *fig. 1.57*. What can you say about the magnitude and the direction of the electric field?**

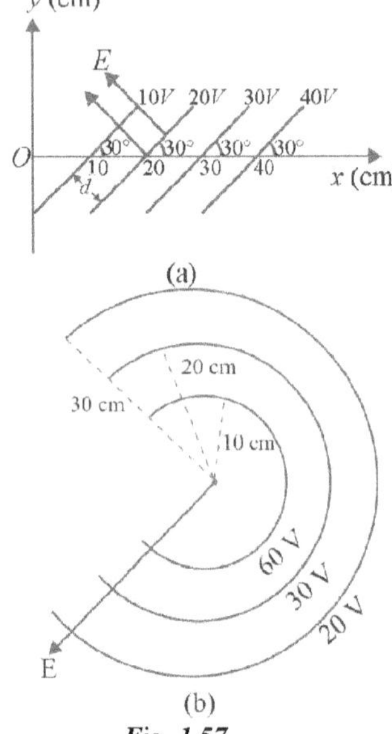

*Fig. 1.57*

**Sol.**

(a) Draw lines perpendicular to equipotential. These are the field lines.

$$\therefore \quad E = \frac{V_{higher} - V_{lower}}{d} = \frac{20-10}{10\sin 30°} = \frac{10\,V}{5\,cm}$$

$$= 200 \text{ V/m},$$

and making an angle 120° with the $x$-axis.

(b) For spherical surface, we have $V = \frac{k}{r}$.

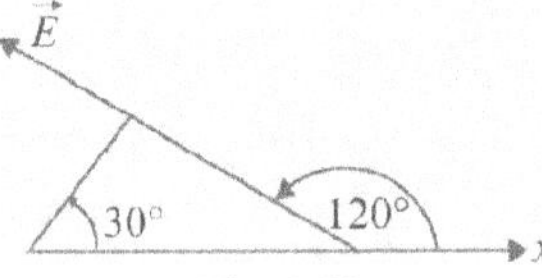

*Fig. 1.58*

Choose any of the equipotential, let of 60V.

$$\therefore \quad 60 = \frac{k}{10} \Rightarrow k = 600 \text{ V-cm}$$

Electric field
$$E = -\frac{dV}{dr} = \frac{k}{r^2}$$

$$= \frac{600 \text{ V-cm}}{r^2}$$

$$= \frac{6}{(0.1)^2} = 600 \text{ V/m}. \quad \textbf{\textit{Ans.}}$$

**Ex. 21** **A test charge $q_0$ is moved from A to $C$ along the path $ABC$ as shown in *fig. 1.59*. Find potential difference between points $D$ and $A$.**

**Sol.**

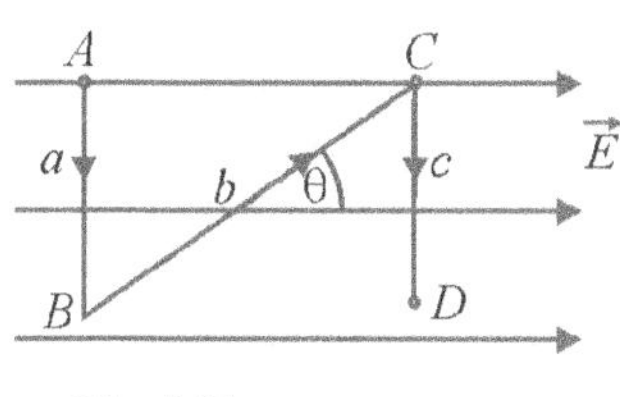


*Fig. 1.59*

Since $AB$ is the equipotential line

$$\therefore \quad V_A = V_B$$

Also
$$V_A - V_D = V_B - V_D = E \times BD$$
$$= E \times b\cos\theta$$
$$= Eb\cos\theta. \qquad \textit{Ans.}$$

## 1.11 ELECTRIC FLUX

The word "flux" comes from the Latin word meaning "to flow". Flow may be of air, water or electric field through any surface.

Electric flux through any surface may be defined as the total field lines crossing that surface.

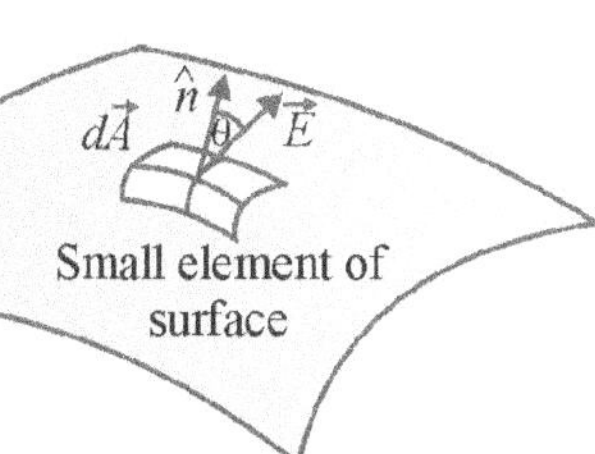


*Fig. 1.60*

The electric flux $d\phi$ through small element of surface $(d\vec{A})$ is defined as

$$d\phi = E_{\perp} dA$$
$$= (E\cos\theta)dA$$
$$= EdA\cos\theta$$

The total flux through the surface

$$\phi = \int EdA\cos\theta$$

or
$$\phi = \int \vec{E}.d\vec{A}$$

If $\vec{E}$ is uniform throughout the surface, then

$$\phi = EA\cos\theta$$

**More about $\phi$ :**

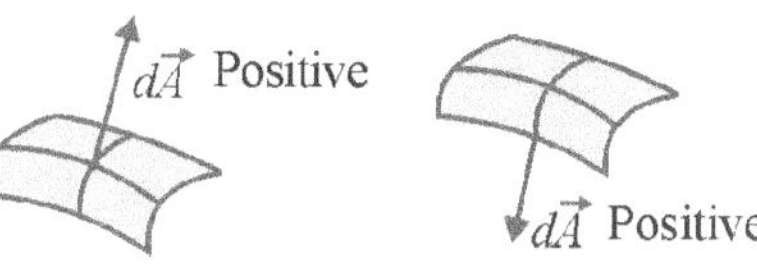


*Fig. 1.61*

1. We may take $d\vec{A}$ positive pointing out of surface.
2. Electric flux is a scalar quantity. It may be negative. Its SI unit is V-m.
3. In finding flux to charge, place the value of charge with the sign in the formula of flux.
4.

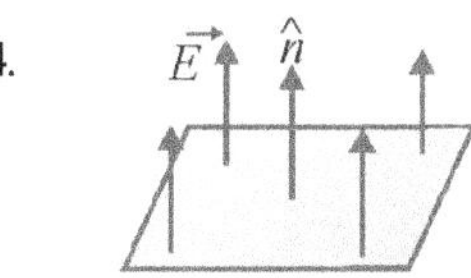
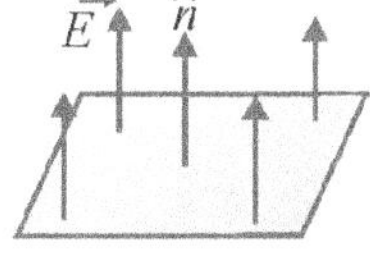


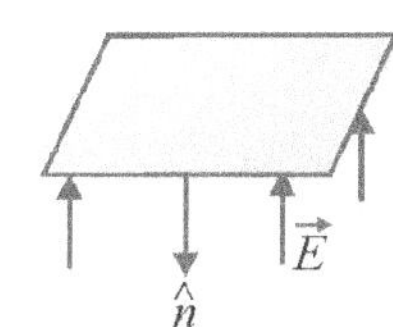


(a) (b) (c)

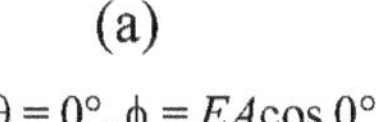

(a) $\theta = 0°, \phi = EA\cos 0°$. $= EA$. This is called emerging flux

(b) $\phi = EA\cos 90°$ $= 0$

(c) $\phi = EA\cos 180°$ $= -EA$. This is called entering flux

*Fig. 1.62*

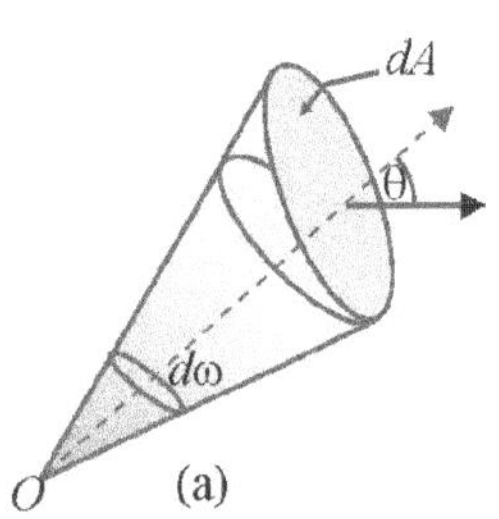


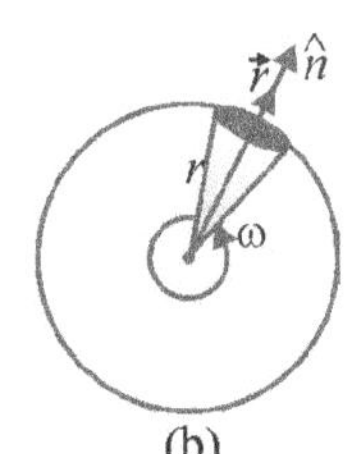


*Fig. 1.63*

## Solid angle (ω)

Solid angle is the analogue in three dimensions of the usual angle in two dimensions. The solid angle subtended by any surface $dA$ at a point $O$ and distance $r$ away is given by

$$d\omega = \frac{dA\cos\theta}{r^2}$$

Total solid angle
$$\omega = \sum \frac{\Delta A\cos\theta}{r^2} \qquad \ldots(1)$$

From the figure (b), $\theta = 0$,
$$\omega = \frac{\sum \Delta A}{r^2} = \frac{4\pi r^2}{r^2}$$

or
$$\omega = 4\pi \text{ steradian} \qquad \ldots(2)$$

**Note:**

The total angle subtended by closed surface always be $4\pi$, regardless of the size and shape of the closed surface.

## Flux due to charge inside closed surface

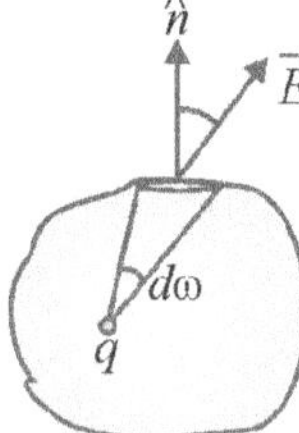


*Fig. 1.65*

Consider a small element of closed surface, which subtended solid angle $d\omega$ at the position of charge $q$. The flux through the element surface,

$$d\phi = \left(\frac{q}{4\pi \epsilon_0}\right) d\omega$$

∴ Total flux
$$\phi = \frac{q}{4\pi \epsilon_0}\int d\omega$$

As $\int d\omega = \omega$, ∴
$$\phi = \frac{q}{4\pi \epsilon_0}\omega$$

Also $\omega = 4\pi$, ∴
$$\phi = \frac{q}{4\pi \epsilon_0} \times 4\pi = \frac{q}{\epsilon_0}$$

**Note:**

The total flux through a closed surface always be $\phi = \frac{q}{\epsilon_0}$, regardless of shape and size of surface and position of charge.

## Flux due to charge out of closed surface

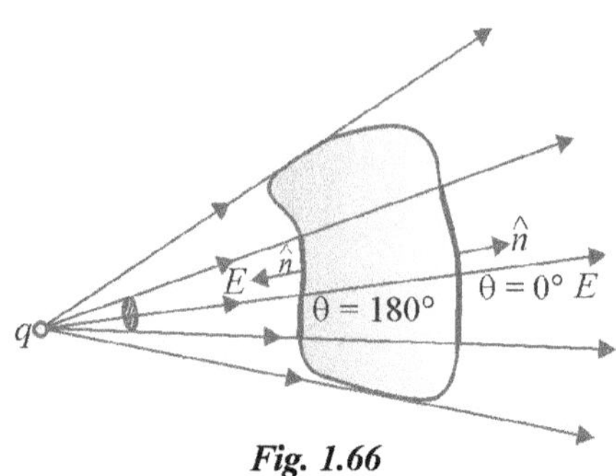


*Fig. 1.66*

Consider a point charge $q$ placed outside the closed surface. If $\phi_{entering}$ and $\phi_{emerging}$ are the entering flux and emerging flux through the close surface, then

$$\phi_{Total} = \phi_{Total} + \phi_{emerging}$$
$$= \phi + \phi = 0.$$

Thus electric flux associated with the closed surface of any shape due to charge out of the surface will be zero.

**Ex. 22** **Consider the system of three charges as shown in *fig. 1.67*. Calculate the total flux associated with the closed surface.**

**Sol.**

The flux associated with charges inside closed surface is

$$\phi_i = (q_1 - q_2)/\in_0 .$$

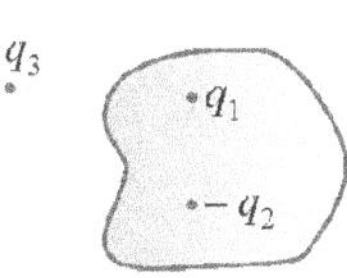


*Fig. 1.67*

Flux associated due to charge out of closed surface $\phi_o = 0$.

$$\therefore \quad \phi_{Total} = \phi_i + \phi_o = (q_1 - q_2)/\in_0 . \quad \textit{Ans.}$$

**Ex. 23** **Find total flux associated with the surfaces shown in *fig. 1.68*.**

**Sol.**

(i)

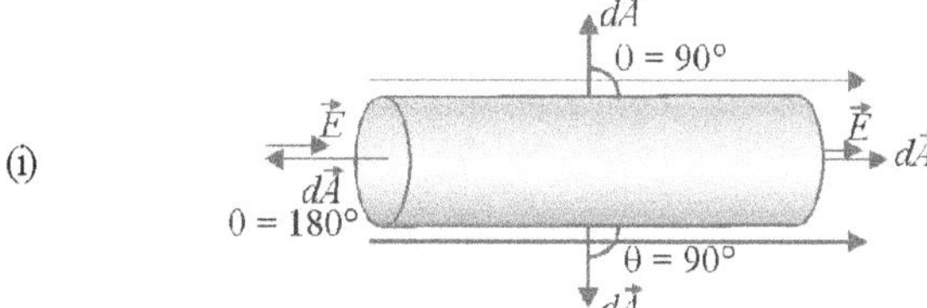


(ii)

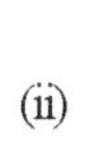

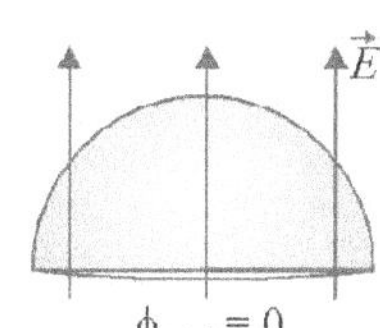


*Fig. 1.68*

$$\phi_{Total} = \int \begin{bmatrix} E\,dA\cos180° + EdA\cos0° \\ +EdA90° + EdA\cos90° \end{bmatrix}$$

$$= 0.$$

Thus the flux through closed surface is zero.

**Ex. 24** **Find the flux due to electric field through the surfaces as shown in *fig. 1.69*.**

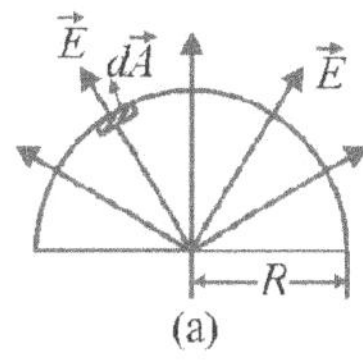


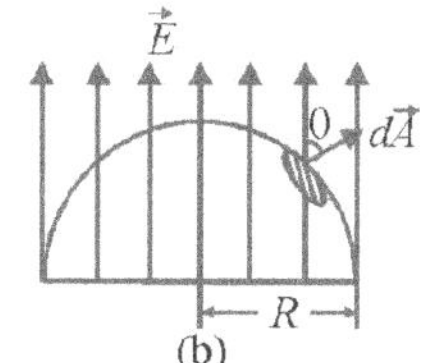


*Fig. 1.69*

**Sol.**

(a) Let us consider small element of surface $d\vec{A}$. The flux through this element surface

$$d\phi = EdA\cos\theta = EdA\cos0 = E\,dA$$

The total flux associated

$$\phi = \int EdA = E\int dA = E \times 2\pi R^2 = 2\pi ER^2$$

(b) The flux through element $d\vec{A}$,

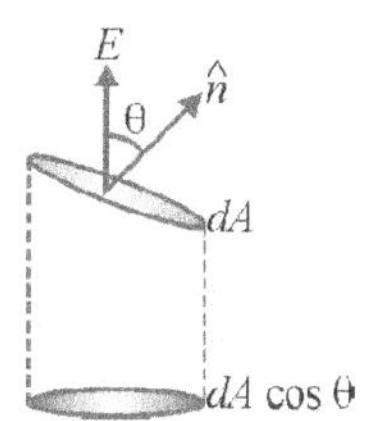


*Fig. 1.70*

$$d\phi = EdA\cos\theta$$

The total flux $\phi = E\int dA\cos\theta$

$$= E\int(\text{horizontal projection of } d\vec{A})$$

$$= E \times \pi R^2$$

$$= \pi ER^2 . \quad \textit{Ans.}$$

**Ex. 25** **A point charge q is placed at the centre of the cubical box. Find, (a) total flux associated with the box (b) flux emerging through each face of the box (c) flux through shaded area of surface**

**Sol.**

(a) Total flux $\phi_0 = \dfrac{q}{\in_0}$.

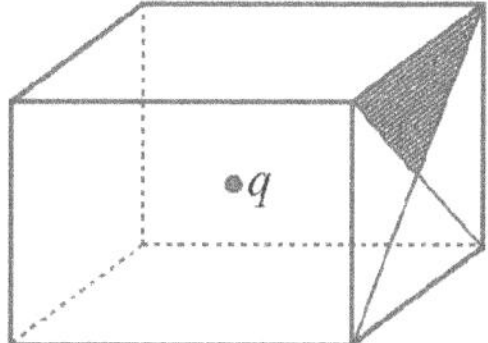


*Fig. 1.71*

(b) This total flux is emerging equally from each face of the box (6 faces). Thus flux through each face,

$$\phi = \frac{q}{6\in_0}$$

(c) The flux through shaded portion

$$\phi' = \frac{\phi}{4} = \frac{q}{24\in_0}.$$

**Ex. 26** **Find flux due to a point charge q placed**

**(a) at centre of the face** **(b) corner of the cubical box.**

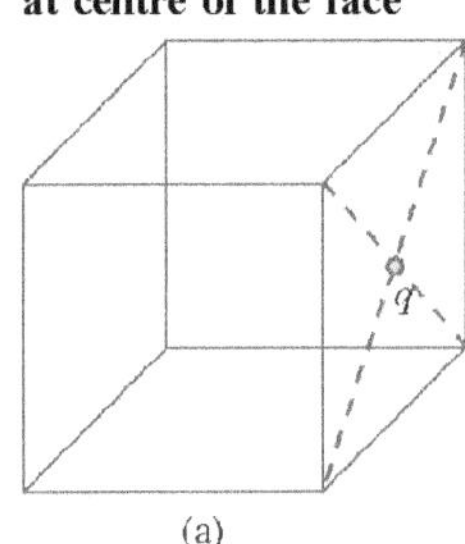


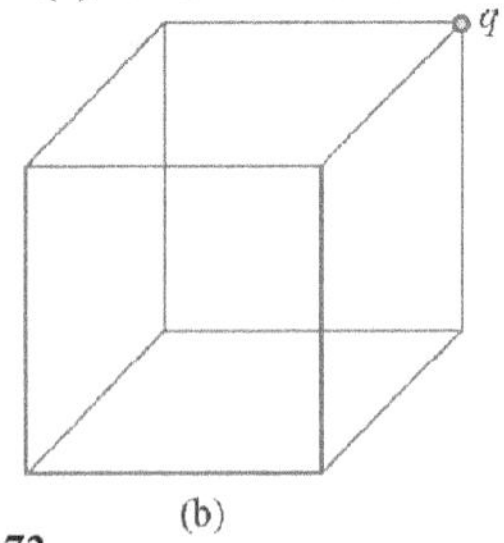


*Fig. 1.72*

**Sol.**

(a) If charge is kept at the centre of a face : First we should enclosed the charge by assuming an identical imaginary cube. The total flux through the cubes $\phi_{total} = \frac{q}{\epsilon_0}$.

Thus the flux through given cube $\phi = \frac{q}{2\epsilon_0}$.

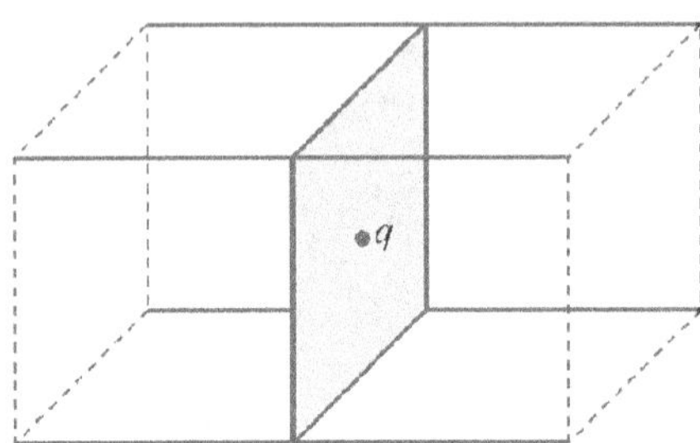


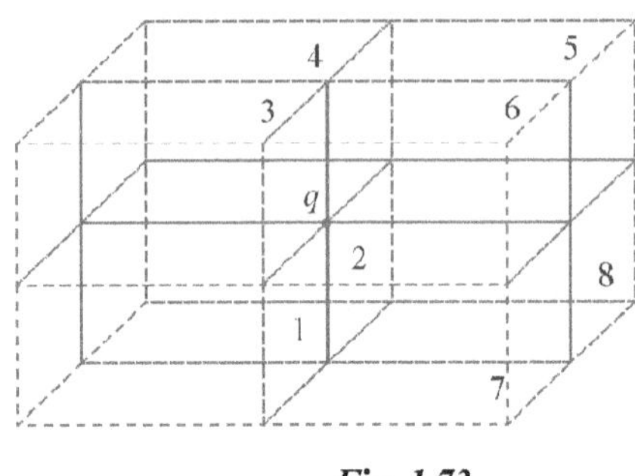


*Fig. 1.73*

(b) If the charge is placed at the corner of a cube, seven more identical cubes are required to enclose the charge completely. The total flux through all the faces of 8 cubes is

$\phi_{total} = \frac{q}{\epsilon_0}$. The contribution of this flux through each cube

$\phi = \frac{q}{8\epsilon_0}$. This flux emerging equally through three front faces of the cube. Other three faces; junction of which charge is placed have no flux. Therefore the flux through the face

$= \frac{q/8\epsilon_0}{3} = \frac{q}{24\epsilon_0}$.

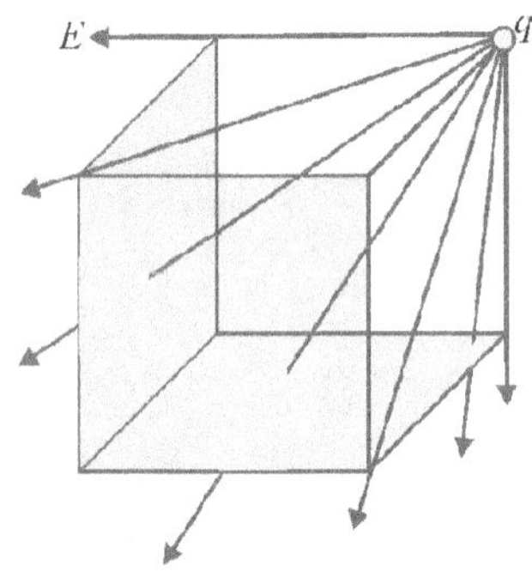


*Fig. 1.74*

**Ex. 27** **Find flux due to the charge *q* placed as shown in *fig. 1.75*.**

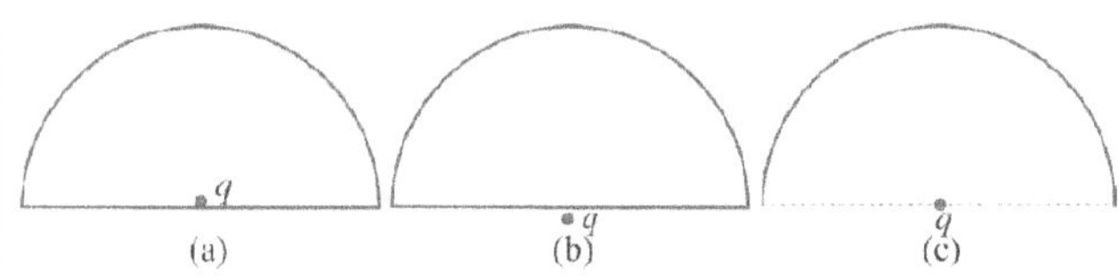


*Fig. 1.75*

**Sol.**

(a) $\phi = \frac{q}{\epsilon_0}$ (b) $\phi = 0$ (c) $\phi = \frac{q}{2\epsilon_0}$

## 1.12 GAUSS'S LAW OR GAUSS'S THEOREM

Gauss's law is the very powerful tool of electrostatics. It can be used to find total flux associated with the closed surface due to charges appearing in the space. By doing this we can calculate electric field at any point of the surface. According to it, the total flux of the net electric field through a closed surface (Gaussian surface) equals the net charge enclosed by the surface divided by $\epsilon_0$. Thus if $q_{in}$ is the total charge inside the closed surface, then

$$\oint \vec{E}.d\vec{A} = \frac{q_{in}}{\epsilon_0}.$$

**Proof of Gauss's law**

Consider charges $q_1, q_2, \ldots\ldots, q_n$ are inside a closed surface and charges $q'_1, q'_2, \ldots\ldots, q'_n$ are outside the surface.

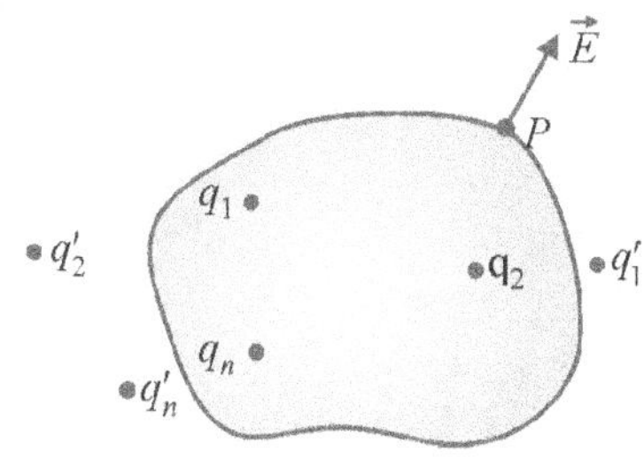


Fig. 1.76

If $\vec{E}_1, \vec{E}_2, \ldots\ldots, \vec{E}_n; \vec{E}'_1, \vec{E}'_2, \ldots\ldots, \vec{E}'_n$ are the fields produced by the respective charges ; inside and outside the closed surface, then resultant electric field at any point $P$ on it

$$\vec{E} = (\vec{E}_1 + \vec{E}_2 + \ldots + \vec{E}_n) + (\vec{E}'_1 + \vec{E}'_2 + \ldots\ldots + \vec{E}'_n)$$

The flux of the resultant electric field through the closed surface

$$\phi = \oint \vec{E}.d\vec{A}$$

$$= \left[\oint \vec{E}_1.d\vec{A} + \oint \vec{E}_2.d\vec{A} + \ldots\ldots + \oint \vec{E}_n.d\vec{A}\right] + \left[\oint \vec{E}'_1.d\vec{A} + \oint \vec{E}'_2.d\vec{A} + \ldots + \oint \vec{E}'_n.d\vec{A}\right] \ldots (1)$$

Here $\oint \vec{E}_1.d\vec{A}$ is the flux due to charge $q_1$ which is $q_1 / \in_0$ and $\oint \vec{E}'_1.d\vec{A}$ is the flux to charge $q'_1$, which is zero, because it is out off the closed surface. Thus equation (1) can be written as ;

$$\oint \vec{E} \times d\vec{A} = \left[\frac{q_1}{\in_0} + \frac{q_2}{\in_0} + \ldots + \frac{q_n}{\in_0}\right] + [0 + 0 + \ldots\ldots + 0]$$

$$= \frac{\Sigma q_i}{\in_0}$$

or $$\oint \vec{E}.d\vec{A} = \frac{q_{in}}{\in_0}. \quad \ldots (2)$$

**Note:**

1. The net charge is the algebraic sum of all the enclosed positive and negative charges, and it can be positive, negative, or zero.
2. The electric field appearing in the Gauss's law is the net electric field due to all the charges present inside as well as outside the closed surface. On the other hand, the charge $q_{in}$ appearing in the law is only the charge inside the closed surface.

**The following observations are useful in calculating total flux**

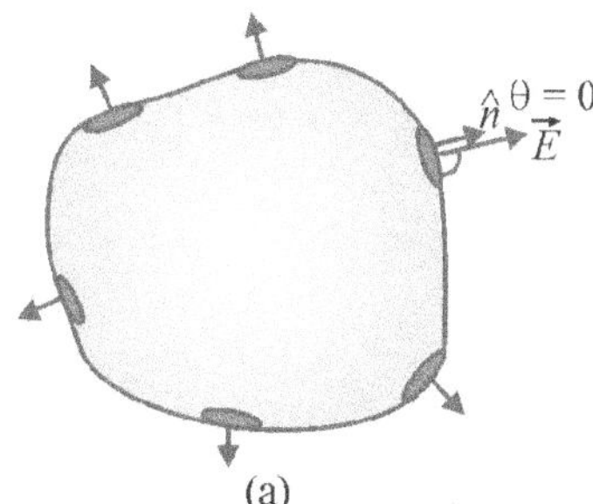


(a)

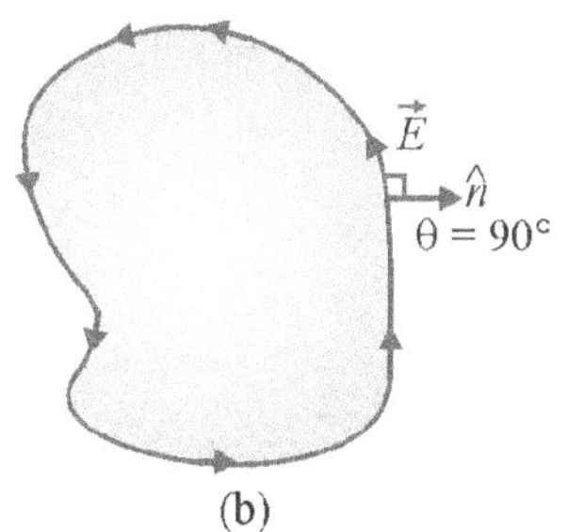


(b)

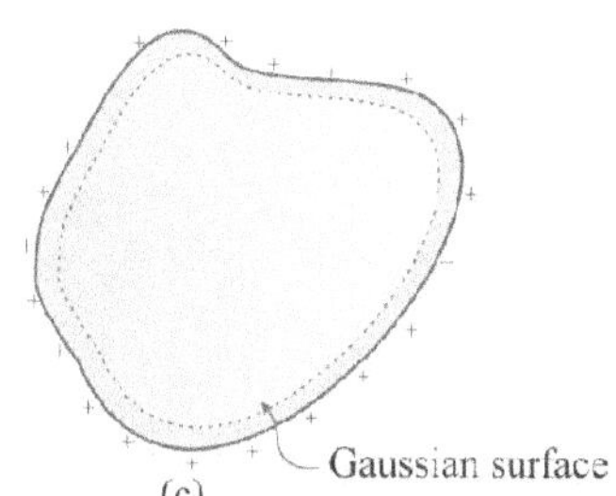


(c)

Fig. 1.77

1. If $\vec{E}$ is perpendicular to a surface area $A(\theta = 0)$ at all points, and has the same magnitude at all points of the surface, then $\oint \vec{E}.d\vec{A} = \oint EA\cos 0 = EA$.

   For spherical surface $EA = E \times 4\pi r^2 = 4\pi E r^2$.

2. If $\vec{E}$ is parallel to a surface at all points, $E_\perp = 0$ *or* $\theta = 90°$ and therefore

   $$\oint \vec{E}.d\vec{A} = \int EA\cos 90° = 0.$$

3. If $\vec{E}$ is zero at all points of a surface, the integral is zero.
4. The surface to which Gauss's law is applied need not be a real physical surface, such as the surface of a solid body. Indeed, in most applications of this law, one considers an imaginary or geometrical surface that may be in empty space, embedded in a solid body, or partly in space and partly within a body.

### Conductor with excess charge

If an excess charge is placed on an isolated conductor, the charge will move entirely over the surface of the conductor. It is because of the fact that like charges repel each other. An internal electric field does appear as the conductor is being charged. However, the excess charge quickly distributes itself such a way that the internal electric field is zero. The movement of charge then ceases, and the net force on each charge is zero; the charges are then in electrostatic equilibrium.

The fact can be verify by Gauss's law. It has explained that the electric field $\vec{E}$ is zero at all points within a conductor when the charges in the conductor are at rest. We may take an imaginary surface in the interior of the conductor as shown in figure. Because $\vec{E}$ is zero everywhere on the surface,

$$\therefore \quad \oint \vec{E}.d\vec{A} = 0$$

By Gauss's law

$$\oint \vec{E}.d\vec{A} = \frac{q_{in}}{\epsilon_0}$$

or

$$0 = \frac{q_{in}}{\epsilon_0}$$

which gives

$$q_{in} = 0.$$

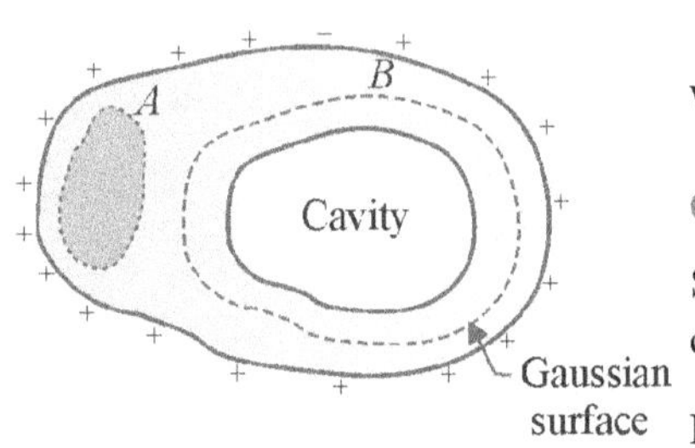


*Fig. 1.78*

### Cavity in the conductor

Suppose there is a cavity in the charged conductor, and there are no charges within the cavity.

For the surface $A$,

$$\oint \vec{E}.d\vec{A} = 0$$

Since $\vec{E}$ is zero in the conductor,

$$\therefore \quad q_{in} = 0.$$

Further more, consideration of a surface such as $B$ shows that the net charge on the surface of the cavity must be zero. Thus the entire charge on the conductor lies on its outer surface, not on the cavity wall.

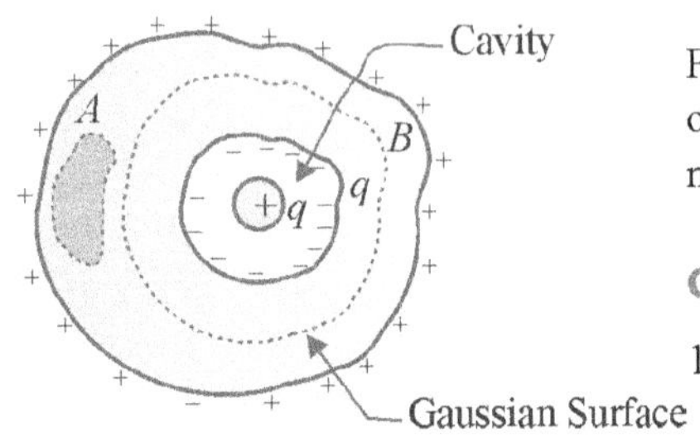


*Fig. 1.79*

### Charge placed inside the cavity

1. Suppose that there is a conductor inside the cavity but insulated from it and that the inner conductor has charge $q$. By Gauss's law

$$\oint \vec{E}.d\vec{A} = \frac{q_{in}}{\epsilon_0}$$

or

$$0 = \frac{q_{in}}{\epsilon_0}$$

Since $\vec{E}$ is zero inside the conductor, which gives $q_{in} = 0$. As the charge inside the cavity is $q$, so there must be a charge on the cavity wall, equal and opposite in sign to the charge $q$. If outer conductor is initially uncharged before the charge $q$ is inserted, there must be a charge on its outer surface, equal and opposite to the charge on the cavity wall, that is $q$.

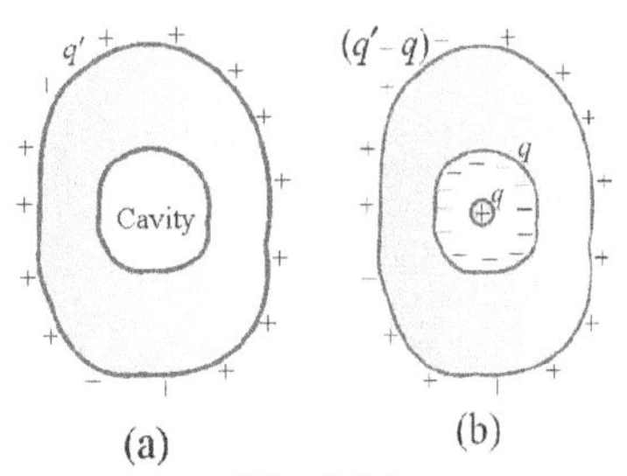


*Fig. 1.80*

2. Consider a charged conductor having charge $q'$ initially. A charge $q$ is placed in a cavity in the conductor. The charge on the outer surface of the conductor = $q' + q$.

3. Lines of field inside cavity due to charge at its centre

**Case 1 : Spherical cavity** **Case 2 : Non-spherical cavity**

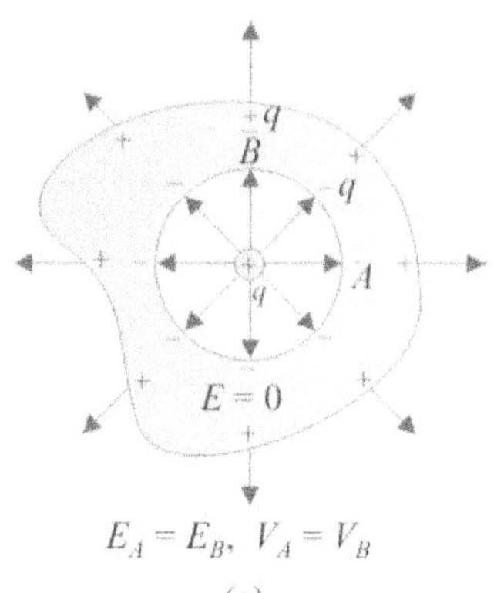


$E_A = E_B$, $V_A = V_B$

(a)

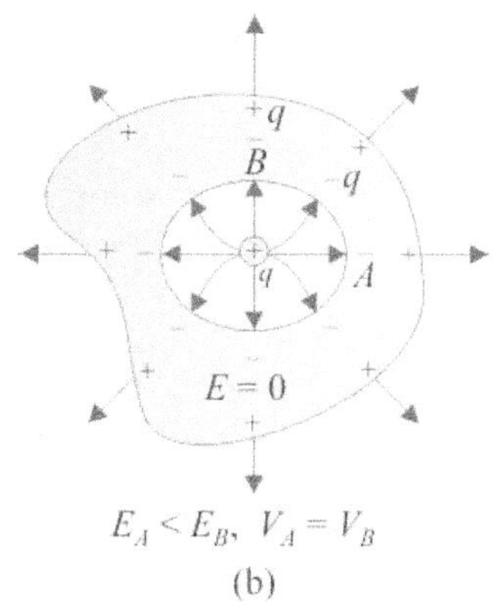


$E_A < E_B$, $V_A = V_B$

(b)

*Fig. 1.81*

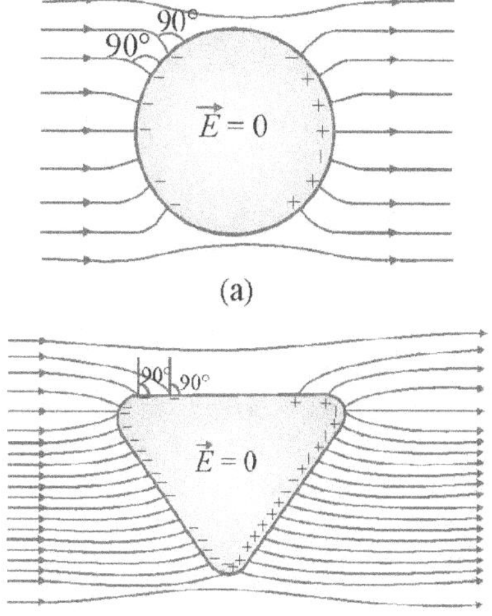


(b)

*Fig. 1.82*

## Conductor in external electric field

Consider an uncharged conductor is placed in an external electric field. The free electrons in the conductor distribute themselves on the surface as shown. Reducing the net electric field inside the conductor to zero and making the net field at the surface perpendicular to the surface.

## Potential of earthed conductor is zero

Let us consider two concentric conducting shells. Inner shell is given a charge $q$. The charges are induced at outer shell, as shown in *fig. 1.83*. The potential of any point on the surface of outer shell

$$V = \frac{1}{4\pi \in_0}\left[\frac{q}{b}-\frac{q}{b}+\frac{q}{b}\right]=\frac{1}{4\pi \in_0}\frac{q}{b}.$$

Now let outer shell is earthed. The charge on outer surface of outer shell neutralise by electrons coming from earth. But negative charge on inner surface of outer shell remain in tact because of attraction of charge of inner shell. Potential at any point on outer shell

$$V = \frac{1}{4\pi \in_0}\left\{\frac{q}{b}-\frac{q}{b}\right\}=0.$$

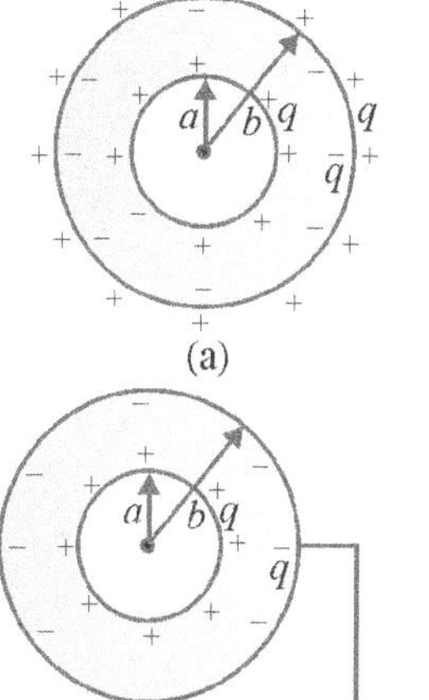


(b)

*Fig. 1.83*

**Ex. 28** **A point charge $q$ is placed on the apex of a cone of semi-vertex angle $\theta$. Show that the electric flux through the base of the cone is $\frac{q}{2\in_0}(1-\cos\theta)$.**

**Sol.**

Consider a Gaussian surface with its centre at the apex of the cone. The flux through the whole sphere is $\frac{q}{\in_0}$, so the flux through the base of the cone $\phi = \frac{A}{A_0}\frac{q}{\in_0}$

where $A$ = area of sphere below the base of the cone

and $A_0$ = area of whole sphere which is $4\pi R^2$.

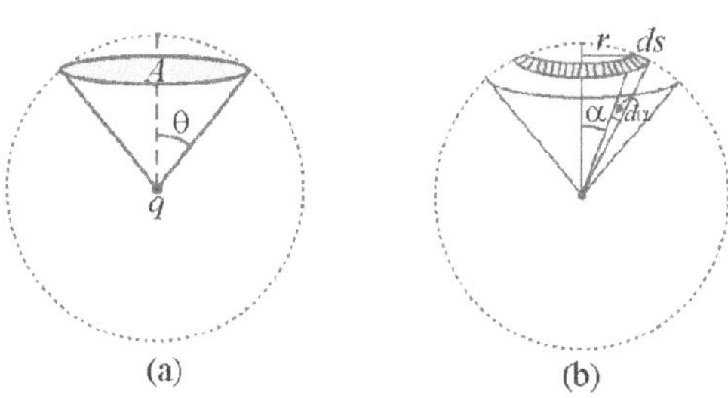


*Fig. 1.84*

To find $A$, choose a surface element confined in angle $d\alpha$ at an angle $\alpha$. The area of the element strip

$$dA = (2\pi r)ds$$

$$= 2\pi R\sin\alpha(Rd\alpha) \quad [r = R\sin\alpha]$$

$$= 2\pi R^2 \sin\alpha\, d\alpha$$

Surface area $\quad A = \int_0^{\theta} 2\pi R^2 \sin\alpha \, d\alpha$

or $\quad A = 2\pi R^2(1-\cos\theta)$

Thus desired flux $\quad \phi = \frac{A}{A_0}\frac{q}{\epsilon_0} = \frac{2\pi R^2(1-\cos\theta)}{4\pi R^2}\cdot\frac{q}{\epsilon_0}$

$$= \frac{q}{2\epsilon_0}(1-\cos\theta).$$

**Ex. 29** **Two charges $+q_1$ and $-q_2$ are placed at $A$ and $B$ respectively. A line of force emanates from $q_1$ at an angle $\alpha$ with the line $AB$. At what angle will it terminate at $-q_2$ ?**

**Sol.**

The number of lines of force emerges is proportional to the amount of charge. The line of force emanating from $q_1$ spread out equally in all directions. Hence lines of force per unit solid angle are $\frac{q_1}{4\pi}$ and the number of lines of force through cone of half angle $\alpha$ is $\frac{q_1}{4\pi}.2\pi(1-\cos\alpha)$.

Similarly the number of lines of force terminating on $-q_2$ at angle $\beta$ is

$$\frac{q_2}{4\pi}2\pi(1-\cos\beta)$$

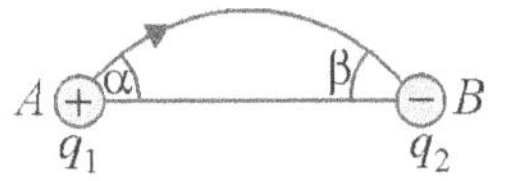

*Fig. 1.85*

As the total lines of force emanating from $q_1$ is equal to the total lines of force terminating to $q_2$, so

$$\frac{q_1}{4\pi}2\pi(1-\cos\alpha) = \frac{q_2}{4\pi}2\pi(1-\cos\beta)$$

or
$$\frac{q_1}{2}.2\sin^2\frac{\alpha}{2} = \frac{q_2}{2}.2\sin^2\frac{\beta}{2}$$

or
$$\sin\frac{\beta}{2} = \sqrt{\frac{q_1}{q_2}}\sin\frac{\alpha}{2}$$

$$\therefore \quad \beta = 2\sin^{-1}\left[\sqrt{\frac{q_1}{q_2}}\sin\frac{\alpha}{2}\right] \qquad \textit{Ans.}$$

## Application of Coulomb's law and Gauss's law

Coulomb's law is the fundamental law of electrostatics, but for symmetric charge distribution Gauss's law can be used. For electrostatics problems, Gauss's law is equivalent to Coulomb's law. In Gauss's law, the closed surface is of any shape. The Gaussian surface will often be a sphere, a cylinder, or some other symmetrical form. But it must always be a closed surface, so that a clear distinction can be made between points that are inside the surface, on the surface, and outside the surface.

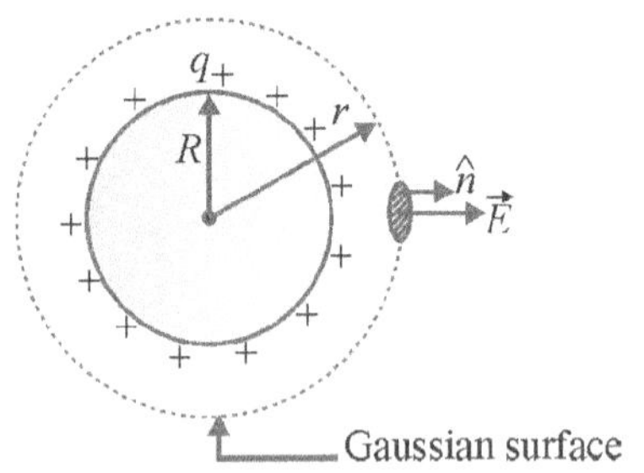


*Fig. 1.86*

## 1.13 APPLYING GAUSS'S LAW : SPHERICAL SYMMETRY

(i) **Charged conducting shell:** *Fig. 1.86* shows a charged spherical shell of total charge $q$ and radius $R$. The charge of the conducting shell will spread uniformly over its outer surface, so charge inside the shell will be zero.

For the Gaussian surface, $r \geq R$,

$$q_{in} = q.$$

By Gauss's law
$$\oint \vec{E}.d\vec{A} = \frac{q_{in}}{\epsilon_0}$$

or
$$\oint \vec{E}.dA\cos 0 = \frac{q}{\epsilon_0}$$

or
$$E\oint dA = \frac{q}{\epsilon_0}$$

or
$$E \times 4\pi r^2 = \frac{q}{\epsilon_0}$$

$$\therefore \quad E = \left(\frac{1}{4\pi\epsilon_0}\right)\frac{q}{r^2}$$

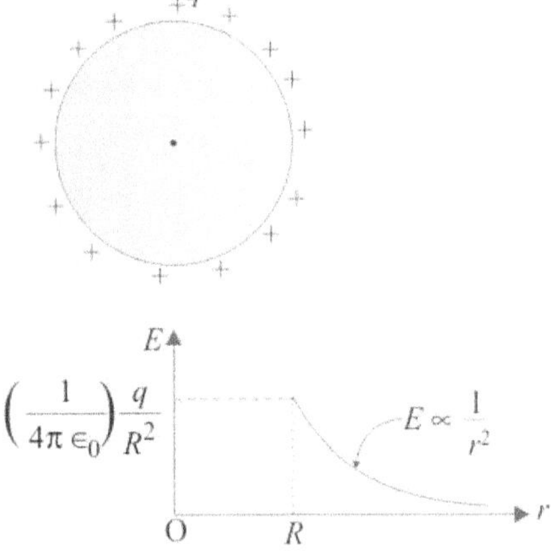


*Fig. 1.87.* Variation of E with r.

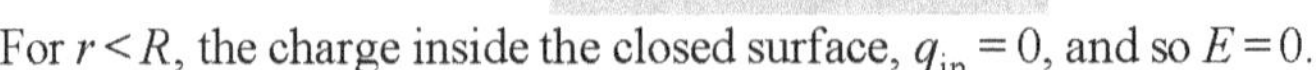

For $r < R$, the charge inside the closed surface, $q_{in} = 0$, and so $E = 0$.

**Note:** Above obtained results are also applicable to the conducting sphere.

**Electric potential :**

For the potential at $r \geq R$, the charge of the shell can be assumed at the centre of the shell, and so electric potential at a distance r from the centre of the shell,

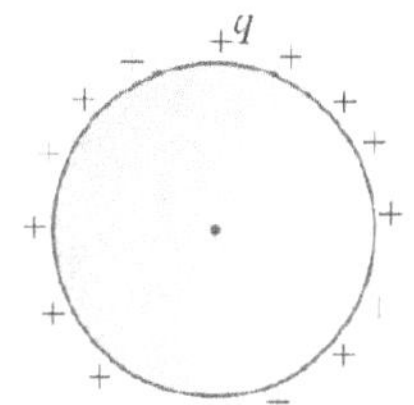


$$V = \left(\frac{1}{4\pi \epsilon_0}\right)\frac{q}{r}, \qquad r > R.$$

At surface of the shell, $r = R$, and so

$$V = \left(\frac{1}{4\pi \epsilon_0}\right)\frac{q}{R}, \qquad r = R$$

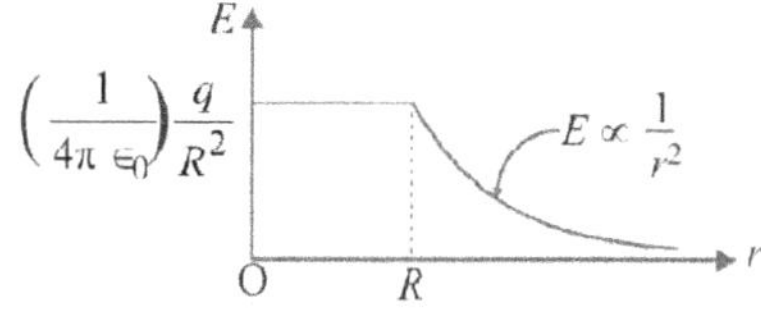


*Fig. 1.87.* Variation of E with r.

*Fig. 1.88*

For $r < R$, the electric field is zero, and so electric potential remain constant from centre to the surface of the shell.

$$\therefore \qquad V = \left(\frac{1}{4\pi \epsilon_0}\right)\frac{q}{R}, \qquad r < R$$

**Self energy :**

The work done in charging the body will store in term of its self energy. In the charging process, the potential of the surface of the shell increases from zero to a value $\left(\frac{1}{4\pi \epsilon_0}\right)\frac{q}{R}$, so the average potential during charging

$$V_{av} = \frac{\left[0 + \frac{1}{4\pi \epsilon_0}\frac{q}{R}\right]}{2} = \frac{1}{8\pi \epsilon_0}\frac{q}{R}$$

Self energy.

$$U = \text{work done in charging}$$
$$= V_{av} \times q$$
$$= \left(\frac{1}{8\pi \epsilon_0}\frac{q}{R}\right)q$$

or

$$U = \frac{1}{8\pi \epsilon_0}\frac{q^2}{R}.$$

As there is no electric field inside the shell, so this energy resides from surface to infinity.

**Note:**

1. A body is given a charge $q$ in air and isolated from the source, its potential

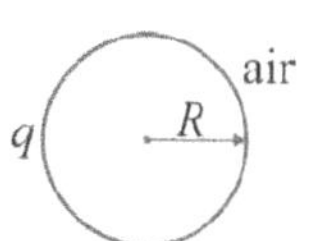


*Fig. 1.89*

$$V = \frac{1}{4\pi \epsilon_0}\frac{q}{R},$$

where $R$ is the radius of the body. When this body is taken into a dielectric medium of constant $k$ (say in water), its potential becomes

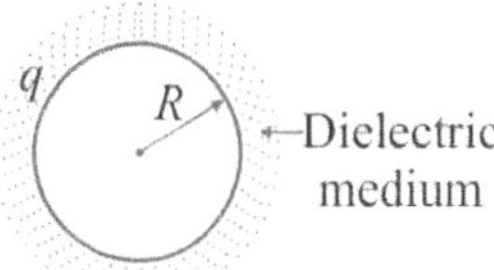


*Fig. 1.90*

$$V' = \frac{1}{4\pi \epsilon_0 k}\frac{q}{R} = \frac{V}{k}$$

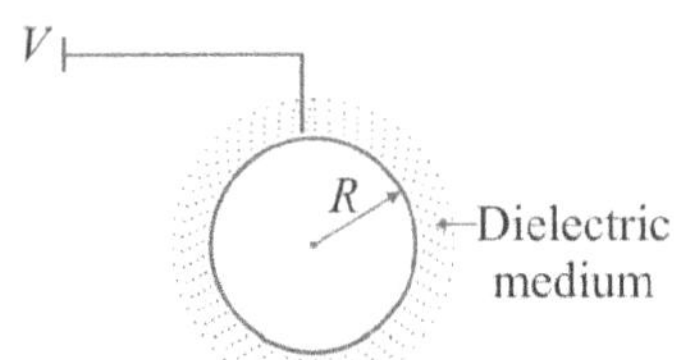


Fig. 1.91

2. A body is charged to a source of potential $V$ and the source remains connected with the body. When this body is taken into a medium its potential remain same but charge increases to $kq$. The new potential of the body

$$V' = \frac{1}{4\pi \epsilon_0 k} \frac{q'}{R}$$

Since $V' = V$,

$$\therefore \quad \frac{1}{4\pi \epsilon_0 k} \frac{q'}{R} = \frac{1}{4\pi \epsilon_0 k} \frac{q}{R}$$

$$\Rightarrow \quad q' = kq.$$

**(ii) Uniformly charged sphere (non conductor)**

Consider a charged sphere of total charge $q$ and radius $R$. Choose a Gaussian surface with $r > R$, the entire charge lies within it. The charge produces an electric field on the Gaussian surface as if the charge were a point charge located at the centre, and so

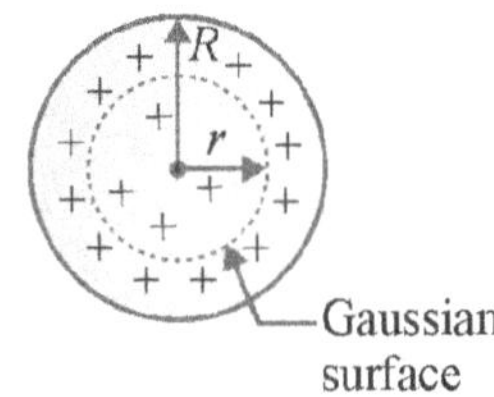


Fig. 1.92

$$E = \left(\frac{1}{4\pi \epsilon_0}\right) \frac{q}{r^2}, \; r > R$$

For the Gaussian surface at $r < R$, charge enclosed in the sphere of radius $r$,

$$q_{in} = \frac{q}{\frac{4}{3}\pi R^3} \times \frac{4}{3}\pi r^3 = \frac{qr^3}{R^3}$$

By Gauss's law

$$\oint \vec{E}.d\vec{A} = \frac{q'_{in}}{\epsilon_0}$$

or

$$E \times 4\pi r^2 = \frac{qr^3 / R^3}{\epsilon_0}$$

$$\therefore \quad E = \left(\frac{1}{4\pi \epsilon_0}\right) \frac{qr}{R^3}$$

At $r = 0, E = 0.$

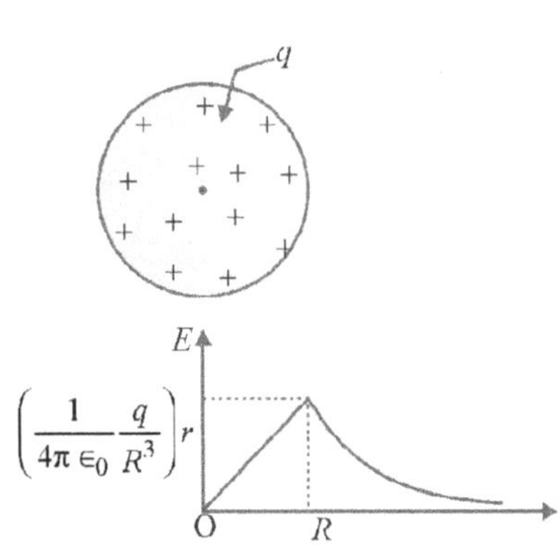


Fig. 1.93

**Electric potential :**

For the potential at $r \geq R$, the charge of the sphere can be assumed at its centre, and so electric potential at a distance r from the centre of the sphere,

$$V = \left(\frac{1}{4\pi \epsilon_0}\right) \frac{q}{r} \quad , \quad r > R$$

At the surface of the shell, $r = R$, and so

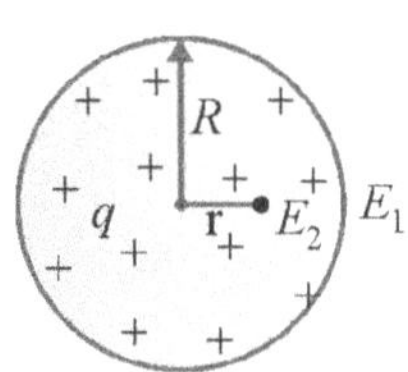


Fig. 1.94

$$V = \left(\frac{1}{4\pi \epsilon_0}\right) \frac{q}{R} \quad , \quad r = R$$

Electric potential at $r < R$ : If $E_1$ and $E_2$ are the electric fields outside and inside the sphere, then

$$E_1 = \left(\frac{1}{4\pi \epsilon_0}\right) \frac{q}{r^2} \text{ and } E_2 = \left(\frac{1}{4\pi \epsilon_0}\right) \frac{qr}{R^3}.$$

Electric potential at any point is defined as,

$$V = -\int_{\infty}^{r} \vec{E}.d\vec{r}$$

$$= -\left[\int_{\infty}^{R} E_1 dr + \int_{R}^{r} E_2 dr\right]$$

$$= -\left[\int_{\infty}^{R}\left(\frac{1}{4\pi \in_0}\frac{q}{r^2}\right)dr + \int_{R}^{r}\left(\frac{1}{4\pi \in_0}\frac{qr}{R^3}\right)dr\right]$$

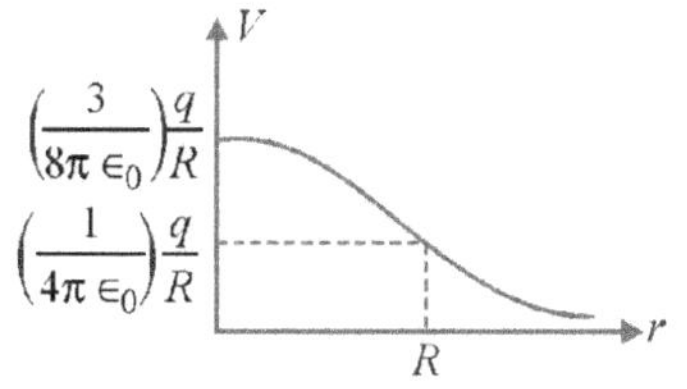

Fig. 1.95

After simplifying, we get $$V = \left(\frac{1}{4\pi \in_0}\right) q \frac{\left[3R^2 - r^2\right]}{2R^3}$$

At the centre of the sphere, $r = 0$, $$V = \left(\frac{1}{4\pi \in_0}\right)\frac{3q}{2R}$$

i.e., $$V_{\text{centre}} = \frac{3}{2}V_{\text{surface}}$$

**Self energy of the charged sphere**

*Fig. 1.95* shows a sphere of total charge $q$ and radius $R$. Take an element of thickness dr at a radial distance r all over the sphere. If $q_1$ and $q_2$ are the charges on the element and the sphere inside, then the energy of this system,

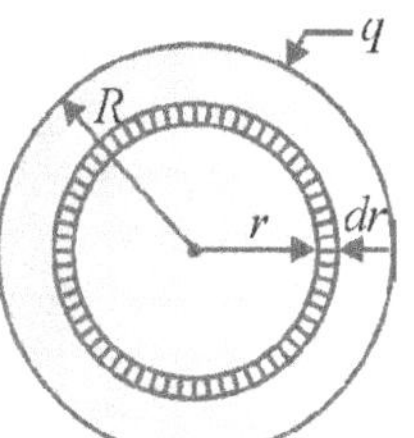

Fig. 1.96

$$dU = \frac{1}{4\pi \in_0}\frac{q_1 q_2}{r}$$

where $$q_1 = \left(\frac{q}{\frac{4}{3}\pi R^3}\right)4\pi r^2 dr = \frac{3q\,r^2 dr}{R^3},$$

and $$q_2 = \left(\frac{q}{\frac{4}{3}\pi R^3}\right)\frac{4}{3}\pi r^3 = \frac{q\,r^3}{R^3}$$

The total energy of the charged sphere

$$U = \int_0^R dU = \left(\frac{1}{4\pi \in_0}\right)\int_0^R \frac{\left(\frac{3q}{R^3}r^2 dr\right)\left(\frac{qr^3}{R^3}\right)}{r}$$

$$= \frac{3}{5}\left(\frac{1}{4\pi \in_0}\right)\frac{q^2}{R}$$

or $$U = \frac{3}{20\pi \in_0}\frac{q^2}{R}.$$

**Ex. 30** **Can a metal sphere of radius 1 cm can hold a charge of 1 coulomb?**

**Sol.**

No. The potential of the surface of the sphere is given by

$$V = \frac{1}{4\pi \in_0}\frac{q}{r}$$

$$= 9\times 10^9 \times \frac{1}{1\times 10^{-2}}$$

$$= 9\times 10^{11}\ V.$$

This potential is very much greater than that required to ionise the air ($3 \times 10^4 V$) and so charge will leak to the surrounding air.

## 1.14 APPLYING GAUSS'S LAW : CYLINDRICAL SYMMETRY

*Fig. 1.97* shows a small part of an infinitely long cylindrical nonconducting rod with a uniform linear charge density $\lambda$. Let us find an expression for the electric field $\vec{E}$ at a distance r from the axis of the rod.

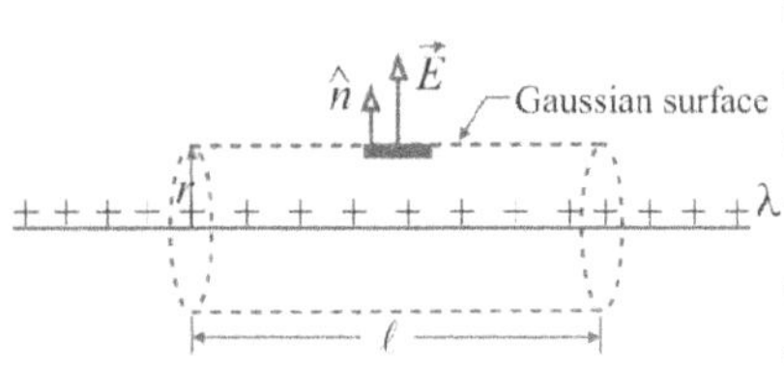


*Fig. 1.97*

Choose a Gaussian surface in the form of a circular cylinder of radius r and length $\ell$, coaxial with the rod. The Gaussian surface must be closed, so we include two end caps as part of the surface. There is no flux through the end caps because $\vec{E}$, being radially directed, and parallel to the end caps at every point.

Using Gauss's law, we have

$$\oint \vec{E}.d\vec{A} = \frac{q_{in}}{\epsilon_0}$$

$$\text{or} \quad \left[\int \vec{E}.d\vec{A}\right]_{\text{end caps}} + \left[\int \vec{E}.d\vec{A}\right]_{\text{cylindrical surface}} = \frac{\lambda\ell}{\epsilon_0}$$

$$\text{or} \quad 0 + \int E\,A\cos 0° = \frac{\lambda\ell}{\epsilon_0}$$

$$\text{or} \quad E\int A = \frac{\lambda\ell}{\epsilon_0}$$

$$\text{or} \quad E \times 2\pi r\ell = \frac{\lambda\ell}{\epsilon_0}$$

$$\therefore \quad E = \frac{\lambda}{2\pi \epsilon_0 r}$$

This is the electric field due to an infinitely long, straight line of charge at a point that is at a radial distance r from the line. The direction of $\vec{E}$ is radially outward from the line of charge if the charge is positive. The result also approximates the field of a finite line of charge, at point that is not too near the ends as compared to the distance from the line.

**Electric potential**

Let us consider an infinite line of charge of uniform linear charge density $\lambda$. The electric field at any point $P$ at a distance r from the line of charge is given by

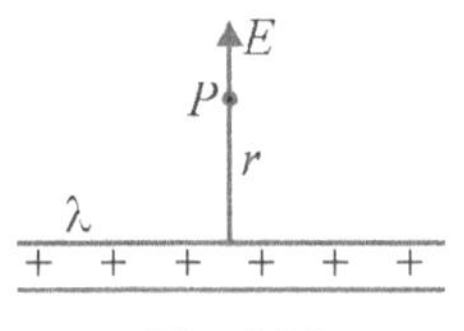


*Fig. 1.98*

$$E = \frac{\lambda}{2\pi \epsilon_0 r}$$

The electric potential at the point

$$V = -\int_{\infty}^{r} \vec{E}.d\vec{r}$$

$$= -\int_{\infty}^{r} \frac{\lambda}{2\pi \epsilon_0 r} dr \cos 0°$$

$$= -\frac{\lambda}{2\pi \epsilon_0} |ln\, r|_{\infty}^{r} = \infty$$

Thus the electric potential due to infinitely long line charge is infinite everywhere. In practical problems, we are interested in potential difference between two points at finite separation. In this case choice of zero potential is arbitrary. If we take $V_Q$ = zero at $r = r_0$, then

$$V_P - V_Q = -\int_{r_0}^{r} \frac{\lambda}{2\pi \epsilon_0 r} dr = \frac{-\lambda}{2\pi \epsilon_0} |lnr|_{r_0}^{r}$$

or
$$V_P - V_Q = -\left[\frac{\lambda}{2\pi \epsilon_0}(ln\,r - ln\,r_0)\right]$$

As $V_Q = 0$

$$\therefore \quad V_P = -\frac{\lambda}{2\pi \epsilon_0}\left[ln\,r - ln\,r_0\right].$$

## 1.15 LINE CHARGE OF FINITE LENGTH

Consider a line charge of uniform linear charge density $\lambda$. Let us find the electric field at a point $P$, distance r from the line charge.

Take an element of length $dx$ at a distance $x$ from the reference point as shown in *Fig. 1.99*

The element subtends an angle $\theta$ from the line of $r$. The charge on the element, $dq = \lambda dx$.

The electric field due to the charge of the element

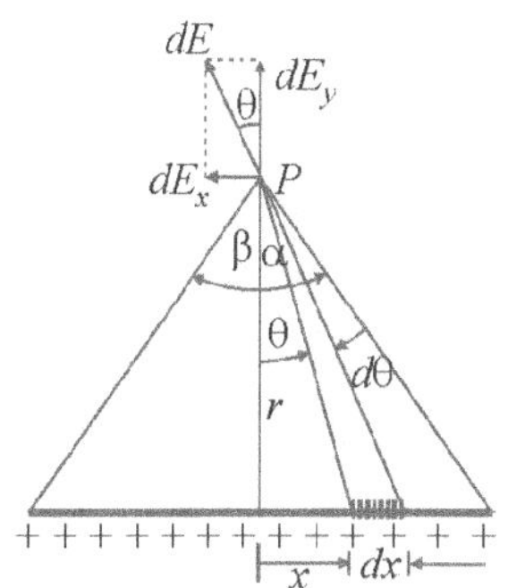

*Fig. 1.99*

$$E = \left(\frac{1}{4\pi \epsilon_0}\right)\frac{dq}{\left(x^2 + r^2\right)} = \frac{1}{4\pi \epsilon_0}\frac{\lambda dx}{\left(x^2 + r^2\right)} \quad ....(i)$$

From the figure $x = r\tan\theta$,

$$\therefore \quad dx = r\sec^2\theta(d\theta)$$

and
$$dE = \left(\frac{1}{4\pi \epsilon_0}\right)\frac{\lambda\left(r\sec^2\theta d\theta\right)}{r^2\tan^2\theta + r^2}$$

$$= \left(\frac{1}{4\pi \epsilon_0}\right)\frac{\lambda r\sec^2\theta d\theta}{r^2\left(\tan^2\theta + 1\right)}$$

$$= \left(\frac{1}{4\pi \epsilon_0}\right)\frac{\lambda d\theta}{r}$$

For the simplicity, we can resolve this field into two perpendicular components;

$$dE_x = dE\sin\theta \text{ and } dE_y = dE\cos\theta$$

The net electric field along $x$ - direction

$$E_x = \int_{-\beta}^{\alpha} dE\sin\theta$$

$$= \frac{\lambda}{4\pi \epsilon_0 r}\int_{-\beta}^{\alpha}\sin\theta\, d\theta$$

$$= \frac{\lambda}{4\pi \epsilon_0 r}\left|-\cos\theta\right|_{-\beta}^{\alpha}$$

or
$$E_x = \frac{\lambda}{4\pi \epsilon_0 r}\left[\cos\beta - \cos\alpha\right]$$

Similarly
$$E_y = \int_{-\beta}^{\alpha} dE\cos\theta$$

$$= \frac{\lambda}{4\pi \in_0 r}\int_{-\beta}^{\alpha} \cos\theta\, d\theta$$

$$= \frac{\lambda}{4\pi \in_0 r}\left|\sin\theta\right|_{-\beta}^{\alpha}$$

or $$E_y = \frac{\lambda}{4\pi \in_0 r}[\sin\alpha + \sin\beta]$$

The resultant field at point $P$ $$E = \sqrt{E_x^2 + E_y^2}$$

The angle made by resultant with direction of $E_y$, $\tan\gamma = \dfrac{E_x}{E_y}$.

## Special cases

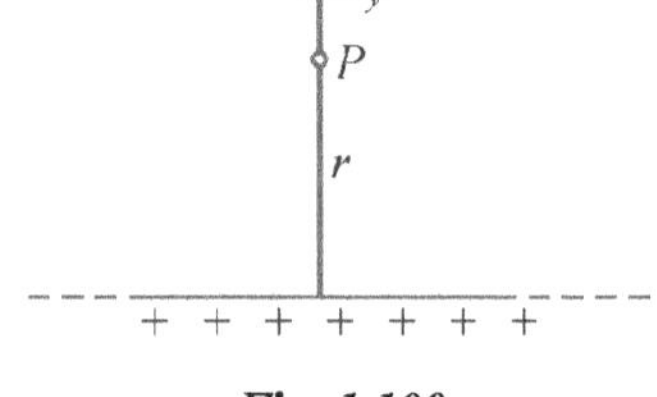


*Fig. 1.100*

1. Infinitely long line charge $\alpha = \dfrac{\pi}{2}$ and $\beta = \dfrac{\pi}{2}$

$\therefore$ $$E_x = 0 \quad \text{and} \quad E_y = \frac{\lambda}{4\pi \in_0 r}\left[\sin\frac{\pi}{2} + \sin\frac{\pi}{2}\right]$$

$$= \frac{\lambda}{2\pi \in_0 r}$$

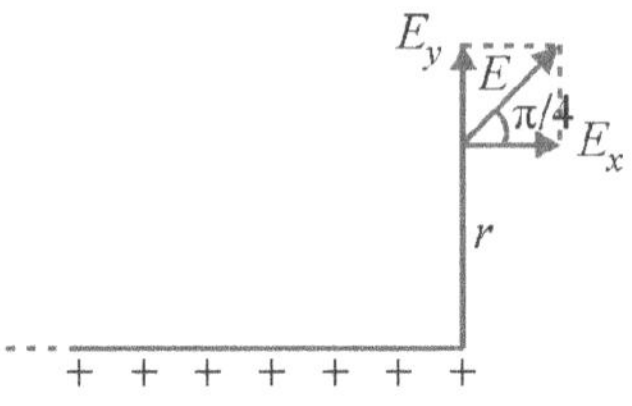

2. Along the end of the line charge $\alpha = \dfrac{\pi}{2}$ and $\beta = 0°$

*Fig. 1.101*

$$E_x = \frac{\lambda}{4\pi \in_0 r}\left[\cos 0° - \cos\frac{\pi}{2}\right]$$

$$= \frac{\lambda}{4\pi \in_0 r}$$

and $$E_y = \frac{\lambda}{4\pi \in_0 r}\left[\sin\frac{\pi}{2} + \sin 0\right]$$

$$= \frac{\lambda}{4\pi \in_0 r}$$

$\therefore$ $$E = \sqrt{E_x^2 + E_y^2} = \frac{\lambda}{2\sqrt{2}\,\pi \in_0 r}$$

$$\tan\gamma = \frac{E_x}{E_y} = 1$$

$\therefore$ $$\gamma = \frac{\pi}{4} \text{ or } 45°.$$

## 1.16 APPLYING GAUSS'S LAW : PLANAR SYMMETRY

(i) **Non conducting sheet :** *Fig. 1.102* shows a portion of a thin, infinite, non conducting sheet with a uniform surface charge density $\sigma$. Let us find the electric field $\vec{E}$ at a distance r in front of the sheet. By symmetry, the field must have the same magnitude and the opposite directions at two points equidistance from the sheet on opposite sides of it. The field lines are directed away from the sheet and perpendicular to it.

A Gaussian surface is a closed cylinder with end caps of area $A$, arranged to penetrate the sheet perpendicular as shown. Because the field lines do not pierce the curved surface. So there is no flux through this portion of the Gaussian surface. Thus the total flux through the Gaussian surface reduces to the flux through end caps, which is simply $EA + EA = 2EA$. Thus by Gauss's law

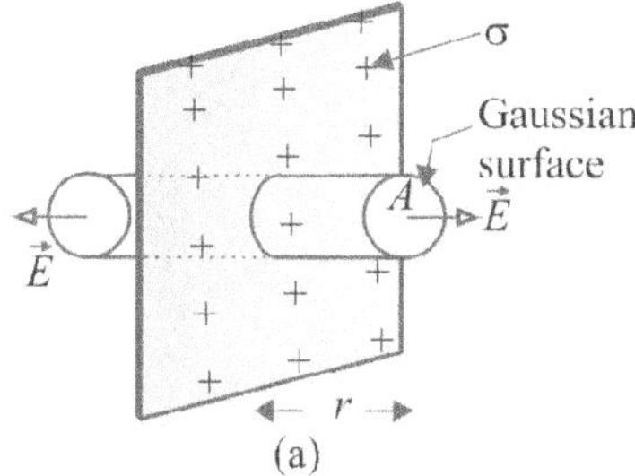

(a)
Fig. (a) Perspective view,

$$\oint \vec{E}.d\vec{A} = \frac{q_{in}}{\epsilon_0}$$

or
$$2EA = \frac{\sigma A}{\epsilon_0}$$

$\therefore$
$$E = \frac{\sigma}{2\epsilon_0}.$$

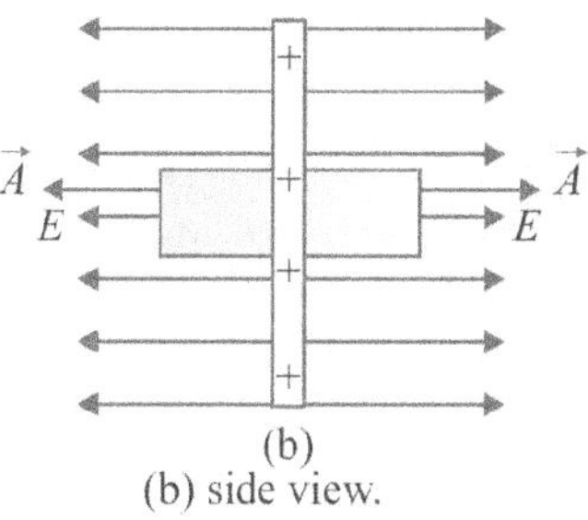

(b)
(b) side view.

*Fig. 1.102*

Thus the magnitude of the field is independent of the distance from the sheet. In practice an infinite sheet of charge does not exist. The above formula can be used for sheet of finite size if points under consideration are not near the edges of the sheet and the distances from the sheet are small compared to the size of the sheet.

(ii) **Conducting sheet :** When a charge is given to a conducting sheet, it distributes itself over the entire outer surface of the sheet. For the thin sheet, the charge distributes on both of its faces. Thus a conducting sheet is equivalent to the combination of two non-conducting sheets, with the same charge density. Suppose $\sigma$ is the surface charge density.

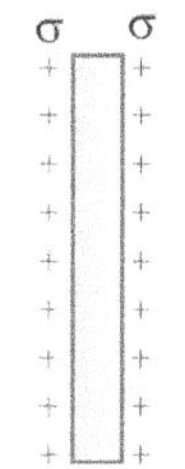

(a) A conducting sheet of charge.

≅

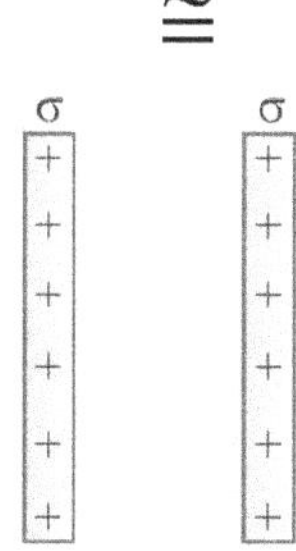

(b) Two non-conducting sheets of charge.

*Fig. 1.104*

The electric field thus arises from the superposition of the fields of two non-conducting charged sheets. Thus field on the right of the plate

$$E_R = \frac{\sigma}{2\epsilon_0} + \frac{\sigma}{2\epsilon_0} = \frac{\sigma}{\epsilon_0}$$

and field at the left of the plate

$$E_L = \frac{\sigma}{2\epsilon_0} + \frac{\sigma}{2\epsilon_0} = \frac{\sigma}{\epsilon_0}$$

Field inside the plate

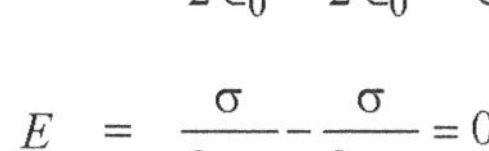

$$E = \frac{\sigma}{2\epsilon_0} - \frac{\sigma}{2\epsilon_0} = 0$$

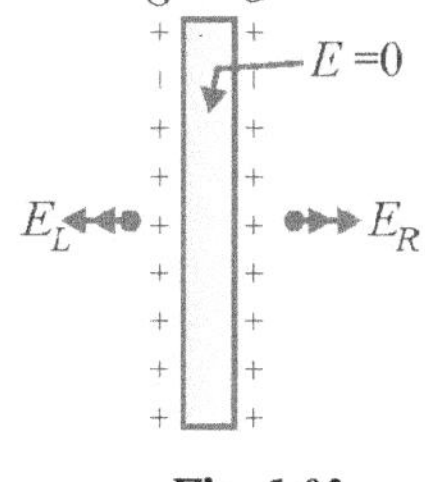

*Fig. 1.03*

**Note :** For surface charge density $\sigma$, the total charge on non-conducting sheet of area $A$, $q = \sigma A$. The total charge on conducting sheet, $q' = 2\sigma A = 2q$.

(iii) **Electric field due to two parallel non-conducting sheets of charge :**

Consider two infinite sheets of charge with surface charge densities $\sigma_1$ and $\sigma_2$ on them.

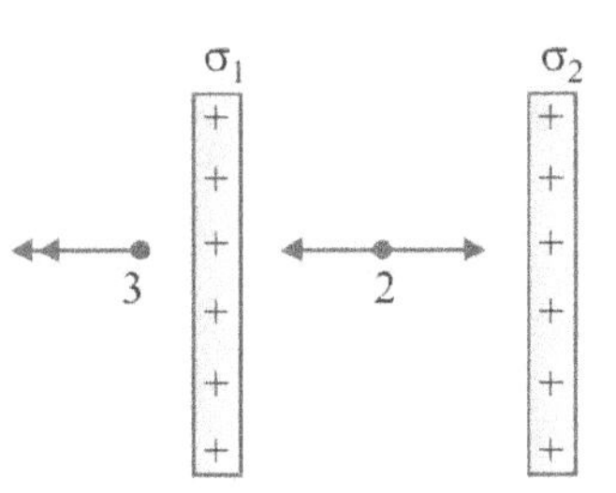


Fig. 1.105

Field at the point 1,
$$E_1 = \frac{\sigma_1}{2\epsilon_0} + \frac{\sigma_2}{2\epsilon_0} = \frac{\sigma_1 + \sigma_2}{2\epsilon_0}$$

2,
$$E_2 = \frac{\sigma_1}{2\epsilon_0} - \frac{\sigma_2}{2\epsilon_0} = \frac{\sigma_1 - \sigma_2}{2\epsilon_0}$$

3,
$$E_3 = \frac{\sigma_1}{2\epsilon_0} + \frac{\sigma_2}{2\epsilon_0} = \frac{\sigma_1 + \sigma_2}{2\epsilon_0}$$

**Special case :** For $\sigma_1 = \sigma$ and $\sigma_2 = -\sigma$

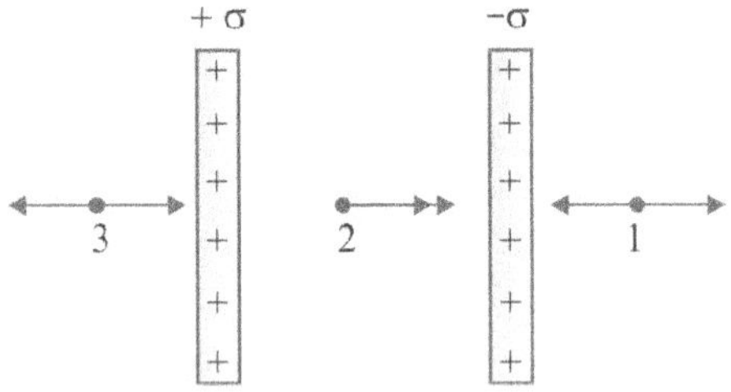

$$E_1 = \frac{\sigma - \sigma}{2\epsilon_0} = 0$$

$$E_2 = \frac{\sigma - (-\sigma)}{2\epsilon_0} = \frac{\sigma}{\epsilon_0}$$

$$E_3 = \frac{\sigma - \sigma}{2\epsilon_0} = 0$$

Fig. 1.106

Thus in case of two parallel sheets with equal and opposite charge densities, the field exists only between the sheets.

**Ex. 31** **(a) Two large thin conducting plates are placed parallel to each other at some separation. One of the plates is given a charge $q$, find the charges on the faces of the other plate.**

**(b) If one of the plates is earthed and other plate is given charge $q$, find charges on the faces of the plates.**

## Sol.

(a) *Fig. 1.107* shows two large conducting plates, left plate has charge $q$. Because of induction of the charge of left plate, the negative charge $-q$ will induce on the front face of the right plate. As net charge of the right plate is zero, so $+q$ will appear on the other face of the plate.

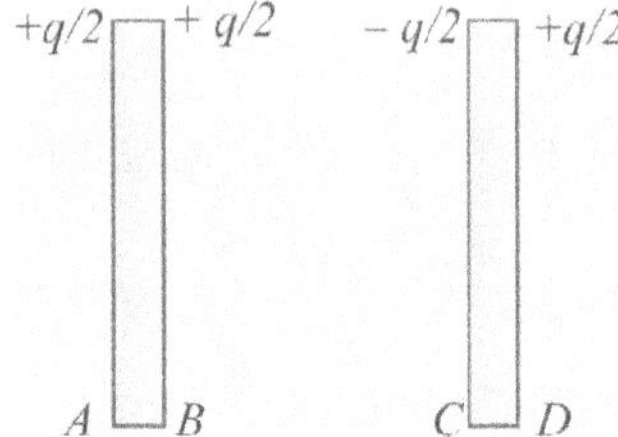


Fig. 1.107

If $A$, $B$, $C$ and $D$ represent the faces of the plates, then

$$q_A = +\frac{q}{2}, \quad q_B = +\frac{q}{2}$$

$$q_C = -\frac{q}{2}, \quad q_D = +\frac{q}{2}$$

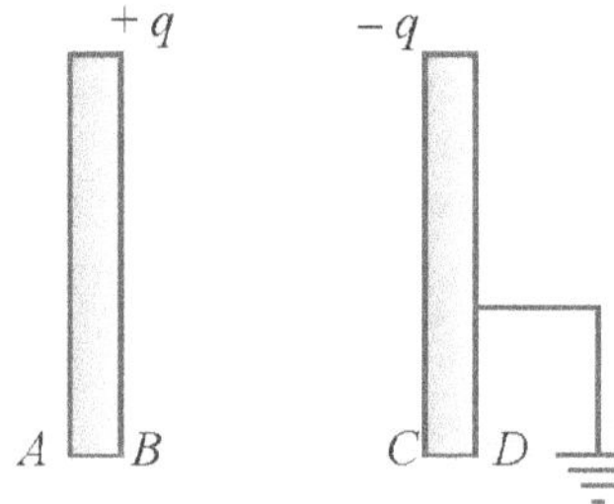


Fig. 1.108

(b) When the plate is earthed the charge of the face D gets neutralise by the electrons coming from the earth, and so

$$q_A = 0, \quad q_B = +q$$
$$q_C = -q, \quad q_D = 0.$$

**Ex. 32** **Two large thin conducting plates with charges, $q_1$ and $q_2$ are placed parallel to each other, find charges on the faces of the plates.**

## Sol.

Charges of the plates will distribute equally on their faces, as shown. In addition to these charges, the charges induce due to mutual interaction. It can be easily understand by the *fig. 1.109* .

If $A$, $B$, $C$ and $D$ represent the faces of the plates, then

$$q_A = \frac{q_1 + q_2}{2}$$

$$q_B = \frac{q_1 - q_2}{2}$$

$$q_C = -\left(\frac{q_1 - q_2}{2}\right)$$

and
$$q_D = \left(\frac{q_1 + q_2}{2}\right)$$

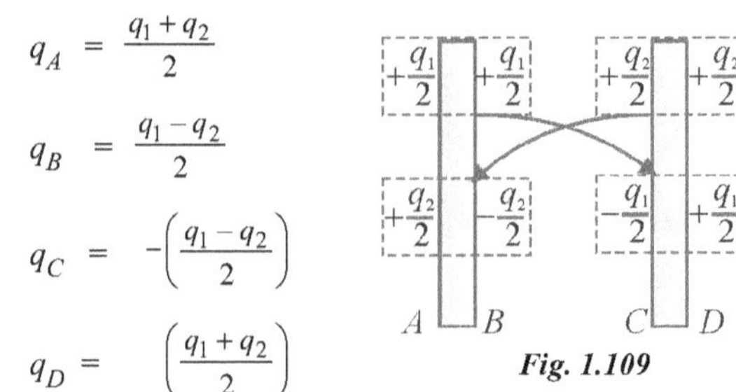


Fig. 1.109

**Special cases :**

1 If $q_1 = +q$ and $q_2 = +q$, then

$$q_A = q$$
$$q_B = 0$$
$$q_C = 0$$
$$q_D = q$$

*Fig. 110*

Thus when equal and same sign of charges are given to the plates, the charges will appear on the far faces of the plates.

2. If $q_1 = +q$ and $q_2 = -q$, then

$$q_A = 0$$
$$q_B = +q$$
$$q_C = -q$$

and $$q_D = 0$$

*Fig. 1.111*

Thus when plates are given equal and opposite charges, the charges will appear on the near faces of the plates.

**Ex. 33 Three identical metal plates with large surface are kept parallel to each other as shown in *fig. 1.112*. The left most plate is given a charge $Q$, the right most a charge $-2Q$ and the middle one remain neutral. Find the charge appearing on the outer surface of the right most plate.**

**Sol.**

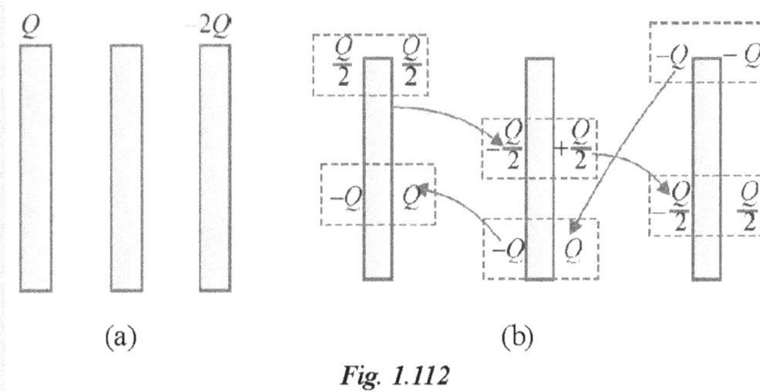

*Fig. 1.112*

Induce charge will appear on the faces on the plates in addition to the charges on the plates. The charge on the outer surface of the right most plate,

$$q_{net} = -Q + \frac{Q}{2} = -\frac{Q}{2}. \qquad \textit{Ans.}$$

## 1.17 CONDUCTOR OF ANY SHAPE

Consider a charged conductor of irregular shape. Surface charge density on it varies from point to point. Take a small element of area A, with surface charge density $\sigma$. Let us construct a Gaussian surface in the shape of a cylinder. Electric field is directed outward and perpendicular to the surface at that point. So curved surface does not contribute to the flux. Thus the contribution to the flux is through the end cap only, which is EA.

From Gauss's law

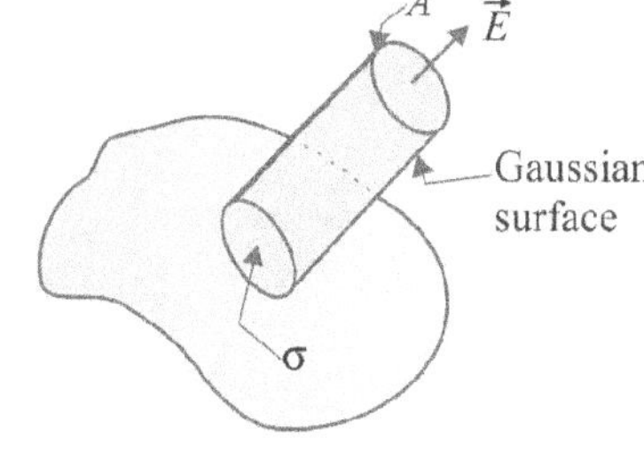


*Fig. 1.113*

$$\oint \vec{E}.d\vec{A} = \frac{q_{in}}{\epsilon_0}$$

or $$EA = \frac{\sigma A}{\epsilon_0}$$

or $$E = \frac{\sigma}{\epsilon_0}.$$

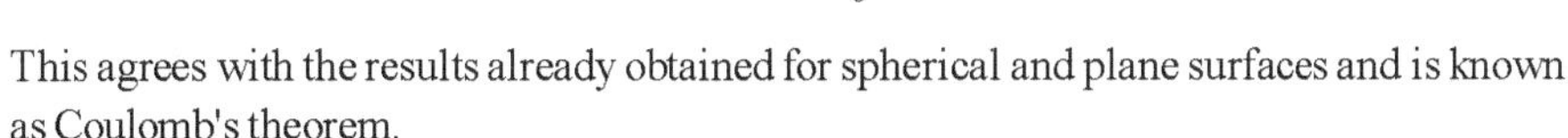

This agrees with the results already obtained for spherical and plane surfaces and is known as Coulomb's theorem.

## 1.18 MECHANICAL FORCE ON THE CHARGED CONDUCTOR

It is known to us that similar charges repel each other, hence the charge on any part of surface of the conductor is repelled by the charge on its remaining part. The surface of the conductor thus experiences a force as the charge is bound to the surface.

Let us consider a small element of conductor of area $\Delta A$. If $\vec{E}_1$ and $\vec{E}_2$ are the fields produced by the element and rest of the conductor, then resultant field at point P outside the conductor

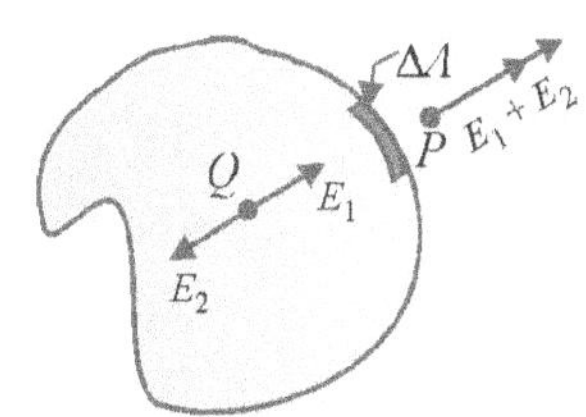


*Fig. 1.114*

$$E = E_1 + E_2 = \frac{\sigma}{\epsilon_0} \quad \ldots(i)$$

and field at point Q inside the conductor

$$-E_1 + E_2 = 0 \quad \ldots(ii)$$

On solving above equations, we get

$$E_1 = E_2 = \frac{\sigma}{2\epsilon_0}$$

Force exerted by rest part of the conductor on the element,

$$\Delta F = E_2 q_1$$

$$= \frac{\sigma}{2\epsilon_0} \times (\sigma \Delta A)$$

or

$$\frac{\Delta F}{\Delta A} = \frac{\sigma^2}{2\epsilon_0} = \frac{\epsilon_0}{2}(\sigma/\epsilon_0)^2 = \frac{1}{2}\epsilon_0 E^2$$

For medium of dielectric constant k,

$$\Delta F / \Delta A = \frac{1}{2}\epsilon_0 k E^2.$$

Thus the mechanical force per unit area on the charged conductor is $\sigma^2 / 2\epsilon_0$.

## 1.19 ENERGY DENSITY

The electrostatic energy due to a charge on a conductor remains in the medium surrounding the conductor. The charge on the conductor simply defines the surface condition existing in the electric field. So the energy is due to electric field which surrounds the medium. The force on the $\Delta A$ area of the charged surface

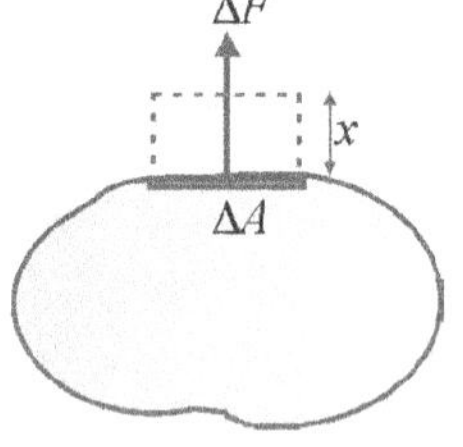

*Fig. 1.115*

$$\Delta F = \left(\frac{\epsilon_0}{2}E^2\right)\Delta A.$$

If the surface is displaced along the direction of force, then

the work done = force × displacement

or

$$\Delta W = \left(\frac{\epsilon_0 E^2}{2}\right)\Delta A x.$$

This work done is stored as energy in the medium. Here $(\Delta A)x$ is the volume swept, and so energy per unit volume or energy density

$$u = \frac{1}{2}\epsilon_0 E^2$$

**Note:**

1. The direction of $\vec{E}$ is immaterial in considering its energy, because it is either positive or negative, $E^2$ is always positive and , so there is always a pull on the charged surface.
2. For a sphere of radius $R$, with charge $q$,

$$E = \frac{1}{4\pi\epsilon_0 k}\frac{q}{R^2}$$

$$\therefore \quad u = \frac{1}{2}\epsilon_0 k\left[\frac{1}{4\pi\epsilon_0 k}\frac{q}{R^2}\right]^2 \text{ in a medium}$$

$$= \left(\frac{1}{32\pi^2\epsilon_0 k}\right)\frac{q^2}{R^4}.$$

### The electron volt

When any charged particle is accelerated through a potential $V$, it acquires a kinetic energy.

$$K = qV \text{ J}$$

For an electron or proton, $q = e = 1.6 \times 10^{-19}$ C

$$\therefore \quad K = (1.60 \times 10^{-19})\, V \text{ J}$$

This amount is very small and is multiple of $1.60 \times 10^{-19}$, hence we introduce a new unit of energy, known as electron volt ($eV$). Thus

$$1eV = 1.6 \times 10^{-19} \text{ J}$$

### Force on an uncharged conductor placed in an electric field

Let a small sphere A of volume $V$ is placed at a distance $r$ from a point charge $q$ at $O$. The dotted lines show the direction of the lines of the force before the introduction of the sphere, while the full lines show the direction of lines of force when sphere is placed in the field. Assuming no distortion of the field occurs due to the presence of the sphere, the intensity of electric field at the centre of the sphere

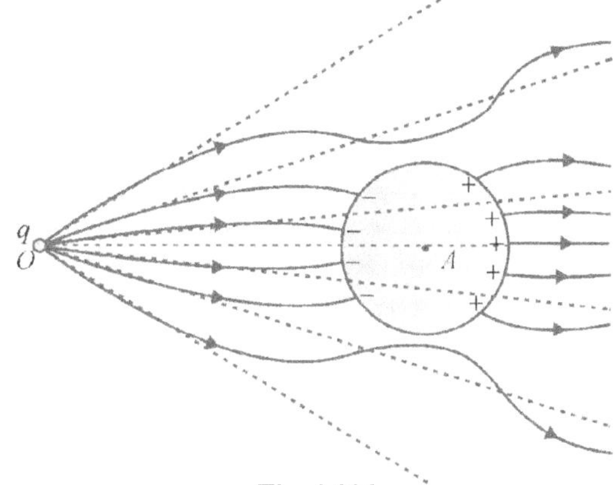

Fig. 1.116

$$E = \left(\frac{1}{4\pi \epsilon_0 k}\right)\frac{q}{r^2}$$

where $k$ is the dielectric constant of the medium between $O$ and $A$.
The potential energy which is confined in volume $V$,

$$U = \frac{1}{2}\epsilon_0 kE^2V = \frac{q^2V}{32\pi^2 \epsilon_0 kr^4}$$

Let $F$ be the force that the sphere experiences due to the field, then

$$F = -\frac{dU}{dr}$$

$$= -\frac{d}{dr}\left[\frac{q^2V}{32\pi^2 \epsilon_0 kr^4}\right]$$

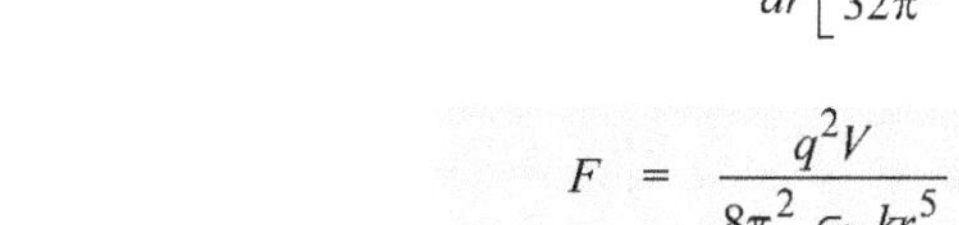

or $$F = \frac{q^2V}{8\pi^2 \epsilon_0 kr^5}.$$

## 1.20 ELECTRIC FIELD DUE TO CHARGED RING

Let us consider a ring of radius $R$ with a uniformly distributed charge of density $\lambda$ per unit length. We may imagine the ring to be made of insulating material, so that the charges can be regarded fixed in place.
Take a small element of ring of length $ds$. Since $\lambda$ is the charge per unit length, so the charge on the element

$$dq = \lambda ds.$$

Assuming $dq$ to be a point charge, the electric field due to this charge at a distance $x$ from the centre of the ring,

$$dE = \left(\frac{1}{4\pi \epsilon_0}\right)\frac{dq}{r^2} = \left(\frac{1}{4\pi \epsilon_0}\right)\frac{\lambda ds}{r^2}$$

From the geometry, $r^2 = R^2 + x^2$

$$\therefore \quad dE = \left(\frac{1}{4\pi \epsilon_0}\right)\frac{\lambda ds}{(R^2 + x^2)}$$

Fig. 1.117

*Fig. 1.117* shows that $d\vec{E}$ is at an angle $\theta$ to the central axis and has components perpendicular to and parallel to that axis. All the perpendicular components get cancel out because they are equal in magnitude but point in different directions. Thus resultant field is due to the parallel components; they all have the same direction, so the net field

$$E = \int dE \cos\theta$$

$$= \frac{\lambda}{4\pi \in_0} \frac{\cos\theta}{(R^2 + x^2)} \int_0^{2\pi R} ds$$

$$= \frac{(\lambda \times 2\pi R)}{4\pi \in_0} \frac{\cos\theta}{(R^2 + x^2)}$$

If $q$ be the total charge on the ring, then

$\lambda \times 2\pi R = q$, also $\quad \cos\theta = \dfrac{x}{\sqrt{R^2 + x^2}}$

$$\therefore \quad E = \left(\frac{1}{4\pi \in_0}\right) \frac{qx}{(R^2 + x^2)^{3/2}}$$

For $x >> R$, $R^2 + x^2 \simeq x^2$

$$\therefore \quad E = \left(\frac{1}{4\pi \in_0}\right) \frac{q}{x^2}.$$

This is the field as the ring "looks like" a point charge.
It is interesting to note that if we place an electron of charge e close to the centre of the ring, it would experience a force

$$F_{rest} = -Ee$$

$$= -\left[\left(\frac{1}{4\pi \in_0}\right) \frac{qx}{(R^2 + x^2)^{3/2}}\right](e)$$

For $x << R$,

$$F_{rest} = \left[\left(\frac{1}{4\pi \in_0}\right) \frac{qe}{R^3}\right](-x)$$

Acceleration $\quad a = \dfrac{F_{rest}}{m} = \left(\dfrac{1}{4\pi \in_0}\right) \dfrac{qe}{mR^3}(-x)$

On comparing with standard equation of SHM, $a = -\omega^2 x$, we get

$$\omega = \sqrt{\left(\frac{1}{4\pi \in_0}\right) \frac{qe}{mR^3}}$$

and $\quad T = \dfrac{2\pi}{\omega} = 2\pi \sqrt{\dfrac{4\pi \in_0 mR^3}{qe}}$

**Maximum value of $E$**

For $E$ to be maximum, $\quad \dfrac{dE}{dx} = 0,$

or $\quad \dfrac{d}{dx}\left[\left(\dfrac{1}{4\pi \in_0}\right) \dfrac{qx}{(R^2 + x^2)^{3/2}}\right] = 0$

After simplification, we get

$$x = \frac{R}{\sqrt{2}}$$

$$\therefore \qquad E_{max} = \frac{1}{4\pi \epsilon_0} \frac{q\dfrac{R}{\sqrt{2}}}{\left[R^2 + \left(\dfrac{R}{\sqrt{2}}\right)^2\right]^{3/2}}$$

$$= \frac{2}{3\sqrt{3}}\left[\frac{1}{4\pi \epsilon_0}\frac{q}{R^2}\right]$$

At the centre of ring, $x = 0$, $\therefore E = 0$

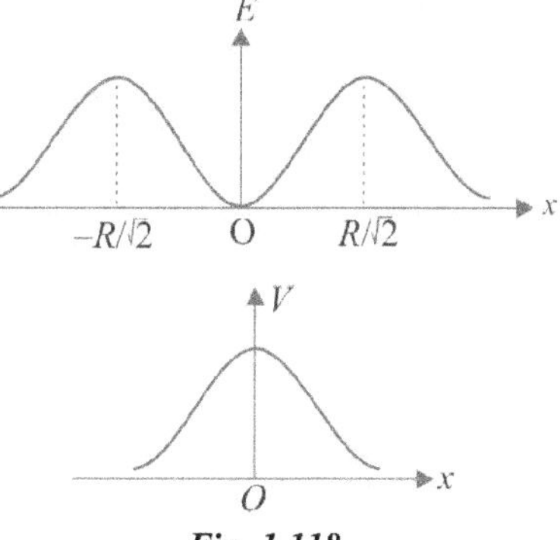

Fig. 1.118

**Electric potential :** Potential at any point on the axis of the ring can be obtained by putting entire charge at any point on the ring. So the distance of the point from the charge $q$ becomes

$$r = \sqrt{R^2 + x^2}$$

$$\therefore \quad \text{Potential} \qquad V = \frac{1}{4\pi \epsilon_0}\frac{q}{r} = \frac{1}{4\pi \epsilon_0}\frac{q}{\sqrt{R^2 + x^2}}$$

**Ex. 34** ***Fig. 1.119*** **shows a plastic rod having a uniformly distributed charge $Q$. The rod has been bent in a $2\theta$ circular arc of radius $R$. What is the electric field $\vec{E}$ and potential due to rod at point $P$.**

**Sol.**

Consider a small element of angular width $d\alpha$ at any angle $\alpha$ above the symmetry axis. The charge on the element

$$dq = \frac{Q}{2\theta}.d\alpha$$

The electric field at $P$ due to this charge

$$dE = \left(\frac{1}{4\pi \epsilon_0}\right)\frac{dq}{R^2}$$

$$= \left(\frac{1}{4\pi \epsilon_0}\right)\frac{\dfrac{Q}{2\theta}(d\alpha)}{R^2}$$

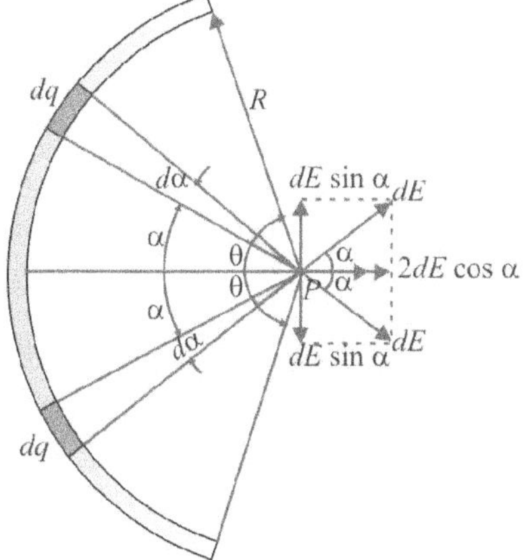

Fig. 1.119

The resultant field due to two such elements = $2dE\cos\alpha$, because parallel components of $dE$, lie in the same direction and perpendicular components get cancelled. Thus effective field due to charge at $P$ is $dE\cos\alpha$. The field due to entire rod

$$E = 2\int_0^\theta dE\cos\alpha$$

$$= 2\int_0^\theta \frac{1}{4\pi \epsilon_0}\frac{\left(\dfrac{Qd\alpha}{2\theta}\right)}{R^2}\cos\alpha$$

$$\text{or} \qquad E = \left(\frac{1}{4\pi \epsilon_0}\right)\frac{Q}{R^2}\left(\frac{\sin\theta}{\theta}\right) \qquad \textit{Ans.}$$

$$\text{Electric potential : } V = \left(\frac{1}{4\pi \epsilon_0}\right)\frac{Q}{R}. \qquad \textit{Ans.}$$

**Ex. 35** **Two charged rings, each of radius $R$ with the charges, $Q_1$ and $Q_2$ are placed parallel with separation $x$, between their centres. Find electric field $\vec{E}$ and potential $V$ at the centres of the rings.**

**Sol.**

Electric field at the centre due to own charge is zero, while due to charge of other ring will be

$$E = \left(\frac{1}{4\pi \epsilon_0}\right)\frac{Qx}{(R^2 + x^2)^{3/2}}$$

Thus field at the centre of the ring 1,

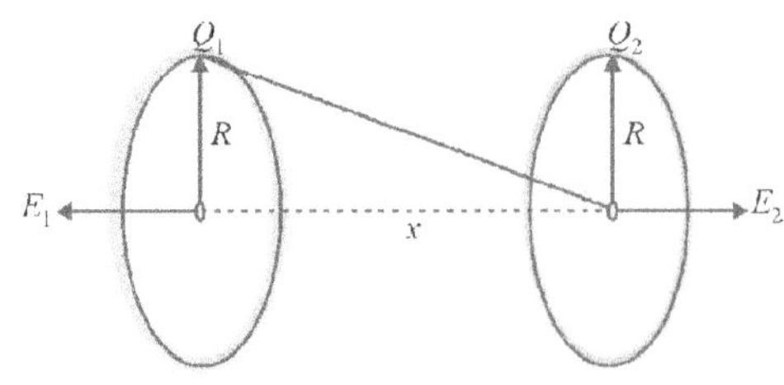


*Fig. 1.120*

$$E_1 = 0+\left(\frac{1}{4\pi \in_0}\right)\frac{Q_2 x}{(R^2+x^2)^{3/2}}$$

$$= \left(\frac{1}{4\pi \in_0}\right)\frac{Q_2 x}{(R^2+x^2)^{3/2}}$$

and field at the centre of the ring 2

$$E_2 = 0+\left(\frac{1}{4\pi \in_0}\right)\frac{Q_1 x}{(R^2+x^2)^{3/2}}$$

$$= \left(\frac{1}{4\pi \in_0}\right)\frac{Q_1 x}{(R^2+x^2)^{3/2}}. \qquad \textbf{Ans.}$$

Electric potential $$V_1 = \left(\frac{1}{4\pi \in_0}\right)\left[\frac{Q_1}{R}+\frac{Q_2}{\sqrt{R^2+x^2}}\right]$$

and $$V_2 = \left(\frac{1}{4\pi \in_0}\right)\left[\frac{Q_2}{R}+\frac{Q_1}{\sqrt{R^2+x^2}}\right].$$

**Ans.**

## 1.21 CHARGED DISC

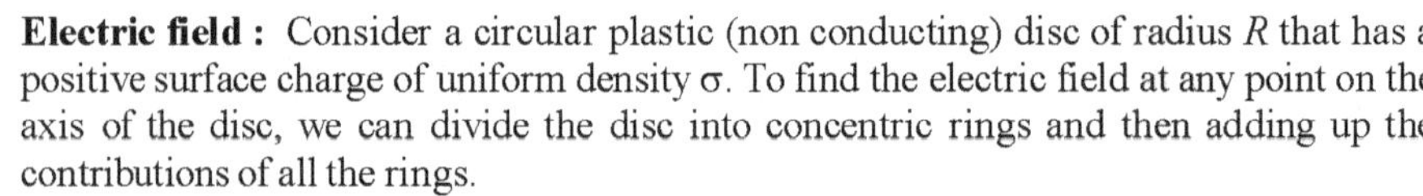

**Electric field :** Consider a circular plastic (non conducting) disc of radius $R$ that has a positive surface charge of uniform density $\sigma$. To find the electric field at any point on the axis of the disc, we can divide the disc into concentric rings and then adding up the contributions of all the rings.

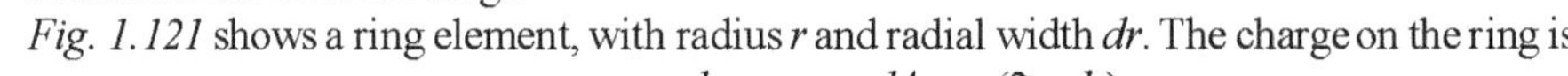

*Fig. 1.121* shows a ring element, with radius $r$ and radial width $dr$. The charge on the ring is

$$dq = \sigma\, dA = \sigma\,(2\pi r dr)$$

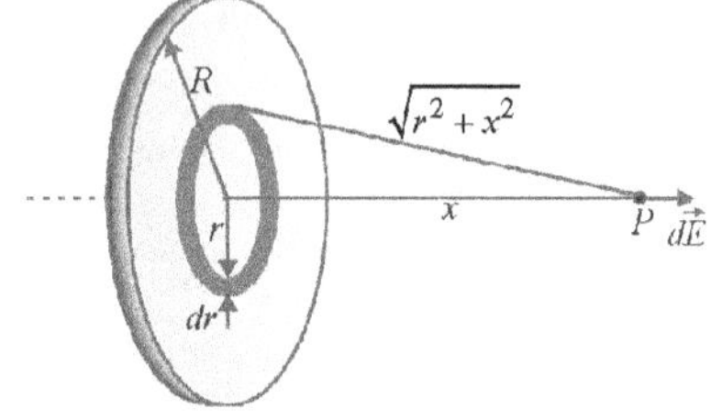


***Fig. 1.121. A disc of radius R and uniform charge density σ.***

The electric field at $P$ due to this element at a distance on the axis of the disc

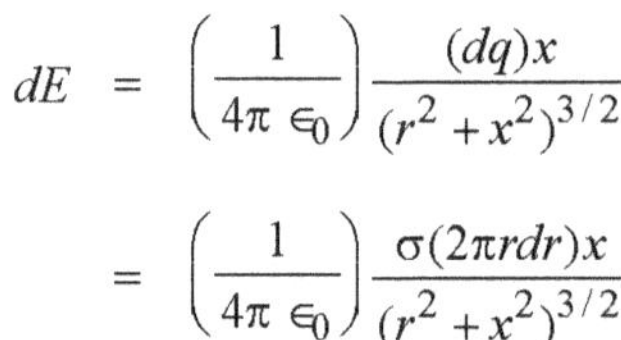

$$dE = \left(\frac{1}{4\pi \in_0}\right)\frac{(dq)x}{(r^2+x^2)^{3/2}}$$

$$= \left(\frac{1}{4\pi \in_0}\right)\frac{\sigma(2\pi r dr)x}{(r^2+x^2)^{3/2}}$$

The field due to whole disc can be find by integrating the above obtained result from r = 0 to $r = R$. Thus

$$E = \frac{\sigma x}{4 \in_0}\int_0^R \frac{2rdr}{(r^2+x^2)^{3/2}}$$

Substituting, $$r^2+x^2 = z$$

On differentiating , we get

$$2r\,dr = dz \qquad (x \text{ is constant})$$

$$\therefore \quad E = \frac{\sigma x}{4 \in_0}\int_0^R \frac{dz}{z^{3/2}}$$

$$= \frac{\sigma x}{4 \in_0}\left|\frac{z^{-1/2}}{(-1/2)}\right|_0^R$$

$$= -\frac{\sigma x}{4 \in_0}\left[\frac{1}{\sqrt{r^2+x^2}}\right]_0^R$$

$$= \frac{\sigma x}{2 \in_0}\left[\frac{1}{x}-\frac{1}{\sqrt{R^2+x^2}}\right]$$

or $$E = \frac{\sigma}{2 \in_0}\left[1-\frac{x}{\sqrt{R^2+x^2}}\right].$$

### Special cases :

(i) For infinitely large non conducting disc, $R \to \infty$, $\therefore\ E = \dfrac{\sigma}{2\epsilon_0}$.

(ii) For conducting disc, the charge spreads on both sides of it, and so

$$E = \frac{\sigma}{2\epsilon_0} + \frac{\sigma}{2\epsilon_0} = \frac{\sigma}{\epsilon_0}.$$

**Note:** The electric field due to a conductor of any shape with surface charge $\sigma$, is always $\dfrac{\sigma}{\epsilon_0}$ on its surface or close to the surface.

### Electric potential

Let us now find the electric potential at any point on the axis of the non-conducting charged disc, having surface charged density $\sigma$. To find the potential, we can divide the disc into large number of concentric rings and then adding up the contributions of all the rings.

*Fig. 1.122* shows a ring element, with radius r with radial width dr, the charge on the ring is

$$dq = \sigma(2\pi r dr)$$

The electric potential at $P$ due to this element at a distance $x$ on the axis of the disc

$$dV = \left(\frac{1}{4\pi\epsilon_0}\right)\frac{dq}{\sqrt{r^2+x^2}}$$

$$= \left(\frac{1}{4\pi\epsilon_0}\right)\frac{\sigma(2\pi r dr)}{\sqrt{r^2+x^2}}$$

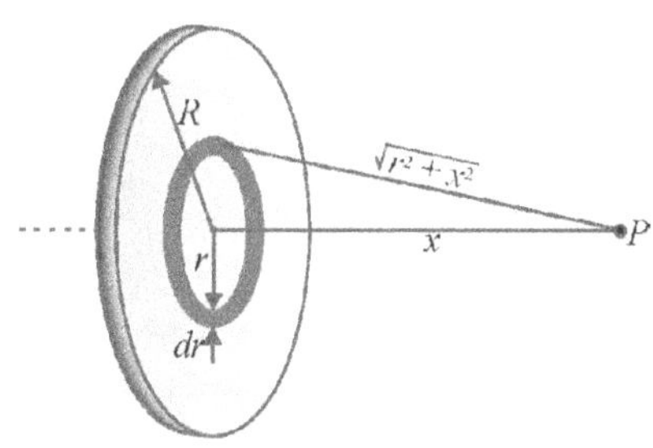

*Fig. 1.122*

Thus the potential due to the charge on the whole disc

$$V = \frac{\sigma}{2\epsilon_0}\int_0^R \frac{r dr}{(r^2+x^2)^{1/2}}$$

or
$$V = \frac{\sigma}{2\epsilon_0}\left[\sqrt{R^2+x^2} - x\right].$$

At the centre of the disc, $x = 0$, $\quad \therefore V = \dfrac{\sigma R}{2\epsilon_0}$.

For $x >> R$, we can write by Binomial

$$V = \frac{\sigma}{2\epsilon_0}[x\left(1+\frac{R^2}{x^2}\right)^{1/2} - x]$$

$$= \frac{\sigma}{2\epsilon_0}\left[x + \frac{R^2}{2x} - x\right]$$

$$= \frac{\sigma R^2}{4\epsilon_0 x} = \frac{\sigma(\pi R^2)}{4\pi\epsilon_0 x}$$

$$= \left(\frac{1}{4\pi\epsilon_0}\right)\frac{q}{x}.$$

Here $q = \sigma(\pi R^2)$ is the total charge of the disc.

## Potential at the edge of the disc :

To calculate the potential at point $P$, we can divide the disc in large number of rings with $P$ as the centre. Figure shows an element of radial width dr at radial position $r$. The arc length $AB = 2r\theta$

The charge on the element,

$$dq = \sigma(2r\theta dr)$$

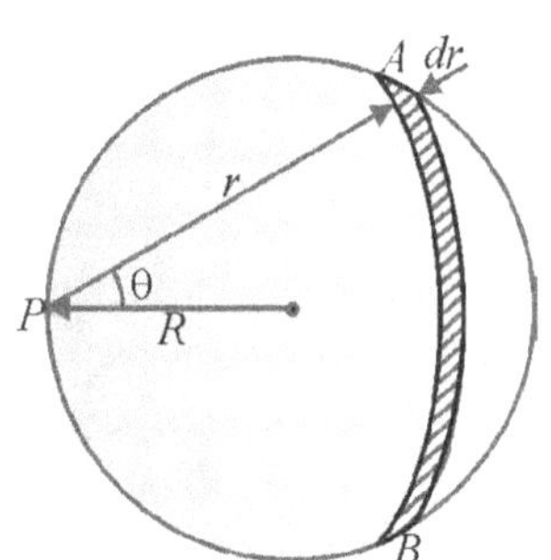

Fig. 1.123

The potential due to this element

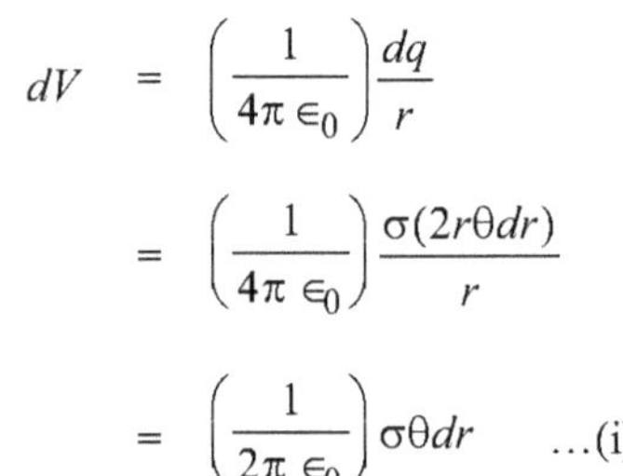
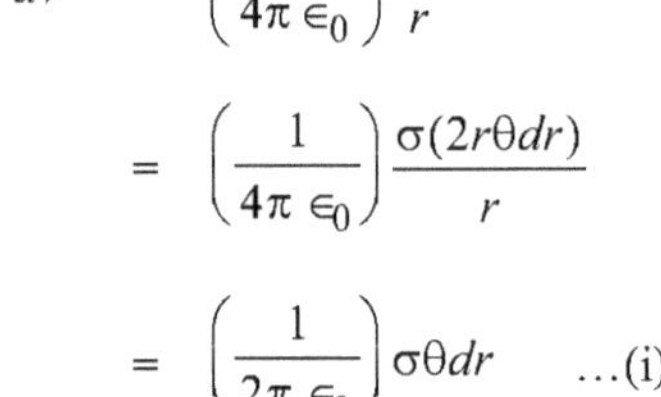

$$dV = \left(\frac{1}{4\pi \epsilon_0}\right)\frac{dq}{r}$$

$$= \left(\frac{1}{4\pi \epsilon_0}\right)\frac{\sigma(2r\theta dr)}{r}$$

$$= \left(\frac{1}{2\pi \epsilon_0}\right)\sigma\theta dr \qquad \ldots(i)$$

Potential due to the whole disc

$$V = \frac{\sigma}{2\pi \epsilon_0}\int_0^{2R} \theta dr$$

From the figure $\quad r = 2R\cos\theta$ and

$$dr = -2R\sin\theta\, d\theta$$

Substituting the value of $dr$ in equation (i), we have

$$V = -\frac{\sigma}{2\pi \epsilon_0}\int_{\theta_1=\pi/2}^{\theta_2=0} 2R\theta\sin\theta d\theta$$

or

$$V = \frac{\sigma R}{\pi \epsilon_0}.$$

## Charged soap bubble

We know that the excess pressure in a soap bubble of radius $r$ due to surface tension $T$ is given by

$$P_O = \frac{4T}{r}$$

If now bubble is given a charge $q$, then the outward mechanical pressure

$$= \frac{\sigma^2}{2\epsilon_0} = \frac{1}{2\epsilon_0}\left(\frac{q}{4\pi r^2}\right)^2 = \frac{q^2}{32\pi^2 \epsilon_0 r^4}$$

For the equilibrium of the bubble $\left(P_i + \frac{\sigma^2}{2\epsilon_0}\right) - P_O = \frac{4T}{r}$

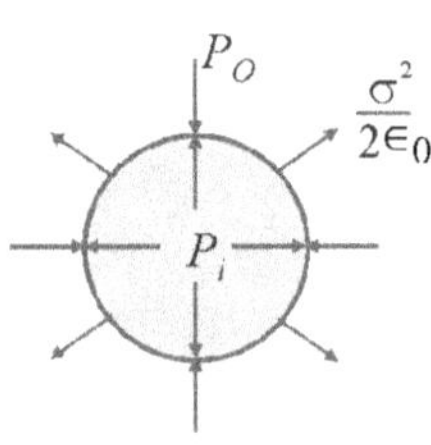

Fig. 1.124

$$\therefore\; P_i - P_O = P = \frac{4T}{r} - \frac{\sigma^2}{2\epsilon_0} = \frac{4T}{r} - \frac{q^2}{32\pi^2 \epsilon_0 r^4} \qquad \ldots(1)$$

Thus decrease in pressure due to charge on the bubble

$$-dP = \frac{q^2}{32\pi^2 \epsilon_0 r^4} \qquad \ldots(2)$$

We see that effective value of pressure decreases therefore bubble will expand. By Boyle's law

$$PV = \text{constant}$$

or $$P \times \frac{4}{3}\pi r^3 = \text{constant}$$

or $$Pr^3 = \text{constant} \quad \ldots(3)$$

Differentiating equation (3), we get

$$\frac{dP}{P} = -\frac{3dr}{r}$$

or $$dr = \frac{r}{3}\left(\frac{-dP}{P}\right) \quad \ldots(4)$$

$$= \frac{r}{3} \times \left(\frac{q^2}{32\pi^2 \epsilon_0 r^4}\right)\frac{1}{P}$$

or $$dr = \frac{q^2}{96\pi^2 \epsilon_0 r^3 P}. \quad \ldots(5)$$

**Special case :** when net excess pressure is to be zero, from equation (1) we have

$$0 = \frac{4T}{r} - \frac{\sigma^2}{2\epsilon_0}$$

which gives $$\sigma = \sqrt{\frac{8T\epsilon_0}{r}}.$$

**Ex. 36** **Two tiny conducting balls of identical mass $m$ and identical charge $q$ hang from non conducting threads of length $L$. Assume that $\theta$ is so small that $\tan\theta$ can be replaced by its approximate equal, $\sin\theta$.**

**(a) Show that for equilibrium,**

$$x = [q^2L/(2\pi\epsilon_0 mg)]^{1/3}$$

**where $x$ is the separation between the balls.**

**(b) What happens to the balls if one of them is discharged, and find the new equilibrium separation $x$.**

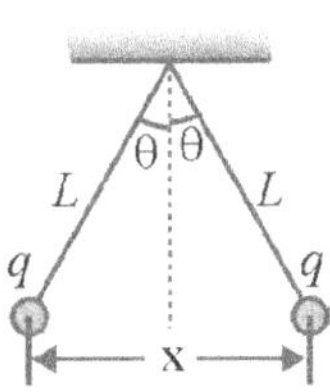


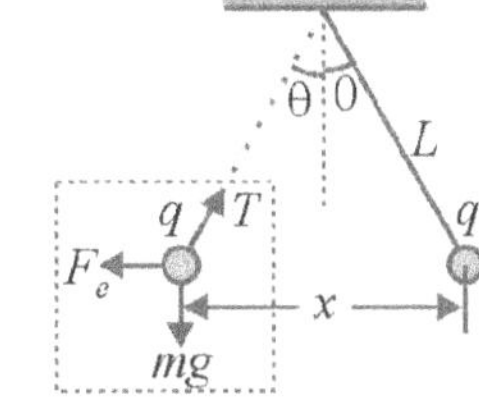


*Fig. 1.125*

**Sol.**

(a) Consider the equilibrium of the either ball. Electric force between the balls

$$F_e = \frac{1}{4\pi\epsilon_0}\frac{q^2}{x^2}$$

From the free body diagram, we have

$$T\sin\theta = \frac{1}{4\pi\epsilon_0}\frac{q^2}{x^2} \quad \ldots(i)$$

and $$T\cos\theta = mg \quad \ldots(ii)$$

Dividing equation (i) by (ii), we get

$$\tan\theta = \frac{q^2}{4\pi\epsilon_0 x^2 mg} \quad \ldots(iii)$$

It is given that $\tan\theta = \sin\theta$

$$= (x/2)/L$$

Substituting this value in (iii) and rearranging for x, we get

$$x = \left[\frac{q^2L}{(2\pi\epsilon_0 mg)}\right]^{1/3}.$$

(b) When one ball is discharged, it will touch the other ball which has charge $q$ on it. Due to conduction the charge divided equally on both the balls (because both the balls are identical). Therefore each ball will have the charge $q/2$. They repel each other, and let they are now have separation $x_0$ between them.

Electric force between them is $$= \frac{1}{4\pi\epsilon_0}\frac{(q/2)^2}{(x_0)^2}$$

$$\therefore \quad \tan\theta = \frac{q^2}{16\pi\epsilon_0 x_0^2 mg}$$

or $$(x_0/2)/L = \frac{q^2}{16\pi\epsilon_0 x_0^2 mg}$$

Solving above equation for $x_0$, we get

$$x_0 = \left[\frac{q^2 L}{8\pi \in_0 mg}\right]^{1/3}.$$

**Ex. 37** ***Fig. 1.126*** **shows a long nonconducting, massless rod of length *L*, pivoted at its centre and balanced with a weight *W* at a distance *x* from the left end. At the left end and right end of the rod are attached small conducting spheres with positive charges *q* and 2*q* respectively. A distance *h* directly beneath each of these spheres is a fixed sphere with positive charge *Q*.**

**(a) Find the distance *x* when the rod is horizontal and balanced.**

**(b) What value should h have so that the rod exerts no vertical force on the bearing when the rod is horizontal and balance?**

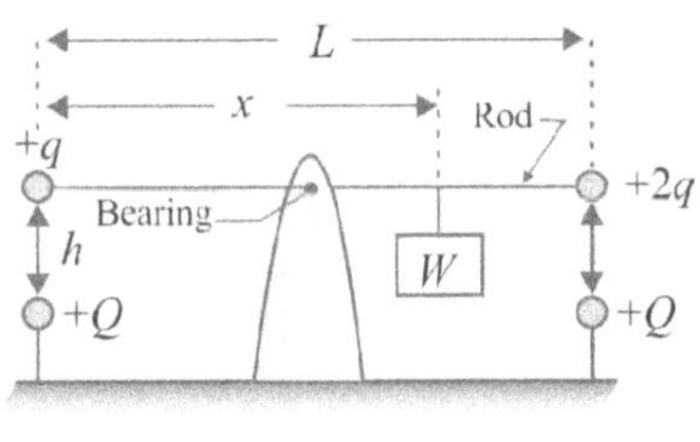


(a)

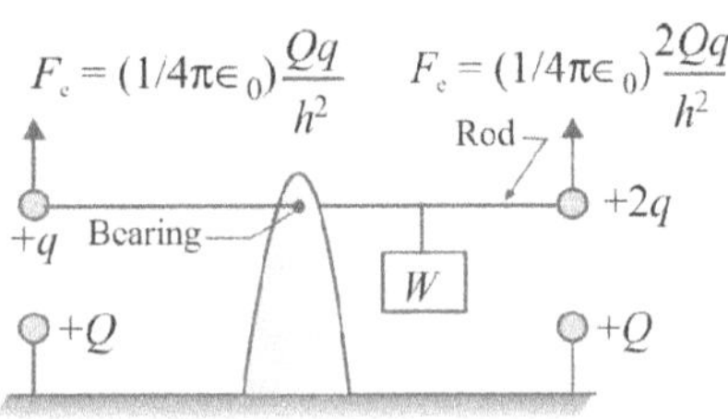


(b)

*Fig. 1.126*

**Sol.**

(a) Forces acting on the rod are shown in *Fig. 1.126(b)*. For the rod to be horizontal ,

$$\Sigma\tau = 0.$$

Taking moment of the forces acting on the rod about the axis passing through bearing (here this point is chosen due to the fact that the moment of the reaction at the bearing becomes zero. We can take any other point about which moments are calculated, provided first the reaction at the bearing must be calculated). Thus

$$\left(\frac{1}{4\pi \in_0}\right)\frac{Qq}{h^2}\cdot\frac{L}{2} + W.(x - L/2) = \left(\frac{1}{4\pi \in_0}\right)\frac{(2Qq)}{h^2}\cdot\frac{L}{2}$$

Solving above equation, we get

$$x = \left[\frac{QqL}{8\pi \in_0 Wh^2} + \frac{L}{2}\right] \quad \textit{Ans.}$$

(b) The rod exerts no vertical force on the bearing, if $\Sigma F_y = 0$,

$$\text{or} \quad \left(\frac{1}{4\pi \in_0}\right)\frac{Qq}{h^2} + \left(\frac{1}{4\pi \in_0}\right)\frac{(2Qq)}{h^2} = W$$

$$\text{or} \quad h = \sqrt{(3qQ/4\pi \in_0 W)}. \quad \textit{Ans.}$$

**Ex. 38** **Find the electric field strength and the potential at the centre of a hemisphere of radius *R* charged uniformly with the surface density σ.**

**Sol.**

**Field :** Choose an elemental ring of thickness $d\theta$ at an angular position $\theta$ from its bisector. The charge on this element,

$$dq = (2\pi r)ds.\ \sigma = (2\pi r)(Rd\theta)\ \sigma = 2\pi(R\sin\theta)Rd\theta\sigma$$

$$= 2\sigma\pi R^2 \sin\theta d\theta.$$

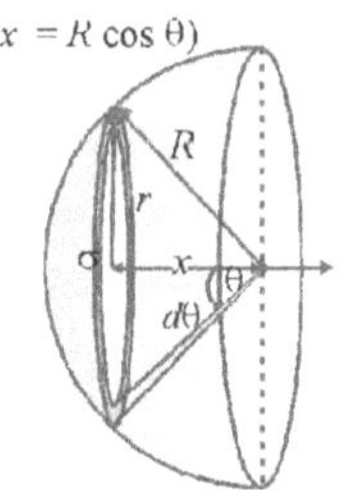


*Fig. 1.127*

The electric field due to this element ring,

$$dE = \left[\frac{1}{4\pi \in_0}\frac{dqx}{R^3}\right].$$

The total field

$$E = \int_0^{\pi/2} \frac{1}{4\pi \in_0}\frac{(R\cos\theta)dq}{R^3}$$

Substituting the value of $dq$ in above equation, we have

$$E = \int_0^{\pi/2}\left(\frac{1}{4\pi \in_0}\right)2\sigma\pi R^2 \frac{\sin\theta d\theta(R\cos\theta)}{R^3}$$

After solving, we get $E = \dfrac{\sigma}{4 \in_0}.$

**Potential :** Potential due to elemental ring

$$dV = \left(\frac{1}{4\pi \in_0}\right)\frac{dq}{R}$$

Potential due to hemisphere,

$$V = \int_0^{\pi/2}\left(\frac{1}{4\pi \in_0}\right)2\sigma\pi R^2 \frac{\sin\theta}{R}$$

After solving, we get $V = \dfrac{\sigma R}{2 \in_0}.$

**Ex. 39** **Two identical particles of mass m carrying a charge $q$ each. Initially one is rest on a smooth horizontal plane and the other is projected along the plane directly towards the first particle from a large distance, with speed $v$. Find the distance of closest approach.**

## Sol.

When one particle approaches towards the other, due to the repulsion, the other will also start moving. In this process the velocity of the first decreases while that of second increases until their velocities become equal. When this happens the distance between the particles become let say $r$. Let $v$ be the velocity of each particle at this instant, then from conservation of momentum, we have

$$mu + 0 = mv + mv \quad \ldots (i)$$

or

$$v = \frac{u}{2}$$

and from conservation of energy, we have

$$\frac{1}{2}mu^2 + 0 = \frac{1}{2}mv^2 + \frac{1}{2}mv^2 + \frac{(1/4\pi \epsilon_0)q^2}{r} \quad .. (ii)$$

Solving above equations, we get

$$r = \frac{4q^2}{(4\pi \epsilon_0 \, mu^2)}$$

**Ex. 40** **A drop of water of mass $18 \times 10^{-6}$ kg falls away from the bottom of a charged conducting sphere of radius 20 cm, carrying with it charge of $10^{-9}$ coulomb and leaving on the sphere a uniformly distributed charge of $2.5 \times 10^{-6}$ coulomb. What is the speed of the drop after it has fallen 30 cm ? [ $\epsilon_0 = 1/(4\pi \times 9 \times 10^9) F/m$ and $g = 9.8 m/s^2$ ]**

## Sol.

Taking reference level at $B_1$ and using principle of conservation of energy, we have

Mechanical energy at $A$ = Mechanical energy at $B$

or $\quad mg \times 0.30 + (1/4\pi \epsilon_0)q_1q_2/0.20$

$$= 0 + \frac{1}{2}mv^2 + (1/4\pi \epsilon_0)q_1q_2/(0.20 + 0.30)$$

where $m = 18 \times 10^{-6}$kg, $q_1 = 2.5 \times 10^{-6}$ C., $q_2 = 10^{-9}$ C.

Substituting these values in above equation and solving for $v$, we get

$$v = 3.65 \text{ m/s} \qquad \textit{Ans.}$$

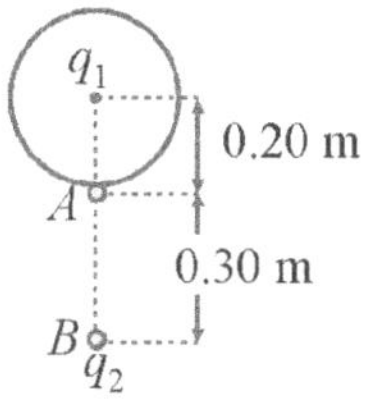

*Fig. 1.128*

**Ex. 41** **A ball of radius $R$ carries a positive charge whose volume density depends only on a separation $r$ from the ball's centre as $\rho = \rho_0\left(1 - \frac{r}{R}\right)$, where $\rho_0$ is a constant. Assuming the permitivities of the ball and the environment to be equal to unity. Find**

**(a) The magnitude of the electric field strength as a function of the distance $r$ both inside and outside the ball;**

**(b) The maximum intensity $E_{max}$ and the corresponding distance $r$.**

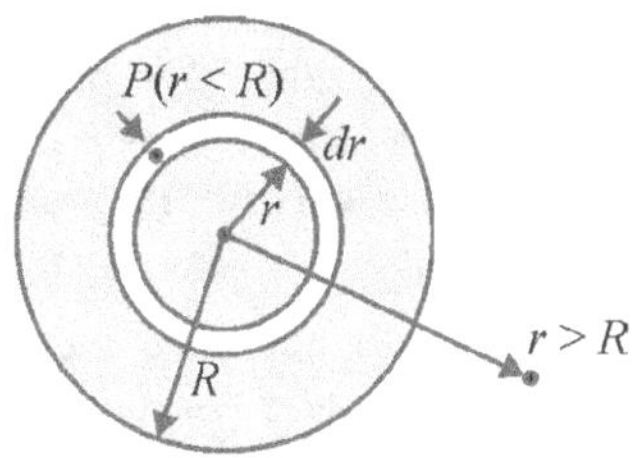


*Fig. 1.129*

## Sol.

(a) Given that $\quad \rho = \rho_0\left(1 - \frac{r}{R}\right)$

Choose an element dr at a distance r from the centre of the ball. The charge on this element will be

$$dq = \rho_0\left(1 - \frac{r}{R}\right) \times (4\pi r^2 dr)$$

The total charge enclosed in the sphere of radius $r$,

$$q = \int_0^r \rho_0\left(1 - \frac{r}{R}\right) \times (4\pi r^2 dr)$$

$$= 4\pi\rho_0\left(\frac{r^3}{3} - \frac{r^4}{4R}\right)$$

Electric field at a point $(r < R)$ is given by

$$E = \frac{1}{4\pi \epsilon_0}\frac{q}{r^2}$$

$$= \frac{\rho_0 r}{3\epsilon_0}\left(1 - \frac{3r}{4R}\right)$$

For $r \geq R$, we have

$$q = \int_0^R \rho_0\left(1 - \frac{r}{R}\right) \times (4\pi r^2 dr)$$

$$= \frac{\pi\rho_0 R^3}{3}$$

$$E = \frac{1}{4\pi \epsilon_0}\frac{q}{r^2}$$

or

$$= \frac{\rho_0 R^3}{12\epsilon_0 r^2}$$

(b) We have $E = \rho_0 r \dfrac{(1-3r/4R)}{3\epsilon_0}$

For electric field to be maximum,

$$\frac{dE}{dr} = 0$$

or $$0 = \frac{\rho_0(1-6r/4R)}{3\epsilon_0}$$

or $$r = \frac{2R}{3}. \quad \textit{Ans.}$$

**Ex. 42** **A thin nonconducting ring of radius $R$ has a linear charge density $\lambda = \lambda_0 \cos\varphi$, where $\lambda_0$ is a constant, $\varphi$ is the azimuthal angle. Find the magnitude of the electric field strength**

**(a) at the centre of the ring,**

**(b) on the axis of the ring as a function of the distance $x$ from its centre investigate the obtained function at $x >> R$.**

**Sol.**

(a) Charge on the ring for the given charge function $\lambda = \lambda_0 \cos\varphi$ may be shown as in the fig.*1.130*. As it is clear from the fig, to find the electric field strength due to this charge distribution, the ring may be divided in two halves and an element $dq$ in arc $ds$ may be taken at angle $\varphi$ measured in anti clockwise direction from $OX$. The field strength at O due to this element is as shown in the fig. It is evident that it has the $dE\cos\varphi$ and $dE\sin\varphi$ component of the electric field intensity due a charge element $dq = \lambda ds$ in the first quadrant. So, now, resultant field due to $dE\sin\varphi$ components of the positive half of the ring is given as

$$dE'_{ry} = dE\sin\varphi$$

or, $$= \frac{1}{4\pi\varepsilon_0}\frac{dq}{R^2}\sin\varphi$$

or, $$= \frac{1}{4\pi\varepsilon_0}\frac{\lambda ds}{R^2}\sin\varphi$$

so, $$dE'_{ry} = \frac{1}{4\pi\varepsilon_0}\frac{\lambda R d\varphi}{R}\sin\varphi$$

or, $$= \frac{1}{4\pi\varepsilon_0}\frac{\lambda_0}{R}\cos\varphi\sin\varphi d\varphi$$

or $$= \frac{1}{4\pi\varepsilon_0}\frac{\lambda_0}{R}\times\frac{\sin 2\varphi}{2}d\varphi$$

so, $$E'_{ry} = \frac{1}{8\pi\varepsilon_0}\frac{\lambda_0}{R}\int_{-\pi/2}^{\pi/2}\sin 2\varphi d\varphi$$

or $$E'_{ry} = \frac{\lambda_0}{8\pi\varepsilon_0 R}\left[-\frac{\cos 2\varphi}{2}\right]_{-\pi/2}^{\pi/2}$$

or $$E'_{ry} = -\frac{\lambda_0}{16\pi\varepsilon_0 R}\left[\cos\pi - \cos\pi\right]$$

or $$E'_{ry} = -\frac{\lambda_0}{16\pi\varepsilon_0 R}\left[-1+1\right]$$

or, $$E'_{ry} = 0$$

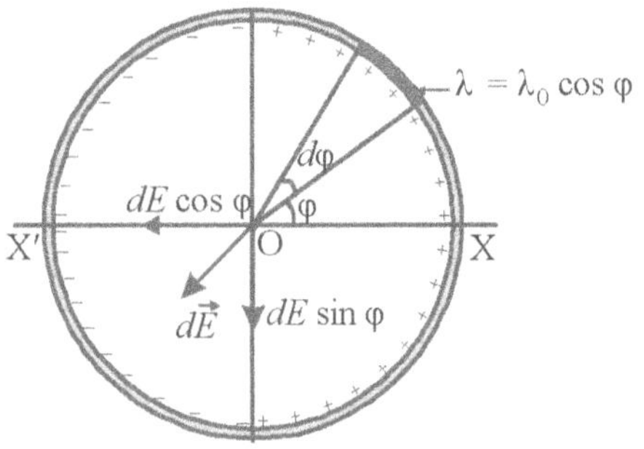

*Fig. 1.130*

Now, field strength due to $dE\cos\varphi$ component of the positive half of the ring is given as

$$dE'_{rx} = dE\cos\varphi$$

or, $$= \frac{1}{4\pi\varepsilon_0}\frac{dq}{R^2}\cos\varphi$$

or, $$= \frac{1}{4\pi\varepsilon_0}\frac{\lambda ds}{R^2}\cos\varphi$$

or, $$= \frac{\lambda_0}{4\pi\varepsilon_0 R}\cos^2\varphi d\varphi$$

(since, $ds = Rd\varphi$ & $\lambda = \lambda_0\cos\varphi$)

or, $$E'_{rx} = \frac{\lambda_0}{4\pi\varepsilon_0 R}\int_{-\pi/2}^{\pi/2}\left[\frac{\cos 2\varphi + 1}{2}\right]d\varphi$$

or, $$E'_{rx} = \frac{\lambda_0}{4\pi\varepsilon_0 R}\left[\frac{\sin 2\varphi}{4} + \frac{\varphi}{2}\right]_{-\pi/2}^{\pi/2}$$

or, $$E'_{rx} = \frac{\lambda_0}{4\pi\varepsilon_0 R}\left[\frac{\pi}{4} - \left(-\frac{\pi}{4}\right)\right]$$

or, $$E'_{rx} = \frac{\lambda_0}{8\varepsilon_0 R}$$

So. $$E'_r = \sqrt{E'^2_{rx} + E'^2_{ry}}$$

or $$E'_r = \frac{\lambda_0}{8\varepsilon_0 R}$$

Similarly, resultant of $dE\sin\varphi$ components due to a charge element in the second 'right half' of the ring is zero and the resultant of

$dE\cos\varphi$ component of other half is same in magnitude and direction as that of $E'_{rx}$. Hence resultant field at the centre

$$E_r = 2E'_r$$

or,
$$E_r = \frac{\lambda_0}{4\varepsilon_0 R}$$

(b) Since, due to the given charge variation $\lambda = \lambda_0\cos\varphi$ one half of the ring lying in the first and fourth quadrant is positive and other half lying in second and third quadrant is negative. So, to calculate the electric field intensity at a point distant $x$ (say) on the axis, we may consider a charge element $dq$ concentrated in small length ds $(= Rd\varphi)$ at an angular position $\varphi$ with respect to diameter $XOX'$. This electric field intensity $dE$ at point $P$ as shown in the fig. has two components; $dE\sin\theta$ and $dE\cos\theta$. $dE\cos\theta$ component due to a charge element in the positive half is cancelled by the cosine component of electric field intensity of $-dq$ charge element which is symmetrically placed in the negative half of the ring. In this way the since components of the electric field intensity due to charge on the positive half and the negative half of the ring contribute to the total field on the axis of the ring. The $dE\sin\theta$ components due to the charge distribution in the lower and upper half of the ring are perpendicular to the axis and also parallel to a diameter which is at an angle of $\varphi$ with the positive $x$-axis. Similarly, all the charge element at different angular positions of $\varphi$ in the lower and upper half of the ring have their electric field intensity components perpendicular to the axis of the ring and parallel to the corresponding diameter. So, if one looks at the centre of the ring along the axis, these electric field intensity vectors seem to be radiating along the radii of a semicircle whose centre is the point $P$ at which resultant field is to be found out. So, to get the resultant electric field at this point $P$, one $dE\sin\theta$ component is resolved at $P$ along two perpendicular components. One component is parallel to XOX' and other component is parallel to YOY'

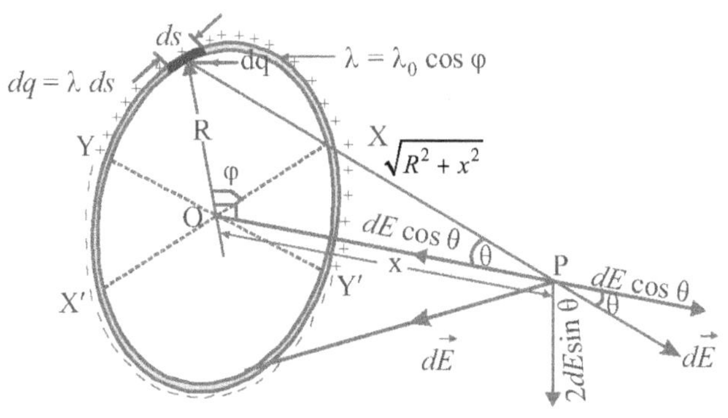


*Fig. 1.131*

So, $\quad dE_x = dE\sin\theta\cos\varphi \quad \ldots$ (i)

and $\quad dE_y = dE\sin\theta\sin\varphi \quad \ldots$ (ii)

Now, when $dE_x$ is integrated for whole ring i.e., from $\varphi = 2\pi$, we get total electric field at point $P$ in $x$-direction.

so, $$E_x = \int_{\varphi=0}^{\varphi=2\pi} dE_x$$

or $$= \int_{\varphi=0}^{\varphi=2\pi} dE\sin\theta\cos\varphi$$

or $$= \int_0^{2\pi} \frac{1}{4\pi\varepsilon_0}\frac{dq}{R^2+x^2}\sin\theta\cos\varphi$$

or $$= \int_0^{2\pi} \frac{1}{4\pi\varepsilon_0}\frac{\lambda ds}{R^2+x^2}\sin\theta\cos\varphi$$

or $$= \int_0^{2\pi} \frac{1}{4\pi\varepsilon_0}\frac{\lambda_0\cos\varphi R d\varphi}{R^2+x^2}\sin\theta\cos\varphi$$

or $$= \frac{1}{4\pi\varepsilon_0}\frac{\lambda_0 R}{R^2+x^2}\sin\int_0^{2\pi}\cos^2\varphi d\varphi$$

or $$= \frac{1}{4\pi\varepsilon_0}\frac{\lambda_0 R}{R^2+x^2}\frac{R}{\sqrt{R^2+x^2}}\int_0^{2\pi}\cos^2\varphi d\varphi$$

or $$= \frac{1}{4\pi\varepsilon_0}\frac{\lambda_0 R}{R^2+x^2}\frac{R}{\sqrt{R^2+x^2}}\int_0^{2\pi}\frac{1+\cos 2\varphi}{2}d\varphi$$

or $$= \frac{1}{4\pi\varepsilon_0}\frac{\lambda_0 R}{R^2+x^2}\frac{R}{\sqrt{R^2+x^2}}\left(\frac{\varphi+\sin 2\varphi}{2}\right)_0^{2\pi}$$

or $$= \frac{\lambda_0 R^2}{4\varepsilon_0(R^2+x^2)^{3/2}}$$

so, $$E_x = \frac{\lambda_0 R^2}{4\varepsilon_0(R^2+x^2)^{3/2}}$$

Now, on integrating $dE_y$ for whole ring, i.e, from $\varphi = 0$ to $\varphi = 2\pi$, we get total electric field in y-direction. So,

$$E_y = \int_{\varphi=0}^{\varphi=2\pi} dE_y$$

or $$= \int_{\varphi=0}^{\varphi=2\pi} dE\sin\theta\sin\varphi$$

or $$= \int_0^{2\pi} \frac{1}{4\pi\varepsilon_0}\frac{dq}{R^2+x^2}\frac{R}{(R^2+x^2)^{1/2}}\sin\varphi$$

or $= \int_0^{2\pi} \frac{1}{4\pi\varepsilon_0} \frac{R\lambda ds}{(R^2+x^2)^{3/2}} \sin\varphi$

[ since, $\lambda = \lambda_0 \cos\varphi$ ]

or $= \int_0^{2\pi} \frac{R}{4\pi\varepsilon_0(R^2+x^2)^{3/2}} \lambda_0 \cos\varphi R d\varphi \sin\varphi$

or $= \int_0^{2\pi} \frac{\lambda_0 R^2}{4\pi\varepsilon_0(R^2+x^2)^{3/2}} \cos\varphi \sin\varphi d\varphi$

or $= \frac{\lambda_0 R^2}{4\pi\varepsilon_0(R^2+x^2)^{3/2}} \int_0^{2\pi} \sin 2\varphi d\varphi / 2$

or $= \frac{\lambda_0 R^2}{4\pi\varepsilon_0(R^2+x^2)^{3/2}} \left[\frac{-\cos 2\varphi}{4}\right]_0^{2\pi}$

or $E_y = \frac{\lambda_0 R^2}{4\varepsilon_0(R^2+x^2)^{3/2}} \left[\frac{-(\cos 4\pi - \cos 0)}{4}\right]$

or $E_y = 0$

so, $E_r = \sqrt{E_x^2 + E_y^2}$

or, $E_r = \frac{\lambda_0 R^2}{4\varepsilon_0(R^2+x^2)^{3/2}}$

**Ex. 43** **A metal sphere of radius $r_1$ with a charge $q$ is placed at the centre of an uncharged thin conducting shell of radius $r_2$. Find electric field and potential at the positions $r > r_2$, $r_1 < r < r_2$ and $r < r_1$ in the following cases.**

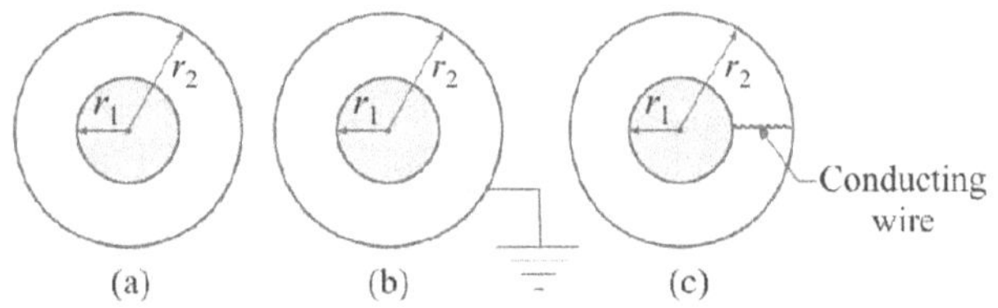


*Fig. 1.132*

## Sol.

(a) When charged metal sphere is placed at the centre of the shell, an equal amount of negative charge will appear at the inner surface and positive charge on the outer surface of the shell. If $A$, $B$ and $C$ are the respective positions, then

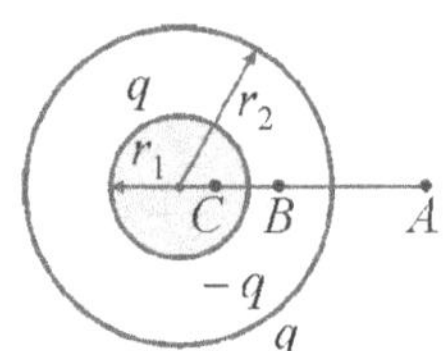


*Fig. 1.133*

For $r > r_2$ :

$E_A = [E_A]_1 + [E_A]_2$

$= \frac{1}{4\pi\epsilon_0}\left[\frac{q}{r^2} + \frac{q-q}{r^2}\right] = \left(\frac{1}{4\pi\epsilon_0}\right)\frac{q}{r^2}$

$V_A = [V_A]_1 + [V_A]_2$

$= \frac{1}{4\pi\epsilon_0}\left[\frac{q}{r} + \frac{q-q}{r}\right] = \left(\frac{1}{4\pi\epsilon_0}\right)\frac{q}{r}$

For $r_1 < r < r_2$ :

$E_B = [E_B]_1 + [E_B]_2$

$= \left(\frac{1}{4\pi\epsilon_0}\right)\frac{q}{r^2} + 0 = \left(\frac{1}{4\pi\epsilon_0}\right)\frac{q}{r^2}$

$V_B = [V_B]_1 + [V_B]_2$

$= \left(\frac{1}{4\pi\epsilon_0}\right)\frac{q}{r}$

For $r < r_1$ :

$E_C = [E_C]_1 + [E_C]_2$

$= 0 + 0 = 0$

$V_C = [V_C]_1 + [V_C]_2$

$= \left(\frac{1}{4\pi\epsilon_0}\right)\frac{q}{r_1} + 0 = \left(\frac{1}{4\pi\epsilon_0}\right)\frac{q}{r_1}$

(b) When outer surface of the shell is earthed, its charge becomes zero.

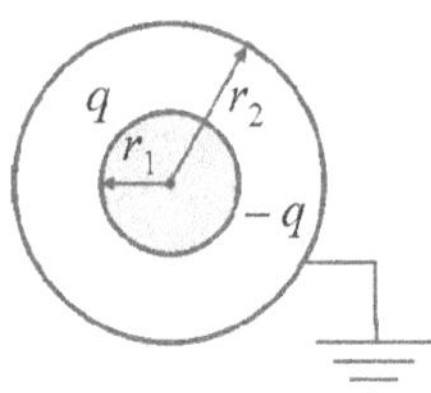


*Fig. 1.134*

For $r > r_2$ :

$E_A = [E_A]_1 + [E_A]_2$

$= \frac{1}{4\pi\epsilon_0}\left[\frac{q}{r^2} - \frac{q}{r^2}\right] = 0$

$V_A = [V_A]_1 + [V_A]_2$

$= \frac{1}{4\pi\epsilon_0}\left[\frac{q}{r} - \frac{q}{r}\right] = 0$

For $r_1 < r < r_2$ :

$E_B = [E_B]_1 + [E_B]_2$

$= \frac{1}{4\pi\epsilon_0}\frac{q}{r^2} + 0 = \left(\frac{1}{4\pi\epsilon_0}\right)\frac{q}{r^2}$

$V_B = [V_B]_1 + [V_B]_2$

$= \frac{1}{4\pi\epsilon_0}\left[\frac{q}{r} - \frac{q}{r_2}\right]$

For $r < r_1$ :

$$E_C = 0 + 0 = 0$$

$$V_C = [V_C]_1 + [V_C]_2$$

$$= \frac{1}{4\pi \epsilon_0}\left[\frac{q}{r_1} - \frac{q}{r_2}\right]$$

(c) When sphere and shell are connected by a conducting wire, the entire charge of the sphere will flow to the outer surface of the shell, so that potential of both becomes equal.

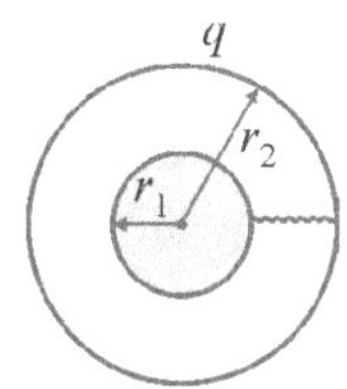


*Fig. 1.135*

For $r > r_2$ :

$$E_A = [E_A]_1 + [E_A]_2$$

$$= 0 + \frac{1}{4\pi \epsilon_0}\frac{q}{r^2} = \left(\frac{1}{4\pi \epsilon_0}\right)\frac{q}{r^2}$$

$$V_A = [V_A]_1 + [V_A]_2$$

$$= 0 + \frac{1}{4\pi \epsilon_0}\frac{q}{r} = \left(\frac{1}{4\pi \epsilon_0}\right)\frac{q}{r}$$

For $r_1 < r < r_2$ :

$$E_B = [E_B]_1 + [E_B]_2$$

$$= 0 + 0 = 0$$

$$V_B = [V_B]_1 + [V_B]_2$$

$$= 0 + \frac{1}{4\pi \epsilon_0}\frac{q}{r_2} = \left(\frac{1}{4\pi \epsilon_0}\right)\frac{q}{r_2}$$

For $r < r_1$ :

$$E_C = [E_C]_1 + [E_C]_2$$

$$= 0 + 0 = 0$$

$$V_C = [V_C]_1 + [V_C]_2$$

$$= 0 + \left(\frac{1}{4\pi \epsilon_0}\right)\frac{q}{r_2}$$

$$= \left(\frac{1}{4\pi \epsilon_0}\right)\frac{q}{r_2}.$$

**Ex. 44** **An uncharged sphere of radius $r_1$ is placed at the centre of a conducting shell of radius $r_2$, having charge $q$. Find charge on the sphere in the following situations.**

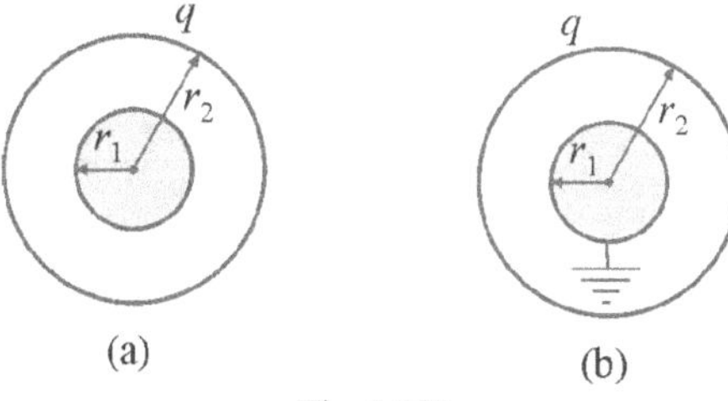


*Fig. 1.136*

**Sol.**

(a) In this case the potential on the surface of the sphere and shell is equal and so no charge will appear on the sphere.

(b) Let $q'$ charge appears on the sphere. The charges on the two surfaces of the shell are shown in the figure.

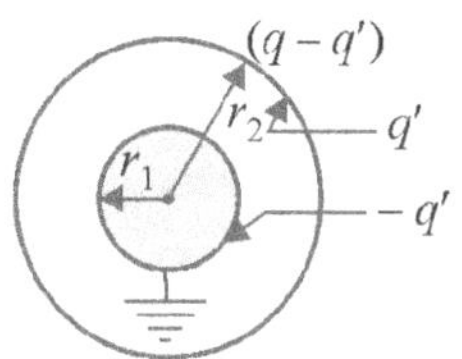


*Fig. 1.137*

As sphere is earthed, so its potential will be zero. i.e.,

$$0 = \frac{1}{4\pi \epsilon_0}\left[\frac{q}{r_2} - \frac{q'}{r_1}\right]$$

$$\therefore \quad q' = q\left(\frac{r_1}{r_2}\right). \qquad \textit{Ans.}$$

**Ex. 45** ***Fig. 1.138* shows three concentric thin spherical shells *A*, *B* and *C* of radii *a*, *b*, *c* respectively. The shells *A* and *C* are given charges *q* and –*q* respectively and the shell *B* is earthed. Find the charges appearing on the surfaces of *B* and *C*.**

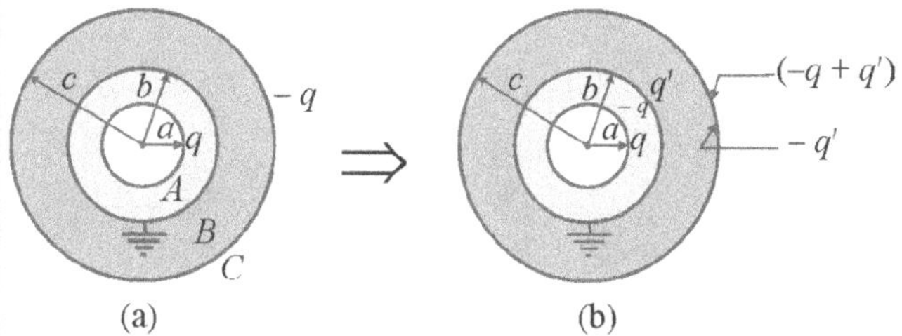


*Fig. 1.138*

**Sol.**

The inner surface of shell *B* will have charge – *q*. Let outer surface of it has charge $q'$. The charges on the surfaces of shell *C* are shown in figure (b). As shell *B* is earthed, so its potential will be zero. Thus

$$0 = \frac{1}{4\pi \epsilon_0}\left[\frac{q}{b} + \frac{q'-q}{b} + \frac{(-q+q'-q')}{c}\right]$$

After solving, we get $q' = q\frac{b}{c}$ *Ans.*

Thus charge on outer surface of shell *B* is $\frac{qb}{c}$. Charge on the inner surface of shell *C* is $-\frac{qb}{c}$ and on outer surface $\left(-q + \frac{qb}{c}\right)$.

**Ex. 46** **A dielectric cylinder of radius a is infinitely long. It is non-uniformly charged such that volume charge density ρ varies directly as the distance from the cylinder. Calculate the electric field intensities due to it, if ρ is zero at the axis and is $\rho_s$ on the surface. Also calculate the potential difference between the axis and the surface.**

**Sol.**

Consider a co-axial shell of radius $x$ and thickness $dx$ and of length $\ell$. The charge on this shell

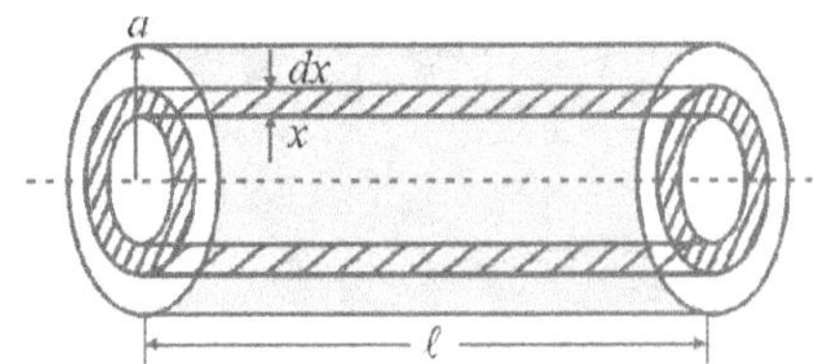


*Fig. 1.139*

$$dq = \rho(2\pi x\ell)dx$$

As $\rho$ varies directly as the distance $x$, hence $\rho$ can be written as $\rho = cx$, where $c$ is a constant given by the relation

$$\rho_s = ca$$

$$\therefore \quad c = \frac{\rho_s}{a}$$

The intensity of electric field at any point $P$ at a distance r from the axis of the cylinder can be obtained as : By Gauss law

$$E \times 2\pi r\ell = \frac{q}{\epsilon_0}$$

$$= \frac{1}{\epsilon_0}\int dq$$

$$= \frac{1}{\epsilon_0}\int \rho(2\pi x\ell)dx$$

$$= \frac{1}{\epsilon_0}\int_0^a (cx)2\pi x\ell dx$$

After putting the value of $\rho_s$ and simplifying, we get

$$E = \frac{\rho_s r^2}{3\epsilon_0 a}$$

At, $r = a$, $E = \frac{\rho_s a}{3\epsilon_0}$. The field in all the cases is radially outward.

We know that

$$V_A - V_B = -\int_B^A \vec{E}.d\vec{r}$$

$$\therefore V_{\text{axis}} - V_{\text{surface}} = -\int_a^0 \frac{\rho_s r^2}{3\epsilon_0 a}dr = \frac{\rho_s}{3a\epsilon_0}\int_0^a r^2 dr$$

$$= \frac{\rho_s a^2}{9\epsilon_0}. \qquad \textbf{Ans.}$$

**Ex. 47** **The electric field in a region is given by $\vec{E} = E_0 \frac{x}{\ell}\hat{i}$. Find the charge contained inside a cubical volume bounded by the surfaces $x = 0$, $x = \ell$ $y = 0$, $y = \ell$, $z = 0$ and $z = \ell$.**

**Sol.** At $x = 0$, $E = 0$ and $x = \ell$, $\vec{E} = E_0\hat{i}$.

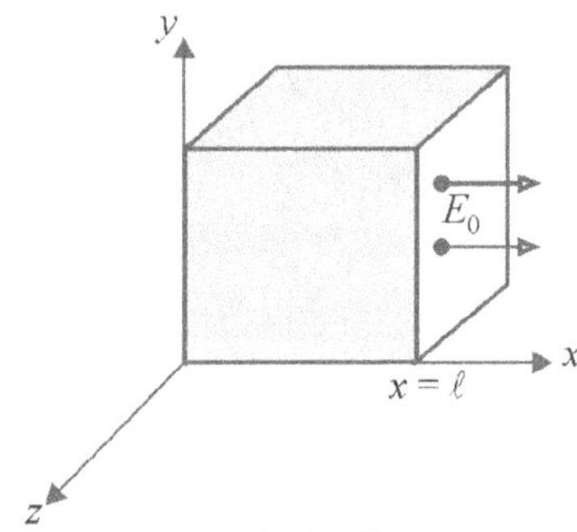


*Fig. 1.140*

The direction of the field is along the x-axis, so it will cross the $yz$ – face of the cube. The flux of this field

$$\phi = \phi_{\text{left face}} + \phi_{\text{right face}}$$

$$= 0 + E_0\ell^2 = E_0\ell^2$$

By Gauss's law,

$$\phi = \frac{q}{\epsilon_0}$$

$$\therefore \quad q = \epsilon_0\phi = \epsilon_0 E_0\ell^2. \qquad \textbf{Ans.}$$

**Ex. 48** ***Fig. 1.141*** **shows two parallel nonconducting rings arranged with their central axes along a common line. Ring 1 has uniform charge $q_1$ and radius $R$; ring 2 has uniform charge $q_2$ and the same radius $R$, rings are separated by a distance $3R$. The net electric field at point P on the common line, at distance $R$ from ring 1 is zero. What is the ratio $\frac{q_1}{q_2}$?**

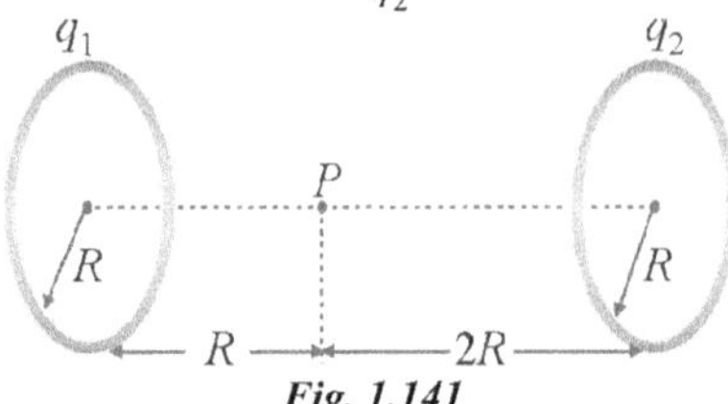


*Fig. 1.141*

**Sol.**

The electric field due to the ring at a distance $x$ from the centre is given by

$$E = \left(\frac{1}{4\pi\epsilon_0}\right)\frac{qx}{(R^2 + x^2)^{3/2}}$$

Thus electric field at P due to ring 1

$$E_1 = \left(\frac{1}{4\pi\epsilon_0}\right)\frac{q_1 R}{(R^2 + R^2)^{3/2}}$$

$$= \left(\frac{1}{4\pi\epsilon_0}\right)\frac{q_1}{2^{3/2}R^2}$$

Electric field at $P$ due to the ring 2

$$E_2 = \left(\frac{1}{4\pi\epsilon_0}\right)\frac{q_2(2R)}{[R^2 + (2R)^2]^{3/2}}$$

$$= \left(\frac{1}{4\pi\epsilon_0}\right)\frac{2q_2}{R^2 5^{3/2}}.$$

For the net field at $P$ to be zero

$$E_1 = E_2$$

or
$$\left(\frac{1}{4\pi\epsilon_0}\right)\frac{q_1}{R^2 2^{3/2}} = \left(\frac{1}{4\pi\epsilon_0}\right)\frac{2q_2}{R^2 5^{3/2}},$$

which on simplification gives

$$\frac{q_1}{q_2} = \frac{2\times 2^{3/2}}{5^{3/2}} = \frac{2^{5/2}}{5^{3/2}}$$

$$= 0.506. \qquad \textit{Ans.}$$

**Ex. 49** **A very thin disc is uniformly charged with surface density $\sigma > 0$. Find the electric field intensity E on the axis of this disc at the point from which the disc is such at an angle $\Omega$.**

**Sol.**

The electric field due to a small element of disc of charge $\sigma$ dA is

$$dE = \frac{1}{4\pi\epsilon_0}\frac{\sigma dA}{r^2}$$

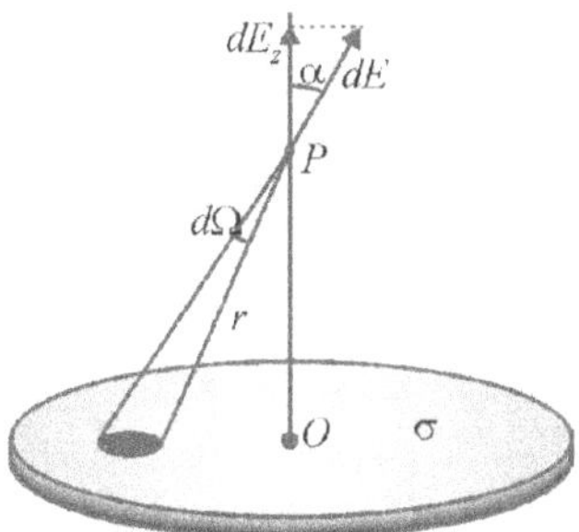


*Fig. 1.142*

The effective field at this point $P$ is dEcos $\alpha$. The total field

$$E_z = \int dE\cos\alpha$$

$$= \frac{1}{4\pi\epsilon_0}\int\frac{\sigma dA}{r^2}\cos\alpha.$$

Here $\int\frac{dA\cos\alpha}{r^2}$ is the total solid angle which $\Omega$. Thus

$$E_z = \left(\frac{1}{4\pi\epsilon_0}\right)\sigma\Omega. \qquad \textit{Ans.}$$

**Ex. 50** **Find the potential of an uncharged conducting sphere provided that a point charge $q$ is located at a distance $r$ from its centre.**

**Sol.**

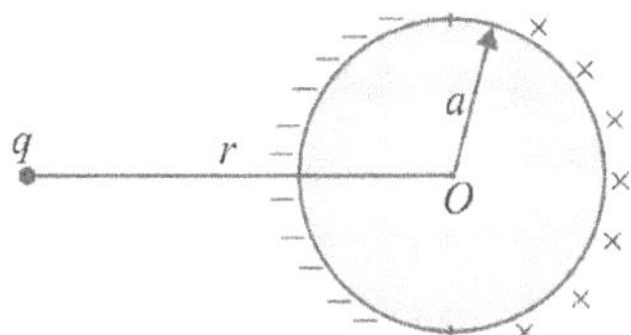


*Fig. 1.143*

Potential $V$ is the same for all points of the sphere.

Thus we can calculate its value at the centre O of the sphere, because only for this point it can be calculated in the most simple way :

$$V = \frac{1}{4\pi\epsilon_0}\frac{q}{r} + V' \qquad \ldots \text{(i)}$$

where first term is the potential due to point charge $q$ and $V'$ is the potential due to induced charge on the surface of the sphere. But entire induced charges are at equal distance a from the point $O$ and the total induced charge is equal to zero, and so $V' = 0$. Thus required potential

$$V = \frac{1}{4\pi\epsilon_0}\frac{q}{r} \qquad \textit{Ans.}$$

**Ex. 51** **A point charge $q$ is within an electrically neutral shell whose outer surface has spherical shape (see *fig. 1.144*). Find the potential at the point $P$ lying outside the shell at a distance $r$ from the centre $O$ of the outer surface.**

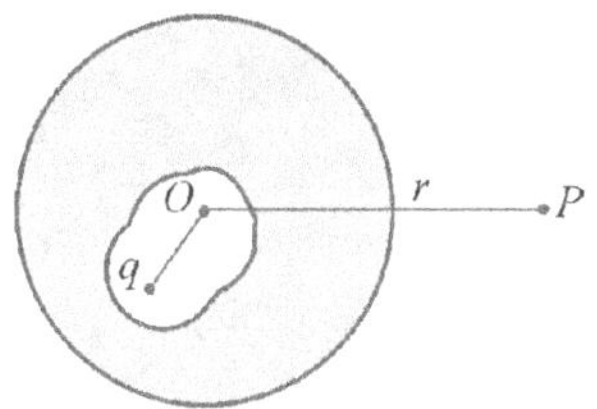


*Fig. 1.144*

**Sol.**

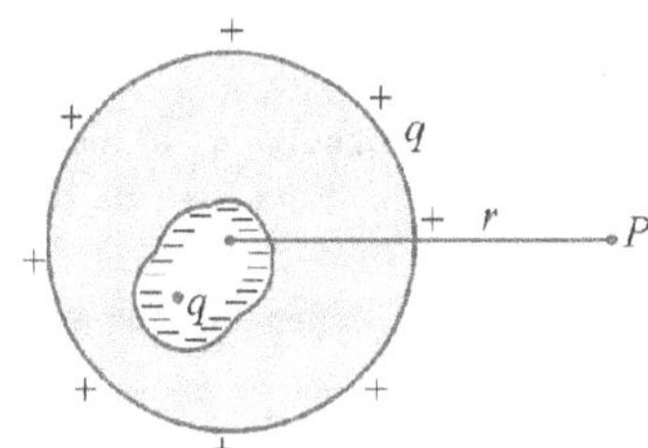


*Fig. 1.145*

The field at the point $P$ is determined only due to induced charges on the outer spherical surface. The field of the point charge $q$ and of the induced charges on the inner surface of the sphere is equal to zero everywhere outside the cavity. Also, the charge on the outer surface of the shell is distributed uniformly and hence potential at $P$

$$V = \frac{1}{4\pi\epsilon_0}\frac{q}{r}. \qquad \textit{Ans.}$$

**Ex. 52** **A point charge $q$ is at a distance $r$ from the centre $O$ of an uncharged spherical conducting layer, whose inner and outer radii are equal to $a$ and $b$ respectively. Find the potential at the point $O$ if $r < a$.**

**Sol.**

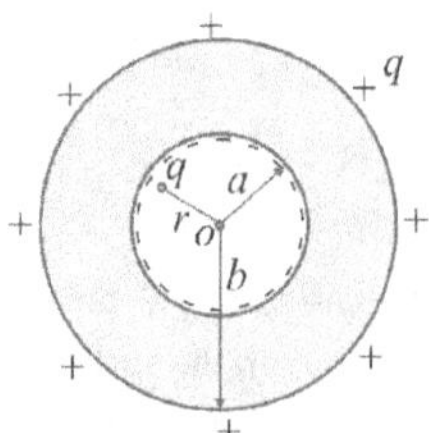


*Fig. 1.146*

Equal amount of charges will induce on the inner and outer surface of the conductor. The each negative charge is at an equal distance a from $O$, and so potential due to this charge at $O$,

$$V_- = \frac{1}{4\pi \in_0} \frac{(-q)}{a}$$

Similarly due to positive charge, potential at $O$

$$V_+ = \frac{1}{4\pi \in_0} \frac{q}{b}$$

Potential due to charge $q$ at $O$

$$V_0 = \frac{1}{4\pi \in_0} \frac{q}{r}$$

Thus total potential

$$V = V_0 + V_- + V_+$$

$$= \frac{q}{4\pi \in_0}\left[\frac{1}{r} - \frac{1}{a} + \frac{1}{b}\right]. \qquad \textit{Ans.}$$

**Ex. 53** **A system consists of two concentric spheres, the inner sphere of radius $R_1$ having a charge $q_1$. What charge $q_2$ must be placed onto the outer sphere of radius $R_2$ to make the potential of the inner sphere equal to zero. What will be the dependence of potential V on the distance $r$ from the centre of the system? Plot schematically the graph of this dependence, assuming that $q_1 < 0$.**

**Sol.**

The potential at the surface of outer sphere

$$V = \frac{1}{4\pi \in_0}\left(\frac{q_1}{R_1} + \frac{q_2}{R_2}\right)$$

It is given that $V = 0$

$$\therefore \quad 0 = \frac{1}{4\pi \in_0}\left(\frac{q_1}{R_1} + \frac{q_2}{R_2}\right)$$

which on solving gives

$$q_2 = -\left(\frac{R_2}{R_1}\right)q_1 \qquad \textit{Ans.}$$

The potential at a distance r from the centre of the system can be written as

$$V_1 = \frac{1}{4\pi \in_0}\frac{q_1 + q_2}{r} \text{ ; for } r > R_2$$

$$= \frac{1}{4\pi \in_0}\frac{q_1 - \left(\frac{R_2}{R_1}\right)q_1}{r}$$

$$= \frac{q_1}{4\pi \in_0}\left[\frac{1 - \frac{R_2}{R_1}}{r}\right]$$

and

$$V_2 = \frac{1}{4\pi \in_0}\left[\frac{q_1}{r} + \frac{q_2}{R_2}\right] \text{ ; for } r < R_1$$

$$= \frac{1}{4\pi \in_0}\left[\frac{q_1}{r} - \frac{R_2}{R_1}\frac{q_1}{R_2}\right]$$

$$= \frac{q_1}{4\pi \in_0}\left[\frac{1}{r} - \frac{1}{R_1}\right].$$

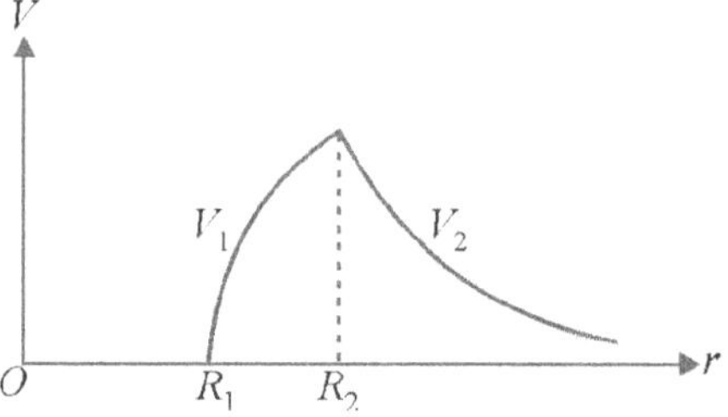


*Fig. 1.147 Variation of V with r.*

**Ex. 54** **A positive charge $q$ is placed in front of a conducting solid cube at a distance $d$ from its centre. Find the electric field at the centre of the cube due to the charges appearing on its surface.**

**Sol.**

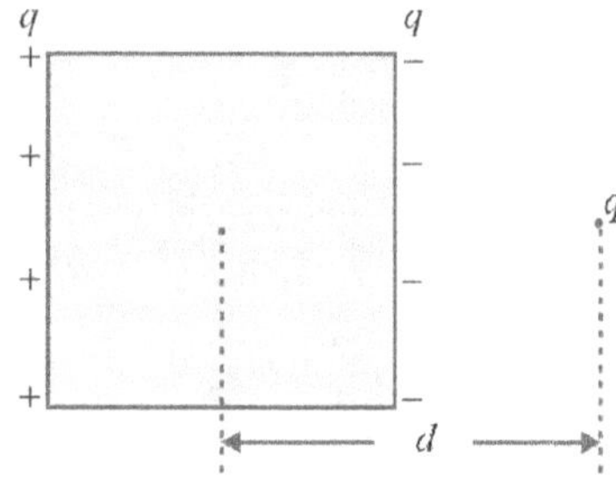


*Fig. 1.148*

Charge will induce on the surface of the cube due to the charge $q$. The net electric field at the centre of the cube due to all the charges must be zero. Let $E_1$ be the electric field due to the charges appearing on the surface of the cube and if $E_2$ is the electric field due to charge $q$, then

$$\vec{E}_1 + \vec{E}_2 = 0$$

or

$$\vec{E}_1 = -\vec{E}_2$$

or

$$E_1 = E_2$$

The electric field due to charge q at the centre of the cube,

$$E_2 = \left(\frac{1}{4\pi\epsilon_0}\right)\frac{q}{d^2}$$

$$\therefore \quad E_1 = \left(\frac{1}{4\pi\epsilon_0}\right)\frac{q}{d^2}. \qquad \textit{Ans.}$$

**Ex. 55** **Calculate the flux of electric field $\vec{E}$ through (i) each of the bases, (ii) the curved surface of a right cylindrical closed surface of radius a and length $\ell$, due to the charge $q$ situated at its geometrical centre.**

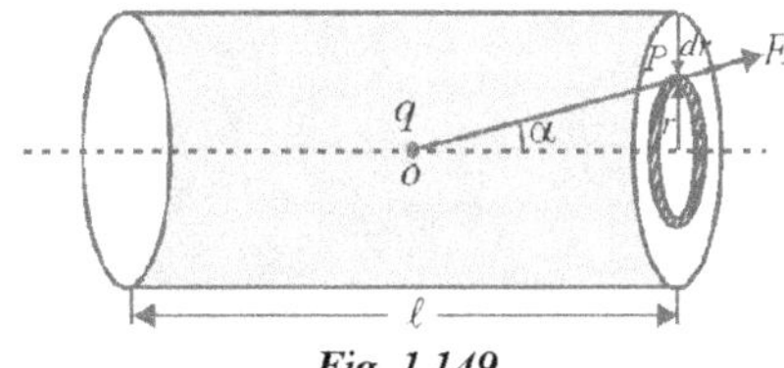


*Fig. 1.149*

## Sol.

Take an element ring of radius $r$ and thickness $dr$ in the right face of the cylinder (see *Fig. 1.149*). The electric field at any point $P$ on an annular ring is

$$E = \left(\frac{1}{4\pi\epsilon_0}\right)\frac{1}{\left(r^2+\frac{\ell^2}{4}\right)} \text{ along } OP$$

The electric flux of this field through the element

$$d\phi = E\cos\alpha \times 2\pi r\, dr$$

$$= \frac{q}{4\pi\epsilon_0} \times \frac{(\ell/2)}{\sqrt{\left(r^2+\frac{\ell^2}{4}\right)}} \times 2\pi r dr$$

$$= \frac{q\ell r dr}{4\epsilon_0\left(r^2+\frac{\ell^2}{4}\right)^{3/2}}$$

$\therefore$ Total flux through the right face of the cylinder

$$\phi_{\text{right}} = \int_0^a \frac{q\ell r dr}{4\epsilon_0\left(r^2+\frac{\ell^2}{4}\right)^{3/2}}$$

$$= \frac{q}{2\epsilon_0}\left[1-\frac{\ell/2}{\left(a^2+\frac{\ell^2}{4}\right)^{1/2}}\right]$$

By symmetry the flux through left face of the cylinder will also be same. Total flux through the cylinder

$$\phi = \frac{q}{\epsilon_0}$$

or $\quad \phi_{curved} + \phi_{right} + \phi_{left} = \dfrac{q}{\epsilon_0}$

or $\phi_{\text{curved}} + 2\phi_{\text{right}} = \dfrac{q}{\epsilon_0}$

$$\therefore \quad \phi_{curved} = \frac{q}{\epsilon_0} - \frac{q}{\epsilon_0}\left[1-\frac{\ell/2}{(a^2+\ell^2/4)^{1/2}}\right]$$

$$= \frac{q\ell}{2\epsilon_0\left(a^2+\frac{\ell^2}{4}\right)^{1/2}}. \qquad \textit{Ans.}$$

**Ex. 56** **Determine the law of variation of potential with distance in an electric field produced between two parallel infinite plates, bearing equal and opposite charges.**

## Sol.

The electric field between such plates is constant. If $E$ is the electric field and $d$ is the separation between the plates, then potential difference between them

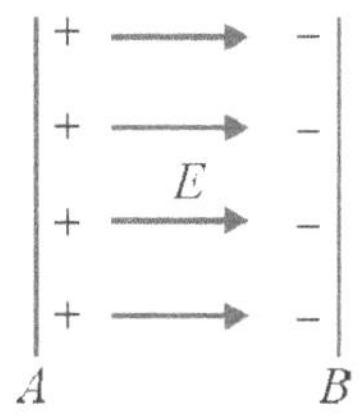

*Fig. 1.150*

$$V_{AB} = V_A - V_B = Ed \Rightarrow E = \frac{V_{AB}}{d} \quad \ldots \text{(i)}$$

If the potential of the negatively charged plate B is assumed zero, then

$$V_A - 0 = Ed$$

or $\quad V_A = Ed$

The potential difference between plate $A$ and an arbitrary point at a distance $x$ from the plate $A$ is given by

$$V_{Ax} = V_A - V_x = Ex \quad \ldots \text{(ii)}$$

From equations (i) and (ii), we get

$$V_x = V_{AB}\left(1-\frac{x}{d}\right) \qquad \textit{Ans.}$$

**Ex. 57** **If the electric potential in a region is represented as $V = 2x + 3y - 4z$, obtain expression for the electric field strength.**

## Sol.

Given $\quad V = 2x+3y-4z$

$$\therefore \quad E_x = -\frac{\partial V}{\partial x} = -\frac{\partial}{\partial x}(2x+3y-4z) = -2$$

$$E_y = -\frac{\partial V}{\partial y} = -\frac{\partial}{\partial y}(2x+3y-4z) = -3$$

and $\quad E_z = -\dfrac{\partial V}{\partial z} = -\dfrac{\partial}{\partial z}(2x+3y-4z) = 4$

Thus $\quad \vec{E} = E_x\hat{i} + E_y\hat{j} + E_z\hat{k}$

$$= -2\hat{i} - 3\hat{j} + 4\hat{k}. \qquad \textit{Ans.}$$

**Ex. 58** **Calculate the potential due to a thin charged rod of length $L$ at the point along and perpendicular to its length.**

**Sol.**

Suppose a thin rod has a uniform linear charge density $\lambda$. To find potential at point $P$, let us divide the rod into a series of small elements of thickness $dx$ each. Consider such an element at a distance $x$ from $O$. The charge on the element

$$dq = \lambda\, dx$$

The potential due to the element at point $P$

$$dV = \left(\frac{1}{4\pi \epsilon_0}\right)\frac{\lambda dx}{r}$$

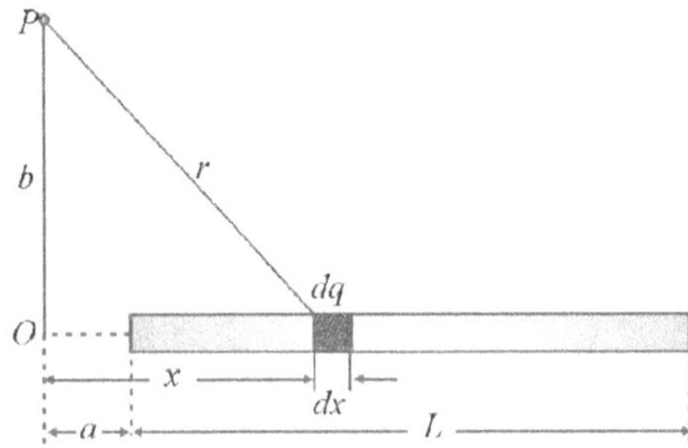


*Fig. 1.151*

The potential due to the entire rod.

$$V = \left(\frac{1}{4\pi \epsilon_0}\right)\int_a^{(L+a)}\frac{\lambda dx}{r}$$

$$= \left(\frac{1}{4\pi \epsilon_0}\right)\int_a^{(L+a)}\frac{\lambda dx}{(b^2+x^2)^{1/2}}$$

$$= \left(\frac{\lambda}{4\pi \epsilon_0}\right)\left[\ln\{x+\sqrt{b^2+x^2}\}\right]_a^{L+a}$$

$$= \left(\frac{\lambda}{4\pi \epsilon_0}\right)\ell n\left[\frac{(L+a)+\sqrt{b^2+(L+a)^2}}{a+\sqrt{b^2+a^2}}\right]$$

*Ans.*

**Ex. 59** **A non-conducting disc of radius *a* and uniform surface charge density σ is placed on the ground, with its axis vertical. A particle of mass m and positive charge q is dropped, along the axis of the disc, from height *H* with zero initial velocity. The particle has** $\frac{q}{m} = \frac{4\pi \epsilon_0 g}{\sigma}$.

**(a) Find the value of *H* if the particle just reaches the disc**

**(b) Sketch the potential energy of the particle as a function of its height and find its equilibrium position.**

**Sol.**

The potential of point $P$ at a distance $H$ from the centre of the disc is given by :

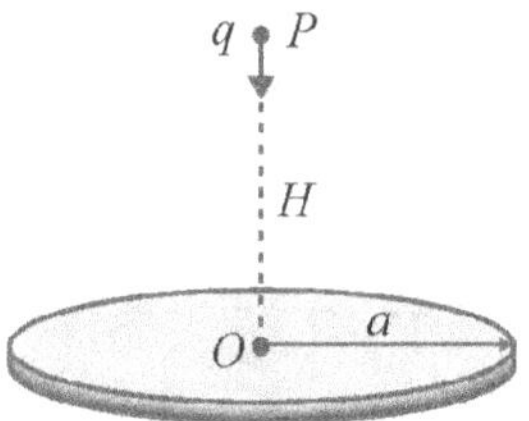


*Fig. 1.152*

$$V_p = \frac{\sigma}{2\epsilon_0}[\sqrt{a^2+H^2} - H]$$

At the centre of the disc, $H = 0$

$$\therefore \quad V_0 = \frac{\sigma a}{2\epsilon_0}$$

(a) For the particle released at $P$ ;

As initial and final K.E. of the particle are zero, so by conservation of mechanical energy, we have

Decrease in gravitational P.E. = Increase in electric P.E.

or $\quad mgH = [V_0 - V_p]\, q$

or $\quad mgH = \frac{\sigma q}{2\epsilon_0}[a - (\sqrt{a^2+H^2} - H)]$

or $\quad gH = \frac{q}{m}\left(\frac{\sigma}{2\epsilon_0}\right)[(a+H) - \sqrt{a^2+H^2}]$

Given $\quad \frac{q}{m} = \frac{4\epsilon_0 g}{\sigma}$

$\therefore \quad gH = \frac{4\epsilon_0 g}{\sigma}\times\frac{\sigma}{2\epsilon_0}[(a+H) - \sqrt{a^2+H^2}]$

or $\quad \frac{H}{2} = (a+H) - \sqrt{a^2+H^2}$

or $\quad \sqrt{a^2+H^2} = a + \frac{H}{2}$

or $\quad a^2 + H^2 = \left(a + \frac{H}{2}\right)^2$

or $\quad a^2 + H^2 = a^2 + \frac{H^2}{4} + aH$

$\therefore \quad H = \frac{4}{3}a$ *Ans.*

(b) Potential energy of the particle at a height H is given by

$$U = \text{Gravitational P.E.} + \text{Electrostatic P.E.}$$

$$= MgH + qV$$

$$= mgH + \frac{\sigma q}{2\epsilon_0}[\sqrt{a^2+H^2} - H] \quad \ldots \text{(i)}$$

$[V = V_f]$

For equilibrium, $F = -\frac{dU}{dH} = 0$

or $$\frac{d}{dH}\left[mgH + \frac{\sigma q}{2\epsilon_0}\left(\sqrt{a^2+H^2} - H\right)\right] = 0$$

or $$mg + \frac{\sigma q}{2\epsilon_0}\left[\frac{H}{\sqrt{a^2+H^2}} - 1\right] = 0$$

As $$\frac{4\epsilon_0 g}{\sigma} = \frac{q}{m} \text{ or } \frac{\sigma q}{2\epsilon_0} = 2mg$$

$$\therefore \quad mg + 2mg\left[\frac{H}{\sqrt{a^2+H^2}} - 1\right] = 0$$

or $$1 + \frac{2H}{\sqrt{a^2+H^2}} - 2 = 0$$

or $$\frac{2H}{\sqrt{a^2+H^2}} = 1$$

or $$\frac{H^2}{a^2+H^2} = \frac{1}{4}$$

or $$4H^2 = a^2 + H^2$$

or $$3H^2 = a^2$$

$$\therefore \quad H = \frac{a}{\sqrt{3}}.$$

From equation (i) at $H = \frac{a}{\sqrt{3}}$

$$U_{min} = mg\frac{a}{\sqrt{3}} + \frac{\sigma q}{2\epsilon_0}\left[\sqrt{a^2 + \left(\frac{a}{\sqrt{3}}\right)^2} - \frac{a}{\sqrt{3}}\right]$$

$$= mg\frac{a}{\sqrt{3}} + 2mg\left[\sqrt{a^2 + \frac{a^2}{3}} - \frac{a}{\sqrt{3}}\right]$$

$$= \sqrt{3}\, mga.$$

Also at $H = 0$, $U = 2\, mga$

The potential energy verses height graph is shown in figure

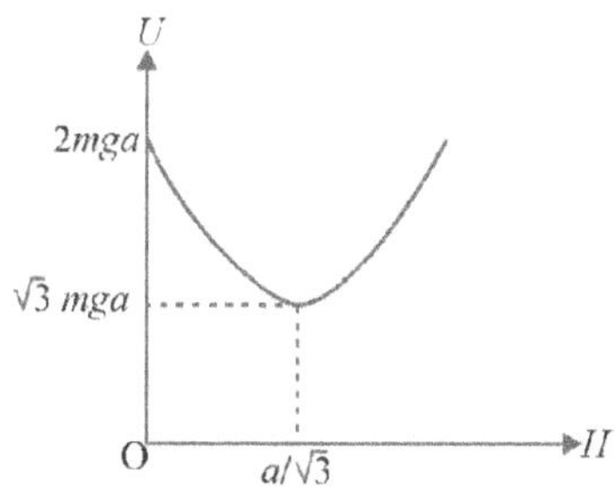


*Fig. 1.153*

**Ex. 60** **There are two large metallic plates $S_1$ and $S_2$ carrying surface charge densities $\sigma_1$ and $\sigma_2$ respectively ($\sigma_1 > \sigma_2$) placed at a distance $d$ apart in vacuum. Find the work done by the electric field in moving a point charge $q$ distant $a$ ($a < d$) from $S_1$ towards $S_2$ along a line making an angle $\pi/4$ with the normal to the plates.**

## Sol.

If $E_1$ and $E_2$ are the respective fields produced by the plates, then net field between the plates

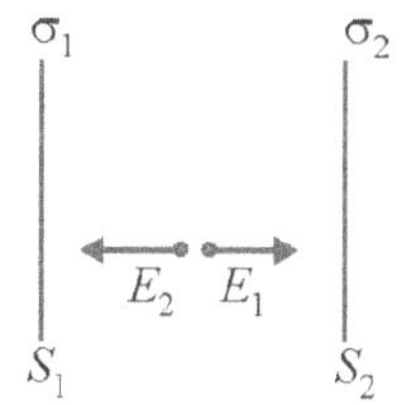


*Fig. 1.154*

$$E = E_1 - E_2$$

$$= \frac{\sigma_1}{\epsilon_0} - \frac{\sigma_2}{\epsilon_0} = \frac{\sigma_1 - \sigma_2}{\epsilon_0}$$

Force on the point charge $F = qE = \frac{q}{\epsilon_0}(\sigma_1 - \sigma_2)$

Work done by the electric field

$$W = Fs\cos\theta$$

$$= \frac{q}{\epsilon_0}(\sigma_1 - \sigma_2)a\cos\frac{\pi}{4}$$

$$= \frac{qa}{\sqrt{2}}(\sigma_1 - \sigma_2).$$ *Ans.*

**Ex. 61** **Two point charges $q$ and $-q$ are separated by distance $2\ell$. Find the flux of the electric field strength vector across a circle of radius $R$.**

## Sol.

Consider a ring element of thickness dr at a distance r from centre. The flux across this element

$$d\phi = E \times 2\pi r dr$$

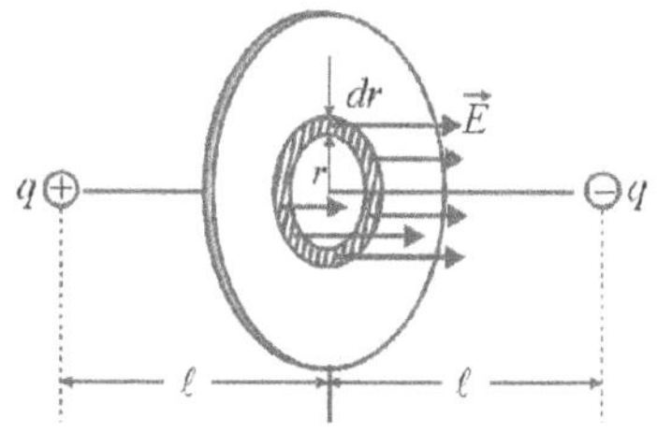


*Fig. 1.155*

Total flux

$$\phi = \int_0^R E \times 2\pi r\, dr$$

where $E = \frac{1}{4\pi \epsilon_0} \frac{P}{(r^2+\ell^2)^{3/2}}$ and $P = q \times 2\ell$.

Substituting these value in above expression, we have

$$\phi = \frac{P}{4\pi \epsilon_0} \int_0^R \frac{2\pi r dr}{(r^2+\ell^2)^{3/2}}$$

Substituting, $r^2 + \ell^2 = z$

also $\quad 2r\,dr = dz$

$$\therefore \quad \phi = \frac{P}{4\epsilon_0} \int_0^R z^{-3/2} dz$$

$$= \frac{P}{4\epsilon_0} \left| \frac{z^{-1/2}}{-\frac{1}{2}} \right|_0^R$$

$$= \frac{-P}{2\epsilon_0} \left| (r^2+\ell^2)^{-1/2} \right|_0^R$$

$$= \frac{-P}{2\epsilon_0} \left| \frac{1}{\sqrt{r^2+\ell^2}} \right|_0^R$$

$$= \frac{-P}{2\epsilon_0} \left( \frac{1}{\sqrt{R^2+\ell^2}} - \frac{1}{\ell} \right)$$

$$= \frac{q\ell}{\epsilon_0} \left( \frac{1}{\ell} - \frac{1}{\sqrt{R^2+\ell^2}} \right). \quad \textit{Ans.}$$

**Ex. 62** **A point charge $q$ is isolated at the centre $O$ of a sphere uncharged conducting layer provided with a small orifice. The inside and outside radii of the layer are equal to $a$ and $b$ respectively. What amount of work has to be performed to slowly transfer the charge $q$ from the point $O$ through the orifice and into infinity.**

**Sol.**

Because of charge $q$, the charge will induce over the conductor as shown in figure.

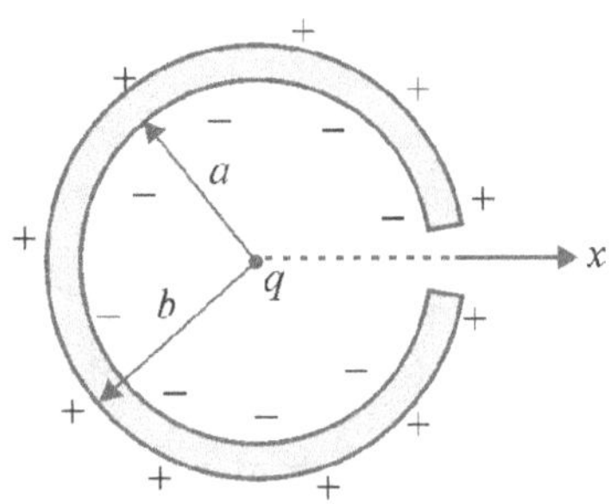


*Fig. 1.156*

The potential at the centre

$$V = \frac{q}{4\pi \epsilon_0} \left( \frac{1}{b} - \frac{1}{a} \right)$$

Potential difference

$$\Delta V = V_\infty - V$$

$$= 0 - \frac{q}{4\pi \epsilon_0} \left( \frac{1}{b} - \frac{1}{a} \right)$$

$$= \frac{q}{4\pi \epsilon_0} \left( \frac{1}{a} - \frac{1}{b} \right)$$

Work done in transferring the charge $dq$, from centre to infinity

$$dW = (\Delta V) dq$$

Total work $\quad W = \int (\Delta V) dq$

$$= \frac{1}{4\pi \epsilon_0} \left( \frac{1}{a} - \frac{1}{b} \right) \int_0^q q\,dq$$

$$= \frac{q^2}{8\pi \epsilon_0} \left( \frac{1}{a} - \frac{1}{b} \right). \quad \textit{Ans.}$$

**Ex. 63** **A conducting spherical bubble of radius a and thickness $t$ ($t << a$) is charged to a potential $V$. Now it collapses to form a spherical droplet. Find the potential of the droplet.**

**Sol.**

As mass and charge of the bubble remain conserved, and if $r$ be the radius of the resulting drop, so

$$\left( \frac{4}{3} \pi r^3 \right) \rho = (4\pi a^2 t) \rho$$

or $\quad r = (3a^2 t)^{1/3}$

The potential of the bubble

$$V = \frac{1}{4\pi \epsilon_0} \frac{q}{a},$$

which gives $\quad q = 4\pi \epsilon_0 aV$

Now potential of the resulting drop

$$V' = \frac{1}{4\pi \epsilon_0} \frac{q}{r}$$

$$= \frac{1}{4\pi \epsilon_0} \frac{4\pi \epsilon_0 aV}{(3a^2 t)^{1/3}}$$

$$= \left( \frac{a}{3t} \right)^{1/3} V. \quad \textit{Ans.}$$

**Ex. 64** **The minimum strength of a uniform electric field which can tear a conducting uncharged thin-walled sphere into two parts is known to be $E_0$. Determine the minimum electric field strength $E_1$ required to tear the sphere of twice as large radius if the thickness of its walls is the same as in the former case.**

**Sol.**

If $\sigma$ is the surface charge density on the sphere and R its radius, then for tearing of the sphere

$$\sigma = \sqrt{\frac{8T \in_0}{R}}$$

or $\quad \sigma^2 R = \text{constant.}$

Here $T$ is the rupture strength of the sphere.

Since $\quad E \propto \sigma,$

$\therefore \quad E^2 R = \text{constant}$

For the sphere of twice the radius, we have

$$E_0^2 R = E_1^2 (2R),$$

which on simplification gives

$$E_1 = \frac{E_0}{\sqrt{2}}. \qquad \textit{Ans.}$$

**Ex. 65** **Two small identical balls lying on a horizontal plane are connected by a weightless spring - One ball is fixed at point $O$ and the other is free. The balls are charged identically, as a result of which the spring length increases two fold. Determine the change in the frequency of harmonic vibrations of the system.**

**Sol.**

If $\ell$ be the length of the spring, then extension of the spring becomes $2\ell$.

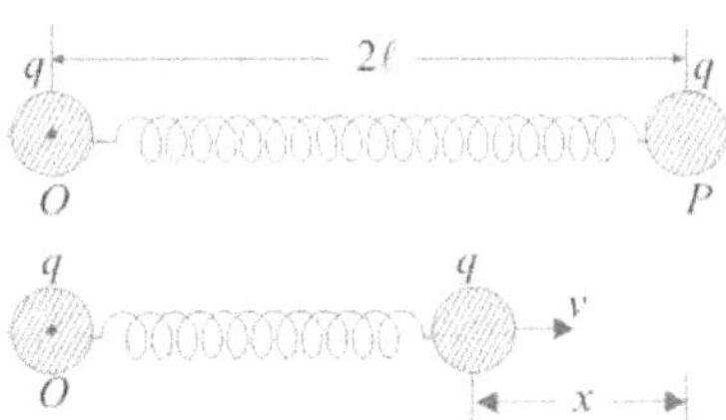


*Fig. 1.157*

Let at any instant free ball is displaced from the mean position by a distance $x$ which is small comparison to $\ell$.

The total mechanical energy of the system

$$E = \frac{1}{2}k(\ell - x)^2 + \frac{1}{4\pi \in_0}\frac{q^2}{(2\ell - x)} + \frac{1}{2}mv^2$$

$$= \frac{1}{2}k(\ell - x)^2 + \frac{1}{4\pi \in_0}q^2(2\ell - x)^{-1} + \frac{1}{2}mv^2$$

$$= \frac{1}{2}k(\ell - x)^2 + \frac{1}{4\pi \in_0}q^2\left[(2\ell)^{-1}\left\{1 - \frac{x}{2\ell}\right\}^{-1}\right] + \frac{1}{2}mv^2$$

$$= \frac{1}{2}k(\ell - x)^2 + \frac{q^2}{4\pi \in_0}\left[\frac{1}{2\ell}\left\{1 + \frac{x}{2\ell}\right\}\right] + \frac{1}{2}mv^2$$

$$= \frac{1}{2}k(\ell - x)^2 + \frac{q^2}{4\pi \in_0}\left[\frac{1}{2\ell} + \frac{x}{4\ell^2}\right] + \frac{1}{2}mv^2 \quad \text{... (i)}$$

At the mean position

$$k\ell = \frac{q^2}{4\pi \in_0 (2\ell)^2} \quad \text{... (ii)}$$

On solving equations (i) and (ii) and simplifying, we get

$$E \simeq \frac{5}{2}k\ell^2 + kx^2 + \frac{1}{2}mv^2 \quad \text{... (iii)}$$

For free oscillations,

$$\frac{dE}{dt} = 0$$

or $$\frac{d}{dt}\left[\frac{5}{2}k\ell^2 + kx^2 + \frac{1}{2}mv^2\right] = 0$$

or $$2kx\frac{dx}{dt} + \frac{m}{2} \times 2v \times \frac{dv}{dt} = 0$$

or $$\frac{dv}{dt} = -\frac{2k}{m}x$$

On comparing with standard equation of SHM, $a = -\omega^2 x$, we get $\omega = \sqrt{\frac{2k}{m}}$. The frequency without charge $\omega_0 = \sqrt{\frac{k}{m}}$. Thus $\omega = \sqrt{2}\omega_0$.

## 1.22 ELECTRIC POTENTIAL ENERGY OF SYSTEM OF CHARGES

For the calculation of potential energy of the system of charged particles, the method is to compute the potential energy for each pair of charges separately and then add these algebraically. Hence for n-charge particle system,

$$U = \frac{1}{4\pi \in_0}\sum_{\text{all pairs}}\frac{q_i q_j}{r_{ij}}$$

or $$U = \frac{1}{2}\left(\frac{1}{4\pi \in_0}\right)\sum_{i=1}^{n}\sum_{j=1}^{n}\frac{q_i q_j}{r_{ij}}; \; (i \neq j)$$

In the expression $\frac{1}{2}$ is introduced as each pair is counted twice. For example, the energy contribution due to charge $q_1$ and $q_2$ is required once only when $i = 1$ and $j = 2$. But in this expression this term comes twice ; once when $i = 1, j = 2$ and other when $i = 2, j = 1$. For $n$ - particle system, there are $N$-pairs, where

$$N = \frac{1}{2}n(n-1)$$

**Ex. 66** **A positively charged sphere of mass $m = 5$ kg is attached by a spring of force constant $k = 10^4$ N/m. The sphere is tied with a thread so that the spring is in its natural length. Another identical, negatively charged sphere is fixed to the floor, vertically below the positively charged sphere as shown in *fig. 1.158*. Initial separation between sphere is $x_0 = 0.50$ m. Now thread is burnt and maximum elongation of the spring is 0.10 m, calculate the charge on each sphere ($g = 10$ m/s²).**

**Sol.**

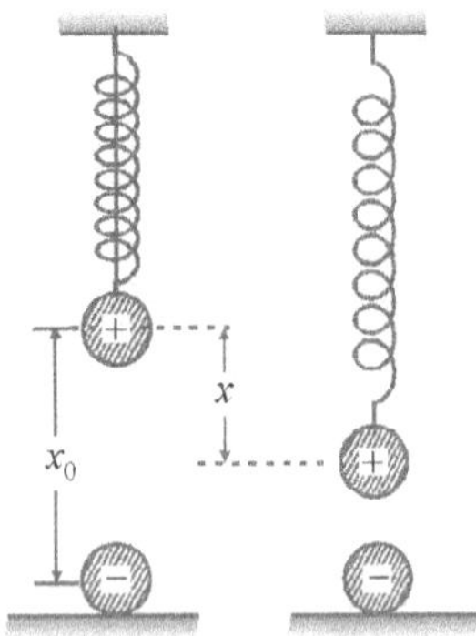


*Fig. 1.158*

In conservative fields the total mechanical energy of the system remains constant. Thus

Mechanical energy at initial position = Mechanical energy at final position

If $x$ be the maximum elongation of the spring and $q$ be the charge on each sphere, then

$$\frac{1}{4\pi\epsilon_0}\frac{q(-q)}{x_0} + mgx_0 + 0 = \frac{1}{4\pi\epsilon_0}\frac{q(-q)}{(x_0 - x)} + mg(x_0 - x) + \frac{1}{2}kx^2$$

or
$$\frac{1}{2}kx^2 = mgx + \frac{1}{4\pi\epsilon_0}q^2\left[\frac{1}{x_0 - x} - \frac{1}{x_0}\right]$$

Given, $x_0 = 0.50$ m, $x = 0.1$ m and $k = 10^4$ N/m

$$\therefore \quad \frac{1}{2}\times 10^4 \times (0.1)^2 =$$

$$5\times 10\times 0.1 + 9\times 10^9 \times q^2\left[\frac{1}{(0.50-0.1)} - \frac{1}{0.5}\right]$$

After simplifying, we get

$$q = 10^{-4}\text{ C}$$ *Ans.*

**Ex. 67** **Eight point charges are placed at the corners of a cube of edge a as shown in *fig. 1.159*. Find the work done in dissembling this system of charges.**

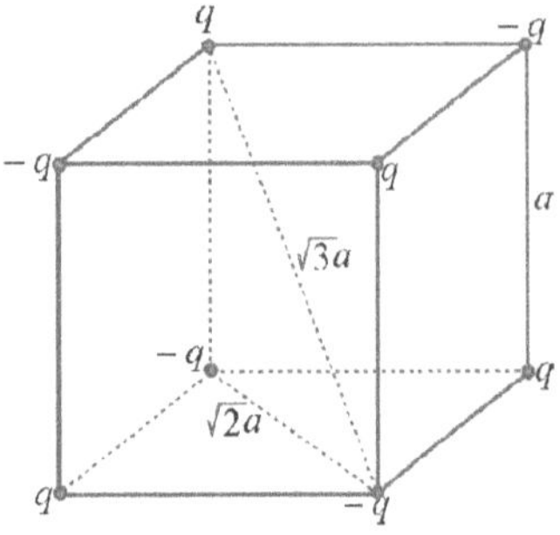


*Fig. 1.159*

**Sol.**

The number of charge-pairs $= \frac{n(n-1)}{2} = \frac{8(8-1)}{2} = 28$

Out of these 28 pairs ;

(i) 12 pairs are of opposite charges at separation a each, with total energy

$$U_1 = 12\left[\frac{1}{4\pi\epsilon_0}\frac{q(-q)}{a}\right]$$

(ii) 12 pairs of similar charges at separation $\sqrt{2}\,a$ each , with total energy

$$U_2 = 12\left[\frac{1}{4\pi\epsilon_0}\frac{qq}{\sqrt{2}\,a}\right]$$

(iii) 4 pairs of opposite charges at separation $\sqrt{3}\,a$ , with total energy

$$U_3 = 4\left[\frac{1}{4\pi\epsilon_0}\frac{q(-q)}{\sqrt{3}\,a}\right].$$

Thus total potential energy of the system of charges

$$U = U_1 + U_2 + U_3$$

$$= \frac{1}{4\pi\epsilon_0}\frac{q^2}{a}\left[-12 + \frac{12}{\sqrt{2}} - \frac{4}{\sqrt{3}}\right]$$

$$= -5.83\left[\frac{1}{4\pi\epsilon_0}\frac{q^2}{a}\right]$$

Thus work done in dissembling the charge $= +\,5.83\left[\frac{1}{4\pi\epsilon_0}\frac{q^2}{a}\right]$. *Ans.*

**Ex. 68** **Four point charges + 8μC, –1μC, –1μC and the + 8μC are fixed at the points $-\sqrt{27/2}$ m , $-\sqrt{3/2}$ m , $+\sqrt{3/2}$ m and $\sqrt{27/2}$ m respectively on the $y$-axis. A particle of mass $6\times 10^{-4}$ kg and a charge + 0.1 μC moves along the -$x$ direction. Its speed at $x = +\infty$ is $v_0$. Find the least value of $v_0$ for which the particle will cross the origin. Find also the kinetic energy of the particle at the origin. Assume that space is gravity free. Given $1/4\pi\epsilon_0 = 9\times 10^9$ Nm²/C²**

**Sol.**

Suppose $q_1 = 8$ μC, $q_2 = 1$μC and $q_0 = 0.1$μC. Because of the symmetric positions of the charges, the force on the charge $q_0$ will be along $x$-direction.

If $P$ be a point at a distance $x$ where net force is zero, then

$$2\times\frac{1}{4\pi\epsilon_0}\frac{q_1q_0}{PC^2}\cos\alpha - 2\times\frac{1}{4\pi\epsilon_0}\frac{q_2q_0}{PD^2}\cos\beta = 0$$

or
$$\frac{q_1\left(\frac{x}{PC}\right)}{PC^2} = \frac{q_2(x/PD)}{PD^2}$$

or
$$\frac{q_1}{q_2} = \frac{PC^3}{PD^3}$$

or
$$\frac{1}{8} = \frac{\left(\frac{3}{2}+x\right)^{3/2}}{\left(\frac{27}{2}+x^2\right)^{3/2}}$$

After solving, we get $x = \sqrt{2.5}\,m$

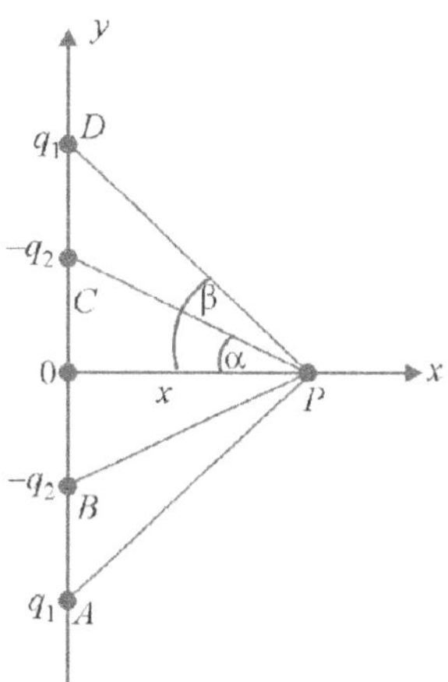


*Fig. 1.160*

If charge $q_0$ crosses the point $P$, then it will move by attractive force of the particle towards the origin, so its speed should be infinitely small at point $P$.

Thus by conservation of mechanical energy, we have

$$[\text{K.E.} + \text{P.E.}]_{\text{at infinity}} \geq [\text{K.E.} + \text{P.E.}]_{\text{at P}}$$

or $$\left[\frac{1}{2}mv_0^2 + 0\right]$$

$$\geq 2 \times \frac{1}{4\pi \in_0}\left[\frac{(8\times10^{-6})(0.1\times10^{-6})}{\sqrt{\frac{27}{2}+2.5}} + \frac{(-1\times10^{-6})(0.1\times10^{-6})}{\sqrt{\frac{3}{2}+2.5}}\right]$$

After solving, we get

$$v_0^2 \geq 9$$

or $$(v_0)_{\min} = 3 \text{ m/s}$$ ***Ans.***

Let $K$ is the K.E. of the charge $q_0$ at the origin, then

$$K + 2\times\frac{1}{4\pi \in_0}\left[\frac{(8\times10^{-6})\times(0.1\times10^{-6})}{\sqrt{27/2}} - \frac{(1\times10^{-6})\times(0.1\times10^{-6})}{\sqrt{3/2}}\right]$$

$$= \left[\frac{1}{2}mv_0^2 + 0\right]$$

Substituting $v_0 = 3$ m/s and simplifying, we get

$$K = 17.2 \times 10^{-4} \text{ J.}$$ ***Ans.***

**Ex. 69** **Two plane parallel conducting plates $1.5 \times 10^{-2}$ m apart are held horizontal one above the other in air. The upper plate is maintained as positive potential of 1.5 k volt while the other plate is earthed. Calculate the number of electrons which must be attached to a small oil drop of mass $4.9 \times 10^{-15}$ kg between the plates to maintain it at rest, assuming that the density of air is negligible in comparison with that of oil. If the potential of above plate is suddenly changed to –1.5 k volt. What is the initial acceleration of the charged drop? Also obtain the terminal velocity of the drop if its radius is 5.0 $\times 10^{-6}$ m and the coefficient of viscosity of air is $1.8 \times 10^{-5}$ N-s/m²**

**Sol.**

For the equilibrium, the drop must have negative charge $q$, and so

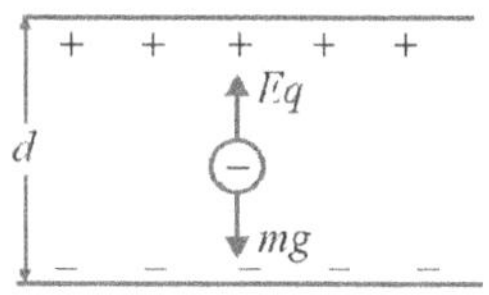

*Fig. 1.161*

$$qE = mg \quad \dots \text{(i)}$$

or $$q = \frac{mg}{E}$$

Here $$E = \frac{V}{d} = \frac{1.5\times10^3}{1.5\times10^{-2}} = 10^5 \text{ V/m}$$

$$m = 4.9 \times 10^{-15} \text{ kg}$$

$$\therefore \quad q = \frac{(4.9\times10^{-15})\times(9.8)}{10^5}$$

$$= 4.8 \times 10^{-19} \text{ C}$$

If $n$ is the number of electrons on the oil drop, the

$$n = \frac{q}{e} = \frac{4.8\times10^{-19}}{1.6\times10^{-19}}$$

$$= 3.$$ ***Ans.***

When polarity of plates is reversed, the electric force also acts in downward direction, and so net force

$$F = mg + qE \quad \dots\text{(ii)}$$

From equations (i) and (ii), we get

$$F = 2\,mg$$

Initial acceleration of the drop

$$a = \frac{F}{m} = \frac{2mg}{m} = 2g \text{ m/s}^2 \text{ downward}$$ ***Ans.***

As drop accelerates in downward direction, its velocity increases and hence viscous force increases in upward direction. At certain moment the net force on the drop becomes zero and thereafter drop will move with constant velocity. If $v$ is the terminal velocity, then

$$2mg = 6\pi\eta rv$$

$$\therefore \quad v = \frac{mg}{3\pi\eta r}$$

$$= \frac{(4.9\times10^{-15})\times9.8}{3\pi\times(1.8\times10^{-5})\times(5.0\times10^{-6})}$$

$$= 5.7 \times 10^{-5} \text{ m/s.}$$ ***Ans.***

**Ex. 70** **Small identical balls with equal charges are fixed at the vertices of a right 1977 -gon with side $a$. At a certain instant, one of the balls is released, and a sufficiently long time interval later, the ball adjacent to the first released ball is freed. The kinetic energies of the released balls are found to differs by $K$ at a sufficiently long distance from the polygon. Determine the charge $q$ of each ball.**

**Sol.**

After a very long time, the potential energy stored in the system will give the kinetic energy to the first released ball, and so

$$\frac{1}{2}mv_1^2 = \frac{q^2}{4\pi\epsilon_0}\left[\frac{1}{a_1}+\frac{1}{a_2}+....+\frac{1}{a_{N-1}}\right] \quad ...\text{(i)}$$

where $a_1$, $a_2$, .......$a_{N-1}$ are the distances from the first ball (before it was released) to the remaining balls in the circle, $a_1$ and $a_{N-1}$ being the distances to the nearest neighbours, i.e, $a_1 = a_{N-1} = a$. Here $N = 1977$. Similar treatment can be made for second ball. Neglecting the influence of the first released ball, then we have

$$\frac{1}{2}mv_2^2 = \frac{q^2}{4\pi\epsilon_0}\left[\frac{1}{a_1}+\frac{1}{a_2}+....+\frac{1}{a_{N-2}}\right] \quad ...\text{(ii)}$$

From equations (i) and (ii), we have

$$\frac{1}{2}mv_1^2 - \frac{1}{2}mv_2^2 = \frac{q^2}{4\pi\epsilon_0 a}$$

or $$K = \frac{q^2}{4\pi\epsilon_0 a}$$

or $$q = \sqrt{4\pi\epsilon_0 aK}$$ ***Ans.***

## 1.23 ELECTRIC DIPOLE

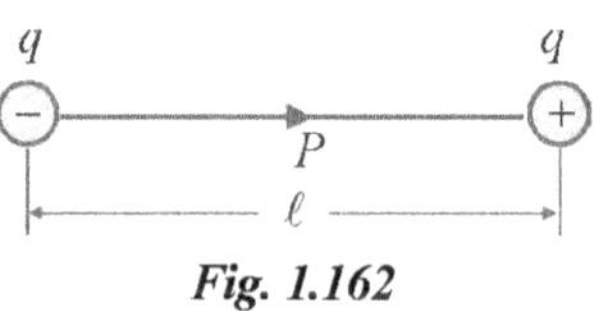

*Fig. 1.162*

A system of two equal and opposite charges fixed at a small distance constitutes a dipole. If $\ell$ is the distance between the charges $+q$ and $-q$, then dipole moment is defined as :

$$\vec{P} = q\vec{\ell}.$$

It is a vector quantity and its direction is from negative to positive charge.

**Potential due to an electric dipole :** Consider a dipole $AB$ of dipole moment, $\vec{P} = q\vec{\ell}$.

We want to calculate the electric potential at a point $P$, at a distance $r$ from the centre of the dipole. Let line $r$ makes an angle $\theta$ with the line of dipole.

The electric potential due to the charges of the dipole at $P$

$$V_p = \left(\frac{1}{4\pi\epsilon_0}\right)\left[\frac{q}{PB} - \frac{q}{PA}\right]$$

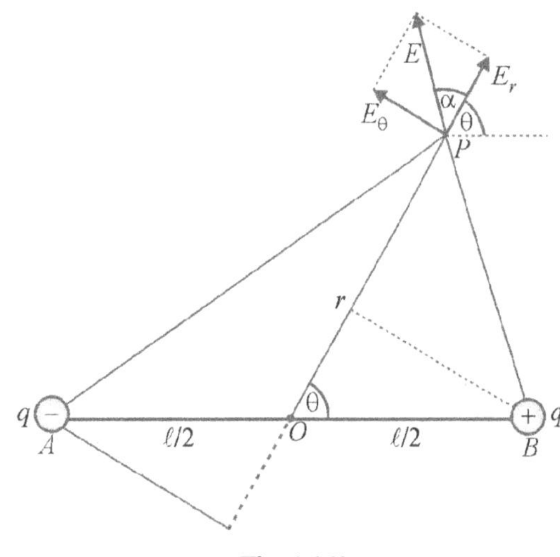

*Fig. 1.163*

From the figure, $PA = r + \frac{\ell}{2}\cos\theta$ and $PB = r - \frac{\ell}{2}\cos\theta$, assuming that $\ell << r$.

$$\therefore \quad V_p = \left(\frac{1}{4\pi\epsilon_0}\right)\left[\frac{q}{\left(r-\frac{\ell}{2}\cos\theta\right)} - \frac{q}{\left(r+\frac{\ell}{2}\cos\theta\right)}\right]$$

$$= \left(\frac{1}{4\pi\epsilon_0}\right)\frac{q\ell\cos\theta}{\left[r^2 - \frac{\ell^2}{4}\cos^2\theta\right]}$$

As $\ell << r$, hence $\frac{\ell^2}{4}\cos^2\theta$ can be neglected and putting $q\ell = P$, we get

$$V_P = \left(\frac{1}{4\pi\epsilon_0}\right)\frac{P\cos\theta}{r^2}. \quad ...(1)$$

In vector notation it can be written as :

$$V_P = \left(\frac{1}{4\pi\epsilon_0}\right)\frac{\vec{P}.\vec{r}}{r^3}.$$

**Electric field due to an electric dipole :** The electric field at point $P$ varies with $r$ and $\theta$ both, so we can not get $\vec{E}$ from the differentiation of $V$ at once. The components of $\vec{E}$ in two perpendicular directions are ; the radial component $E_r$, and transverse component $E_\theta$. Thus

$$E_r = -\frac{\partial V}{\partial r} = -\frac{\partial}{\partial r}\left[\frac{1}{4\pi \epsilon_0}\frac{P\cos\theta}{r^2}\right]$$

$$= \left(\frac{1}{4\pi \epsilon_0}\right)\frac{2P\cos\theta}{r^3} \quad \ldots \text{(i)}$$

and

$$E_\theta = -\frac{1}{r}\frac{\partial V}{\partial \theta} = -\frac{1}{r}\frac{\partial}{\partial \theta}\left[\frac{1}{4\pi \epsilon_0}\frac{P\cos\theta}{r^2}\right]$$

$$= \left(\frac{1}{4\pi \epsilon_0}\right)\frac{P\sin\theta}{r^3} \quad \ldots \text{(ii)}$$

$\therefore$

$$E = \sqrt{E_r^2 + E_\theta^2}$$

or

$$E = \left(\frac{1}{4\pi \epsilon_0}\right)\frac{P\sqrt{3\cos^2\theta + 1}}{r^3} \quad \ldots (2)$$

Dividing equation (ii) by (i), we get

$$\tan\alpha = \frac{\tan\theta}{2}$$

or

$$\alpha = \tan^{-1}\left(\frac{\tan\theta}{2}\right) \quad \ldots (3)$$

Here $\alpha$ is the angle made by the resultant field $\vec{\mathbf{E}}$ with the line of $\vec{\mathbf{r}}$. The direction of $\vec{\mathbf{E}}$ from the direction of dipolemoment is $\theta + \alpha$.

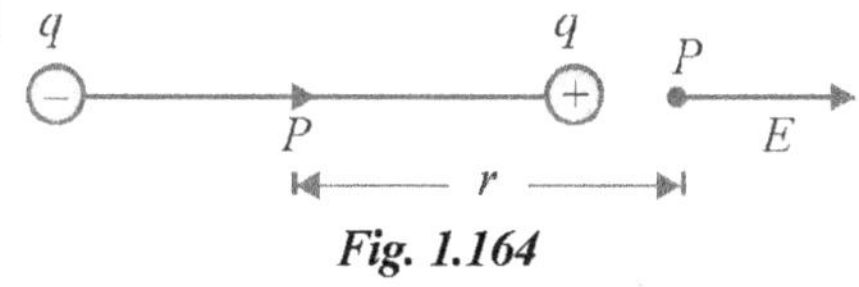

Fig. 1.164

**Special cases :**

1. **End -on position :** At the axis of the dipole, $\theta = 0$, and so

$$E = \left(\frac{1}{4\pi \epsilon_0}\right)\frac{2P}{r^3}$$

and

$$V = \left(\frac{1}{4\pi \epsilon_0}\right)\frac{P}{r^2}$$

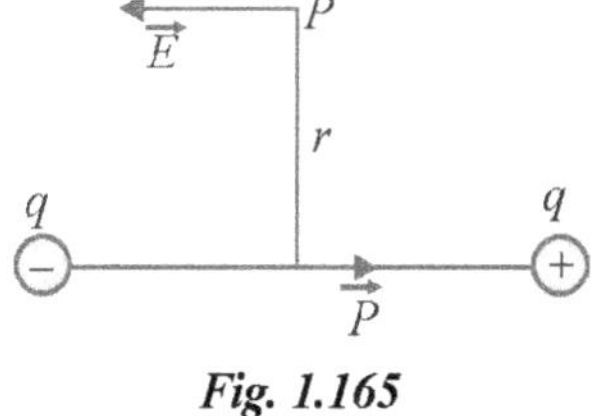

Fig. 1.165

2. **Broad side -on position :** At the equatorial line of the dipole, $\theta = 90°$ and so

$$E = \left(\frac{1}{4\pi \epsilon_0}\right)\frac{P}{r^3}$$

and $V = 0.$

**Electric field and potential due to an electric dipole : Second method**

1. **End-on position :**

   The electric field at any point $P$, at a distance $r$ from the centre of the dipole is the vector sum of the field produced by both the charges. Thus

$$E = E_{(+)} - E_{(-)}$$

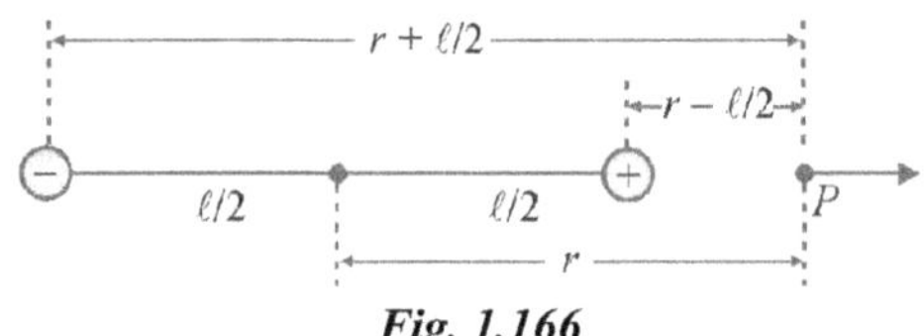

Fig. 1.166

$$= \frac{1}{4\pi \in_0}\left[\frac{q}{\left(r-\frac{\ell}{2}\right)^2} - \frac{q}{\left(r+\frac{\ell}{2}\right)^2}\right]$$

$$= \frac{1}{4\pi \in_0}\frac{2q\ell r}{\left(r^2-\frac{\ell^2}{4}\right)^2}$$

$$= \frac{1}{4\pi \in_0}\frac{2\mathrm{P}\mathrm{r}}{\left(r^2-\frac{\ell^2}{4}\right)^2}$$

As $\ell << r$, $\therefore\ r^2 - \frac{\ell^2}{4} \approx r^2$, and so

$$E = \left(\frac{1}{4\pi \in_0}\right)\frac{2P}{r^3}.$$

**Electric potential :**

$$V = \frac{1}{4\pi \in_0}\left[\frac{q}{r-\ell/2} - \frac{q}{r+\ell/2}\right]$$

$$= \frac{1}{4\pi \in_0}\left[\frac{q\ell}{r^2-\ell^2/4}\right]$$

$$= \frac{1}{4\pi \in_0}\left[\frac{P}{r^2-\ell^2/4}\right]$$

As $\ell << r$,

$$\therefore \quad V = \left(\frac{1}{4\pi \in_0}\right)\frac{P}{r^2}.$$

2. **Broadside -on position :**

The electric field at point $P$ is the vector sum of the fields produced by the two charges. As the distance of the point $P$ is equal for both the charges, and so magnitude of field produced by each charge

$$E' = \frac{1}{4\pi \in_0}\frac{q}{\left(r^2+\ell^2/4\right)}$$

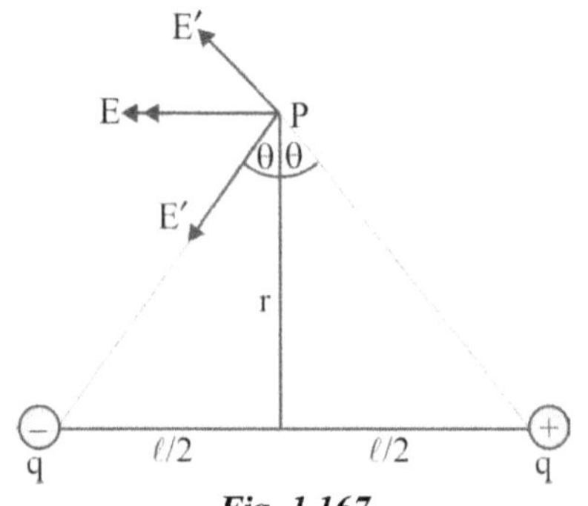

Fig. 1.167

The resultant field at the point $P$

$$E = 2E'\sin\theta$$

$$= 2\left[\left(\frac{1}{4\pi \in_0}\right)\frac{q}{r^2+\ell^2/4}\right]\times\frac{\ell/2}{\sqrt{r^2+\ell^2/4}}$$

$$= \frac{1}{4\pi \in_0}\frac{q\ell}{\left(r^2+\ell^2/4\right)^{3/2}}$$

$$= \frac{1}{4\pi \in_0}\frac{P}{\left(r^2+\ell^2/4\right)^{3/2}}$$

For $\ell << r$, $r^2 + \frac{\ell^2}{4} \approx r^2$, and so

$$E = \left(\frac{1}{4\pi \in_0}\right)\frac{P}{r^3}.$$

**3. At any position :**

Resolve the given dipole moment along OP and perpendicular to it. These are $P\cos\theta$ and $P\sin\theta$ and if $E_1$ and $E_2$ are the respective electric fields produced by them, then

$$E_1 = \frac{1}{4\pi\epsilon_0}\frac{2P\cos\theta}{r^3} \qquad \ldots \text{(i)}$$

and

$$E_2 = \frac{1}{4\pi\epsilon_0}\frac{P\sin\theta}{r^3} \qquad \ldots \text{(ii)}$$

Squaring (i) and (ii) and adding, we get

$$E = \sqrt{E_1^2 + E_2^2} = \frac{1}{4\pi\epsilon_0}\frac{P\sqrt{3\cos^2\theta + 1}}{r^3}$$

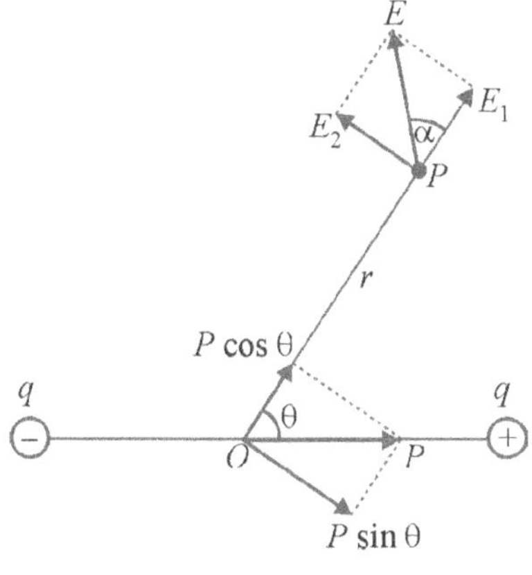


*Fig. 1.168*

**Note:** At end-on position the angle between $\vec{P}$ and $\vec{E}$ is 0°, while at broadside -on position the angle between $\vec{P}$ and $\vec{E}$ is 180°.

## 1.24 A DIPOLE IN AN ELECTRIC FIELD

Consider an electric dipole placed in an uniform field of intensity $\vec{E}$. The ends of the dipole experience equal and opposite forces, each of magnitude $F = Eq$.

Thus, because of uniform field, the net force on the dipole becomes zero and so the centre of mass of the dipole does not move. However, the forces on the charged ends do produce a net torque $\vec{\tau}$ on the dipole about its centre of mass. The magnitude of this torque

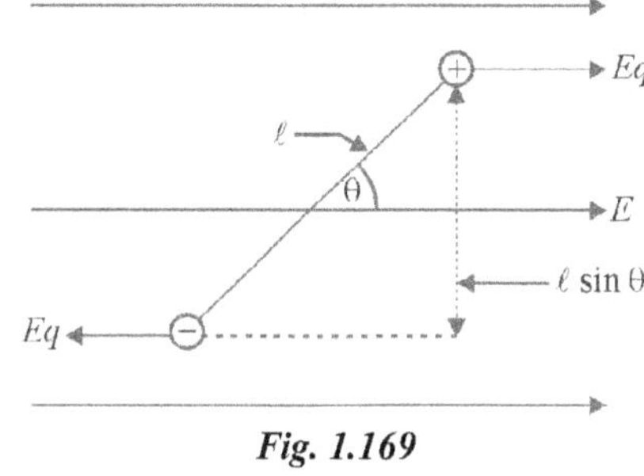


*Fig. 1.169*

$$\tau = \text{[magnitude of either force]} \times \text{[ distance between lines of action of the forces]}$$

$$= F \times \ell\sin\theta$$

$$= Eq \times \ell\sin\theta = E(q\ell)\sin\theta$$

or

$$\tau = PE\sin\theta$$

In vector notation, it can be written as :

$$\vec{\tau} = \vec{P} \times \vec{E} \qquad \ldots (1)$$

**Work done by the agent to increase the angle from $\theta_1$ to $\theta_2$ :**

The torque exerted by the agent to increase the angle

$$\tau_{agent} = PE\sin\theta$$

Work done,

$$W_{agent} = \int_{\theta_1}^{\theta_2} \tau_{agent}\, d\theta$$

$$= \int_{\theta_1}^{\theta_2} PE\sin\theta\, d\theta$$

$$= PE\left|-\cos\theta\right|_{\theta_1}^{\theta_2}$$

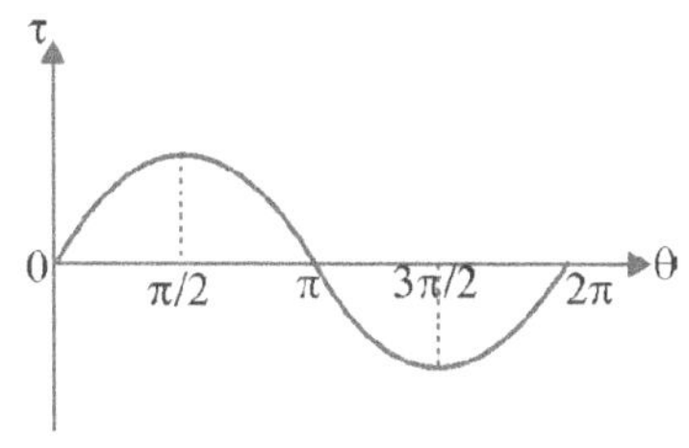


*Fig. 1.170*

or

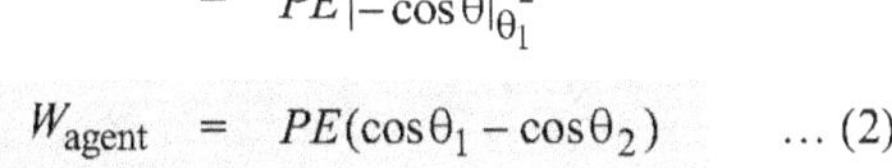

$$W_{agent} = PE(\cos\theta_1 - \cos\theta_2) \qquad \ldots (2)$$

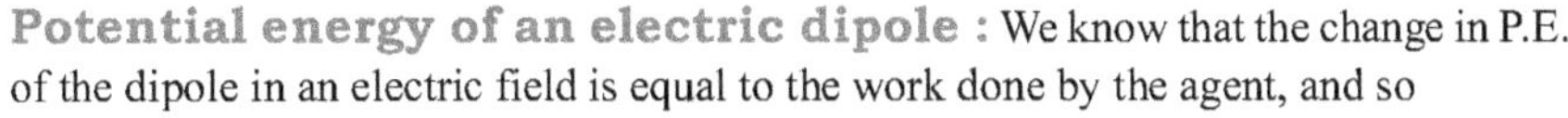

**Potential energy of an electric dipole :** We know that the change in P.E. of the dipole in an electric field is equal to the work done by the agent, and so

$$\Delta U = W_{agent}.$$

In any situation involving *P.E.*, we are free to choose the zero potential energy configuration.

Thus if we choose the potential energy to be zero,when the angle $\theta = 90°$. Therefore

$$U_f - U_i = W_{agent}$$

$$= PE(\cos\theta_1 - \cos\theta_2)$$

For $\theta = 90°$, $U_i = 0$ ; $\theta_2 = \theta$ and $U_f = U$.

$$\therefore \quad U = -PE\cos\theta \quad \ldots (3)$$

In vector notation it can be written as

$$U = -\vec{P}.\vec{E}$$

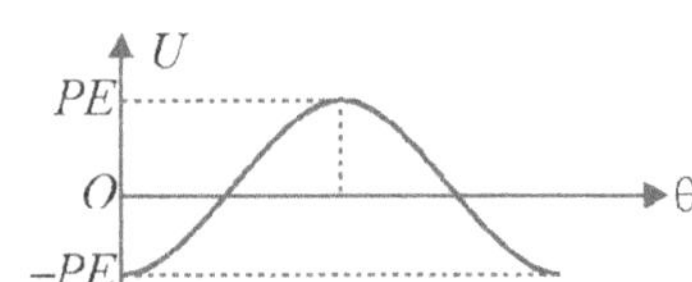

*Fig. 1.171 variation of U with θ.*

## 1.25 FORCE BETWEEN TWO SHORT DIPOLES

1. **When dipoles are placed parallel to each other :**

Suppose dipoles are placed at a separation *r*. The P.E. of dipole $\vec{P}_2$ in the field of dipole $\vec{P}_1$ is,

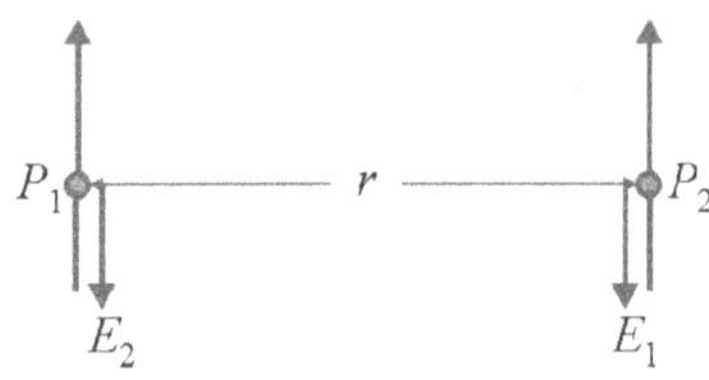

*Fig. 1.172*

$$U = -P_2E_1\cos 180°$$

$$= \left(\frac{1}{4\pi \in_0}\right)\frac{P_1P_2}{r^3}$$

The force between them is given by

$$F = \frac{-dU}{dr} = -\frac{d}{dr}\left[\frac{1}{4\pi \in_0}\frac{P_1P_2}{r^3}\right]$$

$$= \left(\frac{1}{4\pi \in_0}\right)\frac{3P_1P_2}{r^4}$$

As the force is positive, so it is of repulsive nature.

2. **When dipoles are placed on the same axis :**

Suppose the dipoles are placed at a separation *r*. The P.E. of the dipole $\vec{P}_2$ in the field of $\vec{P}_1$ is,

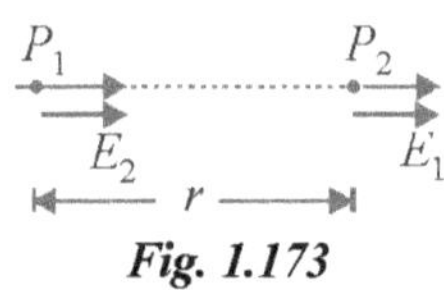

*Fig. 1.173*

$$U = -P_2E_1\cos 0°$$

$$= -\left(\frac{1}{4\pi \in_0}\right)\frac{2P_1P_2}{r^3}$$

The force between them is given by,

$$F = -\frac{dU}{dr} = -\frac{d}{dr}\left[-\frac{1}{4\pi \in_0}\frac{2P_1P_2}{r^3}\right]$$

$$= -\left(\frac{1}{4\pi \in_0}\right)\frac{6P_1P_2}{r^4}$$

Here minus sign of *F* indicates attractive force.

## Equilibrium of a dipole in electric field:

When a dipole is placed along the direction of electric field and disturb slightly from this position, it will return towards initial position. Such a configuration of the dipole is corresponding to stable equilibrium.

When a dipole is placed anti parallel to the electric field and disturb slightly from this position, it will align in the direction of field. Such a configuration of the dipole is corresponding to unstable equilibrium.

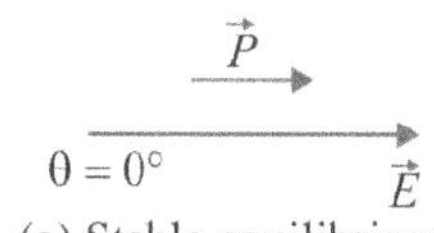


*Fig. 1.174*

## Oscillations of dipole in electric field :

Consider a dipole $\vec{P}$ placed in uniform field $\vec{E}$ at small angle $\theta$ with the direction of $\vec{E}$. The electric field exerts a restoring torque $\tau$ on the dipole. Due to which dipole comes to its mean position, and crosses it due to inertia and repeat this motion again and again. Thus

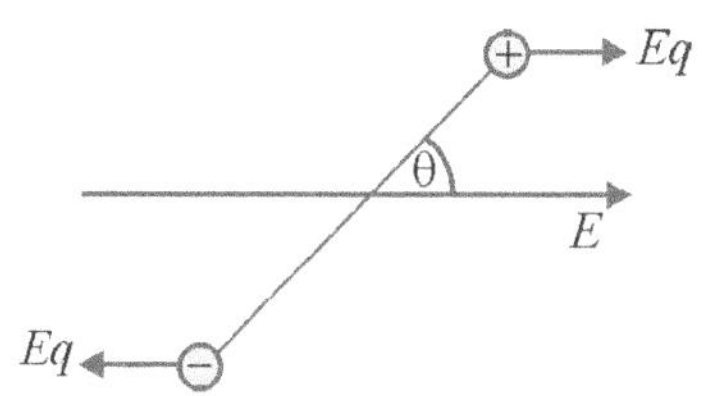


*Fig. 1.175*

$$\tau = -PE\sin\theta$$

For small angle, $\sin\theta \simeq \theta$.

$$\tau = PE(-\theta)$$

and angular acceleration $$\alpha = \frac{\tau}{I} = \frac{PE}{I}(-\theta)$$

Compare this equation with standard equation of SHM, $\alpha = -\omega^2\theta$, we get

$$\omega = \sqrt{\frac{PE}{I}}$$

and $$T = \frac{2\pi}{\omega} = 2\pi\sqrt{\frac{I}{PE}}.$$

Here $I$ is the moment of inertia of the dipole about an axis passing through centre of mass of the dipole.

**Case 1 :** When masses of the charges are equal, the centre of mass will lie at the centre of the dipole, and so

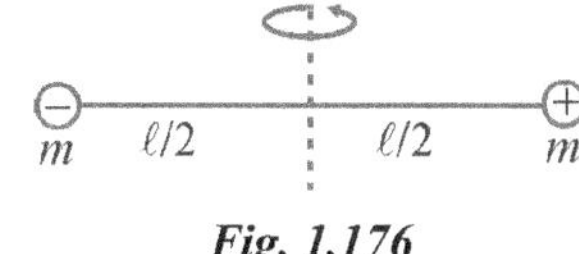


*Fig. 1.176*

$$I = m(\ell/2)^2 + m(\ell/2)^2$$

$$= \frac{m\ell^2}{2}$$

**Case 2 :**When masses of the charges are unequal. Let one of the charges is of mass $m$ and other is of $2m$, if $\bar{x}$ is the c.m. of system from m, then

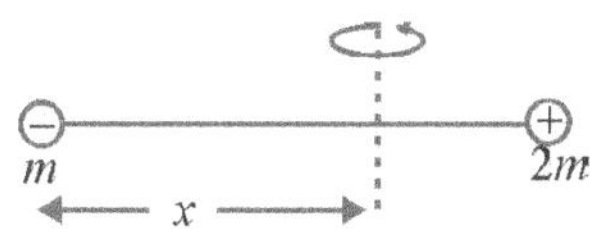


*Fig. 1.177*

$$\bar{x} = \left(\frac{m\times 0 + 2m\times\ell}{m+2m}\right)$$

$$= \frac{2\ell}{3}$$

$$\therefore \quad I = m\left(\frac{2\ell}{3}\right)^2 + 2m\left(\frac{\ell}{3}\right)^2$$

$$= \frac{4}{9}m\ell^2 + \frac{2}{9}m\ell^2$$

$$= \frac{2}{3}m\ell^2.$$

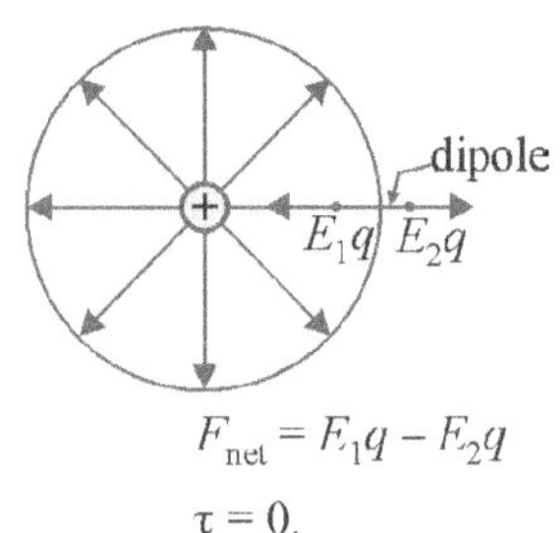


$F_{net} = E_1q - E_2q$

$\tau = 0.$

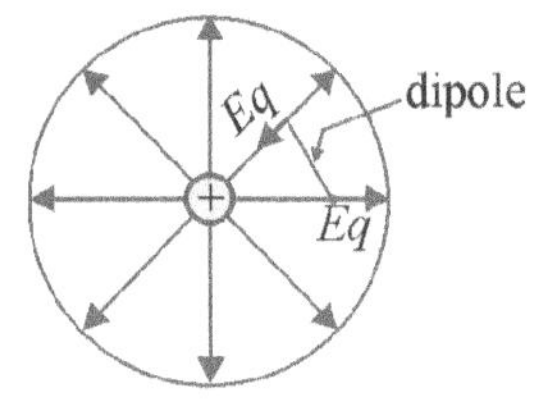


$F_{net} \neq 0, \tau \neq 0.$

*Fig. 1.178*

### A dipole in non-uniform electric field :

Let us consider a small dipole placed in a non-uniform field, such as the field due to a point charge. Here, the forces acting on the two charges of the dipole are not equal in magnitude and also their direction are not exactly opposite to each other. For a short dipole torque can be obtained by the formula,

$$\tau = PE\sin\theta.$$

The dipole experiences a net translatory force and a torque (in some cases it may be zero).

### Electric multipoles :

According to the number of charges in the system, it is called the monopole (one-pole), the dipole (two-poles), the quadrupole (four -poles), the octupole (eight poles) etc. In general the number of poles in a multipole is always $2^n$, where $n = 0, 1, 2, \ldots\ldots$

### Electric quadrupole :

The quadrupole is an arrangement of two parallel dipoles of opposite polarity, but equal otherwise, separated by small distance. We can regard quadrupole as an arrangement of two dipoles. Figure shows few quadrupoles.

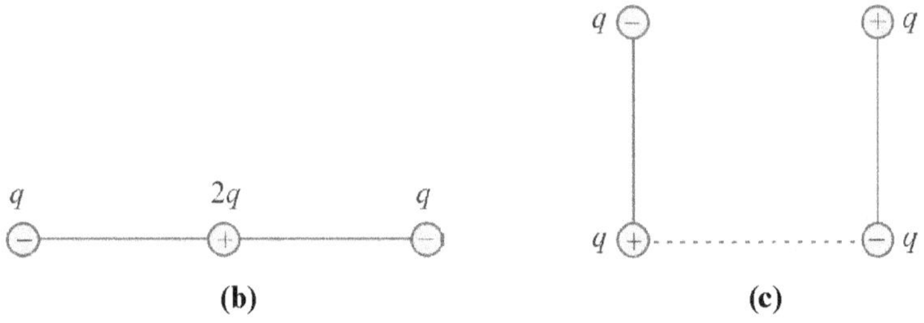


*Fig. 1.179*

## 1.26 QUANTISATION OF CHARGE : MILLIKAN OIL DROP EXPERIMENT

Millikan's apparatus consists of two parallel metal plates $A$ and $B$ (parallel plate capacitor), are insulated from each other with a small gap between them. Oil is sprayed in small drops from an atomiser above the upper plate and a few of the drops are allowed to fall through a small hole in this plate. A light beam is incident between the plates, and a telescope is used to see this motion. Oil drops soonly get terminal velocity. It is found that some of the oil drops are electrically charged because of friction of mouth of atomiser. The drops can also be charged by falling $X$-rays on them. The drops are usually negatively charged.

Suppose a drop has a negative charge $q$ and plates are maintained at a potential difference

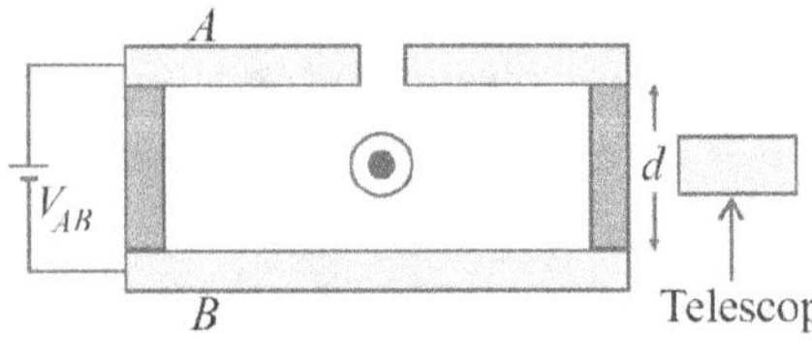


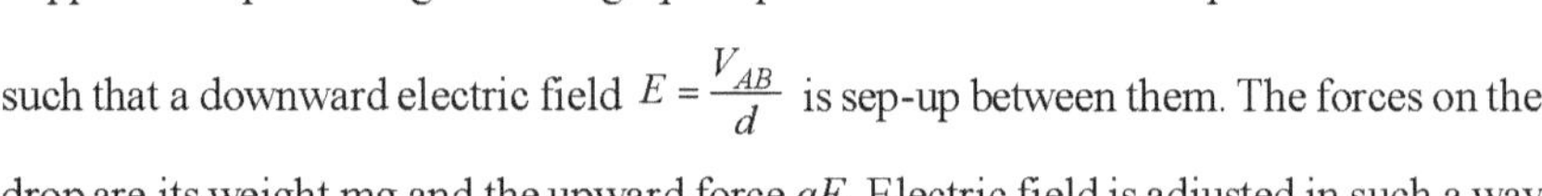

such that a downward electric field $E = \frac{V_{AB}}{d}$ is sep-up between them. The forces on the drop are its weight mg and the upward force $qE$. Electric field is adjusted in such a way that the drop remains at rest. Thus

$$qE = mg$$

or

$$q = \frac{mg}{E}.$$

If $r$ be the radius of the drop, then $m = \rho \times \frac{4}{3}\pi r^3$, and

$$q = \frac{4\pi}{3}\frac{\rho r^3 gd}{V_{AB}} \qquad \ldots (1)$$

$qE$, $mg$; $F_v = 6\pi\eta r v_T$, $mg$

*Fig. 1.180*

### Radius of oil drop

Now switch off the field and allows the drop to fall freely. If $v_T$ is the terminal velocity of the oil drop, then by Stoke's law, viscous force

$$F_v = 6\pi\eta r v_T \quad \ldots (2)$$

As oil drop falls freely , so neglecting buoyant force exerted by air

$$mg = F_v$$

or
$$\frac{4}{3}\pi r^3 \rho g = 6\pi\eta r v_T$$

∴
$$r = 3\sqrt{\eta v_T / 2\rho g}$$

Substituting the value of $r$ in equation (1), we get

$$q = 18\pi \frac{d}{V_{AB}} \sqrt{\frac{\eta^3 v_T^3}{2\rho g}}. \quad \ldots (3)$$

Millikan and his students measured the charges on the different sizes of drops of different oils and found that every drop had a charge equal to some small integral multiple of charge $e$. That is, drops were observed with charges of $e$, $2e$, $3e$, ......... etc.

**Ex. 71** **Find the position, where the electric field due to an electric dipole is perpendicular to the dipole moment.**

**Sol.**

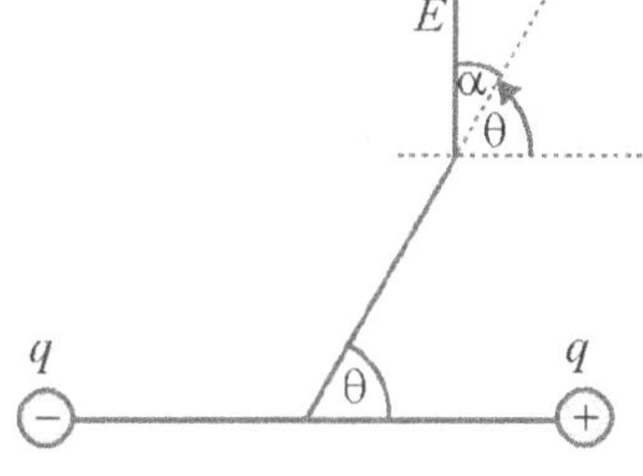


*Fig. 1.181*

From the figure

$$\theta + \alpha = 90°$$

∴
$$\alpha = 90° - \theta$$

We know that
$$\tan\alpha = \frac{\tan\theta}{2}$$

or
$$\tan(90 - \theta) = \frac{\tan\theta}{2}$$

or
$$\cot\theta = \frac{\tan\theta}{2}$$

or
$$\tan\theta = \sqrt{2}$$

∴
$$\theta = \tan^{-1}(\sqrt{2}). \quad \textit{Ans.}$$

**Ex. 72** ***Fig. 1.182*** **shows the deflecting plates of an ink-jet printer, with superposed coordinate axes. An ink drop with a mass m of $1.3 \times 10^{-10}$ kg and a negative charge of magnitude $Q = 1.5 \times 10^{-13}$C enters the region between the plates, initially moving along the $x$-axis with speed $v_x = 18$ m/s. The length L of the plates is 1.6 cm. The plates are charged and thus produce an electric field at all points between them.**

**Assume that field $\vec{E}$ is downward directed, uniform, and has a magnitude of $1.4 \times 10^6$ N/C. What is the vertical deflection of the drop at the far edge of the plate? (The gravitational force on the drop is small relative to the electrostatic force acting on the drop and can be neglected.)**

**Sol.**

The drop is negatively charged and so force on it acts upward and

$$F = EQ.$$

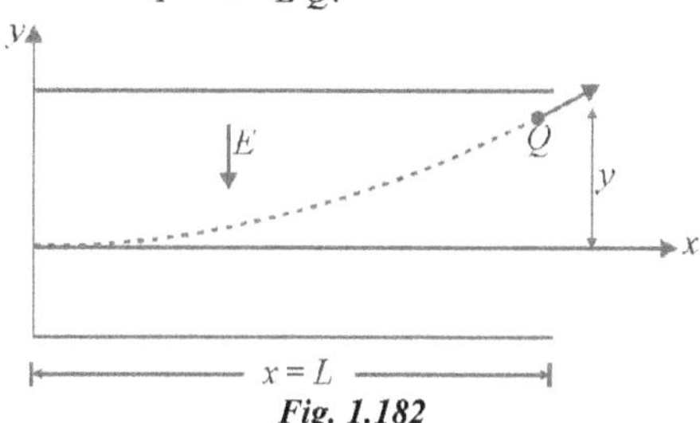


*Fig. 1.182*

By Newton's second law

$$a_y = \frac{F}{m} = \frac{EQ}{m}$$

Let $t$ is the time taken by the drop to travel the distance $L$, so

$$L = v_x t \text{ or } t = \frac{L}{v_x}.$$

The vertical deflection

$$y = \frac{1}{2}a_y t^2 = \frac{1}{2}\left(\frac{EQ}{m}\right)\left(\frac{L}{v_x}\right)^2$$

$$y = \frac{EQL^2}{2mv_x^2}$$

$$= \frac{(1.4\times10^{6})\times(1.5\times10^{-13})\times(1.6\times10^{-2})^2}{2\times(1.3\times10^{-10})(18)^2}$$

$$= 6.4 \times 10^{-4} \text{ m.} \qquad \textit{Ans.}$$

**Ex. 73** **A uniform electric field $E$ is created between two parallel, charged plates as shown in *fig. 1.183*. An electron enters the field symmetrically between the plates with a speed $v_0$. The length of each plate is $\ell$. Find the angle of deviation of the path of the electron as it comes out of the field.**

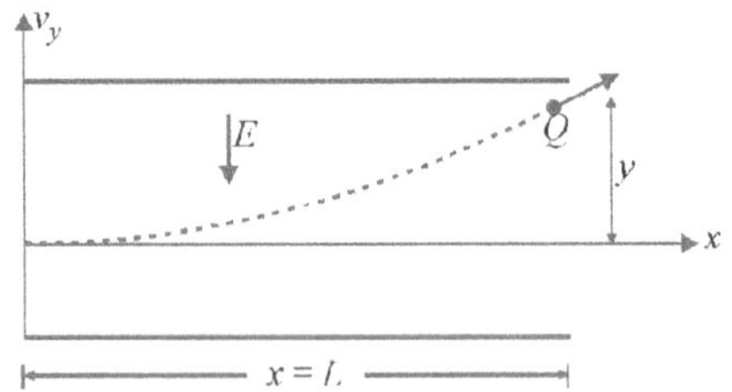


*Fig. 1.183*

**Sol.**

As the field directed in downward direction, so force and hence acceleration of the electron will be in upward direction. Acceleration

$$a_y = \frac{Ee}{m}$$

The time taken in crossing the plate

$$t = \frac{\ell}{v_0}$$

The velocity acquired by the electron in upward direction

$$v_y = a_y t = \frac{Ee\ell}{mv_0}$$

Its horizontal component of velocity remain constant.

If $\theta$ is the angle of deviation of the electron, then

$$\tan\theta = \frac{v_y}{v_x}$$

$$= \frac{(Ee\ell/mv_0)}{v_0}$$

or $$\theta = \tan^{-1}\left(\frac{Ee\ell}{mv_0^2}\right) \qquad \textit{Ans.}$$

**Note:** The path of the charged particle in an electric field will be parabolic, if particle is projected at some angle with the field.

**Image method :** Method of image consists of replacing a complicated charge distribution by a point charge or group of charges, called electrical image, which is equivalent to given system of charges.

**Ex. 74** **A point charge $q$ is at a distance $r$ from an infinite extend earthed conductor. Find force between them.**

**Sol.**

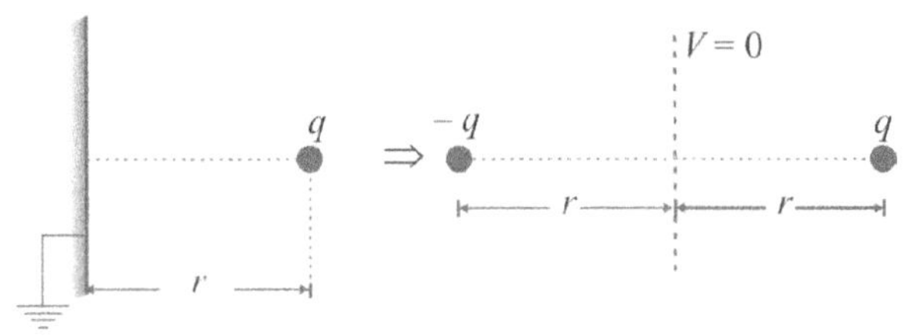


*Fig. 1.184*

The electrical image of charge $q$ is $-q$ at a distance equal to the distance of $q$ from conductor.

The force between the charge and earthed conductor will be same as the force between $q$ and its image $(-q)$.

$$\therefore \qquad F = \frac{1}{4\pi\epsilon_0}\frac{qq}{(2r)^2} = \left(\frac{1}{4\pi\epsilon_0}\right)\frac{q^2}{4r^2}$$

**Work done :** Let charge $q$ is to be displaced from $r_1$ to $r_2$ from earthed conductor, then work done

$$W = \int_{r_1}^{r_2} F\,dx$$

$$= \frac{q^2}{4\pi\epsilon_0}\int_{r_1}^{r_2}\frac{1}{(2x)^2}$$

$$= \frac{q^2}{4\pi\epsilon_0}\frac{1}{4}\left(-\frac{1}{x}\right)_{r_1}^{r_2}$$

$$= \frac{q^2}{16\pi\epsilon_0}\left(\frac{1}{r_1}-\frac{1}{r_2}\right)$$

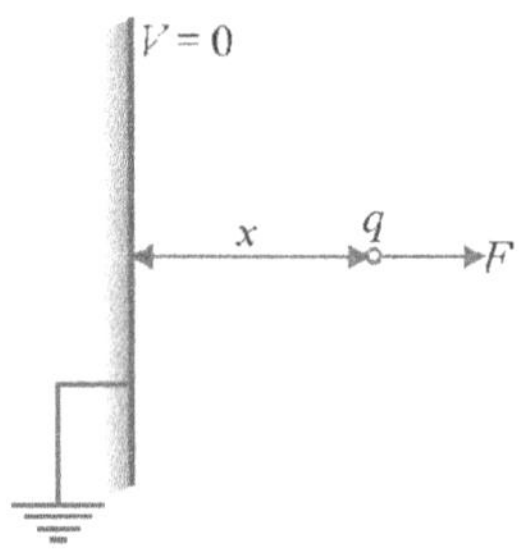

*Fig. 1.185*

If $r_2 = \infty$, and $r_1 = r$ ; $W = \dfrac{q^2}{16\pi\epsilon_0 r}$.

**Ex. 75** **A point charge $q$ is placed between two large parallel conducting plates 1 and 2 separated by a distance $\ell$. Find the total charges $q_1$ and $q_2$ induced on each plate, if the plates are connected by a wire and the charge $q$ is located at a distance $\ell_1$ from the left plate 1 (see *fig. 1.187*).**

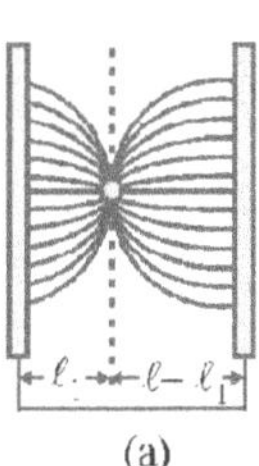
(a)

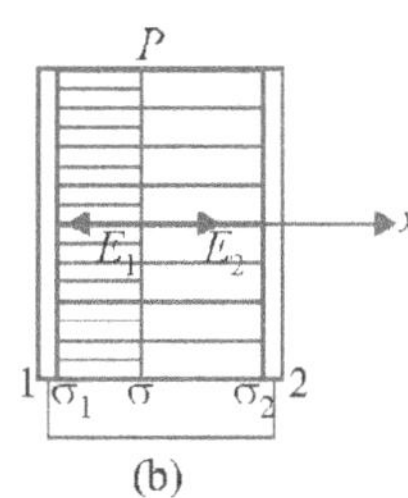

(b)

*Fig. 1.187*

**Sol.**

Suppose $\sigma$ is the charge density on the surface $P$. If $\sigma_1$ and $\sigma_2$ are the surface density on the plates respectively, then net charge density on plane to be zero

$$\sigma + (\sigma_1 + \sigma_2) = 0$$

or
$$\sigma = -(\sigma_1 + \sigma_2) \quad \ldots \text{(i)}$$

The plates are connected by the wire, and hence the potential difference between them is equal to zero, so

$$E_1\ell_1 - E_2(\ell - \ell_1) = 0 \quad \ldots \text{(ii)}$$

where $E_1 = \frac{\sigma_1}{\epsilon_0}$ and $E_2 = \frac{\sigma_2}{\epsilon_0}$

$$\therefore \quad \frac{\sigma_1}{\epsilon_0}\ell_1 - \frac{\sigma_2}{\epsilon_0}(\ell - \ell_1) = 0 \quad \ldots \text{(iii)}$$

Solving equations (i) and (iii), we get

$$\sigma_1 = -\frac{\sigma(\ell - \ell_1)}{\ell} \text{ and } \sigma_2 = -\frac{\sigma\ell_1}{\ell} \qquad \textit{Ans.}$$

# Review of formulae & Important Points

1. **Conductors and insulators :**

   Conductors are the materials which have large number of free electrons. While insulators have no or very few free electrons.

2. By conduction method one can charge metals. The charge on the body will be proportional to its size.

3. By method of induction we can charge metals and non-metals both. The magnitude of induced charge $q'$ is given by

$$q' = q\left(1 - \frac{1}{k}\right),$$

   where $k$ is called dielectric constant. For metals $k = \infty$, and so

$$q' = q.$$

4. **The elementary charge :** Electric charge is quantized : Any charge can be written as $ne$, where $n = \pm 1, \pm 2, \ldots,$ and $e = 1.60 \times 10^{-19}$C. The electric charge is conserved and relativistically not variant.

5. Charge given to metals will always spread on their free surfaces.

6. **Coulomb's law :** The force between two point charges $q_1$ and $q_2$ at rest and placed at a separation $r$ in vacuum or free space is given by

$$F = \frac{1}{4\pi\epsilon_0}\frac{|q_1||q_2|}{r^2}$$

7. If the space of thickness $t$ between the charges is filled with a dielectric of dielectric constant $k$, then

$$F = \frac{1}{4\pi\epsilon_0}\frac{|q_1||q_2|}{\left[(r-t) + t\sqrt{k}\right]^2}$$

8. **Coulomb's law in vector form :** If charges $q_1$ and $q_2$ are placed at the position vectors $\vec{r}_1$ and $\vec{r}_2$ respectively, then force between them

$$\vec{F}_{21} = \frac{1}{4\pi\epsilon_0}\frac{|q_1||q_2|(\vec{r}_2 - \vec{r}_1)}{|\vec{r}_2 - \vec{r}_1|^3}.$$

9. **Electric field :** The electric field $\vec{E}$ at any point is defined as the force experiences by an unit test charge placed at that point. Thus if $\vec{F}$ be the force on charge $q_0$, then

$$\vec{E} = \frac{\vec{F}}{q_0}.$$

   Field due to a point charge $\vec{E}$ set up by a point charge at a distance $r$ from the charge is

$$E = \frac{1}{4\pi\varepsilon_0}\frac{q}{r^2}.$$

10. **Electric potential energy :** The change in electric potential energy $\Delta U$ of the system of charges is defined as

$$\Delta U = -W_{\text{electric force}} = W_{\text{agent}}$$

Also $$U - U_{\infty} = -\left[W_{\text{electric force}}\right]_{\infty}^{\text{any position}}$$

As $$U_{\infty} = 0,$$

$\therefore$ $$U = -\left[W_{\textit{electric force}}\right]_{\infty}^{\textit{any position}}$$

For two charges $q_1$ and $q_2$ placed at a separation $r$,

$$U = \frac{1}{4\pi\varepsilon_0}\frac{q_1 q_2}{r}$$

11. **Electric potential difference :** We can define the potential difference $\Delta V$ between two points $f$ and $i$ in an electric field as :

$$\Delta V = V_f - V_i = \frac{-\left[W_{\textit{electric force}}\right]_i^f}{q_0}$$

Similarly $$V_A - V_B = \frac{-\left[W_{\textit{electric force}}\right]_B^A}{q_0}$$

Potential at any point is defined as

$$V_P = \frac{-\left[W_{\textit{electric force}}\right]_{\infty}^P}{q_0}$$

Potential due to a point charge $q$ at a distance $r$ is given by

$$V = \frac{1}{4\pi\varepsilon_0}\frac{q}{r}.$$

12. **Relationship between $\vec{E}$ and $V$ :** We can get

$$V_A - V_B = -\int_B^A \vec{E}\cdot d\vec{r}$$

$$= \int_A^B \vec{E}\cdot d\vec{r}$$

A B E

Also $$E = \frac{-dV}{dr}$$

For constant field

$$V_A - V_B = Ed$$

13. **Work done from $A$ to $B$ :**

$$W_A^B = (V_B - V_A)q$$

14. **Electric flux :** The electric flux of field $\vec{E}$ can be defined as :

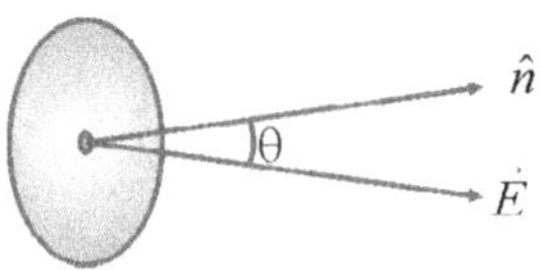


$$\phi_e = \int \vec{E}\cdot d\vec{A}$$

For constant field $E$ over the area $A$, $\phi = EA\cos\theta$.

15. Electric potential, potential energy and flux are scalar quantities but they can be negative. In using formula of these quantities, place the value of charges with the sign. While in using formula of electric field do not place the sign of charge.

16. **Electric flux due to a charge in the closed surface**

$$\phi = \frac{q}{\epsilon_0}$$ ·q

17. **Flux due to the charge out of the closed surface**

$$\phi = 0$$

18. **Gauss's law :** According to it, the total electric flux through a Gaussian surface is equal to $\left(\frac{1}{\epsilon_0}\right)$ times the charge inside the close surface. Thus

$$\oint \vec{E}\cdot d\vec{A} = \left(\frac{1}{\epsilon_0}\right) q_{in}.$$

19. **Application of Gauss's law :** Using Gauss's law we can derive the following results.

(i) An excess charge on a conductor is located entirely on outer surface of the conductor.

(ii) The electric field due to an infinite nonconducting sheet with uniform surface charge density $\sigma$ is perpendicular to the plane of the sheet and has magnitude

$$E = \frac{\sigma}{2\epsilon_0}$$

(iii) The external electric field near the surface of a charged conductor is perpendicular to the surface and has magnitude

$$E = \frac{\sigma}{\epsilon_0}$$

Field $E = 0$ inside the conductor.

(iv) The electric field at any point due to an infinite line of charge with uniform linear charge density $\lambda$ is perpendicular to the line of charge and has magnitude

$$E = \frac{\lambda}{2\pi \in_0 r}$$

(v) The electric field due to a spherical shell of radius $R$ with charge $q$

$$E = \frac{1}{4\pi \in_0} \frac{q}{r^2}, \text{ for } r \geq R$$

$$= 0 \quad , \text{for } r < R.$$

**20. Conducting sphere of radius $R$ with charge $q$ (solid or hollow):**

$$E = \frac{1}{4\pi \in_0} \frac{q}{r^2} \quad (r > R)$$

$$E = \frac{1}{4\pi \in_0} \frac{q}{R^2} \quad (r = R)$$

$$E = 0 \quad (r < R)$$

$$V = \frac{1}{4\pi \in_0} \frac{q}{r} \quad (r > R)$$

$$V = \frac{1}{4\pi \in_0} \frac{q}{R} \quad (r = R)$$

$$V = \frac{1}{4\pi \in_0} \frac{q}{R} \quad (r < R)$$

Potential energy of the spherical conductor of radius $R$ with charge $q$

$$U = \frac{1}{8\pi \in_0} \frac{q^2}{R}$$

**21. Non conducting sphere of radius $R$ with charge $q$ :**

$$E = \frac{1}{4\pi \in_0} \frac{q}{r^2} \quad (r > R)$$

$$E = \frac{1}{4\pi \in_0} \frac{q}{R^2} \quad (r = R)$$

$$E = \frac{1}{4\pi \in_0} \frac{qr}{R^3} \quad (r < R)$$

$$E = 0 \quad (r = 0)$$

$$V = \frac{1}{4\pi \in_0} \frac{q}{r} \quad (r > R)$$

$$V = \frac{1}{4\pi \in_0} \frac{q}{R} \quad (r = R)$$

$$V = \frac{1}{4\pi \in_0} \frac{q(3R^2 - r^2)}{2R^3} \quad (r < R)$$

$$V = \frac{3}{2}\left(\frac{1}{4\pi \in_0} \frac{q}{R}\right) \quad (r = 0)$$

Potential energy of charged sphere of radius $R$ with charge $q$

$$U = \frac{3}{20\pi \in_0} \frac{q^2}{R}$$

**22. Line charge with linear charge density $\lambda$**

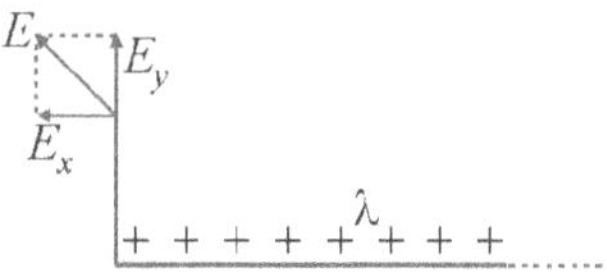

$$E = \frac{\lambda}{2\pi \in_0 r}$$

at the middle of the line charge

$E$ along the end of the line charge

$$E_x = E_y = \frac{\lambda}{4\pi \in_0 r}$$

$$E = \sqrt{E_x^2 + E_y^2}$$

$$= \frac{\lambda}{2\sqrt{2}\pi \in_0 r}$$

**23. Ring of radius $R$ with a uniformly distributed charge $q$ :**

$$E = \frac{1}{4\pi \in_0} \frac{qr}{\left(R^2 + r^2\right)^{3/2}}$$

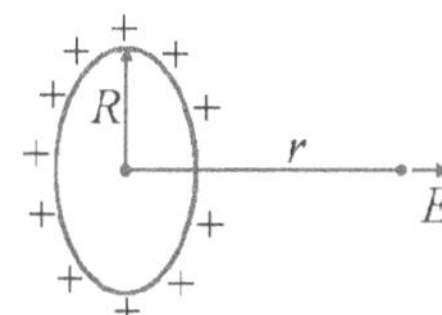

$$E = 0, \quad (r = 0)$$

$$E_{max} = \frac{q}{6\sqrt{3}\, \pi \in_0 R^2} \quad \left(r = \frac{R}{\sqrt{2}}\right)$$

$$V = \frac{1}{4\pi \in_0} \frac{q}{\sqrt{R^2 + r^2}} \quad (r > 0)$$

$$V = \frac{1}{4\pi \epsilon_0} \frac{q}{R} \qquad (r = 0)$$

**24. Energy density in electric field :**

$$u = \frac{1}{2} \epsilon_0 E^2 \qquad \text{(in free space)}$$

**Electric Dipole :** Dipole moment $\vec{P} = q\vec{\ell}$

**Electric field at any position $(r, \theta)$ :**

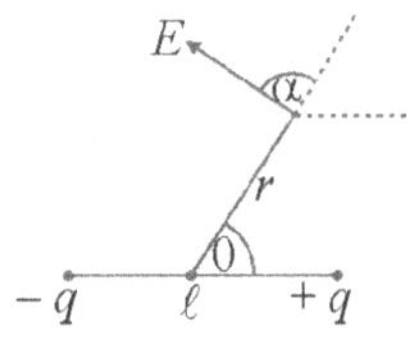


$$E = \frac{1}{4\pi \epsilon_0} \frac{P\sqrt{3\cos^2\theta + 1}}{r^3}$$

$$V = \frac{1}{4\pi \epsilon_0} \frac{P\cos\theta}{r^2}$$

$$\tan\alpha = \frac{\tan\theta}{2}$$

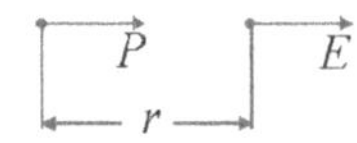


(i) Along the axis of the dipole, $\theta = 0$

$$E = \frac{1}{4\pi \epsilon_0} \frac{2P}{r^3}$$

$$V = \frac{1}{4\pi \epsilon_0} \frac{P}{r^2}.$$

(ii) Along the equator of the dipole, $\theta = 90°$

$$E = \frac{1}{4\pi \epsilon_0} \frac{P}{r^3},$$

$$V = 0.$$

(iii) Force between two short dipoles placed on the same axis

$$F = \frac{1}{4\pi \epsilon_0} \frac{6P_1P_2}{r^4}.$$

Force between two short dipoles placed parallel on different axes

$$F = \frac{1}{4\pi \epsilon_0} \frac{3P_1P_2}{r^4}$$

★★★

Electricity

# MCQ Type 1

Exercise 1.1

## LEVEL - 1

**Only one option correct**

1. Consider a neutral conducting sphere. A positive point charge is placed outside the sphere. The net charge on the sphere is then,
   (a) negative and distributed uniformly over the surface of the sphere
   (b) negative and appears only at the point on the sphere closest to the point charge
   (c) negative and distributed non-uniformly over the entire surface of the sphere
   (d) zero.

2. There is a point charge $+q$ inside a hollow sphere and a point charge $-q$ just outside its surface. The total flux passing through the sphere
   (a) $\frac{-q}{\epsilon_0}$ (b) $\frac{q}{\epsilon_0}$
   (c) $\frac{2q}{\epsilon_0}$ (d) zero.

3. Figure shows three electric field lines. If $F_A$, $F_B$ and $F_C$ are the forces on a test charge $q$ at the positions $A$, $B$ and $C$ respectively, then

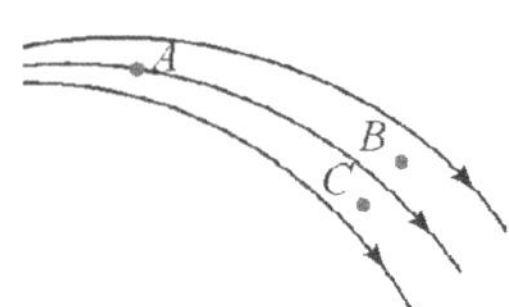


   (a) $F_A > F_B > F_C$ (b) $F_A < F_B < F_C$
   (c) $F_A > (F_B = F_C)$ (d) $F_A < (F_B = F_C)$

4. In the figure the electric lines on the right have twice the separation of those on the left. If a charge particle takes time $t$ to move a distance $x$ in left region, then it will take time to travel the same distance in the right side region is :

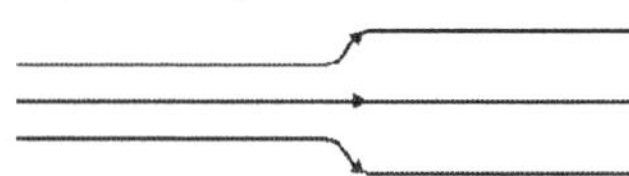

   (a) $\frac{t}{2}$ (b) $t$
   (c) $\sqrt{2}\, t$ (d) $2t$

5. A surface has the area vector $\vec{A} = (2\hat{i} + 3\hat{j})\, m^2$. The flux of an electric field through it if the field is $\vec{E} = 4\hat{i}\frac{V}{m}$ :
   (a) 8 V-m (b) 12 V-m
   (c) 20 V-m (d) zero

6. In figure a close surface encloses two of the four positively charged particles. Which of the particles contribute to the electric field at point $P$ on the surface :
   (a) $q_1, q_2$
   (b) $q_1, q_3$
   (c) $q_1, q_2, q_3$
   (d) $q_1, q_2, q_3, q_4$

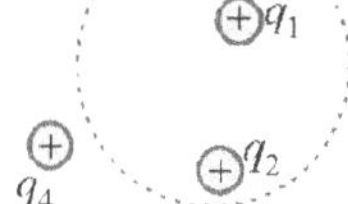


7. Figure shows five charged lumps of plastic and an electrically neutral metal coin. The close surface $S$ is indicated in the figure. The net flux through the surface is :

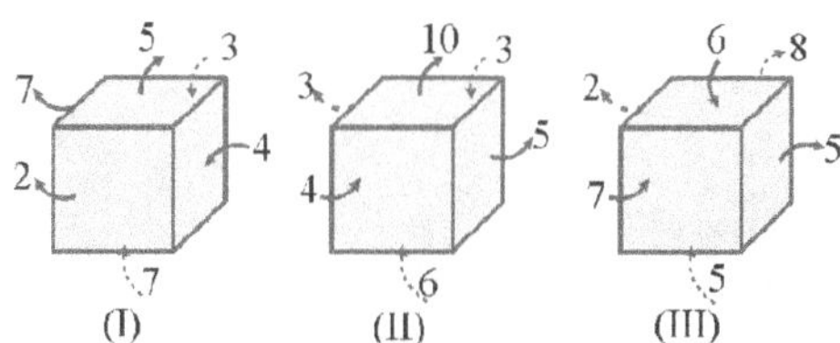


   (a) 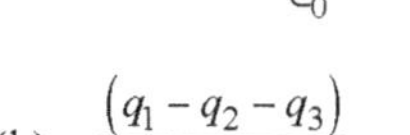 $\frac{(q_1 - q_2 - q_3 - q_4 + q_5)}{\epsilon_0}$
   (b) 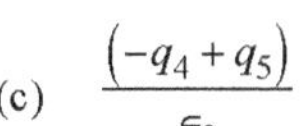 $\frac{(q_1 - q_2 - q_3)}{\epsilon_0}$
   (c)  $\frac{(-q_4 + q_5)}{\epsilon_0}$
   (d) zero

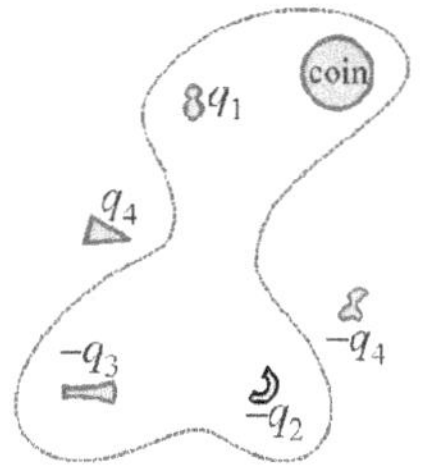

8. The figure shows three situations in which a Gaussian cube sits in an electric field. The arrows and the values indicate the directions of the field lines and the magnitudes (in N-m²/C) of the flux through the six sides of each cube. The dotted arrows are of the hidden faces. In which situation the cube enclose net positive charge :

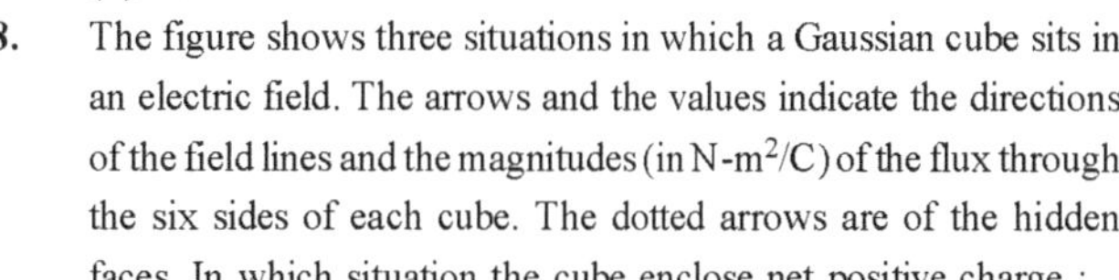


   (a) I (b) II
   (c) III (d) none

| Answer Key | 1 | (d) | 2 | (b) | 3 | (c) | 4 | (c) |
|---|---|---|---|---|---|---|---|---|
| Sol. from page 107 | 5 | (a) | 6 | (d) | 7 | (b) | 8 | (b) |

9. The figure shows three non conducting rods, one circular and two straight. Each has a uniform charge of magnitude $Q$ along its top half and another along its bottom half. Which of them correctly represents the direction of field at point $P$ :

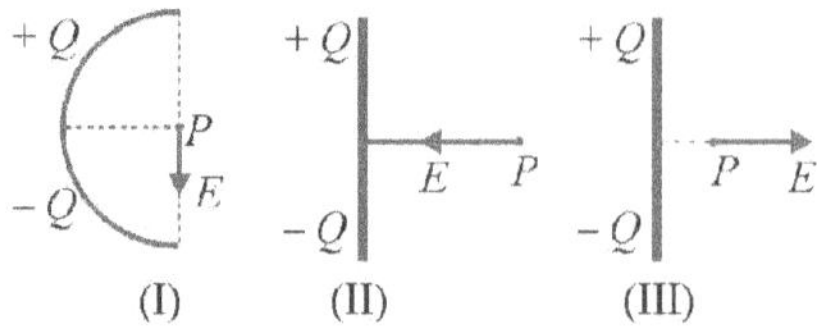


(a) I (b) II
(c) III (d) I and II

10. A long, hollow conducting cylinder is kept coaxially inside another long, hollow conducting cylinder of larger radius. Both the cylinders are initially electrically neutral
(a) A potential difference appears between the two cylinders when a charge density is given to the inner cylinder.
(b) A potential difference appears between two cylinders when a charge density is given to the outer cylinder.
(c) No potential difference appears between the two cylinders when a uniform line charge is kept along the axis of the cylinders.
(d) No potential difference appears between the two cylinders when same charge density is given to both the cylinders.

11. A small metal ball is brought into contact alternatively with points $A$, $B$ and $C$ of the charged body shown in figure. After each contact the charge of the ball is determined approximately by touching it against an electroscope. If $q_A$, $q_B$ and $q_C$ are the charges, then

(a) $q_A > q_B > q_C$ (b) $q_A < q_B < q_C$
(c) $q_A = q_B, q_C = 0$ (d) $q_A = 0, q_B = q_C$

12. An uncharged metal ball is placed in the uniform electric field of a plane capacitor. Which of them correctly represents the field lines on the ball ?

(a) 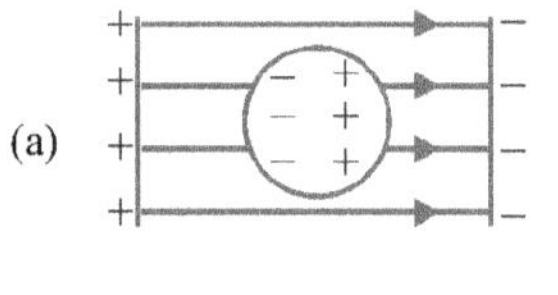 (b) 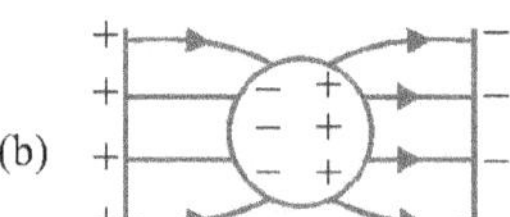

(c) 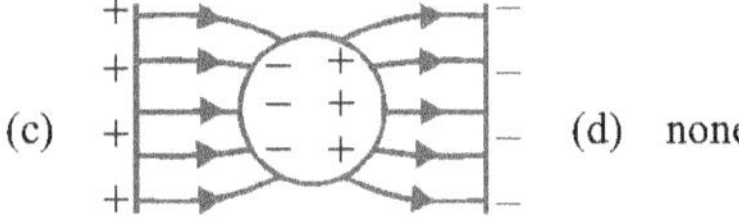 (d) none

13. The equipotential surfaces of a certain field are shown in figure. It is know that $V_1 > V_2$. The direction of electric field is correctly represents in

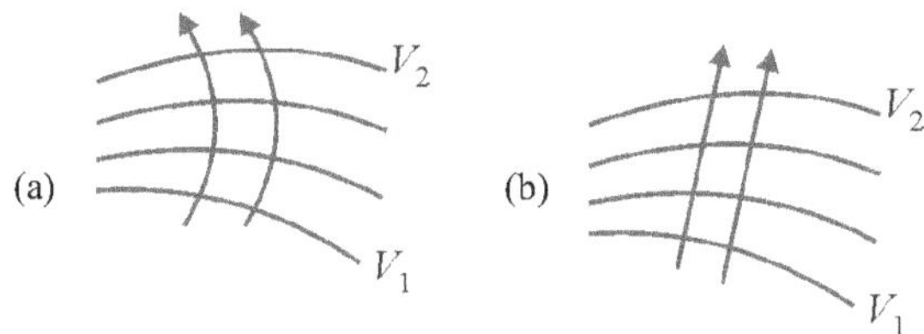


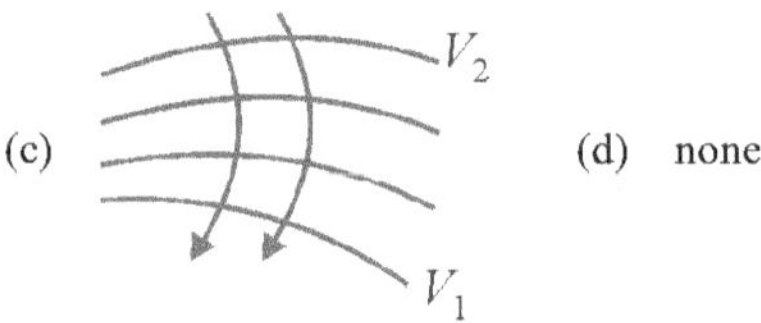


(d) none

14. The intensity of an electric field inside a capacitor is $E$. The work done to move a charge $q$ in a closed rectangular loop is

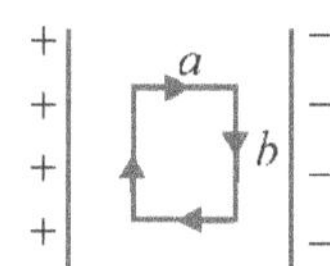


(a) $E(2a + 2b)$ (b) $E(2a)$
(c) $Ea$ (d) zero

15. Figure shows three paths along which we can move positively charged sphere $A$ closer to positively charged sphere $B$ which is fixed in a plane. If $W_1$, $W_2$ and $W_3$ are the work done along the three respective paths, then

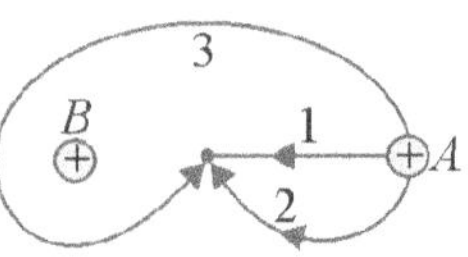


(a) $W_1 > W_2 > W_3$ (b) $W_1 > W_3 > W_2$
(c) $W_1 = W_2 = W_3$ (d) none of these

16. Two equal positive charges are kept at points $A$ and $B$. The electric potential at the points between $A$ and $B$ (excluding these points) is studied while moving from $A$ to $B$. The potential
(a) continuously increases (b) continuously decreases
(c) increases then decreases (d) decreases then increases

| Answer Key | 9 | (a) | 10 | (a) | 11 | (a) | 12 | (c) |
|---|---|---|---|---|---|---|---|---|
| Sol. from page 107 | 13 | (a) | 14 | (d) | 15 | (c) | 16 | (d) |

**17.** Electric charges are distributed in a small volume. The flux of the electric field through a spherical surface of radius 1 m surrounding the total charge is 100 V-m. The flux over the concentric sphere of radius 2 m will be

(a) 25 V-m (b) 50 V-m
(c) 100 V-m (d) 200 V-m

**18.** Charges $Q$ and $-2Q$ are placed at some distance. The locus of points in the plane of the charges where the potential is zero will be

(a) a straight line (b) a circle
(c) a parabola (d) an ellipse

**19.** A conducting sphere $S_1$ intersects a closed surface $S_2$ as shown in the figure. A positive charge $q$ is placed at a point $P$. What is the value of electric flux through the surface $S_2$ ?

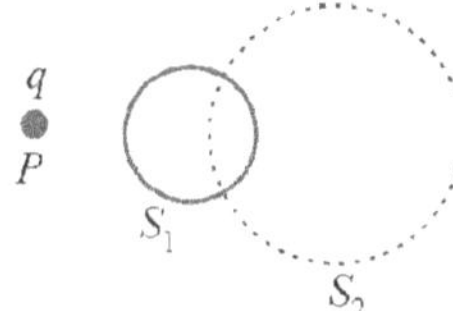


(a) 0 (b) $\frac{q}{\epsilon_0}$

(c) $<\frac{q}{\epsilon_0}$ (d) $>\frac{q}{\epsilon_0}$

**20.** A conducting spherical shell having inner radius $a$ and outer radius $b$ carries a net charge $Q$. If a point charge $q$ is placed at the centre of this shell, then the surface charge density on the outer surface of the shell is

(a) $\frac{Q-q}{4\pi b^2}$ (b) $\frac{Q}{4\pi b^2}$

(c) $\frac{Q+q}{4\pi b^2}$ (d) zero.

**21.** A loop of diameter $d$ is rotated in a uniform electric field until the position of maximum electric flux is found. The flux in this position is measured to be $\phi$. What is the electric field strength ?

(a) $\frac{4\phi}{\pi d^2}$ (b) $\frac{2\phi}{\pi d^2}$

(c) $\frac{\phi}{\pi d^2}$ (d) $\frac{\pi\phi d^2}{4}$

**22.** Out of gravitational, electromagnetic, Vander Waals, electrostatic and nuclear forces; which two are able to provide an attractive force between two neutrons

(a) electrostatic and gravitational
(b) electrostatic and nuclear
(c) gravitational and nuclear
(d) some other forces like Vander Waals

**23.** Two small spheres each having the charge $+Q$ are suspended by insulating threads of length $L$ from a hook. This arrangement is taken in space where there is no gravitational effect, then the angle between the two suspensions and the tension in each will be

(a) $180°, \frac{1}{4\pi\varepsilon_0}\frac{Q^2}{(2L)^2}$ (b) $90°, \frac{1}{4\pi\varepsilon_0}\frac{Q^2}{L^2}$

(c) $180°, \frac{1}{4\pi\varepsilon_0}\frac{Q^2}{2L^2}$ (d) $180°, \frac{1}{4\pi\varepsilon_0}\frac{Q^2}{L^2}$

**24.** A charge $q$ is placed at the centre of the line joining two equal charges $Q$. The system of the three charges will be in equilibrium, if $q$ is equal to

(a) $-\frac{Q}{2}$ (b) $-\frac{Q}{4}$

(c) $+\frac{Q}{4}$ (d) $+\frac{Q}{2}$

**25.** The electric potential $V$ at any point $O$ ($x$, $y$, $z$ all in metres) in space is given by $V=4x^2$ volt. The electric field at the point (1m, 0, 2m) in volt/metre is

(a) 8 along negative $x$–axis (b) 8 along positive $x$-axis
(c) 16 along negative $x$–axis (d) 16 along positive $z$-axis

**26.** Figure shows the electric lines of force emerging from a charged body. If the electric field at $A$ and $B$ are $E_A$ and $E_B$ respectively and if the displacement between $A$ and $B$ is $r$ then

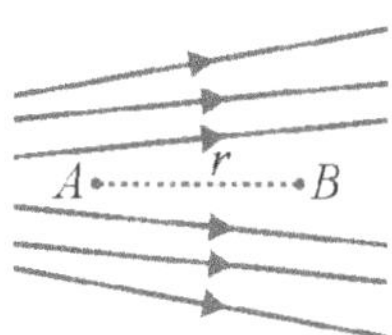


(a) $E_A > E_B$ (b) $E_A < E_B$

(c) $E_A = \frac{E_B}{r}$ (d) $E_A = \frac{E_B}{r^2}$

**27.** In the electric field of a point charge q, a certain charge is carried from point $A$ to $B$, $C$, $D$ and $E$. Then the work done

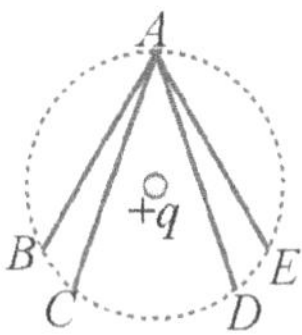


(a) is least along the path $AB$
(b) is least along the path $AD$
(c) is zero along all the paths $AB$, $AC$, $AD$ and $AE$
(d) is least along $AE$

| Answer Key | 17 | (c) | 18 | (a) | 19 | (b) | 20 | (c) | 21 | (a) | 22 | (c) |
|---|---|---|---|---|---|---|---|---|---|---|---|---|
| Sol. from page 107 | 23 | (a) | 24 | (b) | 25 | (a) | 26 | (a) | 27 | (c) | | |

**28.** The magnitude of electric field intensity $E$ is such that, an electron placed in it would experience an electrical force equal to its weight is given by

(a) $mge$ (b) $\frac{mg}{e}$

(c) $\frac{e}{mg}$ (d) $\frac{e^2}{m^2}g$

**29.** A charged particle is free to move in an electric field. It will travel

(a) always along a line of force

(b) along a line of force, if its initial velocity is zero

(c) along a line of force, if it has some initial velocity in the direction of an acute angle with the line of force

(d) none of the above

**30.** Two point charges $Q$ and $-3Q$ are placed at some distance apart. If the electric field at the location of $Q$ is E then at the locality of $-3Q$, it is

(a) $-E$ (b) $E/3$

(c) $-3E$ (d) $-E/3$

**31.** The number of electrons to be put on a spherical conductor of radius 0.1m to produce an electric field of 0.036N/C just above its surface is

(a) $2.7 \times 10^5$ (b) $2.6 \times 10^5$

(c) $2.5 \times 10^5$ (d) $2.4 \times 10^5$

**32.** Four equal charges $Q$ are placed at the four corners of a square of each side is $a$. Work done in removing a charge $-Q$ from its centre to infinity is

(a) 0 (b) $\frac{\sqrt{2}Q^2}{4\pi\varepsilon_0 a}$

(c) $\frac{\sqrt{2}Q^2}{\pi\varepsilon_0 a}$ (d) $\frac{Q^2}{2\pi\varepsilon_0 a}$

**33.** The magnitude of electric field $E$ in the annular region of a charged cylindrical capacitor

(a) is same throughout

(b) is higher near the outer cylinder than near the inner cylinder

(c) varies as $1/r$, where r is the distance from the axis

(d) varies as $1/r^2$, where r is the distance from the axis

**34.** A metallic solid sphere is placed in a uniform electric field. The lines of force follow the path(s) shown in figure as

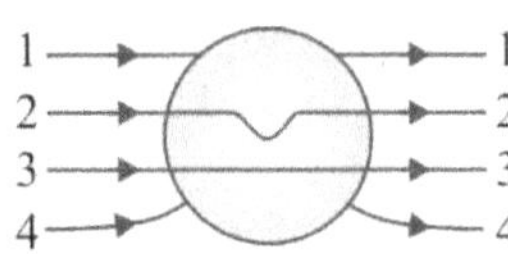


(a) 1 (b) 2

(c) 3 (d) 4

**35.** A particle of mass $m$ and charge $q$ is placed at rest in a uniform electric field $E$ and then released. The kinetic energy attained by the particle after moving a distance $y$ is

(a) $qEy^2$ (b) $qE^2y$

(c) $qEy$ (d) $q^2Ey$

**36.** An electron of mass $m_e$ initially at rest moves through a certain distance in a uniform electric field in time $t_1$. A proton of mass $m_p$ also initially at rest takes time $t_2$ to move through an equal distance in this uniform electric field. Neglecting the effect of gravity, the ratio of $t_2 / t_1$ is nearly equal to

(a) 1 (b) $(m_p/m_e)^{1/2}$

(c) $(m_e/m_p)^{1/2}$ (d) 1836

**37.** If a charged spherical conductor of radius 10 cm has potential $V$ at a point distant 5 cm from its centre, then the potential at a point distant 15 cm from the centre will be

(a) $\frac{1}{3}V$ (b) $\frac{2}{3}V$

(c) $\frac{3}{2}V$ (d) $3V$

**38.** Ten electrons are equally spaced and fixed around a circle of radius $R$. Relative to $V$=0 at infinity, the electrostatic potential $V$ and the electric field $E$ at the centre $C$ are

(a) $V \neq 0$ and $\vec{E} \neq 0$ (b) $V \neq 0$ and $\vec{E} = 0$

(c) $V = 0$ and $\vec{E} = 0$ (d) $V = 0$ and $\vec{E} \neq 0$

**39.** The displacement of a charge $Q$ in the electric field $E = e_1\hat{i} + e_2\hat{j} + e_3\hat{k}$ is $\hat{r} = a\hat{i} + b\hat{j}$. The work done is

(a) $Q(ae_1 + be_2)$ (b) $Q\sqrt{(ae_1)^2 + (be_2)^2}$

(c) $Q(e_1 + e_2)\sqrt{a^2 + b^2}$ (d) $Q\sqrt{(e_1^2 + e_2^2)}(a+b)$

**40.** Three charges $Q$, $+q$ and $+q$ are placed at the vertices of a right-angled isosceles triangle as shown. The net electrostatic energy of the configuration is zero if $Q$ is equal to

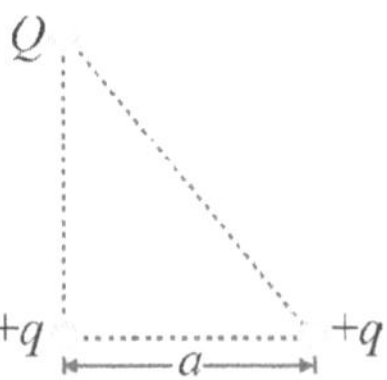


(a) $\frac{-q}{1+\sqrt{2}}$ (b) $\frac{-2q}{2+\sqrt{2}}$

(c) $-2q$ (d) $+q$

| Answer Key | 28 | (b) | 29 | (b) | 30 | (b) | 31 | (c) | 32 | (c) | 33 | (c) | 34 | (d) |
|---|---|---|---|---|---|---|---|---|---|---|---|---|---|---|
| Sol. from page 107 | 35 | (c) | 36 | (b) | 37 | (b) | 38 | (b) | 39 | (a) | 40 | (b) | | |

41. Figures below show regular hexagons, with charges at the vertices. In which of the following cases the electric field at the centre is not zero.

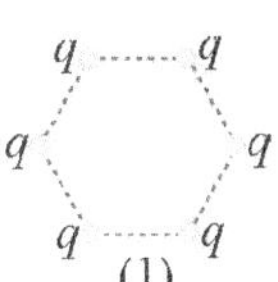
(1)

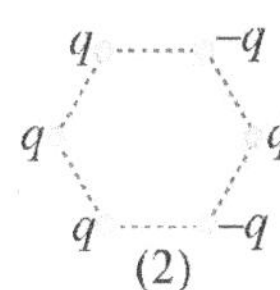
(2)

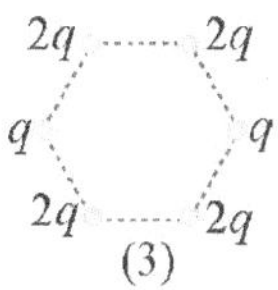
(3)

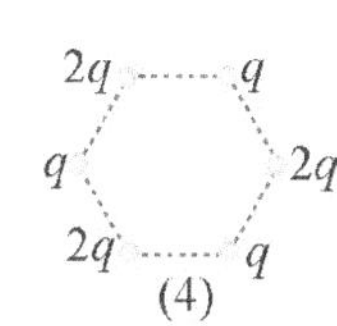
(4)

(a) 1 (b) 2
(c) 3 (d) 4

42. The work done in bringing a 20 coulomb charge from point $A$ to point $B$ for distance 0.2m is 2J. The potential difference between the two points will be (in volt)
(a) 0.2 (b) 8
(c) 0.1 (d) 0.4

43. A thin spherical conducting shell of radius $R$ has a charge $q$. Another charge $Q$ is placed at the centre of the shell. The electrostatic potential at a point $P$ a distance $\frac{R}{2}$ from the centre of the shell is

(a) $\frac{(q+Q)2}{4\pi\varepsilon_0 R}$ (b) $\frac{2Q}{4\pi\varepsilon_0 R}$

(c) $\frac{2Q}{4\pi\varepsilon_0 R}-\frac{2q}{4\pi\varepsilon_0 R}$ (d) $\frac{2Q}{4\pi\varepsilon_0 R}+\frac{q}{4\pi\varepsilon_0 R}$

44. A hollow conducting sphere is placed in an electric field produced by a point charge placed at $P$ as shown in figure. Let $V_A$, $V_B$, $V_C$ be the potentials at point $A$, $B$ and $C$ respectively. Then

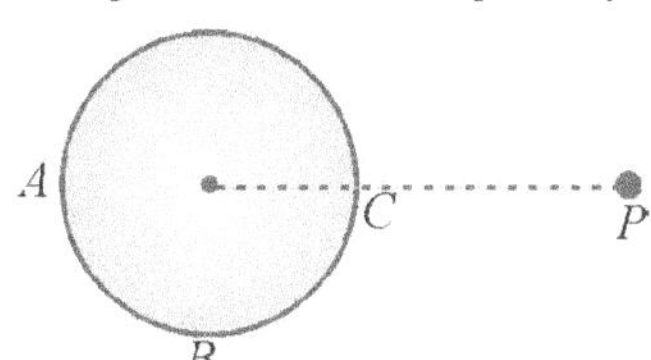


(a) $V_C > V_B$ (b) $V_B > V_C$

(c) $V_A > V_B$ (d) $V_A = V_C$

45. Electric potential of earth is taken to be zero because earth is a good
(a) insulator (b) conductor
(c) semiconductor (d) dielectric

46. Equipotential surfaces associated with an electric field which is increasing in magnitude along the $x$-direction are
(a) planes parallel to $yz$-plane
(b) planes parallel to $xy$-plane
(c) planes parallel to $xz$-plane
(d) coaxial cylinders of increasing radii around the $x$-axis

47. Figure shows three points $A$, $B$ and $C$ in a region of uniform electric field $\vec{E}$. The line $AB$ is perpendicular and $BC$ is parallel to the field lines. Then which of the following holds good. Where $V_A$, $V_B$ and $V_C$ represent the electric potential at points $A$, $B$ and $C$ respectively

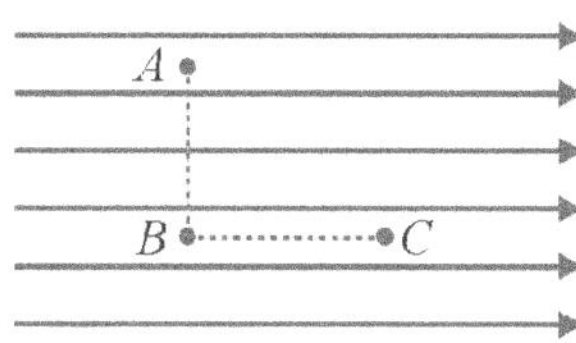


(a) $V_A = V_B = V_C$ (b) $V_A = V_B > V_C$
(c) $V_A = V_B < V_C$ (d) $V_A > V_B = V_C$

48. A charged ball $B$ hangs from a silk thread $S$, which makes an angle $\theta$ with a large charged conducting sheet $P$, as shown in the figure. The surface charge density $\sigma$ of the sheet is proportional to

(a) $\sin\theta$
(b) $\tan\theta$
(c) $\cos\theta$
(d) $\cot\theta$

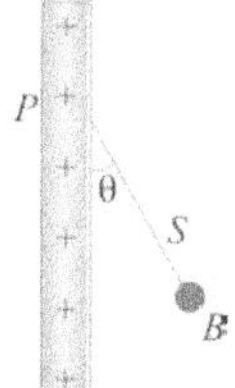


49. Two point charges $+8q$ and $-2q$ are located at $x = 0$ and $x = L$ respectively. The location of a point on the $x$-axis at which the net electric field due to these two point charges is zero
(a) $8L$ (b) $4L$
(c) $2L$ (d) $\frac{L}{4}$

50. For a given surface the Gauss's law is stated as $\oint \vec{E}.d\vec{A} = 0$. From this we can conclude that
(a) E is necessarily zero on the surface
(b) E is perpendicular to the surface at every point
(c) The total flux through the surface is zero
(d) The flux is only going out of the surface

| Answer Key | 41 | (b) | 42 | (c) | 43 | (d) | 44 | (d) | 45 | (b) |
|---|---|---|---|---|---|---|---|---|---|---|
| Sol. from page 107 | 46 | (a) | 47 | (b) | 48 | (b) | 49 | (c) | 50 | (c) |

**51.** Electric charge is uniformly distributed along a long straight wire of radius 1mm. The charge per cm length of the wire is $Q$ coulomb. Another cylindrical surface of radius 50 cm and length 1m symmetrically encloses the wire as shown in the figure. The total electric flux passing through the cylindrical surface is

(a) $\frac{Q}{\varepsilon_0}$

(b) $\frac{100Q}{\varepsilon_0}$

(c) $\frac{10Q}{(\pi\varepsilon_0)}$

(d) $\frac{100Q}{(\pi\varepsilon_0)}$

**52.** $q_1$, $q_2$, $q_3$ and $q_4$ are point charges located at points as shown in the figure and $S$ is a spherical Gaussian surface of radius $R$. Which of the following is true according to the Gauss's law?

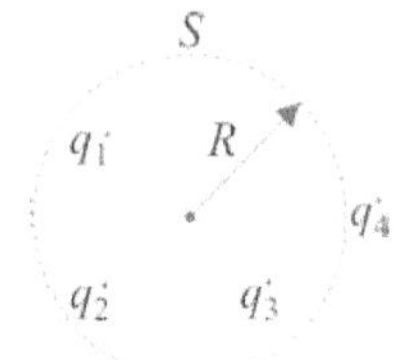


(a) $\oint(\vec{E}_1+\vec{E}_2+\vec{E}_3).d\vec{A}=\frac{q_1+q_2+q_3}{2\varepsilon_0}$

(b) $\oint(\vec{E}_1+\vec{E}_2+\vec{E}_3+\vec{E}_4).d\vec{A}=\frac{(q_1+q_2+q_3)}{\varepsilon_0}$

(c) $\oint(\vec{E}_1+\vec{E}_2+\vec{E}_3).d\vec{A}=\frac{(q_1+q_2+q_3+q_4)}{\varepsilon_0}$

(d) none of the above

**53.** If the electric flux entering and leaving an enclosed surface respectively is $\phi_1$ and $\phi_2$ the electric charge inside the surface will be

(a) $(\phi_1+\phi_2)\varepsilon_0$ (b) $(\phi_2-\phi_1)\varepsilon_0$

(c) $(\phi_1+\phi_2)/\varepsilon_0$ (d) $(\phi_2+\phi_1)/\varepsilon_0$

**54.** An electric line of force in the $xy$ plane is given by equation $x^2+y^2=1$. A particle with unit positive charge, initially at rest at the point $x=1$, $y=0$ in the $xy$ plane

(a) not move at all

(b) will move along straight line

(c) will move along the circular line of force

(d) information is insufficient to draw any conclusion

**55.** If on the concentric hollow spheres of radii $r$ and $R(>r)$ the charge $Q$ is distributed such that their surface densities are same then the potential at their common centre is

(a) $\frac{Q(R^2+r^2)}{4\pi\varepsilon_0(R+r)}$ (b) $\frac{QR}{R+r}$

(c) zero (d) $\frac{Q(R+r)}{4\pi\varepsilon_0(R^2+r^2)}$

**56.** Three positive charges of equal value $q$ are placed at the vertices of an equilateral triangle. The resulting lines of force should be sketched as in

(a) 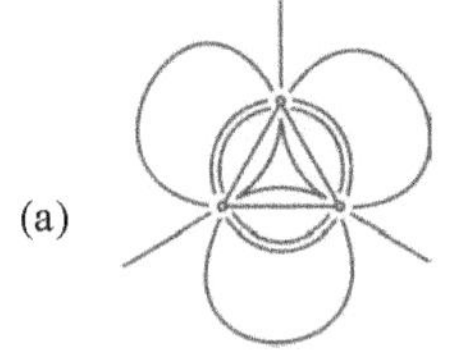

(b) 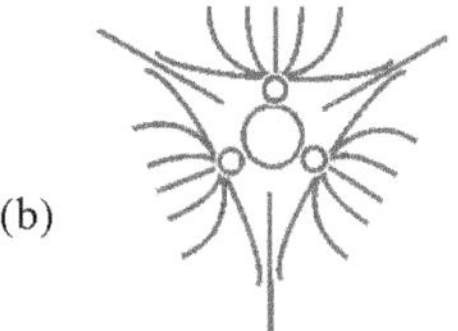

(c) 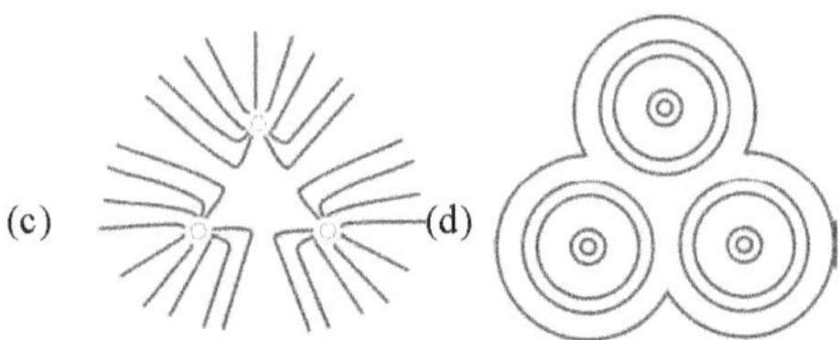
(d)

**57.** A metallic shell has a point charge $q$ kept inside its cavity. Which one of the following diagrams correctly represents the electric lines of forces

(a) 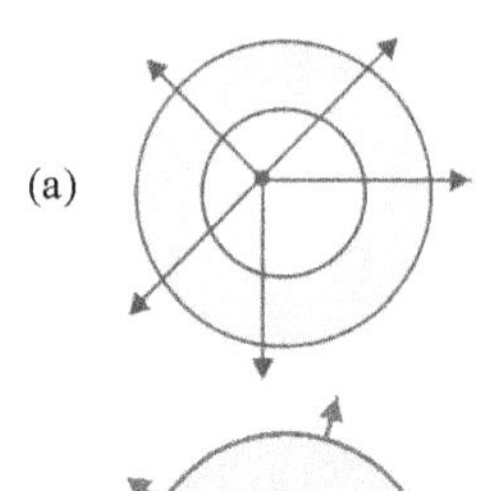

(b) 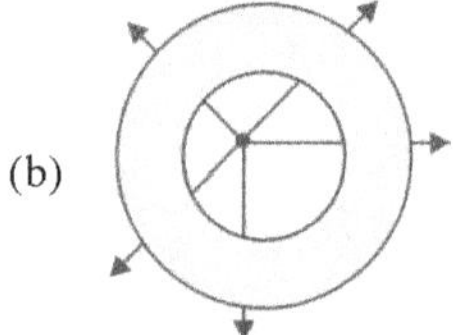

(c) 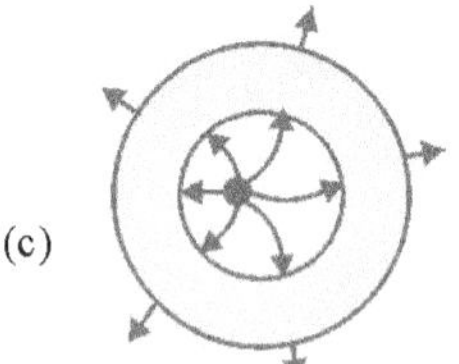

(d) 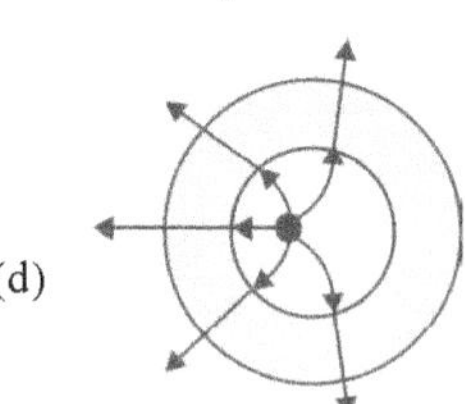

**58.** Two point charges $+q$ and $-q$ are held fixed at $(-d, 0)$ and $(d, 0)$ respectively of a $(x, y)$ coordinate system. Then

(a) $E$ at all points on the $y$-axis is along $\hat{i}$

(b) The electric field $\vec{E}$ at all points on the $x$-axis has the same direction

(c) Dipole moment is $2qd$ directed along $\hat{i}$

(d) Work has to be done in bringing a test charge from infinity to the origin

| Answer Key | 51 | (b) | 52 | (b) | 53 | (b) | 54 | (c) |
|---|---|---|---|---|---|---|---|---|
| Sol. from page 107 | 55 | (d) | 56 | (c) | 57 | (c) | 58 | (a) |

**59.** A charged particle $q$ is shot towards another charged particle $Q$ which is fixed, with a speed $v$. It approaches $Q$ upto a closest distance $r$ and then returns. If $q$ were given a speed $2v$, the closest distances of approach would be

(a) $r$ (b) $2r$

(c) $r/2$ (d) $r/4$

**60.** Point charge $q$ moves from point $P$ to point $S$ along the path $PQRS$ (figure shown) in a uniform electric field $E$ pointing coparallel to the positive direction of the $x$-axis. The coordinates of the points $P,Q,R$ and $S$ are $(a, b, 0)$, $(2a, 0, 0)$, $(a, -b, 0)$ and $(0, 0, 0)$ respectively. The work done by the field in the above process is given by the expression

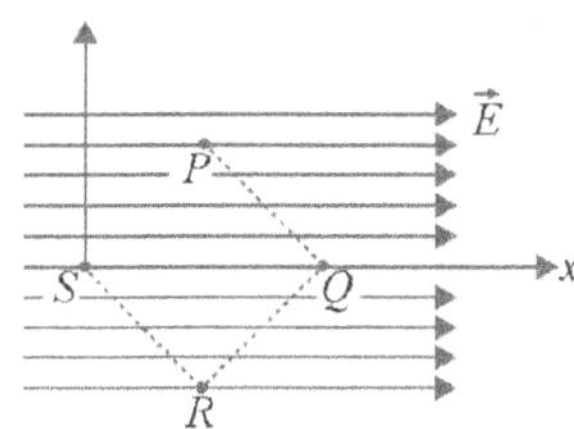


(a) $qEa$ (b) $-qEa$

(c) $qEa\sqrt{2}$ (d) $qE\sqrt{[(2a)^2 + b^2]}$

**61.** The variation of potential with distance $R$ from a fixed point is as shown below. The electric field at $R = 5$m is

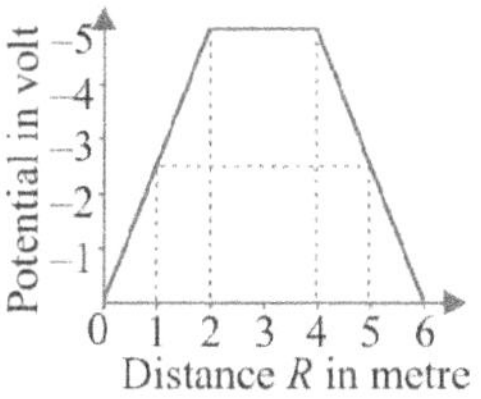

(a) 2.5 volt / m

(b) –2.5 volt / m

(c) 2 / 5 volt / m

(d) –2 / 5 volt / m

Potential in volt: –5, –4, –3, –2, –1

Distance $R$ in metre: 0 1 2 3 4 5 6

**62.** The electric field due to a uniformly charged sphere of radius $R$ as a function of the distance from its centre is represented graphically by

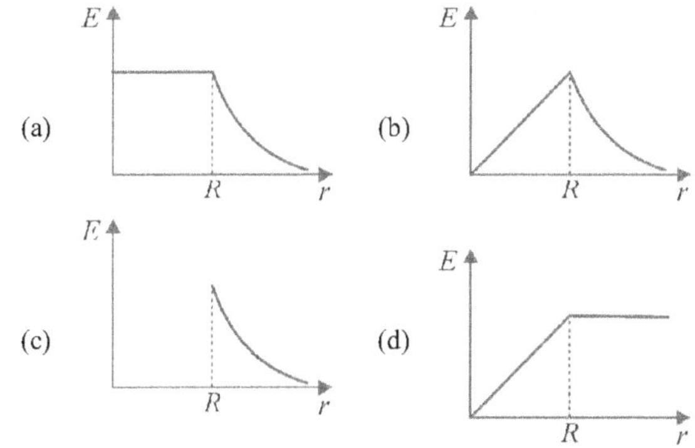


**63.** A point charge $q$ is at a distance d from a conducting plane and is to be moved infinitely away from the plane. The energy required to achieve this is :

(a) $\frac{1}{4\pi\varepsilon_0}\frac{q^2}{d}$ (b) $\frac{1}{4\pi\varepsilon_0}\frac{q}{d}$

(c) $\frac{1}{4\pi\varepsilon_0}\frac{q}{2d}$ (d) $\frac{1}{4\pi\varepsilon_0}\frac{+q^2}{4d}$

**64.** Five balls numbered 1 to 5 are suspended using separate threads. Pairs (1, 2), (2, 4), (4, 1) show electrostatic attraction, while pairs (2, 3) and (4, 5) show repulsion. Therefore ball 1 must be :

(a) positively charged (b) negatively charged

(c) neutral (d) made of metal

**65.** $A$ and $B$ are two concentric spheres. If $A$ is given a charge $Q$ while $B$ is earthed as shown in figure :

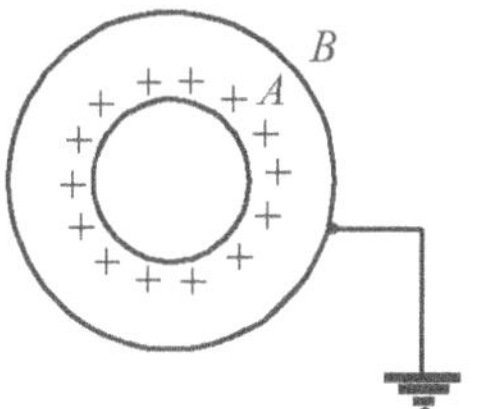


(a) the charge density of $A$ and $B$ are same

(b) the field inside and outside $A$ is zero

(c) the field between $A$ and $B$ is not zero

(d) the field inside and outside $B$ is zero

**66.** Under the influence of the Coulomb field of charge $+Q$, a charge $-q$ is moving around it in an elliptical orbit. Find out the correct statement(s)

(a) the angular momentum of the charge $-q$ is constant

(b) the linear momentum of the charge $-q$ is constant

(c) the angular velocity of the charge $-q$ is constant

(d) the linear speed of the charge $-q$ is constant

**67.** A solid spherical conductor of radius $R$ has a spherical cavity of radius $a$ $(a < R)$ at its centre. A charge $+Q$ is kept at the centre. The charge at the inner surface, outer and at a position $r$ $(a < r < R)$ are respectively

(a) $+Q, -Q, 0$ (b) $-Q, +Q, 0$

(c) $0, -Q, 0$ (d) $+Q, 0, 0$

**68.** One metallic sphere $A$ is given positive charge whereas another identical metallic sphere $B$ of exactly same mass as of $A$ is given equal amount of negative charge. Then

(a) mass of $A$ and mass of $B$ still remain equal

(b) mass of $A$ increases

(c) mass of $B$ decreases

(d) mass of $B$ increases

| Answer Key | 59 | (d) | 60 | (b) | 61 | (a) | 62 | (b) | 63 | (d) |
|---|---|---|---|---|---|---|---|---|---|---|
| Sol. from page 107 | 64 | (c) | 65 | (c) | 66 | (a) | 67 | (b) | 68 | (d) |

69. Three charges are placed at the vertices of an equilateral triangle of side '$a$' as shown in the following figure. The force experienced by the charge placed at the vertex $A$ in a direction normal to $BC$ is

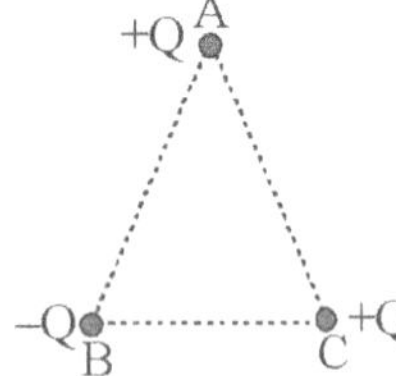


(a) $Q^2/(4\pi\varepsilon_0 a^2)$ (b) $-Q^2/(4\pi\varepsilon_0 a^2)$

(c) zero (d) $Q^2/(2\pi\varepsilon_0 a^2)$

70. An infinite number of charges, each of charge 1μC, are placed on the $x$-axis with co-ordinates $x$ = 1, 2, 4, 8, ......∞. If a charge of 1 C is kept at the origin, then what is the net force acting on 1 C charge

(a) 9000 N (b) 12000 N
(c) 24000 N (d) 36000 N

71. Gauss law of gravitation is

(a) $\oint \vec{g}.d\vec{A} = m$ (b) $\oint \vec{g}.d\vec{A} = Gm$

(c) $\oint \vec{g}.d\vec{A} = -4G\pi m$ (d) all the above

72. There is an electric field $E$ in $x$-direction. If the work done on moving a charge 0.2 C through a distance of 2m along a line making an angle 60° with the $x$-axis is 4.0 J, what is the value of $E$

(a) $\sqrt{3}$ N/C (b) 4 N/C

(c) 5 N/C (d) 20 $N/C$.

73. Two charge $+q$ and $-q$ are situated at a certain distance. At the point exactly midway between them

(a) electric field and potential both are zero
(b) electric field is zero but potential is not zero
(c) electric field is not zero but potential is zero
(d) neither electric field nor potential is zero

74. Two metal pieces having a potential difference of 800V are 0.02 m apart horizontally. A particle of mass $1.96 \times 10^{-15}$kg is suspended in equilibrium between the plates. If $e$ is the elementary charge, then charge on the particle is

(a) $e$ (b) $3e$
(c) $6e$ (d) $8e$

75. Two spheres of radii $a$ and $b$ respectively are charged and joined by a wire. The ratio of electric field of the spheres is

(a) $a/b$ (b) $b/a$
(c) $a^2/b^2$ (d) $b^2/a^2$

76. The ratio of momenta of an electron and an α-particle which are accelerated from rest by a potential difference of 100 volt is

(a) 1 (b) $\sqrt{\frac{2m_e}{m_\alpha}}$

(c) $\sqrt{\frac{m_e}{m_\alpha}}$ (d) $\sqrt{\frac{m_e}{2m_\alpha}}$

77. The dimension of (1/2) $\varepsilon_0 E^2$ ($\varepsilon_0$ : permittivity of free space; $E$ : Electric field ) is

(a) $[MLT^{-}]$ (d) $[ML^2T^{-}]$
(c) $[ML^{-1}T^{-2}]$ (d) $[ML^2T^{-1}]$

78. Two spheres $A$ and $B$ of radius '$a$' and '$b$' respectively are at same electric potential. The ratio of the surface charge densities of $A$ and $B$ is

(a) $\frac{a}{b}$ (b) $\frac{b}{a}$

(c) $\frac{a^2}{b^2}$ (d) $\frac{b^2}{a^2}$

79. A ball of mass 1 g and charge $10^{-8}$C moves from a point $A$, where potential is 600 volt to the point $B$ where potential is zero. Velocity of the ball at the point $B$ is 20 cm/s. The velocity of the ball at the point $A$ will be

(a) 22.8 cm/s (b) 228 cm/s
(c) 16.8 m/s (d) 168 m/s

80. The figure shows the path of a positively charged particle 1 through a rectangular region of uniform electric field as shown in the figure. What is the direction of electric field and the direction of particles 2, 3 and 4 ?

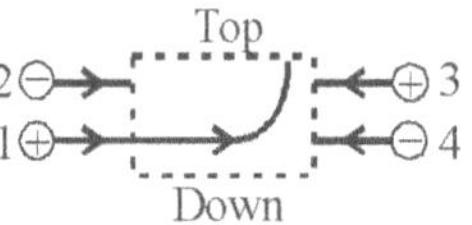


(a) Top, down, top, down (b) Top, down, down, top
(c) Down, top, top, down (d) Down; top, down, down

81. The spatial distribution of the electric field due to charges ($A$, $B$) is shown in figure. Which one of the following statements is correct?

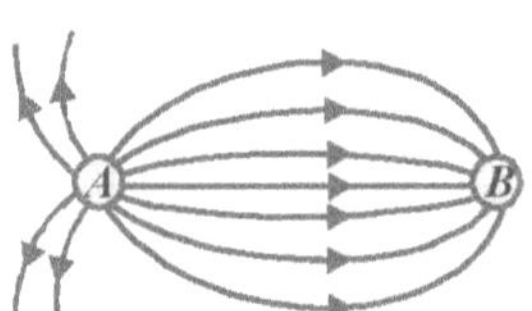


(a) $A$ is +ve and $B$ –ve and $|A| > |B|$
(b) $A$ is –ve and $B$ + ve; $|A| = |B|$
(c) Both are +ve but $A > B$
(d) Both are – ve but $A > B$

| Answer Key | 69 | (c) | 70 | (b) | 71 | (c) | 72 | (d) | 73 | (c) | 74 | (b) | 75 | (b) |
|---|---|---|---|---|---|---|---|---|---|---|---|---|---|---|
| Sol. from page 107 | 76 | (d) | 77 | (c) | 78 | (b) | 79 | (a) | 80 | (a) | 81 | (a) | | |

**82.** Charges are placed on the vertices of a square as shown. Let $E$ be the electric field and $V$ the potential at the centre. If the charges on $A$ and $B$ are interchanged with those on $D$ and $C$ respectively, then.

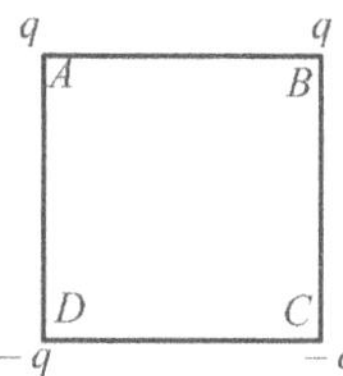


(a) $\vec{E}$ remains unchanged, $V$ changes

(b) Both $\vec{E}$ and $V$ change

(c) $\vec{E}$ and $V$ remains unchanged

(d) $\vec{E}$ changes, V remains unchanged

**83.** An electric dipole of moment $\vec{p}$ is placed normal to the lines of force of electric intensity $\vec{E}$, then the work done in deflecting it through an angle of 180° is

(a) $pE$ (b) $+2pE$
(c) $-2pE$ (d) zero

**84.** The value of electric potential at any point due to any electric dipole is

(a) $k.\frac{\vec{p}\times\vec{r}}{r^2}$ (b) $k.\frac{\vec{p}\times\vec{r}}{r^3}$

(c) $k.\frac{\vec{p}.\vec{r}}{r^2}$ (d) $k.\frac{\vec{p}.\vec{r}}{r^3}$

**85.** Gauss's law should be invalid if

(a) there were magnetic monopoles
(b) the inverse square law were not exactly true
(c) the velocity of light were not a universal constant
(d) none of these

**86.** A square surface of side $L$ meters is in the plane of the paper. A uniform electric field $\vec{E}$ (volt/m), also in the plane of the paper, is limited only to the lower half of the square surface, (see figure). The electric flux in SI units associated with the surface is

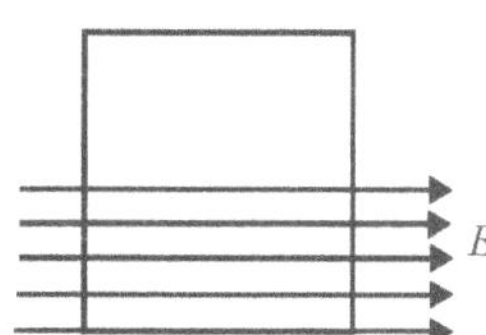


(a) zero (b) $EL^2$
(c) $EL^2 / 2\epsilon_0$ (d) $EL^2/2$

**87.** Consider an electric field $\vec{E} = E_0\hat{x}$ where $E_0$ is a constant. The flux through the shaded area (as shown in the figure) due to this field is

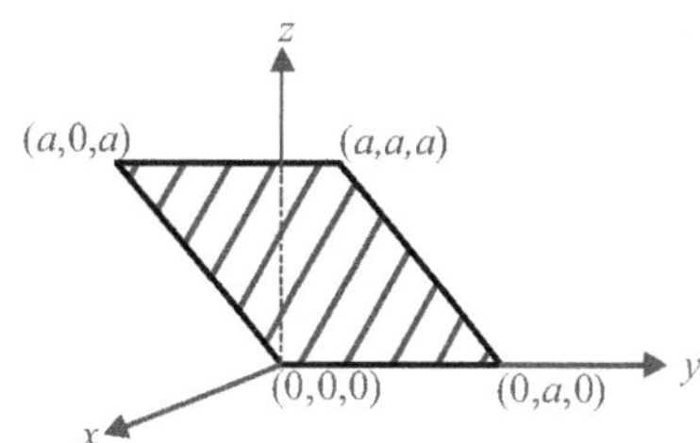


(a) $2E_0a_2$ (b) $\sqrt{2}E_0a^2$

(c) $E_0\, a^2$ (d) $\frac{E_0a^2}{\sqrt{2}}$

**88.** A wooden block performs SHM on a frictionless surface with frequency, $\nu_0$. The block carries a charge $+Q$ on its surface. If now a uniform electric field $\vec{E}$ is switched-on as shown, then the SHM of the block will be

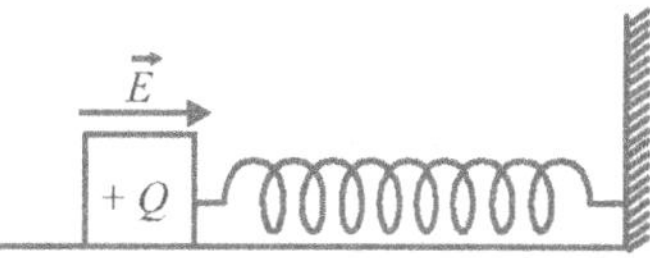


(a) of the same frequency and with shifted mean position.
(b) of the same frequency and with the same mean position
(c) of changed frequency and with shifted mean position.
(d) of changed frequency and with the same mean position.

**89.** Two thin wire rings each having a radius $R$ are placed at a distance $d$ apart with their axes coinciding. The charges on the two rings are $+Q$ and $-Q$. The potential difference between the centres of the two rings is

(a) zero

(b) $\frac{Q}{4\pi\varepsilon_0}\left[\frac{1}{R}-\frac{1}{\sqrt{R^2+d^2}}\right]$

(c) $QR / 4\pi\varepsilon_0 d^2$

(d) $\frac{Q}{2\pi\varepsilon_0}\left[\frac{1}{R}-\frac{1}{\sqrt{R^2+d^2}}\right]$

**90.** Two infinitely long parallel conducting plates having surface charge densities $+\sigma$ and $-\sigma$ respectively, are separated by a small distance. The medium between the plates is vacuum. If $\varepsilon_0$ is the dielectric permittivity of vacuum, then the electric field in the region between the plates is

(a) 0 V/m (b) $\frac{\sigma}{2\varepsilon_0}$ V/m

(c) $\frac{\sigma}{\varepsilon_0}$ V/m (d) $\frac{2\sigma}{\varepsilon_0}$ V/m

| Answer Key | 82 | (d) | 83 | (d) | 84 | (d) | 85 | (b) | 86 | (a) |
|---|---|---|---|---|---|---|---|---|---|---|
| Sol. from page 107 | 87 | (c) | 88 | (a) | 89 | (d) | 90 | (c) | | |

91. The figure shows a charge $q$ placed inside a cavity in an uncharged conductor. Now if an external electric field is switched on then :

(a) only induced charge on outer surface will redistribute.
(b) only induced charge on inner surface will redistribute
(c) both induced charge on outer and inner surface will redistribute.
(d) force on charge $q$ placed inside the cavity will change

92. A given charge is situated at a certain distance from an electric dipole in the end-on position, experiences a force $F$. If the distance of the charge is doubled, the force acting on the charge will be

(a) $2F$ (b) $F/2$
(c) $F/4$ (d) $F/8$

| Answer Key | 91 | (a) | 92 | (d) | | |
|---|---|---|---|---|---|---|
| Sol. from page 107 | | | | | | |

## LEVEL - 2

### Only one option correct

1. Consider a system of three charges $\frac{q}{3}, \frac{q}{3}$ and $-\frac{2q}{3}$ placed at points $A$, $B$ and $C$, respectively, as shown in figure. Take $O$ to be the circle of radius $R$ and angle $CAB = 60°$. Choose the correct one:

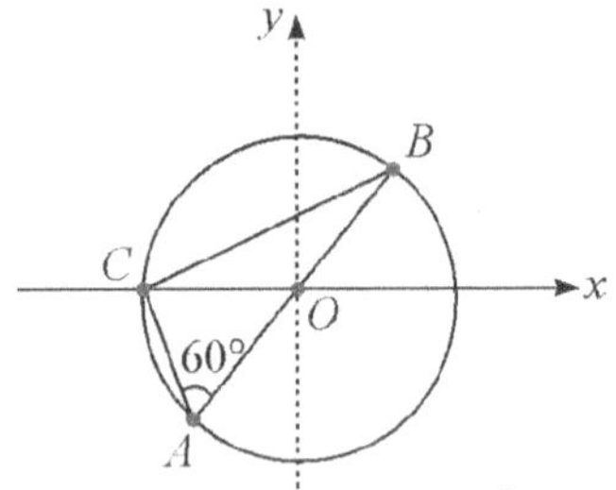

(a) The electric field at point $O$ is $\frac{q}{8\pi \in_0 R^2}$ directed along the negative x-axis.
(b) The potential energy of the system is zero.
(c) The magnitude of the force between the charges at $C$ and $B$ is $\frac{q^2}{54\pi \in_0 R^2}$
(d) The potential at point $O$ is $\frac{q}{12\pi \in_0 R}$

2. Figure shows an electric quadrupole, with quadrupole moment ($Q = 2q\ell^2$). The electric field at a distance from its centre at the axis of the quadrupole is given by

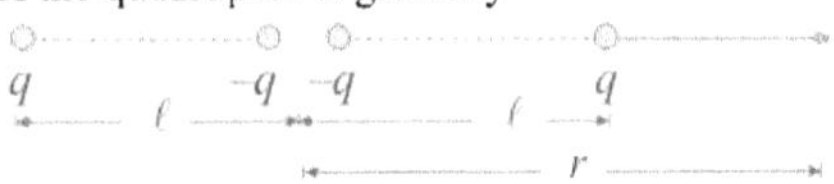

(a) $\left(\frac{1}{4\pi \in_0}\right)\frac{Q}{r^4}$ (b) $\left(\frac{1}{4\pi \in_0}\right)\frac{2Q}{r^4}$
(c) $\left(\frac{1}{4\pi \in_0}\right)\frac{3Q}{r^4}$ (d) none

3. Two small identical metal balls of radius $r$ are at a distance $a$ from each other and are charged, one with a potential $V_1$ and the other with a potential $V_2$. The charges on the balls are :

(a) $q_1 = V_1 a, q_2 = V_2 a$
(b) $q_1 = V_1 r, q_2 = V_2 r$
(c) $q_1 = \left(\frac{V_1 + V_2}{2}\right)a, q_2 = \left(\frac{V_1 + V_2}{2}\right)r$
(d) $q_1 = -\frac{r}{a}(rV_2 - aV_1), q_2 = -\frac{r}{a}(rV_1 - aV_2)$

4. The distance between the plates of a charged plate capacitor disconnected from the battery is 5 cm and the intensity of the field in it is $E$ = 300 V/cm. An uncharged metal bar 1 cm thick is introduced into the capacitor parallel to its plates. The potential difference between the plates now is :

(a) 1500 V (b) 1200 V
(c) 900 V (d) zero.

5. Three infinite long charged sheets of charge densities $-\sigma$, $-2\sigma$ and $\sigma$ are placed parallel to xy-plane at $z = 0, z = a, z = 3a$. Electric field at point $P$ is

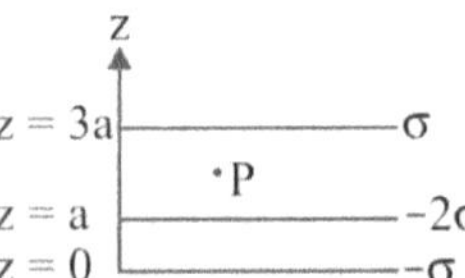


(a) $\frac{-2\sigma}{\epsilon_0}\hat{k}$ (b) $\frac{2\sigma}{\epsilon_0}\hat{k}$
(c) $\frac{-4\sigma}{\epsilon_0}\hat{k}$ (d) $\frac{4\sigma}{\epsilon_0}\hat{k}$

| Answer Key | 1 | (c) | 2 | (c) | 3 | (d) |
|---|---|---|---|---|---|---|
| Sol. from page 110 | 4 | (b) | 5 | (d) | | |

6. Figure shows an imaginary cube of edge $\frac{L}{2}$. An uniformly charged rod of length $L$ moves towards left at a small but constant speed $v$. At $t = 0$, the left end just touches the centre of the face of the cube opposite it. Which of the graphs shown in the figure represents the flux of the electric field through the cube as the rod goes through it

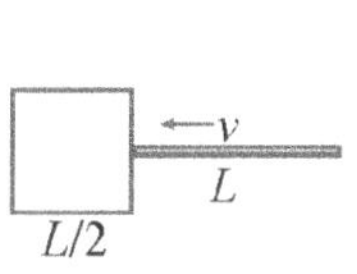


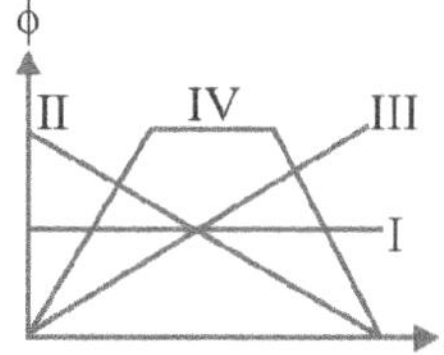


(a) I  (b) II
(c) III  (d) IV

7. A sphere of radius $2R$ has a uniform charge density $\rho$. The difference in the electric potential at $r = R$ and $r = 0$ from the centre is :

(a) $\frac{-\rho R^2}{\epsilon_0}$  (b) $\frac{-2\rho R^2}{\epsilon_0}$

(c) $\frac{\rho R^2}{3\epsilon_0}$  (d) $\frac{-\rho R^2}{6\epsilon_0}$

8. A sphere of radius $R$ carries charge density $\rho$ proportional to the square of the distance from the centre such that $\rho = CR^2$, where $C$ is a positive constant. At a distance $R/2$ from the centre, the magnitude of the electric field is

(a) $\frac{CR^3}{20\epsilon_0}$  (b) $\frac{CR^3}{10\epsilon_0}$

(c) $\frac{CR^3}{5\epsilon_0}$  (d) none of these

9. The work done in moving an electron of charge e and mass m from $A$ to $B$ along the circular path (shown in figure) in the vertical plane in the field of charge $Q$ is

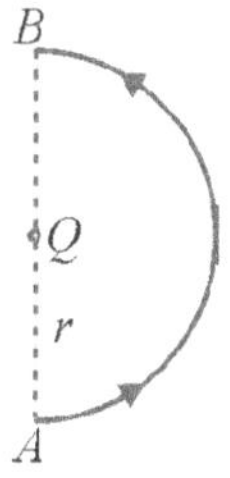

(a) $2\,mg$

(b) $\frac{-2Qe}{r}$

(c) $2mgr + \frac{2Qe}{r}$

(d) zero

10. Two particles $A$ and $B$ having equal charges are placed at a distance $d$ apart. A third charged particle placed on the perpendicular bisection of $AB$ at distance $x$. The third particle experiences maximum force when

(a) $x = \frac{d}{\sqrt{2}}$  (b) $x = \frac{d}{2}$

(c) $x = \frac{d}{2\sqrt{2}}$  (d) $x = \frac{d}{3\sqrt{2}}$

11. Two plane metal plates are placed parallel to each other, one carries a surface density $+\sigma$ and the other $-2\sigma$. A third plate is placed between them and earthed. The charge density on the left face of this plate is :

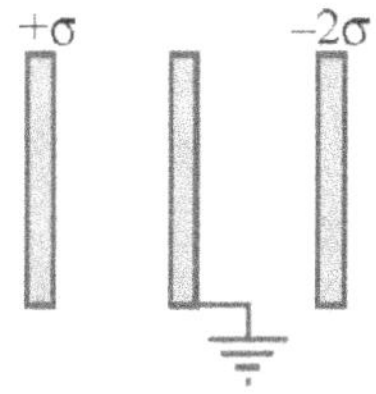

(a) $+\sigma$
(b) $-\sigma$
(c) $+2\sigma$
(d) zero

12. Four similar point charges $q$ are located at the vertices of a tetrahedron with an edge $a$. The energy of the interaction of charges is :

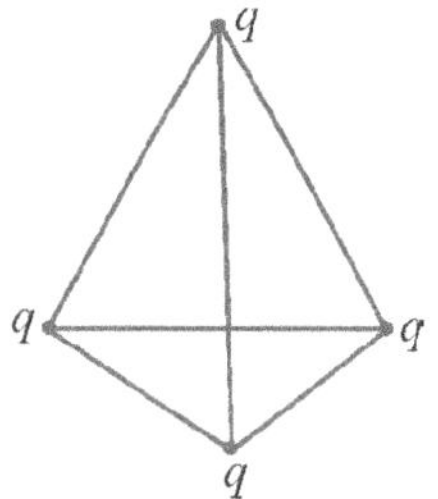


(a) $\frac{6q^2}{4\pi\epsilon_0 a}$  (b) $\frac{4q^2}{4\pi\epsilon_0 a}$

(c) $\frac{3q^2}{4\pi\epsilon_0 a}$  (d) $\frac{q^2}{4\pi\epsilon_0 a}$

13. Two charges are at a distance $d$ apart. If a copper plate (conducting medium) of thickness $\frac{d}{2}$ is placed between them, the effective force will be

(a) $2F$  (b) $F/2$
(c) 0  (d) $\sqrt{2}F$

14. Two spherical conductors $B$ and $C$ having equal radii and carrying equal charges in them repel each other with a force $F$ when kept apart at some distance. A third spherical conductor having same radius as that of $B$ but uncharged is brought in contact with $B$, then brought in contact with $C$ and finally removed away from both. The new force of repulsion between $B$ and $C$ is

(a) $F/4$  (b) $3F/4$
(c) $F/8$  (d) $3F/8$

15. Electric potential at any point is $V = -5x + 3y + \sqrt{15}z$, then the magnitude of the electric field is

(a) $3\sqrt{2}$  (b) $4\sqrt{2}$
(c) $5\sqrt{2}$  (d) 7

| Answer Key | 6 | (d) | 7 | (d) | 8 | (d) | 9 | (a) | 10 | (c) |
|---|---|---|---|---|---|---|---|---|---|---|
| Sol. from page 110 | 11 | (b) | 12 | (a) | 13 | (c) | 14 | (d) | 15 | (d) |

16. Four point +ve charges of same magnitude ($Q$) are placed at four corners of a rigid square frame as shown in figure. The plane of the frame is perpendicular to $z$-axis. If $a$ –ve point charge is placed at a distance z away from the above frame ($z << L$) then

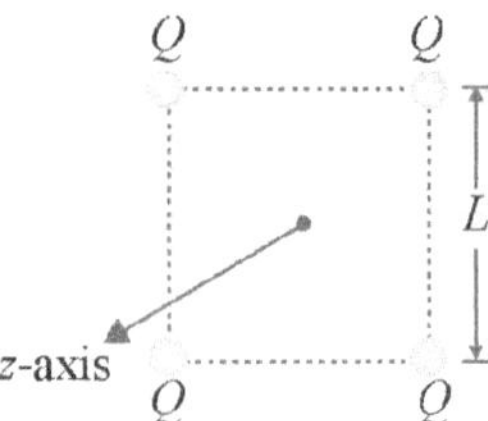


(a) –ve charge oscillates along the $z$-axis.
(b) it moves away from the frame
(c) it moves slowly towards the frame and stays in the plane of the frame
(d) it passes through the frame only once.

17. Two identical thin rings each of radius $R$ meters are coaxially placed at a distance $R$ meters apart. If $Q_1$ coulomb and $Q_2$ coulomb are respectively the charges uniformly spread on the two rings, the work done in moving a charge $q$ from the centre of one ring to that of other is

(a) zero (b) $\dfrac{q(Q_1 - Q_2)(\sqrt{2}-1)}{\sqrt{2}.4\pi\varepsilon_0 R}$

(c) $\dfrac{q\sqrt{2}(Q_1 + Q_2)}{4\pi\varepsilon_0 R}$ (d) $\dfrac{q(Q_1 + Q_2)(\sqrt{2}+1)}{\sqrt{2}.4\pi\varepsilon_0 R}$

18. A charge $+q$ is fixed at each of the points $x = x_0$, $x = 3x_0$, $x = 5x_0$....... infinite, on the $x$-axis and a charge $-q$ is fixed at each of the points $x = 2x_0$, $x = 4x_0$, $x = 6x_0$...... infinite. Here $x_0$ is a positive constant. Take the electric potential at a point due to a charge $Q$ at a distance $r$ from it to be $Q / (4\pi\varepsilon_0 r)$. Then, the potential at the origin due to the above system of charges is

(a) 0 (b) $\dfrac{q}{8\pi\varepsilon_0 x_0 \ln 2}$

(c) $\infty$ (d) $\dfrac{q \ln 2}{4\pi\varepsilon_0 x_0}$

19. A non-conducting ring of radius 0.5 m carries a total charge of $1.11 \times 10^{-10}$C distributed non-uniformly on its circumference producing an electric field $\vec{E}$ everywhere in space. The value of the line integral $\int_{\ell=\infty}^{\ell=0} -\vec{E}.\vec{d\ell}$ ($\ell = 0$ being centre of the ring) in volts is

(a) + 2 (b) –1
(c) –2 (d) zero

20. Charge $q$ is uniformly distributed over a thin half ring of radius $R$. The electric field at the centre of the ring is

(a) $\dfrac{q}{2\pi^2\varepsilon_0 R^2}$ (b) $\dfrac{q}{4\pi^2\varepsilon_0 R^2}$

(c) $\dfrac{q}{4\pi\varepsilon_0 R^2}$ (d) $\dfrac{q}{2\pi\varepsilon_0 R^2}$

21. Two equal point charges are fixed at $x = -a$ and $x = +a$ on the $x$-axis. Another point charge $Q$ is placed at the origin. The change in the electric potential energy of $Q$, when it is displaced by a small distance $x$ along the $x$-axis, is approximately proportional to

(a) $x$ (b) $x^2$
(c) $x^3$ (d) $1 / x$

22. Four charges equal to $-Q$ are placed at the four corners of a square and a charge $q$ is at its centre. If the system is in equilibrium the value of $q$ is

(a) $-\dfrac{Q}{4}(1+2\sqrt{2})$ (b) $\dfrac{Q}{4}(1+2\sqrt{2})$

(c) $-\dfrac{Q}{2}(1+2\sqrt{2})$ (d) $\dfrac{Q}{2}(1+2\sqrt{2})$

23. Two concentric conducting thin spherical shells $A$, and $B$ having radii $r_A$ and $r_B$ ($(r_B > r_A)$ are charged to $Q_A$ and $-Q_B$ ($|Q_B| > |Q_A|$). The electric field along a line (passing through the centre) is

(a) (b)

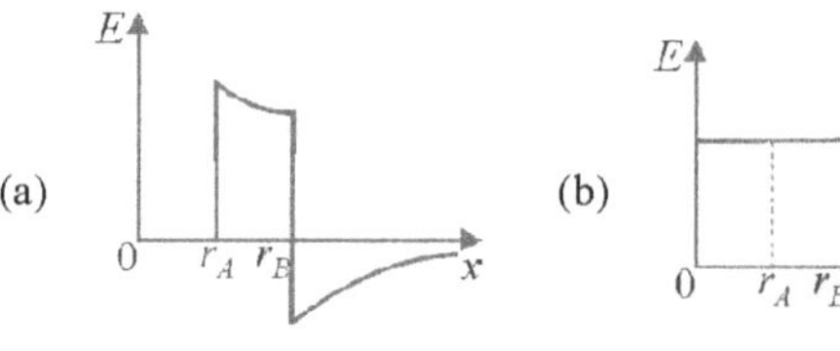


(c)

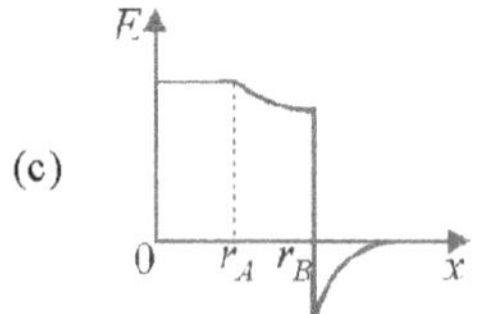


(d)

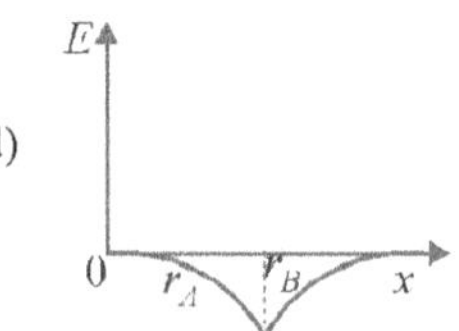


24. A particle of charge -$q$ and mass m moves in a circular orbit of radius $r$ about a fixed charge $+ Q$. The relation between the radius of the orbit r and the time period $T$ is :

(a) $r = \dfrac{Qq}{16\pi^2 \epsilon_0 m} T^2$ (b) $r^3 = \dfrac{Qq}{16\pi^3 \epsilon_0 m} T^2$

(c) $r^2 = \dfrac{Qq}{16\pi^3 \epsilon_0 m} T^3$ (d) $r^2 = \dfrac{Qq}{4\pi^3 \epsilon_0 m} T^3$

| Answer Key | 16 | (a) | 17 | (b) | 18 | (d) | 19 | (a) | 20 | (a) |
|---|---|---|---|---|---|---|---|---|---|---|
| Sol. from page 110 | 21 | (b) | 22 | (b) | 23 | (a) | 24 | (b) | | |

**25.** A thin glass rod is bent into a semicircular shape of radius $R$. A charge $+Q$ is uniformly distributed along the upper half and a charge $-Q$ is uniformly distributed along the lower half as shown in the figure. The electric field at the centre $P$, is :

(a) $\dfrac{Q}{4\pi\varepsilon_0 R^2}$

(b) $\dfrac{Q}{2\pi\varepsilon_0 R^2}$

(c) $\dfrac{Q}{(4\pi\varepsilon_0 R)^2}$

(d) $\dfrac{Q}{\pi^2\varepsilon_0 R^2}$

**26.** A bullet of mass $m$ and charge $Q$ is fired towards a solid uniformly charged sphere of radius $R$ and total charge $Q$. If it strikes the surface of sphere with speed $v$, the minimum speed $v$ so that it can penetrate through the sphere :

(a) $\dfrac{Q}{\sqrt{2\pi\,\epsilon_0\, mR}}$  (b) $\dfrac{Q}{\sqrt{6\pi\,\epsilon_0\, mR}}$

(c) $\dfrac{Q}{\sqrt{4\pi\,\epsilon_0\, mR}}$  (d) $\dfrac{3Q}{\sqrt{4\pi\,\epsilon_0\, mR}}$

**27.** A plastic disk is charged on one side with a uniform surface charge density $\sigma$ and then three quadrant of the disk are removed. The remaining quadrant is shown in figure, with $V = 0$ at infinity, the potential due to the remaining quadrant at point $P$ is :

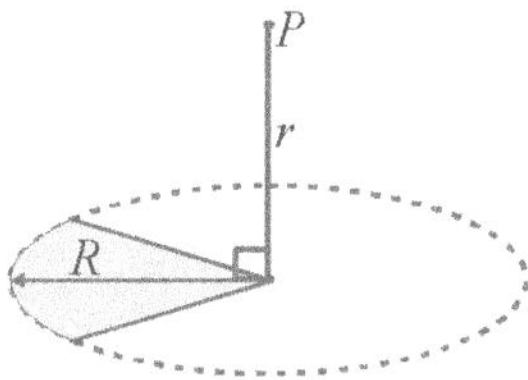


(a) $\dfrac{\sigma}{2\,\epsilon_0}[(r^2 + R)^{1/2} - r]$  (b) $\dfrac{\sigma}{2\,\epsilon_0}[R - r]$

(c) $\dfrac{\sigma}{8\,\epsilon_0}[(r^2 + R^2)^{1/2} - r]$  (d) none of these

**28.** A neutral conducting spherical shell is kept near a charge $q$ as shown. The potential at point $P$ due to the induced charges is :

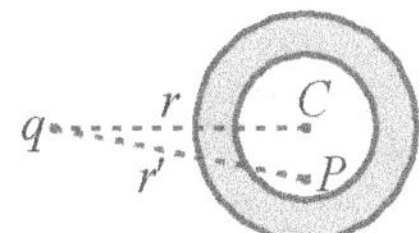


(a) $\dfrac{kq}{r}$  (b) $\dfrac{kq}{r'}$

(c) $\dfrac{kq}{r} - \dfrac{kq}{r'}$  (d) $\dfrac{kq}{CP}$

**29.** A disk of radius $a / 4$ having a uniformly distributed charge 6 C is placed in the $x$ - $y$ plane with its centre at $(-a / 2, 0, 0)$. A rod of length $a$ carrying a uniformly distributed charge 8 C is placed on the $x$ - axis from $x = a/4$ to $x = 5a / 4$. Two point charges $-7$ C and 3 C are placed at $(a / 4, -a/4, 0)$ and $(-3a/4, 3a / 4, 0)$, respectively. Consider a cubical surface formed by six surfaces $x = \pm a / 2$, $y = \pm a / 2$, $z = \pm a / 2$. The electric flux through this cubical surface is

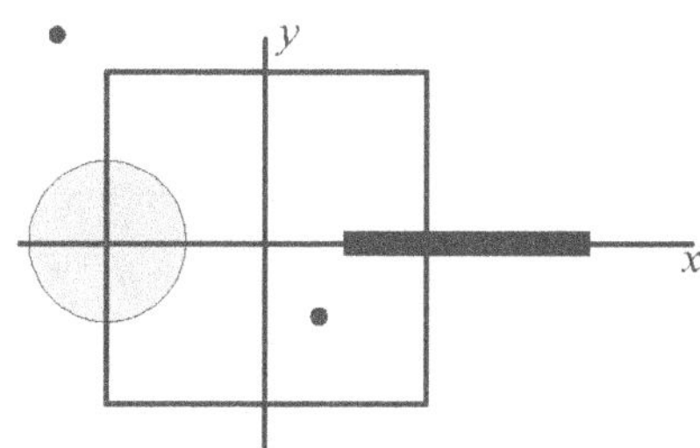


(a) $\dfrac{-2C}{\varepsilon_0}$  (b) $\dfrac{2C}{\varepsilon_0}$

(c) $\dfrac{10C}{\varepsilon_0}$  (d) $\dfrac{12C}{\varepsilon_0}$

**30.** Consider the shown uniform solid insulating sphere with a short and light electric dipole of dipole moment $p\hat{j}$ (embedded at its centre) placed at rest on a horizontal surface. An electric field $E\hat{i}$ is suddenly switched on in the region such that the sphere instantly begins rolling without slipping. Speed of the sphere when the dipole moment becomes horizontal for the first time is ($m$ = Mass of the sphere)

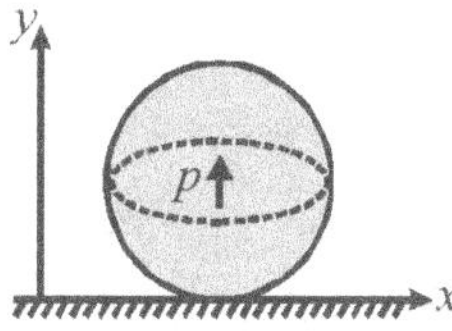


(a) $\sqrt{\dfrac{5pE}{m}}$  (b) $\sqrt{\dfrac{10pE}{7m}}$

(c) $\sqrt{\dfrac{5pE}{2m}}$  (d) zero

| Answer Key | 25 | (d) | 26 | (c) | 27 | (c) |
|---|---|---|---|---|---|---|
| Sol. from page 110 | 28 | (c) | 29 | (a) | 30 | (b) |

**31.** Two small balls of mass $M$ each carrying charges $+Q$ and $-Q$, connected by a massless rigid non-conducting rod of length $L$ lie along $x$-axis as shown. A uniform electric field $\vec{E} = 3\hat{k} + 3\hat{j}$ has been switched on. The angular velocity vector of the dipole when dipole moment aligns with the electric field is

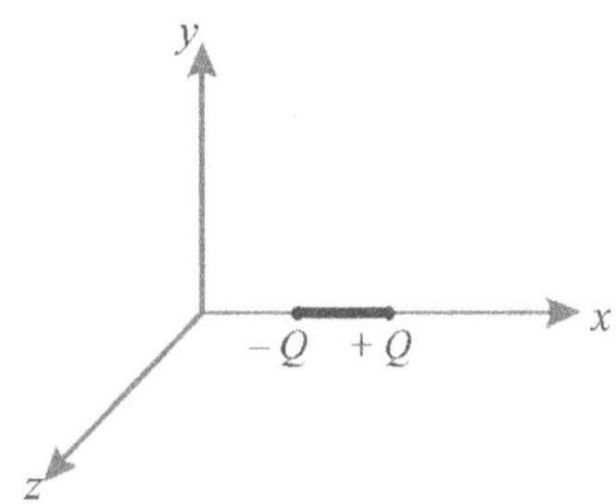


(a) $\sqrt{\frac{3\sqrt{2}\pi Q}{2ML}}\left(-\hat{j}+\hat{k}\right)$  (b) $\sqrt{\frac{6\sqrt{2}Q}{ML}}\left(-\hat{j}+\hat{k}\right)$

(c) $\sqrt{\frac{3\sqrt{2}\pi Q}{ML}}\left(-\hat{j}-\hat{k}\right)$  (d) $\sqrt{\frac{3\sqrt{2}\pi Q}{ML}}\left(-\hat{j}+\hat{k}\right)$

**32.** The grid (each square of 1m × 1m), represents a region in space containing a uniform electric field. If potentials at point O, A, B, C, D, E, F, G, H are respectively 0, –1, –2, 1, 2, 0, –1, 1 and 0 volts. Find the electric field intensity.

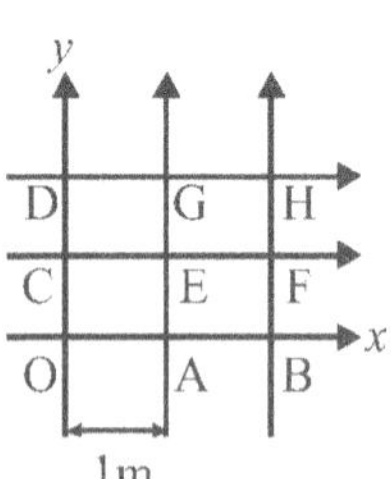


(a) $(\hat{i}+\hat{j})V/m$  (b) $(\hat{i}-\hat{j})V/m$

(c) $(-\hat{i}+\hat{j})V/m$  (d) $(-\hat{i}-\hat{j})V/m$

**33.** Three concentric metallic spherical shells of radii $R$, $2R$, $3R$, are given charges $Q_1$, $Q_2$, $Q_3$, respectively. It is found that the surface charge densities on the outer surfaces of the shells are equal. Then, the ratio of the chrges given to the shells, $Q_1 : Q_2, Q_3$, is

(a) 1 : 2 : 3  (b) 1 : 3 : 5
(c) 1 : 4 : 9  (d) 1 : 8 : 18

**34.** A solid sphere of radius $R_1$ and volume charge density $\rho = \frac{\rho_0}{r}$ is enclosed by a hollow sphere of radius $R_2$ with negative surface charge density $\sigma$, such that the total charge in the system is zero. $\rho_0$ is a positive constant and $r$ is the distance from the centre of the sphere. The ratio $R_2 / R_1$ is

(a) $\frac{\sigma}{\rho_0}$  (b) $\sqrt{\frac{2\sigma}{\rho_0}}$

(c) $\sqrt{\frac{\rho_0}{2\sigma}}$  (d) $\frac{\rho_0}{\sigma}$

**35.** In figure $+Q$ charge is located at one of the edge of the cube. Then electric flux through cube due to $+Q$ charge is

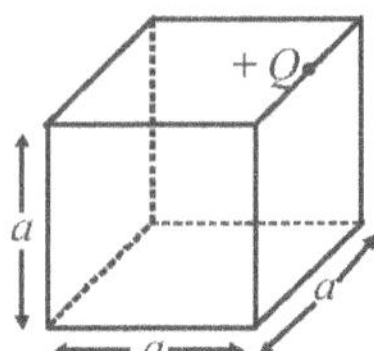


(a) $\frac{+Q}{\epsilon_0}$  (b) $\frac{+Q}{2\epsilon_0}$

(c) $\frac{+Q}{4\epsilon_0}$  (d) $\frac{+Q}{8\epsilon_0}$

**36.** If an insulated non-conducting sphere of radius $R$ has charge density $\rho$. The electric field at a distance $r$ from the centre of sphere $(r < R)$ will be

(a) $\frac{\rho R}{3\epsilon_0}$  (b) $\frac{\rho r}{\epsilon_0}$

(c) $\frac{\rho r}{3\epsilon_0}$  (d) $\frac{3\rho R}{\epsilon_0}$

**37.** Two insulating plates are both uniformly charged in such a way that the potential difference between them is $V_2 - V_1 = 20V$. (i.e. plate 2 is at a higher potential). The plates are separated by $d = 0.1$ m and can be treated as infinitely large. An electron is released from rest on the inner surface of plate 1. What is its speed when it hits plate 2 $(e = 1.6 \times 10^{-19}$ C, $m_e = 9.11 \times 10^{-31}$ kg)?

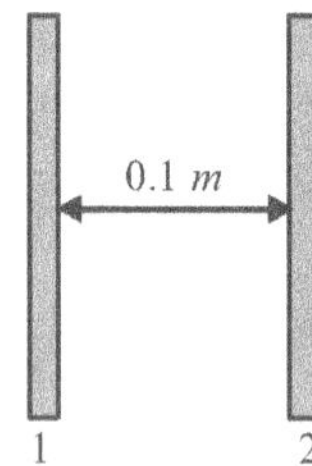


(a) $7.02 \times 10^{12}$ m/s  (b) $1.87 \times 10^{6}$ m/s
(c) $32 \times 10^{-19}$ m/s  (d) $2.65 \times 10^{6}$ m/s

**38.** The potential at a point $x$ (measured in $\mu m$) due to some charges situated on the $x$-axis is given by $V(x) = 20 / (x^2 - 4)$ volts. The electric field $E$ at $x = 4\ \mu m$ is given by

(a) 5/3 volt / $\mu m$ and in the – ve $x$ direction
(b) 5/3 volt / $\mu m$ and in the + ve direction
(c) 10/9 volt / $\mu m$ and in the – ve direction
(d) 10/9 volt / $\mu m$ and in the + ve direction

| Answer Key | 31 | (b) | 32 | (b) | 33 | (b) | 34 | (c) |
|---|---|---|---|---|---|---|---|---|
| Sol. from page 110 | 35 | (c) | 36 | (c) | 37 | (d) | 38 | (d) |

39. The adjacent diagram shows a charge $+Q$ held on an insulating support $S$ and enclosed by a hollow spherical conductor represents the centre of the spherical conductor and $P$ is a point such that $OP = x$ and $SP = r$. The electric field at point $P$ will be

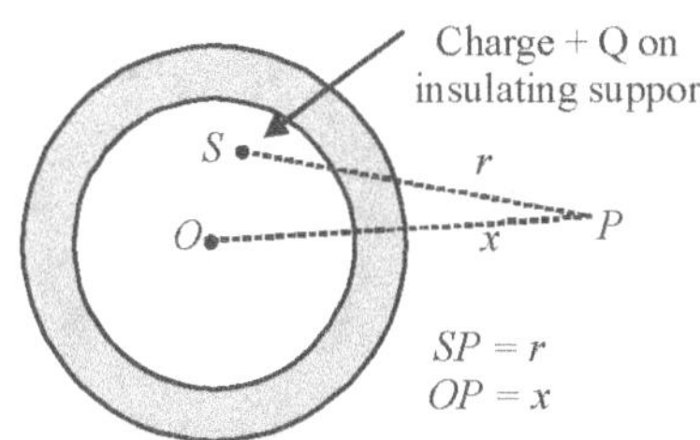


(a) $\frac{Q}{4\pi\varepsilon_0 x^2}$ (b) $\frac{Q}{4\pi\varepsilon_0 r^2}$

(c) 0 (d) none of the above

40. Two equal charges $q$ of opposite sign separated by a distance $2a$ constitute an electric dipole of dipole moment $p$. If $P$ is a point at a distance $r$ from the centre of the dipole and the line joining centre of the dipole to this point makes an angle $\theta$ with the axis of the dipole, then the potential at $P$ is given by $(r >> 2a)$ (where $p = 2qa$) (where $p = 2\ qa$)

(a) $V = \frac{p\cos\theta}{4\pi\varepsilon_0 r^2}$ (b) $V = \frac{p\cos\theta}{4\pi\varepsilon_0 r}$

(c) $V = \frac{p\sin\theta}{4\pi\varepsilon_0 r}$ (d) $V = \frac{p\cos\theta}{2\pi\varepsilon_0 r^2}$

41. A spherical portion has been removed from a solid sphere having a charge distributed uniformly in its volume in the figure. The electric field inside the emptied space is

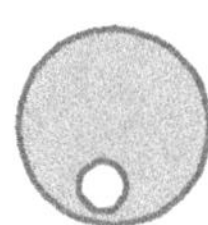

(a) zero everywhere (b) non-zero and uniform
(c) non-uniform (d) zero only at its centre

42. A solid sphere of radius $R$ has a charge $Q$ distributed in its volume with a charge density $\rho = kr^a$, where $k$ and $a$ are constants and $r$ is the distance from its centre. If the electric field at $r = \frac{R}{2}$ is $\frac{1}{8}$ times that at $r = R$, the value of $a$ is.

(a) 3 (b) 5
(c) 2 (d) both (a) and (b)

43. A block of mass $m$ and charge $q$ is connected to a point $O$ with help of an inextensible string. The system is on a horizontal table. An electric field is switched on in direction perpendicular to string. What will be tension in string when it become parallel to electric field?

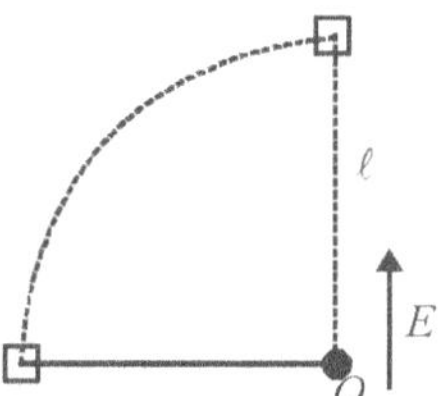


(a) $\frac{qE}{2}$ (b) $3qE$

(c) $\frac{qE}{\ell}$ (d) $\frac{3qE}{5}$

44. Two short dipoles of dipole moment $p$ are placed at two corners of a squares as shown in the figure. What is the ratio of magnitudes of electric field at two points. $O$ & $A$?

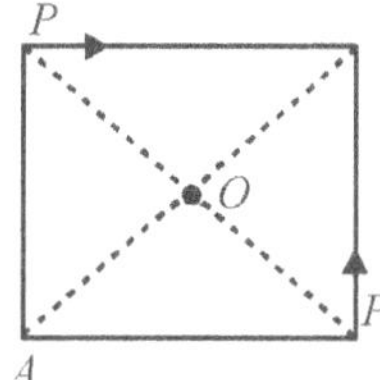


(a) 2 (b) $2\sqrt{2}$
(c) 1 (d) $\sqrt{2}$

45. A point shell of radius $a$ and centre (0, 0, 0). What is flux linked to hemispherical surface? $x^2 + y^2 + z^2 = 4a^2$ & $z > 0$ ?

(a) $\frac{q}{2\varepsilon_0}$ (b) $\frac{q}{\varepsilon_0}$

(c) less than $\frac{q}{2\varepsilon_0}$ (d) zero

46. Two pith balls having charge $3q$ and $2q$ are placed at distance of $a$ from each other. For what value of charge transferred from 1st ball to 2nd ball, force between balls becomes maximum?

(a) $\frac{q}{2}$ (b) $\frac{5q}{2}$

(c) $7q$ (d) $q$

47. Two concentric spherical shells of radii $a$ & $1.2\ a$ have charges $+Q$ and $-2\ Q$ respectively. At what distance from centres potential will be same as that of centre?

(a) $2\ a$ (b) $1.5\ a$
(c) $2.5\ a$ (d) $3\ a$

| Answer Key | 39 | (a) | 40 | (a) | 41 | (b) | 42 | (c) | 43 | (b) |
|---|---|---|---|---|---|---|---|---|---|---|
| Sol. from page 110 | 44 | (b) | 45 | (a) | 46 | (a) | 47 | (b) | | |

**48.** A conduction rod of length $l$ rotates about its one end with angular velocity $\omega$. Potential difference between $A$ and $B$ is ($M$ & $e$ = mass and charge of electron)

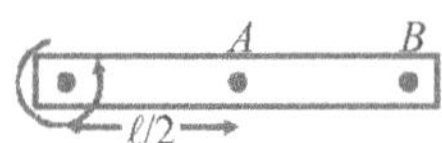


(a) $\frac{M\omega^2 l^2}{e}$ (b) $\frac{3M\omega^2 l^2}{4e}$

(c) $\frac{3}{8}\frac{M\omega^2 l^2}{e}$ (d) zero

**49.** There is *a* dielectric rod between charges $q_1$ and $q_2$. If this rod is removed, then net force on $q_1$.

$q_1$ $q_2$

(a) increases
(b) decreases
(c) remains same
(d) both (1) & (2) are possible, depending on the nature of charges

**50.** Surface charge densities of two concentric spheres of radii, $R_1$ and $R_2$ are $+\sigma_1$ and $-\sigma_2$. Suppose $E_1$ is field at distance $r$ (such that $R_1 < r < R_2$). Now if two spheres are connected by a thin wire, field at same point is $E_2$, where $\left|\frac{E_2}{E_1}\right|$ is

(a) $\frac{R_1}{R_1 + R_2}$ (b) $\frac{R_2}{R_1 + R_2}$

(c) zero (d) infinite

**51.** If electric field between plates of a parallel plate capacitor is 2 N/C and charge on two plates are 10 C and 3 C then force on one of the plates is

(a) 20 $N$ (b) 13 $N$

(c) $\frac{60}{7}N$ (d) $\frac{7}{2}N$

**52.** A solid sphere having uniform charge density $\rho$ and radius $R$ is show in figure. A spherical cavity of radius $\frac{R}{2}$ is hollowed out. What is potential of $O$?(Assuming potential of infinity to be zero)

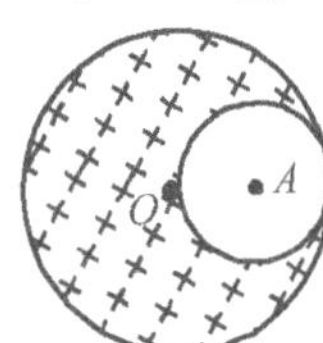


(a) $\frac{11 R^2 \rho}{24 \varepsilon_0}$ (b) $\frac{5}{12}\frac{R^2 \rho}{\varepsilon_0}$

(c) $\frac{7 \rho R^2}{12 \varepsilon_0}$ (d) $\frac{3}{2}\frac{R^2 \rho}{\varepsilon_0}$

**53.** Three charges each of value $Q$ are placed at points $A$ ($-K$, 0), $O$ (0, 0) and b (0, $K$). If force on point charge at $A$ is $a\hat{i} + b\hat{j}$ then force on point charge at $B$ is

(a) $-a\hat{i} - b\hat{j}$ (b) $b\hat{j} + a\hat{j}$

(c) $-b\hat{i} - a\hat{j}$ (d) $-a\hat{j} + b\hat{i}$

**54.** A charged particle enters at point $A$ and comes out from $B$. Its velocity makes angle $\alpha$ & $\beta$ with electric field at these two points. Ratio of kinetic energy of changed particle at these two points will be

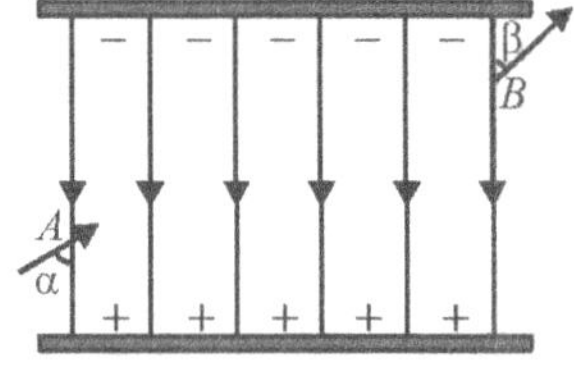


(a) $\frac{\sin^2 \alpha}{\sin^2 \beta}$ (b) $\frac{\sin^2 \beta}{\sin^2 \alpha}$

(c) $\frac{\cos^2 \alpha}{\cos^2 \beta}$ (d) $\frac{\cos^2 \beta}{\cos^2 \alpha}$

**55.** If a point charge is placed at vertex of cube then, flux linked to surface shaded in figure

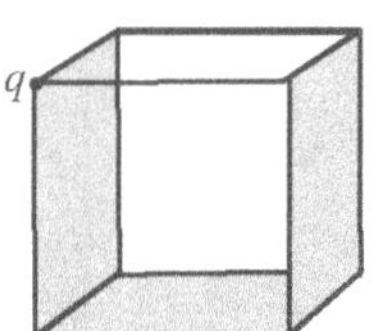

(a) $\frac{q}{8 \varepsilon_0}$ (b) $\frac{q}{3 \varepsilon_0}$

(c) $\frac{q}{12 \varepsilon_0}$ (d) Zero

**56.** Two concentric shells are having radii $R$ and $2R$, charges $q_1$ and $q_2$ and potentials 3 V and V respectively. Now outer shell is earthed,

(a) Potential difference between shell increases
(b) Potential difference between shell decreases
(c) Potential of inner sphere will become 2 V
(d) Potential of common centre will become 2.5 V

| Answer Key | 48 | (c) | 49 | (d) | 50 | (c) | 51 | (c) | 52 | (b) |
|---|---|---|---|---|---|---|---|---|---|---|
| Sol. from page 110 | 53 | (c) | 54 | (b) | 55 | (c) | 56 | (c) | | |

**57.** A thin non-conducting ring of radius $a$ has a linear charge density $\lambda = \lambda_0 \sin\phi$. A uniform electric field $E_0\hat{i} + E_0\hat{i}$ is present there. Net force acting on ring is

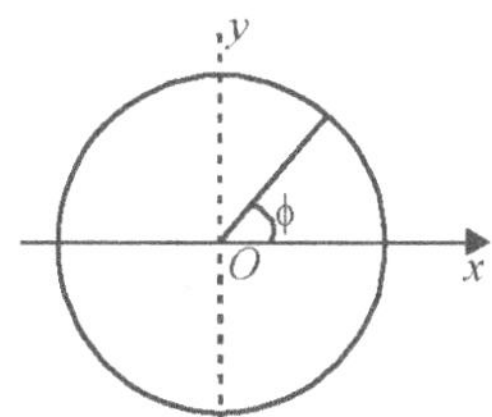


(a) $E_0\sqrt{2}\,\pi a^2\lambda_0$ (b) $E_0\,\pi a^2\lambda_0$

(c) $2E_0\,\pi a^2\lambda_0$ (d) zero

**58.** A uniformly charged thin spherical shell of radius $R$ carries uniform surface charge density of $\sigma$ per unit area. It is made of two hemispherical shells, held together by pressing them with force $F$ (see figure). $F$ is proportional to

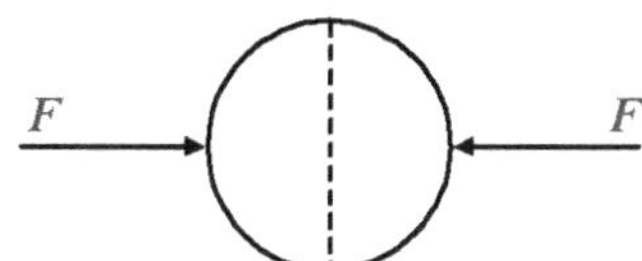


(a) $\frac{1}{\varepsilon_0}\sigma^2 R^2$ (b) $\frac{1}{\varepsilon_0}\sigma^2 R$

(c) $\frac{1}{\varepsilon_0}\frac{\sigma^2}{R}$ (d) $\frac{1}{\varepsilon_0}\frac{\sigma^2}{R^2}$

**59.** A tiny spherical oil drop carrying a net charge $q$ is balanced in still air will a vertical uniform electric field of strength $\frac{81\pi}{7}\times 10^5\ Vm^{-1}$. When the field is switched off, the drop is observed to fall with terminal velocity $2\times 10^{-3} ms^{-1}$. Given $g = 9.8\ m\,s^{-2}$, viscosity of the air $= 1.8\times 10^{-5}\ Ns\,m^{-2}$ and the density of oil = 900 kg $m^{-3}$, the magnitude of $q$ is

(a) $1.6\times 10^{-19}C$ (b) $3.2\times 10^{-19}C$

(c) $4.8\times 10^{-19}C$ (d) $8.0\times 10^{-19}C$

**60.** Let $P(r) = \frac{Q}{\pi R^4}r$ be the charge density distribution for a solid sphere of radius $R$ and total charge $Q$. For a point '$p$' inside the sphere at distance $r_1$ from the centre of the sphere, the magnitude of electric field is :

(a) $\frac{Q}{4\pi\,\epsilon_0\,r_1^2}$ (b) $\frac{Qr_1^2}{4\pi\,\epsilon_0\,R^4}$

(c) $\frac{Qr_1^2}{3\pi\,\epsilon_0\,R^4}$ (d) 0

**61.** Let there be a spherically symmetric charge distribution with charge density varying as $\rho(r) = \rho_0\left(\frac{5}{4} - \frac{r}{R}\right)$ upto $r = R$, and $\rho(r) = 0$ for $r > R$, where $r$ is the distance from the origin. The electric field at a distance $r (r < R)$ from the origin is given by

(a) $\frac{\rho_0 r}{4\varepsilon_0}\left(\frac{5}{3} - \frac{r}{R}\right)$ (b) $\frac{4\pi\rho_0 r}{3\varepsilon_0}\left(\frac{5}{3} - \frac{r}{R}\right)$

(c) $\frac{4\rho_0 r}{4\varepsilon_0}\left(\frac{5}{4} - \frac{r}{R}\right)$ (d) $\frac{\rho_0 r}{3\varepsilon_0}\left(\frac{5}{4} - \frac{r}{R}\right)$

| Answer Key | 57 | (b) | 58 | (a) | 59 | (d) |
|---|---|---|---|---|---|---|
| Sol. from page 110 | 60 | (b) | 61 | (c) | | |

Electricity

# MCQ Type 2

Exercise 1.2

**Multiple correct options**

1. When the separation between two charges is increased, the electric potential energy of the charges
(a) may increase (b) may decrease
(c) increases (d) decreases

2. Which of the following quantities do not depend on the choice of zero potential or zero potential energy ?
(a) potential at a point
(b) potential difference between two points
(c) potential energy of two-charge system
(d) change in potential energy of a two-charge system

3. An electric dipole is placed in an electric field generated by a point charge.
(a) The net force on the dipole never be zero.
(b) The net force on the dipole may be zero.
(c) The torque on the dipole due to the field must be zero.
(d) The torque on the dipole due to the field may be zero.

4. The electric field and the electric potential at a point are $E$ and $V$ respectively.
(a) If $E = 0$, $V$ may be zero
(b) If $V = 0$, $E$ may be zero
(c) If $E \neq 0, V$ may be zero
(d) If $V \neq 0$, E may be zero.

5. The electric potential decreases uniformly from 100 $V$ to 50 $V$ as one moves on the $y$-axis from $y = -1$m to $y = +1$m. The electric field at the origin.
(a) must be equal to 25 V/m
(b) may be equal to 25 V/m
(c) may be less than 25 V/m
(d) may be greater than 25 V/m

6. If the flux of the electric field is zero.
(a) The electric field must be zero everywhere on the surface.
(b) The electric field may be zero everywhere on the surface.
(c) The charge inside the surface must be zero.
(d) The charge in the vicinity of the surface must be zero.

7. An electric dipole is placed at the centre of a sphere.
(a) The flux of the electric field through the sphere is zero
(b) The electric field is zero at every point on the sphere.
(c) The electric field is not zero anywhere on the sphere
(d) The electric field is zero on a circle on the sphere.

8. For spherical symmetrical charge, variation of electric potential with distance from centre is given in diagram. Given that :

$V = \dfrac{q}{4\pi \epsilon_0 R}$ for $r \leq R_0$

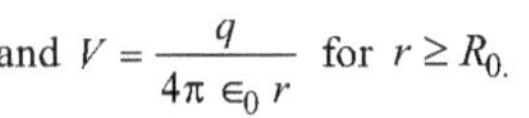

and $V = \dfrac{q}{4\pi \epsilon_0 r}$ for $r \geq R_0$.

Then which option(s) are correct ?
(a) Total charge within $2R_0$ is $q$.
(b) Total electrostatic energy for $r \leq R_0$ is zero.
(c) At $r = R_0$ electric field is discontinuous.
(d) There will be no charge anywhere except $r = R_0$

9. Consider the points lying on a straight line joining two fixed opposite charges. Between the charges there is
(a) no point where electric field is zero
(b) only one point where electric field is zero
(c) no point where potential is zero
(d) only one point where potential is zero

10. An ellipsoidal cavity is carved within a perfect conductor. A positive charge $q$ is placed at the centre of the cavity. The points $A$ and $B$ are on the cavity surface as shown in the figure. Then

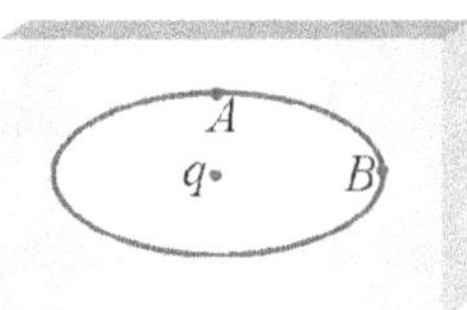


(a) electric field near $A$ in the cavity = Electric field near $B$ in the cavity
(b) charge density at $A$= Charge density at $B$
(c) potential at $A$ = Potential at $B$
(d) total electric field flux through the surface of the cavity is $q/\varepsilon_0$

11. A positively charged thin metal ring of radius $R$ is fixed in the $xy$-plane with its centre at the $O$. A negatively charged particle $P$ is released from rest at the point $(0, 0, z_0)$, where $z_0 > 0$. Then the motion of $P$ is
(a) periodic for all values of $z_0$ satisfying $0 < z_0 < \infty$
(b) simple harmonic for all values of satisfying $0 < z_0 < R$
(c) approximately simple harmonic provided $z_0 << R$
(d) such that $P$ crosses $O$ and continues to move along the negative $z$-axis towards $z = -\infty$

12. A non-conducting solid sphere of radius $R$ is uniformly charged. The magnitude of the electric field due to the sphere at a distance $r$ from its centre
(a) increases as $r$ increases for $r < R$
(b) decreases as $r$ increases for $0 < r < \infty$
(c) decrease as r increases for $R < r < \infty$
(d) is discontinuous at $r = R$

| Answer Key | 1 | (a, b) | 2 | (b, d) | 3 | (a, d) | 4 | (a,b,c,d) | 5 | (b, d) | 6 | (b, c) |
|---|---|---|---|---|---|---|---|---|---|---|---|---|
| Sol. from page 117 | 7 | (a, c) | 8 | (b,d,c,d) | 9 | (a, d) | 10 | (c, d) | 11 | (a, c) | 12 | (a, c) |

**13.** Two point charges $+q$ and $-q$ are held fixed at $(-d, 0)$ and $(d, 0)$ respectively of a $xy$-plane. Then :
(a) The electric field $E$ at all points on the $x$-axis has the same direction.
(b) Electric field at all points on $y$-axis is along $x$-axis.
(c) Work has to be done in bringing a test charge from $\infty$ to the origin
(d) The dipole moment is $2qd$ along $x$-axis.

**14.** Two point charges $Q$ and $-Q/4$ are separated by a distance $x$ then :

Q — $x$ — $-Q/4$

(a) the potential is zero at a point on the axis which is $x/3$ on the right of the charge $-Q/4$
(b) the potential is zero at a point on the axis which is $x/5$ on the left of the charge $-Q/4$
(c) electric field is zero at a point on the axis at a distance $x$ on the right of the charge $-Q/4$
(d) there exist two points on the axis where electric field is zero.

**15.** A non conducting ring of radius R is charged as shown in figure :

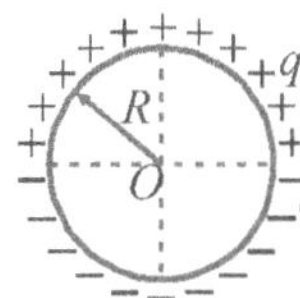


(a) The electric field is zero at the centre of the ring
(b) the electric potential is zero at centre of the ring
(c) the electric potential at the centre is, $V = \dfrac{2q}{4\pi \epsilon_0 R}$
(d) the electric field at the centre is , $E = \dfrac{q}{\pi^2 \epsilon_0 R^2}$

**16.** Figure shows a cross-section of a spherical metal shell of inner radius $R$ and out radius $2R$. A point charge $q$ is located at a distance $R/2$ from the centre of the shell. If the shell is electrically neutral, then :

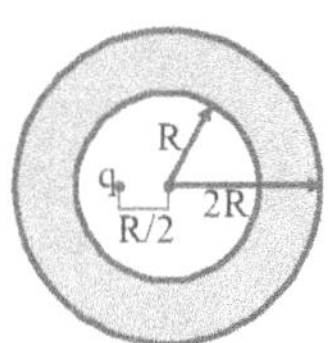


(a) the electrical field at some point inside shell is zero.
(b) the electrical field at point inside shell is non-zero
(c) the electrical field at the outer surface of the shell is $E = \dfrac{1}{4\pi\varepsilon_0}\dfrac{q}{(3R/2)^2}$
(d) the electrical field at the outer surface is $E = \dfrac{1}{4\pi\varepsilon_0}\dfrac{q}{(2R)^2}$

**17.** In the given diagram, a line of force of a particular force field is shown. Out of the following options, it can never represent

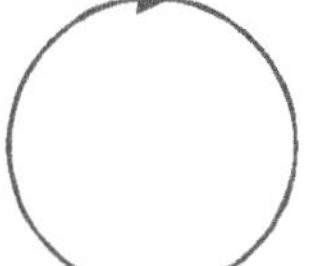

(a) an electrostatic field
(b) a magnetostatic field
(c) a gravitational field of a mass of rest
(d) an induced electric field

**18.** $S_1$ and $S_2$ are two equipotential surfaces on which the potentials are not equal
(a) $S_1$ and $S_2$ cannot intersect
(b) $S_1$ and $S_2$ cannot both be plane surfaces.
(c) in the region between $S_1$ and $S_2$, the field is maximum where they are closest to each other
(d) a line of force from $S_1$ to $S_2$ must be perpendicular to both

**19.** Charges $Q_1$ and $Q_2$ lie inside and outside respectively of a closed surface $S$. Let $E$ be the field at any point on $S$ and $\phi$ be the flux of $E$ over $S$.
(a) If $Q_1$ changes, both $E$ and $\phi$ will changes
(b) If $Q_2$ changes, $E$ will change but $\phi$ will not change
(c) If $Q_1 = 0$ and $Q_2 \neq 0$ then $E \neq 0$ but $\phi = 0$
(d) If $Q_1 \neq 0$ and $Q_2 = 0$ then $E = 0$ but $\phi = 0$

**20.** A ring with a uniform charge $Q$ and radius $R$, is placed in the $yz$ plane with its centre at the origin.
(a) The field at the origin ia zero
(b) The potential at the origin is $\dfrac{1}{4\pi\varepsilon_0}\dfrac{Q}{R}$
(c) The field at the point $(x, 0, 0)$ is $\dfrac{1}{4\pi\varepsilon_0}\dfrac{Q}{x^2}$
(d) The field at the point $(x, 0, 0)$ is $\dfrac{1}{4\pi\varepsilon_0}\dfrac{Q}{R^2 + x^2}$

**21.** Four identical charges are placed at the point $(1, 0, 0)$, $(0, 1, 0)$, $(-1, 0, 0)$ and $(0, -1, 0)$.
(a) The potential at the origin is zero
(b) The field at the origin is zero
(c) The potential at all points on the $z$- axis, other than the origin, is zero
(d) The field at all points on the $z$- *axis*, other than the origin, acts along the $z$-axis

**22.** A few electric field lines for a system of two charges $Q_1$ and $Q_2$ fixed at two different points on the x-axis are shown in the figure. These lines suggest that

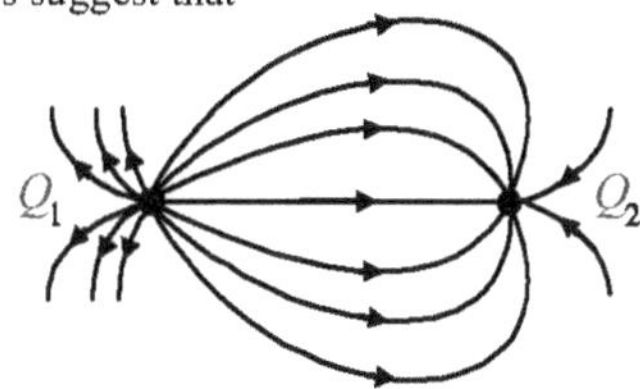


(a) $|Q_1| > |Q_2|$
(b) $|Q_1| < |Q_2|$
(c) at a finite distance to the left of $Q_1$ the electric field is zero
(d) at a finite distance to the right of $Q_2$ the electric field is zero

**23.** A spherical metal shell $A$ of radius $R_A$ and a solid metal sphere $B$ of radius $R_B (< R_A)$ are kept far apart and each is given charge '$+Q$'. Now they are connected by a thin metal wire. Then
(a) $E_A^{inside} = 0$
(b) $Q_A > Q_B$
(c) $\dfrac{\sigma_A}{\sigma_B} = \dfrac{R_B}{R_A}$
(d) $E_A^{on\,surface} < E_B^{on\,surface}$

| Answer Key | 13 | (b, d) | 14 | (a, c) | 15 | (b, d) | 16 | (b, d) | 17 | (a, c) | 18 | (a,c,d) |
|---|---|---|---|---|---|---|---|---|---|---|---|---|
| Sol. from page 117 | 19 | (a,b,c) | 20 | (a, b) | 21 | (b, d) | 22 | (a, d ) | 23 | (a,b,c,d) | | |

Electricity

# Statement Questions

*Exercise 1.3*

Read the two statements carefully to mark the correct option out of the options given below. Select the right choice.

(a) If both the statements are true and the ***Statement* - 2** is the correct explanation of ***Statement* - 1**.

(b) If both the statements are true but ***Statement* - 2** is not the correct explanation of the ***Statement* - 1**.

(c) If ***Statement* - 1** true but ***Statement* - 2** is false.

(d) If ***Statement* - 1** is false but ***Statement* - 2** is true.

**1.** ***Statement* - 1**

Some charge is put at the centre of a conducting sphere. It will move to the surface of the sphere.

***Statement* - 2**

Conducting sphere has no free electrons at the centre.

**2.** ***Statement* - 1**

Charge given to a conductor comes to its outer surface.

***Statement* - 2**

All the electrons of the conductor will move on to the surface.

**3.** ***Statement* - 1**

Gravitational force can be added vectorially to the electric force.

***Statement* - 2**

Gravitational field can be added vectorially to the electric field.

**4.** ***Statement* - 1**

A spherical shell made of plastic, contains a charge q distributed uniformly over its surface gives zero electric field inside the shell.

***Statement* - 2**

The electric field at the centre of the shell is zero.

**5.** ***Statement* - 1**

A charge q is put inside a cavity in a conductor. The electric field outside the surface of the conductor is zero.

***Statement* - 2**

The force on a charge $Q$ placed outside the sphere will be non zero.

**6.** ***Statement* - 1**

Electric lines of field cross each other.

***Statement* - 2**

Electric field at a point superimpose to give one resultant electric field.

**7.** ***Statement* - 1**

If a proton and an electron are placed in the same uniform field. They experience same force but different acceleration.

***Statement* - 2**

By Newton's second law $\vec{F} = m\vec{a}$.

**8.** ***Statement* - 1**

If a point charge q is placed in front of an infinite grounded conducting plane surface, the point charge will experience a force.

***Statement* - 2**

The force is due to the induced charge on the conducting surface which is at zero potential.

**9.** ***Statement* - 1**

A point charge is brought in an electric field, the field at a nearby point will increase or decrease, depending on the nature of charge.

***Statement* - 2**

The electric field is independent of the nature of charge.

**10.** ***Statement* - 1**

The lightening conductor at the top of high building has sharp pointed ends. It is used to prevent the cracks in the building.

***Statement* - 2**

The charge density at sharp ends becomes very much higher than the building.

**11.** ***Statement* - 1**

Electrons move away from a low potential to high potential region.

***Statement* - 2**

Electrons have negative charge.

**12.** ***Statement* - 1**

The tyres of aircraft are slightly conducting.

***Statement* - 2**

If a conductor is connected to ground, the extra charge induced on conductor will flow to ground.

**13.** ***Statement* - 1**

Four charges $q, q, -q, -q$ are placed at the corners of a square. The electric field at the centre of the square is zero.

***Statement* - 2**

The electric potential at the centre of the square is zero.

| Answer Key | 1 | (a) | 2 | (c) | 3 | (c) | 4 | (b) | 5 | (d) | 6 | (d) | 7 | (a) |
|---|---|---|---|---|---|---|---|---|---|---|---|---|---|---|
| Sol. from page 118 | 8 | (a) | 9 | (c) | 10 | (a) | 11 | (a) | 12 | (b) | 13 | (d) | | |

14. ***Statement* - 1**

When two bodies with charges $Q$ and $-Q$ are brought in contact, the charge on each body becomes zero, and hence charge is lost.

***Statement* - 2**

Some energy disappears in the form of heat and light.

15. ***Statement* - 1**

Dielectric breakdown occurs due to the intense electric field.

***Statement* - 2**

Cosmic rays make the ionosphere.

16. ***Statement* - 1**

A metallic shield in form of a hollow shell may be built to block an electric field.

***Statement* - 2**

In a hollow spherical shield, the electric field inside it is zero at every point.

17. ***Statement* - 1**

For practical purposes, the earth is used as a reference at zero potential in electrical circuits.

***Statement* - 2**

The electrical potential of a sphere of radius $R$, with charge $Q$ uniformly distributed on the surface is given by $\frac{Q}{4\pi \epsilon_0 R}$.

18. ***Statement* - 1**

Two metal spheres of radii $R$ and $2R$ with charges $Q$ and $2Q$ are put in contact. The charge flows from sphere of radius $2R$ towards sphere of radius R.

***Statement* - 2**

There is no loss of electrical energy of the system.

19. ***Statement* - 1**

A charged sphere with charge $Q$ is placed inside a conducting shell and they are connected by a metal wire. The entire charge of the sphere will move to the shell.

***Statement* - 2**

The electric potential of the shell becomes equal to the sphere.

20. ***Statement* - 1**

The electric flux of the electric field $\oint \vec{E} \cdot d\vec{A}$ is zero. The electric field is zero everywhere on the surface.

***Statement* - 2**

The charge inside the surface is zero.

21. ***Statement* - 1**

The point charge $q_1$ and $q_2$ produce fields $E_1$ and $E_2$ at any point and potential $V_1$ and $V_2$ at the same point. The electric field due to both the charges at that point must be $E_1 + E_2$.

***Statement* - 2**

The electric potential at that point due to both the charges must be $V_1 + V_2$.

22. ***Statement* - 1**

Gauss's law cannot be used for calculating the electric field due to three equal charges located at the corners of an equilateral triangle.

***Statement* - 2**

Gauss's law is not valid for this case.

23. ***Statement* - 1**

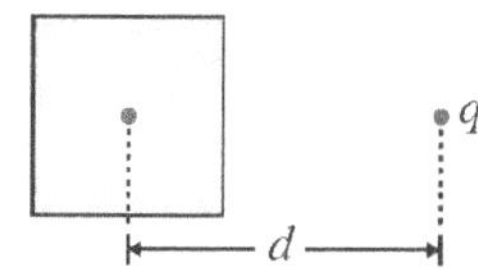


Figure shows a point charge $q$ is placed in front of a metal cube at a distance $d$ from its centre. The electric field due to this charge at the centre of cube is $\frac{1}{4\pi \epsilon_0} \frac{q}{d^2}$.

***Statement* - 2**

The electric field at the centre of the cube is zero.

24. ***Statement-1* :** For a charged particle moving from point $P$ to point $Q$, the net work done by an electrostatic field on the particle is independent of the path connecting point $P$ to point $Q$.

***Statement-2* :** The net work done by a conservative force on an object moving along a closed loop is zero.

| Answer Key | 14 | (d) | 15 | (b) | 16 | (a) | 17 | (a) | 18 | (d) | 19 | (a) |
|---|---|---|---|---|---|---|---|---|---|---|---|---|
| Sol. from page 118 | 20 | (d) | 21 | (d) | 22 | (c) | 23 | (a) | 24 | (a) | | |

Electricity

# Passage & Matrix

Exercise 1.4

## PASSAGES

**Passage for Q. 1 to Q.3**
A long cylinder of radius $a$ is charged with a volume charge density

$\rho \quad = \rho_0 r^3$ for $r \le a$

$\quad = 0 \quad$ for $r > a$

where $\rho_0$ is constant and $r$ is the distance measured from the axis of the cylinder.

1. The charge contained in $\ell$ length of the cylinder for $r > a$ is :

(a) $\dfrac{2\pi\,\rho_0 a^3 \ell}{3}$ (b) $\dfrac{2\pi\,\rho_0 a^5 \ell}{5}$

(c) $\dfrac{4\pi\,\rho_0 a^3 \ell}{3}$ (d) zero

2. The electric field at $r < a$ :

(a) $\dfrac{\rho_0 r^4}{5\,\epsilon_0}$ (b) $\dfrac{\rho_0 r^3}{3\,\epsilon_0}$

(c) $\dfrac{\rho_0 r^5}{5\,\epsilon_0}$ (d) zero

3. The electric field at $r > a$

(a) $\dfrac{\rho_0 a^3}{3\,\epsilon_0\, r}$ (b) $\dfrac{\rho_0 a^5}{3\,\epsilon_0\, r}$

(c) $\dfrac{\rho_0 a^5}{5\,\epsilon_0\, r}$ (d) zero

**Passage for Q. 4 to Q. 6**
The nuclear charge (Ze) is non-uniformly distributed within a nucleus of radius $R$. The charge density $\rho(r)$ (charge per unit volume) is dependent only on the radial distance r from the centre of the nucleus as shown in figure. The electric field is only along the radial direction.

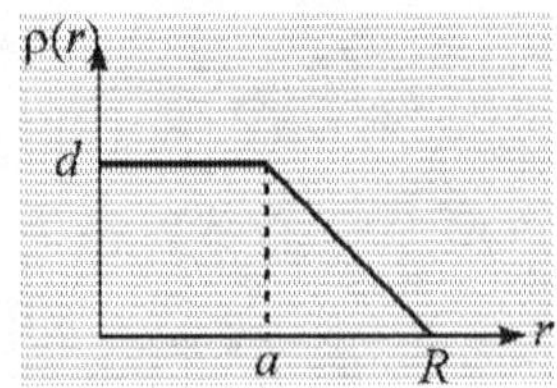


4. The electric field at $r = R$ is

(a) independent of $a$

(b) directly proportional to $a$

(c) directly proportional to $a^2$

(d) inversely proportional to $a$.

5. For $a = 0$, the value $d$ (maximum value of $\rho$ as shown in the figure) is

(a) $\dfrac{3Ze}{4\pi R^3}$ (b) $\dfrac{3Ze}{\pi R^3}$

(c) $\dfrac{4Ze}{3\pi R^3}$ (d) $\dfrac{Ze}{3\pi R^3}$

6. The electric field within the nucleus is generally observed to be linearly dependent on $r$. This implies

(a) $a = 0$ (b) $a = \dfrac{R}{2}$

(c) $a = R$ (d) $a = \dfrac{2R}{3}$

**Passage for Q. 7 to Q. 9**
Two small metallic balls of radii $R_1$ and $R_2$ are in vacuum at a distance $\ell$, which is considerably exceeding their dimensions and have a certain total charge $Q$. It is known to you that electrical energy of this system is $U = U_1 + U_2 + U_{12}$, where $U_1$ and $U_2$ are their self energies and $U_{12}$ is their external energy. $q_1$ and $q_2$ are the charges on the balls. Then :

7. The electrical energy of the system is given by :

(a) $U = \dfrac{1}{4\pi\,\epsilon_0}\left(\dfrac{q_1^2}{2R_1} + \dfrac{q_1 q_2}{R_1 + R_2}\right)$

(b) $U = \dfrac{1}{4\pi\,\epsilon_0}\left(\dfrac{q_1^2}{2R_1} + \dfrac{q_2^2}{2R_2}\right)$

(c) $U = \dfrac{1}{4\pi\,\epsilon_0}\left(\dfrac{q_1^2}{2R_1} + \dfrac{q_2^2}{2R_2} + \dfrac{q_1 q_2}{\ell}\right)$

(d) zero

| Answer Key | 1 | (b) | 2 | (a) | 3 | (c) | 4 | (a) |
|---|---|---|---|---|---|---|---|---|
| Sol. from page 119 | 5 | (b) | 6 | (c) | 7 | (c) | | |

8. For the electrical energy $U$ to be minimum, the charges $q_1$ and $q_2$ on them are :

(a) $q_1 = \frac{Q}{2}, q_2 = \frac{Q}{2}$

(b) $q_1 = Q\frac{R_1}{R_2}, q_2 = Q\frac{R_2}{R_1}$

(c) $q_1 = \frac{QR_1}{R_1 + R_2}, q_2 = \frac{QR_2}{R_1 + R_2}$

(d) $q_1 = \frac{QR_2}{R_1 + R_2}, q_2 = \frac{QR_1}{R_1 + R_2}$

9. The potential difference between the balls when energy of the system is minimum :

(a) $\frac{1}{4\pi \epsilon_0}\left(\frac{q_1}{R_1} - \frac{q_2}{R_2}\right)$ (b) $\frac{1}{4\pi \epsilon_0}\left(\frac{q_1 - q_2}{\ell}\right)$

(c) $\frac{1}{4\pi \epsilon_0}\left(\frac{q_1}{R_1} - \frac{q_2}{\ell}\right)$ (d) zero

**Passage for Q. 10 to Q.12**

There is a fixed semicircular ring of radius $R$, lying in $y$-$z$ plane, with centre of arc at origin and it is uniformly charged with charge $Q$. There is a long hollow pipe of very small radius, inner surface of pipe is smooth and it is made of insulated material. Pipe is fixed along $x$ -axis from origin. A small ball with charge $q$ and mass $m$ is projected in pipe with negligible velocity, ball can smoothly move in pipe. Whole arrangement lies in gravity free space.

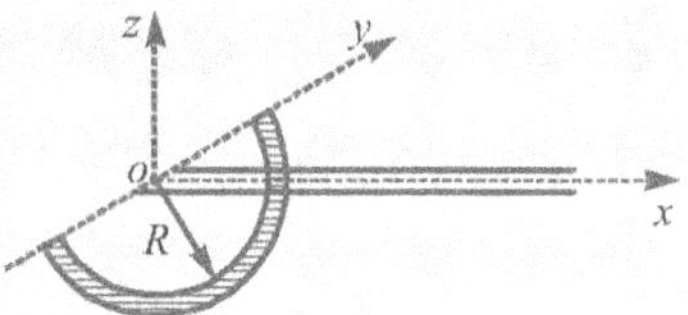


10. The maximum acceleration of ball in pipe is

(a) $\frac{1}{4\pi\varepsilon_0}\frac{Qq}{mR^2}$ (b) $\frac{1}{12\sqrt{3}\pi\varepsilon_0}\frac{Qq}{mR^2}$

(c) $\frac{1}{3\sqrt{3}\pi\varepsilon_0}\frac{Qq}{mR^2}$ (d) None of these

11. The kinetic energy of particle when its acceleration is maximum is

(a) $\frac{1}{4\pi\varepsilon_0}\frac{Qq}{R}\left(1-\sqrt{\frac{2}{3}}\right)$ (b) $\frac{1}{4\pi\varepsilon_0}\frac{Qq}{R}\left(\frac{1}{2}\right)$

(c) $\frac{1}{4\pi\varepsilon_0}\frac{Qq}{R}\left(\frac{1}{\sqrt{2}}\right)$ (d) None of these

12. Normal reaction exerted by pipe on ball when ball is moving in pipe is along

(a) z-axis always (b) –z axis always

(c) initially along y-axis and then along z-axis

(d) y-axis always

## MATRIX MATCHING

13. Column II describe graph for charge distribution given in column I match the description.

**Column I** / **Column II**

A. Uniformly charged ring (p)

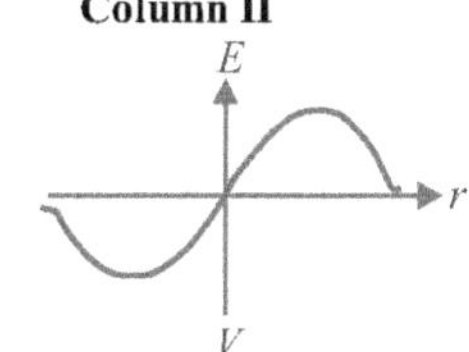


B. Infinitely large charge conducting sheet (q)

C. Infinite non conducting thin sheet (r)

D. Hollow non conducting sphere (s)

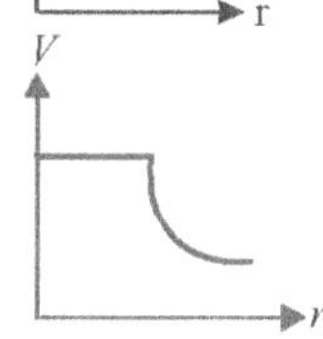


| Answer Key | 8 | (c) | 9 | (d) | 10 | (c) | 11 | (a) |
|---|---|---|---|---|---|---|---|---|
| Sol. from page 119 | 12 | (b) | | | 13 | A.-p, q ; B. - r ; C. - r ; D. - s | | |

**14.** Figure shows three concentric spherical conducting shells A, B, and C of radii $R$, $2R$ and $4R$ respectively. A and C are connected by a conducting wire and $B$ is given charge Match the following columns : $\left[\frac{1}{4\pi \epsilon_0} = K\right]$

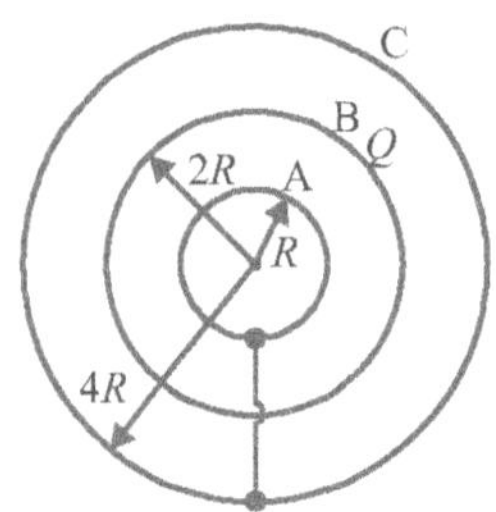


| | Column - I | | Column - II |
|---|---|---|---|
| A. | Charge on shell A | (p) | Q/ 3 |
| B. | Charge on shell C | (q) | – Q/ 3 |
| C. | Potential of A | (r) | Q |
| D. | Potential of C | (s) | $K\frac{Q}{4R}$ |
| | | (t) | none |

**15.** A conducting sphere $A$ of radius $a$, with charge $Q$ is placed concentrically inside a conducting shell $B$ of radius $b$. $B$ is earthed, $C$ is the common centre of $A$ and $B$. If $P$ is point between shells $A$ and $B$ at distance $r$ from centre $C$ then for $(a = 1\text{m}, b = 3\text{m}$ and $r = 2\text{m})$ $\left(K = \frac{1}{4\pi \epsilon_0}\right)$

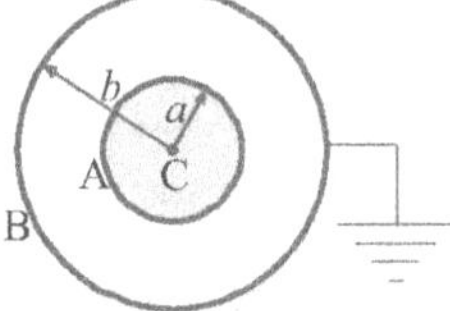


| | Column - I | | Column - II |
|---|---|---|---|
| A. | Electric field at point $P$ is | (p) | $2KQ$ |
| B. | Electrical potential at point $P$ is ($v_\infty = 0$) | (q) | zero |
| C. | Electric potential difference between $A$ and $B$ is | (r) | $\frac{KQ}{4}$ |
| D. | Electric field outside the shell $B$ at distance 5 m from centre $C$ is | (s) | $\frac{KQ}{6}$ |

| Answer Key | 14 | A. - (q) ; B - (p) ; C - (s) ; D. - (t) | 15 | A. - (r) ; B - (s) ; C - (p) ; D. - (q) |
|---|---|---|---|---|
| Sol. from page 119 | | | | |

## Electricity — Subjective Integer Type — Exercise 1.5

*Solution from page 120*

**1.** Two like point charges of 5 cgs electrostatic units each are at some distance from each other. Determine the potential at a point 10 cm from each of the charges. How will this potential change if the space around the charges is filled with a dielectric of permittivity $\epsilon = 2$ ?

**Ans.** $V$ = 300 V and 150 V.

**2.** An electric field of 20 N/C exists along the $x$-axis in space. Calculate the potential difference $V_B - V_A$ where the points $A$ and $B$ are given by,

(a) A = (0, 0); B = (4m, 2m)

(b) A = (4m, 2m); B = (6m, 5m)

(c) A = (0, 0); B = (6m, 5m)

Do you find any relation between the answers of parts (a), (b) and (c) ?

**Ans.** (a) – 80 V (b) – 40 V (c) – 120 V.

3. The electric field in a region is given by $E = \frac{3}{5}E_0 i + \frac{4}{5}E_0 j$ with $E_0 = 2.0 \times 10^3$ N/C. Find the flux of this field through a rectangular surface of area 0.2 m$^2$ parallel to the yz- plane.

**Ans.** 240 N-m$^2$/C.

4. A positron, of charge $1.60 \times 10^{-19}$ C, revolves in a circular path of radius r between and concentric with the cylinders as shown in figure. What must be its kinetic energy K is electron volt? Assume that a = 2.0 cm, b = 3.0 cm, and $\lambda$ = 30 nC/m.

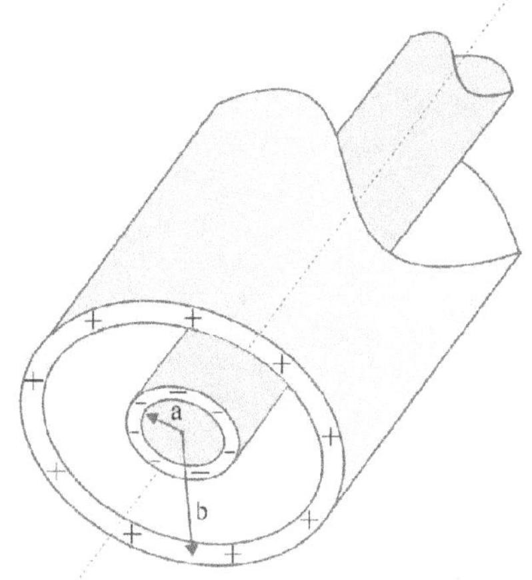


**Ans.** 270 eV

5. A ball of mass of mass $10^{-2}$ kg and having a charge $+3 \times 10^{-6}$C is tied at one end of a 1 m long thread. The other end of the thread is fixed and a charge $-3 \times 10^{-6}$ C is placed at this end. The ball can move in a circular orbit of radius 1 m in the vertical plane. Initially, the ball is at the bottom. Find minimum initial horizontal velocity of the ball so that it will be able to complete the full circle.

**Ans.** $v$ = 762 m/s.

6. In figure, a point charge $+q$ is at a distance $d/2$ directly above the centre of a square of side $d$. The magnitude of the electric flux through the square is $\frac{q}{x \in_0}$. Find the value of $x$.

**Ans.** 6

7. A charged dust particle of radius $5 \times 10^{-7}$ m is located in a horizontal electric field having an intensity of $6.28 \times 10^5$ V/m. The surrounding medium is air with coefficient of viscosity $\eta = 1.6 \times 10^{-5}$ N-s/m$^2$. If this particle moves with a uniform horizontal speed 0.02 m/s, find the number of electrons on it.

**Ans.** 30.

8. Four point charges, each of $+q$, are rigidly fixed at the four corners of a square planar soap film of side 'a'. The surface tension of the soap film is $T$. The system of charges and planar film are in equilibrium, and $a = k\left[\frac{q^2}{T}\right]^{1/N}$, where '$k$' is a constant. Then find the value of N .

**Ans.** 3

Electricity

## Subjective Exercise 1.6

*Solution from page 121*

1. The distance between two fixed positive charges $4e$ and $e$ is $l$. How should a third charge $q$ be arranged for it to be in equilibrium ? Under what conditions will the equilibrium of the charge $q$ be stable and when will it be unstable ?

***Ans.*** At a distance $\frac{l}{3}$ from the smaller charge. The equilibrium will be stable during longitudinal displacements, if the charge $q$ is positive and unstable if $q$ is negative.

2. Two free positive charges $4e$ and e are a distance $a$ apart. What charge is needed to achieve equilibrium for the entire system and where should it be placed ?

***Ans.*** The negative charge $q = \frac{4e}{9}$ should be placed at a distance $\frac{a}{3}$ from the charge e.

3. A negative point charge $2e$ and a positive charge $e$ are fixed at a distance $l$ from each other. Where should a positive test charge q be placed on the line connecting the charges for it to be in equilibrium ? What is the nature of equilibrium of the test charge with respect to longitudinal motions. Plot the dependence of the force acting on this charge on the distance between it and the charge $+e$.

***Ans.*** The test charge should be placed at a distance $a = l(1 + \sqrt{2})$ behind the positive charge. The equilibrium will be stable.

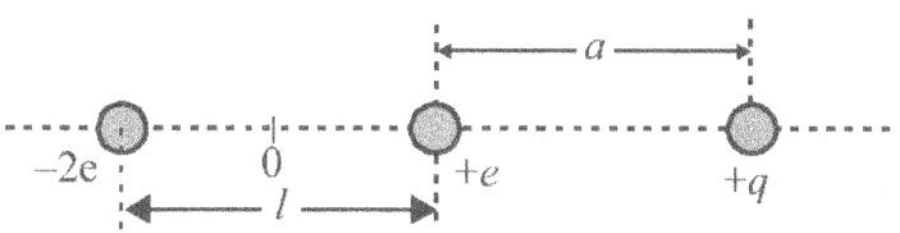


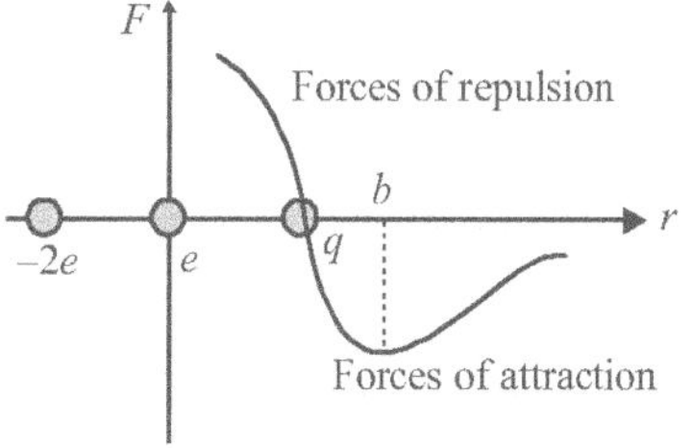


4. Two small equally charged conducting balls are suspended from long threads secured at one point. The charges and masses of the balls are such that they are in equillibrium when the distance between them is $a$ = 10 cm (the length of the threads $L >> a$). One of the balls is then discharged. How will the balls behave after this ? What will be the distance $b$ between the balls when equilibrium is restored ?

***Ans.*** The balls will first go down, touch each other and then move apart a distance $b = \frac{a}{\sqrt[3]{4}}$ .

5. A charge is uniformly distributed over the surface of two concentric conductive spheres (with the same density $\sigma$). What is the magnitude of this charge if a quantity of work of $V$ is required to transfer one positive unit of electricity from infinity to the common centre of the spheres ? The radii of the spheres are $r$ and $R$.

**Ans.** $Q = \frac{r^2 + R^2}{r + R} V$ .

6. Suppose all the electrons of 100 g water are lumped together to form a negatively charged particle and all the nuclei are lumped together to form a positively charged particle. If these two particles are placed 10.0 cm away from each other, find the force of attraction between them. Compare it with your weight.

**Ans.** 2.56 x $10^{25}$ N.

7. Two identical pith balls are charged by rubbing against each other. They are suspended from a horizontal rod through two strings of length 20 cm each, the separation between the suspension points being 5 cm. In equilibrium, the separation between the balls in 3 cm. Find the mass of each ball and the tension in the strings. The charge on each ball has a magnitude $2.0 \times 10^{-8}$ C.

**Ans.** 8.2 g, 8.2 x $10^{-2}$ N.

8. A wire is bent in the form of a regular hexagon and a total charge $q$ is distributed uniformly on it. What is the electric field at the centre ? You may answer this part without making any numerical calculations.

**Ans.** zero.

9. A circular wire -loop of radius $a$ carries a total charge $Q$ distributed uniformly over its length. A small length $dL$ of the wire is cut off. Find the electric field at the centre due to the remaining wire.

**Ans.** $\frac{QdL}{8\pi^2\varepsilon_0 a^3}$ .

10. A nonconducting sheet of large surface area and thickness $d$ contains uniform charge distribution of density $\rho$. Find the electric field at a point $P$ inside the plate, at a distance $x$ from the central plane. Draw a qualitative graph of $E$ against $x$ for $0 < x < d$.

**Ans.** $\frac{\rho x}{\varepsilon_0}$ .

11. (a) Two similar point charges $q_1$ and $q_2$ are placed at a distance $r$ apart in air. If a dielectric slab of thickness $t$ ($<< r$) and dielectric constant $k$ is put between the charges, calculate the Coulomb force of repulsion.

(b) If the thickness of slab covers half the distance between the charges, the coulomb repulsive force is reduced in the ratio 9 : 4, calculate the dielectric constant of the slab.

**Ans.** (a) $F = \frac{1}{4\pi\varepsilon_0}\frac{q_1 q_2}{(r - t + t\sqrt{k})^2}$ (b) $k = 4$.

12. A thin non conducting ring of radius $R$ has a linear charge density $\lambda = \lambda_0 \cos\phi$, where $\lambda_0$ is a constant $\phi$ is the azimuthal angle. Find the magnitude of the electric field strength

(a) at the centre of the ring;

(b) on the axis of the ring as a function of the distance $r$ from its centre. Investigate the obtained function at $r >> R$

**Ans.** (a) $E = \frac{\lambda_0}{4 \epsilon_0 R}$ (b) $E = \frac{\lambda_0 R^2}{4 \epsilon_0 (R^2 + r^2)^{3/2}}$

13. A charge $+ 10^{-9}$C is located at the origin in free space and another charge $Q$ at (2, 0, 0). If the $x$ component of the electric field at (3, 1, 1) is zero, calculate the value of $Q$. Is the y component is zero at (3, 1, 1)? **Ans.** $Q = -3^{5/2}/(11^{3/2} \times 10^{-9})$C ; not zero

14. A very long uniform charged thread oriented along the axis of a circle of radius $R$ rests on its centre with one of the ends. The charge per unit length of the thread is equal to $\lambda$. Find the flux of the vector $E$ across the circle area. **Ans.** $\lambda R / 2\varepsilon_0$

15. A thin glass rod is bent into a semicircle of radius $R$. A charge $+ Q$ is uniformly distributed along the upper half and a charge $- Q$ is uniformly distributed along the lower half, as shown in figure. Find the electric field $E$ at $P$, the centre of the semicircle.

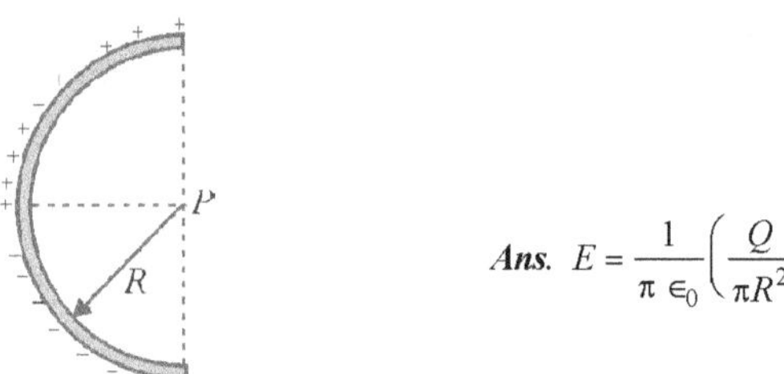


**Ans.** $E = \frac{1}{\pi \epsilon_0}\left(\frac{Q}{\pi R^2}\right)$

16. One end of a 10 cm long silk thread is fixed to a large vertical non conducting plate and the other end is fastened to a small ball having a mass of 10 g and a charge of $4.0 \times 10^{-6}$C. In equilibrium, the thread makes an angle of 60° with the vertical. (a) Find the tension in the thread in equilibrium (b) Suppose the ball is slightly pushed aside and released. Find the time period of the small oscillations.

**Ans.** (a) 0.20 N (b) 0.45 s.

17. In figure, a uniform upward-pointing electric field $E$ of magnitude $2.00 \times 10^3$ N/C has been set up between two horizontal plates by charging the lower plate positively and the upper plate negatively. The plates have length $L = 10.0$ cm and separation $d = 2.00$ cm. An electron is then shot between the plates from the left edge of the lower plate. The initial velocity $v_0$ of the electron makes an angle $\theta = 45°$ with the lower plate and has a magnitude of $6.00 \times 10^6$ m/s.

(a) Will the electron strikes one of the plate ?

(b) If so, which plate and how far horizontally from the left edge?

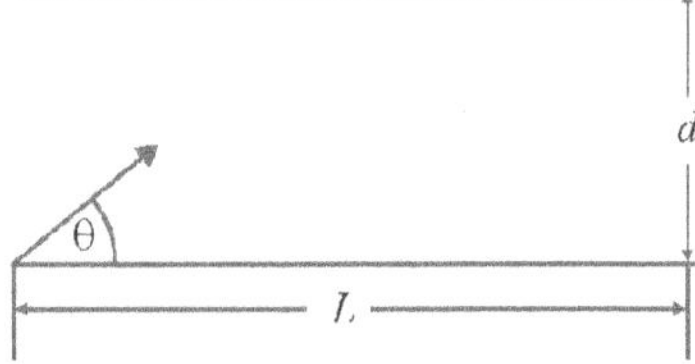


**Ans.** (a) Electron hits the upper plate (b) x = 2.72 cm

18. In figure, the charge on a neutral isolated conductor is separated by a nearly positively charged rod. What is the flux through the five Gaussian surfaces shown in cross section ? Assume that the charges enclosed by $S_1$, $S_2$, and $S_3$ are equal in magnitude.

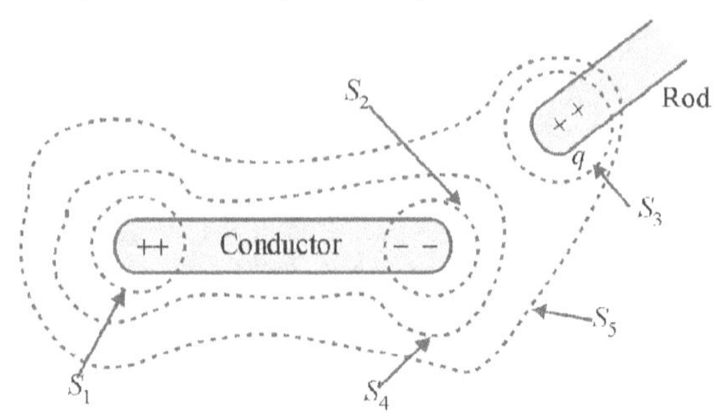


**Ans.** $\phi_1 = \frac{q}{\epsilon_0}$, $\phi_2 = -\frac{q}{\epsilon_0}$, $\phi_3 = \frac{q}{\epsilon_0}$, $\phi_4 = 0$, $\phi_5 = \frac{q}{\epsilon_0}$

19. In figure, a sphere of radius a and a charge $+q$ uniformly distributed throughout its volume, is concentric with a spherical conducting shell of inner radius $b$ and outer radius $c$. This shell has a net charge of $-q$. Find an expression for the electric field as a function of the radius $r$ (a) within the sphere ($r < a$); (b) between the sphere and the shell ($a < r < b$); (c) inside the shell ($b < r < c$); and (d) outside the shell ($r > c$). (e) what are charges on the inner and outer surfaces of the shell?

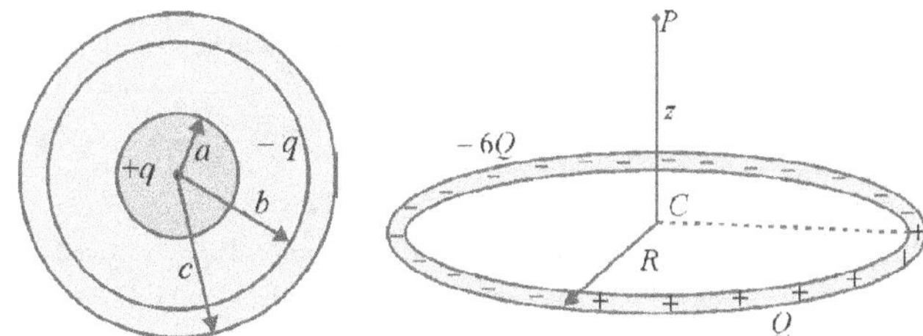


*Ans.* (a) $E = \frac{1}{4\pi \epsilon_0} \frac{qr}{a^3}$ (b) $E = \frac{1}{4\pi \epsilon_0} \frac{q}{r^2}$ (c) $E = \frac{1}{4\pi \epsilon_0 r^2} \frac{q(c^3 - r^3)}{(c^3 - b^3)}$

(d) $E = 0$ (e) $-q$ and zero.

20. A circular plastic rod of radius $R$ has a positive charge $+Q$ uniformly distributed along one-quarter of its circumference and a negative charge of $-6Q$ uniformly distributed along the rest of the circumference. With $V = 0$ at the infinity, what is the electric potential (a) at the centre $C$ of the circle and (b) at point $P$, which is on the axis of the circle at a distance $z$ from the centre ?

*Ans.* (a) $\frac{(1/4\pi\varepsilon_0)(-5Q)}{R}$. (b) $\frac{(1/4\pi\varepsilon_0)(-5Q)}{(z^2 + R^2)^{1/2}}$

21. Point charges $q$ and $-q$ are located at the vertices of a square with diagonals $2\ell$ as shown in figure. Find the magnitude of the electric field at a point located symmetrically with respect to the vertices of the square at a distance $x$ from its centre.

*Ans.* $E = \frac{q\ell}{\sqrt{2}\pi\varepsilon_0(\ell^2 + x^2)^{3/2}}$.

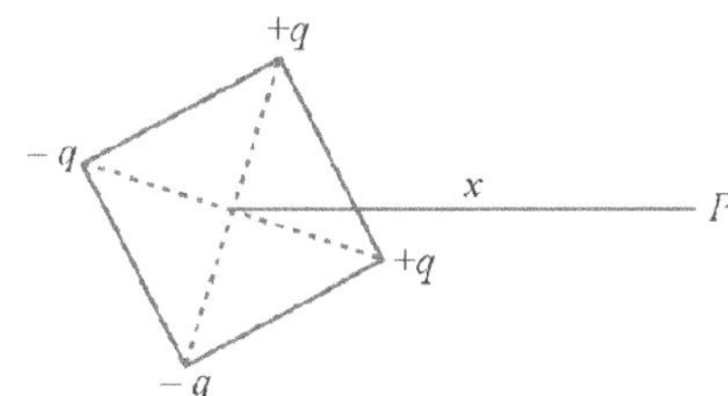


22. A system consists of a thin ring of radius $R$ and a very long uniformly charged thread oriented along the axis of the ring, with one of its end coinciding with the centre of the ring. The total charge on the ring is equal to $q$. The charge of the thread (per unit length) is equal to $\lambda$. Find the interaction force between the ring and the thread.

*Ans.* $\frac{q\lambda}{4\pi\varepsilon_0 R}$.

23. A thread carrying a uniform charge $\lambda$ per unit length has the configuration shown in figure. Assuming a curvature radius $R$ to be considerably less than the length of the thread, find the electric field strength at the point $O$.

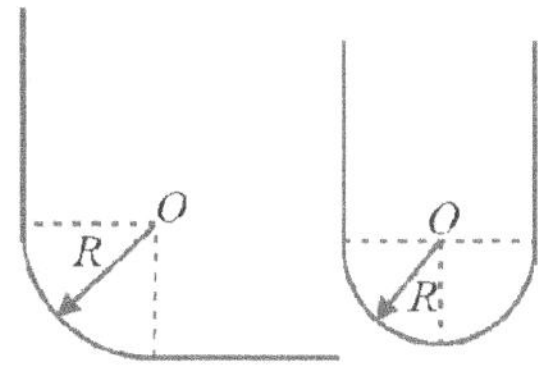


*Ans.* (a) $E = \frac{\lambda\sqrt{2}}{4\pi \epsilon_0 R}$ (b) $E = 0$.

24. Three charges of 0.1 C each are placed on the corners of an equilateral triangle of side 1.0 m. If the energy is supplied to this system at the rate of 1.0 kW, how much time would be required to move one of the charges onto the mid point of the line joining the other two? *Ans.* $1.8 \times 10^5$ s

25. Three point charges $q$, $2q$ and $8q$ are to be placed on a 9 cm long straight line. Find the position where the charges should be places such that the potential energy of the system is minimum. In this situation, what is the electric field at the position of the charge $q$ due to the other two charges?

*Ans.* $2q$ and $8q$ at the ends and $q$ is at a distance 3 cm from $2q$, $E = 0$.

26. An inclined plane is making an angle $\alpha = 30°$ with the horizontal electric field of 100 V/m as shown in figure. A particle of mass 1 kg and charge 0.01 C is allowed to slide down from a height of 1 m. If the coefficient of friction is 0.2, find the time it will take the particle to reach the bottom.

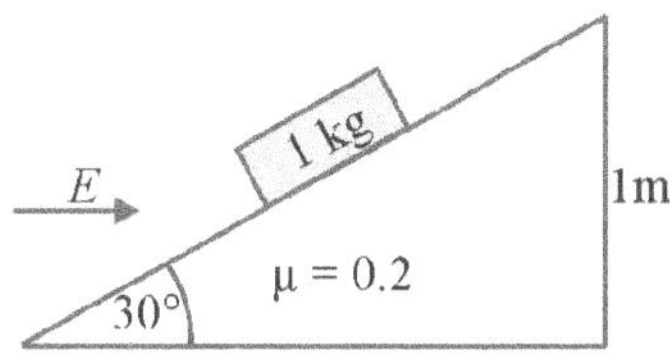


*Ans.* $t = 1.345$s

27. An electron is constrained to the central axis of the ring of charge of radius $R$. Show that the electrostatic force exerted on the electron can cause it to oscillate through the centre of the ring with an angular frequency of $\omega = \sqrt{(eq/4\pi\varepsilon_0 mR^3)}$, where $q$ is the charge on the ring, and $m$ is the mass of the electron.

28. In figure two plastic rods, one of charge $+q$ and the other of charge $-q$, form a circle of radius $R$ in an xy plane. An $x$ axis passes through their connecting points, and charge is distributed uniformly on both rods. What are the magnitude and direction of the electric field $E$ produced at the centre of the circle?

*Ans.* $E = \frac{1}{\pi \epsilon_0}\left(\frac{q}{\pi R^2}\right)$

**29.** In figure, a pendulum is hung from the higher of two large horizontal plates. The pendulum consists of a small insulating sphere of mass m and charge $+q$ and an insulating thread of length $\ell$. What is the period of the pendulum if a uniform electric field $E$ is set up between the plates by

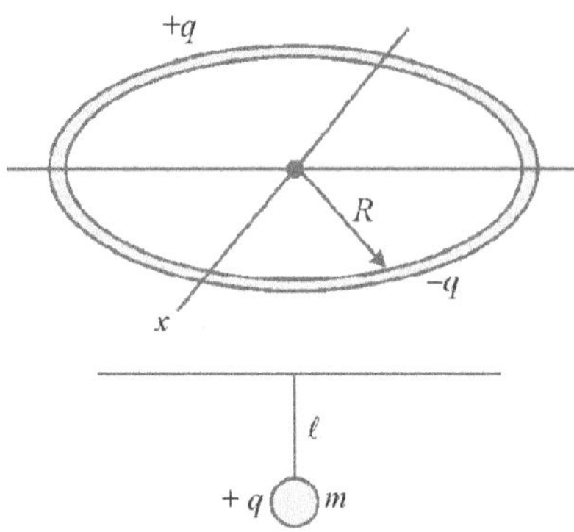


(a) charging the top plate negatively and the lower plate positively and

(b) vice versa? In both cases, the field points away from one plate and directed towards the other plate.

*Ans.* (a) $T = 2\pi\sqrt{\ell/(g - qE/m)}$ (b) $T = 2\pi\sqrt{\ell/(g + qE/m)}$ .

**30.** Figure shows a section through a long, thin walled metallic tube of radius $R$, carrying a charge per unit length $\lambda$ on its surface. Derive expressions for $E$ in terms of distance $r$ from the tube axis, considering both (a) $r > R$ and (b) $r < R$.

*Ans.* (a) $\lambda/2\pi\varepsilon_0 r$, (b) 0

**31.** Charge is distributed uniformly throughout the volume of an infinitely long cylinder of radius $R$. (a) Show that $E$ at a distance $r$ from the cylinder axis ($r < R$) is given by $E = \rho r/2\varepsilon_0$, where $\rho$ is the volume charge density. (b) Write an expression for $E$ when $r > R$.

**32.** A very long conducting cylindrical rod of length $L$ with a total charge $+q$ is surrounded by a conducting cylindrical shell (also of length $L$) with total charge $-2q$, as shown in figure. Find

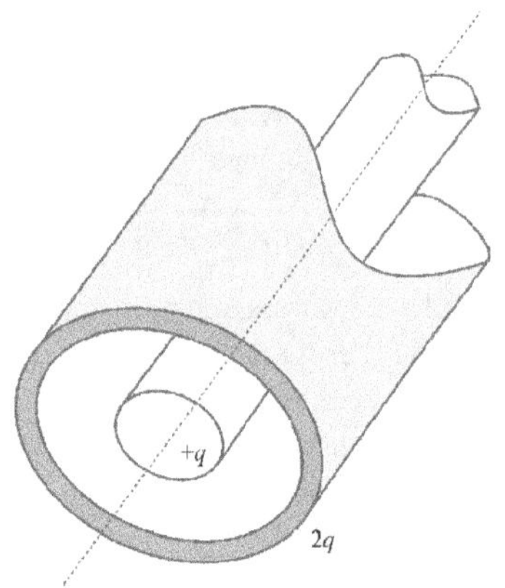


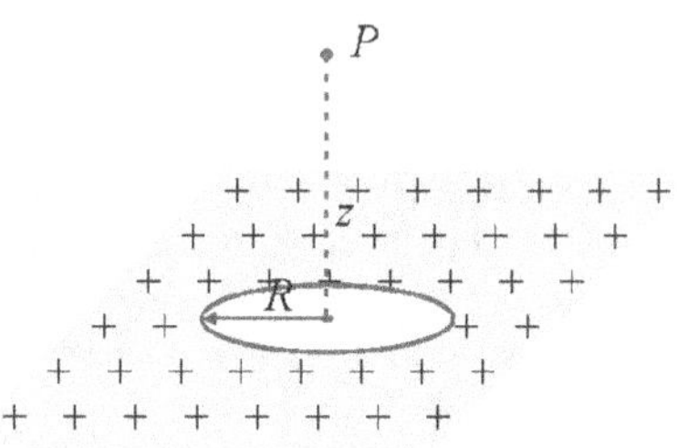


(a) the electric field at points outside the conducting shell.

(b) the distribution of the charge on the conducting shell, and

(c) the electric field between shell and rod.

*Ans.* (a) $E = q/2\pi\varepsilon_0 Lr$, radially inward (b) $-q$ on both inner and outer surfaces (c) $E = q/2\pi\varepsilon_0 Lr$

**33.** A large flat nonconducting surface has a uniform charge density $\sigma$. A small circular hole of radius R has been cut in the middle of the sheet, as shown in figure. Ignore fringing of the field lines around all edges. Calculate the electric field at point $P$, a distance $z$ from the centre of the hole along its axis.

*Ans.* $E = \sigma/2\varepsilon_0(z^2 + R^2)^{1/2}$

**34.** A solid nonconducting sphere of radius $R$ has a non uniform charge distribution of volume charged density $\rho = \rho_s r/R$, where $\rho_s$ is a constant and $r$ is the distance from the centre of the sphere. Show that (a)the total charge on the sphere is $Q = \pi\rho_s R^3$ and

(b) the electric field inside the sphere has a magnitude given by $E = Qr^2/4\pi\varepsilon_0 R^4$ .

**35.** A nonconducting spherical shell, of inner radius a and outer radius b, has a volume charge density $\rho = A/r$, where A is a constant and r is the distance from the centre of the shell. In addition a point charge $q$ is located at the centre. What value should $A$ have if the electric field in the shell $(a \le r \le b)$ is to be uniform?

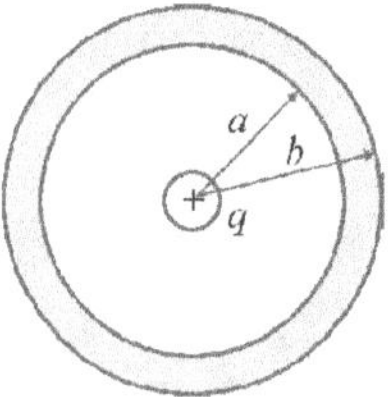


*Ans.* $q/2\pi a^2$

**36.** What is the potential at point $P$ due to the charge distribution as given in the figure. Rank the situation according to the magnitude of the electric field that is set up at $P$ from greatest to least.

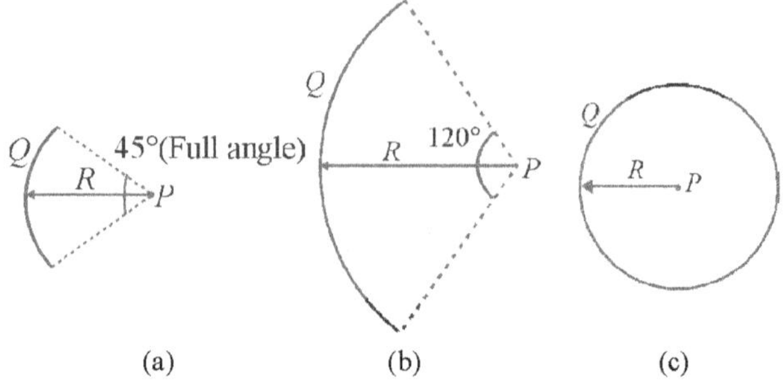

*Ans.* $\frac{(1/4\pi\varepsilon_0)Q}{R}$ in each case, Maximum in (a) Minimum in (c)

**37.** A radioactive source in the form of a metal sphere of radius $10^{-2}$m, emits beta particles (electrons) at the rate of $5 \times 10^{10}$ particles per second. The source is electrically insulated. How long will it take for its potential to be raised by 2 volts assuming that 40 % of the emitted beta particles escape the source.

*Ans.* 700 μs.

**38.** Three particles, each of mass 1 g and carrying a charge $q$ are suspended from a common point by insulated massless strings, each 100 cm long. If the particles are in equilibrium and are located at the corners of an equilateral triangle of side length 3 cm, calculate the charge $q$ on each particle. (Take g = 10 m/s$^2$).

*Ans.* $3.162 \times 10^{-9}$ C.

**39.** Two identical balls each of mass 0.10 g and carrying identical charges are suspended by two insulating threads of equal length from a common point. At equilibrium they arrange themselves at the corners of an equilateral triangle with the apex at the centre of suspension. The distance of the balls from each other is 40 cm. Assuming the line joining the balls as horizontal, find the amount of charge on each ball.

*Ans.* $q = 1.01 \times 10^{-7}$ C.

**40.** A point particle of mass $M$ is attached to one end of a massless rigid nonconducting rod of length L. Another point particle of the same mass is attached to the other end of the rod. The two particles carry charges $+q$ and $-q$ respectively. This arrangement is held in a region of a uniform electric field $E$ such that the rod makes a small angle θ (say of about 5 degrees) with the field direction. Find an expression for the minimum time needed for the rod to become parallel to the field after it is set free.

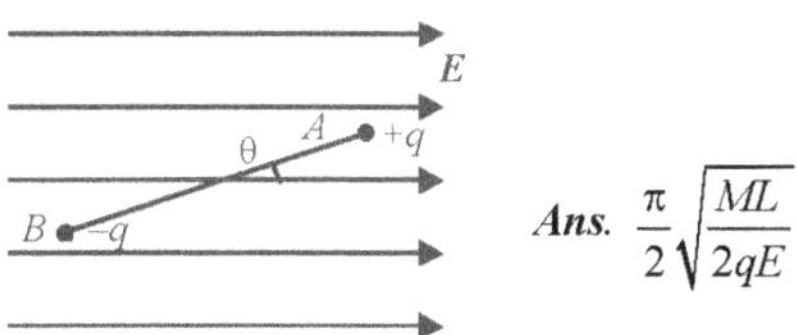


*Ans.* $\frac{\pi}{2}\sqrt{\frac{ML}{2qE}}$.

**41.** A drop of water of mass $18 \times 10^{-3}$ g falls away from the bottom of charged conducting sphere of radius 20 cm, carrying it with a charge of $10^{-9}$ coulomb and leaving on the sphere a uniformly distributed charge of $2.5 \times 10^{-6}$ coulomb. What is the speed of the drop after it has fallen 30 cm ? $(4\pi\varepsilon_0)^{-1} = 9 \times 10^9$ J-m /C $^2$.

*Ans.* 3.658 m/s.

**42.** Two circular wire loops of radii 0.05 m and 0.09 m, respectively are put such that their axes coincide and their centres are 0.12 m apart. Charge of $10^{-6}$ C is spread uniformly on each loop. Find the potential difference between the centres of the loops.

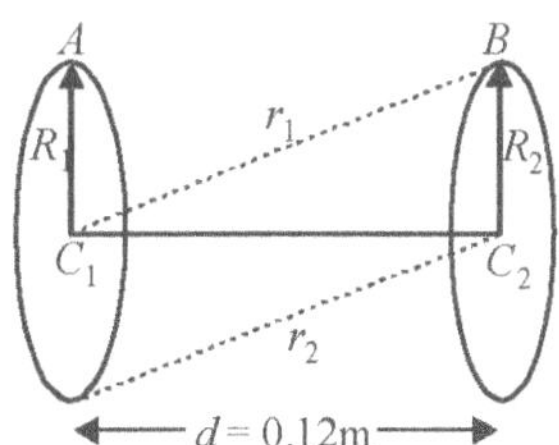


*Ans.* $7.08 \times 10^4$ V.

**43.** Two equal charges $q$ are kept fixed at $-a$ and a along the $x$-axis. A particle of mass m and charge $q/2$ is brought to the origin and given a small displacement along the (i) $x$-axis and (ii) $y$-axis. Describe the motion in the two cases.

*Ans.* (i) $T = 2\pi\sqrt{\frac{4\pi\varepsilon_0 ma^3}{2q^2}}$.

(ii) This motion is not oscillatory.

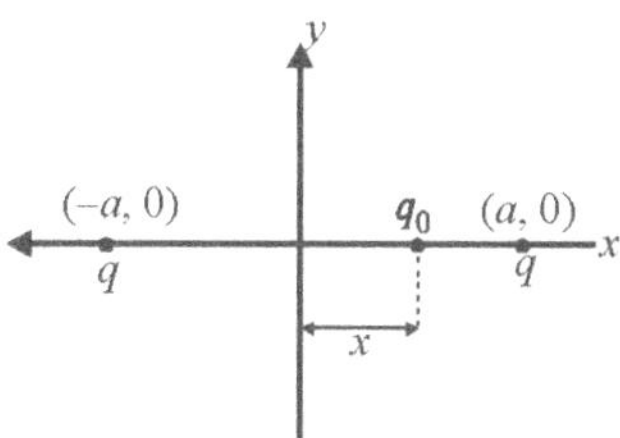


**44.** A circular ring of radius $R$ with uniform positive charge density λ per unit length is located in the $yz$- plane with its centre at the origin $O$. A particle of mass m and positive charge $q$ is projected from the point $P(R\sqrt{3}, 0, 0)$ on the positive $x$-axis directly towards $O$, with an initial speed $v$. Find the smallest (non-zero) value of the speed $v$ such that the particle does not return to $P$.

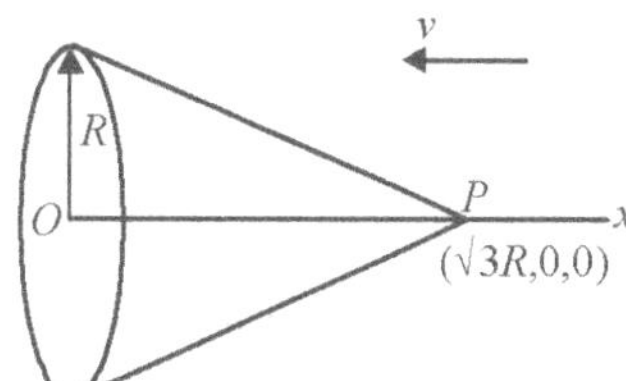


*Ans.* $v = \sqrt{\frac{\lambda q}{2\varepsilon_0 m}}$.

**45.** A long charged cylinder of radius $a$ and linear charge density λ is surrounded by an earthed hollow co-axial conducting cylinder of radius $b$. What is the electric field in the space between the two cylinders ?

*Ans.* $\frac{1}{4\pi\varepsilon_0}.\frac{2\lambda}{r}$.

**46.** Three point charges of 1$C$, 2$C$ and 3$C$ are placed at the corners of an equilateral triangle of side 1 m. Calculate the work required to move these charges to the corners of a smaller equilateral triangle of sides 0.5 m as shown in figure.

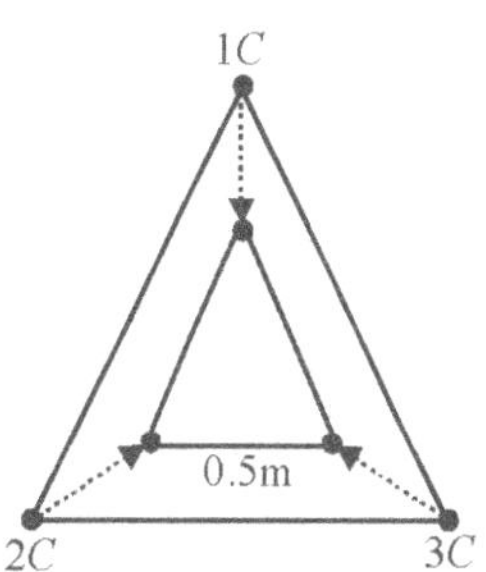


*Ans.* $99 \times 10^9$ J.

**47.** Three concentric spherical metal shells $A$, $B$ and $C$ of radii $a$, $b$ and $c$ $(a < b < c)$ have surface charge densities $+\sigma, -\sigma$ and $+\sigma$ respectively.

(i) Find the potentials of three shells $A$, $B$ and $C$.

(ii) If the shells $A$ and $C$ are at the same potential, obtain the relation between the radii $a$, $b$ and $c$.

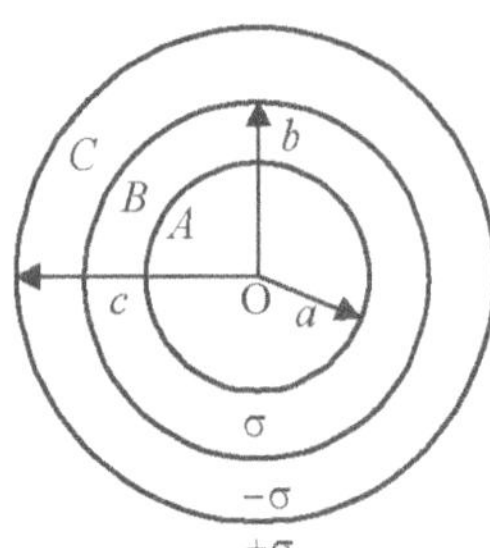


*Ans.* (i) $V_A = \frac{\sigma}{\varepsilon_0}(a - b + c)$,

$$V_B = \frac{\sigma}{\varepsilon_0}\left(\frac{a^2 - b^2}{b} + c\right), V_C = \frac{\sigma}{\varepsilon_0}\left(\frac{a^2 - b^2 + c^2}{c}\right)$$

(ii) $c = a + b$.

**48.** A proton moves with speed of $7.45 \times 10^5$ m/s directly towards a free proton originally at rest. Find the distance of closest approach for the two protons.

*Ans.* $9.94 \times 10^{-13}$ m

**49.** A charge of $4 \times 10^{-9}$ coulomb is uniformly distributed over a surface of a ring-shaped conductor of radius 0.3 m. Calculate the intensity of electric field at a point on the axis of the ring at a distance 0.4 m from the plane of conductor and specify its direction. What is the intensity at the centre of the ring ?

*Ans.* $E = 115.2$ N/C, along the axis of ring, at centre $E = 0$.

**50.** Find the potential $V(x, y)$ of an electrostatic field $E = a(y\boldsymbol{i} + x\boldsymbol{j})$, where a is a constant, $\boldsymbol{i}$ and $\boldsymbol{j}$ are the unit vectors of the $x$ and $y$ axes.

*Ans.* $V = -a\,xy +$ const.

**51.** Find the potential $V(x, y)$ of an electrostatic field $E = 2\,axy\,\boldsymbol{i} + a(x^2 - y^2)\boldsymbol{j}$, where a is a constant, $\boldsymbol{i}$ and $\boldsymbol{j}$ are the unit vectors of the $x$ and $y$ axes.

*Ans.* $V = ay\left(\frac{y^2}{3} - x^2\right) + const.$

**52.** A point charge $q$ is located at a distance $r$ from the centre $O$ of an uncharged conducting spherical layer whose inside and outside radii are equal to $R_1$ and $R_2$ respectively. Find the potential at the point $O$ if $r < R_1$.

*Ans.* $V = \frac{q}{4\pi\varepsilon_0}\left(\frac{1}{r} - \frac{1}{R_1} + \frac{1}{R_2}\right)$.

**53.** A ball of radius $R$ carries a positive charge whose volume density depends only on a separation $r$ from the ball's centre as $\rho = \rho_0(1 - r/R)$, where $\rho_0$ is a constant. Assuming the permittivities of the ball and the environment to be equal to unity, find :

(a) the magnitude of the electric field strength as a function of the distance $r$ both inside and outside the ball;

(b) the maximum intensity $E_{max}$ and the corresponding distance $r_m$.

*Ans.* (a) $E = \frac{\rho_0 r}{3\varepsilon_0}\left(1 - \frac{3r}{4R}\right)$ for $r \le R$, $E = \frac{\rho_0 R^3}{12\varepsilon_0 r^2}$ for $r \ge R$ ;

(b) $E_{max} = \frac{1}{9}\frac{\rho_0 R}{\varepsilon_0}$ for $r_m = \frac{2}{3}R$.

**54.** A space is filled up with a charge with volume density $\rho = \rho_0 e^{-\alpha r^3}$, where $\rho_0$ and $\alpha$ are positive constants, $r$ is the distance from the centre of this system. Find the magnitude of the electric field strength vector as a function of $r$. Investigate the obtained expression for the small and large values of $r$, i.e. at $\alpha r^3 << 1$ and $\alpha r^3 >> 1$.

*Ans.* $E = \frac{\rho_0}{3\varepsilon_0 \alpha r^2}(1 - e^{-\alpha r^3})$. Accordingly, $E \approx \frac{\rho_0 r}{3\varepsilon_0}$ and

$E \approx\approx \frac{\rho_0}{3\varepsilon_0 \alpha r^2}$.

**55.** Inside a ball charged uniformly with volume density $\rho$ there is a spherical cavity. The centre of the cavity is displaced with respect to the centre of the ball by a distance $a$. Find the field strength $\boldsymbol{E}$ inside the cavity, assuming the permittivity equal to unity.

*Ans.* $\frac{1}{3}\frac{a\rho}{\varepsilon_0}$.

**56.** A soap bubble of radius r and surface tension $T$ is given a potential $V$. Show that the new radius $R$ of the bubble is related with the initial radius by the equation

$$P(R^3 - r^3) + 4T(R^2 - r^2) = \frac{\varepsilon_0 V^2 R}{2}.$$

where $P$ is the atmospheric pressure.

☆☆☆

# Hints & Solutions

## Solutions EXERCISE 1.1 LEVEL -1

1. (d) Equal and opposite charges will appear on the sphere. So net charge in the sphere becomes zero.

2. (b) The total flux passing through the sphere

$$\phi = \frac{q_{in}}{\epsilon_0} = \frac{q}{\epsilon_0}$$

3. (c) With the increase in the spacing between the field lines, intensity of electric field decreases. So

$$F_A > (F_B = F_C)$$

4. (c) $$x = \frac{1}{2}at^2 = \frac{1}{2}\left(\frac{Eq}{m}\right)t^2$$

and $$x = \frac{1}{2}\left(\frac{Eq}{2m}\right)t'^2$$

∴ $$t' = \sqrt{2}\,t.$$

5. (a) $\phi = \vec{E}.\vec{A} = 4\hat{i}.(2\hat{i} + 3\hat{j}) = 8$ V-m

6. (d) Electric field at $P$ is due to all the charges; either inside or outside the close surface.

7. (b) $\phi = \frac{q_{in}}{\epsilon_0} = \frac{q_1 - q_2 - q_3}{\epsilon_0}.$

8. (b) We know that $\phi = \frac{q_{in}}{\epsilon_0}$

∴ $$q = \epsilon_0 .\phi$$

For positive charge, $\phi$ must be positive. In case II, total field lines are $(10 + 5 + 3) - (4 + 6 + 3) = 5$, are coming out of the cube.

9. (a) As shown in the figure the direction of electric field in case I is correctly represented.

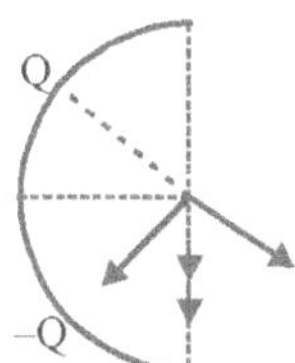

10. (a) When charge is given to inner cylinder, an electric field will be in between the cylinders. So there is potential difference between the cylinders.

11. (a) The charge density nearby $A$ is greatest and at $C$, it is least.

12. (c) Electric field lines at each point of the ball must crosses normally.

13. (a) Electric field will be from higher to lower potential and must be perpendicular to the equapotential surfaces.

14. (d) The displacement of the charge particles is zero, and so work done will be zero.

15. (c) Work done, $W_{AB} = (V_B - V_A)q$. In all the three cases, potential difference is same and so $W_1 = W_2 = W_3$.

16. (d) The variation of potential is shown in the figure.

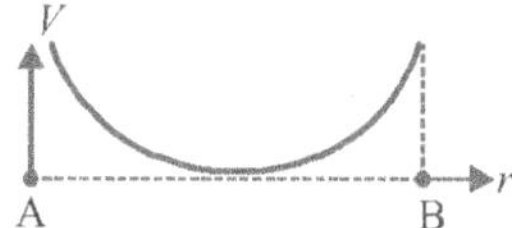

17. (c) Flux does not depend on the size and shape of the close surface, and so, it remains same.

18. (a) The potential of this system of charges will be zero at any point on the line perpendicular to the line joining the charges.

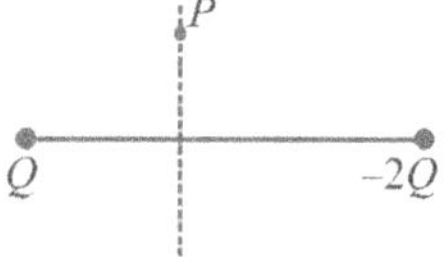

19. (b) The positive charge of magnitude $q$ will appear of the part of the sphere which is inside close surface.

20. (d) The total charge on the outer surface will be $Q + q$. So charge density will be $\left[\frac{Q+q}{4\pi b^2}\right]$

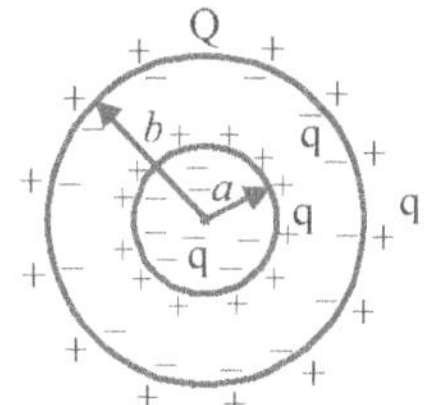

21. (a) $$\phi = EA\cos 0°$$

$$= E \times \frac{\pi d^2}{4},$$

$$\therefore\ E = \frac{4\phi}{\pi d^2}.$$

22. (c) Gravitational force is universal force, so it is present everywhere. Strong nuclear force also acts between nucleons.

23. (a) In the absence of gravitational force, the only force acts on the spheres is electrostatic repulsion and so the angle between two suspension becomes 180°. So force between the sphere

$$F = \frac{1}{4\pi\epsilon_0}\frac{Q^2}{(2L)^2}.$$

24. (b) For the equilibrium of charge $Q$,

$$k\frac{Q^2}{\ell^2} + k\frac{qQ}{(\ell/2)^2} = 0$$

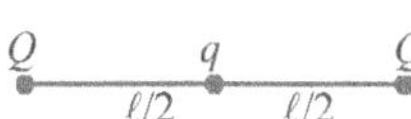

∴ $$q = -\frac{Q}{4}.$$

25. (a) $E = -\frac{dV}{dx} = -\frac{d(4x^2)}{dx} = -8x$

At $x = 1, E = -8 \times 1 = -8$ V/m.

26. (a) With the increase in spacing between the field lines, the intensity of field decreases.

27. (c) The potential difference between either of $B$, $C$, $D$, $E$ and $A$ is zero, and so work done along all the paths is zero.

28. (b) $E\ell = mg$

or $E = mg/\ell$

29. (b) If charge particle is put at rest in electric field, then it will move along line of force.

30. (b) Field due to $Q$ at $B$

$$E_B = \frac{1}{4\pi\epsilon_0}\frac{Q}{r^2}$$

Now field due to $-3Q$ at $A$

$$E = \frac{1}{4\pi\epsilon_0}\frac{3Q}{r^2}$$

$\therefore$ $E_B = E/3$.

Q ——— r ——— −3Q
A ————————— B

31. (c) $E = \frac{1}{4\pi\epsilon_0}\frac{q}{r^2}$

or $0.036 = 9\times10^9 \frac{(ne)}{(0.1)^2}$

or $n = 2.5 \times 10^5$.

32. (c) $W = U_f - U_i$

$$= 0 - \left[4\times\frac{1}{4\pi\epsilon_0}\frac{-Q^2}{a/\sqrt{2}}\right]$$

$$= \frac{\sqrt{2}Q^2}{\pi\epsilon_0 a}.$$

33. (c) $E = \frac{\lambda}{2\pi\epsilon_0 r}$.

34. (d) Electric field line will be perpendicular to the surface of the sphere and so line number 4 is correct.

35. (c) $K$ = work done = $F \times s = Eqy$.

36. (b) $x = \frac{1}{2}at^2$

or $t = \sqrt{\frac{2x}{a}} = \sqrt{\frac{2x}{(Ee/m)}}$

$\therefore$ $\frac{t_2}{t_1} = \sqrt{\frac{m_p}{m_c}}$

37. (b) Potential of the surface of the spherical conductor is also $V$, and so

$$V = \frac{1}{4\pi\epsilon_0}\frac{q}{(10)}$$

and $V' = \frac{1}{4\pi\epsilon_0}\frac{q}{(15)}$

$\therefore$ $V' = \frac{2}{3}V$

38. (b) Electric field, $E = 0$ and potential, $V = 10\times\frac{1}{4\pi\epsilon_0}\left(\frac{e}{R}\right)$.

39. (a) $W = \vec{F}.\vec{s} = \vec{E}Q.\vec{s} = Q(e_1\hat{i} + e_2\hat{j} + e_3\hat{k}).(a\hat{i} + b\hat{j})$

$= Q(e_1 a + e_2 b)$.

40. (b) $U = \frac{1}{4\pi\epsilon_0}\left[\frac{q^2}{a} + \frac{Qq}{a} + \frac{Qq}{\sqrt{2}a}\right] = 0$

$\therefore$ $Q = -\frac{2q}{(2+\sqrt{2})}$.

41. (b) In second case net electric field is not zero, see figure.

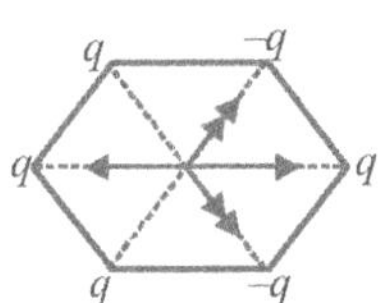


42. (c) $V = \frac{W}{q} = \frac{2}{20} = 0.1$ volt.

43. (d) $V = \frac{1}{4\pi\epsilon_0}\left[\frac{q}{R} + \frac{Q}{R/2}\right]$

$= \frac{1}{4\pi\epsilon_0}\left[\frac{q}{R} + \frac{2Q}{R}\right]$.

44. (d) The potential of each point of the sphere will be same.

45. (b)

46. (a) Equipotential associated with the field along $x$-direction will be perpendicular to $x$-direction i.e., parallel to $yz$-plane.

47. (b) Electric field runs from higher to lower potential and so $V_A = V_B$ also $V_A > V_C$.

48. (b) The electric field due to the sheet,

$$E = \frac{\sigma}{\epsilon_0}.$$

Now for the equilibrium of the ball

$T\sin\theta = Eq$

and $T\cos\theta = mg$

$\therefore$ $\tan\theta = \frac{Eq}{mg} = \frac{\sigma q}{\epsilon_0 mg}$.

Thus $\sigma \propto \tan\theta$.

49. (c) $E_1 = E_2$

or $\frac{1}{4\pi\epsilon_0}\frac{8q}{(L+x)^2} = \frac{1}{4\pi\epsilon_0}\frac{2q}{x^2}$

$\therefore$ $x = L$

Thus distance from origin is $= L + L = 2L$

8q ——L—— −2q ——x——

50. (c) $\oint \vec{E}.d\vec{A} = 0$, represents charge inside close surface is zero.

Electric field as any point on the surface may be zero.

51. (b) The change inside cylinder is, $q_{in} = Q \times 100$.

Now $\phi = \frac{q_{in}}{\epsilon_0}$

$= \frac{100Q}{\epsilon_0}$.

52. (b) Electric field at any point of the close surface is due to all the charges. So it is

$$\oint(\vec{E}_1+\vec{E}_2+\vec{E}_3+\vec{E}_4).d\vec{A}=\frac{q_1+q_2+q_3}{\epsilon_0}.$$

53. (b) Net flux, $\phi=\phi_2-\phi_1$.

So, $\phi_2-\phi_1=\frac{q_{\text{in}}}{\epsilon_0}$, $\therefore\ q_{in}=(\phi_2-\phi_1)\epsilon_0$.

54. (c) The equation $x^2+y^2=1$, represents a circle, and so particle will move along circular line of force.

55. (d) $q_1+q_2=Q$

and $\frac{q_1}{4\pi r^2}=\frac{q_2}{4\pi R^2}$

$\therefore\ q_1=\frac{Qr^2}{R^2+r^2}$ and $q_2=\frac{QR^2}{R^2+r^2}$

Now $V=\frac{1}{4\pi\epsilon_0}\left(\frac{q_1}{r}+\frac{q_2}{R}\right)$

$=\frac{1}{4\pi\epsilon_0}\frac{Q(R+r)}{(R^2+r^2)}.$

56. (c)

57. (c) Electric lines of force must crosses the shell surface normally at each point of it.

58. (a) It can be seen that electric field at $y$ axis is along $\hat{i}$.

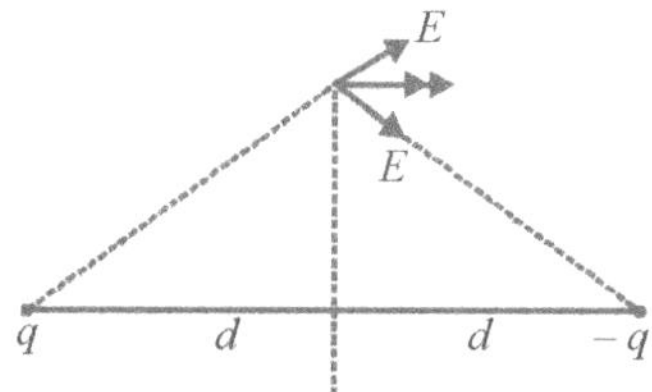


59. (d) $\frac{1}{2}mv^2=\frac{1}{4\pi\epsilon_0}\frac{Qq}{r}$

and $\frac{1}{2}m(2v)^2=\frac{1}{4\pi\epsilon_0}\frac{Qq}{r'}$

$\therefore\ r'=\frac{r}{4}.$

60. (b) $W=\vec{F}.\vec{s}=Eq\hat{i}.(-a\hat{i}-b\hat{j})$
$=-Eqa.$

61. (a) $E=-\frac{\Delta V}{\Delta r}=-\left(\frac{V_2-V_1}{r_2-r_1}\right)=-\left(\frac{0-5}{6-4}\right)=2.5\,V/m.$

62. (b) See theory.

63. (d) $W=\int_d^\infty Fdx=\frac{1}{4\pi\epsilon_0}\int_d^\infty\frac{q^2}{(2x)^2}dx$

$=\frac{1}{16\pi\epsilon_0}\frac{q^2}{d}.$

64. (c) If ball 1 has positive charge, then ball 2 will have negative and 4 must be positive. Again ball 1 will have negative charge. It shows that ball 1 must be neutral.

65. (c) The electric field at a distance $r$ in between $A$ and $B$ will be,

$$E=\frac{1}{4\pi\epsilon_0}\frac{q}{r^2}.$$

66. (a) The torque of the centripetal force about axis of rotation is zero and so angular momentum of the charge $-q$ remains constant.

67. (b) There will be no charge inside material of the conductor.

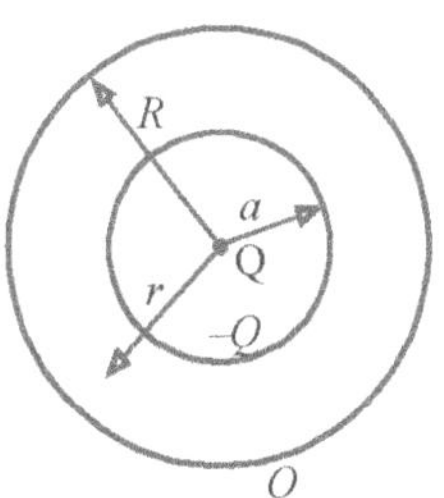


68. (d) When negative charge is given to the sphere, electrons are put on it, and so its mass will increase.

69. (c) The resultant force on the charge at $A$ is parallel to $BC$.

70. (b) $F=\frac{10^{-6}}{4\pi\epsilon_0}\left[\frac{1}{1^2}+\frac{1}{2^2}+\frac{1}{4^2}+\frac{1}{8^2}+.......\infty\right]$

$=9\times10^9\times10^{-6}\frac{1}{\left(1-\frac{1}{4}\right)}=12000$ N.

71. (c) Gravitational force, $F=\frac{Gm_1m_2}{r^2}$,

and electric force, $F=\frac{1}{4\pi\epsilon_0}\frac{q_1q_2}{r^2}.$

So, $\frac{1}{4\pi\epsilon_0}=G$ or $\frac{1}{\epsilon_0}=4\pi G.$ Thus Gauss law of gravitation can be written as, $\oint\vec{g}.d\vec{A}=\frac{1}{\epsilon_0}(-m)=-4\pi Gm.$ Here (–) represents attraction.

72. (d) $W=Fd\cos60°$
$=Eqd\cos60°$

2m
60°
E
2cos 60°

or $4=E\times0.2\times2\times\frac{1}{2}$

$\therefore\ E=20$ N/C.

73. (c)

74. (b) $E=\frac{V}{d}=\frac{800}{0.02}=40000\,V/m.$

For the equilibrium of the particle

$mg=Eq$
$=E(ne)$

$\therefore\ n=\frac{mg}{Ee}=\frac{1.96\times10^{-15}\times9.8}{40000\times1.6\times10^{-19}}$
$=3$

75. (b) For the connected spheres, we have

$$V_1 = V_2$$

or $$\frac{1}{4\pi\epsilon_0}\frac{q_1}{a} = \frac{1}{4\pi\epsilon_0}\frac{q_2}{b}$$

$\therefore$ $$\frac{q_1}{q_2} = \frac{a}{b}$$

Now $$\frac{E_1}{E_2} = \frac{q_1/a^2}{q_2/b^2} = \frac{a}{b}\times\frac{b^2}{a^2} = \frac{b}{a}.$$

76. (d) $K_{electron} = eV$, and $K_{alpha} = (2e)V$

Now $$\frac{P_{electron}}{P_{alpha}} = \frac{\sqrt{2m_e K_{electron}}}{\sqrt{2m_\alpha K_{alpha}}} = \sqrt{\frac{m_e}{m_\alpha}\times\frac{1}{2}}$$

77. (c) The dominant of $\frac{1}{2}\epsilon_0 E^2$ are of energy density. So these are

$$J/m^3 = \frac{mL^2T^{-2}}{L^3} = ML^{-1}T^{-2}.$$

78. (b) Given $$\frac{1}{4\pi\epsilon_0}\cdot\frac{q_A}{a} = \frac{1}{4\pi\epsilon_0}\cdot\frac{q_B}{b}$$

or $$\frac{q_A}{q_B} = \frac{a}{b}$$

Now $$\frac{\sigma_A}{\sigma_B} = \frac{q_A/4\pi a^2}{q_B/4\pi b^2} = \frac{q_A}{q_B}\times\frac{b^2}{a^2}$$

$$= \frac{a}{b}\times\frac{b^2}{a^2} = \frac{b}{a}.$$

79. (c) Work done = change in K.E.

$$(V_A - V_B)q = \frac{1}{2}mV_A^2 - \frac{1}{2}mV_B^2$$

$$600\times 10^{-8} = \frac{1}{2}\times 10^{-3}(V_A^2 - 0.20^2)$$

$\therefore$ $V_A = 22.8$ cm/s.

80. (a) Positive charge particle moves in the direction of field and so the right trend is : Top, down, top, down.

81. (a) Spacing between the lines of field increases from $A$ to $B$, and so magnitude of charge at $B$ will be less than $A$.

82. (d) Potential at the centre in both the cases is zero. But field will be different.

83. (d) $W = \text{PE}(\cos 90° - \cos 270°) = 0$.

84. (d) $$V = k\frac{\vec{p}.\vec{r}}{r^3} = \frac{k\,pr\cos\theta}{r^3}$$

$$= k\frac{p\cos\theta}{r^2}.$$

85. (b)

86. (a) $\phi = EA\cos 90° = 0$.

87. (c) The surface area normal to the field is $A = a^2$. So electric flux,

$$\phi = EA = Ea^2.$$

88. (c) Due to the electric field spring compresses and so the mean portion of the block will shift by $QE/K$.

89. (d) $$V_1 = \frac{1}{4\pi\epsilon_0}\left[\frac{Q}{R} - \frac{Q}{\sqrt{R^2+d^2}}\right]$$

and $$V_2 = \frac{1}{4\pi\epsilon_0}\left[\frac{-Q}{R} + \frac{Q}{\sqrt{R^2+d^2}}\right]$$

Thus, $$V_1 - V_2 = \frac{Q}{2\pi\epsilon_0}\left[\frac{1}{R} - \frac{1}{\sqrt{R^2+d^2}}\right].$$

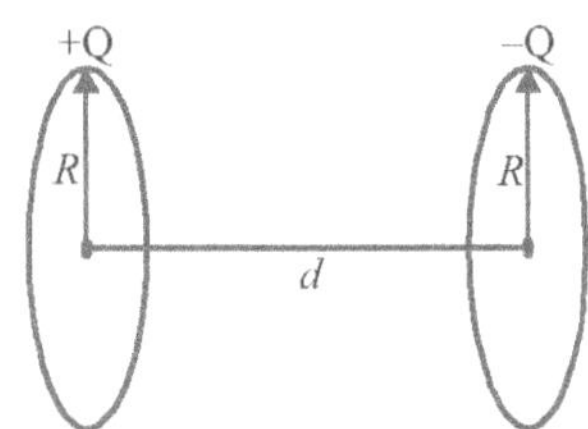


90. (c) $$E = \frac{\sigma}{2\epsilon_0} + \frac{\sigma}{2\epsilon_0} = \frac{\sigma}{\epsilon_0}.$$

91. (a)

92. (d)

## Solutions EXERCISE 1.1 LEVEL -2

1. (c) Electric field at the centre.

$$E = \frac{1}{4\pi\epsilon_0}\frac{(2q/3)}{R^2} = \frac{q}{6\pi\epsilon_0 R^2}.$$

Potential energy of the system,

$$U = \frac{1}{4\pi\epsilon_0}\left[\frac{\frac{q}{3}\times\frac{q}{3}}{2R} + \frac{\frac{q}{3}\left(-\frac{2q}{3}\right)}{\sqrt{3R}} + \frac{\frac{q}{3}\left(-\frac{2q}{3}\right)}{R}\right] \neq 0$$

Force, $$F_{BC} = \frac{1}{4\pi\epsilon_0}\left[\frac{\frac{q}{3}\times\left(\frac{2q}{3}\right)}{(\sqrt{3R})^2}\right] = \frac{q^2}{54\pi\epsilon_0 R^2}.$$

2. (c) $$E = \frac{1}{4\pi\epsilon_0}\left[\frac{2p}{(r-\ell/2)^3} - \frac{2p}{(r+\ell/2)^3}\right]$$

$$= \frac{1}{4\pi\epsilon_0}\frac{3Q}{r^4}.$$

P P r

3. (d) $$V_1 = \frac{1}{4\pi\epsilon_0}\left[\frac{q_1}{r} + \frac{q_2}{a}\right]$$

and $$V_2 = \frac{1}{4\pi\epsilon_0}\left[\frac{q_2}{r} + \frac{q_1}{a}\right]$$

After solving above equations, and neglecting $r^2$ in comparison to $a$, we get

$$q_1 = -\frac{r}{a}(rV_2 - aV_1), \text{ and } q_2 = -\frac{r}{a}(rV_1 - aV_2)$$

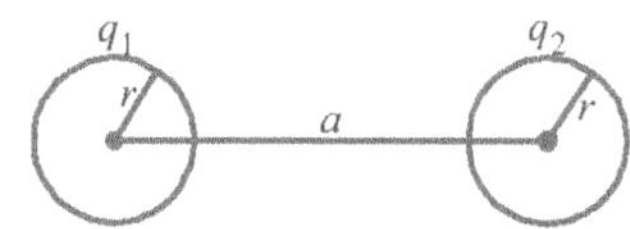


4. (b) $V = V_{air} + V_{metal}$
$= E_{air} \times 4 + E_{metal} \times 1$
$= 300 \times 4 + 0 \times 1$
$= 1200$ V.

5. (a) $$\vec{E} = \left(\frac{\sigma}{2\epsilon_0} + \frac{2\sigma}{2\epsilon_0} + \frac{\sigma}{2\epsilon_0}\right)(-\hat{k})$$
$$= -\frac{2\sigma}{\epsilon_0}\hat{k}.$$

6. (d) If $\lambda$ be the linear charge density of the rod, then in time $t$,

$$q_{in} = \lambda x = \lambda vt, \text{ and so } \phi = \frac{q_{in}}{\epsilon_0} = \frac{\lambda vt}{\epsilon_0}.$$

The flux of the charge increases till $vt = L/2$. i.e., $\phi_{max} = \frac{\lambda L}{2\epsilon_0}$

when rod comes out from left side of the cube, the flux then starts decreasing. So option (d) is correct.

7. (d) The charge on the sphere

$$Q = \rho \times \frac{4}{3} \times \pi (2R)^3 = \frac{32}{3}\pi\rho R^3.$$

At, $r = 0$, $$V_1 = \frac{3}{2} \times \frac{1}{4\pi\epsilon_0}\frac{Q}{(2R)} = \frac{3}{2} \times \frac{1}{4\pi\epsilon_0} \times \frac{\left(\frac{32}{3}\pi\rho R^3\right)}{2R}$$

$$= \frac{2\rho R^2}{\epsilon_0}.$$

At, $r = R$, $$V_2 = \frac{1}{4\pi\epsilon_0}Q\left[\frac{3(2R)^2 - R^2}{2(2R)^3}\right]$$

$$= \frac{11\rho R^2}{6\epsilon_0}.$$

Thus, $$V_2 - V_1 = \frac{11\rho R^2}{6\epsilon_0} - \frac{2\rho R^2}{\epsilon_0}$$

$$= \frac{-\rho R^2}{6\epsilon_0}$$

8. (d) For, $r = R/2$
Using Gauss's law, we have

$$\oint \vec{E}.d\vec{A} = \frac{q_{in}}{\epsilon_0}$$

or $$E \times 4\pi r^2 = \int_0^{R/2} \frac{\rho 4\pi r^2 dr}{\epsilon_0}$$

or $$E = \frac{Cr^3}{5\epsilon_0} = \frac{CR^3}{40\epsilon_0}.$$

9. (a) $W = W_{gravity} + W_{electric}$
$= mg \times 2r + 0$
$= 2\,mgr.$

10. (c) $$F = \frac{1}{4\pi\epsilon_0}\frac{qq'}{\left[\left(\frac{d}{2}\right)^2 + x^2\right]}\cos\theta$$

$$= \frac{1}{4\pi\epsilon_0}\frac{qq'x}{\left[\left(\frac{d}{2}\right)^2 + x^2\right]^{3/2}}$$

For $F$ to be maximum, $\frac{dF}{dx} = 0$

or $$x = \frac{d}{2\sqrt{2}}.$$

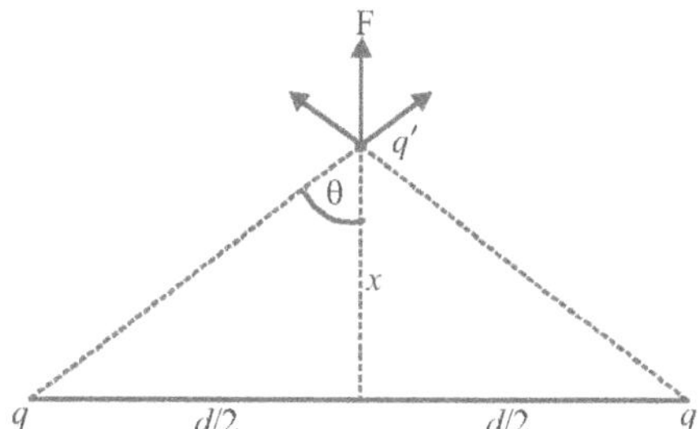


11. (b) See figure.

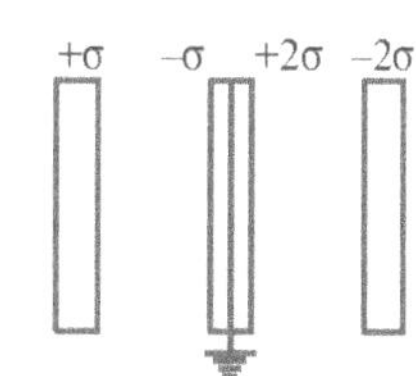


12. (a) $$U = 6 \times \frac{1}{4\pi\epsilon_0}\frac{q^2}{a}.$$

13. (a) The force between the charges becomes zero, because copper plate will not transfer the field lines of one charge to the other.

14. (d) $$F_{BC} = k\frac{qq}{r^2} = F.$$

The charge on third conductor in two contacts; one with $B$ and other with $C$ becomes, $\frac{q}{2}$ and $\frac{3q}{4}$.

Thus, $q_B = \frac{q}{2}$, $q_C = \frac{3q}{4}$.

Now, $$F'_{BC} = k\frac{\left(\frac{q}{2}\right)\left(\frac{3q}{4}\right)}{r^2} = \frac{3F}{8}.$$

15. (d) $E_x = \frac{-\partial V}{\partial x} = \frac{-\partial}{\partial x}(-5x + 3y + \sqrt{15}z)$

$= 5$

$E_y = \frac{-\partial V}{\partial y} = -3$, and $E_z = -\sqrt{15}$.

Now, $E = \sqrt{E_x^2 + E_y^2 + E_z^2}$

$= \sqrt{5^2 + (-3)^2 + (\sqrt{15})^2}$

$= 7$.

16. (a) The electric field on the $z$-axis

$$E = 4 \times \frac{1}{4\pi \epsilon_0} \frac{Qz}{\left(\frac{L^2}{2} + z^2\right)^{3/2}}.$$

The restoring force, $F = -Eq = -\frac{Qqz}{\pi \epsilon_0 \left(\frac{L^2}{2} + z^2\right)^{3/2}}$

For $z << L$, $F = -\frac{Qqz}{\sqrt{8}\pi \epsilon_0 L^3}$. As $F \propto (-z)$, so it represents SHM.

17. (b) $W_{21} = (V_1 - V_2)q$

$V = \frac{1}{4\pi \epsilon_0}\left[\frac{Q_1}{R} + \frac{Q_2}{\sqrt{2}R}\right]$

and $V_2 = \frac{1}{4\pi \epsilon_0}\left[\frac{Q_2}{R} + \frac{Q_1}{\sqrt{2}R}\right]$

Thus, $W_{21} = \frac{q(Q_1 - Q_2)(\sqrt{a} - 1)}{\sqrt{2}.4\pi \epsilon_0 R}$.

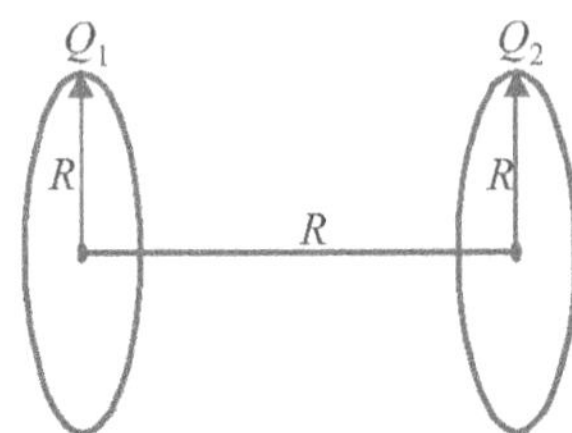


18. (d) $V = \frac{1}{4\pi \epsilon_0}\left[\frac{q}{x_0} - \frac{q}{2x_0} + \frac{q}{3x_0} - \frac{q}{4x_0} + .....\infty\right]$

$= \frac{q}{4\pi \epsilon_0 x_0} \ell n(1+1) = \frac{q \ell n2}{4\pi \epsilon_0 x_0}$.

+q −q +q −q ........∞
$x_0$ $2x_0$ $3x_0$ $4x_0$

19. (a) $\int_{\ell=\infty}^{\ell=0} -\vec{E}.d\ell = V = \frac{1}{4\pi \epsilon_0 x_0} \frac{q}{R}$

$= \frac{9 \times 10^9 \times 1.11 \times 10^{-10}}{0.5} = 2$ volt.

20. (a) $E = \frac{1}{4\pi \epsilon_0} \frac{q}{R^2}\left(\frac{\sin\theta}{\theta}\right)$

$= \frac{1}{4\pi \epsilon_0} \frac{q}{R^2}\left(\frac{\sin\theta}{\pi/2}\right)$

$= \frac{q}{2\pi^2 \epsilon_0 R^2}$.

21. (b) $U_i = k\left[\frac{2Qq}{a} + \frac{q^2}{2a}\right]$.

and $U_f = k\left[\frac{Qq}{(a+x)} + \frac{Qq}{(a-x)} + \frac{q^2}{2a}\right]$

Now, $U_f - U_i = \frac{2Qqx^2}{a(a^2 - x^2)}$

For small value of $x$, $(a^2 - x^2) \longrightarrow a^2$, and so

$U_f - U_i \propto x^2$.

q Q q
x

22. (b) For the system to be in equilibrium, net force on each of the charges must be zero. Net for on any of $-Q$ to be zero, we have

$\sqrt{2}k\frac{Q^2}{Q^2} + k\frac{Q^2}{2a^2} - \frac{kQq}{a^2/2} = 0$ $\quad \therefore \; q = \frac{Q}{4}(1 + 2\sqrt{2})$

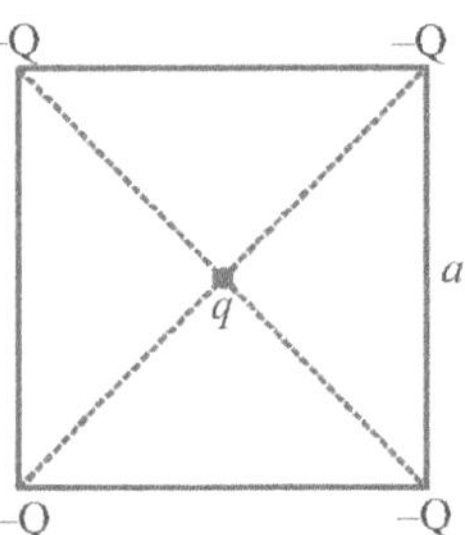


23. (a) For, $r < r_A$, $E = 0$

$r = r_A$, $\quad E = \frac{1}{4\pi \epsilon_0} \frac{Q_A}{r_A^2}$.

$r_A < r < r_B$, $\quad E = \frac{1}{4\pi \epsilon_0} \frac{Q_A}{r^2}$

$r = r_B$, $\quad E = \frac{1}{4\pi \epsilon_0}\left(\frac{Q_A - Q_B}{r_B^2}\right)$.

$= -\frac{1}{4\pi \epsilon_0}\left(\frac{Q_B - Q_A}{r_B^2}\right)$

These values are correctly represent in option (a).

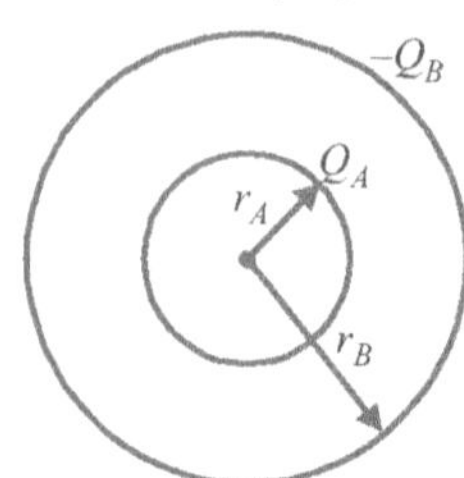

24. (b) By Newton's second law,

$$\frac{1}{4\pi\epsilon_0}\frac{Qq}{r^2} = \frac{mv^2}{r},$$

or $$v = \sqrt{\frac{Qq}{4\pi\epsilon_0 mr}}$$

Now time period, $$T = \frac{2\pi r}{v} = \frac{2\pi r}{\sqrt{\dfrac{Qq}{4\pi\epsilon_0 mr}}}$$

or $$r^3 = \left(\frac{Qq}{16\pi^3\epsilon_0 m}\right)T^2.$$

25. (d) $$E = \frac{1}{4\pi\epsilon_0}\frac{Q}{R^2}\frac{\sin\frac{\pi}{4}}{(\pi/4)}$$

$$= \frac{Q}{\sqrt{2}\pi^2\epsilon_0 R^2}.$$

Now resultant field at $P = \sqrt{2}E$

$$= \frac{Q}{\pi^2\epsilon_0 R^2}.$$

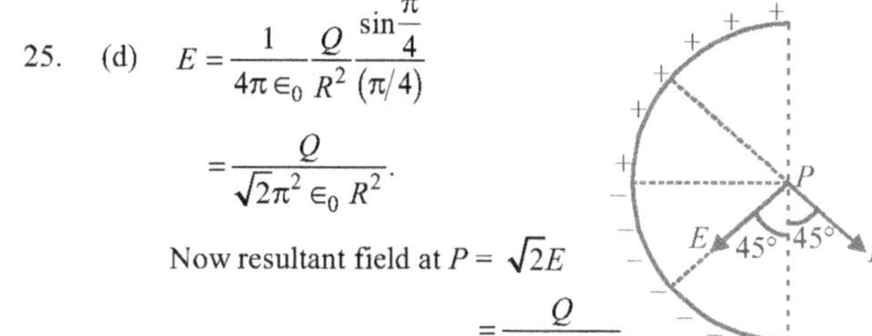


26. (c) $$\frac{1}{2}mv^2 = (V_{\text{centre}} - V_{\text{surface}})Q$$

$$= \left(\frac{Q}{8\pi\epsilon_0 R}\right)Q$$

or $$v = \frac{Q}{\sqrt{4\pi\epsilon_0 mR}}.$$

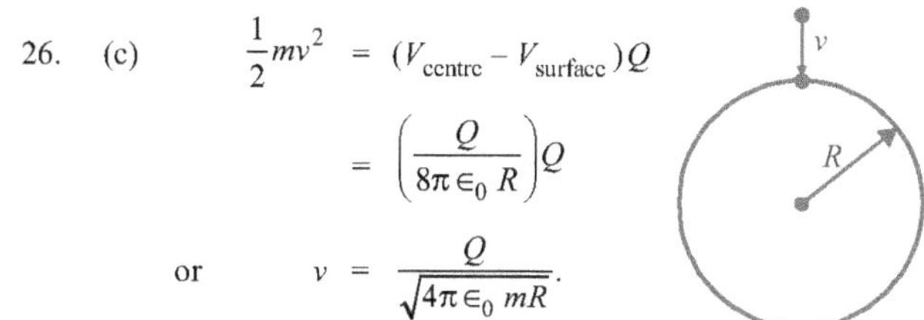


27. (c) The potential at $P$ due to whole disc is

$$V = \frac{\sigma}{2\epsilon_0}\left[\sqrt{R^2+r^2} - r\right].$$

Now potential due to quarter disc,

$$V = \frac{V}{4} = \frac{\sigma}{8\epsilon_0}\left[\sqrt{R^2+r^2} - r\right].$$

28. (c) Inside conducting shell,

$$V_C = V_P$$

or $$\frac{1}{4\pi\epsilon_0}\left[\frac{q}{r} + \left(\frac{q}{R} - \frac{q}{R}\right)\right] = \frac{1}{4\pi\epsilon_0}\left[\frac{q}{r'} + V'\right]$$

∴ $$V' = \frac{1}{4\pi\epsilon_0}\left(\frac{q}{r} - \frac{q}{r'}\right)$$

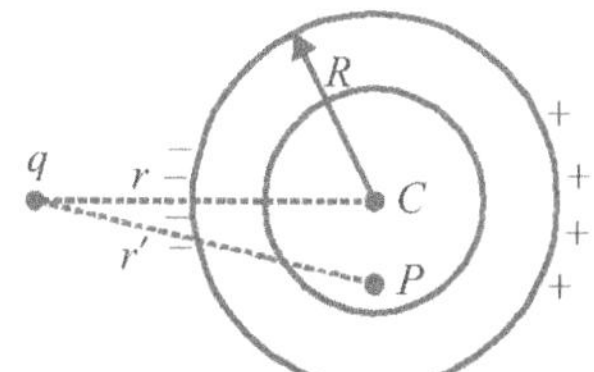


29. (a) Total flux through the cubical surface,

$$\phi = \frac{q_{\text{in}}}{\epsilon_0}$$

$$= \left[\frac{3+2+(-7)}{\epsilon_0}\right]C = -\frac{2C}{\epsilon_0}$$

30. (b) $$W = \Delta K$$

or $$-PE(\cos 90° - \cos 0°) = \frac{1}{2}mv^2 + \frac{1}{2}I\omega^2$$

or $$+PE = \frac{1}{2}mv^2 + \frac{1}{2}\left(\frac{2}{5}mR^2\right)\times\frac{v^2}{R^2}$$

∴ $$v = \sqrt{\frac{10PE}{7m}}.$$

31. (b) $$\vec{P} = (QL)\hat{i}.$$

The angle between $\vec{P}$ and $\vec{E}$;

$$\theta_i = 90°, \text{ and } \theta_4 = 0.$$

Now $$W = \Delta K$$

$$-\text{PE}(\cos 90° - \cos 0°) = \frac{1}{2}I\omega^2$$

or $$+\text{PE} = \frac{1}{2}\left(\frac{ML^2}{2}\right)\omega^2$$

or $$\omega = \sqrt{\frac{12\sqrt{2}Q}{ML}}$$

Angular velocity vector,

$$\vec{\omega} = \omega(\hat{r})$$

$$= \sqrt{\frac{12\sqrt{2}Q}{ML}}\frac{(-\hat{j}+\hat{k})}{\sqrt{2}}$$

$$= \sqrt{\frac{6\sqrt{2}Q}{ML}}(-\hat{j}+\hat{k})$$

32. (b) $$E_x = \frac{V_o - V_A}{x} = \frac{0-(-1)}{1} = 1\text{ V/m}$$

and $$E_y = \frac{V_o - V_B}{y} = \frac{0-1}{1} = -1\text{ V/m}$$

Thus $\vec{E} = E_x\hat{i} + E_y\hat{j} = (\hat{i} - \hat{j})$ V/m.

33. (b) Charge on their outer surfaces are ; $Q_1$, $Q_1 + Q_2$ and $Q_1 + Q_2 + Q_3$ respectively.

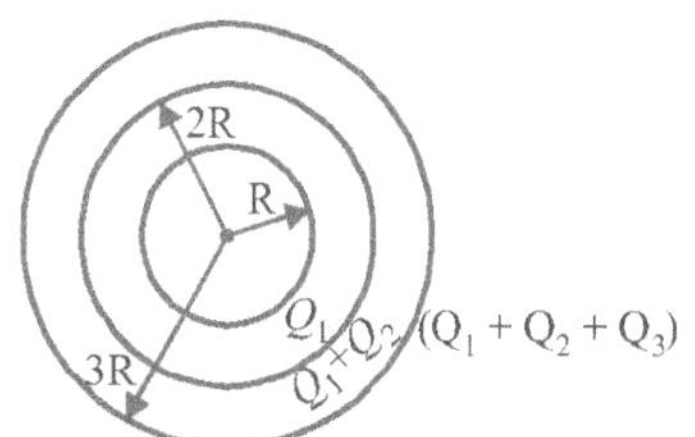


Now $$\frac{Q_1}{4\pi R^2} = \frac{Q_1+Q_2}{4\pi(2R)^2} = \frac{Q_1+Q_2+Q_3}{4\pi(3R)^2}$$

After simplifying, we get

$$Q_1 : Q_2 : Q_3 = 1 : 3 : 5$$

34. (c) $q_1 = \int_0^{R_1} \rho \times 4\pi r^2 dr$

$= 4\pi \int_0^{R_1} \frac{\rho_0}{r} \times r^2 dr$

$= 2\pi\rho_0 R_1^2$

and $q_2 = -\sigma \times 4\pi R_2^2$

Given $q_1 + q_2 = 0$

or $2\pi\rho_0 R_1^2 - \sigma \times 4\pi R_2^2 = 0$

$\therefore \quad \frac{R_2}{R_1} = \sqrt{\frac{\rho_0}{2\sigma}}$.

35. (c) The flux of this charge will pass through such four identical cubes, and so

$\phi_{total} = \frac{q}{\epsilon_0}$.

$\therefore \quad \phi_{each} = \frac{q}{\epsilon_0}$.

36. (c) $E = \frac{1}{4\pi\epsilon_0}\frac{qr}{R^3} = \frac{1}{4\pi\epsilon_0}\frac{\rho \times \frac{4}{3}\pi R^3 r}{R^3}$

$= \frac{\rho r}{3\epsilon_0}$.

37. (d) $e(V_2 - V_1) = \frac{1}{2}mv^2$

On substituting the given values, we get

$v = 2.65 \times 10^6$ m/s

38. (d) $V = \left[\frac{20}{x^2 - 4}\right]$

$E = -\frac{dV}{dx} = +20(x^2-4)^{-2} \times 2x$

$= +\frac{40x}{(x^2-4)^2}$.

At $x = 4$ μm, $E = \frac{40 \times 4}{(4^2-4)^2}$

$= \frac{10}{9}$ V/μm.

39. (a) Using Gauss's law, we have

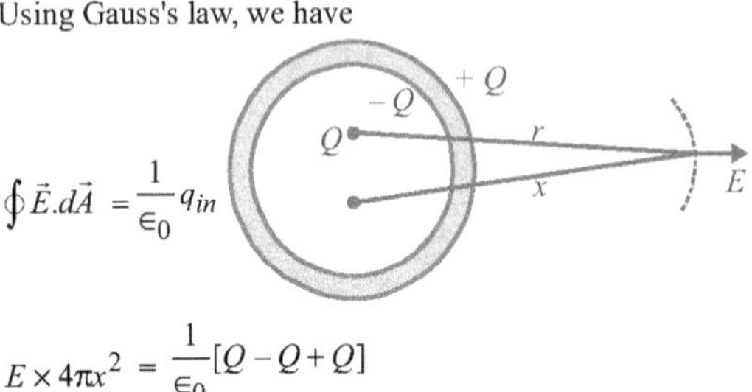

$\oint \vec{E}.d\vec{A} = \frac{1}{\epsilon_0} q_{in}$

$E \times 4\pi x^2 = \frac{1}{\epsilon_0}[Q - Q + Q]$

$\therefore \quad E = \frac{1}{4\pi\epsilon_0}\frac{Q}{x^2}$.

40. (a)

41. (b) Electric field inside cavity,

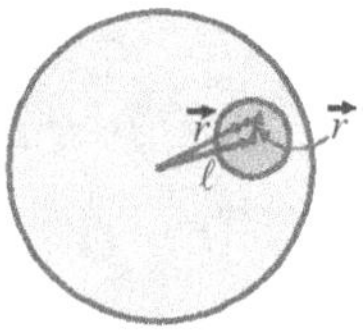

$\vec{E} = \vec{E}_{sphere} = \vec{E}_{cavity}$

$= \frac{\rho\vec{r}}{3\epsilon_0} - \frac{\rho\vec{r}}{3\epsilon_0}$

$= \frac{\rho}{3\epsilon_0}(\vec{r} - \vec{r}\,')$

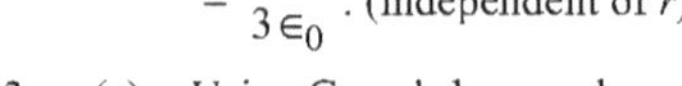

$= \frac{\rho\vec{\ell}}{3\epsilon_0}$. (independent of $r$).

43. (c) Using Gauss's law, we have

$\oint \vec{E}.d\vec{A} = \frac{1}{\epsilon_0}\int(\rho dv) = \frac{1}{\epsilon_0}\int_0^R kr^a \times 4\pi r^2 dr$

or $E \times 4\pi R^2 = \left(\frac{4\pi k}{\epsilon_0}\right)\frac{R^{(a+3)}}{(a+3)}$

$\therefore \quad E_1 = \frac{kR^{(a+1)}}{\epsilon_0 (a+3)}$

For $r = \frac{R}{2}$. $E_2 = \frac{k\left(\frac{R}{2}\right)^{a+1}}{\epsilon_0(a+3)}$

Given, $E_2 = \frac{E_1}{8}$

or $\frac{k\left(\frac{R}{2}\right)^{a+1}}{\epsilon_0(a+3)} = \frac{1}{8}\frac{kR^{(a+1)}}{\epsilon_0(a+3)}$

$\therefore \quad \frac{1}{2^{a+1}} = \frac{1}{8}$

or $a = 2$.

44. (b) $W = \Delta K$

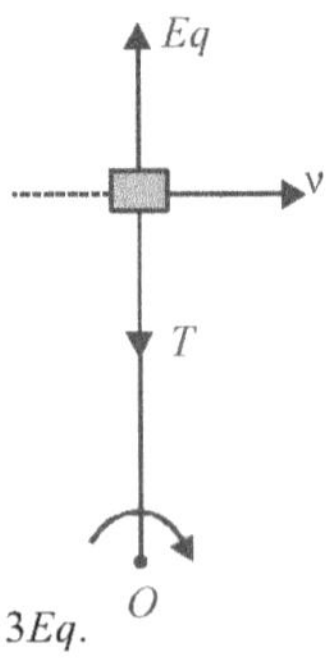

or $Eql = \frac{1}{2}mv^2 - 0$

$\therefore \quad v^2 = \frac{2Eql}{m}$

Non $T - Eq = \frac{mv^2}{l}$

or $T = Eq + \frac{mv^2}{l}$

$= Eq + 2Eq = 3Eq$.

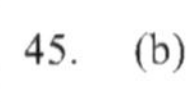

45. (b)

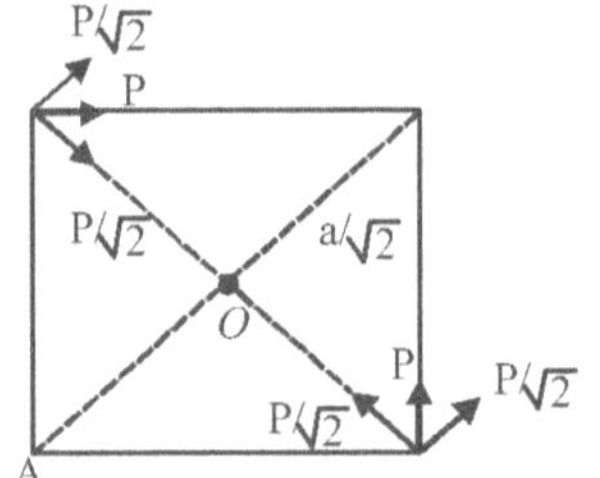

$$E_o = 2\frac{1}{4\pi E_0}\frac{\frac{P}{\sqrt{2}}}{\left(\frac{a}{\sqrt{2}}\right)^3} = \frac{1}{4\pi E_0}\frac{2P}{a^3}$$

and $E_A = \sqrt{2}\frac{1}{4\pi E_0}\frac{P}{a^3}$

$\therefore \frac{E_o}{E_A} = 2\sqrt{2}.$

46. (a) The total flux linked to the shell $\phi = \frac{q}{\epsilon_0}$. The flux through the hemisphere will be $\frac{q}{2\epsilon_0}$.

47. (a) If x the charge transferred between the balls, then force between them

$$F = k\frac{(3q-x)(2q+x)}{r^2}$$

$$= k\frac{(6q^2+qx-x^2)}{r^2}$$

$F$ to be maximum, $\frac{dF}{dx} = 0$

or $\frac{dF}{dx}(6q^2+qx-x^2) = 0$

or $q - 2x =$

$\therefore \quad x = \frac{q}{2}.$

48. (b) $\frac{1}{4\pi E_0}\left[\frac{Q}{a} - \frac{2Q}{1.2a}\right] = \frac{1}{4\pi E_0}\left[\frac{Q-2Q}{r}\right]$

$\therefore \quad r = \frac{3a}{2}.$

49. (c)

ω A e B

$3\frac{l}{4}$

The mechanical force on A,

$$F_A = m\omega^2\left(\frac{3l}{4}\right)$$

$$= \frac{3}{4}m\omega^2 l.$$

If $E$ is the electric field, then

$$Ee = \frac{3}{4}m\omega^2 l$$

or $$E = \frac{3m\omega^2 l}{4e}$$

$$\therefore V_A - V_B = E\frac{l}{2} = \frac{3}{8e}m\omega^2 l.$$

50. (d) .

51. (c)

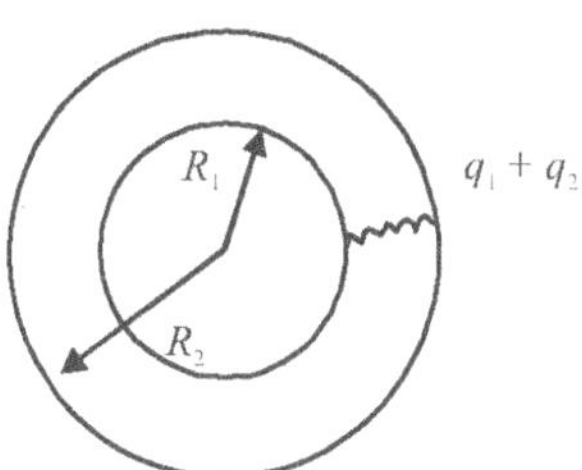


When both the spheres are connects by the wire, the entire charge will flow out on the outer sphere. So the electric field $E_2 = 0$

52. (c) $E = E_1 - E_2 = 2$

10 C 3 C

2 N/C

or $2 = \frac{\frac{q_1}{A}}{2\epsilon_0} - \frac{\frac{q_2}{A}}{2\epsilon_0}$

or $2 = \frac{10}{2A\epsilon_0} - \frac{3}{2A\epsilon_0} \Rightarrow \frac{1}{A\epsilon_0} = \frac{2}{3.5}$

$$F_{21} = E_1 q_2 = \frac{\left(\frac{q_1}{A}\right)}{2\epsilon_0}q_2$$

$$= \frac{10\times 3}{2AE_0} = \frac{10\times 3}{2}\times\frac{2}{3.5} = \frac{60}{7}N.$$

53. (b) Change of the whole sphere, $Q = \left(\frac{4}{3}\pi R^3\right)\rho$

Change of the cavity, $q = \frac{4}{3}\pi\left(\frac{R}{2}\right)^2\rho = \frac{Q}{8}$

Now,

$$V_o = \left[(V_{\text{whole sphere}})_o - (V_{\text{cavity}})_o\right]$$

$$= \frac{3}{8\pi\varepsilon_0}\frac{Q}{R} - \frac{1}{4\pi\varepsilon_0}\frac{\left(\frac{Q}{8}\right)}{\frac{R}{2}}$$

$$= \frac{5}{16\pi\varepsilon_0}\frac{Q}{R}$$

$$= \frac{5}{16\pi\varepsilon_0 R}\times\left(\frac{4}{3}\pi R^3\rho\right)$$

$$= \frac{5}{12}\frac{R^2\rho}{\varepsilon_0}.$$

54. (c)

$F_A = (F' + F\cos\theta)(-\hat{i}) - F\sin\theta\,\hat{j}$

$F_B = F\sin\theta\,\hat{i} + (F' + F\cos\theta)\,\hat{j}$

If $F_A = a\hat{i} + b\hat{j}$, then $F_B = -b\hat{i} + a\hat{j}$

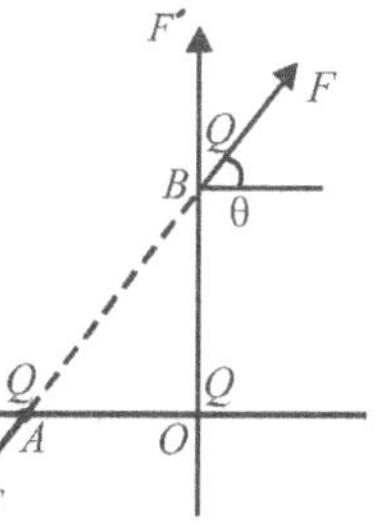

55. (b) $v_A \sin\alpha = v_A \sin\beta$

or $\frac{v_A}{v_B} = \frac{\sin\beta}{\sin\alpha}$

$\therefore \frac{K_A}{K_B} = \frac{\frac{1}{2}mv_A^2}{\frac{1}{2}mv_B^2} = \frac{v_A^2}{v_B^2}$

$= \frac{\sin^2\beta}{\sin^2\alpha}$

56. (c) Flux through face 1 is zero and through each of the two faces 2 and 3 is $\frac{q}{24\varepsilon_0}$. So total flux through shaded surface, $\phi = 0 + 2 \times \frac{q}{24\varepsilon_0} = \frac{q}{12\varepsilon_0}$

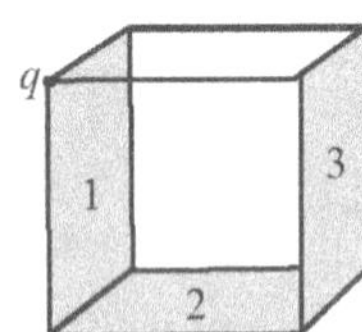


57. (c) Previously, if $V_1$ and $V_2$ are the potentials of inner and outer shells due to own charge respectively, then

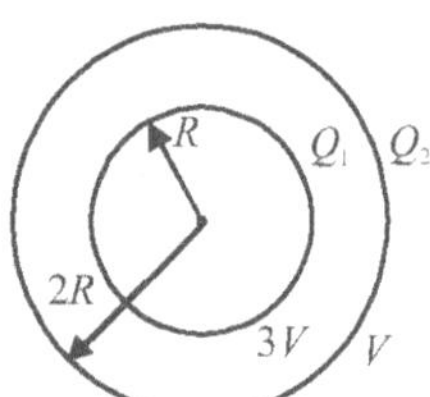


$V_1 + V_2 = 3V$

$\therefore V_1 + V = 3V$ or $V_1 = 2V$

When outer shell is earthed, its potential becomes zero, and so potential of inner becomes

$V_1' = 2V + 0 = 2V$

58. (b) $dq = (\lambda_0 \sin\theta)\, a d\theta$

$dp = dq \times 2a$

$= 2a\lambda_0 \sin\theta d\theta$

or $d\vec{p} = 2a\lambda_0 \sin\theta d\theta\, [-\cos\theta\, \hat{i} - \sin\theta\, \hat{j}\,]$

Now $\vec{\tau} = \int_0^{\pi} d\vec{p} \times \vec{E}$

$= 2\pi\lambda_0 \int_0^{\pi}\left(-\cos\theta\sin\theta\hat{i} - \sin^2\theta\hat{j}\right) \times \left(E_0\hat{j} + E_0\hat{j}\right)$

$= E_0 \pi a^2 \lambda_0$

59. (a) The electrostatic pressure at a point on the surface of a uniformly charged sphere $= \frac{\sigma^2}{2\epsilon_0}$

$\therefore$ The force on a hemispherical shell $= \frac{\sigma^2}{2\epsilon_0} \times \pi R^2$

60. (d) **When the electric field is on**

Force due to electric field = weight

$qE = mg$

$qE = \frac{4}{3}\pi R^3 \rho g$

$\therefore q = \frac{4\pi R^3 \rho g}{3E}$ ...(i)

**When the electric field is switched off**

Weight = viscous drag force

$mg = 6\pi\eta R v_t$

$\frac{4}{3}\pi R^3 \rho g = 6\pi\eta R v_t$

$\therefore R = \sqrt{\frac{9\eta v_t}{2\rho g}}$ ...(ii)

From (i) & (ii), $q = \frac{4}{3}\pi\left[\frac{9\eta v_t}{2\rho g}\right]^{\frac{3}{2}} \times \frac{\rho g}{E}$

$= \frac{4}{3} \times \pi\left[\frac{9 \times 1.8 \times 10^{-5} \times 2 \times 10^{-3}}{2 \times 900 \times 9.8}\right]^{\frac{3}{2}} \times \frac{900 \times 9.8 \times 7}{81\pi \times 10^5}$

$= 7.8 \times 10^{-19}$ C

61. (b)

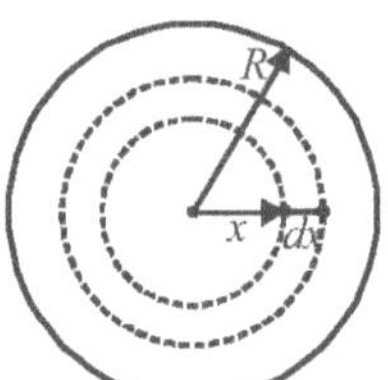


Let us consider a spherical shell of thickness $dx$ and radius $x$.

The volume of this spherical shell $= 4\pi x^2 dx$. The charge enclosed within shell

$= \left[\frac{Qx}{\pi R^4}\right][4\pi x^2 dx] = \frac{4Q}{R^4}x^3 dx$

The charge enclosed in a sphere of radius $r_1$ is

$= \frac{4Q}{R^4}\int_0^{r_1} x^3 dx = \frac{4Q}{R^4}\left[\frac{x^4}{4}\right]_0^{r_1} = \frac{Q}{R^4}r_1^4$

$\therefore$ The electric field at point $p$ inside the sphere at a distance $r_1$ from the centre of the sphere is

$E = \frac{1}{4\pi\epsilon_0}\frac{\left[\frac{Q}{R^4}r_1^4\right]}{r_1^2}$

$= \frac{1}{4\pi\epsilon_0}\frac{Q}{R^4}r_1^2$

62. (c) Let us consider a spherical shell of radius $x$ and thickness $dx$. Charge on this shell

$dq = \rho.4\pi x^2 dx = \rho_0\left(\frac{5}{4} - \frac{x}{R}\right).4\pi x^2 dx$

$\therefore$ Total charge in the spherical region from centre to $r$ ($r < R$) is

$$q = \int dq = 4\pi\rho_0 \int_0^r \left(\frac{5}{4} - \frac{x}{R}\right) x^2 dx$$

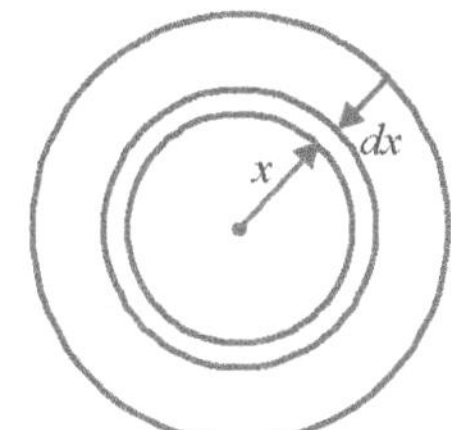


$$= 4\pi\rho_0 \left[\frac{5}{4}.\frac{r^3}{3} - \frac{1}{R}.\frac{r^4}{4}\right] = \pi\rho_0 r^3 \left(\frac{5}{3} - \frac{r}{R}\right)$$

$\therefore$ Electric field at $r$, $E = \frac{1}{4\pi \in_0}.\frac{q}{r^2}$

$$= \frac{1}{4\pi \in_0}.\frac{\pi\rho_0 r^3}{r^2}\left(\frac{5}{3} - \frac{r}{R}\right) = \frac{\rho_0 r}{4 \in_0}\left(\frac{5}{3} - \frac{r}{R}\right)$$

## Solutions EXERCISE 1.2

1. (a, b) Potential energy $U = \frac{1}{4\pi \in_0}\frac{q_1 q_2}{r}$. If charges are of same sign, then potential energy will decrease with increase in $r$, and if charges are of opposite sign, then potential energy will increase with increase in $r$.
2. (b, d)
3. (a, d) The electric field of point charge is non-uniform and so net force on the dipole for any orientation is not zero. The torque on the dipole may be zero, if it is placed parallel to line of field.
4. (a, b, c, d)
   (a, b) $E = 0$ and $V = 0$, due to a point charge at infinity.
   (c) At the equator of the dipole $E \neq 0$, but $V = 0$.
   (d) Inside conductor, $E = 0$, $V \neq 0$.
5. (b, d) $E_y = \frac{100 - 50}{2} = 25 \text{ V/m}$

   As $E = \sqrt{E_x^2 + E_y^2 + E_z^2}$, so $E$ may be greater than 25 V/m.
6. (b, c) $\phi = EA\cos\theta = \frac{q_{in}}{\in_0}$, and so electric field may be either zero at each point of the surface or $\theta = 90°$. Also if $q_{in} = 0$, $\phi$ must be zero.
7. (a, c) The net charge of the dipole is $q_{in} = q - q = 0$, and so $\phi = \frac{q_{in}}{\in_0} = 0$.

   The electric field of dipole is not zero anywhere of its vicinity.
8. (a, b, c, d)
   Given $V$–$r$ graph is of charged conducting sphere, and so all the options are possible.
9. (a, d) The electric field due to a system of equal and opposite charge will not be zero in vicinity of this system, but potential is zero at the equatorial line of these charges.
10. (c, d) Electric field at each point of the cavity is normal to its surface and potential is same on each point of it.
11. (a, c) $F = -Eq$

$$= -\frac{1}{4\pi \in_0}\frac{Qzq}{(R^2 + z^2)^{3/2}}.$$

For $z << R$, $R^2 + z^2 \simeq R^2$, and so

$F \propto (-z)$. It represents SHM.

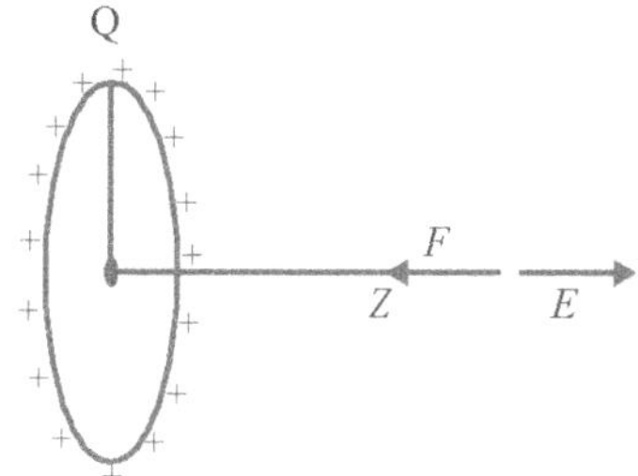


12. (a, c) For, $r \leq R$; $E = \frac{1}{4\pi \in_0}\frac{qr}{R^3}$ ; so $E \propto r$.

    For, $r > R$; $E = \frac{1}{4\pi\in_0}\frac{q}{r^2}$; and so $E \propto \frac{1}{r^2}$.
13. (b, d) The electric field at any point on the $y$-axis in along $x$-axis. The dipole moment, $P = q \times 2d$.

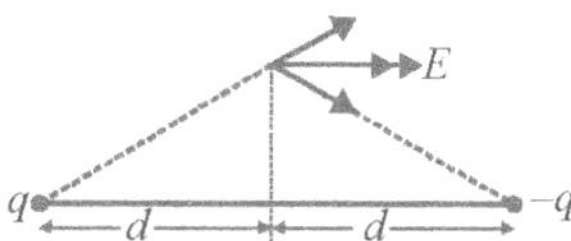


14. (a, c) $V = 0 = \frac{1}{4\pi \in_0}\left[\frac{Q}{x + x'} - \frac{Q/4}{x'}\right]$

    or $x' = x/3$.

    Also $E = 0 = \frac{1}{4\pi\in_0}\left[\frac{Q}{(x + x')^2} - \frac{Q/4}{x'^2}\right]$

    or $x' = x$

    Q x –Q/4 x'
15. (b, d) $V = \frac{1}{4\pi\in_0}\left[\frac{q}{R} - \frac{q}{R}\right] = 0$

    and $E = 2 \times \frac{1}{4\pi\in_0}\frac{q}{R^2}\left(\frac{\sin \pi/2}{\pi/2}\right) = \frac{q}{\pi^2 \in_0 R^2}$.

16. (b, d) The electric field at any point inside the shell, $E = \frac{1}{4\pi\epsilon_0}\frac{q}{R^2}$.

The electric field at the outer surface

$$E = \frac{1}{4\pi\epsilon_0}\frac{q}{(2R)^2}.$$

17. (a, c)
18. (a, c, d)
(a) $S_1$ and $S_2$ can't intersect because their potentials are not same.
(c) $|\vec{E}| = \left|\frac{\Delta V}{\Delta r}\right|$
(d) Field lines are always perpendicular to equipotential surface.
19. (a, b, c) Flux through the close surface,

$$\phi = \frac{q_{in}}{\epsilon_0} = \frac{Q_1}{\epsilon_0}$$

or $EA\cos\theta = \frac{Q_1}{\epsilon_0}$.

Here $E$ is due to both the charges. But flux is only due to $Q_1$.

20. (a, b) The electric field, $E = 0$, and $V = \frac{1}{4\pi\epsilon_0}\frac{Q}{R}$.
21. (b, d) Electric field at the origin, $E = 0$.
The direction of electric field on the any point on $z$-axis is along $z$-axis.

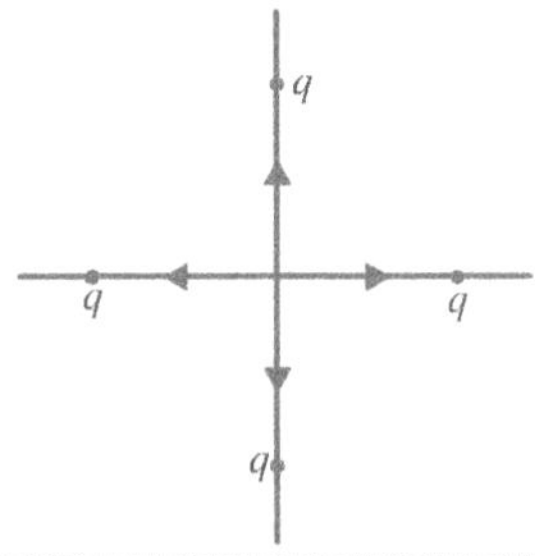


22. (a,d) The electric field lines are originating from $Q_1$ and terminating on $Q_2$. Therefore $Q_1$ is positive and $Q_2$ is negative.
As the number of lines associated with $Q_1$ is greater than that associated with $Q_2$, therefore $|Q_1| > |Q_2|$.
Option (a) is correct.
At a finite distance on the left of $Q_1$, the electric field intensity cannot be zero because the electric field created by $Q_1$ will be greater than $Q_2$. This is because the magnitude of $Q_1$ is greater and the distance smaller $\left[E \propto \frac{Q}{r^2}\right]$
At a finite distance to the right of $Q_2$, the electric field is zero. Here, the electric field created by $Q_2$ at a particular point will cancel out the electric field created by $Q_1$.
23. (a, b, c, d) $Q = Q_A + Q_B$

Also $k\frac{Q_A}{R_A} = k\frac{Q_B}{R_B}$

$\therefore$ $Q_A = \frac{QR_A}{R_A + R_B}$,

and $Q_B = \frac{QR_B}{R_A + R_B}$.

As $R_A > R_B$, and so $Q_A > Q_B$. The electric field inside shell, $E = 0$.

Now $\frac{\sigma_A}{\sigma_B} = \frac{Q_A/4\pi R_A^2}{Q_B/4\pi R_B^2} = \frac{R_B}{R_A}$.

As $E_A = \frac{1}{4\pi\epsilon_0}\frac{Q_A}{R_A^2}$ and $E_B = \frac{1}{4\pi\epsilon_0}\frac{Q_B}{R_B^2}$

$\therefore$ $\frac{E_A}{E_B} = \frac{Q_A}{Q_B}\times\frac{R_B^2}{R_A^2} = \frac{R_B}{R_A}$.

As, $R_A > R_B$, $\therefore E_B > E_A$.

## Solutions EXERCISE-1.3

1. (a) Because of repulsion, the free electrons will more to the outer surface.
2. (c) Only electrons corresponding to charge given will move to the outer surface of the conductor.
3. (c) Gravitational force and electric force are same type of quantities while gravitational field and electric field are different quantities.
4. (b) Both the statements are independently correct.
5. (d) The electric field on the surface of the conductor will be

$E = \frac{1}{4\pi\epsilon_0}\frac{q}{R^2}$, where $R$ be the radius of the conductor. The force on the charge outside the conductor will be $EQ$.

6. (d) Two field lines never intersect.
7. (a) Both the particles have same amount of charge and so force on each of them $F = Ee$. As mass of proton is greater than mass of electron, and so its acceleration will be smaller.
8. (a) There produced an electric field due to the induced charge and so it attract the point charge $q$.
9. (c) The electric field will increase if positive charge is brought in an electric field.
10. (a) Statement-2 correctly explains the statement-1.
11. (a) Negative charge moves from low potential to higher potential.
12. (b) Both the statements are independently correct.
13. (d) The electric field at the centre of the square,

$$E = 2\sqrt{2}\left(\frac{1}{4\pi\epsilon_0}\right)\frac{q}{a^2/2}.$$

And electric potential at the centre

$$V = \frac{1}{4\pi\epsilon_0}\left[\frac{q+q-q-q}{a/\sqrt{2}}\right] = 0.$$

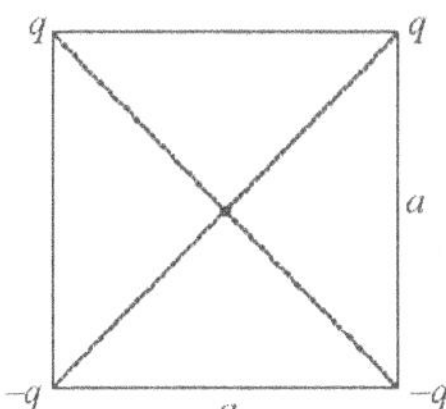


14. (d) The initial and final charge on the system is zero.
15. (b) Both the statements are independently correct.
16. (a) The electrostatic shielding is possible by metallic conductor.
17. (a) The net charge on the earth remains zero. As $Q \to 0$, and so $V = 0$.
18. (d) $V_1 = k\frac{Q}{R}$ and $V_2 = k\frac{(2Q)}{2R}$. Both the spheres have equal potential and so no charge will flow in between them.
19. (a) When charge of sphere moves to the shell, the potential of both of them become equal.
20. (d) $\oint \vec{E}.\vec{A} = EA\cos\theta$, this value can be zero, if either E is zero or $\theta = 90°$. But it must show that net charge inside close surface is zero.
21. (d) The electric field at the point will be the vector sum of $E_1$ and $E_2$, and so electric field at the point $(E_1 - E_2) < E < (E_1 + E_2)$. While electric potential is the scalar sum, so it will be $V = V_1 + V_2$.
22. (c) Gauss's law is valid for the case but mathematically it can not be evaluated.
23. (a) The electric field due to point charge and induced charge at the centre of the cube will be zero, and so $\vec{E}_1 + \vec{E}_2 = 0$. So $E_2 = E_1$. Also $E_1 = \frac{1}{4\pi\epsilon_0}\frac{q}{d^2}$.
24. (a) Statement-2, correctly explains the statement-1.

## Solutions EXERCISE-1.4

**Passage for Q. 1 to Q. 3**

1. (b)

$$q = \int_0^a \rho \times 2\pi r dr\ell$$

$$= 2\pi\ell \int_0^a \rho_0 r^3 \times r dr$$

$$= \frac{2\pi\ell\rho_0}{5}a^5.$$

2. (a)

$$\oint \vec{E}.d\vec{A} = \frac{1}{\epsilon_0}q_{in}$$

$$\text{or } E \times 2\pi r\ell = \frac{2\pi\ell}{5}\rho_0 r^5$$

$$\therefore \quad E = \frac{\rho_0 r^4}{5\epsilon_0}.$$

3. (c) For $r > a$ :

$$E \times 2\pi r\ell = \frac{2\pi\ell\rho_0 a^5}{5}$$

$$\text{or} \quad E = \frac{\rho_0 a^5}{5\epsilon_0 r}.$$

**Passage for Q. 4 to Q. 6**

4. (a) When the point of observation is on the surface of sphere then the whole charge inside the sphere (when distributed symmetrically about the centre) behaves as a point charge on the centre. Therefore until the charge distribution is symmetrical about the centre it does not matter what is the ratio $a/R$. The electric field remains constant and is equal to

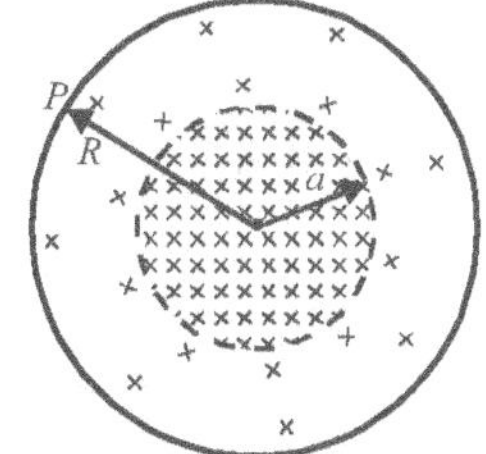


$$E = \frac{1}{4\pi\epsilon_0}.\frac{Ze}{R}$$

5. (b) For $a = 0$, the graph is as shown. The equation for the graph line is

$$\rho = d - \frac{r}{R}dr$$

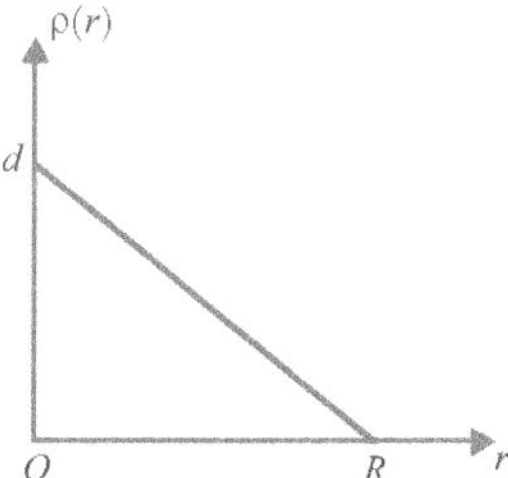


The charge in the dotted element shown in Fig is

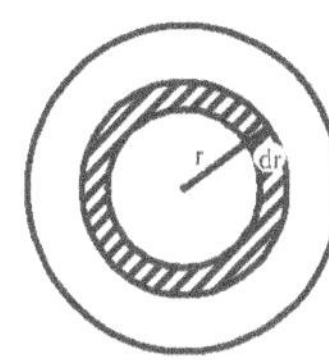


$$dq = \rho \times 4\pi r^2 dr$$

$$\therefore \quad dq = \left(d - \frac{d}{R}r\right)4\pi r^2 dr$$

$$\Rightarrow \quad Ze = \int_0^R 4\pi d r^2 dr - \int_0^R \frac{4\pi d}{R}r^3 dr$$

$$Ze = 4\pi d\frac{R^3}{3} - \frac{4\pi d}{R}\frac{R^4}{4}$$

$$\therefore \quad \frac{Ze.}{4\pi dR^3} = \frac{1}{3} - \frac{1}{4} = \frac{1}{12} \qquad \therefore d = \frac{3Ze}{\pi R^3}$$

6. (c) If the volume charge density is constant then $E \propto r$.

**Passage for Q. 7 to Q. 9**

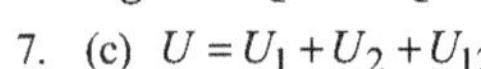

7. (c) $U = U_1 + U_2 + U_{12}$

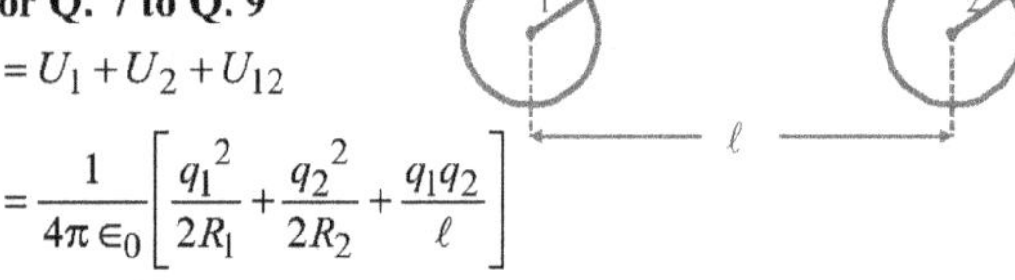


$$= \frac{1}{4\pi\epsilon_0}\left[\frac{q_1^2}{2R_1} + \frac{q_2^2}{2R_2} + \frac{q_1 q_2}{\ell}\right]$$

8. (c) For minimum potential energy

$$V_1 = V_2$$

or $$\frac{q_1}{R_1} = \frac{q_2}{R_2}$$

Also $q_1 + q_2 = Q$

After solving, we get

$$q_1 = \frac{QR_1}{R_1 + R_2} \text{ and } q_2 = \frac{QR_2}{R_1 + R_2}.$$

9. (d)

**Passage for Q. 10 to Q. 12**

**10. (c) 11. (a) 12. (b)**

Potential on $x$-axis is just like on axis of ring

$$V = \frac{1}{4\pi\varepsilon_0}\frac{Q}{(R^2 + x^2)^{1/2}}$$

Since in pipe ball can move only along $x$-axis field along x-axis moves the ball

$$E_x = -dV/dx = \frac{Q}{4\pi\varepsilon_0}\frac{2x}{(R^2 + x^2)^{3/2}}$$

The potential where acceleration is maximum is a point where field is maximum means $\frac{dE_x}{dx} = 0$

$$\Rightarrow x = \frac{R}{\sqrt{2}}$$

Maximum field $E = \frac{Q}{4\pi\varepsilon_0}\frac{\sqrt{2}}{3\sqrt{3}R^2}$

Maximum acceleration $= \frac{qE}{m}$

Velocity at $x = R/\sqrt{2}$ is obtained from conservation of energy (sum of electrostatic potential energy and kinetic energy remains constant)

$$\frac{Qq}{4\pi\varepsilon_0 R} = \frac{1}{4\pi\varepsilon_0}\frac{\sqrt{2}}{\sqrt{3}R} + \frac{1}{2}mv^2$$

component of electric field normal to pipe is along z-axis thus to oppose it normal reaction is along -z-axis.

13. See theory of the chapter.

14. A-r ; B- p ; C-s ; D -t.

If $q_A$ and $q_C$ are the charge on $A$ and $C$ respectively, then

$q_A + q_C = 0$, or $q_A = -q_C$

Also $V_A = V_C$

or $$\frac{1}{4\pi\epsilon_0}\left[\frac{q_A}{R} + \frac{Q}{2R} + \frac{q_C}{4R}\right] = \frac{1}{4\pi\epsilon_0}\left[\frac{q_A}{4R} + \frac{Q}{4R} + \frac{q_C}{4R}\right]$$

or $q_A = -\frac{Q}{3}$ and $q_C = \frac{Q}{3}$

Also $$V_A = \frac{1}{4\pi\epsilon_0}\left(\frac{Q}{4R}\right)$$

and $$V_c = \frac{1}{4\pi\epsilon_0}\frac{5Q}{12}$$

15. A – r : $E = \frac{1}{4\pi\epsilon_0}\frac{Q}{z^2} = \frac{KQ}{4}$

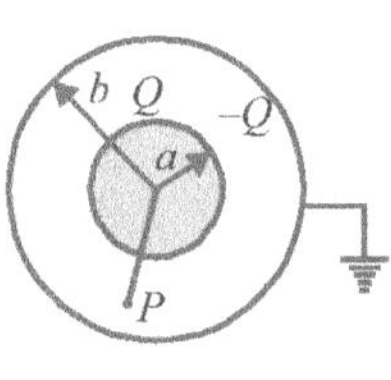


B – r : $V = \frac{1}{4\pi\epsilon_0}\left[\frac{Q}{2} - \frac{Q}{3}\right]$

$$= \frac{1}{4\pi\epsilon_0}\frac{Q}{6} = \frac{KQ}{6}.$$

C – P : $V = \frac{Q}{4\pi\epsilon_0} - 0 = \frac{Q}{4\pi\epsilon_0} = kQ$

D – q : $E \times 2\pi r = \frac{1}{\epsilon_0}(q_{in})$

$$= 0$$

$\therefore \quad E = 0$

## Solutions EXERCISE-1.5

1. The potential

$$V = \frac{1}{4\pi\epsilon_0}\left[\frac{q}{r} + \frac{q}{r}\right]$$

$$= 2\times9\times10^9 \times \frac{\left[\frac{5}{(3\times10^9)}\right]}{0.1}$$

$$= 300 \text{ V}$$ **Ans.**

$$V' = \frac{V}{k} = \frac{300}{2} = 150 \text{ V}.$$

2. (a) We can write

$$V_B - V_A = -\int_A^B \vec{E}\cdot d\vec{r}$$

$$= -\int_{(0,0)}^{(4,2)} 20\hat{i}\cdot(dx\hat{i} + dy\hat{j})$$

$$= -20|x|_0^4$$

$$= -80 \text{ V}$$ **Ans.**

Do the other parts similarly.

3. The electric flux $\phi$ is given by

$$\phi = \vec{E}\cdot\vec{A}$$

$$= \left(\frac{3}{5}E_0\hat{i} + \frac{4}{5}E_0\hat{j}\right)\cdot(0.2\hat{i})$$

$$= \frac{3}{5}\times0.2\times E_0$$

$$= \frac{3}{5}\times0.2\times2\times10^3 = 240 \text{ N}-\text{m}^2/\text{C}.$$

4. The electric field between the cylinders,

$$E = \frac{\lambda}{2\pi\epsilon_0 r},$$

which is only due to inner cylinder. For the motion of the positron, we have

$$Eq = \frac{mv^2}{r}$$

or $$mv^2 = Eqr$$

$$\therefore \quad K = \frac{1}{2}mv^2 = \frac{Eqr}{2} = \frac{\lambda qr}{4\pi\epsilon_0 r} = \frac{\lambda q}{4\pi\epsilon_0}$$

After substituting the values, we can get

$$K = 270 \text{ eV.}$$ **Ans.**

5. The *FBD* of the device shown in figure. At lowest position of the ball,

$$(T_A + F_e) - mg = \frac{mv_A^2}{\ell} \quad ...(i)$$

At highest position of the ball

$$(T_B + mg) + F_e = \frac{mv_B^2}{\ell}$$

To just complete the circle, $T_B = 0$

$$\therefore \quad mg - F_e = \frac{mv_B^2}{\ell} \quad ...(ii)$$

where $$F_e = \frac{1}{4\pi\epsilon_0}\frac{q^2}{l^2}$$

Also $$\frac{1}{2}mv_A^2 = \frac{1}{2}mv_B^2 + mg\,(2\ell) \quad ...(iii)$$

After solving above equations and substituting the values, we get

$$v_A = 7.62 \text{ m/s}$$ **Ans.**

6. The given charge can be completely covered by six identical plates, so total flux

$$\phi = \frac{q}{\epsilon_0}$$

The flux through each plate $= \dfrac{q}{6\epsilon_0}$. **Ans.**

7. The electric force on the dust particle

$$F_e = qE,$$

and viscous force, $F_v = 6\pi\eta rv$.

For constant velocity,

$$F_e - F_v = 0$$

or $$qE = 6\pi\eta rv$$

$$\therefore \quad q = \frac{6\pi\eta rv}{E}$$

$$= \frac{6\pi \times 1.6\times10^{-5} \times 5\times10^{-17} \times 0.02}{6.28\times10^{5}}$$

$$= 0.48\times10^{-17} \text{ C}$$

$$= 48\times10^{-19} \text{ C}$$

If $n$ be the number of electrons on the dust particle, then

$$n = \frac{q}{e} = \frac{48\times10^{-19}}{1.6\times10^{-19}} = 30$$ **Ans.**

8. If $F$ is the force between two charges at the corner of the side then

$$F = \frac{1}{4\pi\epsilon_0}\frac{q^2}{a^2}$$

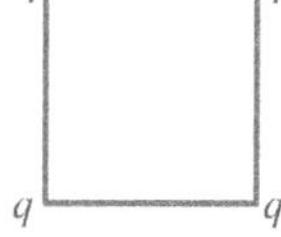


For equilibrium of the film,

$$F + \frac{F}{2}\cos 45° = T \times a$$

After solving above equation

$$a = k\left(\frac{q^2}{T}\right)^{1/3}$$

## Solutions EXERCISE-1.6

1. Let charge $q$ be placed at a distance $x$ from smaller charge. Then For the equilibrium of this charge we have

$$\frac{(4e)q}{(\ell - x)^2} = \frac{qe}{x^2}$$

$$\therefore \quad x = \frac{\ell}{3}.$$ **Ans.**

2. For the equilibrium of charge $q$, we have $x = \dfrac{a}{3}$, and for the equilibrium of charge $e$, we have

$$\frac{(4e)e}{a^2} + \frac{qe}{(a/3)^2} = 0$$

$$\therefore \quad q = -\frac{4e}{9}.$$ **Ans.**

3. For the equilibrium of the charge $q$

$$\frac{eq}{a^2} = \frac{(2e)q}{(a+\ell)^2}$$

$$\therefore \quad a = \frac{\ell}{(\sqrt{2}-1)} = \ell(\sqrt{2}+1)$$ **Ans.**

4. For small $\theta$, we have

$$\tan\theta = \sin\theta$$

$$= \frac{a}{2L}$$

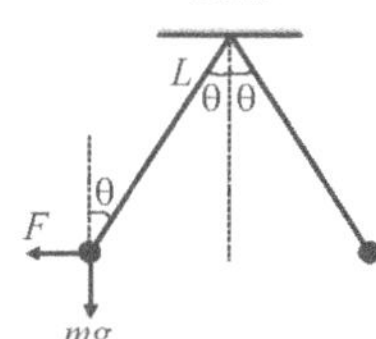


For the equilibrium of either ball, we can write,

$$\frac{e^2}{a^2} = mg\tan\theta = mg\frac{a}{2L} \quad \ldots (i)$$

On contact the charge e still remaining on one of the balls will be equally distributed between both balls and condition for the new equilibrium of the balls will be

$$\frac{e^2}{4b^2} = mg\tan\theta' = mg\frac{b}{2L} \quad \ldots (ii)$$

Hence from (i) and (ii), we get

$$b = \frac{a}{\sqrt[3]{4}}.$$ **Ans.**

5. If $\sigma$ is the charge density on each of the sphere, then

$$Q = q_1 + q_2 = (4\pi r^2 + 4\pi R^2)\sigma$$

The work needed to transfer one positive charge to the common centre of the system is equal to the potential $V$ at the centre of the system.

$$\therefore \quad V = \frac{1}{4\pi\epsilon_0}\left[\frac{q_1}{r} + \frac{q_2}{R}\right]$$

After solving above equations, we get

$$q_1 = \frac{r^2V}{R+r}, \quad q_2 = \frac{R^2V}{R+r}$$

and $$Q = \left[\frac{r^2 + R^2}{r+R}\right]V.$$ **Ans.**

6. The number of molecules in 100 g of water

$$= \left[6.02\times10^{23}\times\frac{100}{18}\right]$$

Each molecule of water has 10 electrons, so total charge

$$q = 6.02\times10^{23}\times\frac{100}{18}\times10\times1.6\times10^{-19}$$

$$= 5.35\times10^{6}\text{C}$$

The force, $$F = \frac{1}{4\pi\epsilon_0}\cdot\frac{q^2}{r^2}$$

$$= 9\times10^9\times\frac{(5.35\times10^6)^2}{0.1^2}$$

$$= 2.56\times10^{25}\text{ N}$$ **Ans.**

7. $$\sin\theta = \frac{1}{20}$$

The force between the balls

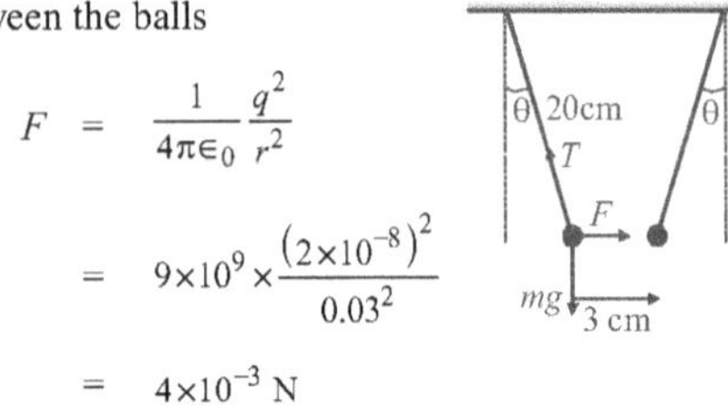


$$F = \frac{1}{4\pi\epsilon_0}\frac{q^2}{r^2}$$

$$= 9\times10^9\times\frac{(2\times10^{-8})^2}{0.03^2}$$

$$= 4\times10^{-3}\text{ N}$$

For the equilibrium of the ball,

$$T\sin\theta = F$$

$$\therefore \quad T = \frac{F}{\sin\theta} = \frac{4\times10^{-3}}{\frac{1}{20}} = 0.08\text{ N}$$ **Ans.**

and $$T\cos\theta = mg$$

$$\therefore \quad m = \frac{0.08\cos\theta}{9.8} = 8.2\text{ g.}$$ **Ans.**

8. As the charge has symmetric distribution about the centre of the hexagon, so net electric field at that point must be zero.

9. The charge on the element

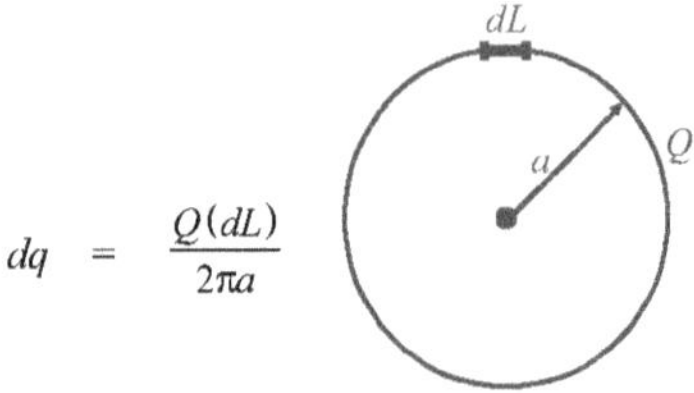


$$dq = \frac{Q(dL)}{2\pi a}$$

The electric field due to the charge of the element at the centre,

$$E_1 = \frac{1}{4\pi\epsilon_0}\frac{dq}{a^2} = \frac{1}{4\pi\epsilon_0}\left[\frac{QdL}{2\pi a^3}\right]$$

The electric field at the centre of the circular loop, $\vec{E} = 0$. If $E_2$ be the electric field of the remaining wire loop, then

$$\vec{E} = \vec{E}_1 + \vec{E}_2 = 0$$

$$\therefore \quad \vec{E}_2 = -\vec{E}_1$$

or $$E_2 = E_1$$

$$= \frac{Q\,dL}{8\pi^2\epsilon_0 a^3}.$$ **Ans.**

10. Using Gauss's law, we have

$$\oint \vec{E}\cdot d\vec{A} = \frac{q_{in}}{\epsilon_0}$$

$$2EA = \frac{2Ax\rho}{\epsilon_0}$$

$$\therefore \quad E = \frac{\rho x}{\epsilon_0}.$$

11. (a) The force between the charges,

$$F = \frac{1}{4\pi\epsilon_0}\frac{q_1q_2}{[(r-t)+\sqrt{kt}]^2}$$

(b) The force in air

$$F_{air} = \frac{1}{4\pi\epsilon_0}\cdot\frac{q_1q_2}{r^2} \quad \text{...(i)}$$

and force in the presence of dielectric

$$F_{med} = \frac{1}{4\pi\epsilon_0}\cdot\frac{q_1q_2}{\left[\left(r-\frac{r}{2}\right)+\sqrt{k}\frac{r}{2}\right]^2} \quad \text{...(ii)}$$

Given, $$\frac{F_{air}}{F_{med}} = \frac{9}{4}$$

$$\therefore \quad k = 4$$ **Ans.**

12. (a) Take an element of angular width $d\phi$ at $\phi$. The charge

$$dq = \lambda(Rd\phi) = \lambda_0\cos\phi Rd\phi$$

The electric field due to this element at the centre of the ring

$$dE = \frac{1}{4\pi\epsilon_0}\frac{dq}{R}.$$

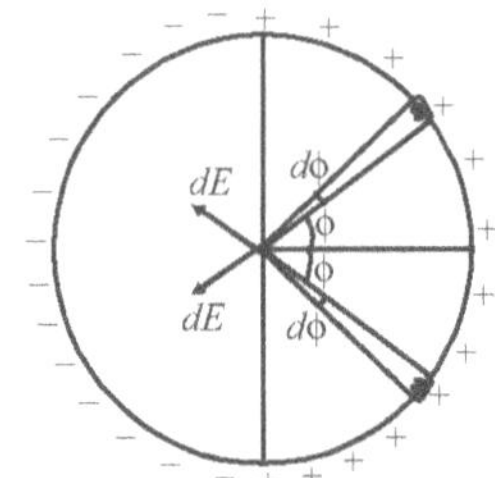


The $x$ components of this field get added while $y$ components cancel each other.

Thus the magnitude of the net electric field

$$E = 4\int_0^{\pi/2} dE\cos\phi$$

$$= 4\left(\frac{1}{4\pi\epsilon_0}\right)\int_0^{\pi/2}\left(\frac{\lambda_0\cos\phi\,Rd\phi}{R^2}\right)\cos\phi$$

$$= \frac{4\lambda_0}{4\pi\epsilon_0 R}\int_0^{\pi/2}\cos^2\phi\,d\phi$$

$$= \frac{\lambda_0}{4\epsilon_0 R}.$$ **Ans.**

(b) The electric field due to charge $dq$, at $P$

$$dE = \frac{1}{4\pi\epsilon_0}\frac{\lambda Rd\phi}{(R^2+r^2)}$$

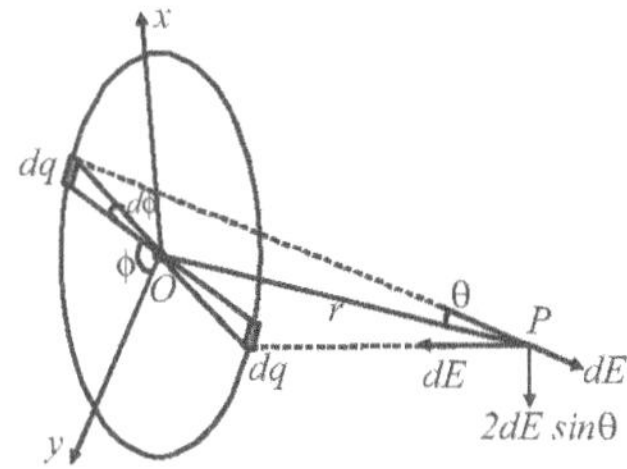


The resultant of two diametrically opposite point is $2dE\cos\phi\sin\theta$

So resultant field $= 2\times2\int_{0}^{\pi/2} dE\cos\phi\sin\theta$

After simplifying, we get

$$E_1 = \frac{\lambda_0 R^2}{4\epsilon_0\left(R^2+r^2\right)^{3/2}} \qquad \textbf{Ans.}$$

13. The position vector of $P$

$$\vec{r}_1 = \left(3\hat{i}+\hat{j}+\hat{k}\right)\text{m}$$

and $$r_1 = \sqrt{3^2+1^2+1^2} = \sqrt{11}\text{ m}$$

The position vector of $\vec{r}_2$ relative to $A$

$$\vec{r}_2 = \left(3\hat{i}+\hat{j}+\hat{k}\right)-2\hat{i} = \left(\hat{i}+\hat{j}+\hat{k}\right)\text{m}$$

and $$r_2 = \sqrt{1^2+1^2+1^2} = \sqrt{3}\text{ m}$$

The net electric field at $P$

$$\vec{E} = \vec{E}_1+\vec{E}_2$$

$$= \frac{1}{4\pi\epsilon_0}\left[\frac{Q_1\left(3\hat{i}+\hat{j}+\hat{k}\right)}{11^{3/2}}+\frac{Q\left(\hat{i}+\hat{j}+\hat{k}\right)}{3^{3/2}}\right]$$

$E_x$ to be zero, we have

$$\frac{1}{4\pi\epsilon_0}\left[\frac{Q\times(3)}{11^{3/2}}+\frac{Q_1\times1}{3^{3/2}}\right] = 0$$

$$\therefore \quad Q = -\left(\frac{3}{11}\right)^{3/2}(3Q_1)$$

$$= -\left[\frac{3^{5/2}}{11^{3/2}\times10^{-9}}\right]\text{C}$$

14. The electric field due to the thread at a distance $r$ from the end

$$\vec{E} = -E_x\hat{i}+E_y\hat{j}$$

where $$E_x = E_y = \frac{\lambda}{4\pi\epsilon_0 R}$$

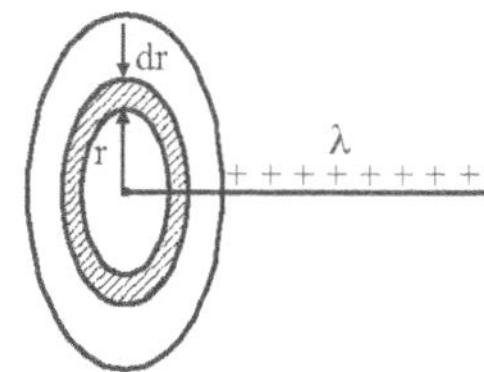


The flux of this field through the area, $dA = 2\pi r dr$ is

$$d\phi = \left(-E_x\hat{i}+E_y\hat{j}\right)\cdot d\vec{A}$$

$$\therefore \quad \phi = \int_0^{2\pi R}\left(-E_x\hat{i}+E_y\hat{j}\right)\cdot(2\pi r dr)\left(-\hat{i}\right)$$

After substituting the values and simplifying, we get

$$\phi = \left[\frac{\lambda R}{2\epsilon_0}\right] \qquad \textbf{Ans.}$$

15. The charge density of each half, $\lambda = \dfrac{Q}{\pi/2} = \dfrac{2Q}{\pi}$

The charge on the element

$$dq = \frac{2Q}{\pi}d\theta$$

Its electric field at $P$

$$dE = \left(\frac{1}{4\pi\epsilon_0}\right)\frac{dq}{R^2}$$

The resultant field of the two elements is

$$= 2dE\sin\theta$$

The resultant field of the semicircle

$$E = \int_0^{\pi/2} 2dE\sin\theta$$

$$= 2\int_0^{\pi/2}\frac{1}{4\pi\epsilon_0}\frac{\left(\frac{2Qd\theta}{\pi}\right)}{R^2}\sin\theta$$

$$= \frac{Q}{\pi^2\epsilon_0 R^2}. \qquad \textbf{Ans.}$$

16. (a) For the equilibrium of the ball, we have

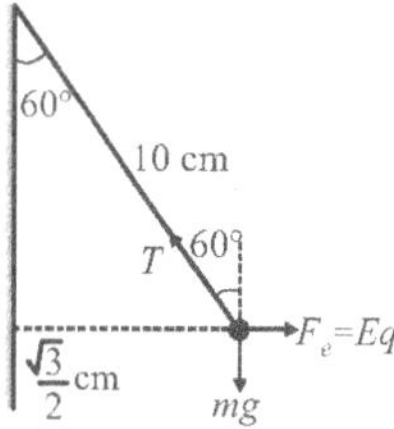


$$T\cos60^\circ = mg$$

$$\therefore \quad T = \frac{mg}{\cos60^\circ} = \frac{0.01\times10}{\frac{1}{2}}$$

$$= 0.2\text{ N}$$

Also $$T\sin60^\circ = Eq$$

or $$0.2\times\frac{\sqrt{3}}{2} = E\times4\times10^{-6}$$

$$\therefore \quad E = 4.33\times10^4\text{ V/m.}$$

(b) The time period of the oscillations is given by

$$T = 2\pi\sqrt{\frac{\ell}{a_{\text{net}}}},$$

where $$a_{\text{net}} = \sqrt{g^2+\left(\frac{Eq}{m}\right)^2}$$

$$= \sqrt{10^2 + \left(\frac{(4.33\times10^4)\times4\times10^{-6}}{0.01}\right)^2}$$

$$= 20 \text{ m/s}^2$$

$$\therefore \quad T = 2\pi\sqrt{\frac{0.1}{20}} = 0.45 \text{ s}$$ **Ans.**

17. The $x$ and $y$ components of electron's velocity are

$$v_x = v_0 \cos 45^\circ = \frac{6}{\sqrt{2}}\times10^6 = 3\sqrt{2}\times10^6 \text{ m/s}$$

and $v_y = v_0 \sin 45^\circ = 3\sqrt{2}\times10^6$ m/s

Acceleration, $a_x = 0$,

and $$a_y = \frac{-Ee}{m} = -\frac{2\times10^3\times1.6\times10^{-19}}{9.1\times10^{-31}}$$

$$= -0.35\times10^{15} \text{ m/s}^2$$

Suppose $t$ is the time to hit the plate, then

$$y = d = v_y t + \frac{1}{2}a_y t^2$$

or $$0.02 = 3\sqrt{2}\times10^6 t + \frac{1}{2}(-0.35\times10^{15})t^2 \quad ...(i)$$

If $x$ is the distance, then

$$x = v_x t = 3\sqrt{2}\times10^6\, t \quad ...(ii)$$

After solving above equations, we get $x = 2.72$ cm.

18. By Gauss's law, we have

$$\oint \vec{E}\cdot d\vec{A} = \frac{q_{in}}{\epsilon_0}$$

For the closed surface

$$S_1, q_{in} = q$$

$$S_2, q_{in} = -q$$

$$S_3, q_{in} = q$$

$$S_4, q_{in} = 0$$

$$S_5, q_{in} = q$$

After substituting the values, we can get the required answers.

19. (a) By using Gauss's law, we have

$$\oint \vec{E}\cdot d\vec{A} = \frac{q_{in}}{\epsilon_0}$$

For $r < a$ : $q_{in} = \dfrac{qr^3}{a^3}$

or $$E\times4\pi r^2 = \frac{qr^3}{a^3}$$

$$\therefore \quad E = \frac{1}{4\pi\epsilon_0}\frac{qr}{a^3}$$

(b) For $a < r < b$ :

$$q_{in} = q,$$

$$\therefore \quad E = \frac{1}{4\pi\epsilon_0}\frac{q}{r^2}$$

(c) For $b < r < c$ :

$$q_{in} = q - \frac{q\left[\frac{4}{3}\pi(r^3 - b^3)\right]}{\left[\frac{4}{3}\pi(c^3 - b^3)\right]}$$

After substituting the value of $q_{in}$ in Gauss's law, we get

$$E = \frac{1}{4\pi\epsilon_0 r^2}\frac{q(c^3 - r^3)}{(c^3 - b^3)}$$ **Ans.**

20. (a) The potential at the centre of the circle

$$V = \frac{1}{4\pi\epsilon_0}\left[\frac{Q}{R} - \frac{6Q}{R}\right]$$

$$= \frac{1}{4\pi\epsilon_0}\frac{(-5Q)}{R}.$$

(b) The potential at point $P$, a distance, $r = \sqrt{R^2 + z^2}$

$$V = \frac{1}{4\pi\epsilon_0}\frac{(-5Q)}{\sqrt{R^2 + z^2}}.$$ **Ans.**

21. The given system of charges is equivalent to, two electric dipoles, each of the moment, $P = q\times2\ell$, placed perpendicular to each other. The field of the dipole at a distance $x$ from its centre is given by

$$E = \frac{1}{4\pi\epsilon_0}\frac{P}{(\ell^2 + x^2)^{3/2}}$$

Thus resultant field,

$$E_r = \sqrt{2}\,E = \frac{\sqrt{2}\,P}{4\pi\epsilon_0(\ell^2 + x^2)^{3/2}}$$

$$= \frac{\sqrt{2}\times2q\ell}{4\pi\epsilon_0(\ell^2 + x^2)^{3/2}} = \frac{q\ell}{\sqrt{2}\,\pi\epsilon_0(\ell^2 + x^2)^{3/2}}$$ **Ans.**

22. The electric field due to the charged thread has two equal components :

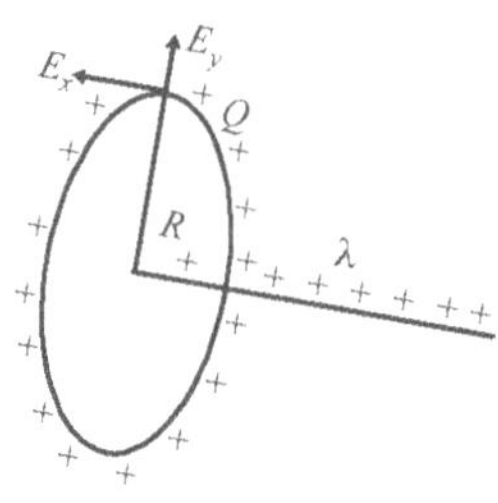


$$E_x = E_y = \frac{\lambda}{4\pi\epsilon_0 R}.$$

The force on the ring due to $E_y$ component becomes zero. So the force due to $E_x$ component is

$$F_x = E_x q = \frac{\lambda q}{4\pi\epsilon_0 R}.$$ **Ans.**

23. (a) The electric field due to the straight parts of the thread becomes zero. Because each part produces electric field; $E_x$ & $E_y$, which will be cancelled out by the field of the other part. So electric field at 0 is only due to the curved part. It is given by

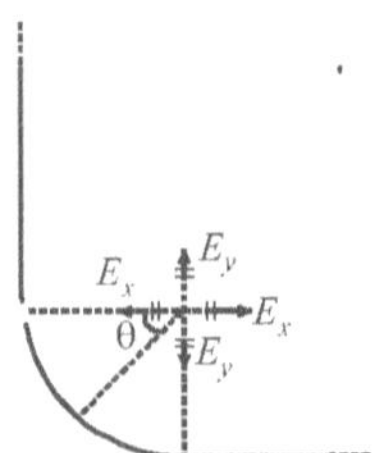

$$E = \frac{1}{4\pi\epsilon_0}\frac{q}{R^2}\left[\frac{\sin\theta}{\theta}\right]$$

$$= \frac{1}{4\pi\epsilon_0}\left(\frac{\lambda\times\frac{\pi}{2}R}{R^2}\right)\frac{\sin\frac{\pi}{4}}{\left(\frac{\pi}{4}\right)}$$

$$= \frac{\sqrt{2}\lambda}{4\pi\epsilon_0 R}.$$

(b) The electric field due to straight parts of the thread is $2E_y$, where $E_y = \frac{\lambda}{4\pi\epsilon_0}$.

The electric field due to curved part,

$$E = \frac{1}{4\pi\epsilon_0}\frac{q}{R^2}\left(\frac{\sin\theta}{\theta}\right)$$

$$= \frac{1}{4\pi\epsilon_0}\frac{\lambda\pi R}{R^2}\frac{\sin\frac{\pi}{2}}{\frac{\pi}{2}}$$

$$= \frac{\pi}{2\pi\epsilon_0 R}$$

Clearly the resultant field at O due to whole thread becomes zero.

24. The initial potential energy of the system

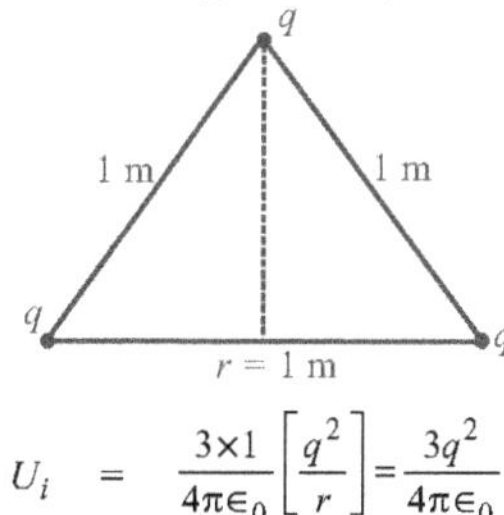


$$U_i = \frac{3\times1}{4\pi\epsilon_0}\left[\frac{q^2}{r}\right] = \frac{3q^2}{4\pi\epsilon_0}$$

Final energy of the system

$$U_f = \frac{1}{4\pi\epsilon_0}\left[\frac{q^2}{1}+\frac{q^2}{0.5}+\frac{q^2}{0.5}\right]$$

$$= \frac{5q^2}{4\pi\epsilon_0}$$

The work done in the process,

$$W = U_f - U_i$$

$$= \frac{5q^2}{4\pi\epsilon_0}$$

If $t$ is the required time, then

$$Pt = W$$

$$\therefore \quad t = \frac{W}{P} = \frac{\left(\frac{12q^2}{4\pi\epsilon_0}\right)}{10^3}$$

$$= \frac{2\times9\times10^9\times(0.1)^2}{10^3}$$

$$= 1.8\times10^5 \text{ s.}$$ ***Ans.***

25. For minimum potential energy, the charges of larger magnitudes should be placed farther. Let charge $q$ is placed at a distance $x$ from $2q$. Thus potential energy of the system.

$$U = \frac{1}{4\pi\epsilon_0}\left[\frac{(2q)q}{x}+\frac{q(8q)}{(9-x)}+\frac{(2q)(8q)}{9}\right]$$

$U$ to be minimum, $\frac{dU}{dx} = 0$

$$\therefore \quad x = 3 \text{ cm.}$$ ***Ans.***

Electric field at the position of $q$

$$\vec{E} = \vec{E}_1 + \vec{E}_2$$

$$= \frac{1}{4\pi\epsilon_0}\left[\frac{2q}{(3\times10^{-2})^2} - \frac{8q}{(6\times10^{-2})^2}\right] = 0$$

26. The *FBD* is shown in figure.

The normal reaction

$$N = mg\cos\theta + Eq\sin\theta \quad \text{...(i)}$$

The acceleration

$$a = \frac{F_{\text{net}}}{m}$$

$$= \left[\frac{mg\sin\theta - (\mu N + qE\cos\theta)}{m}\right] \quad \text{...(iii)}$$

After solving equations (i) and (ii) and substituting the values, we get

$$a = 2.13 \text{ m/s}^2$$

Distance moved,

$$s = \frac{1}{\sin 30^\circ} = 2\text{m}$$

By second equation of motion

$$s = 0 + \frac{1}{2}at^2$$

$$\therefore \quad t = \sqrt{\frac{2s}{a}} = 1.345 \text{ s.}$$ ***Ans.***

27. Let electron is at a distance $x$ from the centre of the ring. The force on the electron,

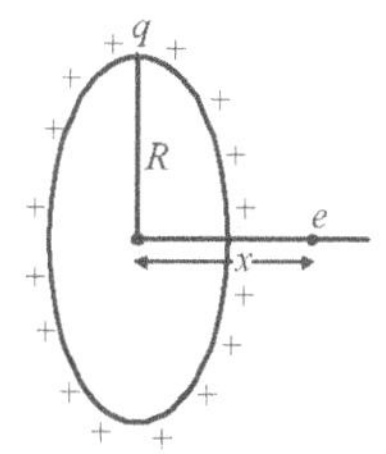


$$F = -E\,e$$

$$= -\left[\frac{1}{4\pi\epsilon_0}\frac{qx}{(R^2+x^2)^{3/2}}\right]e$$

For $x << R$,

$$F = -\left[\frac{1}{4\pi\epsilon_0}\frac{q\,e}{R^3}\right]x$$

Acceleration, $a = \frac{F}{m} = \frac{1}{4\pi\epsilon_0}\frac{qe}{mR^3}(-x)$

Compare with standard equation of SHM, $a = -\omega^2 x$, we get

$$\omega = \sqrt{\frac{qe}{4\pi\epsilon_0 mR^3}}. \quad \textbf{Ans.}$$

28. The electric field due to any half semicircular rod is given by

$$E = \frac{1}{4\pi\epsilon_0}\frac{q}{R^2}\left[\frac{\sin\theta}{\theta}\right]$$

$$= \frac{1}{4\pi\epsilon_0}\frac{q}{R^2}\left[\frac{\sin\frac{\pi}{2}}{\frac{\pi}{2}}\right]$$

$$= \frac{1}{2\pi\epsilon_0}\left(\frac{q}{\pi R^2}\right)$$

The resultant electric field at the centre of the circle

$$E_r = 2E = \frac{1}{\pi\epsilon_0}\left(\frac{q}{\pi R^2}\right) \quad \textbf{Ans.}$$

29. The time period of oscillation of simple pendulum is given by

$$T = 2\pi\sqrt{\frac{\ell}{a_{net}}}$$

(a) In this case, $a_{\text{net}} = \left(g - \frac{Eq}{m}\right)$,

$$\therefore \quad T = 2\pi\sqrt{\frac{\ell}{\left(g - \frac{Eq}{m}\right)}}$$

(b) In this case, $a_{\text{net}} = \left(g + \frac{Eq}{m}\right)$,

$$\therefore \quad T = 2\pi\sqrt{\frac{\ell}{\left(g + \frac{Eq}{m}\right)}}. \quad \textbf{Ans.}$$

30. (a) For $r > R$:

Using Gauss's law, we have $\oint \vec{E}\cdot d\vec{A} = \frac{q_{\text{in}}}{\epsilon_0}$

$$\text{or} \quad E \times 2\pi r\ell = \frac{\lambda\ell}{\epsilon_0}$$

$$\Rightarrow \quad E = \frac{\lambda}{2\pi\epsilon_0 r}.$$

(b) For, $r < R$, $q_{\text{in}} = 0$

$$\therefore \quad E = 0. \quad \textbf{Ans.}$$

31. Using Gauss's law, we have

$$\oint \vec{E}.d\vec{A} = \frac{q_{\text{in}}}{\epsilon_0}$$

$$= \int_0^r \frac{\rho\, 2\pi r\ell dr}{\epsilon_0}$$

$$\text{or} \quad E \times 2\pi r\ell = \frac{2\pi\ell r^2}{2\epsilon_0}$$

$$\therefore \quad E = \frac{\rho r}{2\epsilon_0}$$

32. (a) By Gauss's law

$$\oint \vec{E}\cdot d\vec{A} = \frac{q_{\text{in}}}{\epsilon_0}$$

$$E \times 2\pi rL = \left(\frac{q - 2q}{\epsilon_0}\right)$$

$$\therefore \quad E = \frac{-q}{2\pi\epsilon_0 Lr}$$

(b) $$\oint \vec{E}\cdot d\vec{A} = \frac{q_{\text{in}}}{\epsilon_0}$$

$$\text{or} \quad E \times 2\pi rL = \frac{q}{\epsilon_0}$$

$$\therefore \quad E = \frac{q}{2\pi\epsilon_0 Lr} \quad \textbf{Ans.}$$

33. The electric field due to the given charge sheet

$$E = E_{\text{conducting surface}} - E_{\text{hole}}$$

$$= \frac{\sigma}{2\epsilon_0} - \frac{\sigma}{2\epsilon_0}\left[1 - \frac{x}{\sqrt{R^2 + z^2}}\right]$$

$$= \frac{\sigma}{2\epsilon_0}\left[1 - 1 + \frac{x}{\sqrt{R^2 + z^2}}\right]$$

$$= \frac{\sigma}{2\epsilon_0 (R^2 + z^2)^{1/2}} \quad \textbf{Ans.}$$

34. (a) The total charge on the sphere

$$Q = \int \rho(dV)$$

$$= \int_0^R \left(\rho_s \frac{r}{R}\right) 4\pi r^2 dr$$

$$= \pi\rho_s R^3. \quad \textbf{Ans.}$$

(b) By Gauss's law, we have

$$\oint \vec{E}\cdot d\vec{A} = \frac{q_{\text{in}}}{\epsilon_0} = \int_0^r \frac{\left(\rho_s \frac{r}{R}\right) 4\pi r^2 dr}{\epsilon_0}$$

$$\text{or} \quad E \times 4\pi r^2 = \frac{\pi\rho_s r^4}{\epsilon_0 R}$$

$$\text{or} \quad E = \frac{\rho_s r^2}{4\epsilon_0 R} = \frac{\left(\frac{Q}{\pi R^3}\right) r^2}{4\epsilon_0 R}$$

$$= \frac{Qr^2}{4\pi\epsilon_0 R^4}.$$

35. By Gauss's law, we have $\oint \vec{E}\cdot d\vec{A} = \frac{q_{\text{in}}}{\epsilon_0}$

$$\text{or} \quad E \times 4\pi r^2 = \left[\frac{q + \int_a^r \left(\frac{A}{r}\right) 4\pi r^2 dr}{\epsilon_0}\right]$$

$$= \frac{(q - 2\pi A a^2)}{\epsilon_0} + \frac{2\pi A r^2}{\epsilon_0}$$

$$\text{or} \quad E = \left[\frac{q - 2\pi A a^2}{4\pi r^2}\right] + \frac{A}{2\epsilon_0}$$

For $E$ to be uniform,

$$q - 2\pi A a^2 = 0$$

or $$A = \frac{q}{2\pi a^2}.$$ **Ans.**

36. The potential at any point $P$ is given by

$$V = \frac{1}{4\pi\epsilon_0} \cdot \frac{Q}{R}$$

The result does not depend on the angle subtended. Electric field at any point $P$ is given by

$$E = \frac{1}{4\pi\epsilon_0}\frac{Q}{R^2}\left[\frac{\sin\theta}{\theta}\right]$$

Clearly the $E$ is maximum when $\theta$ is small, so $E$ is minimum in $C$; it is zero.

37. If $q$ be the required charge for the potential then

$$V = \frac{1}{4\pi\epsilon_0}\frac{q}{R}$$

or $$q = 4\pi\epsilon_0 VR$$

The charge emitted per second through the source

$$n = (5\times10^{10})e\times0.40$$

If $t$ is the required time, then

$$t = \frac{q}{n} = \frac{4\pi\epsilon_0 VR}{(5\times10^{10})e\times0.40}$$

After substituting the values, we get

$$t = 700\ \mu\text{s}.$$ **Ans.**

38. The magnitude of the forces between two charges,

$$f = \frac{1}{4\pi\epsilon_0}\frac{q^2}{x^2};\ x = 3\text{ cm} \quad \text{...(i)}$$

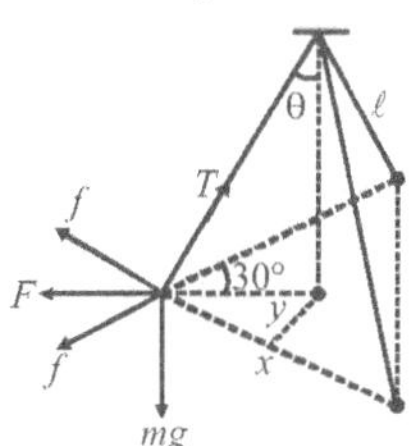


The resultant electric force on any charge particle

$$F = 2f\cos30^\circ = \sqrt{3}f. \quad \text{...(ii)}$$

From the geometry of the figure $\dfrac{x/2}{y} = \cos30^\circ$

$$\therefore \quad y = \frac{x}{\sqrt{3}}$$

Also $$\frac{y}{\ell} = \sin\theta$$

or $$\frac{x/\sqrt{3}}{y} = \sin\theta$$

or $$\sin\theta = \frac{3\sqrt{3}}{100} = \frac{\sqrt{3}}{100} \approx \tan\theta \quad \text{...(iii)}$$

For the equilibrium of the charge, we have

$$T\sin\theta = F$$

and $$T\cos\theta = mg$$

or $$\tan\theta = \frac{F}{mg} \quad \text{...(iv)}$$

After solving above equations and substituting the values, we get

$$q = 1.01\times10^{-7}\text{ C}$$ **Ans.**

39. If $q$ be the charge on each ball, then force between them

$$F_e = \frac{1}{4\pi\epsilon_0}\frac{q^2}{x^2};\ x = 40\text{ cm}$$

For the equilibrium of either ball, we have

$$T\sin\theta = F_e$$

and $$T\cos\theta = mg$$

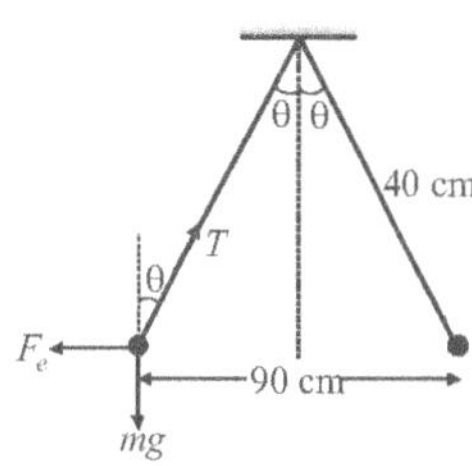


$$\therefore \quad \tan\theta = \frac{F_e}{mg}$$

From the geometry, $\tan\theta = \dfrac{20}{\sqrt{40^2 - 20^2}}$

After substituting the values, we get

$$q = 1.01\times10^{-7}\text{ C}$$ **Ans.**

40. The restoring torque on the dipole so formed,

$$\tau = -PE\sin\theta$$

$$\therefore \quad \alpha = \frac{\tau}{I} = \frac{PE(-\theta)}{I} \quad [\text{For small } \theta, \sin\theta \approx \theta]$$

Comparing with standard equation of SHM, we get

$$\omega = \sqrt{\frac{PE}{I}},$$

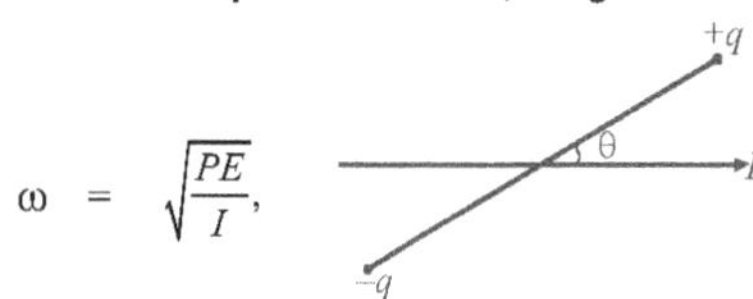


and $$T = \frac{2\pi}{\omega} = 2\pi\sqrt{\frac{I}{PE}}$$

$$= 2\pi\sqrt{\frac{2M\left(\frac{L}{2}\right)^2}{(qL)E}} = 2\pi\sqrt{\frac{ML}{2qE}},$$

The required time, $t = \dfrac{T}{4} = \dfrac{\pi}{2}\sqrt{\dfrac{ML}{2qE}}.$ **Ans.**

41. Mechanical energy at $A$ = mechanical energy at $B$

or $$mg\times0.30 + \frac{1}{4\pi\epsilon_0}\frac{q_1q_2}{0.20}$$

$$= 0 + \frac{1}{2}mv^2 + \frac{1}{4\pi\epsilon_0}\frac{q_1q_2}{(0.20+0.30)}$$

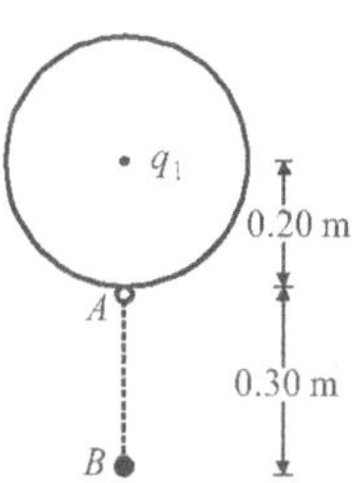


After substituting and simplifying, we get

$$v = 3.65\text{ m/s}$$

42. Given, $R_1 = 0.05$ m, $R_2 = 0.09$ m, $d = 0.12$m, $q = 10^{-6}$ C.

Potential of the centre of first loop

$$V_1 = \frac{1}{4\pi\epsilon_0}\left[\frac{q}{R_1}+\frac{q}{\sqrt{d^2+R_2^2}}\right]$$

and

$$V_2 = \frac{1}{4\pi\epsilon_0}\left[\frac{q}{R_2}+\frac{q}{\sqrt{d^2+R_1^2}}\right]$$

$\therefore \quad V_1 - V_2 =$

$$\frac{1}{4\pi\epsilon_0}\left[\left(\frac{q}{R_1}+\frac{q}{\sqrt{d^2+R_2^2}}\right)-\left(\frac{q}{R_2}+\frac{q}{\sqrt{d^2+R_1^2}}\right)\right]$$

After substituting the values and simplifying, we get

$$V_1 - V_2 = 7.08\times10^4\text{ V}.$$ **Ans.**

43. (i) The restoring force

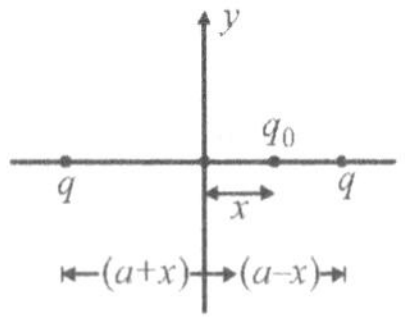

$$F = -\left[\frac{1}{4\pi\epsilon_0}\frac{qq_0}{(a-x)^2}-\frac{1}{4\pi\epsilon_0}\frac{qq_0}{(a+x)^2}\right]$$

$$= -\frac{qq_0}{4\pi\epsilon_0}\left[\frac{1}{(a-x)^2}-\frac{1}{(a+x)^2}\right]$$

$$= \frac{aqq_0(-x)}{\pi\epsilon_0(a^2-x^2)^2}$$

For $x << a$, $F = \frac{qq_0}{\pi\epsilon_0 a^3}(-x)$

The acceleration of the charge $q_0$,

$$\alpha = \frac{F}{m} = \frac{qq_0(-x)}{m\pi\epsilon_0 a^3}$$

Compare with standard equation of SHM, $\alpha = -\omega^2 x$, we have

$$\omega = \sqrt{\frac{qq_0}{m\pi\epsilon_0 a^3}}.$$

Time period, $T = \frac{2\pi}{\omega} = 2\pi\sqrt{\frac{m\pi\epsilon_0 a^3}{qq_0}}.$

For $q_0 = \frac{q}{2}$, $T = 2\pi\sqrt{\frac{2m\pi\epsilon_0 a^3}{q^2}}.$ **Ans.**

(ii) In this case net force is not along the mean position, so the motion is not oscillatory.

44. The electric field at the centre of the ring is zero, so the force on the charged particle at the centre is zero. Hence if the particle reaches at the centre of the ring, then it will not return to $P$. For minimum value of velocity $v$, the speed at the centre must be zero.

By conservation of mechanical, we have

$$(K+U)_P = (K+U)_0$$

or

$$\frac{1}{2}mv^2+\frac{1}{4\pi\epsilon_0}\frac{(2\pi R\lambda)q}{\sqrt{(\sqrt{3}R)^2+R^2}} = 0+\frac{1}{4\pi\epsilon_0}\cdot\frac{(2\pi R\lambda)q}{R}$$

or

$$v = \sqrt{\frac{\lambda q}{2\epsilon_0 m}}.$$ **Ans.**

45. By Gauss's law, we have

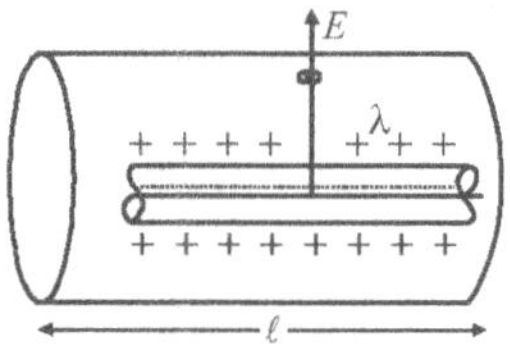

$$\oint \vec{E}\cdot d\vec{A} = \frac{q_{in}}{\epsilon_0}$$

or

$$E\times2\pi r\ell = \frac{\lambda\ell}{\epsilon_0}$$

$$\therefore \quad E = \frac{\lambda}{2\pi\epsilon_0 r}.$$ **Ans.**

46. The initial potential energy of the system

$$U_i = \frac{1}{4\pi\epsilon_0}\left[\frac{q_1q_2}{r_i}+\frac{q_2q_3}{r_i}+\frac{q_1q_3}{r_i}\right]$$

$$= 9\times10^9\left[\frac{2\times3}{1}+\frac{3\times1}{1}+\frac{2\times1}{1}\right]$$

$$= 99\times10^9\text{ J}$$

Final potential energy of the system

$$U_f = \frac{1}{4\pi\epsilon_0}\left[\frac{q_1q_2}{r_f}+\frac{q_2q_3}{r_f}+\frac{q_1q_3}{r_f}\right]$$

$$= 9\times10^9\left[\frac{2\times3}{0.5}+\frac{3\times1}{0.5}+\frac{2\times1}{0.5}\right]$$

$$= 198\times10^9\text{ J.}$$

Work done, $W = U_f - U_i$

$$= 99\times10^9\text{ J.}$$ **Ans.**

47. The charge on the shells are :

$$q_A = \sigma\times4\pi a^2,\ q_B = -\sigma\times4\pi a^2$$

and

$$q_C = \sigma\times4\pi C^2.$$

(i) The potential,

$$V_A = \frac{1}{4\pi\epsilon_0}\left[\frac{q_A}{a}+\frac{q_B}{b}+\frac{q_C}{c}\right]$$

$$= \frac{1}{4\pi\epsilon_0}\left[\frac{4\pi\sigma a^2}{a}-\frac{4\pi\sigma b^2}{b}+\frac{4\pi\sigma c^2}{c}\right]$$

$$= \frac{\sigma}{\epsilon_0}(a-b+c)$$

$$V_B = \frac{1}{4\pi\epsilon_0}\left[\frac{q_A}{b}+\frac{q_B}{b}+\frac{q_C}{c}\right]$$

$$= \frac{1}{4\pi\epsilon_0}\left[\frac{4\pi\sigma a^2}{b}-\frac{4\pi\sigma b^2}{b}+\frac{4\pi\sigma c^2}{c}\right]$$

$$= \frac{\sigma}{\epsilon_0}\left[\frac{a^2-b^2}{b}+c\right]$$

$$V_C = \frac{1}{4\pi\epsilon_0}\left[\frac{q_A}{c}+\frac{q_B}{c}+\frac{q_C}{c}\right]$$

$$= \frac{1}{4\pi\epsilon_0}\left[\frac{4\pi\sigma a^2}{c}-\frac{4\pi\sigma b^2}{c}+\frac{4\pi\sigma c^2}{c}\right]$$

$$= \frac{\sigma}{\epsilon_0}\left[\frac{a^2-b^2+c^2}{c}\right].$$ **Ans.**

(ii) For $V_A = V_C$,

$$\Rightarrow \quad C = (a+b)$$ **Ans.**

48. If $r_0$ be the distance of closest approach, then by conservation of momentum, we have

$$mv + 0 = mv' + mv'$$

$$\therefore \quad v' = \frac{v}{2}.$$

By conservation of mechanical energy, we have

$$0 + \frac{1}{2}mv^2 = \frac{1}{4\pi\epsilon_0}\frac{ee}{r_0} + 2\left(\frac{1}{2}mv'^2\right)$$

After substituting the values and simplifying, we get

$$r_0 = 9.94\times10^{-13}\text{ m.}$$ **Ans.**

49. The electric field at a distance $r$ from the centre of ring is

$$E = \frac{1}{4\pi\epsilon_0}\frac{qr}{(R^2+r^2)^{3/2}}.$$

50. The potential, $V = -\int \vec{E}\cdot d\vec{r}$

$$= -\int a(y\hat{i} + x\hat{j})\cdot(dx\hat{i} + dy\hat{j})$$

$$= -a\int(ydx + xdy)$$

$$= -a\int d(xy)$$

$$= -axy + \text{constant.}$$

51. The potential, $V = -\int \vec{E}\cdot d\vec{r}$

$$= -\int\left[2axy\hat{i} + a(x^2 - y^2)\hat{j}\right]\cdot(dx\hat{i} + dy\hat{j})$$

$$= ay\left[\frac{y^2}{3} - x^2\right] + \text{constant.}$$

52. The induced charges on the hollow sphere are shown in figure.

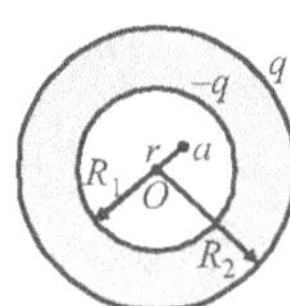


$$V_0 = \frac{1}{4\pi\epsilon_0}\left[\frac{q}{r} - \frac{q}{R_1} + \frac{q}{R_2}\right].$$ **Ans.**

53. (a) Using Gauss's law

$$\oint \vec{E}\cdot d\vec{A} = \frac{q_{in}}{\epsilon_0},$$

where $q_{in} = \int_0^r \rho\times4\pi r^2 dr$

$$= \int_0^r \rho_0\left(1 - \frac{r}{R}\right)\times4\pi r^2 dr$$

$$= 4\pi\rho_0\left(\frac{r^3}{3} - \frac{r^4}{4R}\right).$$

Thus $E\times4\pi r^2 = \left[\dfrac{4\pi\rho_0\left(\dfrac{r^3}{3} - \dfrac{r^4}{4R}\right)}{\epsilon_0}\right]$

$$\therefore \quad E = \frac{\rho_0 r}{3\epsilon_0}\left(1 - \frac{3r}{4R}\right).$$

For $r \geq R$: $q_{in} = \int_0^R \rho_0\left(1 - \frac{r}{R}\right)\times4\pi r^2 dr$

$$= \frac{\pi\rho_0 R^3}{3}.$$

$$\therefore \quad E\times4\pi r^2 = \frac{\pi\rho_0 R^3}{3\epsilon_0}$$

or $$E = \frac{\rho_0 R^3}{12r^3\epsilon_0}$$

(b) For maximum value of $E$, $\frac{dE}{dr} = 0$.

or $$\frac{d}{dr}\left[\frac{\rho_0 r}{3\epsilon_0}\left(1 - \frac{3r}{4R}\right)\right] = 0$$

$$\therefore \quad r = \frac{2R}{3}.$$

and $$E_{max} = \frac{\rho_0 R}{9\epsilon_0}.$$ **Ans.**

54. Using Gauss's law, we have

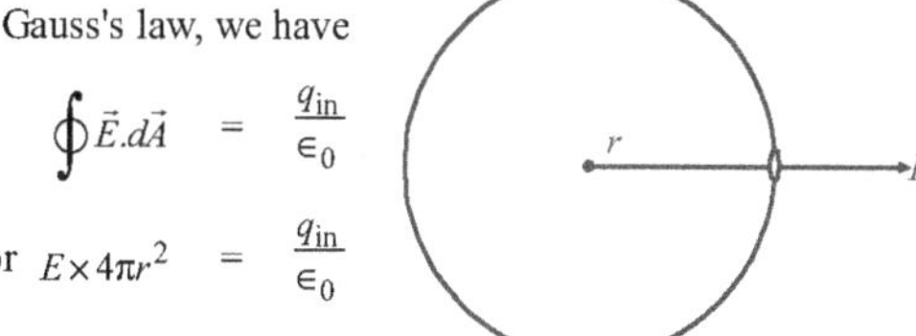


$$\oint \vec{E}.d\vec{A} = \frac{q_{in}}{\epsilon_0}$$

or $$E\times4\pi r^2 = \frac{q_{in}}{\epsilon_0}$$

where $q_{in} = \int_0^r \rho_0 e^{-\alpha r^3}\times4\pi r^2 dr$

$$= \frac{4\pi\rho_0}{3\alpha}\left(1 - e^{-\alpha r^3}\right)$$

$$\therefore \quad E\times4\pi r^2 = \frac{4\pi\rho_0}{3\alpha\epsilon_0}\left(1 - e^{-\alpha r^3}\right)$$

or $$E = \frac{\rho_0}{3\alpha r^2\epsilon_0}\left(1 - e^{-\alpha r^3}\right).$$

For $\alpha r^3 >> 1$, $E = \dfrac{\rho}{3\alpha\epsilon_0 r^2}$

For $\alpha r^3 << 1$, $E = \dfrac{\rho_0}{3\alpha r^2\epsilon_0}\left[1 - 1 + \alpha r^3 + 0(\alpha^2 r^4)\right]$

$$= \frac{\rho_0 r}{3\epsilon_0}.$$ **Ans.**

55. By using Gauss's law, we have

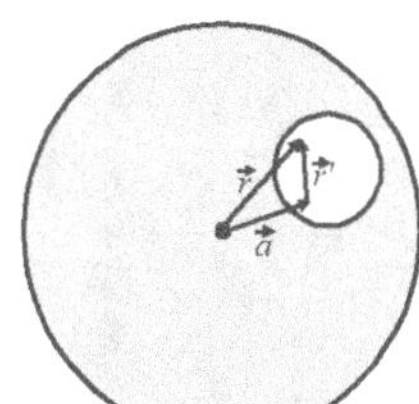

$$\oint \vec{E} \cdot d\vec{A} = \frac{q_{in}}{\epsilon_0}$$

or $$E \times 4\pi r^2 = \frac{\rho \times \frac{4}{3}\pi r^3}{\epsilon_0}$$

$\therefore$ $$E = \frac{\rho r}{3\epsilon_0}.$$

In position vector, it can be written as

$$\vec{E} = \frac{\rho \vec{r}}{3\epsilon_0}.$$

The electric field due to charge of cavity at a distance $\vec{r}$.

$$\vec{E}' = \frac{\rho \vec{r}\,'}{e\epsilon_0}.$$

The net electric field at any point inside the cavity

$$\vec{E}_{net} = \vec{E} - \vec{E}'$$

$$= \frac{\rho \vec{r}}{3\epsilon_0} - \frac{\rho \vec{r}\,'}{3\epsilon_0}$$

$$= \frac{\rho}{3\epsilon_0}(\vec{r} - \vec{r}\,')$$

or $$\vec{E} = \frac{\rho \vec{a}.}{3\epsilon_0}$$ $[As\ \vec{a} + \vec{r}\,' = \vec{r}]$ ***Ans.***

56. If $P_1$ is the initial excess pressure inside the bubble, then

$$P_1 = P + \frac{4T}{r},$$

and volume of the bubble, $V_1 = \frac{4}{3}\pi r^3$. When bubble is charged, its electric field becomes, $E = \frac{V}{R}$ and outward pressure due to this is $\frac{1}{2}\epsilon_0 E^2$. Thus if $P_2$ is the final pressure, then

$$P_2 = P + \left(\frac{4T}{R} - \frac{1}{2}\epsilon_0 E^2\right),$$

and volume, $V_2 = \frac{4}{3}\pi R^3$.

According to Boyle's law, we have

$$P_1 V_1 = P_2 V_2$$

After solving above equations, we get

$$P(R^3 - r^3) + 4T(R^2 - r^2) = \frac{\epsilon_0 V^2 R}{2}.$$

# CHAPTER 2

# Capacitance & Capacitor (131-216)

## 2.1 CAPACITOR OR CONDENSER : AN INTRODUCTION

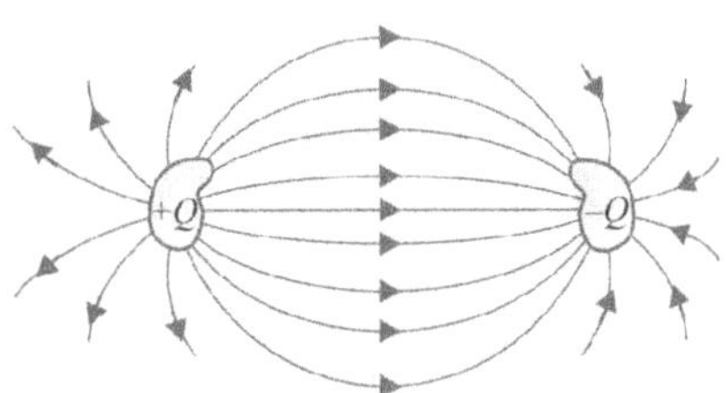


*Fig. 2.1 Capacitor*

A capacitor is an electrical device which is used to store electrical energy in the same way that a bucket is a container for storing water or a tank is a container for storing gas. Each of these devices has fixed capacity which does not depend on the quantity to be stored.

A system consisting of two conductors of any shape, called plates placed at some separation constitutes a **capacitor.** When a capacitor is charged, its plates have equal and opposite charges of $+Q$ and $-Q$. The charge of capacitor means the charge on positive plate. (Note that $Q$ is not the net charge on the capacitor, which is zero). The symbol that we use to represent a capacitor is ⊣⊢.

*Fig. 2.1* shows a capacitor which consists of two conductors, isolated electrically from each other having charges $+Q$ and $-Q$.

## 2.2 CAPACITANCE OR CAPACITY

We know that the potential of a charged conductor is proportional to the charge given to it. Thus for any capacitor we can write

$$Q = CV$$

or

$$C = Q/V$$

The proportionality constant $C$ is called the capacitance of the capacitor. Its value depends only on the shape and size of the conductors not on the charge or potential difference. The SI unit of capacitance is coulomb/volt ($C/V$). It is called 1 farad (1F), a unit in honour of Michael Faraday.

### Why plates with opposite charges?

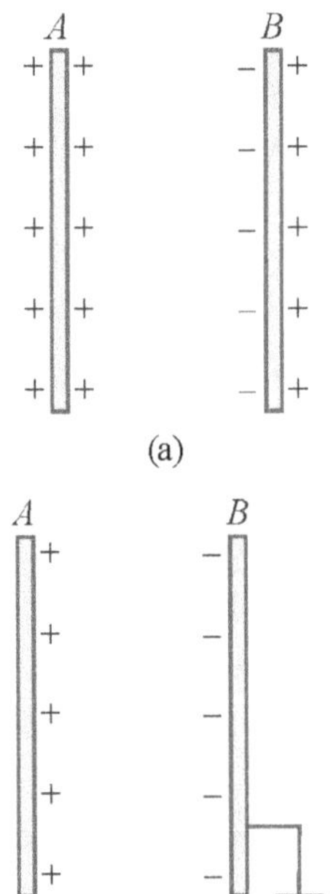


*Fig. 2.2*

When a plate $B$ is brought near a charged plate $A$, the near face of $B$ will have an induce charge (negative) and far face a positive charge. This negative charge tends to lower the potential of $A$ and the positive charge on $B$ tends to raise it. The effect of these charges on $A$ nearly counteract each other, but the negative charge has little greater influence as it is nearer to the plate $A$, thus lowers the potential of $A$. If the plate $B$ is now earthed, the positive charge on $B$ disappears and negative charge does not go to the earth as it is attracted by the positive charge on the plate $A$. Hence the potential of plate $A$ is much lowered due to the presence of the negative charge on plate $B$. Thus the potential of an insulated charged plate be considerably decreased and hence its capacitance can be considerably increased when an earthed plate is brought near it.

**Note :**

1. By making such an arrangement of plates, the entire electric field and hence electric potential energy resides only between the plates. This is the prime requirement of the capacitor.
2. The plate B need not necessarily be earthed. The only requirement is that B must have an equal and opposite charge.
3. Each isolated conductor has capacity, but it is not a capacitor.

### Uses of capacitors

1. As we know that capacitor can be used for storing electrical energy. Energy stored in a large capacitor is used to accelerate the electrons in a cyclotron.
2. Capacitors are very useful to reduce voltage fluctuations in electronic power supplies, to transmit signals, to detect electro-magnetic oscillations at radio frequencies and to other important electronic circuits.

## 2.3 CHARGING A CAPACITOR

Take a capacitor and connect it in an electric circuit with a battery. The energy provided by the battery pulls the electrons from the plate $A$ and send them to plate $B$ of the capacitor. Due to which positive charge on the plate $A$ and negative charge on plate $B$ start increasing. As the plates become oppositely charged, the potential difference between them increases until it equals the potential difference $V$ between the terminals of the battery. Then plate $A$ and the positive terminal of the battery are at the same potential, and there is no longer an electric field in the connecting wires. Similarly, plate $B$ and the negative terminal reach the same potential and there is then no electric field in the wire between them. Thus, with the field zero, there is no further drive of electrons in the connecting wires. The capacitor is then said to be fully charged, with a potential difference $V$ and charge $Q$.

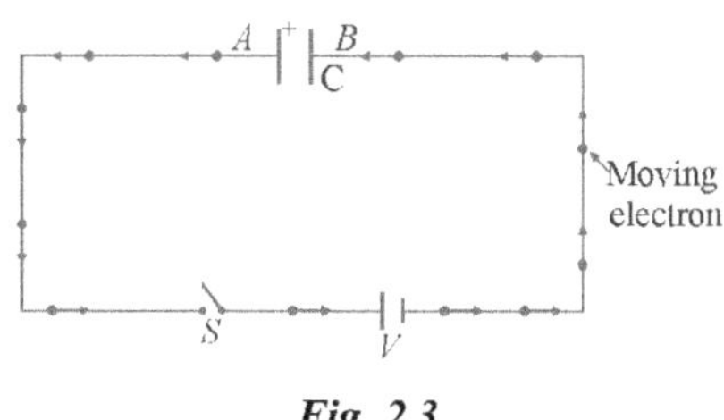


*Fig. 2.3*

### Displacement current

During the charging process of the capacitor, there is an electric current through the connecting wire due to the movement of electrons. This current is called conduction current. According to Maxwell, there must be an equal amount of current between the plates of the capacitor. This current which is due to changing electric field between the plates of capacitor, is called displacement current ($i_d$). If $\sigma$ is the charge density on the plates of the capacitor, then the electric field between them is given by

$$E = \frac{\sigma}{\epsilon_0}$$

$$\therefore \quad \sigma = \epsilon_0 E$$

If $A$ be the area of each plate, then charge on the plate,

$$q = \sigma A = \epsilon_0 EA.$$

The displacement current,

$$i_d = \frac{dq}{dt}$$

$$= \frac{d(\epsilon_0 EA)}{dt}$$

$$= \epsilon_0 A\left(\frac{dE}{dt}\right)$$

$$= \epsilon_0 \frac{d\phi_e}{dt}$$

Thus

$$i_d = \epsilon_0 A\frac{dE}{dt} = \epsilon_0 \frac{d\phi_e}{dt}.$$

## 2.4 CALCULATING CAPACITANCE

**Step I** : First propose any charge $Q$ on one of the plates of the capacitor.

**Step II** : Find potential difference between the plates of the capacitor, keeping other plate earthed.

**Step III** : To find capacitance, use

$$C = \frac{Q}{V}$$

### Capacitance of isolated spherical conductor

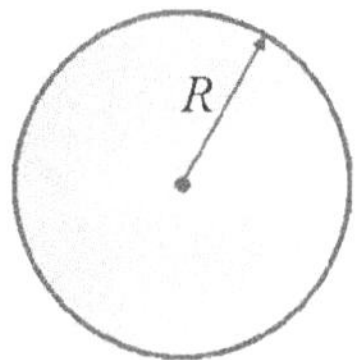


*Fig. 2.4*

Consider a spherical conductor of radius R. It is given charge Q. The potential of its surface

$$V = \frac{1}{4\pi \epsilon_0} \frac{Q}{R}$$

$$\therefore \text{ Capacity} \quad C = \frac{Q}{V} = \frac{Q}{\frac{1}{4\pi \epsilon_0}\frac{Q}{R}}$$

or

$$C = 4\pi \epsilon_0 R.$$

### Radius of 1F isolated conductor

Putting C = 1F in above formula, we have

$$1 = 4\pi \epsilon_0 R$$

or

$$R = \frac{1}{4\pi \epsilon_0}$$

$$= 9 \times 10^9 \text{ m.}$$

This size is more than 1000 times the radius of the earth. Thus a capacitance of 1F in practice is not possible.

### Redistribution of charges

If a conductor of capacitance $C_1$ at potential $V_1$ be connected to another conductor of capacitance $C_2$ at potential $V_2$, the charge flows from the conductor of higher potential towards the conductor at lower potential until their potentials become equal. Thus common potential

*Fig. 2.5*

$$V = \frac{\text{Total charge}}{\text{total capacity}}$$

$$= \frac{Q_1 + Q_2}{C_1 + C_2}$$

or

$$V = \frac{C_1V_1 + C_2V_2}{C_1 + C_2} \quad \ldots (1)$$

If $Q'_1$ and $Q'_2$ are the final charges on them, then

$$Q'_1 = C_1V \text{ and } Q'_2 = C_2V$$

$$\therefore \quad \frac{Q'_1}{Q'_2} = \frac{C_1}{C_2} \quad \ldots (2)$$

Also

$$Q'_1 + Q'_2 = Q_1 + Q_2 \quad \ldots (3)$$

In the process of flowing of charge, there becomes loss of some electrical energy due to the resistance of the flowing medium (wire) which will convert into heat and light. Thus:

$$\text{Loss of electrical energy} = U_i - U_f$$

or

$$U_L = \left[\frac{1}{2}C_1V_1^2 + \frac{1}{2}C_2V_2^2\right] - \frac{1}{2}[C_1 + C_2]V^2$$

$$U_L = \frac{C_1C_2(V_1 - V_2)^2}{2(C_1 + C_2)} \quad \ldots (4)$$

If a conductor of capacitance $C_1$ and charge $Q$ is connected to an uncharged conductor of capacitance $C_2$, then

$$V = \frac{Q}{(C_1 + C_2)},$$

and $$U_L = \frac{Q^2 C_2}{C_1(C_1 + C_2)}$$

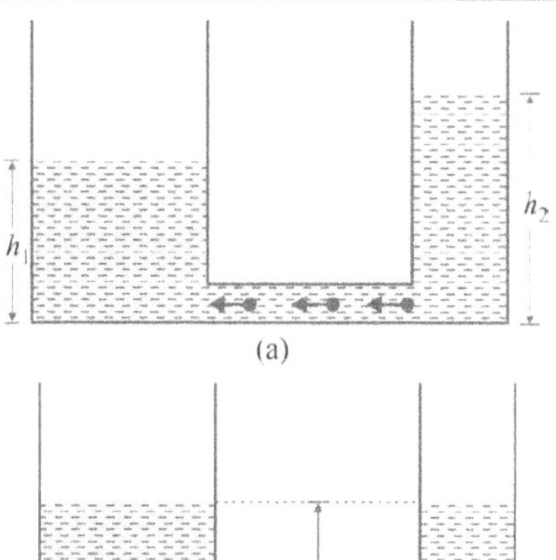

Fig. 2.6

**Analogy with mechanical device**

When two containers having different levels of water are connected by a pipe, water flows from the container having higher level towards the container having water at lower level, until levels in both the containers become equal.

After redistribution, the container of larger capacity will have large amount of water. Here also some part of mechanical energy will convert into heat by the friction (resistance) of the connecting pipe.

**Ex. 1** **Two conductors carrying equal and opposite charges produce a non-uniform electric field as shown in *fig. 2.7.* What is the capacitance of the capacitor if the electric field along y-axis varies as**

$$E = \frac{Q}{\epsilon_0 A}(1 + by^2)$$

**where *b* is a constant. The separation between conductors along *y*-axis is *d*.**

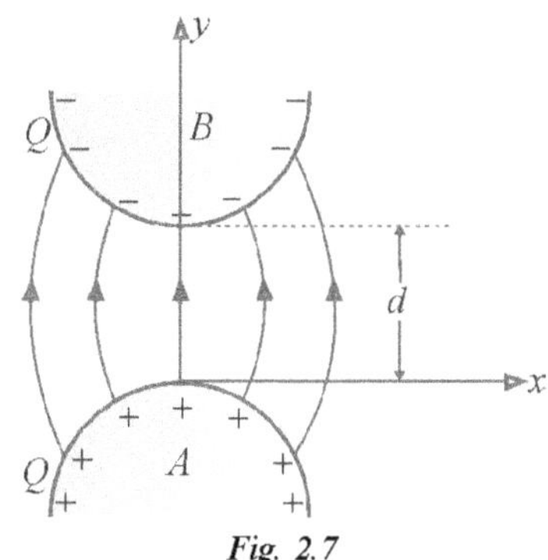

Fig. 2.7

**Sol.** The potential difference between the conductors is given by

$$V = V_A - V_B = \int_A^B E\,dy$$

$$= \int_0^d \frac{Q}{\epsilon_0 A}(1 + by^2)dy$$

$$= \frac{Q}{\epsilon_0 A}\left| y + \frac{by^3}{3} \right|_0^d$$

$$= \frac{Q}{\epsilon_0 A}\left( d + \frac{bd^3}{3} \right)$$

$$= \frac{Qd}{\epsilon_0 A}\left( 1 + \frac{bd^2}{3} \right)$$

The capacitance $$C = \frac{Q}{V} = \frac{\epsilon_0 A}{d\left(1 + \frac{bd^2}{3}\right)}.$$ ***Ans.***

## 2.5 CAPACITANCE OF PARALLEL PLATE CAPACITOR

It consists of two metallic plates of any shape but of equal size and placed at some separation. This constitutes a parallel plate capacitor. Suppose a charge $Q$ is given to plate $A$; it will induce a charge $-Q$ to the other plate $B$, which is earthed. If $d$ is the separation between the plate, then potential difference between the plates

$$V = Ed.$$

Here $E = \frac{\sigma}{\epsilon_0}$. If A is the area of each plate, then $\sigma = \frac{Q}{A}$.

$$V = \frac{(Q/A)d}{\epsilon_0}$$

Capacitance $$C = \frac{Q}{V}$$

or $$C = \frac{\epsilon_0 A}{d}. \quad \ldots(1)$$

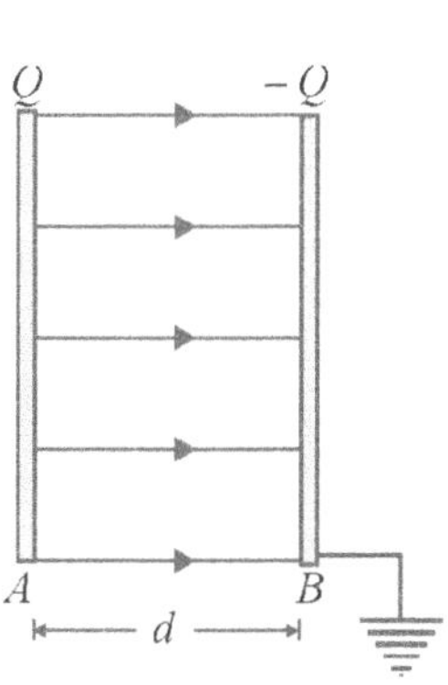

Fig. 2.8

### Effect of dielectric

Above obtained expression for the capacitance holds only when the plates are in vacuum or air. Michael Faraday, first investigated and found that, when a conductor is charged in the presence of dielectric, the charge on the conductor

$$[Q]_{\text{in dielectric medium}} = k[Q]_{\text{air}}, \text{ keeping V constant.}$$

Thus $$[C]_{\text{in dielectric medium}} = k[C]_{\text{air}} \quad \ldots (2)$$

**Note:**

If there are $n$ identical plates at equal distances from each other and the alternate plates are connected together, then the capacitance of the arrangement will be $C = (n-1)\dfrac{\epsilon_0 A}{d}$.

### Capacitance of parallel plate capacitor with a compound dielectric

On introduction of dielectric in the space between the plates of a capacitor, there is decrease in the potential difference between the plates. The potential difference between the plates

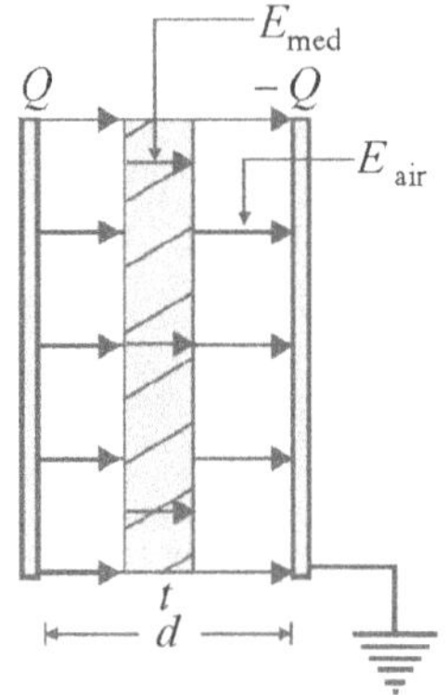

*Fig. 2.9*

$$V = V_{air} + V_{med}$$

$$= E_{air}(d-t) + E_{med}\, t$$

$$= \left[\frac{\sigma}{\epsilon_0}(d-t) + \frac{\sigma}{k\,\epsilon_0}t\right]$$

Capacity $$C = \frac{Q}{V} = \frac{\sigma A}{\left[\dfrac{\sigma}{\epsilon_0}(d-t) + \dfrac{\sigma t}{k\,\epsilon_0}\right]}$$

or $$C = \frac{\epsilon_0 A}{\left[(d-t) + \dfrac{t}{k}\right]}$$

### Other cases :

1. If a metal slab is introduced, then $k = \infty$ and $C = \dfrac{\epsilon_0 A}{(d-t)}$.
2. On introducing the dielectric slab, the potential difference between the plates falls and the capacity is increased. Hence to have the same capacity as before, we must increase the distance between the plates by

$$x = \left(\frac{k-1}{k}\right)t.$$

3. If there are two dielectrics $k_1$ and $k_2$ of thickness $t_1$ and $t_2$ respectively, then

$$C = \frac{\epsilon_0 A}{\left[d - (t_1 + t_2) + \dfrac{t_1}{k_1} + \dfrac{t_2}{k_2}\right]}$$

4. If dielectrics $k_1$, $k_2$, .... of thickness $t_1$, $t_2$, .... respectively are filled the space between the plates, then

$$C = \frac{\epsilon_0 A}{\left[\dfrac{t_1}{k_1} + \dfrac{t_2}{k_2} + \ldots\ldots\ldots + \dfrac{t_n}{k_n}\right]}$$

5. If unequal charges are placed on the plates, then charge on the right face of the plate $A$

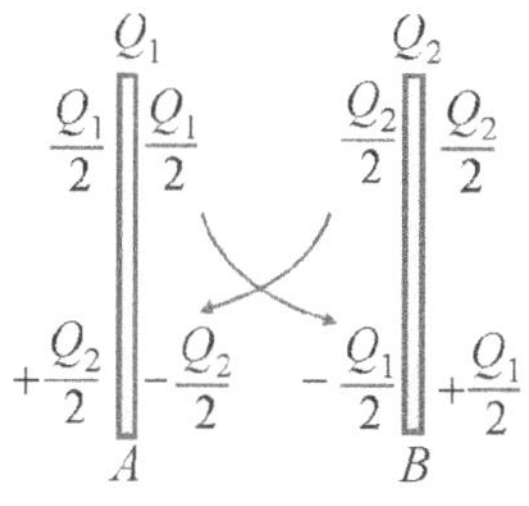

*Fig. 2.10*

$$Q_A = \left[\frac{Q_1 - Q_2}{2}\right]$$

$$V_{AB} = E\,d$$

$$= \frac{\sigma}{\epsilon_0} d$$

$$= \frac{(Q_A / A)}{\epsilon_0} d$$

or

$$V_{AB} = \left(\frac{Q_1 - Q_2}{2 \epsilon_0 A}\right) d$$

Capacitance does not depend on the charges, and so it remains constant.

### Leakage current

Dielectric is not a perfectly insulating material. So when the space between the plates is completely filled with a dielectric, there flows some charge through the dielectric medium. The flow of charge per unit time through a dielectric medium is called leakage current. Consider a dielectric of constant $k$ and resistivity $\rho$. The capacitance

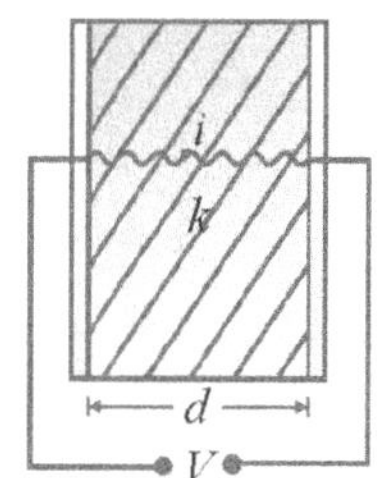

*Fig. 2.11*

$$C = \frac{k \epsilon_0 A}{d}$$

and resistance

$$R = \frac{\rho d}{A}$$

If $V$ is the potential difference between the plates of capacitor, then current

$$i = \frac{V}{R}$$

$$= \frac{V}{\rho \frac{d}{A}} = \frac{VA}{\rho d}$$

$$= \frac{V}{k \epsilon_0 \rho}\left(\frac{k \epsilon_0 A}{d}\right) = \frac{VC}{k \epsilon_0 \rho}$$

or

$$i = \frac{VC}{k \epsilon_0 \rho}$$

## 2.6 ENERGY STORED IN A CAPACITOR

When we stretch the spring, the elastic potential energy will store in the spring. On the similar way, when we charge the capacitor, an electric potential energy stores in it. This energy can be recovered if the capacitor is allowed to discharge. If the charging is done by a battery, the electrical energy is stored at the expense of chemical energy of the battery. In charging the capacitor the work is done by the external agent against the repulsion of the charge which has already gone to the capacitor. This work done will store in terms of electrical potential energy.

Suppose at any time $t$, charge $q$ has gone to the capacitor. If $C$ is the capacitance, then potential

$$v = \frac{q}{C}.$$

If $dq$ amount of charge is brought against the repulsion, then work done

$$dW = v dq = \frac{q}{C} dq$$

Total work done in charging the capacitor to a charge Q

$$W = \int dW = \int_0^Q \frac{q}{C}\,dq$$

or

$$W = \frac{Q^2}{2C}$$

$\therefore$ Energy stored in the capacitor $U = \frac{Q^2}{2C} = \frac{1}{2}QV = \frac{1}{2}CV^2 \quad \left[V = \frac{Q}{C}\right]$ ....(1)

This relation is analogous to the elastic potential energy stored in the spring i.e., $U = \frac{1}{2}kx^2$.

Consider a parallel plate capacitor of area $A$ and plate separation $d$. The electric field is uniform in the region between the plates and the fringing effects are neglected. Energy stored in the capacitor

$$U = \frac{1}{2}CV^2$$

$$= \frac{1}{2}\frac{\epsilon_0 A}{d}V^2$$

$$= \frac{1}{2}\epsilon_0\left(\frac{V}{d}\right)^2(Ad)$$

or

$$U = \frac{1}{2}\epsilon_0 E^2 \times \text{volume} \quad ...(2)$$

or

$$\frac{U}{\text{volume}} = \frac{1}{2}\epsilon_0 E^2$$

or

$$u = \frac{1}{2}\epsilon_0 \vec{E}\cdot\vec{E} \quad ...(3)$$

If the capacitor is filled with a dielectric of constant $k$, then

$$u = \frac{1}{2}k\,\epsilon_0 E^2 \quad ...(4)$$

**Note:**

1. Above relations are derived for a parallel plate capacitor, but they are true for others also. If electric field E is not uniform in the total volume, then we can write

$$U = \frac{1}{2}k\,\epsilon_0 \int E^2 d(vol)$$

2. If a battery is used to charge the capacitor, and $Q$ is the charge delivered by it, then work done by the battery

$$W = VQ.$$

But the energy stored in the capacitor

$$U = \frac{1}{2}QV$$

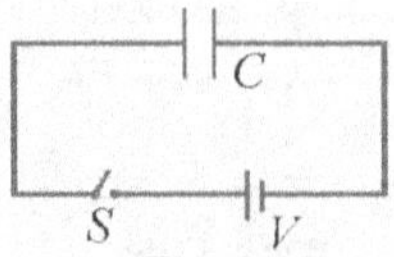

C S V

*Fig. 2.12*

The remaining energy $= VQ - \frac{1}{2}QV = \frac{1}{2}QV$ is lost as heat and light. Thus we can write

$$W_{\text{external source}} = 2U.$$

## 2.7 FORCE BETWEEN THE PLATES OF A CAPACITOR

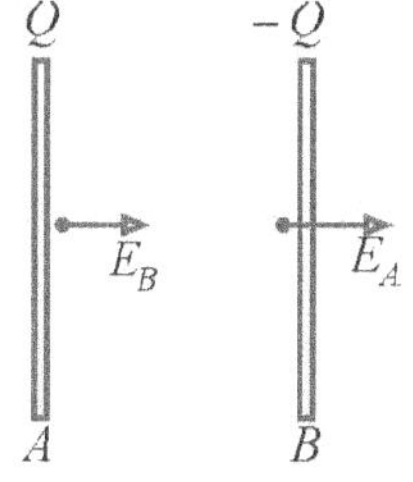

Fig. 2.13

**Method I :** Consider a parallel plate capacitor with plate area $A$. Suppose a charge $Q$ is given to one plate and $-Q$ to the other plate. The force on plate $B$ due to plate $A$ (or vice-versa)

$$F_{BA} = E_A Q_B.$$

The electric field at the position of plate $B$ due to the plate $A$ is

$$E_A = \frac{\sigma}{2\epsilon_0} = \frac{Q}{2\epsilon_0 A}$$

$$\therefore \quad F_{BA} = \frac{Q}{2\epsilon_0 A} \times Q$$

or $$F_{BA} = F_{AB} = F = \frac{Q^2}{2\epsilon_0 A} \quad ...(1)$$

If $E$ is the electric field between the plates, then

$$E = \frac{\sigma}{\epsilon_0} = \frac{Q}{\epsilon_0 A}$$

$$\therefore \quad F = \frac{1}{2}\epsilon_0 E^2 A \quad ...(2)$$

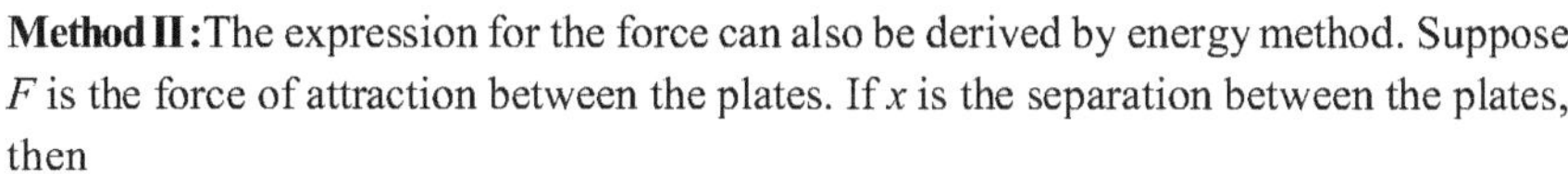

**Method II :** The expression for the force can also be derived by energy method. Suppose $F$ is the force of attraction between the plates. If $x$ is the separation between the plates, then

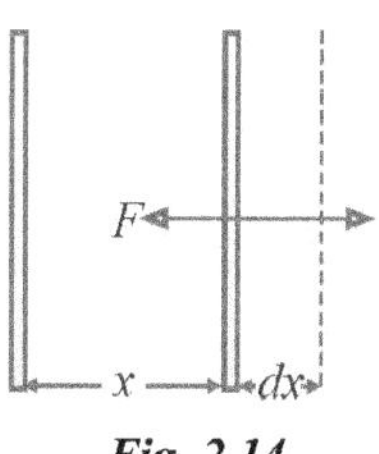

Fig. 2.14

$$U = \frac{1}{2}\epsilon_0 E^2 (Ax)$$

and $$\frac{dU}{dx} = \frac{1}{2}\epsilon_0 E^2 A$$

By the definition $$F = -\frac{dU}{dx}$$

$$= -\frac{1}{2}\epsilon_0 E^2 A$$

**Note:**

1. For isolated capacitor with constant charge, $F = \frac{Q^2}{2\epsilon_0 A}$. This force does not depend on the separation between the plates, and so the constant amount of force is needed.
2. For a capacitor having constant p.d. across the plates, the force

$$F = \frac{(CV)^2}{2\epsilon_0 A} = \left(\frac{\epsilon_0 A}{d}\right)^2 \frac{V^2}{2\epsilon_0 A} = \frac{1}{2}\epsilon_0 \frac{V^2}{d^2} A$$

In this case force depends on the separation (d) between the plates. Thus if we change the separation now, the variable force is needed.

**Ex. 2** **A capacitor has square plates, each of side a making an angle θ with each other as shown in *fig. 2.15*. Show that for small θ, the capacitance *C* is given by**

$$C = \frac{\epsilon_0 a^2}{d}\left(1-\frac{a\theta}{2d}\right).$$

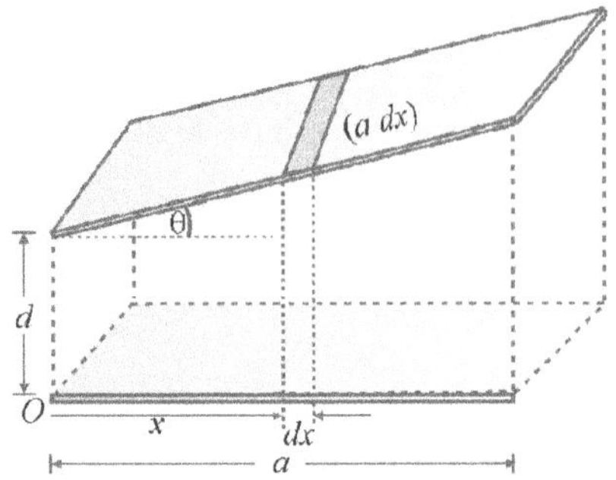

*Fig. 2.15*

**Sol.**

The given capacitor may be supposed to be made up of large number of differential capacitors. Consider one such capacitor of width $dx$ at a distance $x$ from $O$. The area of the element capacitor $dA = adx$. If $d'$ is the separation between the plates at the position of element, then

$$d' = d + x\tan\theta \simeq d + x\theta$$

The capacitance of the element

$$dC = \frac{\epsilon_0 (dA)}{d'} = \frac{\epsilon_0 (adx)}{(d+x\theta)}$$

$$\therefore \quad dC = \frac{\epsilon_0 (adx)}{d\left(1+\frac{x\theta}{d}\right)}$$

$$= \left[\frac{\epsilon_0}{d}(adx)\left(1+\frac{x\theta}{d}\right)^{-1}\right]$$

$$= \left[\frac{\epsilon_0}{d}(adx)\left(1-\frac{x\theta}{d}\right)\right]$$

The total capacitance

$$C = \int_0^a \left[\frac{\epsilon_0}{d}(adx)\left(1-\frac{x\theta}{d}\right)\right]$$

$$= \frac{\epsilon_0 a}{d}\left|x-\frac{\theta}{d}\frac{x^2}{2}\right|_0^a$$

$$= \frac{\epsilon_0 a}{d}\left[a-\frac{\theta a^2}{2d}\right]$$

$$= \frac{\epsilon_0 a^2}{d}\left(1-\frac{\theta a}{2d}\right).$$

**Ex. 3** **Two isolated metallic solid spheres of radii *R* and 2*R* are charged such that both of these have same charge density σ. The spheres are located far away from each other, and connected by a thin conducting wire. Find the new charge density on the bigger sphere.**

**Sol.**

**Method I:** Charge on the smaller sphere

$$Q_1 = \sigma \times 4\pi R^2 = 4\pi R^2\sigma$$

Charge of the bigger sphere

$$Q_2 = \sigma \times 4\pi(2R)^2 = 16\pi R^2\sigma$$

If $Q'_1$ and $Q'_2$ are the charges after connected them, then

$$Q'_1 + Q'_2 = Q_1 + Q_2 = 4\pi R^2\sigma + 16\pi R^2\sigma$$

$$\text{or} \quad Q'_1 + Q'_2 = 20\pi R^2\sigma \qquad \text{...(i)}$$

There potential becomes equal, and so

$$\frac{1}{4\pi\epsilon_0}\frac{Q'_1}{R} = \frac{1}{4\pi\epsilon_0}\frac{Q'_2}{2R}$$

$$\text{or} \quad Q'_2 = 2Q'_1 \qquad \text{...(ii)}$$

Solving equations (i) and (ii), we get

$$Q'_1 = \frac{20}{3}\pi R^2\sigma$$

$$\text{and} \quad Q'_2 = \frac{40}{3}\pi R^2\sigma$$

∴ Surface density of bigger sphere

$$\sigma'_2 = \frac{Q'_2}{4\pi(2R)^2} = \frac{\frac{40}{3}\pi R^2\sigma}{4\pi(2R)^2}$$

$$= \frac{5}{6}\sigma \qquad \textit{Ans.}$$

**Method II :** After connection, the common potential

$$V = \frac{Q_1+Q_2}{C_1+C_2}$$

$$= \left(\frac{20\pi R^2\sigma}{4\pi\epsilon_0 R + 4\pi\epsilon_0 (2R)}\right)$$

$$= \frac{5}{3}\frac{R\sigma}{\epsilon_0}$$

The new charge on bigger sphere

$$Q'_2 = C_2 V = 4\pi\epsilon_0(2R)\times\left(\frac{5R\sigma}{3\epsilon_0}\right)$$

$$= \frac{40}{3}\pi R^2\sigma. \qquad \textit{Ans.}$$

**Ex. 4** **Two parallel plate condensers *A* and *B* having capacitances of 1μF and 5μF are charged separately to the same potential of 100V. Now the positive plate of *A* is connected to the negative plate of *B* and negative plate of *A* to the positive plate of *B*. Find the final charge on each condenser and total loss of electrical energy in the condensers.**

## Sol.

The charge on condenser $A$,

$$Q_1 = C_1V = 1\times10^{-6}\times100$$

$$= 100\times10^{-6}C$$

The charge on condenser $B$,

$$Q_2 = C_2V = 5\times10^{-6}\times100$$

$$= 500\times10^{-6}\ C$$

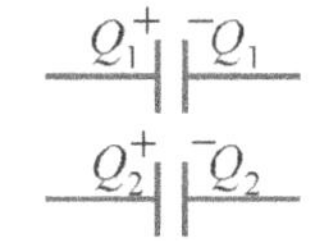

(a) Before connection (b) After connection

*Fig. 2.16*

If $V$ is the common potential of the plates, then

$$V = \frac{Q_1+Q_2}{C_1+C_2}$$

$$= \frac{100\times10^{-6}-500\times100^{-6}}{1\times10^{-6}+5\times10^{-6}}$$

or $$|V| = \frac{200}{3}V$$

If $Q'_1$ and $Q'_2$ are the charges after connection, then

$$Q'_1 = C_1V = 1\times10^{-6}\times\frac{200}{3}$$

$$= \frac{200}{3}\mu C$$

and $$Q'_2 = 5\times10^{-6}\times\frac{200}{3}$$

$$= \frac{1000}{3}\mu C \qquad \textit{Ans.}$$

Initial energy on the condensers

$$U_i = \frac{1}{2}C_1V_1^2+\frac{1}{2}C_2V_2^2$$

$$= \frac{1}{2}\times10^{-6}\times100^2+\frac{1}{2}\times5\times10^{-6}\times100^2$$

$$= 0.03\text{ J}$$

Final energy $$U_f = \frac{1}{2}(C_1+C_2)V^2$$

$$= \frac{1}{2}\left(10^{-6}+5\times10^{-6}\right)\times\left(\frac{200}{3}\right)^2$$

$$= \frac{0.04}{3}J$$

$\therefore$ Loss in electrical energy $$= 0.03-\frac{0.04}{3}$$

$$= \left(\frac{0.05}{3}\right)J. \qquad \textit{Ans.}$$

**Ex. 5** **A conductor is charged from an electrophorous by repeated contacts with a plate which after each contact is recharged with a quantity $Q$ of electricity from the electrophorous. If $q_1$ is the charge of the conductor after the first operation, calculate the ultimate charge.**

## Sol.

**Method I :** Suppose $C_1$ and $C_2$ are the capacitances of conductor and electrophorous respectively. On the first contact, the charge taken by the conductor is $q$, and the charge left on electrophorous plate is $Q-q_1$.

Since in contact, the potentials become equal, so

$$\frac{Q-q_1}{C_2} = \frac{q_1}{C_1}$$

or $$q_1 = \frac{QC_1}{C_1+C_2}$$

In the second contact, let $q_2$ be the charge taken up by the conductor, then $q_1+q_2$ becomes the total charge over the conductor and the charge left over $C_2$ is $Q-q_2$. Again

$$\frac{Q-q_2}{C_2} = \frac{q_1+q_2}{C_1}$$

or $$q_2 = \frac{q_1C_1^2}{(C_1+C_2)^2} = \frac{q_1^2}{Q}$$

Similarly the charge on the conductor on the third contact is $\frac{q_1^3}{Q}$ and so on. Hence the ultimate charge

$$q_{max} = q_1+\frac{q_1^2}{Q}+\frac{q_1^3}{Q}+\ldots\ldots..\infty$$

$$= \frac{q_1Q}{Q-q_1}. \qquad \textit{Ans.}$$

**Method II :** We have got $\frac{q_1}{Q-q_1} = \frac{C_1}{C_2}$

Let $q_{max}$ be the maximum charge which can be given to the conductor. When potential of conductor becomes equal to the potential of the electrophorous plate, thereafter no charge flows between them, so

$$V_{Plate} = V_{Conductor}$$

$$\frac{Q}{C_2} = \frac{q_{max}}{C_1}$$

$$\Rightarrow \quad q_{max} = \frac{C_1}{C_2}Q = \frac{q_1Q}{Q-q}. \qquad \textit{Ans.}$$

## 2.8 CAPACITORS IN SERIES AND PARALLEL

In some circuits, there are many capacitors connected together, we can sometimes replace that combination with an equivalent capacitor. Here we are discussing two basic combinations of capacitors.

(a) Three capacitors connected in series.

⇓

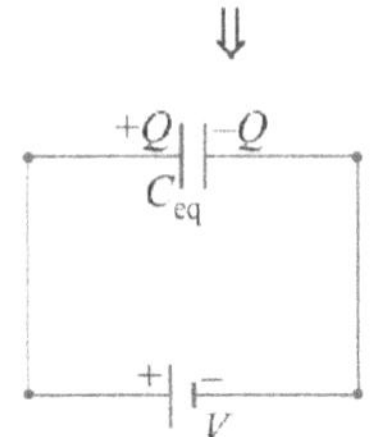


(b) The equivalent capacitor.

*Fig. 2.17*

### Capacitors in series

*Fig. 2.17* shows three capacitors connected in series with a battery. In series means that the capacitors are connected by a wire and there is no other way of flowing of charge. When a potential $V$ is applied across them, the same amount $Q$ of charge will appear on each of the capacitor. The sum of the potential differences across all the capacitors is equal to the applied potential difference $V$. Thus, if $V_1$, $V_2$ and $V_3$ are the potential differences across the capacitors $C_1$, $C_2$ and $C_3$ respectively, then

$$V = V_1 + V_2 + V_3.$$

Here $V_1 = \frac{Q}{C_1}$, $V_2 = \frac{Q}{C_2}$ and $V_3 = \frac{Q}{C_3}$. If $C_{eq}$ is the equivalent capacitance, then

$$V = Q/C.$$

$$\therefore \quad \frac{Q}{C} = \frac{Q}{C_1} + \frac{Q}{C_2} + \frac{Q}{C_3}$$

or

$$\frac{1}{C_{eq}} = \frac{1}{C_1} + \frac{1}{C_2} + \frac{1}{C_3} \quad ...(1)$$

For n-capacitors, we can write

$$\frac{1}{C_{eq}} = \sum_{i=1}^{n} \left( \frac{1}{C_i} \right) \quad ...(2)$$

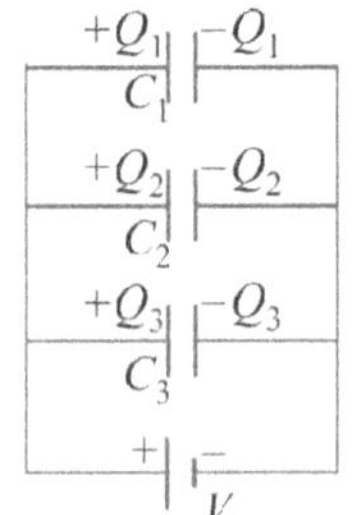


Fig. (a) Three capacitors are connected in parallel

⇓

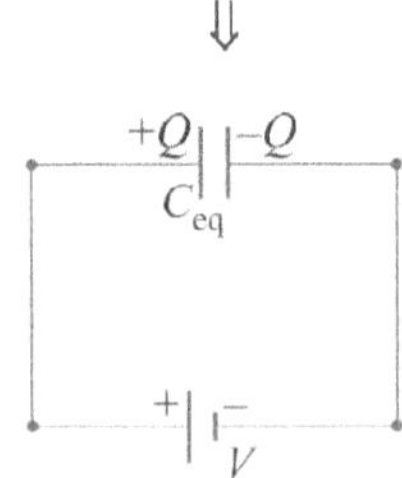


(b) The equivalent capacitor

*Fig. 2.18*

### Capacitors in parallel

*Fig. 2.18* shows three capacitors are connected in parallel with a battery. In parallel connection, one plate of all the capacitors are connected to the wire through the positive terminal of the battery and similarly second plates are connected together through negative terminal of the battery. Thus, each capacitor in parallel has the same potential difference V, which produces charge on the capacitor. If $Q_1$, $Q_2$ and $Q_3$ are the charges on the capacitors $C_1$, $C_2$ and $C_2$ respectively, then

$$Q = Q_1 + Q_2 + Q_3.$$

Here $Q_1 = C_1V$, $Q_2 = C_2V$ and $Q_3 = C_3V$. If $C_{eq}$ is the equivalent capacitance, then total charge $Q = C_{eq}\, V$.

or

$$C_{eq}\, V = C_1V + C_2V + C_3V$$

$$\therefore \quad C_{eq} = C_1 + C_2 + C_3 \quad ...(3)$$

For n-capacitors, we can write

$$C_{eq} = \sum_{i=1}^{n} C_i \quad ...(4)$$

**Ex. 6** **Calculate the capacitance of a parallel plate condenser, with plate area $A$ and distance between plates $d$, when filled with a dielectric whose dielectric constant varies as :**

$$\in(x) = \in_0 + \beta x \qquad 0 < x < \frac{d}{2}$$

$$\in(x) = \in_0 + \beta(d-x), \quad \frac{d}{2} < x < d.$$

**For what value of $\beta$ would the capacity of the condenser twice that when it is without any dielectric ?**

**Sol.**

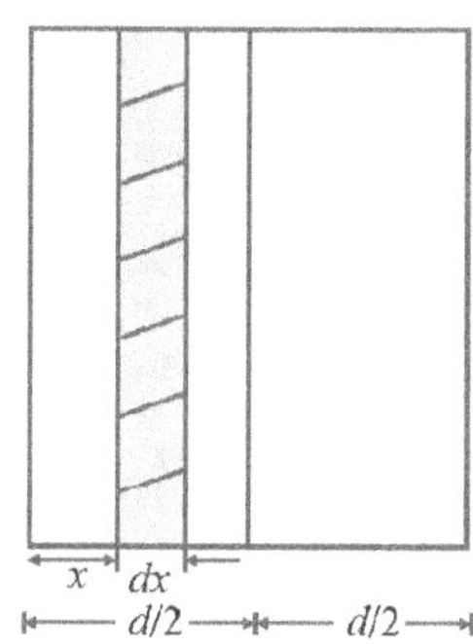


*Fig. 2.19*

The given capacitor is equivalent to two condensers in series. If $C_1$ and $C_2$ are their capacities, then

$$\frac{1}{C} = \int\left[\frac{1}{dC_1} + \frac{1}{dC_2}\right] \qquad ...(i)$$

Take an element of width dx at a distance x from the left plate. Its capacity

$$dC_1 = \frac{(\in_0 + \beta x)A}{dx} \qquad x \le d/2$$

and

$$dC_2 = \frac{(\in_0 + \beta(d-x))A}{dx} \qquad \frac{d}{2} < x \le d$$

Substituting these values in equation (i), we have

$$\frac{1}{C} = \frac{1}{A}\left[\int_0^{\frac{d}{2}} \frac{dx}{(\in_0 + \beta x)} + \int_{\frac{d}{2}}^{d} \frac{dx}{\in_0 + \beta(d-x)}\right]$$

$$= \frac{1}{A\beta}\left[\{\ell n(\in_0 + \beta x)\}_0^{\frac{d}{2}} - \{\ell n(\in_0 + \beta(d-x))\}_{\frac{d}{2}}^{d}\right]$$

$$= \frac{1}{A\beta}\left[\left\{\ell n\left(\in_0 + \beta\frac{d}{2}\right) - \ell n \in_0\right\} - \left\{\ell n \in_0 - \ell n\left(\in_0 + \beta\frac{d}{2}\right)\right\}\right]$$

$$= \frac{2}{A\beta}\left[\ell n\left(\in_0 + \beta\frac{d}{2}\right) - \ell n \in_0\right]$$

$$= \frac{2}{A\beta}\ell n\left(\frac{\in_0 + \beta\frac{d}{2}}{\in_0}\right) \qquad \textit{Ans.}$$

The capacitance $C$ of a condenser without dielectric is

$$C' = \frac{\in_0 A}{d}$$

According to the given condition

$$C = 2C'$$

or

$$\frac{1}{C} = \frac{1}{2C'}$$

or

$$\frac{2}{A\beta}\ell n\left(\frac{\in_0 + \frac{\beta d}{2}}{\in_0}\right) = \frac{d}{2\in_0 A}$$

or

$$\beta = \frac{4\in_0}{d}\ell n\left(\frac{\in_0 + \beta\frac{d}{2}}{\in_0}\right). \qquad \textit{Ans.}$$

**Ex. 7** **Calculate the capacitance of a capacitor filled with two dielectrics of same dimensions but of dielectric constant $k_1$ and $k_2$ respectively.**

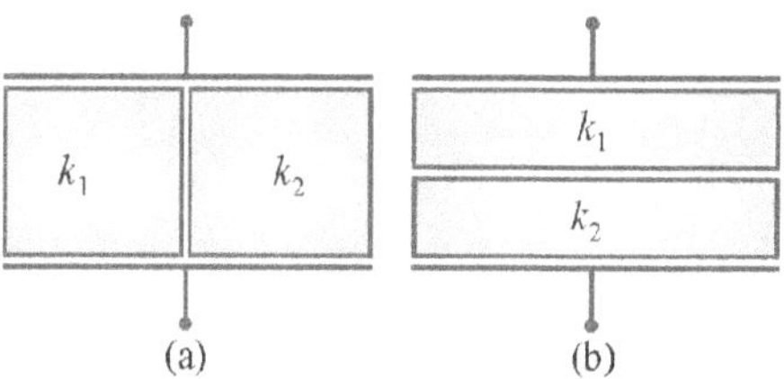


*Fig. 2.20*

**Sol.**

(a) The arrangement can be assumed as two capacitors in parallel. If $d$ is the separation and A is the area of each plate, then each capacitor will occupy area $\frac{A}{2}$. If $C_1$ and $C_2$ are the respective capacitances, then

$$C = C_1 + C_2$$

$$= \frac{\in_0 k_1\left(\frac{A}{2}\right)}{d} + \frac{\in_0 k_2\left(\frac{A}{2}\right)}{d}$$

$$= \frac{\in_0 (k_1 + k_2)A}{2d}. \qquad \textit{Ans.}$$

(b) This arrangement can be assumed as two capacitors in series. Each capacitor will be of area $A$ and separation $\frac{d}{2}$. If $C_1$ and $C_2$ are their respective capacitances, then

$$\frac{1}{C} = \frac{1}{C_1} + \frac{1}{C_2}$$

$$= \frac{\frac{d}{2}}{\in_0 k_1 A} + \frac{\frac{d}{2}}{\in_0 k_2 A}$$

or

$$C = \frac{2\in_0 A}{d}\left(\frac{k_1 k_2}{k_1 + k_2}\right). \qquad \textit{Ans.}$$

**Ex. 8** **A capacitor is formed by two square metal-plates of edge $a$, separated by a distance $d$. Dielectrics of dielectric constant $k_1$ and $k_2$ are filled in the gap shown in *fig. 2.21*. Find the capacitance.**

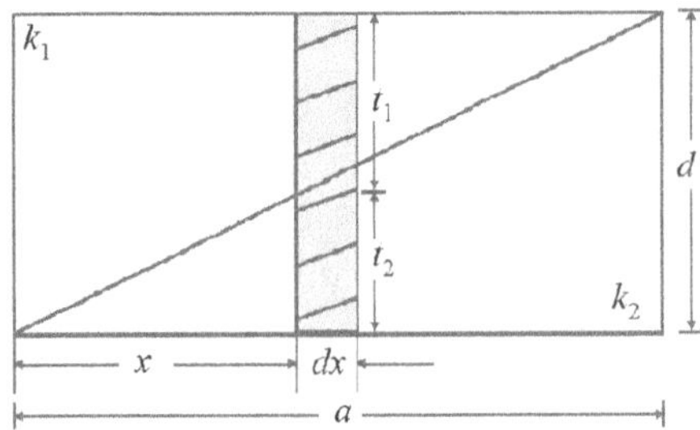


*Fig. 2.21*

## Sol.

Take a small element of the plate of length $dx$ at a distance $x$ from the left end of the plate. If $t_1$ and $t_2$ are the thicknesses of the dielectrics of $k_1$ and $k_2$ respectively, then

$$t_1 = \frac{d(a-x)}{a} \text{ and } t_2 = \frac{xd}{a}$$

The capacitance of element capacitor

$$dC = \frac{\epsilon_0 (dA)}{\frac{t_1}{k_1}+\frac{t_2}{k_2}}$$

$$= \frac{\epsilon_0\, adx}{\left[\frac{d(a-x)}{k_1 a}+\frac{xd}{k_2 a}\right]}$$

$$= \frac{\epsilon_0 a^2}{d}\frac{dx}{\left[\frac{a-x}{k_1}+\frac{x}{k_2}\right]}$$

The total capacitance

$$C = \int_0^a \frac{\epsilon_0 a^2}{d}\frac{dx}{\left[\frac{a-x}{k_1}+\frac{x}{k_2}\right]}$$

$$= \int_0^a \frac{\epsilon_0 a^2}{d}\frac{dx}{\left[\frac{a}{k_1}+x\left(\frac{k_1-k_2}{k_1k_2}\right)\right]}$$

$$= \frac{\epsilon_0 a^2}{d}\left|\frac{\ell n\left[\frac{a}{k_1}+x\left(\frac{k_1-k_2}{k_1k_2}\right)\right]}{\left(\frac{k_1-k_2}{k_1k_2}\right)}\right|_0^a$$

$$= \frac{\epsilon_0 a^2}{d}\left(\frac{k_1k_2}{k_1-k_2}\right)\left[\ell n\left[\left(\frac{a}{k_1}\right)+a\frac{(k_1-k_2)}{k_1k_2}\right]-\ell n\frac{a}{k_1}\right]$$

$$= \frac{\epsilon_0 a^2}{d}\left(\frac{k_1k_2}{k_1-k_2}\right)\left[\ln\left(\frac{a}{k_2}\right)-\ln\left(\frac{a}{k_1}\right)\right]$$

$$= \frac{\epsilon_0 a^2}{d}\left(\frac{k_1k_2}{k_1-k_2}\right)\ell n\frac{k_1}{k_2}$$ **Ans.**

**Ex. 9** **A parallel plate capacitor is constructed using three different dielectric materials as shown in *fig. 2.22*. The parallel plates across which a potential difference is applied are of area $A$ and are separated by a distance $d$. Find the capacitance across $A$ and $B$.**

| $A$ | $2k$ / $4k$ | $k$ | $B$ |
|---|---|---|---|
| | $d/2$ | $d/2$ | |

*Fig. 2.22*

## Sol.

If $C_1$, $C_2$ and $C_3$ are the capacitances of the parts with dielectrics $2k$, $4k$ and $k$ respectively, then

$$C_1 = \frac{(2k)\epsilon_0 \frac{A}{2}}{\frac{d}{2}} = \frac{2k\,\epsilon_0 A}{d} = C$$

$$C_2 = \frac{(4k)\epsilon_0 \frac{A}{2}}{\frac{d}{2}} = \frac{4k\,\epsilon_0 A}{d} = 2C$$

and

$$C_3 = \frac{k\,\epsilon_0 A}{\frac{d}{2}} = \frac{2k\,\epsilon_0 A}{d} = C$$

Here $C_1$ and $C_2$ are in parallel and $C_3$ in series with them, so

$$\frac{1}{C_{AB}} = \frac{1}{C_1+C_2}+\frac{1}{C_3}$$

$$\frac{1}{C_{AB}} = \frac{C_1+C_2+C_3}{(C_1+C_2)C_3}$$

$$= \frac{C+2C+C}{(C+2C)C} = \frac{4C}{3C^2}$$

$$= \frac{4}{3C}$$

or

$$C_{AB} = \frac{3}{4}C = \frac{3}{4}\frac{(2k\,\epsilon_0 A)}{d}$$

$$= \frac{3}{2}\frac{k\,\epsilon_0 A}{d}$$ **Ans.**

**Ex. 10** **Find the capacitance of the following combinations between $A$ and $B$. Area of the each plate is $A$ and separation between nearest two plates is $d$.**

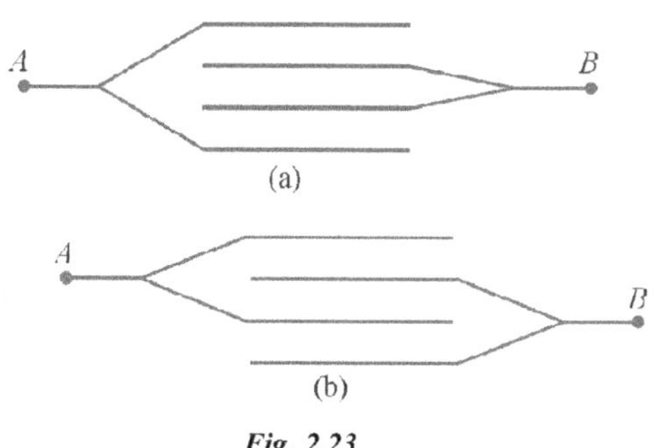


*Fig. 2.23*

## Sol.

When $A$ and $B$ are connected to the positive and negative terminals of the battery respectively, the charges will appear on them as :

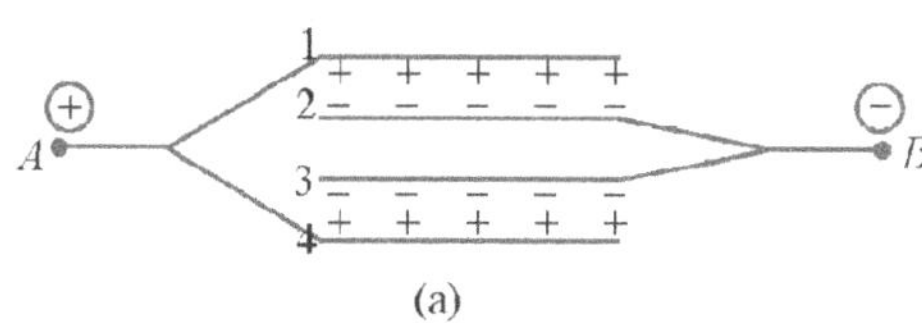


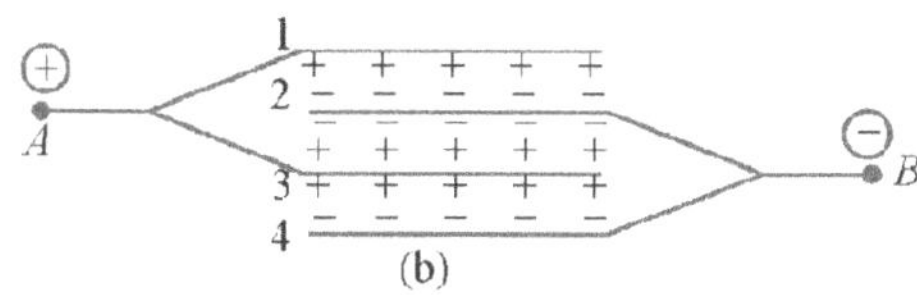


*Fig. 2.24*

(a) It is clear from the figure that there forms two capacitors which are in parallel. Thus $C_{AB} = 2C = 2\frac{\epsilon_0 A}{d}$

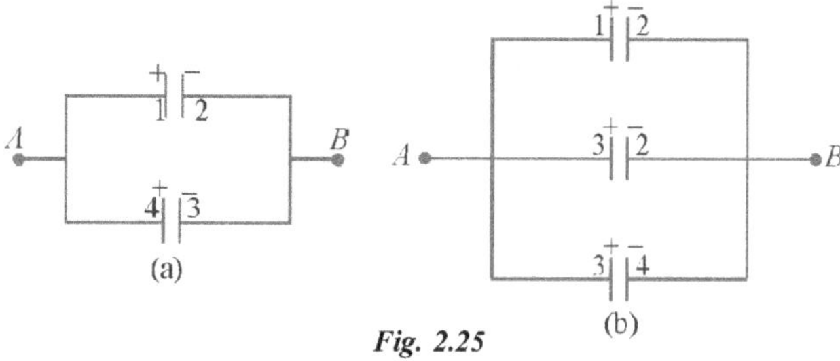


*Fig. 2.25*

(b) There are three capacitors in parallel. Thus $C_{AB} = 3C = 3\frac{\epsilon_0 A}{d}$

**Ex. 11** **Four identical metal plates are located in air at equal distance $d$ from one another. The area of each plate is equal to A. Find the capacitance of the system between points $A$ and $B$ if the plates are interconnected as shown in *fig. 2.26*.**

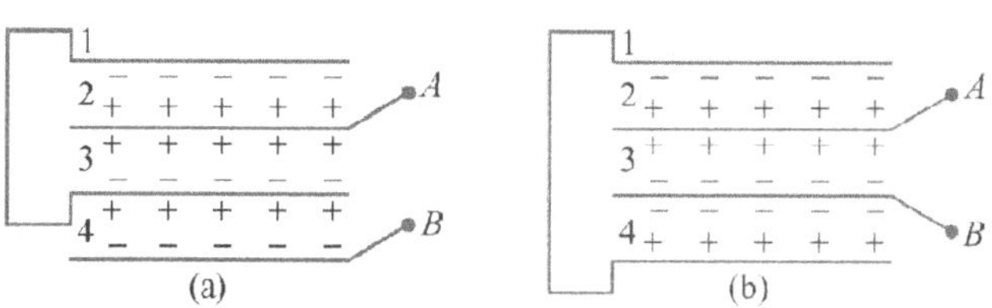


*Fig. 2.26*

## Sol.

(a) $A$ and $B$ are connected to the positive and negative terminals of the battery. The charge appear on the plates are shown in figure. The equivalent arrangement of the plates is shown in figure (a). There forms three capacitors.

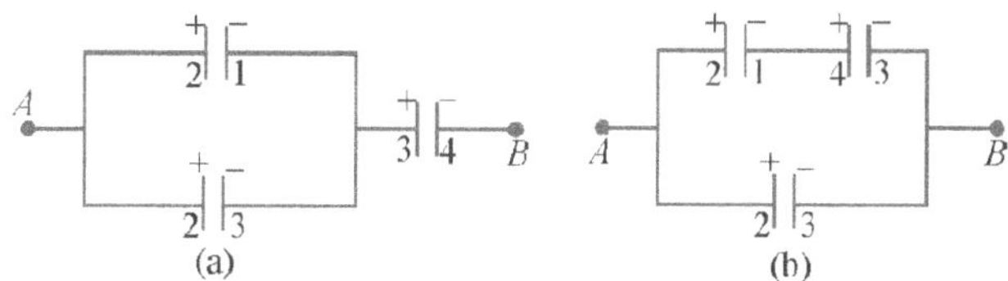


*Fig. 2.27*

If $C$ is the capacitance of the each capacitor then

$$C_{AB} = \frac{(2C)C}{2C+C} = \frac{2C}{3}$$

$$= \frac{2}{3}\frac{\epsilon_0 A}{d}$$

(b) The equivalent arrangement of the plates is shown in figure (b). There forms three capacitors. If $C$ is the capacitance of each capacitor, then

$$C_{AB} = \frac{C}{2} + C = \frac{3C}{2}$$

$$= \frac{3}{2}\frac{\epsilon_0 A}{d}$$ ***Ans.***

**Ex. 12** **Five identical conducting plates 1, 2, 3, 4 and 5 are fixed parallel to and equidistant from each other as shown in *fig. 2.28*. Plates 2 and 5 are connected by a conductor while 1 and 3 are joined by another conductor. The junction of 1 and 3 and the plate 4 are connected to a source of constant emf $V_0$. Find :**

**(i) The effective capacity of the system between the terminals of the source.**

**(ii) The charge on plates 3 and 5.**

**Given $d$ = distance between any two successive plates and $A$ = area of either face of each plate.**

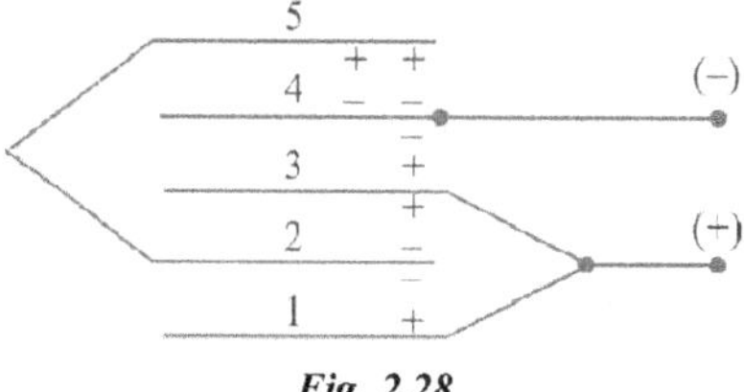


*Fig. 2.28*

**Note:** In solving this type of problem, first mark the charges on the plates. It should be remembered that :

(i) The plate/plates connected to the positive terminal of the battery will have net positive charge and similarly for the negative terminal.

(ii) The plate/plates which are not connected to any terminal of the battery will have induced charge. The net induced charge of the plates together must be zero.

## Sol.

The equivalent arrangement of the plates is shown in *Fig. 2.29*. From these five plates, there forms four identical capacitors. These are $C_{12}$, $C_{32}$, $C_{34}$ and $C_{54}$. The capacitance of each capacitor $C = \frac{\epsilon_0 A}{d}$.

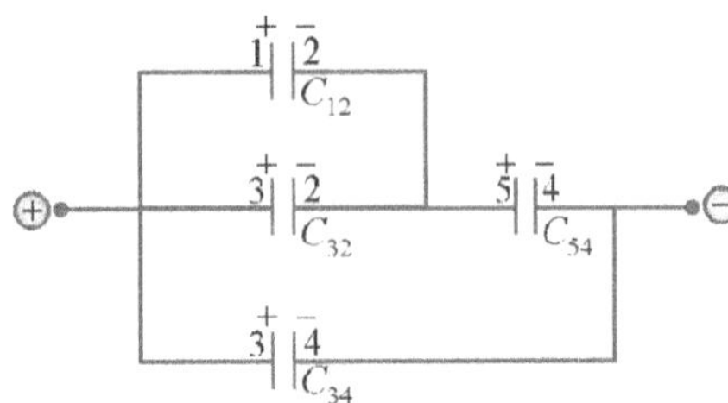

*Fig. 2.29*

Capacitors $C_{12}$ and $C_{32}$ are in parallel and so their capacitance becomes $2C$. Now $2C$ is in series with capacitor $C_{54}$, and so equivalent capacitance becomes $\frac{2C}{3}$. And this now is in parallel with $C_{34}$. Thus effective capacitance between the terminals becomes

$$C_{eq} = C + \frac{2C}{3} = \frac{5C}{3}$$

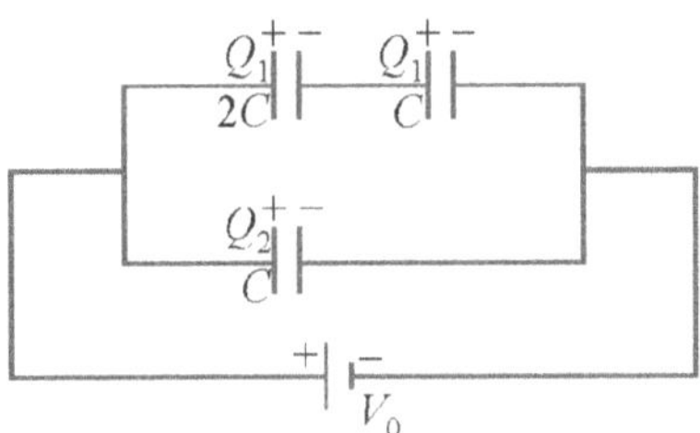

*Fig. 2.30*

Charge on the capacitor $C_{34}$ :

$$Q_{34} = CV_0.$$

Charge on the capacitors $C_{54}$, $C_{12}$ and $C_{32}$ :

$$Q_{54} = \frac{2C}{3}V_0$$

This charge equally divided on to $C_{12}$ and $C_{32}$, so

$$Q_{12} = Q_{32} = Q = \frac{CV_0}{3}$$

The charge on plate 1 : $Q_1 = +Q_{12} = +\frac{CV_0}{3}$

The charge on plate 2 : $Q_2 = -(Q_{12} + Q_{32})$

$$= -2\frac{CV_0}{3} = -2\frac{\epsilon_0 AV_0}{3d}$$

The charge on plate 3 : $Q_3 = +(Q_{32} + Q_{34}) = \left(CV_0 + \frac{CV_0}{3}\right)$

$$= \frac{4}{3}CV_0 = \frac{4}{3}\frac{\epsilon_0 AV_0}{d}$$

The charge on plate 4 : $Q_4 = -(Q_{34} + Q_{54})$

$$= -\left(CV_0 + \frac{2CV_0}{3}\right)$$

$$= -\frac{5CV_0}{3} = -\frac{5\epsilon_0 AV_0}{3d}$$

The charge on plate 5 : $Q_5 = +Q_{54}$

$$= \frac{2CV_0}{3} = \frac{2\epsilon_0 AV_0}{3d}$$ ***Ans.***

**Ex. 13** **The distance between the parallel plates of a charged condenser is $d = 5$ cm and the intensity of the field $E = 300$ V/cm. A slab of dielectric constant $k = 5$ and 1 cm wide is inserted parallel to the plates. Determine the potential difference between the plates, before and after the slab is inserted. If the slab is replaced by a metal plates so that the final potential difference remains unchanged, what be the thickness of the plate ?**

## Sol.

Potential difference across the plates of condenser without slab

$$V = Ed = 300 \times 5 = 1500 \text{ V}$$

and

$$C = \frac{\epsilon_0 A}{d} = \frac{\epsilon_0 A}{0.05}$$

After the slab is inserted, the capacitance

$$C' = \frac{\epsilon_0 A}{(d-t) + \frac{t}{k}}$$

$$= \frac{\epsilon_0 A}{(0.05 - 0.01) + \frac{0.01}{5}} = \frac{\epsilon_0 A}{0.042}$$

If $V'$ is the p.d. now, then for isolated condenser

$$CV = C'V'$$

$$\therefore \quad V' = \frac{CV}{C'} = \frac{\left(\frac{\epsilon_0 A}{0.05}\right) \times 1500}{\left(\frac{\epsilon_0 A}{0.042}\right)}$$

$$= 1260 \, V$$ ***Ans.***

Let $x$ be the thickness of the metal plate. Now the capacitance

$$C'' = \frac{\epsilon_0 A}{(0.05 - x)}$$

If $V''$ is the p.d. now, across the condenser, then

$$C''V'' = CV$$

$$\therefore \quad V'' = \frac{CV}{C''} = \frac{\left(\frac{\epsilon_0 A}{0.05}\right) \times 1500}{\frac{\epsilon_0 A}{0.05 - x}}$$

or

$$1260 = \left(\frac{0.05 - x}{0.05}\right) \times 1500$$

After simplifying, we get $x = 0.8$ cm ***Ans.***

## 2.9 SPHERICAL CAPACITOR

It consists of two concentric conducting shells. Let $a$ and $b$ are the radii of the shells $(b > a)$. If charge $Q$ is given to the inner shell, an induce charge-$Q$ will appear on the inner surface of the outer shell. Its outer surface is earthed. We know that the electric field inside the inner shell is zero and between the shells it is due to the charge of inner shell. Thus electric field at a distance $r$ from the centre of the shells,

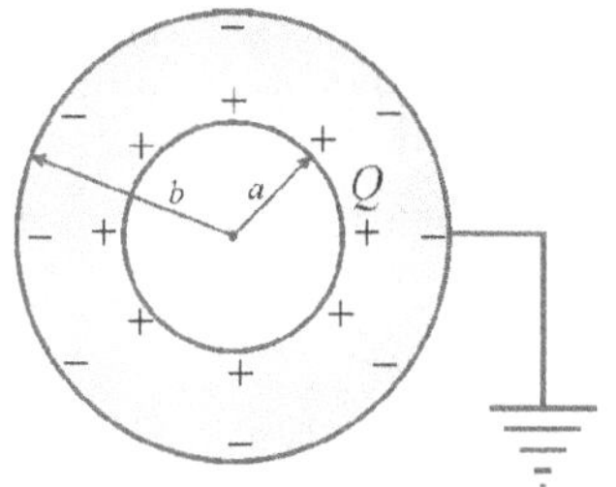

*Fig. 2.31*

$$E = \frac{1}{4\pi \epsilon_0} \frac{Q}{r^2} \qquad (a < r < b)$$

The p.d. between inner and outer shells,

$$V = V_a - V_b = -\int_b^a E dr$$

$$= \int_a^b E dr = \frac{Q}{4\pi \epsilon_0} \int_a^b \frac{dr}{r^2}$$

$$= \frac{Q}{4\pi \epsilon_0} \left( \frac{1}{a} - \frac{1}{b} \right)$$

Capacitance
$$C = \frac{Q}{V}$$

$$= \frac{Q}{\frac{Q}{4\pi \epsilon_0} \left( \frac{1}{a} - \frac{1}{b} \right)}$$

or
$$C = 4\pi \epsilon_0 \left( \frac{ab}{b-a} \right).$$

### Capacity of an earthed sphere enclosed by a concentric spherical shell

Let $a$ is the radius of the sphere and $b$ and $c$ are the inner and outer radius of the shell. Suppose the charge $Q$ is given to the outer shell $B$ and the induced charge on the inner sphere is $-Q_1$. Thus $+Q_1$ charge will appear on the inner face of the shell B and remaining charge $Q - Q_1$ will appear on its outer surface. In this way the system works as the combination of two capacitors :

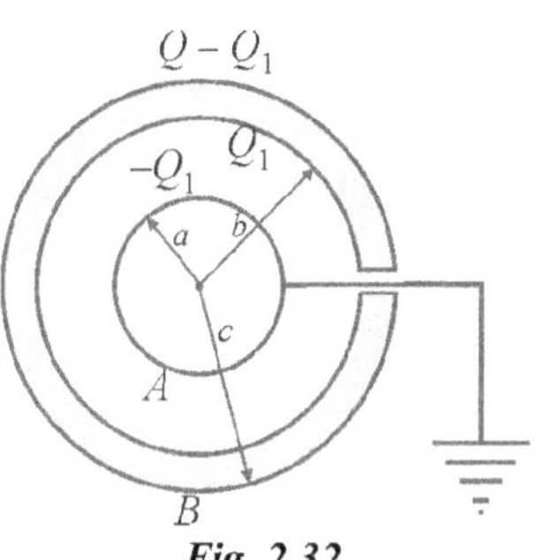

*Fig. 2.32*

(i) that between sphere $A$ and the inner surface of shell $B$, with capacitance

$$C_1 = 4\pi \epsilon_0 \left( \frac{ab}{b-a} \right)$$

(ii) and between outer surface of shell $B$ and infinity, with capacitance

$$C_2 = 4\pi \epsilon_0 c$$

$\therefore$ Total capacity
$$C = C_1 + C_2$$

$$= 4\pi \epsilon_0 \left[ \frac{ab}{b-a} + c \right]$$

### Special cases :

1. For thin shell $c \approx b$, $\therefore$ $C = 4\pi \epsilon_0 \left[ \frac{ab}{b-a} + b \right] = 4\pi \epsilon_0 \left( \frac{b^2}{b-a} \right)$

2. As sphere $A$ is earthed, so $V_A = 0$,

or
$$\frac{1}{4\pi \epsilon_0} \left( -\frac{Q_1}{a} + \frac{Q}{b} \right) = 0$$

$\therefore$
$$Q_1 = \frac{a}{b} Q.$$

**Ex. 14** **Three concentric thin spherical shells are of radii *a*, *b*, *c* ($a < b < c$). The first and third are connected by a fine wire through a small hole in the second and the second is connected to earth through a small hole in the third. Show that the capacity of the condensers so formed is** $4\pi \epsilon_0 \left[\frac{ab}{b-a}+\frac{c^2}{c-b}\right]$.

**Sol.**

If charge $Q$ is given to the outer most shell $C$, then some of the charge will go to the outer surface of the shell A because they are connected together by a wire. The charge $Q_1$ on the inner shell will induce a charge $-Q_1$ on the inner surface of the shell $B$ and $+Q_1$ on its outer surface. Shell C also induces the shell B, so net charge on its outer surface becomes different from $Q_1$, let it becomes $+Q_2$. Thus charge on inner surface of shell $C$ becomes $-Q_2$. In this way three condensers are formed, one by the outer surface of A and inner surface of $B$, second by the outer surface $B$ and inner surface of $C$ and the third by the outer surface of $C$ and infinity. If $C_1$, $C_2$ and $C_3$ are their respective capacities, then

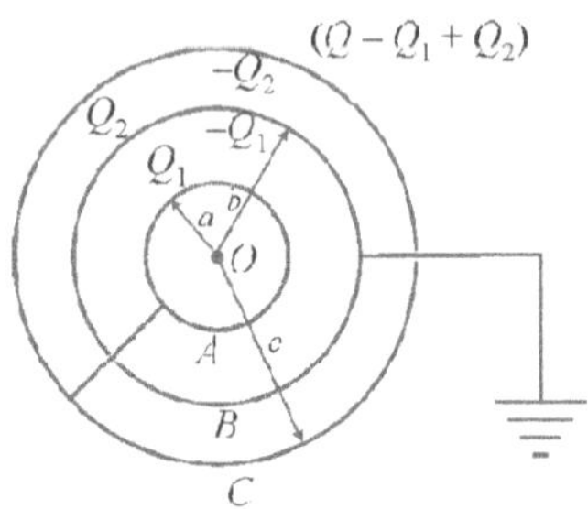


*Fig. 2.33*

$$C_1 = 4\pi \epsilon_0 \left(\frac{ab}{b-a}\right),$$

$$C_2 = 4\pi \epsilon_0 \left(\frac{bc}{c-b}\right)$$

and $$C_3 = 4\pi \epsilon_0 c$$

The total capacity $$C = C_1 + C_2 + C_3$$

$$= 4\pi \epsilon_0 \left[\frac{ab}{b-a}+\frac{bc}{c-b}+c\right]$$

$$= 4\pi \epsilon_0 \left[\frac{ab}{b-a}+\frac{c^2}{c-b}\right]$$

**Ex. 15** **(a) Find the capacitance of spherical capacitor having concentric shells of radii *a* and *b* ($b > a$). The space between the shells is completely filled by a dielectric of constant k.**

**(b) If dielectric is filled upto radius *c* ($a < c < b$) between the shells.**

**Sol.**

(a) When the space between the shells is completely filled by a dielectric, its capacitance

$$C = 4\pi \epsilon_0 k\left(\frac{ab}{b-a}\right)$$

(b)

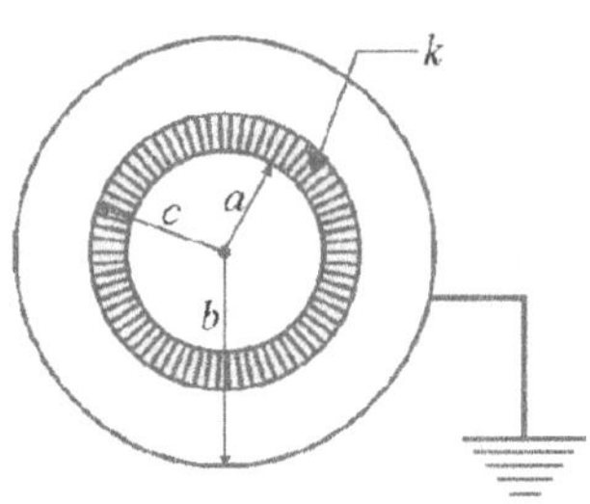


*Fig. 2.34*

The given capacitor is equivalent to two capacitors of capacitances $C_1$ and $C_2$ in series, where

$$C_1 = 4\pi \epsilon_0 k\frac{ac}{c-a}$$

and $$C_2 = 4\pi \epsilon_0 \frac{bc}{b-c}$$

If $C$ is the total capacitance, then

$$\frac{1}{C} = \frac{1}{C_1}+\frac{1}{C_2}$$

or $$C = \frac{C_1C_2}{C_1+C_2}$$

On substituting and simplifying, we get

$$C = \left[\frac{k\,abc}{ka(b-c)+b(c-a)}\right]. \quad \textit{Ans.}$$

**Ex. 16** **If half the space between two concentric conducting spheres be filled with dielectric of dielectric constant *k* and the rest is filled with air. Show that the capacitance of the capacitor thus formed will be same as if the whole part is filled with the dielectric of dielectric constant** $\frac{1}{2}(1+k)$.

**Sol.**

Suppose $\sigma$ is the charge density on the inner sphere and air in between the spheres of radii $a$ and $b$. The p.d. between them

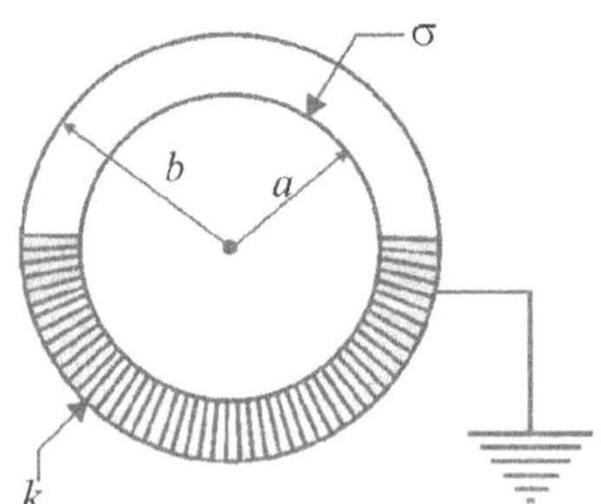


*Fig. 2.35*

$$V = V_a - V_b = \frac{Q}{4\pi \epsilon_0}\left[\frac{1}{a}-\frac{1}{b}\right]$$

$$= \frac{\sigma \times 4\pi a^2}{4\pi \epsilon_0}\left[\frac{1}{a}-\frac{1}{b}\right] = \frac{\sigma a^2}{\epsilon_0}\left[\frac{1}{a}-\frac{1}{b}\right]$$

Capacitance $$C = \frac{Q}{V} = 4\pi \epsilon_0 \left[\frac{ab}{b-a}\right]$$

When the medium is filled with dielectric of constant $\frac{1}{2}(1+k)$, its capacitance becomes

$$C' = \frac{1+k}{2} \times 4\pi \epsilon_0 \left[\frac{ab}{b-a}\right]$$

$$= \left(\frac{1+k}{2}\right) 4\pi \epsilon_0 \left[\frac{ab}{b-a}\right]$$

Now if half the space is filled with dielectric of dielectric constant k and half with air then in order to maintain the same potential difference between the spheres, the surface charge density over one half of the inner sphere will become $k\sigma$ and over the other half remains $\sigma$. Thus

$$C'' = \frac{\text{Total charge}}{\text{p.d.}} = \frac{2\pi a^2 \sigma k + 2\pi a^2 \sigma}{\frac{\sigma a^2}{\epsilon_0}\left[\frac{1}{a} - \frac{1}{b}\right]}$$

$$= \left(\frac{1+k}{2}\right) 4\pi \epsilon_0 \left(\frac{ab}{b-a}\right)$$

$$= C'.$$

## 2.10 CYLINDRICAL CAPACITOR

It consists of two co-axial long cylindrical conductors. Let $a$ and $b$ be the radii of inner and outer cylinders respectively.

If charge $Q$ is given to the inner cylinder, an induced charge $-Q$ will appear on the inner surface of the outer cylinder. The outer cylinder is earthed. Suppose length of the cylinder which is obviously be the length of the capacitor is $\ell$. The electric field between the cylinders is due to the charge of the inner cylinder. If $\lambda$ is the charge per unit length of the cylinder, then electric field at a radial distance $r$ from the axis of the cylinder is

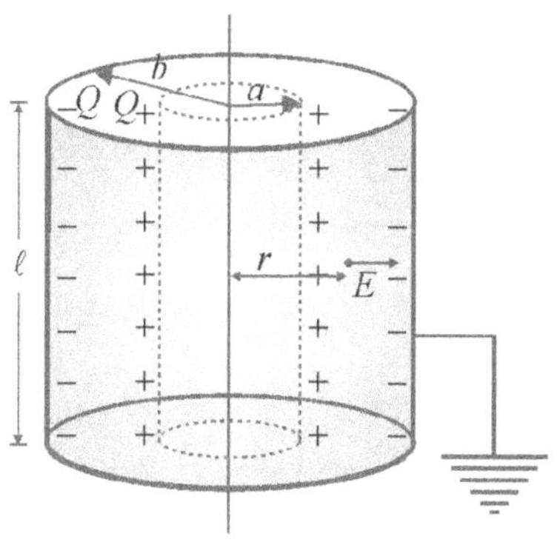


Fig. 2.36

$$E = \frac{\lambda}{2\pi \epsilon_0 r}$$

Potential difference between the cylinders

$$V = V_a - V_b = -\int_b^a E dr$$

$$= \int_a^b E dr$$

$$= \frac{\lambda}{2\pi \epsilon_0} \int_a^b \frac{dr}{r}$$

$$= \frac{\lambda}{2\pi \epsilon_0} \ell n \left(\frac{b}{a}\right)$$

The capacitance $C = \frac{Q}{V}$

$$= \frac{\lambda \ell}{\frac{\lambda}{2\pi \epsilon_0} \ell n \frac{b}{a}}$$

or

$$C = \left[\frac{2\pi \epsilon_0 \ell}{\ell n \frac{b}{a}}\right].$$

### Capacitance between two long parallel conductors

Let $\lambda$ be the charge per unit length on each conductor. Thus for a conductor of length $\ell$, charge $Q = \lambda \ell$. Consider a point $P$ at a distance $x$ from the axis of conductor $A$. Electric field at $P$

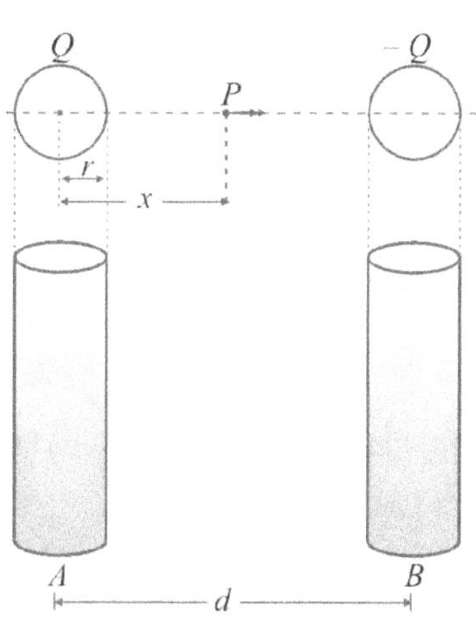


Fig. 2.37

$$E = E_A + E_B$$

$$= \frac{\lambda}{2\pi \epsilon_0 x} + \frac{\lambda}{2\pi \epsilon_0 (d-x)}$$

$$= \frac{\lambda}{2\pi \in_0}\left[\frac{1}{x}+\frac{1}{d-x}\right]$$

Potential difference between the conductors

$$V = V_A - V_B = \int_r^{(d-r)} E dx$$

$$= \frac{\lambda}{2\pi \in_0}\int_r^{(d-r)}\left[\frac{1}{x}+\frac{1}{d-x}\right]dx$$

$$= \frac{\lambda}{2\pi \in_0}\left[\ell n x - \ell n(d-x)\right]_r^{(d-r)}$$

$$= \frac{\lambda}{2\pi \in_0}\left[\{\ell n(d-r) - \ell n r\} - \{\ell n r - \ell n(d-r)\}\right]$$

$$= \frac{\lambda}{\pi \in_0}\ell n\left[\frac{(d-r)}{r}\right]$$

$\therefore$ Capacitance $$C = \frac{Q}{V} = \frac{\lambda \ell}{\frac{\lambda}{\pi \in_0}\ell n\left[\frac{d-r}{r}\right]}$$

or $$C = \frac{\pi \in_0 \ell}{\ell n\left(\frac{d-r}{r}\right)}$$

**Work done in inserting a dielectric slab between the plates of the capacitor**

Consider a capacitor of capacitance $C$ and charged to a potential $V$. The charge on the capacitor is $Q = CV$. The energy stored $U = \frac{1}{2}CV^2$. Let $V'$, $Q'$ and $U'$ are the corresponding values when dielectric is inserted between the plates.

**Case 1 :** After charging the capacitor, battery is disconnected and dielectric is inserted between the plates, then

$$Q' = Q$$

$$C' = kC$$

$$V' = \frac{Q'}{C'} = \frac{Q}{kC} = \frac{V}{k}$$

$$U' = \frac{1}{2}C'V'^2 = \frac{1}{2}(kC)\left(\frac{V}{k}\right)^2 = \frac{1}{2}\frac{CV^2}{k}$$

$$= \frac{U}{k}$$

Thus work done $$W = U_f - U_i = U' - U$$

$$= \frac{1}{2}\frac{CV^2}{k} - \frac{1}{2}CV^2$$

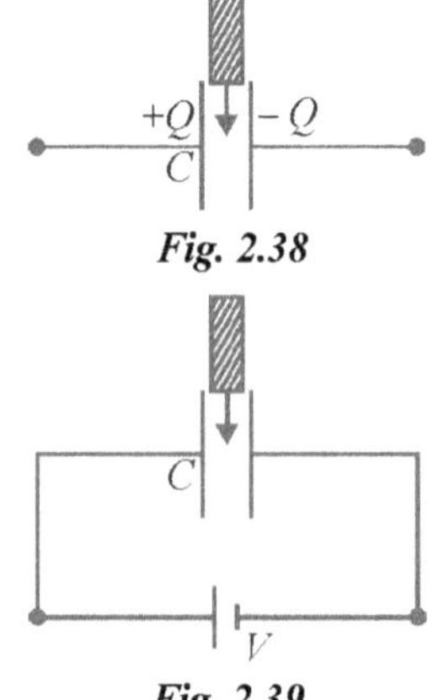

Fig. 2.38

Fig. 2.39

$$= \frac{1}{2}CV^2\left(\frac{1}{k}-1\right)$$

$$= -\frac{1}{2}CV^2\left(\frac{k-1}{k}\right)$$

**Case 2 :** After charging the capacitor, if battery remain connected, then

$$V' = V$$

$$C' = kC$$

$$Q' = C'V' = kCV = kQ$$

$$U' = \frac{1}{2}C'V'^2 = \frac{1}{2}(kC)V^2$$

$$= kU$$

The work done $W = U_f - U_i = U' - U$

$$= \frac{1}{2}CV^2(k-1)$$

**Ex. 17** **A capacitor consists of two stationary plates shaped as a semicircle of radius $R$ and a movable plate made of dielectric with relative permittivity $\in$ and capable of rotating about an axis $O$ between the stationary plates (figure). The thickness of the movable plate is equal to $d$ which is practically the separation between the stationary plates. A potential difference $V$ is applied to the capacitor. Find the magnitude of the moment of forces relative to the axis $O$ acting on the movable plate in the position shown in the figure.**

**Sol.**

The area of dielectric which is out of plates is

$$= \frac{R\phi \times R}{2} = \frac{R^2\phi}{2} \quad \text{(Assuming a triangle of small } \phi)$$

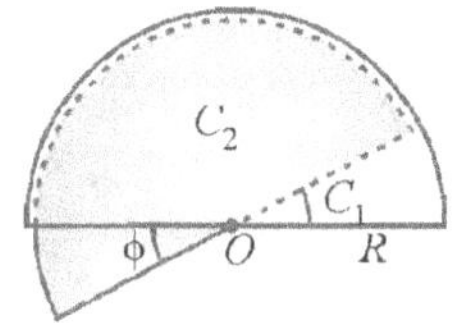


*Fig. 2.40*

The area of dielectric inside the plates is

$$= \frac{\pi R^2}{2} - \frac{R^2\phi}{2} = \frac{(\pi-\phi)R^2}{2}$$

The capacitance of the system

$$C = C_1 + C_2$$

$$= \frac{\epsilon_0\left(\frac{R^2\phi}{2}\right)}{d} + \frac{\in\epsilon_0(\pi-\phi)R^2}{2d}$$

Because of charges on the plates of capacitor, the charge will induce on the dielectric. Due to which it experience a force towards the plates which constitutes a torque about $O$. Let this torque rotates the dielectric by $d\phi$, the work done by the field

$$dW = -dU = \tau d\phi$$

$$\therefore \quad \tau = -\frac{dU}{d\phi}$$

where $U = \frac{1}{2}CV^2$

$$\therefore \quad \tau = -\frac{dU}{d\phi} = -\frac{d}{d\phi}\left(\frac{1}{2}CV^2\right)$$

$$= -\frac{V^2}{2}\left(\frac{dC}{d\phi}\right)$$

$$= -\frac{V^2}{2}\frac{d}{d\phi}\left[\frac{\epsilon_0 R^2\phi}{2d} + \frac{\in\epsilon_0(\pi-\phi)R^2}{2d}\right]$$

$$= -\frac{V^2}{2}\left[\frac{\epsilon_0 R^2}{2d} + \frac{\in\epsilon_0(-1)R^2}{2d}\right]$$

$$= \frac{(\in-1)\epsilon_0 R^2V^2}{4d}. \qquad \textit{Ans.}$$

**Ex. 18** **The gap between the plates of a parallel-plate capacitor is filled with isotropic dielectric whose permittivity $\in$ varies linearly from $\in_1$ to $\in_2$ $(\in_2 > \in_1)$ in the direction perpendicular to the plates. The area of each plate is equal to $S$, the separation between the plates is equal to $d$. Find the capacitance of the capacitor.**

**Sol.**

The value of permittivity of the medium at a distance x from left plate $\in_x = \in_1 + \frac{\in_2 - \in_1}{d}x$. The potential difference between the plates

$$V = \int_0^d E\,dr$$

$$= \int_0^d \left(\frac{\sigma}{\epsilon_0\in_x}\right)dx$$

$$= \frac{\sigma}{\epsilon_0}\int_0^d \frac{dx}{\left(\in_1 + \frac{\in_2-\in_1}{d}\right)x}$$

$$= \frac{\sigma d}{\epsilon_0(\in_2-\in_1)}\ell n\left(\frac{\in_2}{\in_1}\right)$$

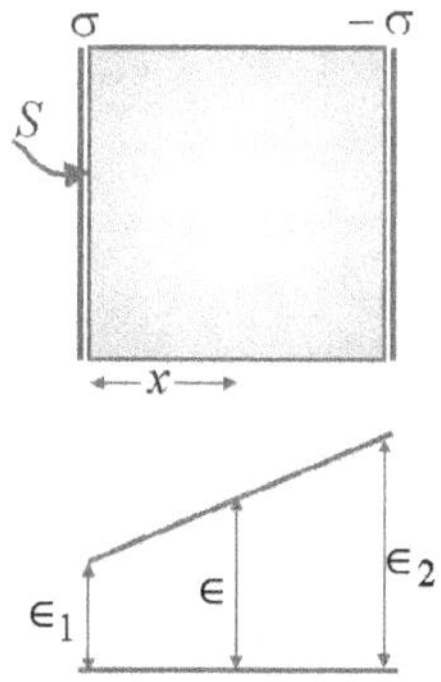

*Fig. 2.41*

Therefore capacitance $C = \frac{Q}{V}$

$$= \frac{\sigma S}{\left[\frac{\sigma d}{\epsilon_0(\epsilon_2 - \epsilon_1)}\ell n\left(\frac{\epsilon_2}{\epsilon_1}\right)\right]}$$

$$= \frac{(\epsilon_2 - \epsilon_1)\epsilon_0 S}{d\,\ell n\frac{\epsilon_2}{\epsilon_1}}. \quad \textit{Ans.}$$

**Ex. 19** **Find the capacitance of a system of two identical metal balls of radius $a$ if the distance between their centres is equal to $b$, with $b>>a$. The system is located in a uniform dielectric with permittivity $\in$.**

**Sol.**

Suppose the charges $q$ and $-q$ are imparted to the balls. Then

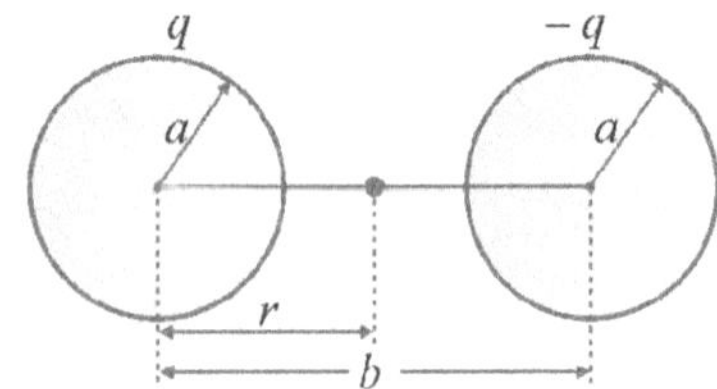


*Fig. 2.42*

$$V_1 = V_{ball} - V_\infty = V$$

$$V_2 = V_{ball} - V_\infty = -V$$

The potential difference between the balls

$$V_1 - V_2 = 2V$$

$$= 2\int_a^{b-a} E dr$$

$$= 2$$

$$\int_a^{b-a}\left(\frac{1}{4\pi\epsilon_0\in}\frac{q}{r^2}\right)dr = \frac{q}{2\pi\epsilon_0\in}\left[\frac{1}{a} - \frac{1}{b-a}\right]$$

$$= \frac{q}{2\pi\epsilon_0\in}\frac{(b-2a)}{a(b-a)}$$

Hence, the required capacitance is

$$C = \frac{q}{V_1 - V_2} = \frac{q}{\left[\frac{q}{2\pi\epsilon_0\in}\frac{(b-2a)}{a(b-a)}\right]}$$

$$= \frac{2\pi\epsilon_0\in a(b-a)}{(b-2a)}$$

For $b >> a$, we can write

$$C \simeq 2\pi\epsilon_0\in a. \quad \textit{Ans.}$$

**Ex. 20** **Three capacitors of capacitances 0.002, 0.004 and 0.006 μF are connected in series.**

**Can a potential of 11,000 V be applied to this battery ? What voltage will be received by each capacitor in the battery. The puncture voltage of each capacitor is 4000 V.**

**Sol.**

In series connection, the charge across each capacitor is equal, and so if $V_1$, $V_2$ and $V_3$ are their potentials then

$$C_1V_1 = C_2V_2 \quad ...(i)$$

$$C_2V_2 = C_3V_3 \quad ...(ii)$$

and $$V_1 + V_2 + V_3 = 11000 \quad ...(iii)$$

Substituting and solving above equations, we get

$$V_1 = 6000\text{ V},$$

$$V_2 = 3000\text{ V}$$

and $$V_3 = 2000\text{ V}$$

So, it is not possible to give 11000 V without puncture of any of the capacitors, because $V_1 > 4000$V.

**Ex. 21** ***Fig. 2.43*** **given below shows two identical parallel plate capacitors connected to a battery with switch *S* closed. The switch is now opened and the free space between the plates of capacitors is filled with a dielectric of dielectric constant 3. What will be the ratio of total electrostatic energy stored in both capacitors before and after the introduction of the dielectric.**

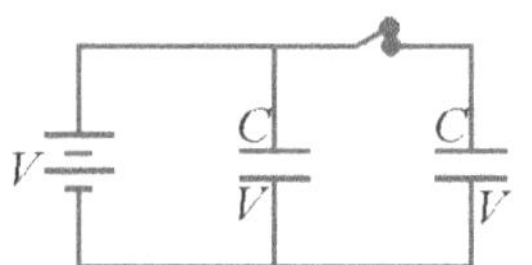


(a) When switch is closed.

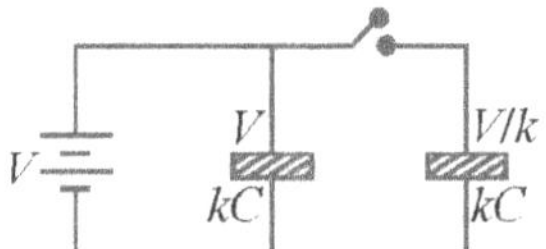


(b) After opening the switch.

*Fig. 2.43*

**Sol.**

Both the capacitors are in parallel across the source. Therefore p.d. across each is $V$

$$\therefore \quad U_i = \frac{1}{2}CV^2 + \frac{1}{2}CV^2$$

$$= CV^2$$

When switch is opened and dielectric is inserted between the plates of capacitors, the capacitance of each is increased to $kC$ while their potentials become $V$ and $\frac{V}{k}$.

$$\therefore \quad U_f = \frac{1}{2}(kC)V^2 + \frac{1}{2}kC\left(\frac{V}{k}\right)^2$$

$$= CV^2\left(\frac{k}{2} + \frac{1}{2k}\right)$$

Now $$\frac{U_i}{U_f} = \frac{1}{\left(\frac{k}{2} + \frac{1}{2k}\right)} = \frac{1}{\left(\frac{3}{2} + \frac{1}{2\times 3}\right)}$$

$$= \frac{3}{5}. \quad \textit{Ans.}$$

**Ex. 22** **Find the steady state charge on the capacitor in the circuit shown in *fig. 2.44*.**

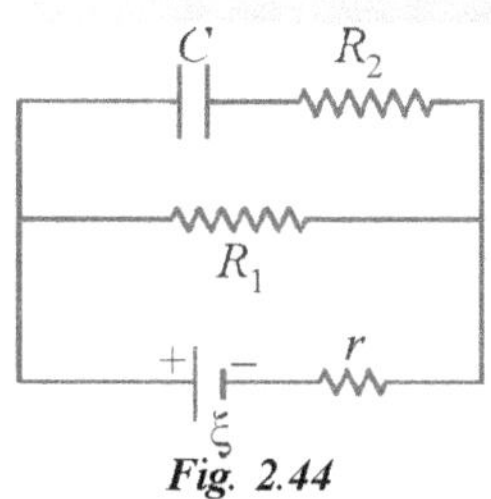

Fig. 2.44

**Sol.** Capacitor after charging stops the current. Therefore there is no current in the arm of capacitor. The entire current will pass through resistor $R_1$.

$$\therefore \quad i = \frac{\xi}{R_1 + r}$$

Since there is no current in $R_2$, therefore no p.d. across it. The p.d. across capacitor is equal to p.d. across $R_1$. i.e.,

$$V = iR_1 = \frac{\xi}{R_1 + r} R_1$$

Charge on capacitor $q = CV = \frac{C\xi R_1}{R_1 + r}$ **Ans.**

**Ex. 23 Three identical metallic plates are kept parallel to one another at a separation of *a* and *b*. The outer plates are connected by a thin conducting wire and a charge *Q* is placed on the central plate. Find final charges on all the six plate's surfaces.**

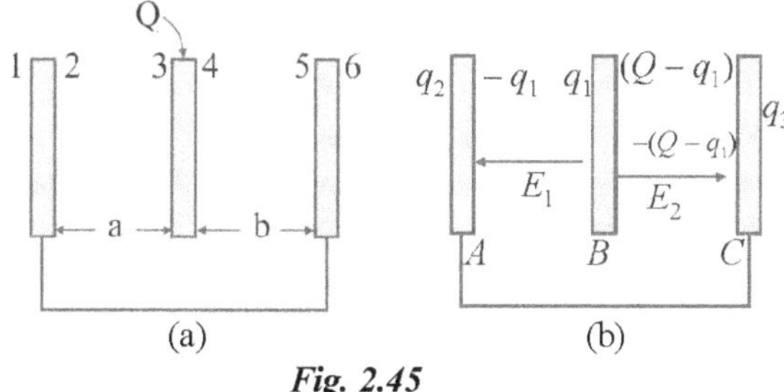

Fig. 2.45

**Sol.**

Suppose charge on left face of $B$ is $q_1$, then right face has charge $Q - q_1$. The charges on other plates are shown in figure. The plates $A$ and $C$ are connected each other, and so the net induced charge on them will be zero.

$$\therefore \quad (q_2 - q_1) + q_3 - (Q - q_1) = 0$$

$$\text{or} \quad q_2 + q_3 = Q \qquad \text{...(i)}$$

Since $A$ and $C$ are at same potential

$$\therefore \quad V_B - V_A = V_B - V_C$$

$$\text{or} \quad E_1 a = E_2 b$$

$$\frac{q_1}{A \epsilon_0} a = \frac{(Q - q_1)}{A \epsilon_0} b$$

$$\text{or} \quad q_1 = \left(\frac{Qb}{a+b}\right) \qquad \text{...(ii)}$$

Electric field due to all the charges inside any plate (say $C$) is zero. Therefore

$$\frac{q_2}{2\epsilon_0 A} - \frac{q_1}{2\epsilon_0 A} + \frac{q_1}{2\epsilon_0 A} + \frac{Q - q_1}{2\epsilon_0 A} - \frac{q_1 - Q}{2\epsilon_0 A} - \frac{q_3}{2\epsilon_0 A} = 0$$

After simplifying, we get

$$q_2 = q_3 \qquad \text{...(iii)}$$

Solving equations (i), (ii) and (iii), we get

$$q_1 = \frac{Qb}{(a+b)}$$

$$q_2 = \frac{Q}{2}$$

$$q_3 = \frac{Q}{2}$$

The charges on all the six faces of the plates are as :

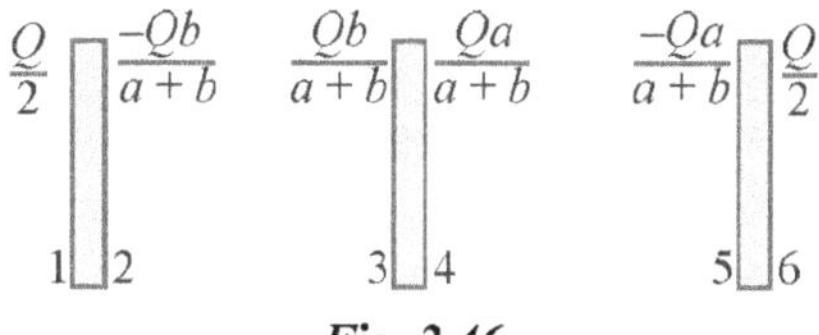

Fig. 2.46

## 2.11 DIELECTRICS

### (a) Polar dielectrics :

Molecule of dielectric material has permanent dipole moment $(\vec{P})$ in the absence of electric field, is known as polar dielectric molecules. But the dipole moments of molecules of substance are randomly oriented, and in the absence of field their net dipole moment is zero. Example : $H_2O$, $NH_3$, HCl etc.

### (b) Non-Polar dielectrics :

Molecule of dielectric has zero dipole moment in its normal state is called non-polar dielectric. Example : $O_2$, $N_2$ etc.

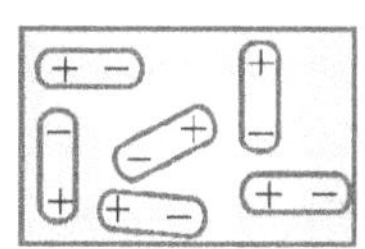
$\vec{E} = 0, \vec{P} = 0$

(a)

Polar molecule

Non -polar molecule

(b)

Fig. 2.47

### Polarisation of dielectrics

When a dielectrics is placed in an electric field, dipole moment induces in each part of it.

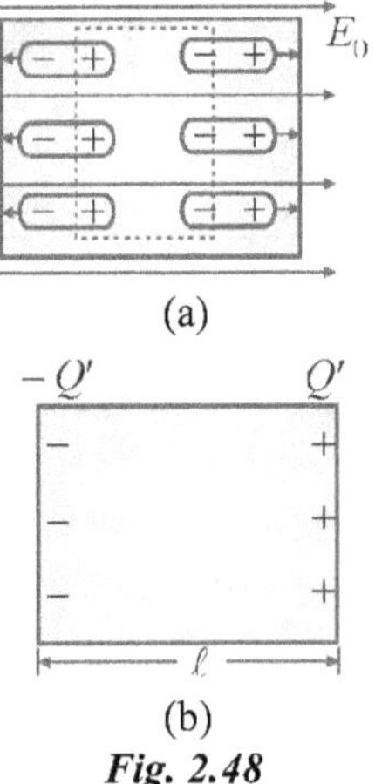

(a)

(b)

*Fig. 2.48*

This is called polarisation. The polarisation $\vec{P}$ is defined as the dipole moment per unit volume. Figure shows a dielectric placed in uniform field. Because of it, an induced charge will appear on the faces of the dielectric, which constitute a dipole moment.

$$\therefore \quad P = \frac{\text{dipole moment}}{\text{volume}}$$

$$= \frac{Q'\ell}{A\ell} = \frac{Q'}{A} = \sigma'$$

### Dielectric strength and dielectric breakdown

If high electric field is applied across a dielectric, then electrons get separate from molecules and dielectric behaves like a conductor. This is known as dielectric breakdown. The maximum value of electric field that a material can withstand without breakdown is called dielectric strength. Its SI unit is V/m.

Dielectric strength of air is $E_0 = 3\times10^6 \text{ V/m}$ at one atmosphere.
The maximum charge the sphere of radius 1 m can have

$$E_0 = \frac{1}{4\pi \in_0} \frac{Q_{max}}{R^2}$$

or
$$3\times10^6 = 9\times10^9 \times \frac{Q_{max}}{1^2}$$

which gives
$$Q_{max} = \frac{1}{3}\times10^{-3} \text{ C} = 0.33 \text{ mC}.$$

## 2.12 INDUCED OR BOUND CHARGE

Consider a parallel plate capacitor with charge $Q$ on its positive plate and $-Q$ charge on its other plate. The electric field between the plates $E_0 = \frac{\sigma}{\in_0} = \frac{Q}{A \in_0}$.

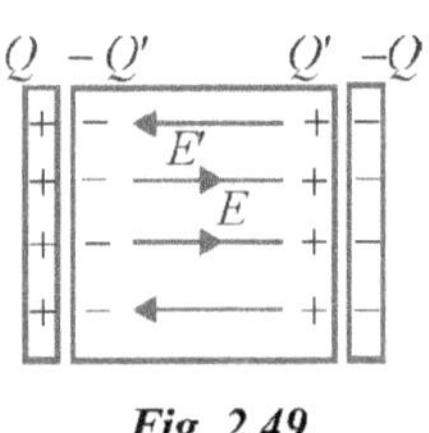

*Fig. 2.49*

When dielectric is placed between the plates it gets polarised and charge is induced on its faces as shown in *fig. 2.49*. Let induced charge is $Q'$ in magnitude. Due to the induced charge the electric field induces inside the dielectric, which opposes the external field. The electric field due to induced charge

$$E' = \frac{\sigma'}{\in_0} = \frac{Q'}{A \in_0}$$

The net electric field inside dielectric is

$$\vec{E}_{med} = \vec{E} + \vec{E}'$$

or
$$E_{med} = E_0 - E'$$

Since
$$E_{med} = \frac{\sigma}{k \in_0} = \frac{Q}{Ak \in_0}$$

$$\therefore \quad \frac{Q}{Ak \in_0} = \frac{Q}{A \in_0} - \frac{Q'}{A \in_0}$$

o
$$Q' = Q\left(1 - \frac{1}{k}\right).$$

### An alternating form of Gauss's law

Let us consider a parallel-plate capacitor filled with a dielectric slab of dielectric constant $k$. The charge on the capacitor is $Q$. Let us take a close surface (by dotted lines) as shown in figure. The charge enclosed by surface is $(Q-Q')$. From Gauss's law

$$\oint \vec{E}\cdot d\vec{A} = \frac{q_{in}}{\epsilon_0}$$

$$= \frac{(Q-Q')}{\epsilon_0}$$

$$= \frac{\left[Q-Q\left(1-\frac{1}{k}\right)\right]}{\epsilon_0}$$

$$= \frac{Q}{k\epsilon_0}$$

or $$\oint k\vec{E}\cdot d\vec{A} = \frac{Q_{free}}{\epsilon_0}$$

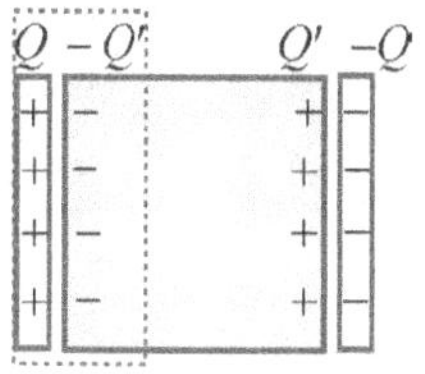

*Fig. 2.50*

**Displacement vector :** The field due to polarisation $E' = \frac{\sigma'}{\epsilon_0} = \frac{P}{\epsilon_0}$.

As $P$ is the polarisation (dipole moment per unit volume) which is opposite to the field $E'$. Thus

$$\vec{E}' = -\frac{\vec{P}}{\epsilon_0}$$

The net field inside dielectric $$\vec{E} = \vec{E}_0 + \vec{E}'$$

$$= \vec{E}_0 - \frac{\vec{P}}{\epsilon_0}$$

or $$\epsilon_0\vec{E} + \vec{P} = \epsilon_0\vec{E}_0$$

The quantity $\epsilon_0\vec{E} + \vec{P} = \vec{D}$, is known as the displacement vector.

$\therefore$ $$\vec{D} = \epsilon_0\vec{E}_0$$

or $$\oint \vec{D}\cdot d\vec{A} = \oint \epsilon_0\vec{E}_0\cdot d\vec{A}$$

Since $$\oint \vec{E}_0\cdot d\vec{A} = \frac{Q_{free}}{\epsilon_0}$$

or $$\oint \epsilon_0\vec{E}_0\cdot d\vec{A} = Q_{free}$$

$\therefore$ $$\oint \vec{D}\cdot d\vec{A} = Q_{free}$$

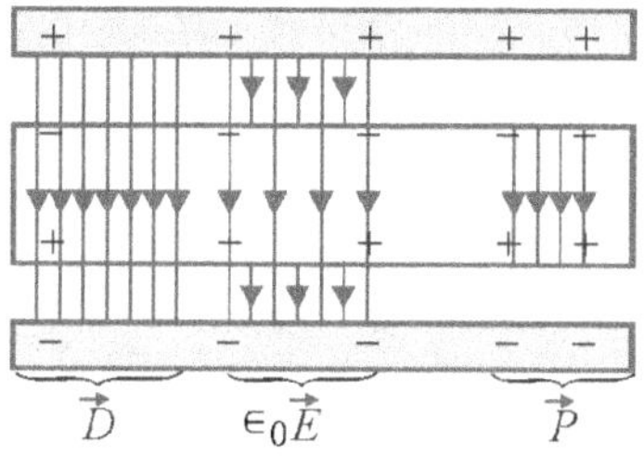


*Fig. 2.51*

This is the another form of Gauss's law.

**Note:**

Invariance of Gauss's law : From the generalization of experimental results, the Gauss's law $\oint \vec{E}\cdot d\vec{A} = \frac{q}{\epsilon_0}$ is valid not only for fixed charges but for moving charges also. In the latter case, the surface integral must be taken for a definite instant of time in a given reference system. Gauss's law is valid for all inertial systems of reference.

## High voltage breakdown or corona or point discharge

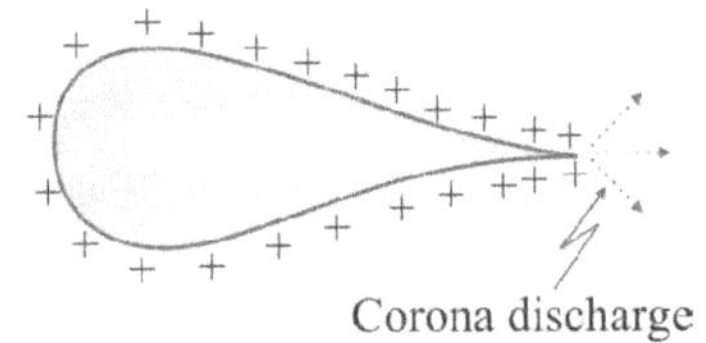


A glowing region of the air near a conductor when the electric field near it exceeds the dielectric strength ($E_0 = 3 \times 10^6$ V/m) of air. It is called by ionization of the air and may be accompanied by hissing sounds. Corona discharge occurs at sharp points where the charge density is high

Let us consider two conducting spheres $A$ and $B$, connected by a conducting wire. A charge $Q$ is given to the system. This charge will share by them in such a way that their potentials become equal. Let $q_1$ and $q_2$ be the charges on them. Thus

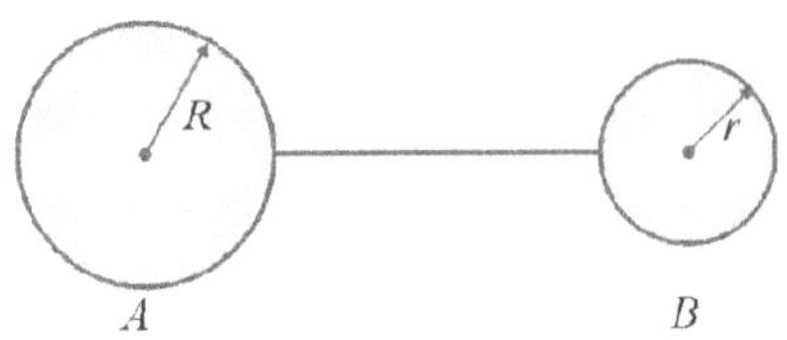


Fig. 2.52

$$V_A = V_B$$

or $$\frac{1}{4\pi \in_0}\frac{q_1}{R} = \frac{1}{4\pi \in_0}\frac{q_2}{r}$$

or $$\frac{q_1}{q_2} = \frac{R}{r}$$

and $$\frac{\sigma_1}{\sigma_2} = \frac{\dfrac{q_1}{4\pi R^2}}{\dfrac{q_2}{4\pi r^2}} = \frac{r^2}{R^2}\times\frac{q_1}{q_2}$$

or $$\frac{\sigma_1}{\sigma_2} = \frac{r^2}{R^2}\times\frac{R}{r} = \frac{r}{R}$$

or we can say $$\sigma \propto \frac{1}{r}.$$

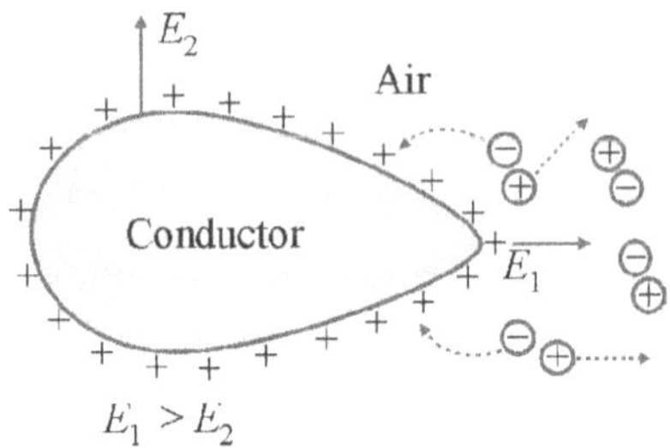


Fig. 2.53

It shows that the field is higher at the surface of small sphere. The same can be explained with a conductor having sharp end. It can be shown by simple knowledge of lines of force that field around this sharp end is much higher than the field in the other regions. Due to this very high field at the sharp ends of the conductor, the air near these points breakdown, and conductor starts discharging. This is known as corona discharge.

## Force on a dielectric slab

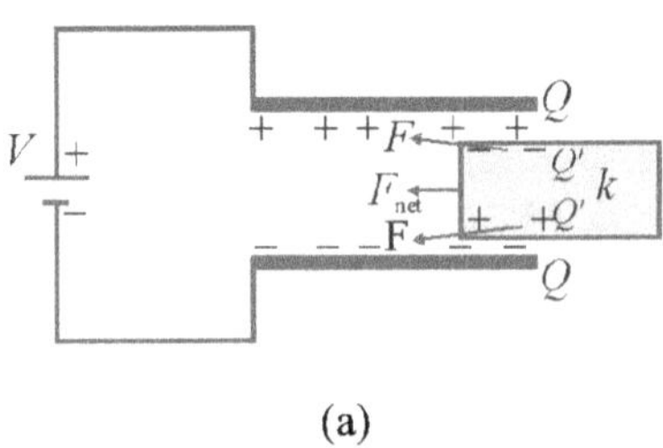


(a)

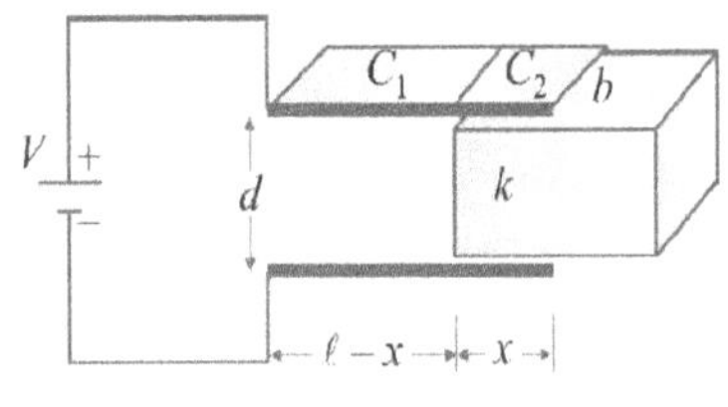


(b)

Fig. 2.54

When a dielectric is placed partially inside a capacitor, it experiences a force towards the plates. If dielectric is left free, it will move into the capacitor. The reason is that, because of charges of plates, the opposite charges are induced on the opposite faces of the dielectric. Because of attraction between opposite charges, a net force acts on the dielectric towards the capacitor.

**(a) When capacitor is kept at constant potential (Mathematical method) :**

Consider a parallel-plate capacitor with plate area $(\ell \times b)$ and separation between the plates is $d$, this is practically the thickness of dielectric slab. The capacitor is connected to a battery of emf $V$. Let $x$ length of the dielectric is inside the plates, then capacitance

$$C = C_1 + C_2$$

$$= \frac{\in_0 b(\ell - x)}{d} + \frac{\in_0 k\, bx}{d}$$

Let the dielectric displaces by $dx$ due to the electrostatic force $F$ exerted by the capacitor (field produced by capacitor) the work done,

$$dW = -dU = F\,dx$$

or $$F = -\frac{dU}{dx}. \qquad ...(i)$$

**Note:** This formula we have already studied in mechanics.

Since, $U = \frac{1}{2}CV^2$

$\therefore$
$$F = -\frac{dU}{dx} = -\frac{d\left(\frac{1}{2}CV^2\right)}{dx}$$

$$= -\frac{V^2}{2}\left(\frac{dU}{dx}\right) \quad \text{[As } V \text{ is constant]}$$

or
$$= -\frac{V^2}{2}\frac{d}{dx}\left[\frac{\epsilon_0 b(\ell - x)}{d} + \frac{\epsilon_0 kbx}{d}\right]$$

$$= -\frac{V^2}{2}\left[\frac{\epsilon_0 b}{d}(-1) + \frac{\epsilon_0 kb}{d}\right]$$

$$= \frac{\epsilon_0 bV^2}{2d}(k-1)$$

Thus, the electric field attract the dielectric with a force $\frac{\epsilon_0 bV^2(k-1)}{2d}$, which is independent of $x$.

**(b) When capacitor has constant charge :**

For constant charge $U = \frac{Q^2}{2C}$

From equation (i), we have $F = -\frac{dU}{dx}$

$$= -\frac{d}{dx}\left[\frac{Q^2}{2C}\right]$$

$$= -\frac{Q^2}{2}\frac{d}{dx}\left(\frac{1}{C}\right) \quad \text{[As Q is constant]}$$

$$= -\frac{Q^2}{2}\frac{d}{dx}\left[\frac{1}{\frac{\epsilon_0 b(\ell - x)}{d} + \frac{\epsilon_0 kbx}{d}}\right]$$

$$= -\frac{Q^2 d}{2\epsilon_0 b}\frac{d}{dx}\left[\frac{1}{\ell + x(k-1)}\right]$$

$$= -\frac{Q^2 d}{2\epsilon_0 b}(-1)\left[\frac{1}{\ell + x(k-1)}\right]^{-2} \times (k-1)$$

$$= \frac{Q^2 d(k-1)}{2\epsilon_0 b}\left[\frac{1}{\ell + x(k-1)}\right]^{-2}$$

*Note:* This time force is a function of $x$.

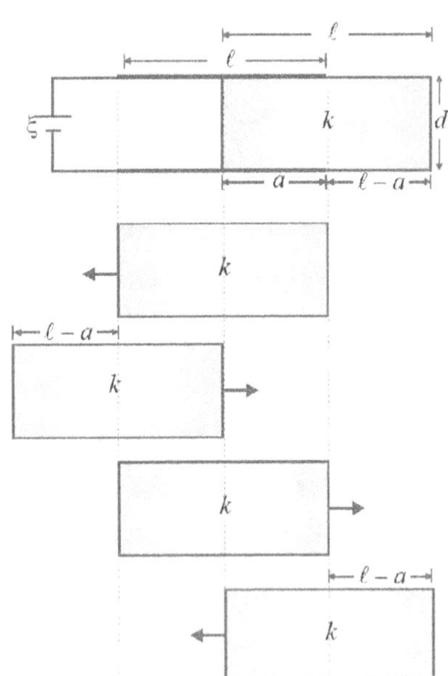

Fig. 2.55

### Oscillations of dielectric slab between the plates of capacitor

Consider the situation shown in figure. The plates of a capacitor have plate area $A$ and are clamped in the laboratory. The dielectric slab is released from rest with a length $a$ inside the capacitor. Neglect any effect of friction or gravity, show that the slab execute periodic motion and find its time period.

The force acting on the dielectric slab $F = \dfrac{\epsilon_0 b\xi^2}{2d}(k-1)$ [As calculated earlier]

and acceleration of slab $a' = \dfrac{F}{m} = \dfrac{\epsilon_0 b\xi^2 (k-1)}{2md}$

The time taken to travel distance $(\ell - a)$

$$(\ell - a) = \frac{1}{2}a' t^2$$

which gives $t = \sqrt{\dfrac{2(\ell - a)}{a'}}$

The time period to complete the oscillation

$$T = 4t = 4\sqrt{\frac{2(\ell-a)}{a'}}$$

$$= 4\sqrt{\frac{2(\ell-a)\times 2md}{\epsilon_0 b\xi^2 (k-1)}}$$

$$= 8\sqrt{\frac{(\ell-a)md}{\epsilon_0 b\xi^2 (k-1)}}$$

As $A = b\ell$ $\quad \therefore \; b = \dfrac{A}{\ell}$

Now $T = 8\sqrt{\dfrac{(\ell-a)m\ell d}{\epsilon_0 A\xi^2 (k-1)}}$.

**Ex. 24 A parallel-plate capacitor is placed in such a way that its plates are horizontal and the lower plate is dipped into a liquid of dielectric constant $k$ and density $\rho$. Each plate has area $A$. The plates now connected to a battery which supplies a positive charge of magnitude $Q$ to the upper plate. Find the rise in the level of the liquid in the space between the plates.**

**Sol.**

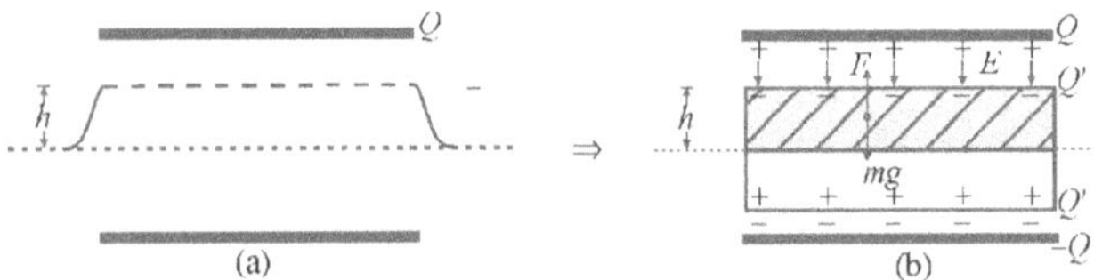

Fig. 2.56

Because of the charges of the plates of capacitor, the charge will induce on the upper and lower layer (which in contact with negative plate of capacitor) of the liquid. The force on upper layer of liquid is $F = EQ'$ in upward direction. Because of this force liquid rises till force equal to weight of liquid rises. Thus

$$F = EQ' = mg$$

where $Q' = Q\left(1 - \dfrac{1}{k}\right)$

and $mg = Ah\rho g$

Charge on lower plate $= -Q + Q' = -Q + Q\left(1 - \dfrac{1}{k}\right)$

$$= -\frac{Q}{k}$$

The electric field due to both the plates of capacitor

$$E = \frac{\sigma}{2\epsilon_0} + \frac{\sigma'}{2\epsilon_0}$$

$$= \frac{Q}{2\epsilon_0 A} + \frac{Q}{2k\epsilon_0 A}$$

$$= \frac{Q}{2\epsilon_0 A}\left(1 + \frac{1}{k}\right)$$

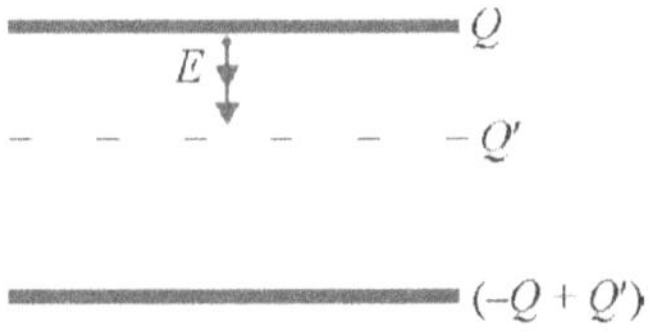

Fig. 2.57

We have $EQ' = mg$

$$\therefore \quad \left[\frac{Q}{2\in_0 A}\left(1+\frac{1}{k}\right)\right]Q\left(1-\frac{1}{k}\right) = Ah\rho g$$

or $$h = \frac{\left(k^2-1\right)Q^2}{2A^2k^2 \in_0 \rho g}. \quad \textit{Ans.}$$

**Ex. 25** **A capacitor of capacitance $C$ is charged by connecting it to a battery of emf $\xi$. The capacitor is now disconnected and reconnected to the battery with the polarity reversed. Calculate the heat developed in the connecting wire.**

**Sol.**

When capacitor is connected to the battery, a charge $Q = C\xi$ appears on one plate and $-Q$ on the other plate. With the polarity reversed, the charge $-Q$ appear on the first plate and $Q$ on the other plate. Thus charge $2Q$, flows through the battery. The work done by battery

$$W = Vq$$

$$= \xi \times 2Q = 2C\xi^2$$

The energy stored in the capacitor in both the cases is $\frac{1}{2}C\xi^2$. Therefore by conservation of energy

$$U_i + W = U_f + \text{heat generated}$$

$$\therefore \quad \text{heat generated} = W$$

$$= 2C\xi^2. \quad \textit{Ans.}$$

## 2.13 TOTAL ENERGY OF THE SYSTEM

Total energy of the system includes self energies (internal energy) of all the charges in the system ($U_i$) and energy due to all possible mutual interactions ($U_e$).
Therefore, total energy of the system $U = U_i + U_e$
There are two methods of finding the total energy of the system.

**Method I:** By using energy density : We know the energy density $u = \frac{1}{2}\in_0 E^2$, where $E$ is the electric field due to all the charges in the system, then total energy of the system (including $U_i$ & $U_e$)

$$U = \int_{V_1}^{V_2} u\,dV$$

**Method II:** By this method, we have to calculate $U_i$ and $U_e$ separately and sum of these gives total energy of the system.

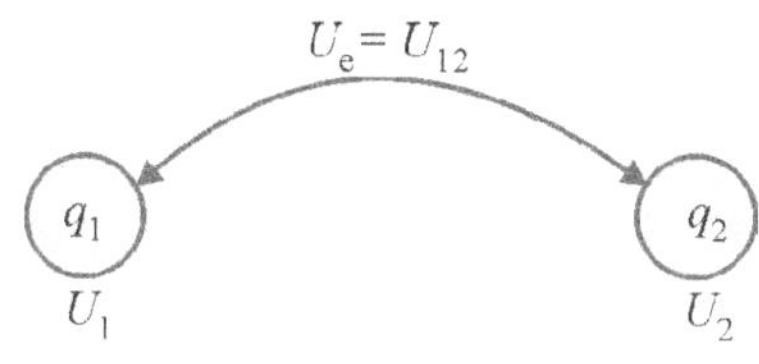

*Fig. 2.58*

Self energy $$U_i = \int_0^q V\,dq$$

Energy due to mutual interaction, let for two charges $q_1$ and $q_2$

$$U_e = q_1(V_{12})$$
$$= q_2(V_{21})$$

where, $V_{12}$ is the potential due to $q_2$ at position of 1, $V_{21}$ is the potential due to $q_1$ at position of 2

Now $$U = U_i + U_e.$$

**Note:** For an isolated charged body, $U_e = 0$, $\quad \therefore U = U_i$.

**Ex. 26** **A spherical conducting thin shell of radius $R$ given charge $q$. Find its total energy.**

**Sol.**

**Method 1 :** The energy of shell resides in the space from $r = R$ to $r = \infty$, because field of charge on shell extend upto infinity. The field at a distance $r$ from the centre of shell ($r > R$), $E = \frac{1}{4\pi\in_0}\frac{q}{r^2}$ and energy density

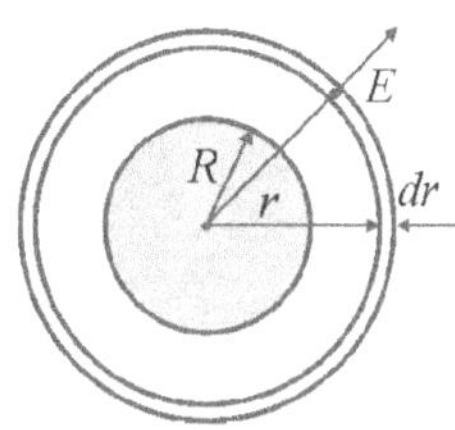

*Fig. 2.59*

$$u = \frac{1}{2}\in_0 E^2 = \frac{1}{2}\in_0\left(\frac{1}{4\pi\in_0}\frac{q}{r^2}\right)^2$$

The energy contained in small volume

$$dU = u \times 4\pi r^2 dr$$

$$= \frac{1}{2}\epsilon_0\left(\frac{1}{4\pi\epsilon_0}\frac{q}{r^2}\right)^2 \times 4\,\pi r^2\,dr$$

Total energy $\quad U = \int_R^{\infty} dU$

$$= \int_R^{\infty}\frac{1}{2}\epsilon_0\left(\frac{1}{4\pi\epsilon_0}\frac{q}{r^2}\right)^2 \times 4\pi r^2 dr$$

$$= \frac{1}{2}\epsilon_0\left(\frac{q}{4\pi\epsilon_0}\right)^2 \times 4\pi\int_R^{\infty}\frac{dr}{r^2}$$

$$= \frac{1}{2}\epsilon_0\left(\frac{q}{4\pi\epsilon_0}\right)^2 \times 4\pi \times \left|-\frac{1}{r}\right|_R^{\infty}$$

or $\quad U = \dfrac{q^2}{8\pi\epsilon_0 R}.$

**Method II :** Let some charge is given to the shell, its corresponding potential becomes $v$. The energy stored on it is equal to the work done, i.e.,

$$dU = v dq$$

Total energy of shell

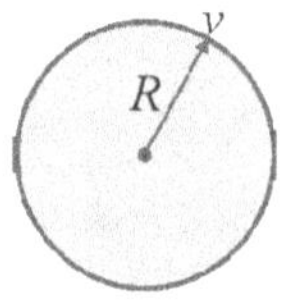

$$U = \int_0^q v\,dq$$

$$= \frac{1}{4\pi\epsilon_0}\int_0^q \frac{q}{R}dq$$

*Fig. 2.60*

$$= \frac{q^2}{8\pi\epsilon_0 R}.$$

**Method III :** To understand easily, let suffix 1, 2, 3 are used for them as shown in *fig. 2.62*.

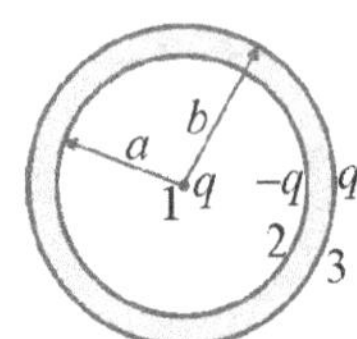


*Fig. 2.61*

$$U = U_1 + U_2 + U_3 + U_{12} + U_{13} + U_{23}$$

$$= U_1 + U_2 + U_3 + q_1(V_{12}) + q_1(V_{13}) + q_2(V_{23})$$

$$= 0 + \frac{(-q)^2}{8\pi\epsilon_0 a} + \frac{q^2}{8\pi\epsilon_0 b} + q\left(\frac{1}{4\pi\epsilon_0}\frac{(-q)}{a}\right)$$

$$+ q\left(\frac{1}{4\pi\epsilon_0}\frac{q}{b}\right) + (-q)\frac{1}{4\pi\epsilon_0}\frac{q}{b}$$

$$= \frac{q^2}{8\pi\epsilon_0}\left(\frac{1}{a} - \frac{1}{b}\right).$$

**Ex. 27 Find total energy of the system having two thin concentric shells with charges $q_1$ and $q_2$.**

**Sol.**

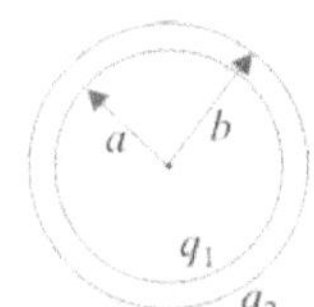


*Fig. 2.62.* Two concentric conducting shell with charges $q_1$ & $q_2$

$$U = U_1 + U_2 + U_{12} = U_1 + U_2 + q_1(V_{12})$$

$$= \frac{q_1^2}{8\pi\epsilon_0 a} + \frac{q_2^2}{8\pi\epsilon_0 b} + q_1\left(\frac{1}{4\pi\epsilon_0}\frac{q_2}{b}\right)$$

$$= \frac{1}{4\pi\epsilon_0}\left[\frac{q_1^2}{2a} + \frac{q_2^2}{2b} + \frac{q_1 q_2}{b}\right]. \quad \textit{Ans.}$$

**Ex. 28 A spherical shell of radius $R_1$ with a uniform charge $q$ has a point charge $q_0$ at its centre. Find the work performed by the electric forces during the shell expansion from radius $R_1$ to radius $R_2$.**

**Sol.**

The total energy of the system

$$U_{\text{initial}} = U_i + U_e = U_s + q_0 V_0$$

$$= \frac{q^2}{8\pi\epsilon_0 R_1} + \frac{q_0 q}{4\pi\epsilon_0 R_1}$$

$$= \frac{q}{4\pi\epsilon_0}\frac{\left(q_0 + \frac{q}{2}\right)}{R_1}$$

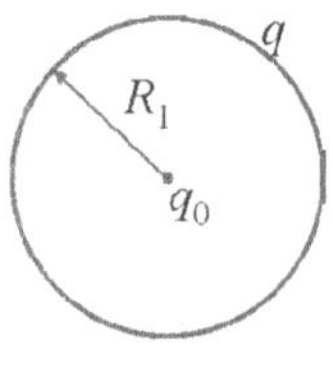

and final energy

*Fig. 2.63*

$$U_{\text{final}} = \frac{q}{4\pi\epsilon_0}\frac{\left(q_0 + \frac{q}{2}\right)}{R_2}$$

$\therefore$ Workdone by electric force in expansion

$$W = -\Delta U = U_{\text{initial}} - U_{\text{final}}$$

$$= \frac{q\left(q_0 + \frac{q}{2}\right)}{4\pi\epsilon_0}\left[\frac{1}{R_1} - \frac{1}{R_2}\right]. \quad \textit{Ans.}$$

## 2.14 VAN DE GRAFF GENERATOR

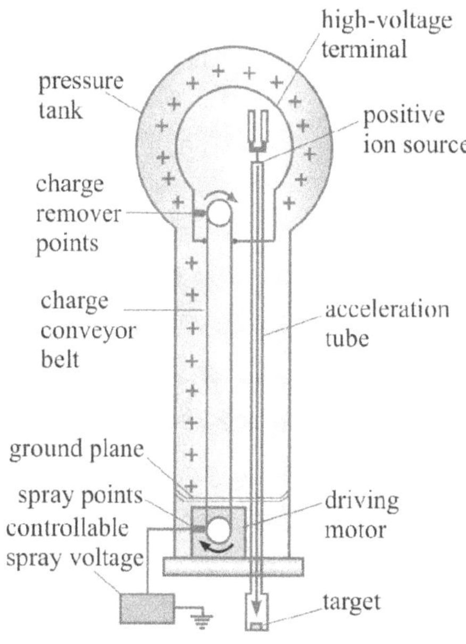

Fig. 2.64

It is an instrument which is used to produce very high voltage of the order of million volt. If a charged conductor is brought in contact to the hollow conductor, its entire charge will transfer to the hollow conductor no matter how high the potential of the latter may be. It consist of hollow metallic conductor A mounted on a stand and a belt made of non-conducting material which runs by means of a high speed rotor over two pulleys. Because of the large electric field near the comb D, air ionises and whose positive ions are repelled by the comb. These positive ions attach to the surface of the moving belt and are carried by the belt to the terminal where they are removed by the another corona discharge to the comb E. This comb is connected with the inner surface of the hollow conductor mounted on the insulating supports. The charge is thus transferred to the conductor and increases its potential.
If the electric field just outside the conductor A is sufficient for dielectric breakdown of air, no more charge can be transferred to it. For a conductor of radius R, the electric field just outside it is $E=\dfrac{Q}{4\pi \epsilon_0 R^2}$ and $V=\dfrac{Q}{4\pi \epsilon_0 R}$. Thus $V=ER$.

Dielectric strength of air $E=3\times10^6 V/m$, and for $R=1$m; $V=3\times10^6\times1=3\times10^6 V$.

Thus, the potential of a conducting sphere of radius 1m can be raised to $3\times10^6$ V by this method.

## 2.15 KIRCHHOFF'S LAWS

Kirchhoff's laws are very useful in analysing multiloops circuits. He provided two laws. These are :

**Junction rule :**

The algebraic sum of the charges or currents at any junction is zero.

For charge : $\Sigma q = 0$

At junction $A$ as shown in *fig. 2.66*,

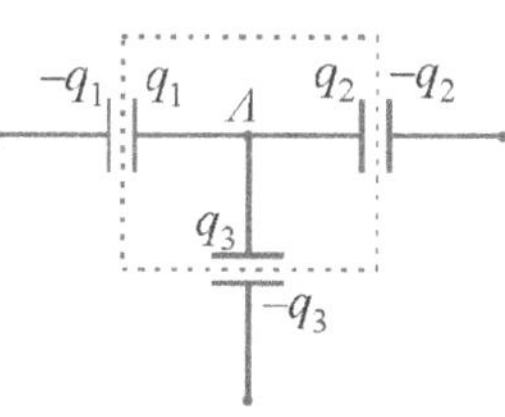

Fig. 2.65

$$q_1+q_2+q_3 = 0$$

or $$q_3 = -(q_1+q_2).$$

For current : $$\Sigma i = 0$$

At $A$, $$i_1+i_2+i_3 = 0$$

or $$i_3 = -(i_1+i_2).$$

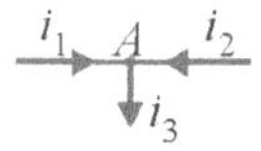

Fig. 2.66

**Loop rule:**

The algebraic sum of the potential differences across all the circuit elements in a closed loop including with emfs must equal to zero.

or $$\Sigma V = 0.$$

(a) Circuit having resistors and cells, then

$$\Sigma\xi+\Sigma iR = 0$$

(b) Circuit having capacitors and cells, then

$$\Sigma\xi+\Sigma\frac{q}{C} = 0$$

(c) Circuit having resistors, capacitors and cells, then

$$\Sigma\xi+\Sigma\frac{q}{C}+\Sigma iR = 0.$$

The juction rule is an application of the principle of conservation of charge. The loop rule is a consequence of conservation of energy.

For circuit analysis, the following procedures should be followed carefully.

First of all label all the known and unknown carefully, including an assumed sense of direction for each unknown. Often one does not know in advance the actual direction or sign of an unknown current, emf or charge, but this does not matter. The solution is carried out using the assumed directions, and if the actual direction of a particular quantity is opposite to the assumed direction, the value of the quantity found with negative sign.

### The following guidelines and sign conventions are useful in analysing circuit problems.

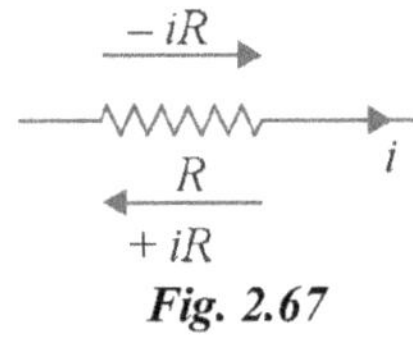

*Fig. 2.67*

1. One must remember that, the current in any resistor or charge on any capacitor is the net response of all the sources present in the circuit. Don't think that only nearest one is sending the current or charge.
2. Choose any closed loop in the network, and designate a direction (clockwise or anticlockwise) to traverse the loop for loop rule.
3. Close loop may or may not have any cell, but one of the close loop must include the cell. For a circuit having only one cell, choose a close loop, which include this cell.
4. (a) The p.d. across any resistor can be taken negative when moves along the direction of current and positive for reverse direction of current.

   (b) The p.d. across capacitor can be taken negative when moves from positive plate of capacitor to negative plate and positive for reverse sense.

$-q/C$ $\quad q \quad -q \quad C \quad$ $+q/C$

*Fig. 2.68*

**Note:** See the sign of charge of first coming plate of capacitor only.

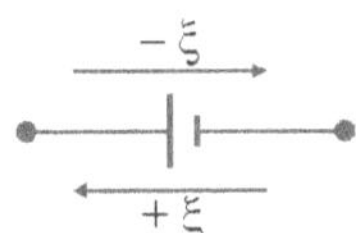

*Fig. 2.69*

   (c) The emf of any cell/battery is taken as negative from its positive terminal to negative terminal and positive for reverse sense.

5. It must be remembered that capacitor in steady state stop the direct current, and so there will be no current in the branch in which capacitor is connected.
6. If capacitors are connected in series with the sources as shown, the charge on each capacitor will be same. It must be remembered that the net charge supply by cell will be zero.
7. Finally, the number of equations obtained must always be equal to the number of unknows.

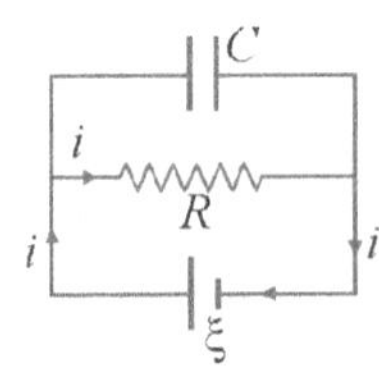

*Fig. 2.70*

### The R-C series circuit

**(a) Charging**

Consider the circuit as shown in *fig. 2.73*. If the capacitor is initially has no charge, then the initial p.d. across the capacitor is zero, and the entire emf appears across resistor, causing an initial current $i_0 = \frac{\xi}{R}$. As the capacitor charges, its potential increases, and p.d. across resistor decreases, corresponding to a decrease in current. After a long time when capacitor becomes fully charged, the entire potential will occur across capacitor and the current becomes zero.

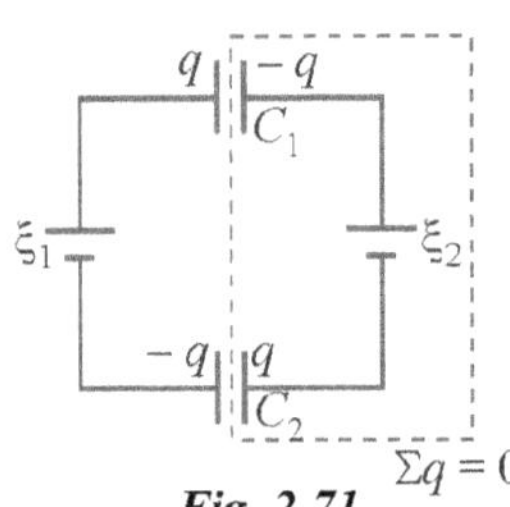

*Fig. 2.71*

Let at any instant the current in the resistor is $i$, then by loop rule

$$-iR - \frac{q}{C} + \xi = 0$$

or

$$-\frac{dq}{dt}R - \frac{q}{C} + \xi = 0$$

$$\frac{dq}{dt}R = \xi - \frac{q}{C}$$

$$\therefore \quad \frac{dq}{\left(\xi - \frac{q}{C}\right)} = \frac{dt}{R}$$

*Fig. 2.72*

Integrating above expression, we have

$$\int_0^q \frac{dq}{\left(\xi - \frac{q}{C}\right)} = \int_0^t \frac{dt}{R}$$

or $$\left|\frac{\ell n\left(\xi - \frac{q}{C}\right)}{-\frac{1}{C}}\right|_0^q = \frac{t}{R}$$

or $$\ell n\left(\xi - \frac{q}{C}\right) - \ell n\xi = \frac{-t}{RC}$$

or $$\ell n\left[1 - \frac{q}{C\xi}\right] = -\frac{t}{RC}$$

Substituting, $C\xi = q_0$, the maximum or steady state charge on the capacitor and $RC = \tau$, capacitive time constant

$\therefore$ $$\ell n\left(1 - \frac{q}{q_0}\right) = -\frac{t}{\tau}$$

or $$q = q_0\left(1 - e^{-t/\tau}\right)$$

**Current :** $$i = \frac{dq}{dt} = q_0 \times e^{-t/\tau} \times \left(\frac{1}{\tau}\right)$$

$$= \frac{q_0}{RC} e^{-t/\tau}$$

$$= \frac{C\xi}{RC} e^{-t/\tau}$$

or $$i = i_0 e^{-t/\tau} \qquad \left[as\ i_0 = \frac{\xi}{R}\right]$$

At $t = 0$, $$i = i_0 e^{-0} = i_0$$

and at $t = \infty$, $$i = i_0 e^{-\infty}$$

$$= 0$$

It means initially capacitor offers no resistance in the circuit. But after charging fully, it offers infinite resistance.

**Potential of capacitor :**

Potential, $$V = \frac{q}{C} = \frac{q_0\left(1 - e^{-t/\tau}\right)}{C}$$

or $$= V_0\left(1 - e^{-t/\tau}\right)$$

**Energy stored :**

$$U = \frac{1}{2}CV^2$$

$$= \frac{1}{2}C\left[V_0\left(1 - e^{-t/\tau}\right)\right]^2$$

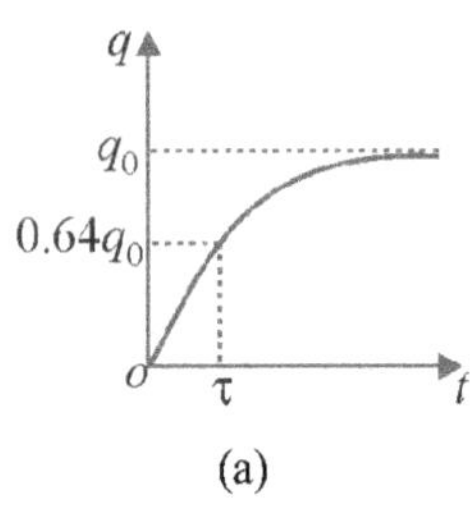

(a)

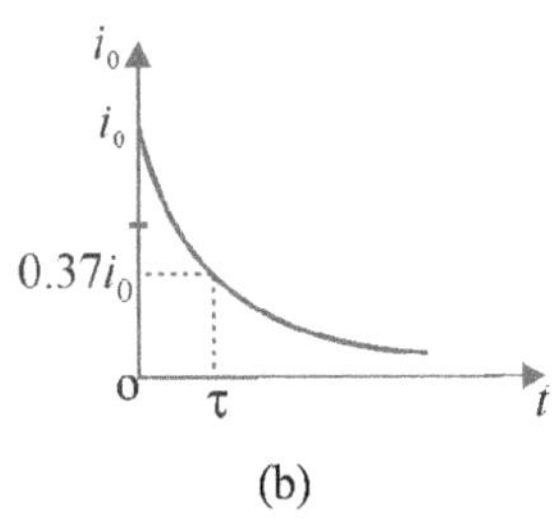

(b)

*Fig. 2.73*

$$= \frac{1}{2}CV_0^2\left(1-e^{-t/\tau}\right)^2$$

or $$U = U_0\left(1-e^{-t/\tau}\right)^2$$

$$q = q_0(1-e^{-t/\tau}); i = i_0e^{-t/\tau}; V = V_0(1-e^{-t/\tau}); U = U_0(1-e^{-t/\tau})^2$$

**Capacitive time constant (τ) :**

At $t = \tau$, $$q = q_0\left(1-e^{-1}\right)$$
$$\simeq 0,64\, q_0$$

or at $t = \tau$, $$i = i_0e^{-1}$$
$$\simeq 0.37\, i_0$$

Therefore time constant is the time in which charge on the capacitor grows to 0.64 times the maximum charge or current decreases to 0.37 times the maximum current.

**(b) Discharging**

After charging the capacitor, let now source is removed from the circuit.

The energy stored in capacitor now used to flow the current. At $t = 0$, we have

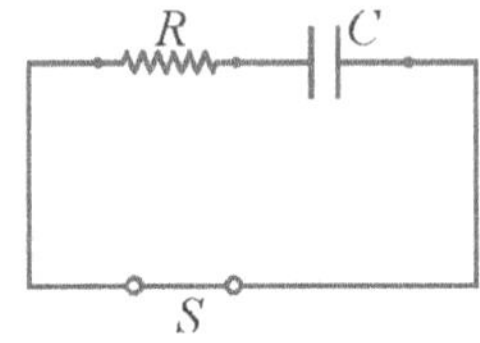

*Fig. 2.74*

$q = q_0$ and $$U = U_0 = \frac{q_0^2}{2C}.$$

Again by loop rule,

$$-iR - \frac{q}{C} = 0$$

where $q$ is the charge on capacitor at any time $t$

or $$-\frac{dq}{dt}R = \frac{q}{C}$$

or $$\frac{dq}{q} = -\frac{dt}{RC}$$

Integrating above expression, we get

$$\int_{q_0}^{q}\frac{dq}{q} = -\int_0^t\frac{dt}{RC}$$

or $$|\ell n\, q|_{q_0}^{q} = -\frac{t}{RC}$$

or $$\ell n\frac{q}{q_0} = -\frac{t}{\tau} \qquad [\text{As } RC = \tau]$$

or $$q = q_0e^{-t/\tau}$$

**Current :** $$i = \frac{dq}{dt} = \frac{d}{dt}\left(q_0e^{-t/\tau}\right)$$

$$= q_0e^{-t/\tau} \times \left(-\frac{1}{\tau}\right)$$

$$= \frac{C\xi}{CR}e^{-t/\tau}$$

$$= -i_0e^{-t/\tau}\left[As\ \frac{\xi}{R} = i_0\right]$$

**Potential :**

$$V = \frac{q}{C} = \frac{q_0}{C}e^{-t/\tau}$$

$$= V_0 e^{-\frac{t}{\tau}}$$

**Energy :**

$$U = \frac{1}{2}CV^2$$

$$= \frac{1}{2}C\left(V_0 e^{-t/\tau}\right)^2$$

$$= \frac{1}{2}CV_0^2 e^{-2t/\tau}$$

$$= U_0 e^{-2t/\tau}.$$

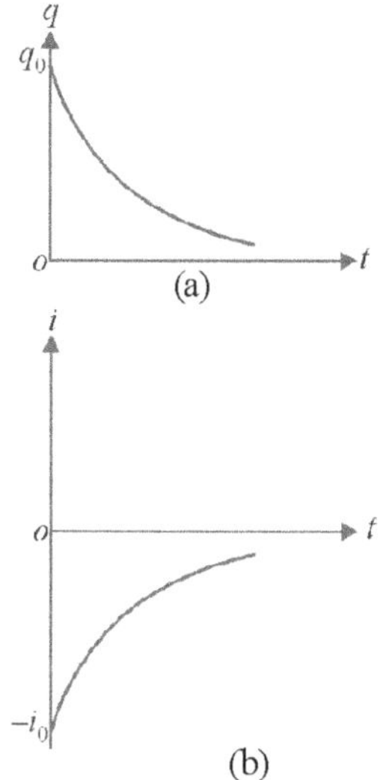


*Fig. 2.75*

## Finding the time constant

If there are many resistors and capacitors are connected in the circuit, then time constant can be obtained by using following steps;

(i) make short circuit at the place of battery.

(ii) Find equivalent capacitance, if there are many capacitors in the circuit. Assuming equivalent capacitor is $C_{net}$.

(iii) Find net resistance across the capacitor, say it is $R_{net}$.

(iv) Finally $\tau_{net} = R_{net} C_{net}$.

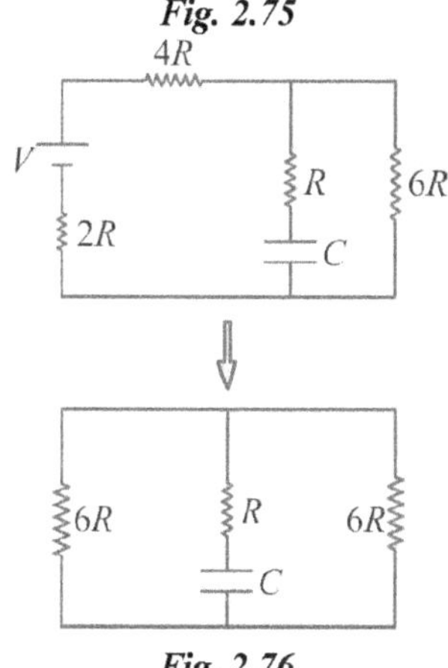


*Fig. 2.76*

## Finding the potential difference between any two points in a circuit

Let we have to find the potential difference between $P$ and $R$ in above circuit

**Step 1 :** Connect an imaginary battery between the points, let it is $V_{PR}$.

**Step 2 :** Choose close loop including the imaginary battery.

**Step 3 :** Use loop rule to find $V_{PR}$.

Choose close loop $P-R-y-x-P$ and applying loop rule, we have

$$\frac{q}{C} + 10 + V_{PR} = 0$$

or

$$-\frac{10}{1} + 10 + V_{PR} = 0$$

or

$$V_{PR} = 0.$$

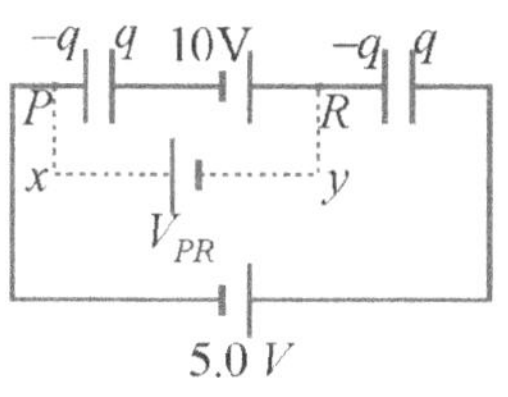


*Fig. 2.77*

## Heat generated

It can be obtained by using conservation of total energy of the system. That is

Initial energy stored in capacitors + work done by sources

= Final energy stored in capacitors + heat generated

or

$$U_i + W = U_f + H$$

or

$$H = (U_i - U_f) + W$$

**Note:** Work done will be positive if work is done by the sources and negative if work is done on the sources.

**(a) Positive work done by source :**

If a capacitor $C$ of potential $V$ ($V$ may be zero) is connected to a source of emf $\xi$ ($\xi > V$)

The work done by source will be $= \xi(\Delta q)$

$$= \xi(q_f - q_i)$$

$$= \xi(C\xi - CV)$$

$$= C\xi(\xi - V).$$

**(b) Negative work done by source :**

If a capacitor $C$ of potential $V$ is connected to a source of emf $\xi$ ($\xi < V$)

The work done by source will be $= \xi\Delta q$

$$= \xi(q_f - q_i)$$

$$= \xi(C\xi - CV)$$

$$= -C\xi(V - \xi).$$

**Case 1.** If $U_f = U_i$, the heat generated $H = W$.

**Case 2.** If capacitors remain the part of same circuit then there always be a positive work.

**Ex. 29** **A capacitor of capacitance $C$ is given a charge $Q$. At $t = 0$, it is connected to an uncharged capacitor of equal capacitance through a resistance R. Find the charge on the second capacitor as a function of time.**

## Sol.

Let at any instant the charge on the uncharged capacitor is $q$. The charge on charged capacitor remains $(Q - q)$.

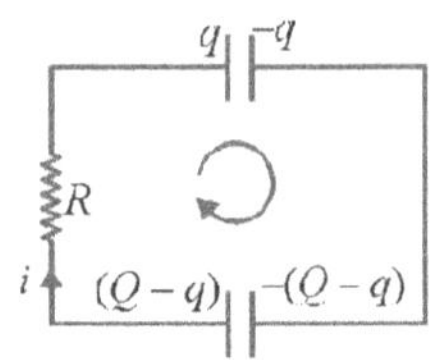


*Fig. 2.78*

Now by loop rule,

$$-iR - \frac{q}{C} + \frac{(Q-q)}{C} = 0$$

or $$-\frac{dq}{dt}R + \left(\frac{Q-2q}{C}\right) = 0$$

or $$\frac{dq}{(Q-2q)} = \frac{dt}{CR}$$

Integrating on both sides of above expression,we get

$$\int_0^q \frac{dq}{Q-2q} = \int_0^t \frac{dt}{RC}$$

$$\left|\frac{\ell n(Q-2q)}{-2}\right|_0^q = \frac{t}{RC}$$

or $$\ell n(Q-2q) - \ell n Q = -\frac{2t}{RC}$$

or $$\ell n\left(\frac{Q-2q}{Q}\right) = -\frac{2t}{RC}$$

or $$\ell n\left(1 - \frac{2q}{Q}\right) = \frac{-2t}{RC}$$

$$\therefore \quad q = \frac{Q}{2}\left(1 - e^{-\frac{2t}{RC}}\right). \quad \textbf{Ans.}$$

**Note:** In above case the time constant $\tau' = \frac{RC}{2}$

**Ex. 30** **There are two uncharged identical metallic spheres of radius $a$, separated a distance $d$. A charged metallic sphere (charge $q$) of same radius is brought and touches sphere 1. After some time it is moved away to a far off distance. After this, the sphere 2 is earthed. Find the charge on sphere 2.**

## Sol.

When sphere with charge $q$ touches metallic sphere 1, the charge on 1 comes out to be $\frac{q}{2}$. The potential due to sphere 1 at the surface of 2 is

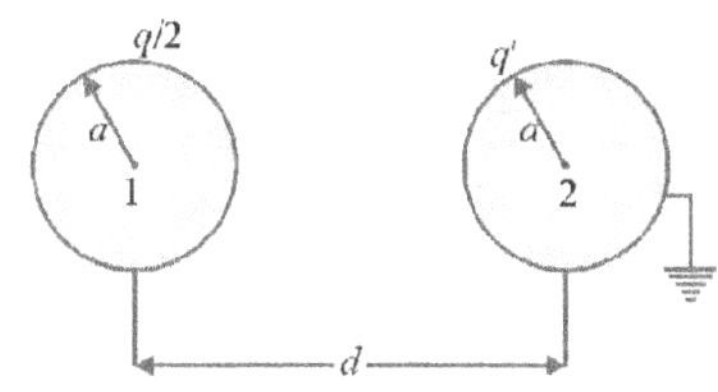


Fig. 2.79

$$V_{21} = \frac{1}{4\pi \in_0} \frac{q_1}{d} = \frac{1}{4\pi \in_0}\left(\frac{q}{2d}\right)$$

When sphere 2 is earthed, its potential becomes zero. Let induced charge on it is $q'$, then

$$V_2 = 0 = \frac{1}{4\pi \in_0} \frac{q}{2d} + \frac{1}{4\pi \in_0} \frac{q'}{a}$$

which gives $$q' = -\frac{qa}{2d}. \qquad \textit{Ans.}$$

**Ex. 31** **Find the time constant of circuit shown in *fig. 2.79*.**

**Sol.**

After short circuit, the net resistance across capacitor

$$C = \frac{6R \times 6R}{6R + 6R} + R = 4R$$

Now $\tau_c = R_{net} \quad C_{net} = 4RC$ *Ans.*

**Ex. 32** **Find the time constant of the circuits shown in figure.**

**Sol.**

(a)

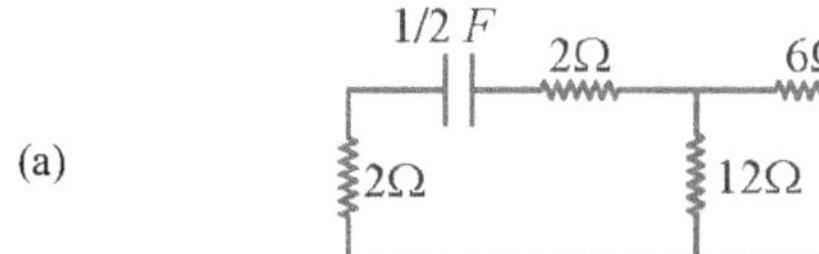


Fig. 2.80

$$R_{net} = \frac{6 \times 12}{6 + 12} + 2 + 2 = 8\ \Omega$$

$$\tau_{net} = R_{net}\ C_{net}$$

$$= 8 \times \frac{1}{2}$$

$$= 4\ s$$

(b)

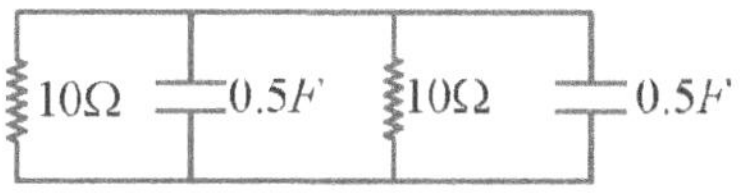

Fig. 2.81

$$C_{net} = 0.5 + 0.5 = 1F$$

$$R_{net} = \frac{10 \times 10}{10 + 10} = 5\ \Omega$$

$$\tau_{net} = R_{net}\ C_{net}$$

$$= 5 \times 1$$

$$= 5\ s$$

**Ex. 33** **A circuit has a section $AB$ as shown in *fig. 2.82*. The emf of the source $\xi$ = 10 V, the capacitor capacitances are equal to $C_1$ = 1.0 μF, $C_2$ = 2.0 μF, and the potential difference $V_A - V_B$ = 5.0 V. Find voltage across each capacitor.**

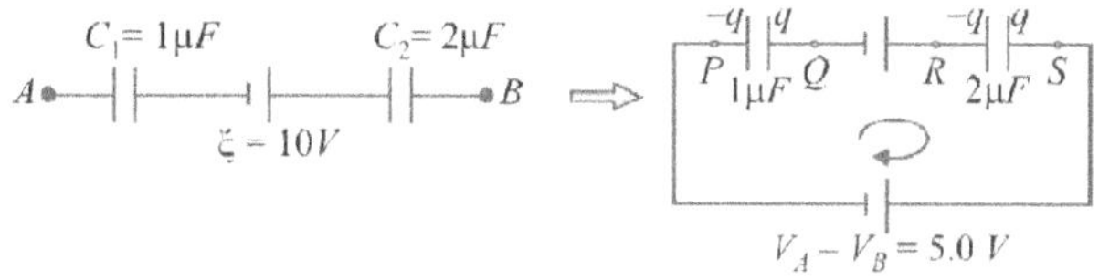

Fig. 2.82

**Sol.**

Both the capacitors are in series, therefore they will have same charges. Let charge on each is $q$. By loop rule,

$$+5 + \frac{q}{1} + 10 + \frac{q}{2} = 0$$

or $$q = -10\ \mu C$$

Potential difference across 1μF, $V_P - V_Q$

$$= -\frac{q}{C} = \frac{-(-10)}{1} = 10\ V \qquad \textit{Ans.}$$

and potential difference across 2μF,

$$V_R - V_S = -\frac{q}{C}$$

$$= \frac{-(-10)}{2}$$

$$= 5V \qquad \textit{Ans.}$$

**Ex. 34** **Find the potential difference $V_a - V_b$ between the points *a* and *b* shown in *fig. 2.84*.**

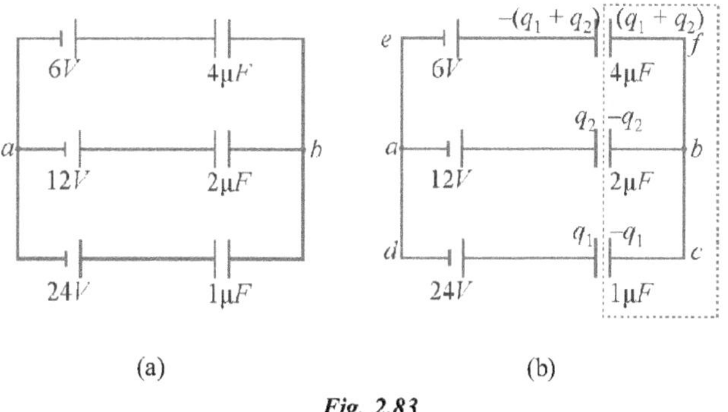


Fig. 2.83

**Sol.**

Suppose the charges on $1\mu F$ and $2\mu F$ are $q_1$ and $q_2$ respectively. By junction rule the charge at junction $b$ must be zero. Therefore the charge on 4 $\mu F$ capacitor be $(q_1 + q_2)$. The proposed charges are shown in figure. We have introduced two unknowns and therefore we require two equations, which can be obtained by loop rule.

In close loop aefba, we have

$$+6+\frac{(q_1+q_2)}{4}+\frac{q_2}{2}-12 = 0$$

or $$q_1+3q_2 = 24 \quad ....(i)$$

Now in close loop *abcda* ,

$$+12-\frac{q_2}{2}+\frac{q_1}{1}-24 = 0$$

or $$2q_1-q_2 = 24 \quad ...(ii)$$

Solving equations (i) and (ii), we get

$$q_1 = 13.7\ \mu C \text{ and } q_2 = 3.4\ \mu C$$

To find $V_a - V_b$, connect an imaginary battery between *a* and *b*, as shown in *fig. 2.85*.

Now in close loop abxya, we have

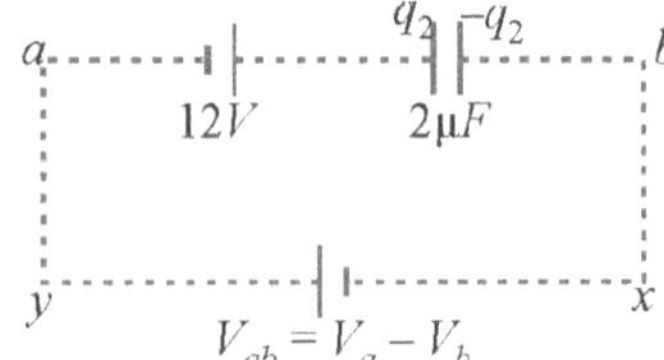

*Fig. 2.84*

$$+12-\frac{q_2}{2}+(V_a-V_b) = 0$$

or $$V_a - V_b = -12+\frac{q_2}{2}$$

$$= -12+\frac{3.4}{2}$$

$$= -10.3 \text{ V.} \qquad \textbf{\textit{Ans.}}$$

**Finding flow of charges :** This can be understand by following example:

**Ex. 35 What charges will flow after the shortening of the switch $S_w$ in the circuit illustrated in *fig. 2.85* through sections 1 and 2 in directions indicated by the arrows ?**

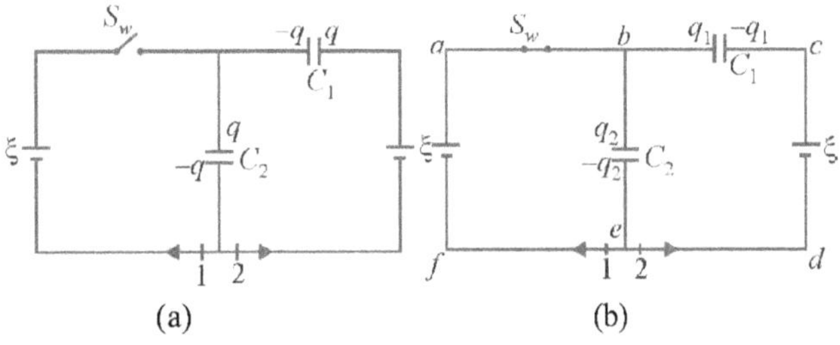

*Fig. 2.85*

**Sol.**

Before shortening of switch both the capacitors are in series with the cell.

Thus charge on each capacitor is $q = \left(\frac{C_1C_2}{C_1+C_2}\right)\xi$

After shortening of switch, let charges on them are as shown in *fig. 2.86*(b).

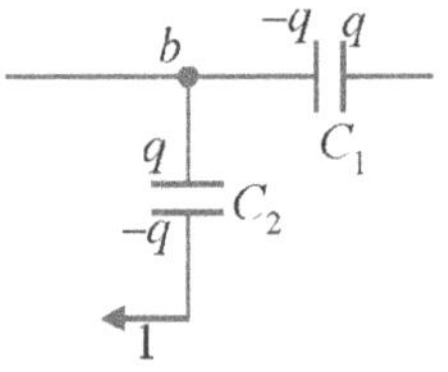

*Fig. 2.86*

In close loop *a b e f a*, we have

$$\frac{-q_2}{C_2}+\xi = 0 \quad ...(i)$$

and in close loop b c d e b

$$\frac{-q_1}{C_1}-\xi+\frac{q_2}{C_2} = 0 \quad ...(ii)$$

Solving equations (i) and (ii), we get

$$q_1 = 0 \text{ and } q_2 = \xi C_2$$

**Flow of charge through section 1 :**

Initially charge of capacitors joining at *b* is $= q - q = 0$

After shortening of switch the charge on them are

$$= q_1+q_2 = 0+C\xi_2 = C\xi_2$$

Therefore flow of charge through section 1

= final charge at junction *b* – initial charge at junction *b*

$$= (q_1+q_2)-(q-q)$$

$$= C\xi_2 - 0 = C\xi_2$$

**Flow of charge through section 2 :**

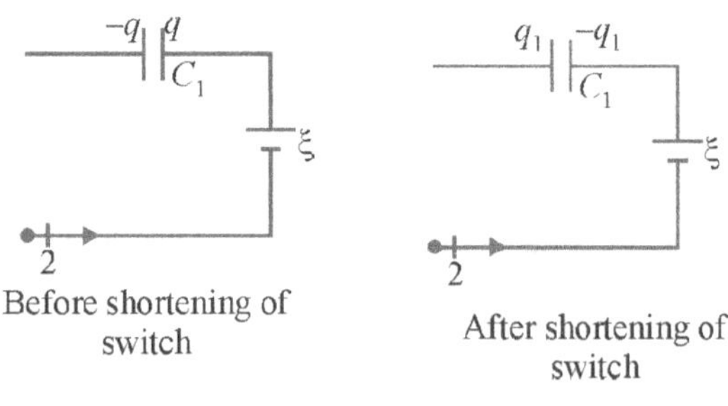

*Fig. 2.87*

It is clear from figure,

the flow of charge through section 2.

=Final charge on capacitor $C_1$

– initial charge on capacitor $C_1$

$$= -q_1-q$$

$$= -(q_1+q)$$

$$= -\left(0+\frac{C_1C_2}{C_1+C_2}\xi\right)$$

$$= -\frac{C_1C_2}{(C_1+C_2)}\xi \qquad \textit{Ans.}$$

**Ex. 36** **What amount of heat will be generated in the circuit shown in *fig. 2.88* after the switch $S_w$ is shifted from position 1 to position 2 ?**

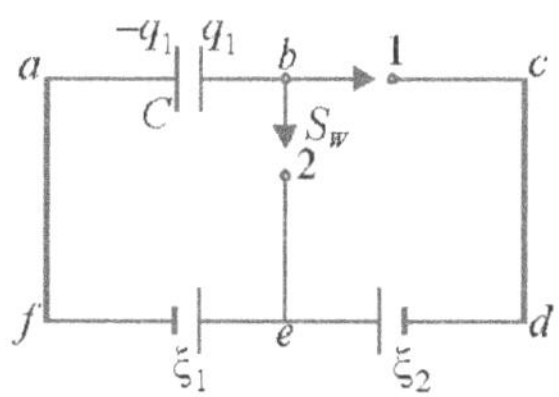

Switch is at position 1

(a)

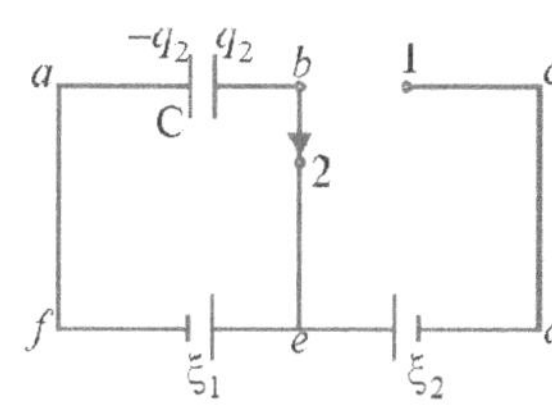

Switch shifted to position 2

(b)

*Fig. 2.88*

**Sol.**

Let $q_1$ and $q_2$ are the charges on the capacitor in the positions of switch 1 and 2 respectively.

Choose close loop $a\ b\ c\ d\ e\ f\ a$ in figure (a),

$$\frac{q_1}{C}+\xi_2-\xi_1 = 0$$

or $$q_1 = C(\xi_1-\xi_2) = C\xi_1 - C\xi_2$$

Now choose close loop $a\ b\ e\ f\ a$ in figure (b),

$$\frac{q_2}{C}-\xi_1 = 0$$

or $$q_2 = C\xi_1$$

It is clear from above calculators that, the charge supplied by battery 1 is as such while charge supplied by battery 2 is increased by

$\Delta q_2 = 0-(-C\xi_2) = C\xi_2$

Therefore work is done only by battery 2 , which is

$$= (\Delta q_2)\xi_2$$

$$= (C\xi_2)\xi_2$$

$$= C\xi_2^2$$

$\therefore$ Heat generated $= \dfrac{C\xi_2^2}{2}$. *Ans.*

### Short in series

Short ideally has zero resistance, and so potential difference across short will be zero.When a short is used acrosse the capacitor the entire charge will pass through the short; no charge comes on the capacitor connected with a short.

Consider the circuit shown in figure.

The charge on capacitor $C_1 = C_1\xi$.

The charge on capacitor $C_2 = 0$

The equivalent capacitance $C_{eq} = C_1$

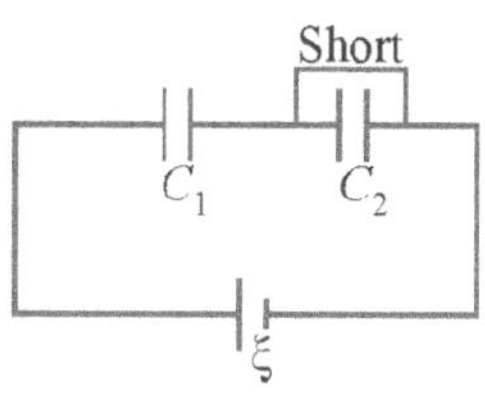

*Fig. 2.89*

**Finding equivalent capacitance :** Wheat stone bridge type circuit

**(a) Balanced circuit : $C_{PQ}$ = ?**

If $\dfrac{C_1}{C_2} = \dfrac{C_3}{C_4}$, the circuit is called balanced. This happens

when $\qquad V_A = V_B$.

The capacitor in arm $AB$ will have no charge, and therefore it can be ignored in finding $C_{PQ}$.

$$\therefore \qquad C_{PQ} = \left(\frac{C_1C_2}{C_1+C_2}\right)+\left(\frac{C_3C_4}{C_3+C_4}\right)$$

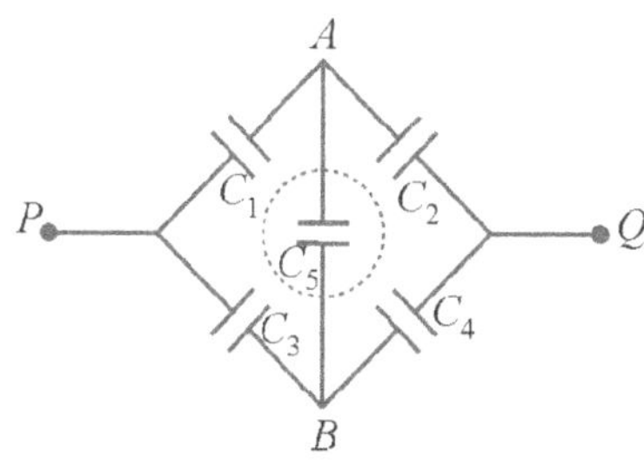

*Fig. 2.90*

**Ex. 37** **Find equivalent capacitance between $P$ and $Q$.**

**Sol.**

(a)

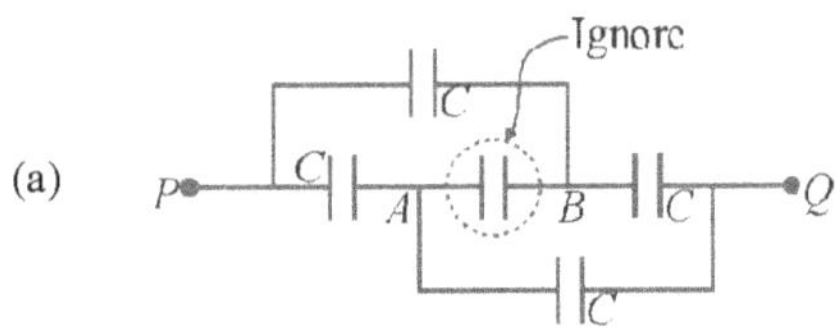


*Fig. 2.91*

The capacitance in dotted circle can be ignored.

$$\therefore \quad C_{PQ} = \frac{C}{2} + \frac{C}{2} = C$$

(b)

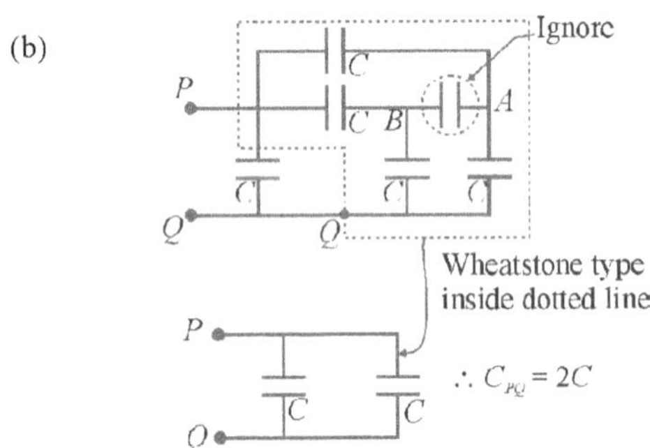


*Fig. 2.92*

**Ex. 38** **Find equivalent capacitance between points $P$ and $Q$ as shown in *fig. 2.93*.**

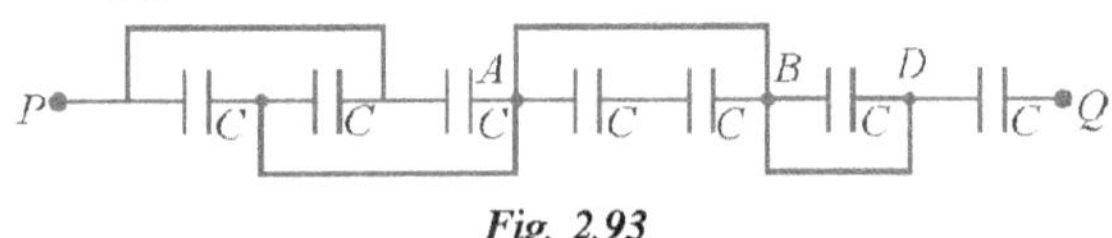


*Fig. 2.93*

**Sol.** In the circuit $V_A = V_B = V_D$. Therefore capacitors connected between $A$ & $B$ and $B$ & $D$ have no charge. So they can be ignored. The effective circuit is as follows :

(a)

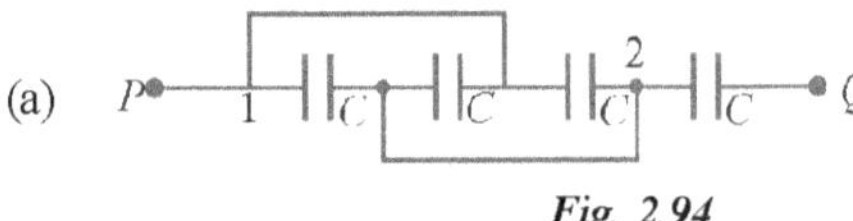


*Fig. 2.94*

(b)

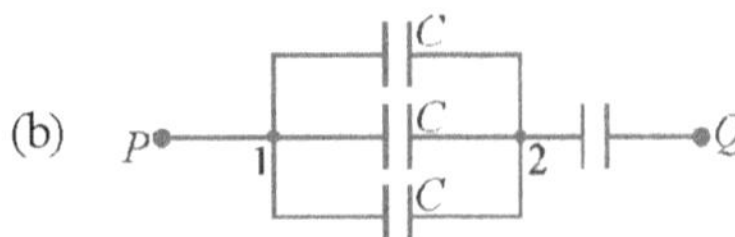


*Fig. 2.95*

(c) $P$ —| 3C |—| C |— $Q$

*Fig. 2.96*

$$\text{Now } C_{PQ} = \frac{3C \times C}{3C + C} = \frac{3}{4}C \qquad \textit{Ans.}$$

**(b) Unbalanced wheat stone bridges :**

This type of problems can be solved by circuit analysis. The method can be understand by the following example:

**Ex. 39** **Find the equivalent capacitance between the points $P$ and $Q$ as shown in *fig. 2.97*.**

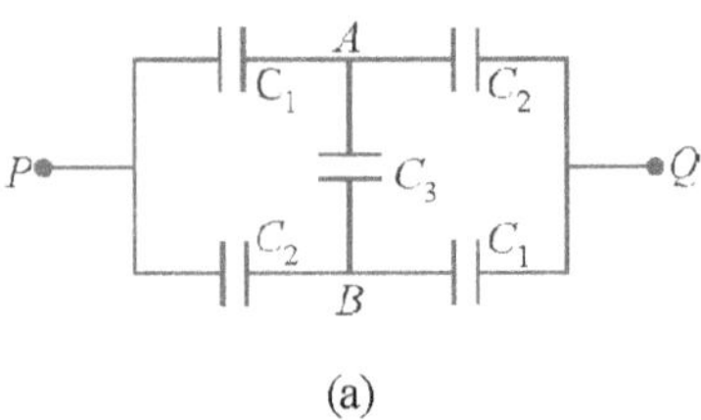


(a)

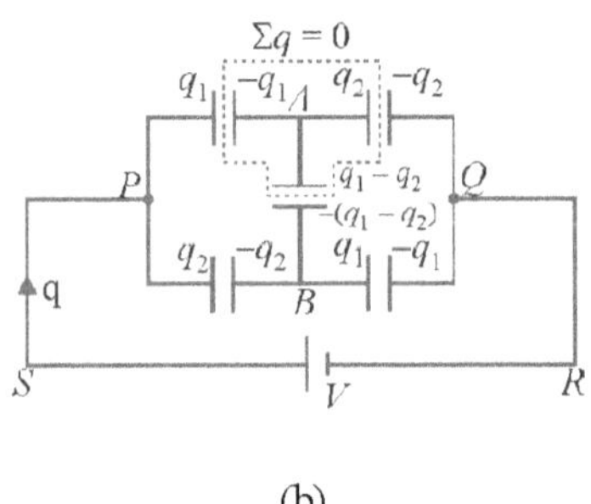


(b)

*Fig. 2.97*

**Sol.**

**Method I :** Let us connect a battery between $P$ and $Q$. The charge distribution is shown in *fig. 2.98*. The charge coming from positive terminal is $(q_1 + q_2)$. The same amount of charge comes from negative terminal of the battery. Due to cross-symmetry, the charge on $C_1$ in both arms will be same. Similarly charge on $C_2$ in both arms will be same.

The charge on capacitor $C_3$ : Let $q_3$ be the charge on capacitor $C_3$. By junction rule

$$q_3 - q_1 + q_2 = 0 \Rightarrow q_3 = (q_1 - q_2)$$

Let total charge drawn from the battery is $q$, then equivalent capacitance between $P$ and $Q$

$$C = \frac{q}{V_{PQ}} = \frac{q_1 + q_2}{V} \qquad \text{...(i)}$$

Now we have to find the value of $q_1$ & $q_2$. Choose a close loop $P\,A\,B\,P$, we have

$$-\frac{q_1}{C_1} - \frac{(q_1 - q_2)}{C_3} + \frac{q_2}{C_2} = 0$$

$$\text{or} \quad -\frac{q_1}{C_1} - \frac{q_1}{C_3} + \frac{q_2}{C_3} + \frac{q_2}{C_2} = 0$$

$$\text{or} \quad q_1\left(\frac{1}{C_1} + \frac{1}{C_3}\right) = q_2\left(\frac{1}{C_2} + \frac{1}{C_3}\right) \qquad \text{...(ii)}$$

Now in close loop $PAQRSP$

$$\frac{-q_1}{C_1} - \frac{q_2}{C_2} + V = 0$$

or $$\frac{q_1}{C_1} + \frac{q_2}{C_2} = V \quad ...(iii)$$

From equations (ii) and (iii), we get

$$\frac{q_1}{C_1} + \frac{q_1\left(\frac{1}{C_1} + \frac{1}{C_3}\right)}{C_2\left(\frac{1}{C_2} + \frac{1}{C_3}\right)} = V$$

or $$q_1\left[\frac{1}{C_1} + \frac{(C_1 + C_3)}{C_1(C_2 + C_3)}\right] = V$$

or $$q_1 = \frac{C_1(C_2 + C_3)}{C_1 + C_2 + 2C_3}V \quad ...(iv)$$

From equation (ii), $$q_2 = \frac{C_2(C_1 + C_3)}{C_1 + C_2 + 2C_3} \quad ...(v)$$

Equivalent capacitance $$C = \frac{q_1 + q_2}{V}$$

$$= \frac{C_1(C_2 + C_3) + C_2(C_1 + C_3)}{C_1 + C_2 + 2C_3}$$

or $$C = \frac{2C_1C_2 + C_1C_3 + C_2C_3}{C_1 + C_2 + 2C_3}.$$

**Method II :** $$V_P - V_Q = (V_P - V_A) + (V_A - V_Q)$$

$$= \frac{q_1}{C_1} + \frac{q_2}{C_2}$$

$$= \frac{q_1}{C_1} + \frac{q - q_1}{C_2} \quad ...(i)$$

Also $$V_P - V_Q = (V_P - V_A) + (V_A - V_B) + (V_B - V_Q)$$

$$= \frac{q_1}{C_1} + \frac{q_1 - q_2}{C_3} + \frac{q_1}{C_1}$$

$$= \frac{q_1}{C_1} + \frac{2q_1 - q}{C_3} + \frac{q_1}{C_1} \quad ...(ii)$$

Eliminate $q_1$ from above equations (i) and (iii) to get

$$C = \frac{q}{V_P - V_Q}$$

The equation (i) can be written as

$$V_P - V_Q = q_1\left(\frac{1}{C_1} - \frac{1}{C_2}\right) + \frac{q}{C_2}$$

or $$\frac{C_1C_2}{C_2 - C_1}(V_P - V_Q) = q_1 + \left(\frac{C_1}{C_2 - C_1}\right)q \quad ...(iii)$$

The equation (ii) can be written as

$$V_P - V_Q = 2q\left(\frac{1}{C_1} + \frac{1}{C_3}\right) - \frac{q}{C_3}$$

or $$\frac{C_1C_3(V_P - V_Q)}{2(C_1 + C_3)} = q_1 - \frac{C_1 q}{2(C_1 + C_3)} \quad ...(iv)$$

Subtracting equation (iv) from (iii), we have

$$(V_P - V_Q)\left(\frac{C_1C_2}{C_2 - C_1} - \frac{C_1C_3}{2(C_1 + C_3)}\right) = \left(\frac{C_1}{C_2 - C_1} + \frac{C_1}{2(C_1 + C_3)}\right)q$$

or $$(V_P - V_q)\left[2C_1C_2(C_1 + C_3) - C_1C_3(C_2 - C_1)\right]$$

$$= C_1\left[2(C_1 + C_3) + (C_2 - C_1)\right]q$$

or $$C = \frac{q}{(V_P - V_Q)} = \frac{2C_1C_2 + C_1C_3 + C_2C_3}{C_1 + C_2 + 2C_3}.$$

**Note:** Students are advised to use method 1.

**Ex. 40** **Find the equivalent capacitance of the combination shown in *fig. 2.98* between *P* and *Q*.**

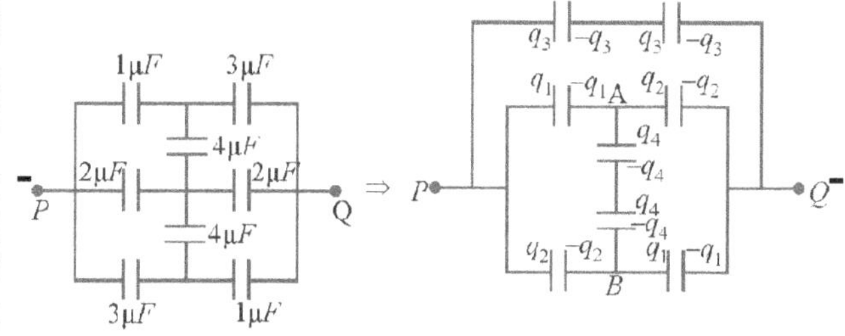

*Fig. 2.98*

## Sol.

It is clear from charge distribution that, there is no exchange of charge between connected arms at the junction. Therefore they can be separated as shown. The above circuit now reduces to

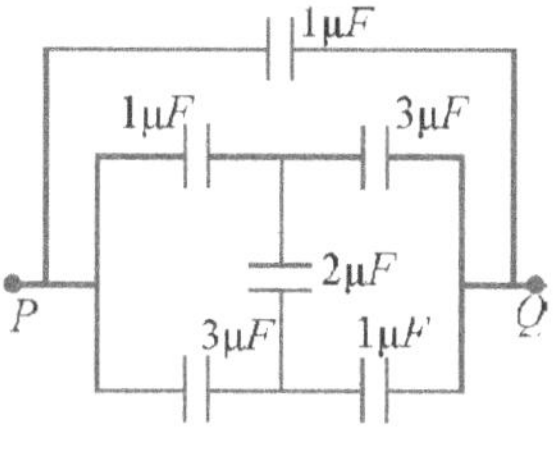

*Fig. 2.99*

For further treatment, go through previous problem answer $\frac{11}{4}\mu F$

***Ans.***

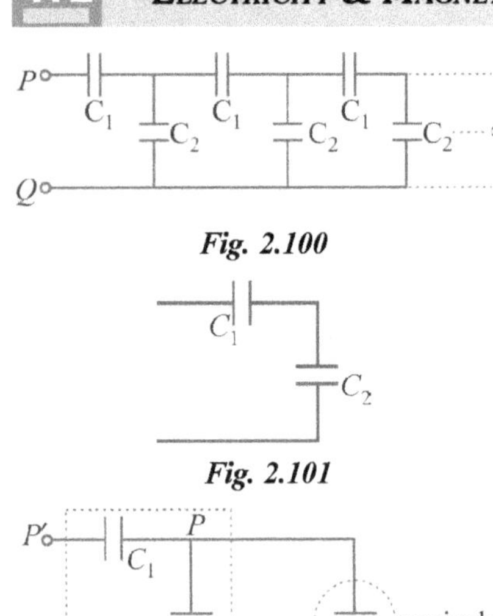

Fig. 2.100

Fig. 2.101

Fig. 2.102

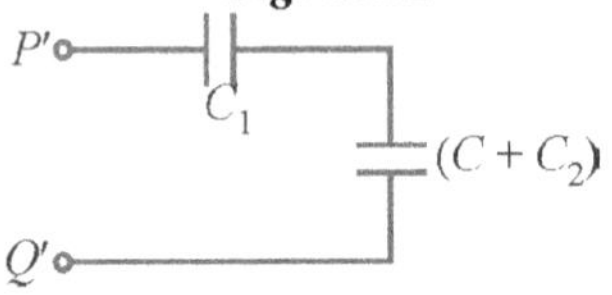

Fig. 2.103

**Infinite ladder :** In the ladder shown in *fig. 2.101*, there is repetation of capacitance $C_1$ and $C_2$. The capacitors $C_1$ and $C_2$ connected in the figure *fig. 2.102* constitute a unit cell.

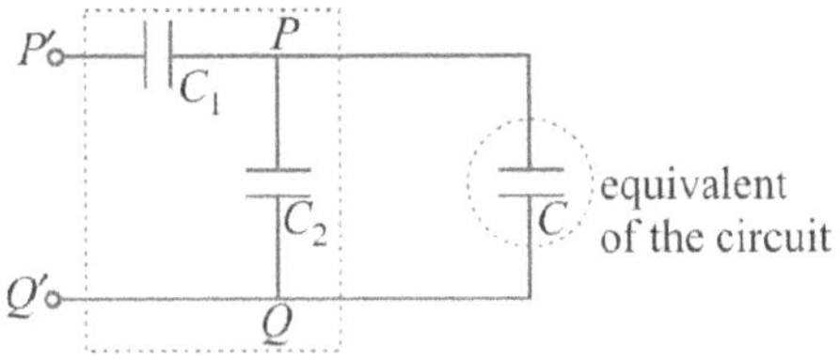

Assume the equivalent capacitance between given points is $C$. Since there are infinite unit cells in the circuit, so we may add one more unit cell or deduct from the circuit, the equivalent of resulting circuit will remain same, i.e., $C$. Finally reduce the circuit to find $C$. In above problem, we add one more unit cell as follows :

It is clear from above theory that $C_{PQ} = C_{P'Q'} = C$. The circuit now reduces to

Now equivalent capacitance $C$

$$\frac{1}{C} = \frac{1}{C_1} + \frac{1}{C + C_2}$$

$$\frac{1}{C} = \frac{C_1 + C_2 + C}{C_1(C + C_2)}$$

or $$C_1C + C_1C_2 = CC_1 + CC_2 + C^2$$

or $$C^2 + CC_2 - C_1C_2 = 0$$

$\therefore$ $$C = \frac{-C_2 \pm \sqrt{C_2^2 + 4 \times C_1C_2}}{2}$$

Take positive value of $C$ because it can not be negative

$\therefore$ $$C = \frac{-C_2 + \sqrt{C_2^2 + 4C_1C_2}}{2}.$$ **Ans.**

**Ex. 41** **A finite ladder is constructed by connecting several sections of 2μF and 4 μF capacitor combinations as shown in *fig. 2.104*. It is terminated by a capacitor of capacitance *C*. What value should be chosen for *C*, such that the equivalent capacitance of the ladder between the points *A* and *B* becomes independent of the number of sections in between ?**

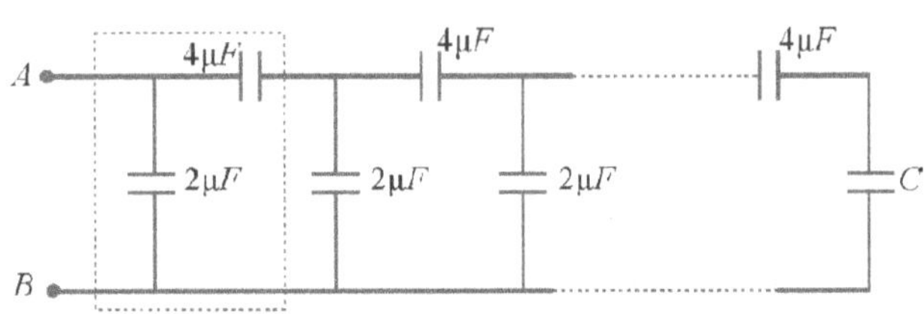


Fig. 2.104

## Sol.

Unit cell comprises 2μF and 4μF as in dotted box.

We can add, zero unit cell with $C$ or one unit cell with $C$ or two unit cells etc; the equivalent capacitance between $A$ and $B$ should be equal in each case.

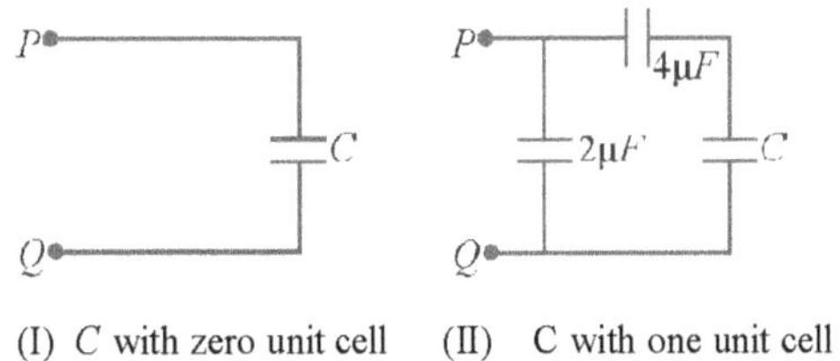


(I) $C$ with zero unit cell (II) C with one unit cell

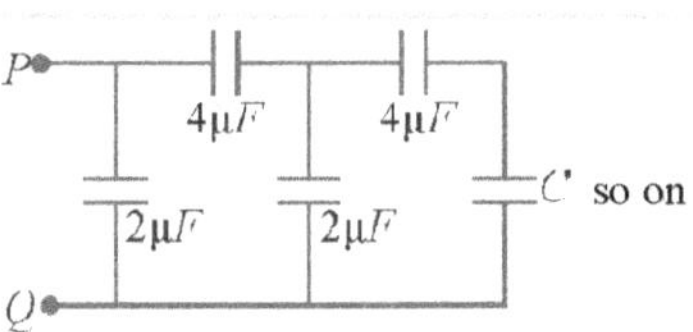


(III) $C$ with two unit cells

Fig. 2.105

To get value of $C$, we may equate any two from above. But for simplicity in calculation, we equate I and II.

$\therefore$ $$C = 2 + \left(\frac{4C}{4 + C}\right)$$

or $$C = \frac{8 + 2C + 4C}{4 + C}$$

or $$C^2 - 2C - 8 = 0$$

$\therefore$ $$C = 4 \text{ μF.}$$ **Ans.**

**Ex. 42** **Twelve capacitors, each having a capacitance *C*, are connected to form a cube (*fig. 2.106*). Find the equivalent capacitance between diagonally opposite corners such as *P* and *Q*.**

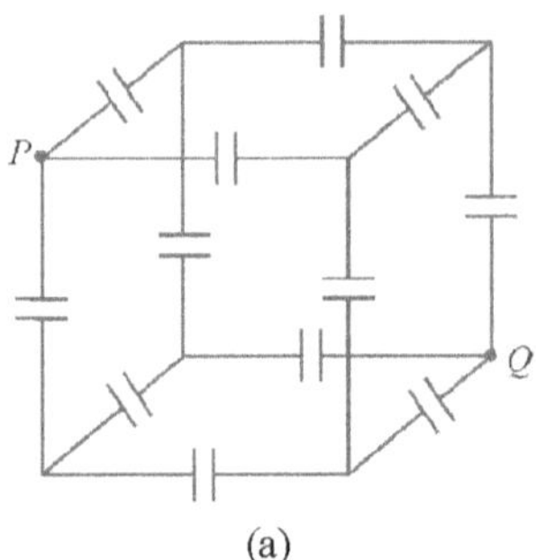


(a)

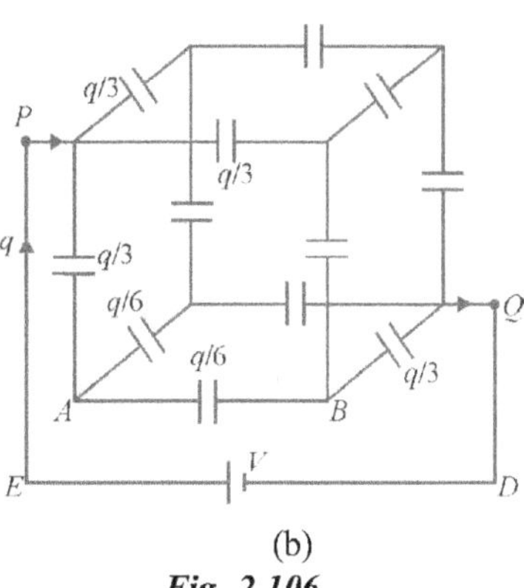

(b)
*Fig. 2.106*

## Sol.

Let a battery is connected between $P$ and $Q$. The circuit has symmetry about diagonal $PQ$. Therefore charge provided by battery say $q$ at $P$ equally distributed into three parts. Similarly the $-q$ provided by negative terminals at $Q$ is equally distributed in three parts. Again at each junction this charge divided into two equal parts. The charge distribution is shown in *fig. 2.107(b)*.

The equivalent capacitance $C_{PQ} = \dfrac{q}{V}$.

Choose close loop $PABQDEP$, we have

$$\frac{\left(\frac{-q}{3}\right)}{C}+\frac{\left(\frac{-q}{6}\right)}{C}+\frac{\left(\frac{-q}{3}\right)}{C}+V = 0$$

or $$\frac{q}{V} = \frac{6C}{5}$$

or $$C_{PQ} = \frac{6C}{5}.$$ **Ans.**

**Ex. 43** **Two capacitors $A$ and $B$ with capacities 3μF and 2μF are charged to a potential difference of 100V and 180V respectively. The plates of the capacitors are connected as shown in *fig. 2.108* with one wire from each capacitor free. The upper plate $A$ is positive and that of $B$ is negative.**

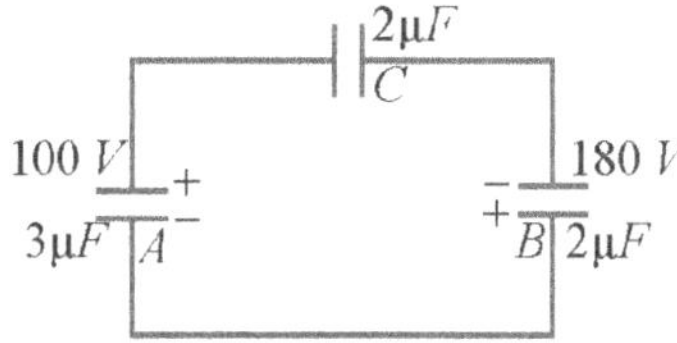

*Fig. 2.107*

**An uncharged 2μF capacitor C with lead wires falls on the free ends to complete the circuit. Calculate:**

**(i) The final charge on the three capacitors and**

**(ii) The amount of electrostatic energy stored in the system before and after the completion of the circuit.**

## Sol.

(i) Let $q$ be the charge flowing during redistribution of charge. By Kirchhoff's loop rule, we have

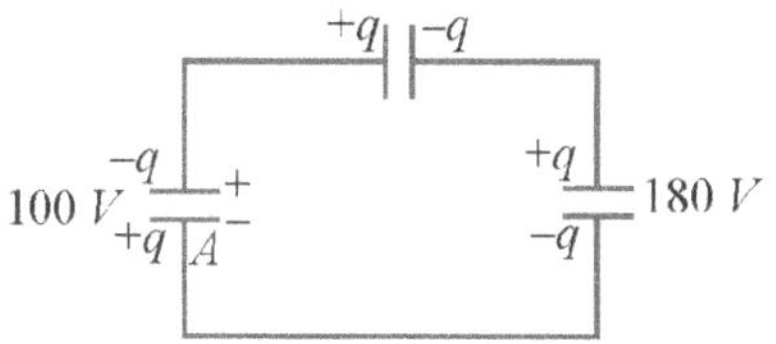

*Fig. 2.108*

$$\frac{q}{2}+\frac{q}{2}+\frac{q}{3}-180-100 = 0$$

or $$q = 210\ \mu C$$

The final charges on the capacitors are

$$q_A = CV-q$$
$$= 3\times 100-210 = 90\ \mu C$$
$$q_B = 2\times 180-210 = 150\ \mu C$$

and $$q_C = 0+210 = 210\ \mu C$$

(ii) Initial electric potential energy

$$U_i = \frac{1}{2}\times\left(3\times 10^{-6}\right)\times 100^2+\frac{1}{2}\times\left(2\times 10^{-6}\right)\times 180^2$$
$$= 47.4\ \text{mJ}$$

$$U_f = \frac{1}{2}\frac{\left(90\times 10^{-6}\right)^2}{\left(3\times 10^{-6}\right)}+\frac{1}{2}\frac{\left(150\times 10^{-6}\right)^2}{\left(2\times 10^{-6}\right)}+\frac{1}{2}\frac{\left(210\times 10^{-6}\right)^2}{\left(2\times 10^{-6}\right)}$$

$= 18$ mJ. **Ans.**

**Ex. 44** **Three capacitors $C_1$, $C_2$, $C_3$ are connected as shown in *fig. 2.109*. The potentials of $P$, $Q$ and $R$ are $V_1$, $V_2$, $V_3$ respectively. Find the potential $V_O$ at the junction $O$.**

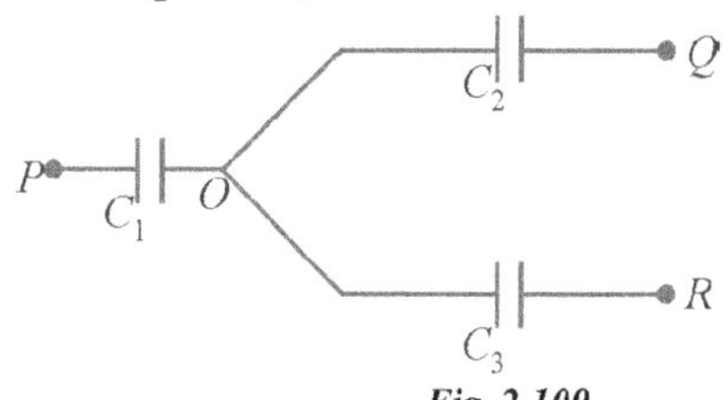

*Fig. 2.109*

## Sol.

Let $q_1$, $q_2$ and $q_3$ be the charges on the capacitors $C_1$, $C_2$ and $C_3$ respectively. Then we have

$$V_1 - V_O = \frac{q_1}{C_1},$$

$$V_O - V_2 = \frac{q_2}{C_2},$$

and $$V_O - V_3 = \frac{q_3}{C_3}.$$

By Kirchhoff's I law at juction O

$$q_1 = q_2 + q_3$$

or $$C_1(V_1 - V_O) = C_2(V_O - V_2) + C_3(V_O - V_3)$$

After simplifying, we get

$$V_O = \left[\frac{C_1V_1 + C_2V_2 + C_3V_3}{C_1 + C_2 + C_3}\right].$$ **Ans.**

**Ex. 45** **In *fig. 2.110*, find the potential difference between the points *A* and *B* and between the points *B* and *C* in the steady state.**

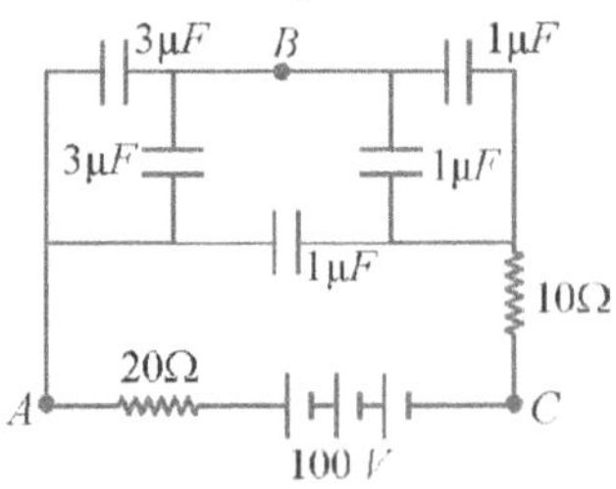
Fig. 2.110

**Sol.**

The equivalent circuit can be drawn as in *fig. 2.112*.

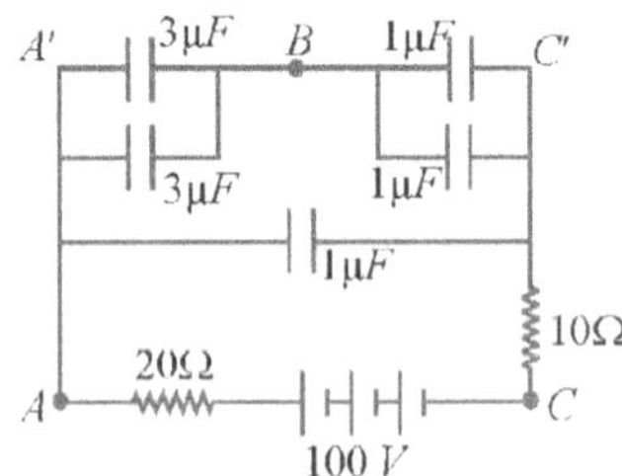
Fig. 2.111

At steady state, there is no current in the resistors, so the potential difference of the battery will appear entirely across the capacitors.

The potential of point $A$ is equal to $A'$ and that of $C$ is equal to $C'$. Thus if $V_1$ and $V_2$ are the required potential difference, then

$$V_1 + V_2 = 100 \quad ...(i)$$

and $$6V_1 = 2V_2 \quad ...(ii)$$

Solving equations (i) and (ii), we get

$$V_1 = 25\text{ V}$$

and $$V_2 = 75\text{ V.} \qquad \textit{Ans.}$$

**Ex. 46** **What is the equivalent capacitance of the capacitor network between *A* and *B* shown in the *fig. 2.112*. Each capacitor in the network is of value *C*.**

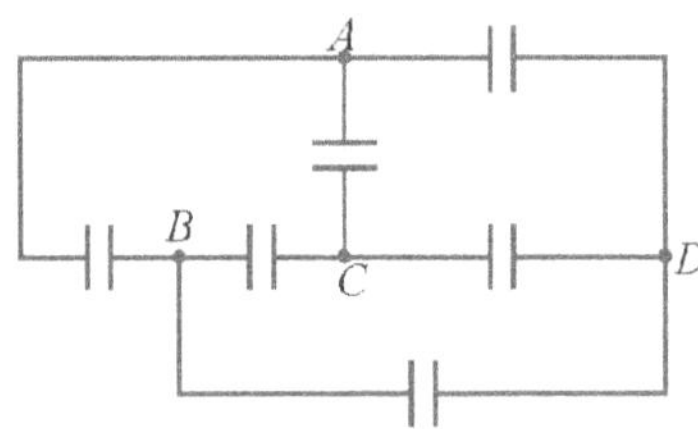
Fig. 2.112

**Sol.**

The equivalent circuit can be drawn as :

From the symmetry considerations, the potentials of the points $C$ and $D$ are equal, and so capacitor connected in arm $CD$ remain uncharged, and therefore can be ignored.

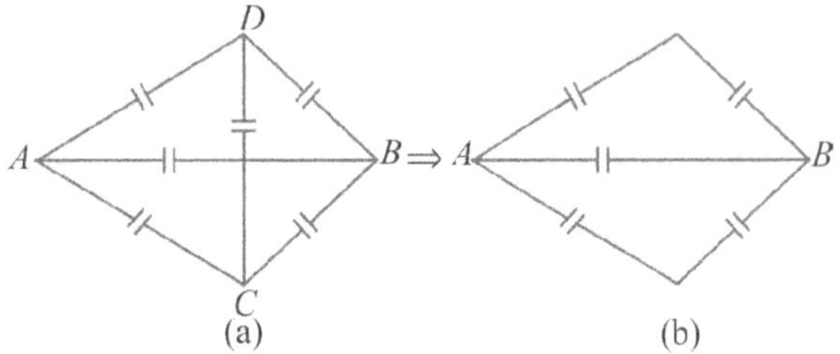
Fig. 2.113

Thus equivalent capacitance between $A$ and $B$ is

$$C_{AB} = \frac{C}{2} + C + \frac{C}{2} = 2C \qquad \textit{Ans.}$$

**Ex. 47** **Two small balls of mass m, bearing a charge q each, are connected by a nonconducting thread of length $2\ell$. At a certain instant, the middle of the thread starts moving at a constant velocity v perpendicular to the direction of the thread at the initial instant. Determine the minimum distance d between the balls.**

**Sol.** Initially the velocity of each ball will be $v$.

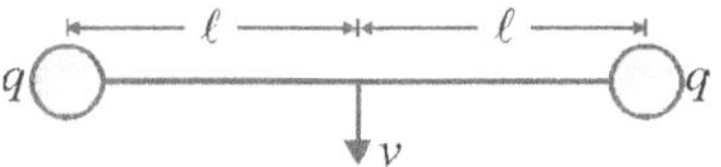
Fig. 2.114

The initial energy of the system

$$U_i = \left(\frac{1}{4\pi \epsilon_0}\right)\frac{q^2}{2\ell} + 2\left(\frac{1}{2}mv^2\right)$$

If $d$ is the minimum distance between the balls, then final energy is only potential energy of the balls, and therefore

$$U_f = \left(\frac{1}{4\pi \epsilon_0}\right)\frac{q^2}{d}$$

By conservation of mechanical energy, we have

$$U_i = U_f$$

or $$\left(\frac{1}{4\pi \epsilon_0}\right)\frac{q^2}{2\ell} + 2\left(\frac{1}{2}mv^2\right) = \left(\frac{1}{4\pi \epsilon_0}\right)\frac{q^2}{d}$$

After simplifying, we get

$$d = \left[\frac{2\ell q^2}{q^2 + 8\pi \epsilon_0 \ell m v^2}\right]. \qquad \textit{Ans.}$$

**Ex. 48** **Two parallel-plate capacitors are arranged perpendicular to the common axis. The separation *d* between the capacitor is much larger than the separation $\ell$ between their plates and than their size. The capacitors are charged to $q_1$ and $q_2$ respectively (see *fig. 2.115*). Find the force *F* of interaction between the capacitors.**

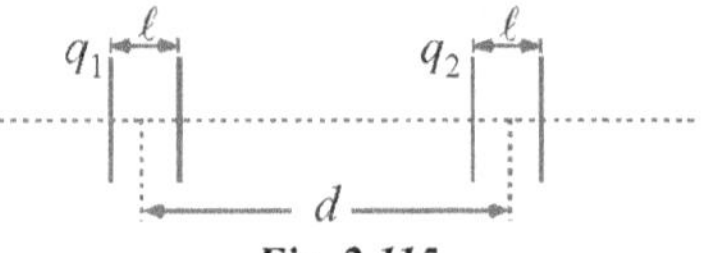
Fig. 2.115

**Sol.**

Let us first take the case when the capacitor are placed so that the plates with like charges face each other.

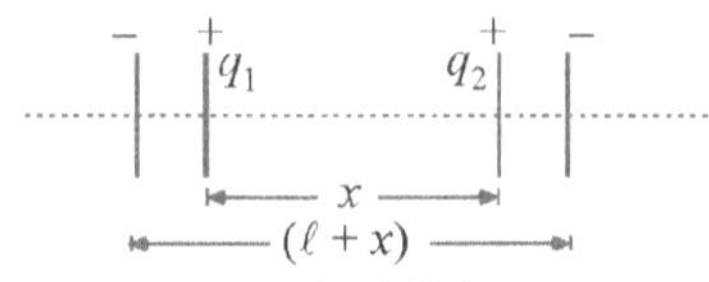
Fig. 2.116

The field produced by first capacitor on the axis at a distance $x$ from the positive plate is

$$E_x = \frac{q_1}{4\pi \epsilon_0}\left[\frac{1}{x^2} - \frac{1}{(\ell + x)^2}\right] \simeq \frac{2q_1\ell}{4\pi \epsilon_0 x^3} \quad (x >> \ell)$$

The force acting on the second capacitor situated at a distance d from the first is

$$F = E_d q_2 - E_{(d+\ell)} q_2 = q_2\left[E_d - E_{(d+\ell)}\right]$$

$$= q_2\left[\frac{2q_1\ell}{4\pi \epsilon_0 d^3} - \frac{2q_1\ell}{4\pi \epsilon_0 (\ell+d)^3}\right]$$

$$= \frac{q_1 q_2 \ell}{4\pi \epsilon_0}\left[\frac{1}{d^3} - \frac{1}{(\ell+d)^3}\right]$$

$$\simeq \frac{3q_1 q_2 \ell^2}{2\pi \epsilon_0 d^4}.$$ ***Ans.***

In this case capacitors will repel-each other with a force $F$. A similar analysis can be made for the case when capacitors are placed so that the plates with opposite charges face each other. Then the capacitors will attract each other with the same amount of force.

**Ex. 49** **Condensers with capacities $C$, $2C$, $3C$ and $4C$ are charged to the voltage $V$, $2V$, $3V$ and $4V$ correspondingly. The circuit is closed. Find the voltage on all condensers in the equilibrium.**

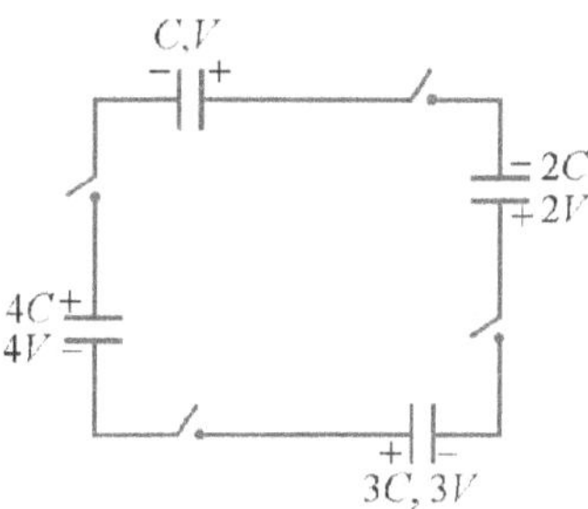


*Fig. 2.117*

**Sol.**

The initial charges on the capacitors are shown in *fig. 2.118* (a)

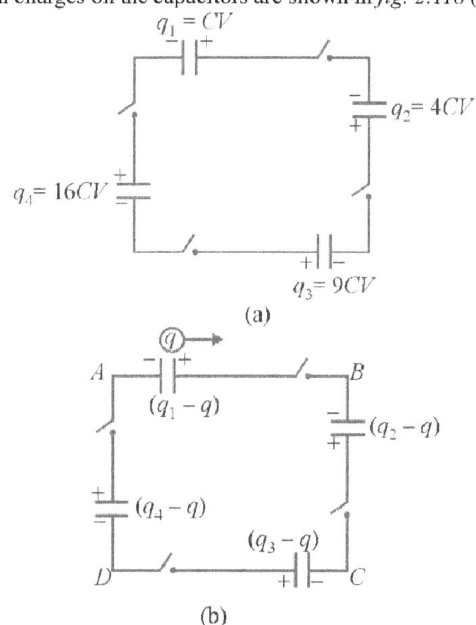


(b)

*Fig. 2.118*

Suppose $q$ amount of charge flows in the circuit after closing it. The net charge on each capacitor is shown in figure (b).

Applying loop rule in $ABCDA$, we have

$$\frac{q_1 - q}{C} + \frac{q_2 - q}{2C} + \frac{q_3 - q}{3C} + \frac{q_4 - q}{4C} = 0$$

or $$\frac{CV - q}{C} + \frac{4CV - q}{2C} + \frac{9CV - q}{3C} + \frac{16CV - q}{4C} = 0$$

After simplifying, we get $$q = \frac{24}{5}CV$$

**Potential difference across the capacitors :**

$$|V_1| = \left|\frac{q_1 - q}{C}\right| = \left|\frac{CV - \frac{24}{5}CV}{C}\right| = \frac{19}{5}V$$

$$|V_2| = \left|\frac{q_2 - q}{2C}\right| = \left|\frac{4CV - \frac{24}{5}CV}{2C}\right| = \frac{2}{3}V$$

$$|V_3| = \left|\frac{q_3 - q}{3C}\right| = \left|\frac{9CV - \frac{24}{5}CV}{3C}\right| = \frac{7V}{5}$$

and $$|V_4| = \left|\frac{q_4 - q}{4C}\right| = \left|\frac{16CV - 24CV}{4C}\right| = \frac{14C}{5}.$$ ***Ans.***

**Ex. 50** **In *fig. 2.119*, all the capacitors have a capacitance of 6.0 μF, and all the batteries have an emf 10 V. What is the charge on capacitor $C$?**

**Sol.**

Suppose $Q$ is the charge on the capacitor. Choose a close loop $a\ b\ c\ d\ e\ f\ g\ h\ i\ j\ k\ l\ m\ n\ a$, and apply loop rule, we have

$$-\frac{Q}{C} + \xi = 0,$$

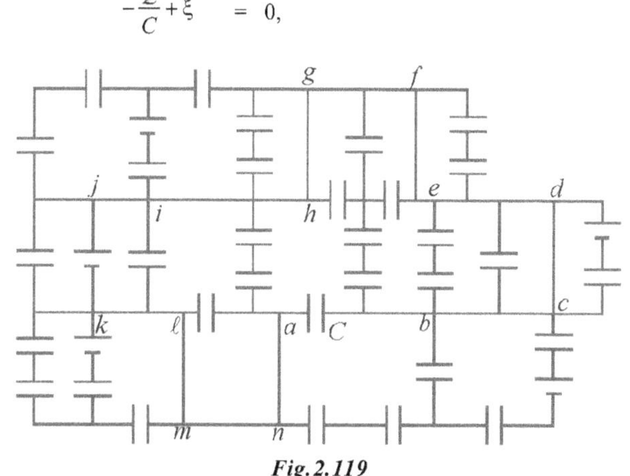


*Fig. 2.119*

which on solving gives

$$Q = C\xi$$

$$= 6 \times 10 = 60\ \mu C.$$ ***Ans.***

**Ex. 51** **Three capacitors $C_1 = 3\ \mu F$, $C_2 = 6\ \mu F$ and $C_3 = 6\ \mu F$ have equal charge $q = 30\ \mu C$ each. $C_1$ and $C_2$ are connected in series as shown in *fig. 2.120*. If $C_3$ is connected across the series combination by connecting $A$ with $C$ and $B$ with $D$ and if resistance of connecting wire is $R = 10\ \Omega$, calculate initial current in the circuit and also heat generated.**

**Sol.**

Let after connection the initial current in the circuit is $i_0$.

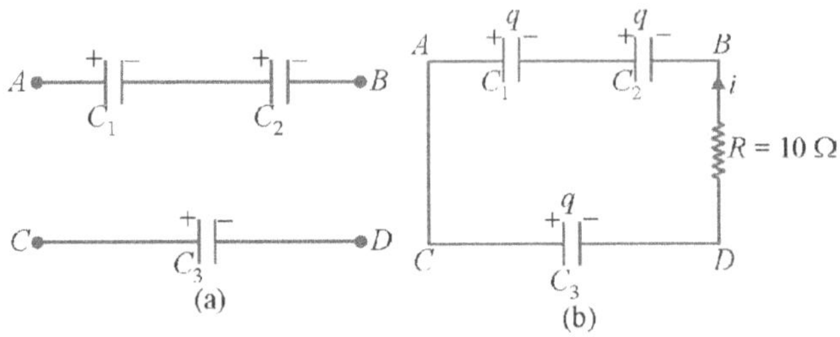


*Fig. 2.120*

Applying loop rule in $A\ C\ D\ B\ A$, we have

$$\frac{q}{C_1}+\frac{q}{C_2}-\frac{q}{C_3}-i_0R = 0$$

or

$$\frac{30}{3}+\frac{30}{6}-\frac{30}{6}-i_0\times 10 = 0$$

$\therefore$ $\qquad i_0 = 1\text{A}$ $\qquad$ ***Ans.***

Heat through the wire is generated till charge flows through it. After getting steady state, no charge will flow. Let $q'$ be the amount of charge flows, then net charge on each capacitor is shown in *fig. 2.121*. By loop rule, we have

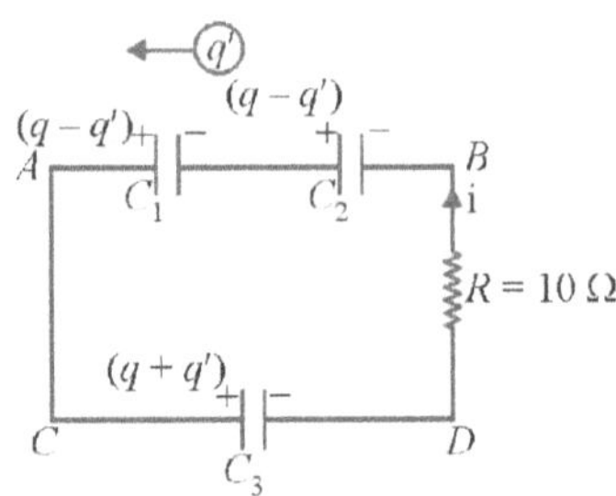


*Fig. 2.121*

$$\frac{q-q'}{C_1}+\frac{q-q'}{C_2}-\frac{q+q'}{C_3} = 0$$

or

$$\frac{30-q'}{3}+\frac{30-q'}{6}-\frac{30+q'}{6} = 0$$

After simplifying, we get

$$q' = 15\ \mu C.$$

The final charges on the capacitors are :

$$q_1 = q-q' = 30-15 = 15\ \mu C$$

$$q_2 = q-q' = 30-15 = 15\ \mu C$$

and

$$q_3 = q+q' = 30+15 = 45\ \mu C$$

The initial energy stored on the capacitors

$$U_i = \frac{q^2}{2}\left[\frac{1}{C_1}+\frac{1}{C_2}+\frac{1}{C_3}\right]$$

$$= \frac{30^2}{2}\left[\frac{1}{3}+\frac{1}{6}+\frac{1}{6}\right]$$

$$= 300\ \mu\ \text{J}.$$

Final energy

$$U_f = \frac{q_1^2}{2C_1}+\frac{q_2^2}{2C_2}+\frac{q_3^2}{2C_3}$$

$$= \frac{15^2}{2\times 3}+\frac{15^2}{2\times 6}+\frac{45^2}{2\times 6}$$

$$= 225\ \mu\ \text{J}$$

Heat generated $= U_i - U_f$

$= 300 - 225 = 75\ \mu\ \text{J}.$ $\qquad$ ***Ans.***

**Ex. 52** **The capacitors shown in *fig. 2.122* has been charged to a potential difference of $V$ volt so that it carries a charge $CV$ with both the switches $S_1$ and $S_2$ remaining open. Switch $S_1$ is closed at $t = 0$. At $t = R_1C$ switch $S_1$ is opened and $S_2$ is closed. Find the charge on the capacitor at $t = (2R_1C + R_2C)$.**

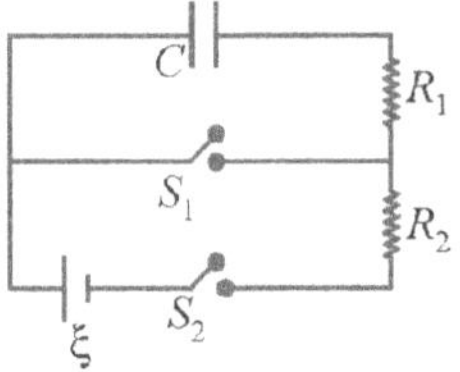


*Fig. 2.122*

**Sol.**

When switch $S_1$ is closed and $S_2$ is open. The circuit is as shown in figure (a).

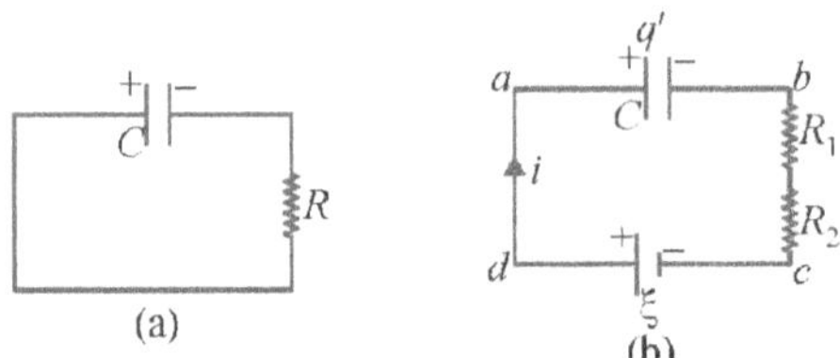


*Fig. 2.123*

The charge stored on the capacitor $q_0 = CV$. Thus

$$q = q_0e^{-\frac{t}{R_1C}}$$

or

$$q = CVe^{-\frac{t}{R_1C}}$$

At $t = R_1C$, the charge on the capacitor is

$$q_1 = CVe^{-1} = \frac{CV}{e}$$

When switch $S_2$ is closed and $S_1$ is open the circuit is shown in figure (b). Applying loop rule in close loop $a\ b\ c\ d\ a$, we have

$$\frac{-q'}{C}-i(R_1+R_2)+\xi = 0$$

or $$i = \frac{C\xi - q'}{C(R_1 + R_2)}$$

or $$\frac{dq'}{dt} = \frac{C\xi - q'}{C(R_1 + R_2)}$$

or $$\frac{dq'}{C\xi - q'} = \frac{dt}{C(R_1 + R_2)}$$

On integrating above equation, we have

$$\int_{\frac{CV}{e}}^{q'} \frac{dq'}{C\xi - q'} = \int_{R_1C}^{t=(2R_1C+R_2C)} \frac{dt}{C(R_1 + R_2)}$$

or $$-\left|\ell n(C\xi - q')\right|_{\frac{CV}{e}}^{q'} = \left|\frac{t}{C(R_1 + R_2)}\right|_{R_1C}^{(2R_1C+R_2C)}$$

or $$\ell n(C\xi - q') - \ell n\left(C\xi - \frac{CV}{e}\right) = -\left[\frac{2R_1C + R_2C - R_1C}{C(R_1 + R_2)}\right]$$

or $$\ell n\left[\frac{C\xi - q'}{C\xi - \frac{CV}{e}}\right] = -1$$

or $$C\xi - \frac{CV}{e} = e(C\xi - q')$$

$$\therefore \quad q' = \left[C\xi\left(1 - \frac{1}{e}\right) + \frac{CV}{e^2}\right].$$ ***Ans.***

**Ex. 53 In the following *RC*-circuit, the capacitor is in the steady state. The initial separation of the capacitor plates is $x_0$. If at $t = 0$, the separation between the plates starts changing so that a constant current flows through *R*. Find the velocity of the moving plates as a function of time. The plate area is *A*.**

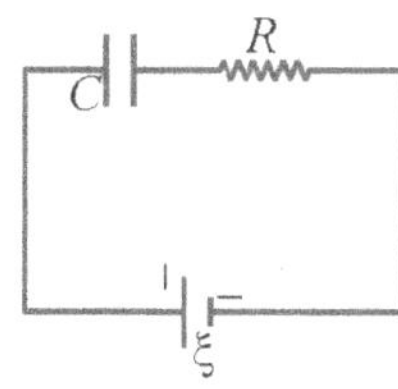


*Fig. 2.124*

## Sol.

For any separation $x$ between the plates, the capacitance

$$C = \frac{\epsilon_0 A}{x}$$

Let $q$ be the instantaneous charge on the capacitor when current $i$ flows through the circuit, by Kirchhoff's law, we have

$$\frac{-q}{C} - iR + \xi = 0$$

or $$\xi = \frac{q}{C} + iR$$

$$\xi = \frac{qx}{\epsilon_0 A} + iR \quad \text{...(i)}$$

Here $q$ and $x$ are variables while $\xi$, $i$ and $R$, A are constants. Differentiating equation (i) w.r.t. time we have

$$0 = \frac{q}{\epsilon_0 A}\frac{dx}{dt} + \frac{x}{\epsilon_0 A}\frac{dq}{dt}$$

Putting $\frac{dq}{dt} = i$ and $\frac{dx}{dt} = v$, we get

$$q = -\frac{ix}{\left(\frac{dx}{dt}\right)}$$

Substituting the value of $q$ in equation (i), we have

$$\xi = \frac{i\,x^2}{\epsilon_0 A\left(\frac{dx}{dt}\right)} + iR$$

or $$\frac{dx}{dt} = v = \left(\frac{-\frac{i}{\epsilon_0 A}}{\xi - iR}\right)x^2$$

or $$-\frac{dx}{x^2} = \left(\frac{\frac{i}{\epsilon_0 A}}{\xi - iR}\right)dt \quad \text{...(ii)}$$

Integrating equation (ii), we have

$$\int_{x_0}^{x} \frac{dx}{x^2} = -\int_0^t \left(\frac{i/\epsilon_0 A}{\xi - iR}\right)dt$$

or $$\frac{1}{x} - \frac{1}{x_0} = -\left(\frac{i/\epsilon_0 A}{\xi - iR}\right)t \quad \text{...(iii)}$$

Again differentiating w.r.t. time

$$-\frac{1}{x^2}\frac{dx}{dt} = -\left(\frac{i/\epsilon_0 A}{\xi - iR}\right)$$

or $$-\frac{1}{x^2}(v) = -\left(\frac{i/\epsilon_0 A}{\xi - iR}\right)$$

$$\therefore \quad v = \left(\frac{i/\epsilon_0 A}{\xi - iR}\right)x^2 \quad \text{...(iv)}$$

Substituting the value of $x$ from equation (iii) in (iv), we get

$$v = \left(\frac{i/\epsilon_0 A}{\xi - iR}\right)\frac{1}{\left[\left(\frac{i/\epsilon_0 A}{\xi - iR}\right)t + \frac{1}{x_0}\right]^2}.$$

***Ans.***

**Ex. 54** **The voltage applied across a capacitor having a capacitance of 10 μF is varies as shown in *fig. 2.125.* Calculate**

(a) **the charge and**

(b) **the energy stored in the capacitor when the terminal voltage is 600 V.**

## Sol.

The charging current is given by

(a) $$i = \frac{dq}{dt} = \frac{d(CV)}{dt} = C\frac{dV}{dt}$$

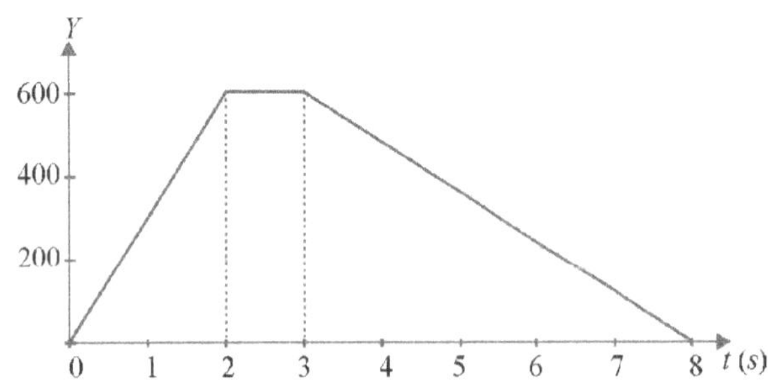


*Fig. 2.125*

From 0 to 2 s : $$i = 10\times10^{-6}\times\frac{600}{2} = 3 \text{ m A}.$$

From 2 to 3 s : $$\frac{dV}{dt} = 0, \quad \therefore i = 0$$

From 3 to 8 s : $$i = 10\times10^{-6}\times\frac{0-600}{5} = -1.2 \text{ m A}$$

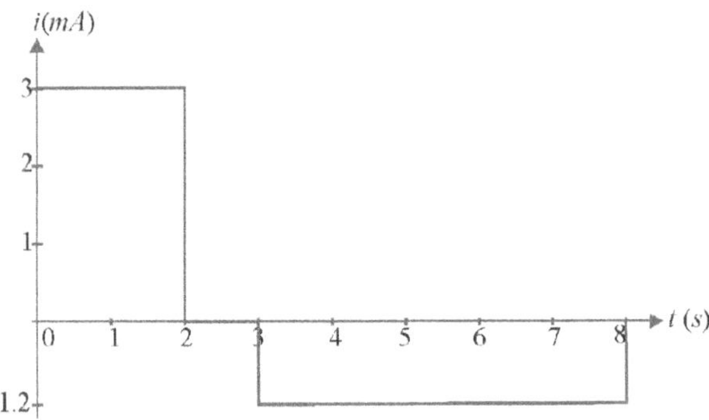


*Fig. 2.126*

(a) Charge when a steady voltage of 600 $V$ is applied

$$= CV = 10\times10^{-6}\times600 = 6\times10^{-3}\ C$$

(b) Energy stored $$U = \frac{1}{2}CV^2 = \frac{1}{2}\times10\times10^{-6}\times600^2 = 1.8\ J$$

***Ans.***

## *Review of formulae & Important Points*

1. **Capacitor and capacitance :** A capacitor is a device which is used to store electrical energy. A capacitor consists of two isolated conductors (plates) with equal and opposite charges $+q$ and $-q$. Its capacitance $C$ is defined as :

$$C = \frac{q}{V},$$

where $V$ is the potential difference between the plates. The SI unit of capacitance is the farad.

2. **Capacitance with a dielectric :** If the space between the plates of a capacitor is completely filled with a dielectric material, the capacitance $C$ is increased by a factor $k$. Thus

$$C_{med} = k\,C_{air}.$$

In a region that is completely filled by a dielectric, all electrostatic equations containing $\epsilon_0$ must be modified by replacing $\epsilon_0$ with $k\,\epsilon_0$.

3. **Electric potential energy of the capacitor :** The electric potential energy $U$ of a charged capacitor is given by

$$U = \frac{q^2}{2C} = \frac{1}{2}CV^2.$$

This energy is associated with the capacitor's electric field $\vec{E}$ between the plates. The energy density within an electric field of magnitude is given by

$$u = \frac{1}{2}\epsilon_0 E^2 \quad \text{(In vacuum)}$$

4. **Redistribution of charges :** When two charged conductors are connected by a conducting wire, charge flows from the conductor of higher potential towards the conductor at lower potential, until their potentials become equal. If $q_1$ and $q_2$ are the charges on the conductors of capacitances $C_1$ and $C_2$, then common potential

$$V = \frac{q_1+q_2}{C_1+C_2} = \frac{C_1V_1+C_2V_2}{C_1+C_2}$$

If $q_1'$ and $q_2'$ are the final charges on them, then

$$q_1' = C_1V \text{ and } q_2' = C_2V$$

$$\text{Loss of energy} = U_i - U_f$$

$$= \left(\frac{1}{2}C_1V_1^2+\frac{1}{2}C_2V_2^2\right) - \frac{1}{2}(C_1+C_2)V^2$$

**5. Combinations of capacitors :**

(i) In series : $\frac{1}{C}=\frac{1}{C_1}+\frac{1}{C_2}+....$

(ii) In parallel : $C = C_1 + C_2 + ...$

**6. Capacitance of spherical conductor of radius *R***

$$C = 4\pi \in_0 R$$

**7. Parallel plate capacitor :**

$$C = \frac{\in_0 A}{d}$$

(Vacuum between the plates)

$$C = \frac{k \in_0 A}{d}$$

(When dielectric $k$ is placed between the plates)

If t is the thickness of the dielectric placed between the plates, then

$$C = \frac{\in_0 A}{\left[(d-t)+\frac{t}{k}\right]}$$

Force between the plates of capacitor $F = \frac{q^2}{2 \in_0} A.$

**8. Spherical capacitor :**

$$C = 4\pi \in_0 \frac{ab}{b-a},$$

when outer shell is earthed

$$C = 4\pi \in_0 \frac{b^2}{b-a},$$

when inner shell is earthed.

**9. Cylindrical capacitor :**

$$C = \frac{2\pi \in_0 \ell}{\ell n b/a}.$$

**10. Dielectrics :**

(i) Induced charge $q' = q\left(1-\frac{1}{k}\right)$

(ii) Polarisation $P = \frac{\text{Induced charge}}{\text{area}} = \frac{q'}{A}$

(iii) Electric displacement

$$\vec{D} = \in_0 \vec{E} + \vec{P}$$

(iv) Electric susceptibility

$$\alpha = \frac{\vec{P}}{E} = 1 + \frac{\chi}{\in_0}$$

**11. Kirchhoff's laws for capacitors :**

(i) Junction rule : The algebraic sum of charges at any junction is equal to zero i.e., $\Sigma q = 0$.

(ii) Loop rule : The algebraic sum of the p.d. across all circuit elements is equal to zero i.e.,

$$\Sigma\xi + \Sigma\frac{q}{C} = 0.$$

(iii) Sign conventions : $-\xi$, $+\xi$ ; $-q/C$, $q$ | $-q$, $+q/C$

**12. In unbalanced wheat stone bridge, the equivalent capacitance between *A* and *B***

$$C_{AB} = \left[\frac{2C_1C_2 + C_2C_3 + C_3C_1}{C_1 + C_2 + 2C_3}\right]$$

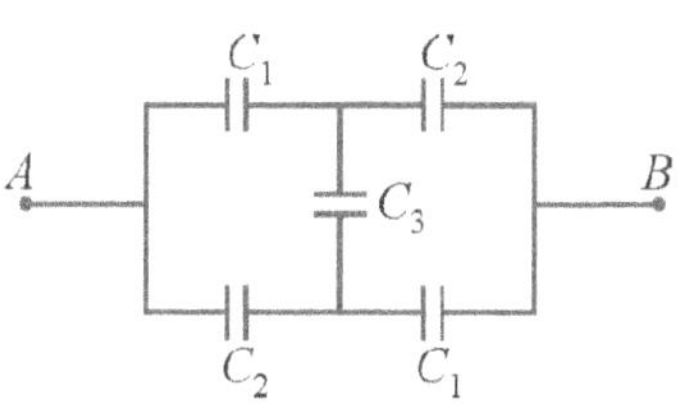


**13. Charging of a capacitor through resistor :**

Charge $q = q_0\left(1-e^{-t/\tau}\right)$

Current $i = i_0 e^{-t/\tau},$

where $q_0 = C\xi$ and $\tau = CR$.

Potential $V = \xi\left(1-e^{-t/\tau}\right)$

Energy $U = U_0\left(1-e^{-t/\tau}\right)^2$

**14. Discharging of a capacitor :**

Charge $q = q_0 e^{-t/\tau},$

Current $i = -i_0 e^{-t/\tau}$

Potential $V = \xi e^{-t/\tau}$

Energy $U = U_0 e^{-2t/\tau}$

★★★

ELECTRICITY

# MCQ Type 1

Exercise 2.1

## LEVEL - 1

**Only one option correct**

1. For each circuit in figure are in :

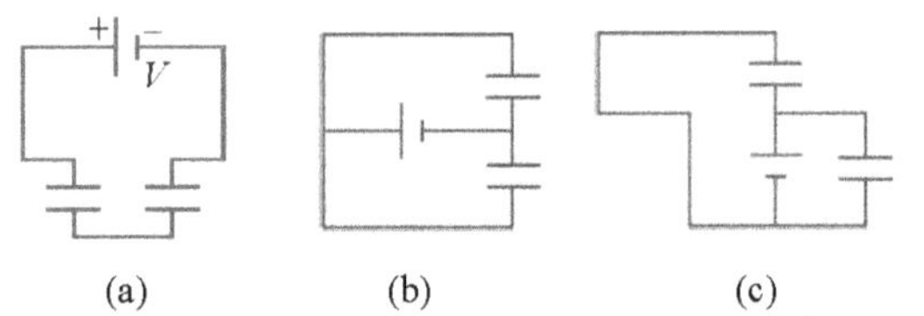


(a) series, series, parallel (b) series, parallel, parallel
(c) parallel, series, parallel (d) none

2. Four ways of making a network of five capacitors of the same value are shown here. Three out of four are identical. The one which is different is :

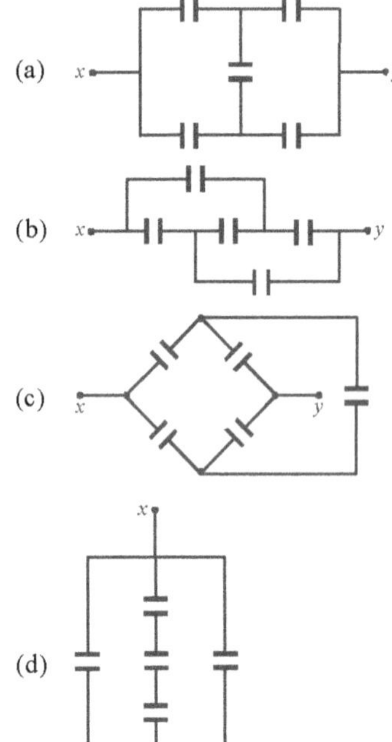


3. Capacitors $C_1$ and $C_2$ ($C_1 > C_2$) are connected to a battery, first individually, then in series. If $q_1$, $q_2$ and $q_3$ are the charges stored on them, then
(a) $q_1 = q_2 = q_3$ (b) $q_1 = q_2 < q_3$
(c) $q_1 > q_2 = q_3$ (d) $q_1 > q_2 > q_3$

4. Two identical capacitors are connected in series with a source of potential $V$. If $Q$ is the charge on one of the capacitors, the capacitance of each capacitor is
(a) $Q/2V$ (b) $Q/V$
(c) $2Q/V$ (d) none of these

5. The capacitance of a parallel plate capacitor is $C$. If one of its plates is removed, then capacitance of the isolated plate will be
(a) $C$ (b) $2C$
(c) Infinite (d) zero

6. The capacitance of the two identical capacitors placed in series is $2C$. Their capacitance when they are placed in parallel is :
(a) $C$ (b) $2C$
(c) $4C$ (d) $8C$

7. A parallel plate air capacitor is connected to a battery. After charging fully, the battery is disconnected and the plates are fulled further apart. Which of the following statements is correct ?
(a) The electric field between the plates of capacitor decreases.
(b) The electric field between the plates of capacitor increases.
(c) The electric field between the plates of capacitor remains same.
(d) Potential difference between the plates remains the same.

8. Two identical capacitors $A$ and $B$ shown in the given circuit are joined in series with a battery. If a dielectric slab of dielectric constant $K$ is slipped between the plates of capacitor $B$ and battery remain connected, then the energy of capacitor A will

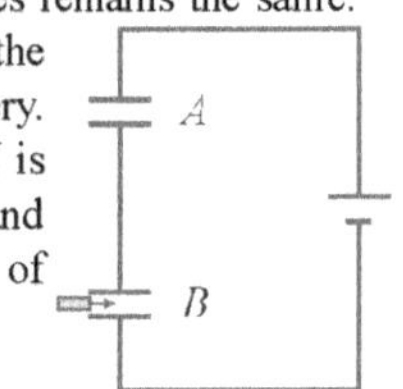


(a) decrease (b) increase
(c) remain the same (d) becomes zero

9. The capacity of a parallel plate condenser is 5μF. When a glass plate is placed between the plates of the conductor, its potential becomes 1/8th of the original value. The value of dielectric constant will be
(a) 1.6 (b) 5
(c) 8 (d) 40

10. The insulated spheres of radii $R_1$ and $R_2$ having charges $Q_1$ and $Q_2$ respectively are connected to each other. There is
(a) no change in the energy of the system
(b) an increase in the energy of the system
(c) always a decrease in the energy of the system
(d) a decrease in the energy of the system unless $Q_1R_2 = Q_2R_1$

11. In a charged capacitor, the energy resides
(a) the positive charges
(b) both the positive and negative charges
(c) the field between the plates
(d) around the edge of the capacitor plates

12. Eight drops of mercury of equal radii possessing equal charges combine to form a big drop. Then the capacitance of bigger drop compared to each individual small drop is
(a) 8 times (b) 4 times
(c) 2 times (d) 32 times

| Answer Key | 1 | (b) | 2 | (d) | 3 | (d) | 4 | (c) | 5 | (d) | 6 | (d) |
|---|---|---|---|---|---|---|---|---|---|---|---|---|
| Sol. from page 201 | 7 | (c) | 8 | (b) | 9 | (c) | 10 | (d) | 11 | (c) | 12 | (c) |

13. Between the plates of a parallel plate condenser, a plate of thickness $t_1$ and dielectric constant $k_1$ is placed. In the rest of the space, there is another plate of thickness $t_2$ and dielectric constant $k_2$. The potential difference across the condenser will be

(a) $\frac{Q}{A\varepsilon_0}\left(\frac{t_1}{k_1}+\frac{t_2}{k_2}\right)$ (b) $\frac{\varepsilon_0 Q}{A}\left(\frac{t_1}{k_1}+\frac{t_2}{k_2}\right)$

(c) $\frac{Q}{A\varepsilon_0}\left(\frac{k_1}{t_1}+\frac{k_2}{t_2}\right)$ (d) $\frac{\varepsilon_0 Q}{A}(k_1t_1+k_2t_2)$

14. There is an air filled $1pF$ parallel plate capacitor. When the plate separation is doubled and the space is filled with wax, the capacitance increases to $2pF$. The dielectric constant of wax is

(a) 2 (b) 4
(c) 6 (d) 8

15. A 6μF capacitor is charged from 10 volts to 20 volts. Increase in energy will be

(a) $18\times10^{-4}$ J (b) $9\times10^{-4}$ J
(c) $4.5\times10^{-4}$ J (d) $9\times10^{-6}$ J

16. A frictionless dielectric plate $S$ is kept on a frictionless table $T$. A charged parallel plate capacitance $C$ (of which the plates are frictionless) is kept near it. The plate $S$ is between the plates. When the plate $S$ is left between the plate

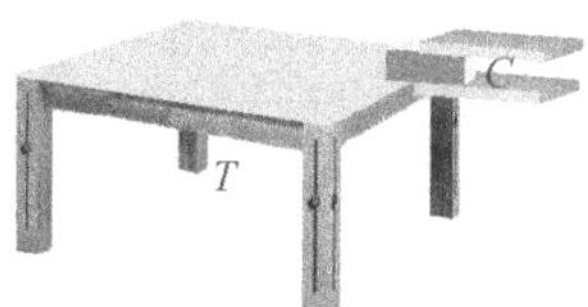


(a) it will remain stationary on the table
(b) it is pulled by the capacitor and will pass on the other end
(c) it is pulled between the plates and start oscillating between the plates
(d) all the above statements are false

17. A parallel plate capacitor is charged and the charging battery is then disconnected. If the plates of the capacitor are moved further apart by means of insulating handles, then

(a) the charge on the capacitor increases
(b) the voltage across the plates decreases
(c) the capacitance increases
(d) the electrostatic energy stored in the capacitor increases.

18. Work done by an external agent in separating the parallel plate capacitor is

(a) $CV$ (b) $\frac{1}{2}C^2V$
(c) $\frac{1}{2}CV^2$ (d) none of these

19. If there are n capacitors in parallel connected to V volt source, then the energy stored is equal to

(a) $CV$ (b) $\frac{1}{2}nCV^2$
(c) $CV^2$ (d) $\frac{1}{2n}CV^2$

20. The work done in placing a charge of $8\times10^{-18}$ coulomb on a condenser of capacity 100 micro-farad is

(a) $32\times10^{-32}$ J (b) $16\times10^{-32}$ J
(c) $3.1\times10^{-26}$ J (d) $4\times10^{-10}$ J

21. Two identical capacitors are joined in parallel, charged to a potential $V$ and then separated and then connected in series i.e. the positive plate of one is connected to negative of the other

(a) the charges on the free plates connected together are destroyed
(b) the charges on the free plates are enhanced
(c) the energy stored in the system increases
(d) the potential difference in the free plates becomes $2V$

22. Seven capacitors each of capacity $2\mu F$ are to be so connected to have a total capacity $\frac{10}{11}\mu F$. Which will be the necessary figure as shown

(a)
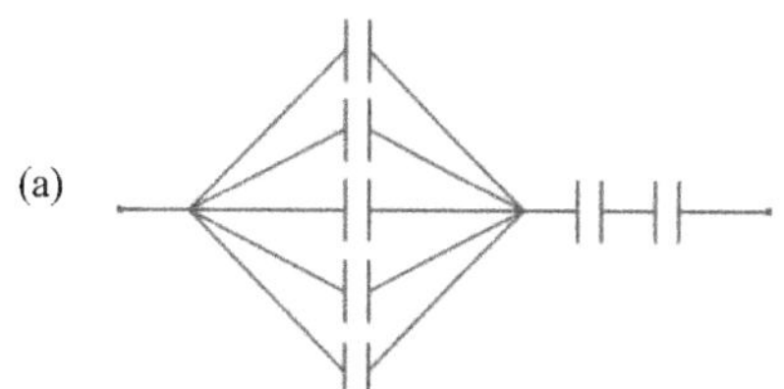

(b)
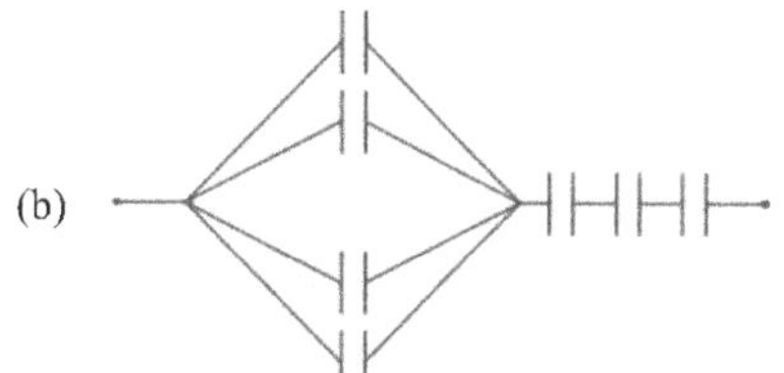

(c)
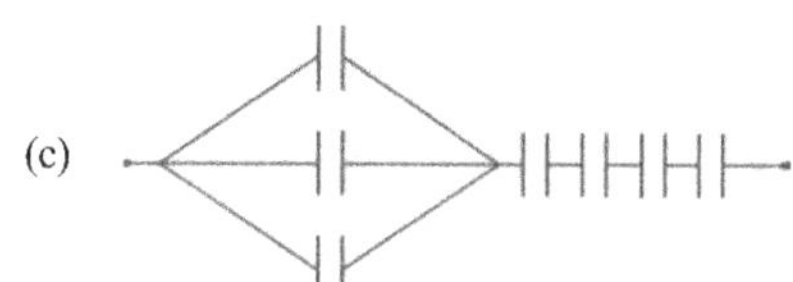

(d)
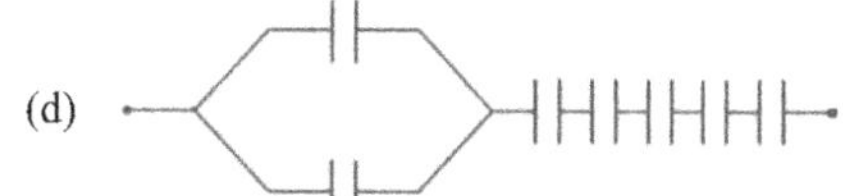

| Answer Key | 13 | (a) | 14 | (b) | 15 | (b) | 16 | (c) | 17 | (d) |
|---|---|---|---|---|---|---|---|---|---|---|
| Sol. from page 201 | 18 | (c) | 19 | (b) | 20 | (a) | 21 | (d) | 22 | (a) |

23. In an adjoining figure are shown three capacitors $C_1$, $C_2$ and $C_3$ joined to a battery. The correct condition will be (symbols have their usual meanings)

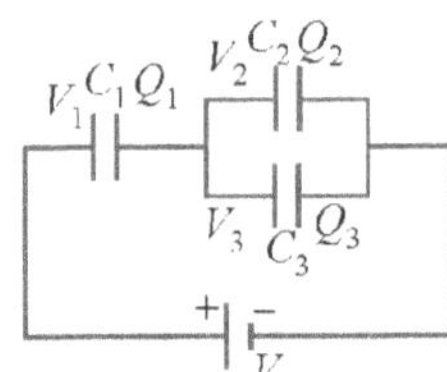


(a) $Q_1 = Q_2 = Q_3$ and $V_1 = V_2 = V_3 = V$

(b) $Q_1 = Q_2 + Q_3$ and $V = V_1 + V_2 + V_3$

(c) $Q_1 = Q_2 + Q_3$ and $V = V_1 + V_2$

(d) $Q_2 = Q_3$ and $V_2 = V_3$

24. Four condensers are joined as shown in the adjoining figure. The capacity of each is 8μF. The equivalent capacity between the points $A$ and $B$ will be

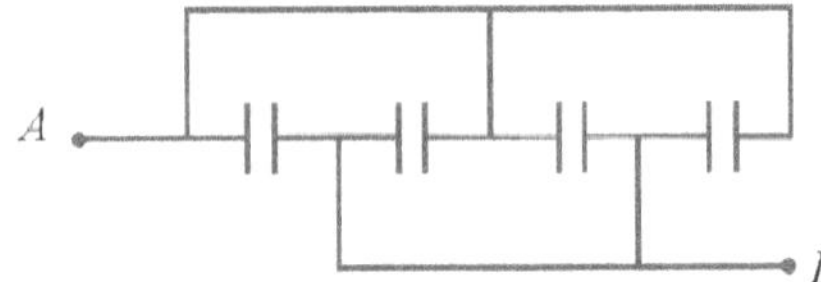


(a) 32μF (b) 2μF
(c) 8μF (d) 16μF

25. In the following circuit, the resultant capacitance between $A$ and $B$ is $1\mu F$. Then value of $C$ is

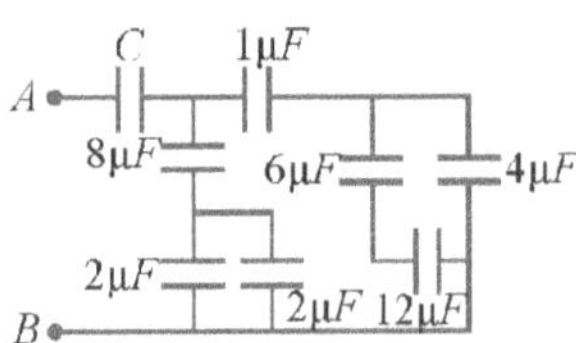


(a) $\frac{32}{11}\mu F$ (b) $\frac{11}{32}\mu F$

(c) $\frac{23}{32}\mu F$ (d) $\frac{32}{23}\mu F$

26. The effective capacitance between the points $P$ and $Q$ of the arrangement shown in the figure is

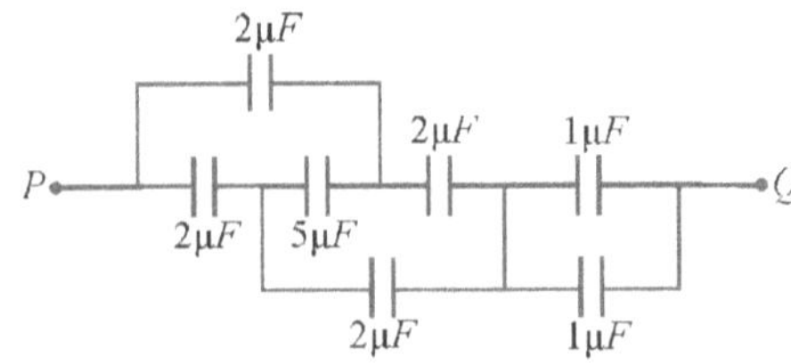


(a) $\frac{1}{2}\mu F$ (b) $1\mu F$

(c) $2\mu F$ (d) $1.33\mu F$

27. The resultant capacitance of given circuit is

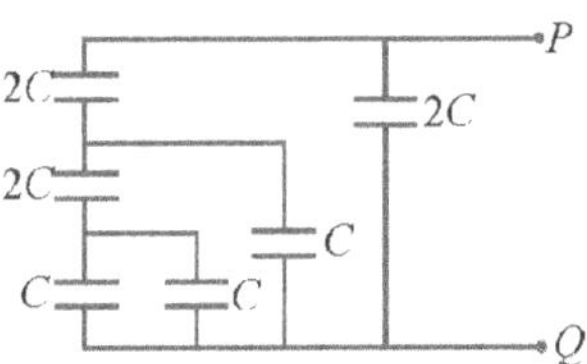


(a) $3C$ (b) $2C$

(c) $C$ (d) $\frac{C}{3}$

28. In the circuit shown in figure, each capacitor has a capacity of $3\mu F$. The equivalent capacity between $A$ and $B$ is

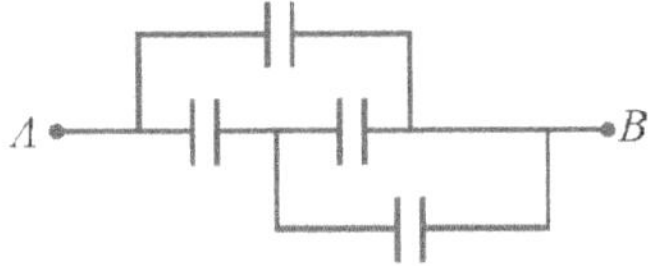


(a) $\frac{3}{4}\mu F$ (b) 3μF

(c) 6μF (d) 5μF

29. Two identical capacitors, have the same capacitance $C$. One of them is charged to potential $V_1$ and the other to $V_2$. The negative ends of the capacitors are connected together. When the positive ends are also connected, the decrease in energy of the combined system is

(a) $\frac{1}{4}C\left(V_1^2 - V_2^2\right)$ (b) $\frac{1}{4}C\left(V_1^2 + V_2^2\right)$

(c) $\frac{1}{4}C\left(V_1 - V_2\right)^2$ (d) $\frac{1}{4}C\left(V_1 + V_2\right)^2$

30. Consider the situation shown in the figure. The capacitor $A$ has a charge $q$ on it whereas $B$ is uncharged. The charge appearing on the capacitor $B$ a long time after the switch is closed is

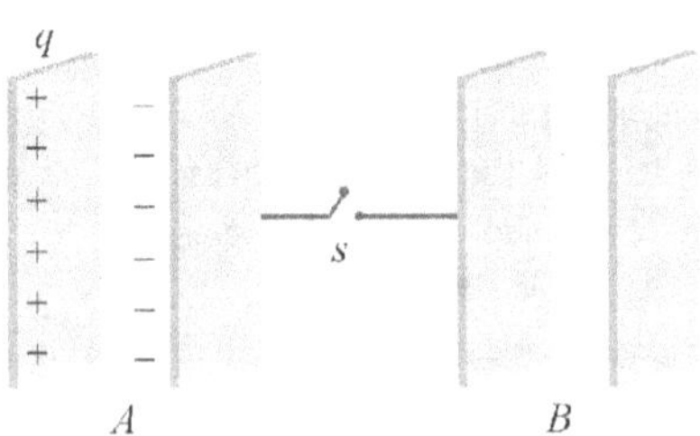


(a) zero (b) $q/2$

(c) $q$ (d) $2q$

31 Two oppositely charged metal spheres of the same radius ($R$) are placed far apart. The capacitance of these two spheres is :

(a) $4\pi\varepsilon_0 R$ (b) $8\pi\varepsilon_0 R$

(c) $2\pi\varepsilon_0 R$ (d) $\pi\varepsilon_0 R$

| Answer Key | 23 | (c) | 24 | (a) | 25 | (d) | 26 | (b) | 27 | (a) |
|---|---|---|---|---|---|---|---|---|---|---|
| Sol. from page 201 | 28 | (d) | 29 | (c) | 30 | (a) | 31 | (c) | | |

**32.** Two conducting shells of radius $a$ and $b$ are connected by conducting wire as shown in figure. The capacity of system is :

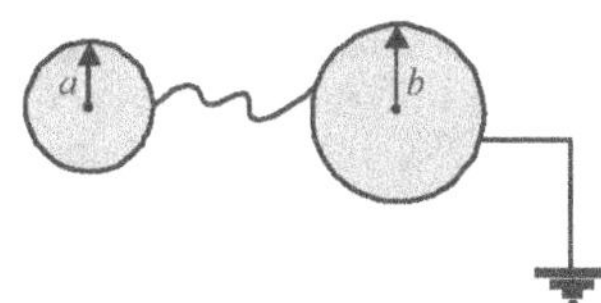


(a) $4\pi\varepsilon_0 \frac{ab}{b-a}$ (b) $4\pi\varepsilon_0 (a+b)$

(c) zero (d) infinite

**33.** A capacitor of capacitance $\frac{1}{5}$ $F$ is initially charged to a potential difference of 10 $V$, and then the switch $S$ is closed. The potential difference across the capacitor at $t = 1$ s is :

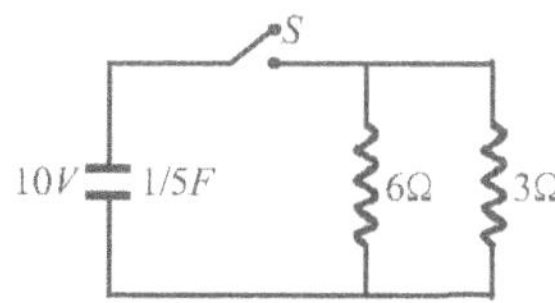


(a) 2.0 $V$ (b) 4.0 $V$

(c) 8 $V$ (d) 0.4 $V$

**34.** A circuit element is placed in a black box. At $t = 0$, a switch is closed and the current flowing through the circuit element and the voltage across its terminals are recorded to have the wave shapes shown in the figure here. The type of element and its magnitude are :

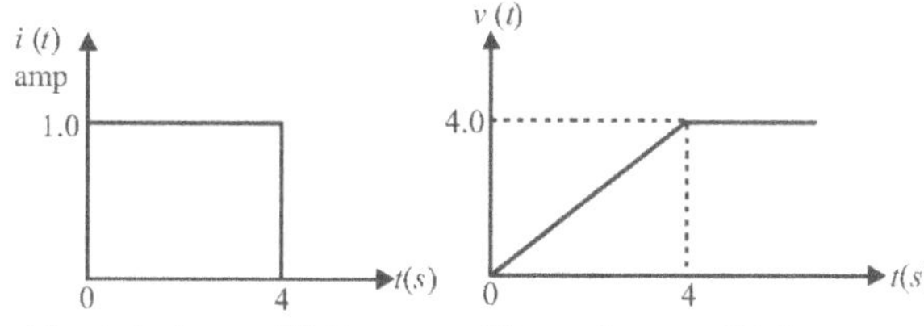


(a) inductance of 4 H (b) resistance of 4 Ω

(c) capacitance of 1 F (d) a voltage source of emf 4 V

**35.** A capacitor is charged by using a battery which is then disconnected. A dielectric slab is then slipped between the plates, which results in

(a) reduction of charge on the plates and increase of potential difference across the plates.

(b) increase in the potential difference across the plate, reduction in stored energy; but no change in the charge on the plates.

(c) decrease in the potential difference across the plates reduction in the stored energy, but no change in the charge on the plates.

(d) none of the above

**36.** Capacitors are used in electrical circuits where appliances need more

(a) current (b) voltage

(c) watt (d) resistance

**37.** Two spherical conductors each of capacity C are charged to potentials $V$ and $-V$. These are then connected by means of a fine wire. The loss of energy will be

(a) zero (b) $\frac{1}{2}CV^2$

(c) $CV^2$ (d) $2CV^2$

**38.** A $2\mu F$ capacitor is charged to 100 volt and then its plates are connected by a conducting wire. The heat produced is

(a) 1 J (b) 0.1 J

(c) 0.01 J (d) 0.001 J

**39.** A 40 $mF$ capacitor in a defibrillator is charged to 3000 $V$. The energy stored in the capacitor is sent through the patient during a pulse of duration $2ms$. The power delivered to the patient is

(a) 45 kW (b) 90 kW

(c) 180 kW (d) 360 kW

**40.** In a given network the equivalent capacitance between $A$ and $B$ is $[C_1 = C_4 = 1\ \mu F,\ C_2 = C_3 = 2\mu F$

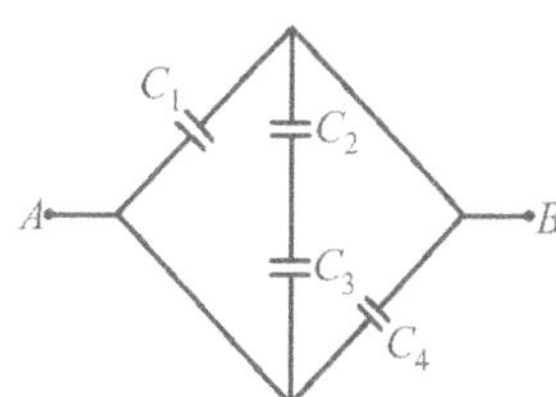


(a) 3 $\mu F$ (b) 6 $\mu F$

(c) 4.5 $\mu F$ (c) 2.5 $\mu F$

**41.** In the figure a potential of + 1200 $V$ is given to point $A$ and point $B$ is earthed, what is the potential at the point $P$

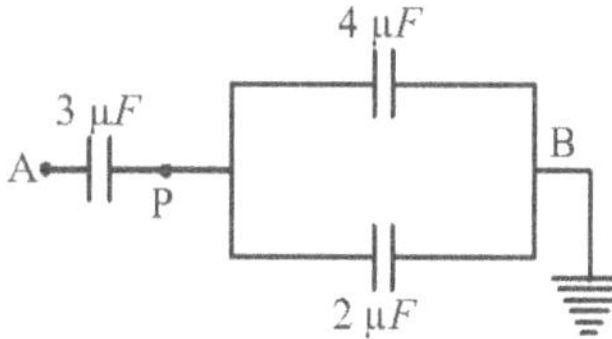


(a) 100 $V$ (b) 200 $V$

(c) 400 $V$ (d) 600 $V$

| Answer Key | 32 | (c) | 33 | (c) | 34 | (c) | 35 | (a) | 36 | (a ) |
|---|---|---|---|---|---|---|---|---|---|---|
| Sol. from page 201 | 37 | (c) | 38 | (c) | 39 | (b) | 40 | (b) | 41 | (c) |

42. A circuit consists of a current source of emf $\xi$ and internal resistance $r$, capacitors, each of capacitance $C$ and resistors, each of value $R$. The voltage across either capacitor is :

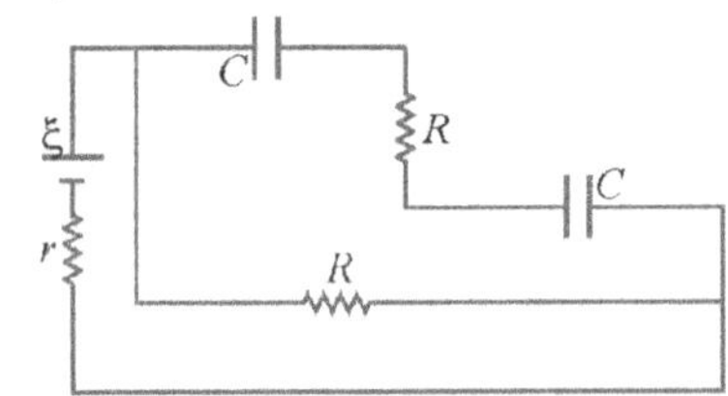


(a) $\frac{\xi R}{2(R+r)}$ (b) $\frac{\xi R}{(R+r)}$

(c) $\frac{\xi(R+r)}{2R}$ (d) zero

43. Two parallel plate capacitor of capacitance C and $2C$ are connected in parallel and charged to a potential difference $V$. The battery is then disconnected and the region between the plates of the capacitor $C$ is completely filled with a material of dielectric constant $k$. The potential difference across the capacitors now becomes :

(a) $\frac{2V}{k}$ (b) $\frac{3V}{k}$

(c) $\frac{3V}{k+2}$ (d) $\frac{2V}{k+3}$

| Answer Key | 42 | (c) | 43 | (c) | | |
|---|---|---|---|---|---|---|
| Sol. from page 201 | | | | | | |

## LEVEL -2

**Only one option correct**

1. In circuit shown in the figure, what is potential of point $A$?

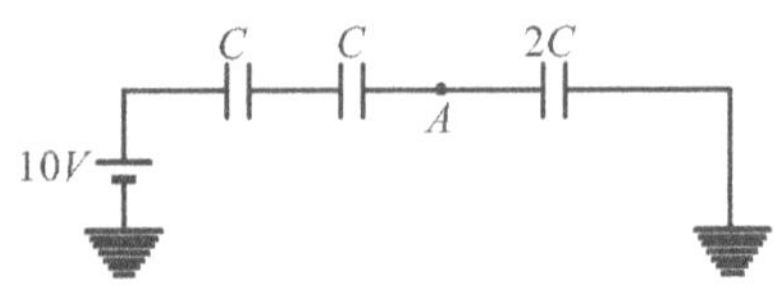


(a) 2 V (b) 5 V
(c) 8 V (d) 4 V

2. Two long cylindrical metal tubes stand on insulating floor. A dielectric oil is filled between plates. Two tubes are maintained with potential difference $V$. A small hole is opened at bottom then

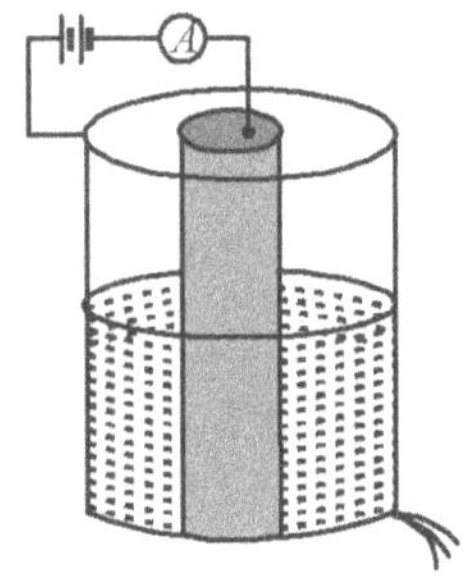


(a) Reading of ammeter decreases
(b) Capacitance of system increases
(c) Current in circuit is dependent on area of hole
(d) Current in circuit is inversely proportional to dielectric constant

3. Given $R_1 = 1\,\Omega, R_2 = 2\,\Omega,\ C_1 = 2\mu F$ and $C_2 = 4\mu F$. The time constant (in μs) for the circuits I, II, III are respectively

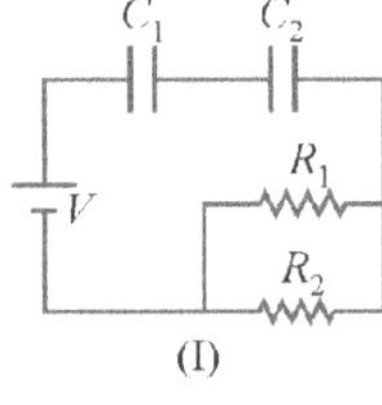


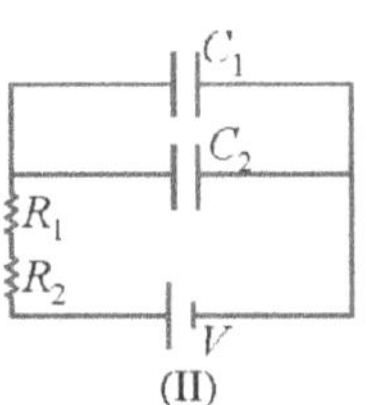


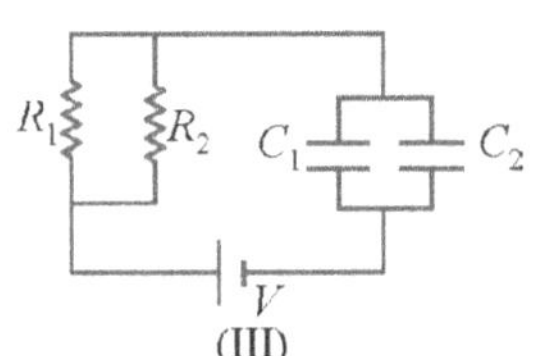


(a) 18, 8 / 9, 4 (b) 18, 4, 8 / 9
(c) 4, 8 / 9, 18 (d) 8 / 9, 18, 4

| Answer Key | 1 | (a) | 2 | (c) | 3 | (d) |
|---|---|---|---|---|---|---|
| Sol. from page 203 | | | | | | |

4. Two plates of equal area $A$ : one square of sides $2L \times 2L$ and other rectangular of sides $4L \times L$ are used to construct a parallel plate capacitor with plates separation $d$. If $C$ is the capacitance, then

(a) $\frac{\epsilon_0 A}{2d}$ (b) $\frac{\epsilon_0 A}{d}$

(c) $\frac{2\epsilon_0 A}{d}$ (d) none of these

5. The graph given below the variation of electric field $E$ (in MV / m) with time t (in μs).

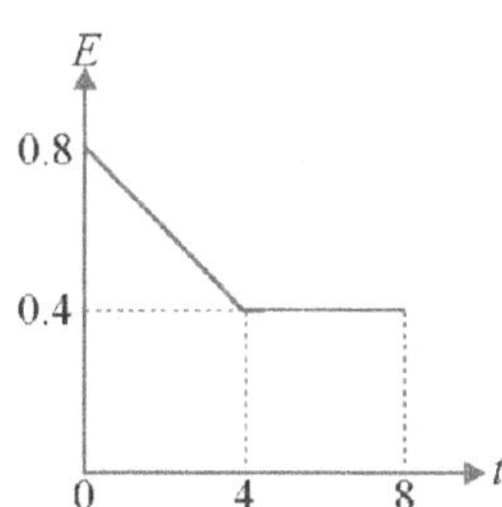


Consider the following statements :

1. The displacement current through a $1\text{m}^2$ region perpendicular to the field during the time interval $t$ = 0 to $t$ = 4 μs is 0.885 A

(given $\epsilon_0 = 8.85 \times 10^{-12}$ SI unit)

2. The displacement current through 1 $\text{m}^2$ region perpendicular to the field during the time interval $t$ = 4μs to 8μs is zero.

Which of the statements given above is/are correct

(a) 1 only (b) 2 only
(c) both 1 and 2 (d) neither 1 nor 2.

6. A parallel plate capacitor of plate area $A$ and plate separation d is charged to potential $V$ and then the battery is disconnected. A slab of dielectric constant k is then inserted between the plates of the capacitors so as to fill the space between the plates. If $Q$, $E$ and $W$ denote respectively, the magnitude of charge on each plate, the electric field between the plates (after the slab is inserted) and work done on the system in question in the process of inserting the slab, then state incorrect relation from the following

(a) $Q = \frac{\varepsilon_0 AV}{d}$ (b) $W = \frac{\varepsilon_0 AV^2}{2kd}$

(c) $E = \frac{V}{kd}$ (d) $W = \frac{\varepsilon_0 AV^2}{2d}\left(1 - \frac{1}{k}\right)$

7. A capacitor of capacity $C_1$ is charged to the potential of $V_0$. On disconnecting with the battery, it is connected with a capacitor of capacity $C_2$ as shown in the adjoining figure. The ratio of energies before and after the connection of switch $S$ will be

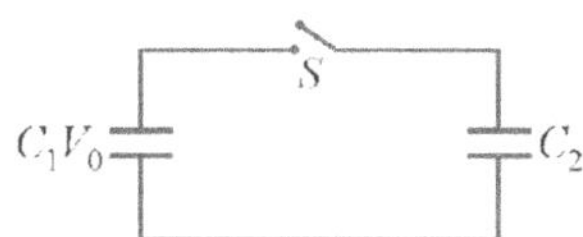


(a) $(C_1 + C_2)/C_1$ (b) $C_1/(C_1 + C_2)$

(c) $C_1C_2$ (d) $C_1/C_2$

8. The capacities and connection of five capacitors are shown in the adjoining figure. The potential difference between the points $A$ and $B$ is 60 volts. Then the equivalent capacity between $A$ and $B$ and the charge on 5μF capacitance will be respectively

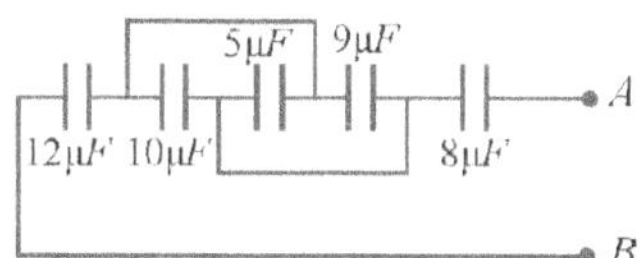


(a) 44μF; 300μC (b) 16μF; 150μC
(c) 15μF; 200μC (d) 4μF; 50μC

9. In the circuit shown here $C_1$ = 6μF, $C_2$ = 3μF and battery $B$ = 20 V. The switch $S_1$ is first closed. It is then opened and afterwards $S_2$ is closed. What is the charge finally on $C_2$

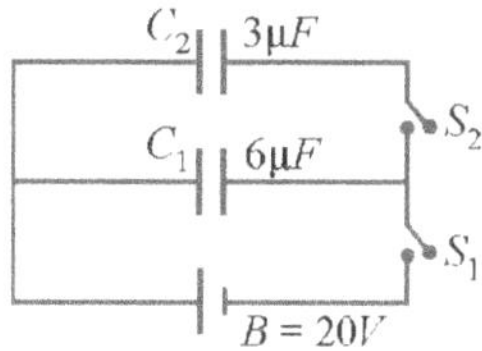


(a) 120μC (b) 80μC
(c) 40μC (d) 20μC

10. Two condensers $C_1$ and $C_2$ in a circuit are joined as shown in figure. The potential of point $A$ is $V_1$ and that of $B$ is $V_2$. The potential of point $D$ will be



(a) $\frac{1}{2}(V_1 + V_2)$ (b) $\frac{C_2V_1 + C_1V_2}{C_1 + C_2}$

(c) $\frac{C_1V_1 + C_2V_2}{C_1 + C_2}$ (d) $\frac{C_2V_1 - C_1V_2}{C_1 + C_2}$

11. The charge on a capacitor of capacitance 10μF connected as shown in the figure is

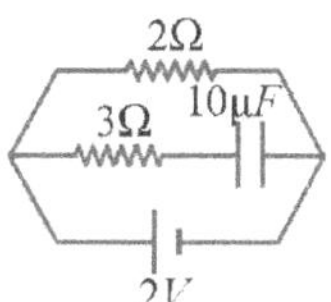


(a) 20μC (b) 15μC
(c) 10μC (d) zero

| Answer Key | 4 | (a) | 5 | (c) | 6 | (b) | 7 | (a) |
|---|---|---|---|---|---|---|---|---|
| Sol. from page 203 | 8 | (d) | 9 | (c) | 10 | (c) | 11 | (a) |

**12.** Three plates $A$, $B$, $C$ each of area 50 $cm^2$ have separation 3mm between $A$ and $B$ and 3mm between $B$ and $C$. The energy stored when the plates are fully charged is

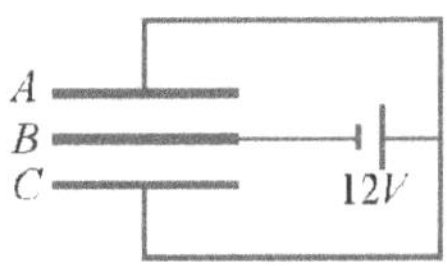


(a) $1.6\times10^{-9}$ J (b) $2.1\times10^{-9}$ J
(c) $5\times10^{-9}$ J (d) $7\times10^{-9}$ J

**13.** In the circuit here, the steady state voltage across capacitor $C$ is a fraction of the battery e.m.f. The fraction is decided by

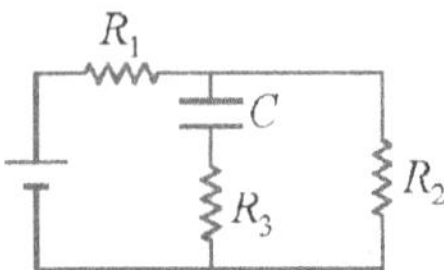


(a) $R_1$ only (b) $R_1$ and $R_2$ only
(c) $R_1$ and $R_3$ only (d) $R_1$, $R_2$ and $R_3$

**14.** Two capacitors $C_1$ and $C_2 = 2C_1$ are connected in a circuit with a switch between them as shown in the figure. Initially the switch is open and $C_1$ holds charge $Q$. The switch is closed. At steady state, the charge on each capacitor will be

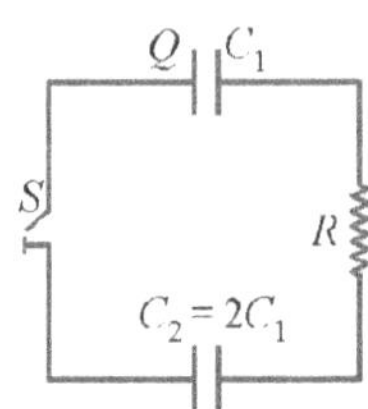


(a) $Q, 2Q$ (b) $Q/3, 2Q/3$
(c) $3Q/2, 3Q$ (d) $2Q/3, 4Q/3$

**15.** To form a composite 16 μF, 1000 V capacitor from a supply of identical capacitors marked 8μF, 250 V, we require a minimum number of n capacitors, where $n$ is

(a) 2 (b) 8
(c) 16 (d) 32

**16.** Five identical plates each of area $A$ are joined as shown in the figure. The distance between the plates is $d$. The plates are connected to a potential difference of $V$ volts. The charge on plates 1 and 4 will be

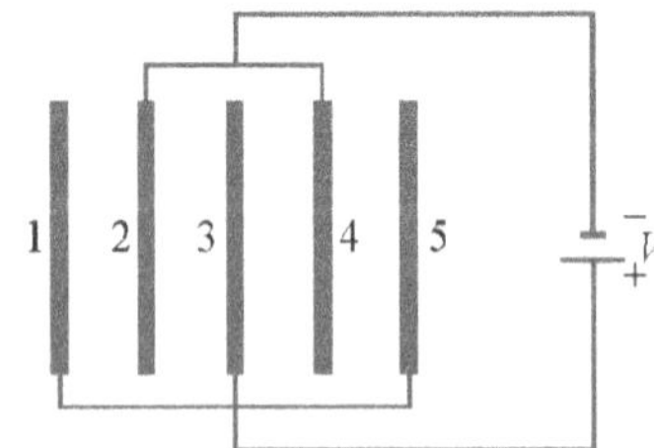


(a) $\frac{\varepsilon_0 AV}{d}, \frac{\varepsilon_0 AV}{d}$ (b) $\frac{\varepsilon_0 AV}{d}, \frac{2\varepsilon_0 AV}{d}$

(c) $\frac{\varepsilon_0 AV}{d}, \frac{-2\varepsilon_0 AV}{d}$ (d) $\frac{-\varepsilon_0 AV}{d}, \frac{-2\varepsilon_0 AV}{d}$

**17.** In the figure below, what is the potential difference between the point $A$ and $B$ and between $B$ and $C$ respectively in steady state

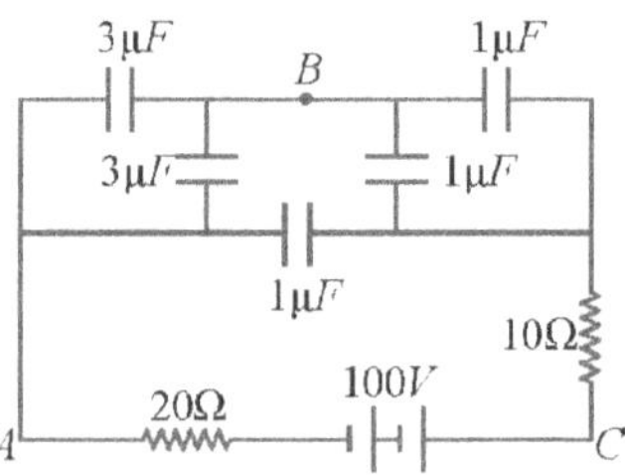


(a) $V_{AB} = V_{BC} = 100V$ (b) $V_{AB} = 75V, V_{BC} = 25V$
(c) $V_{AB} = 25V, V_{BC} = 75V$ (d) $V_{AB} = V_{BC} = 50V$

**18.** A parallel plate capacitor of capacitance $C$ is connected to a battery and is charged to a potential difference $V$. Another capacitor of capacitance $2C$ is connected to another battery and is charged to potential difference $2V$. The charging batteries are now disconnected and the capacitors are connected in parallel to each other in such a way that the positive terminal of one is connected to the negative terminal of the other. The final energy of the configuration is

(a) zero (b) $\frac{25CV^2}{6}$

(c) $\frac{3CV^2}{2}$ (d) $\frac{9CV^2}{2}$

**19.** Condenser $A$ has a capacity of 15μF when it is filled with a medium of dielectric constant 15. Another condenser $B$ has a capacity of 1μF with air between the plates. Both are charged separately by a battery of 100 $V$. After charging, both are connected in parallel without the battery and the dielectric medium being removed. The common potential now is

(a) 400 $V$ (b) 800 $V$
(c) 1200 $V$ (d) 1600 $V$

**20.** In an isolated parallel plate capacitor of capacitance $C$, the four surface have charges $Q_1$, $Q_2$, $Q_3$ and $Q_4$ as shown. The potential difference between the plates is

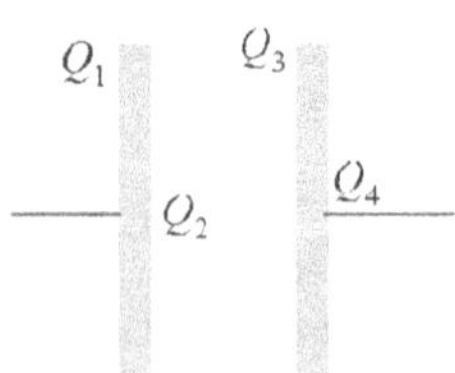


(a) $\frac{Q_1+Q_2+Q_3+Q_4}{2C}$ (b) $\frac{Q_2+Q_3}{2C}$

(c) $\frac{Q_2-Q_3}{2C}$ (d) $\frac{Q_1+Q_4}{2C}$

| Answer Key | 12 | (b) | 13 | (b) | 14 | (b) | 15 | (d) | 16 | (c) |
|---|---|---|---|---|---|---|---|---|---|---|
| Sol. from page 203 | 17 | (c) | 18 | (c) | 19 | (b) | 20 | (c) | | |

21. For the circuit shown, which of the following statements is true?

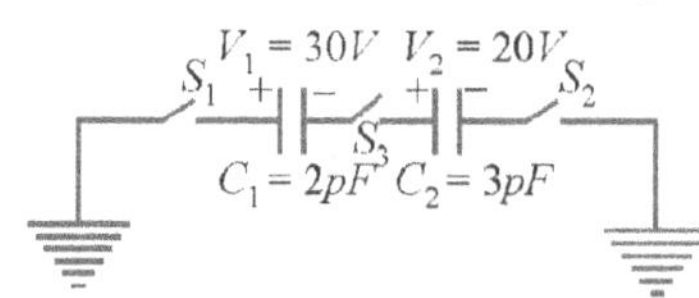


(a) With $S_1$ closed, $V_1 = 15\ V$, $V_2 = 20\ V$
(b) With $S_3$ closed, $V_1 = V_2 = 25\ V$
(c) With $S_1$ and $S_2$ closed $V_1 = V_2 = 0$
(d) With $S_1$ and $S_3$ closed, $V_1 = 30\ V$, $V_2 = 20V$

22. A fully charged capacitor has a capacitance $C$. It is discharged through a small coil of resistance wire embedded in a thermally insulated block of specific heat capacity $s$ and mass $m$. If the temperature of the block is raised by $\Delta T$, the potential difference $V$ across the capacitance is

(a) $\frac{ms\Delta T}{C}$ (b) $\sqrt{\frac{2ms\Delta T}{C}}$

(c) $\sqrt{\frac{2mC\Delta T}{s}}$ (d) $\frac{mC\Delta T}{s}$

23. A 4 $\mu F$ capacitor, a resistance of 2.5 $M\Omega$ is in series with 12 $V$ battery. Find the time after which the potential difference across the capacitor is 3 times the potential difference across the resistor. [Given $\ell n(2) = 0.693$]
(a) 13.86 $s$ (b) 6.93 $s$
(c) 7 $s$ (d) 14 $s$

24. Figure (a) shows two capacitors connected in series and joined to a battery. The graph in figure (b) shows the variation in potential as one moves from left to right on the branch containing the capacitors. Then :

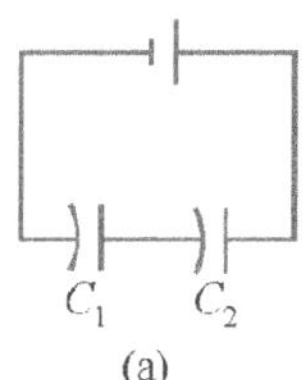

(a)

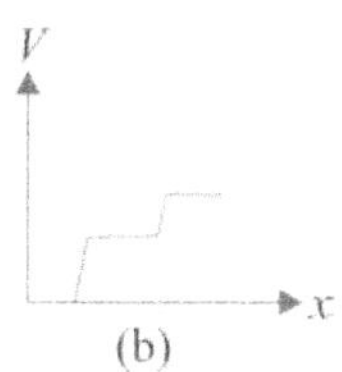

(b)

(a) $C_1 > C_2$ (b) $C_1 = C_2$
(c) $C_1 < C_2$
(d) the information is not sufficient to decide the relation between $C_1$ and $C_2$

25. In an $RC$ circuit while charging, the graph of log $i$ versus time is as shown by the dotted line in the figure, where i is the current. When the value of the resistance is doubled, which of the solid curve best represents the variation of log $i$ versus time

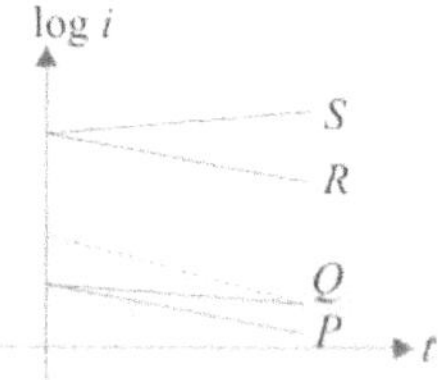


(a) $P$ (b) $Q$
(c) $R$ (d) $S$

26. The given circuit consists of a capacitor and resistors. The time constant of the circuit is :

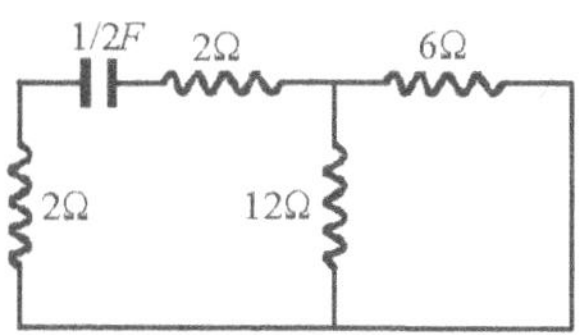


(a) $\frac{1}{4}s$ (b) 4 s
(c) 2 s (d) 1 s

27. When a dc voltage is applied to a capacitor, the voltage across its terminals is found to build up in accordance with $V_c = 150\,(1 - e^{-20t})$. If the current is 1.14 mA after 0.05 s, the capacitance of the capacitor is
(a) 3.01 μF (b) 0.03 μF
(c) 1.03 μF (d) 10.3 μF

28. A parallel plate capacitor with air between the plates has a capacitance of 9 $pF$. The separation between the plates is '$d$'. The space between the plates is now filled with two dielectrics. One of the dielectric has dielectric constant $k_1 = 3$ and thickness $d/3$ while the other one has dielectric constant $k_2 = 6$ and thickness $2d/3$. Capacitance of the capacitor is now
(a) 45 $pF$ (b) 40.5 $pF$
(c) 20.25 $pF$ (d) 1.8 $pF$

29. Seven capacitor, each of capacitance 1μF are connected as shown. The equivalent capacitance between $A$ and $B$ is :

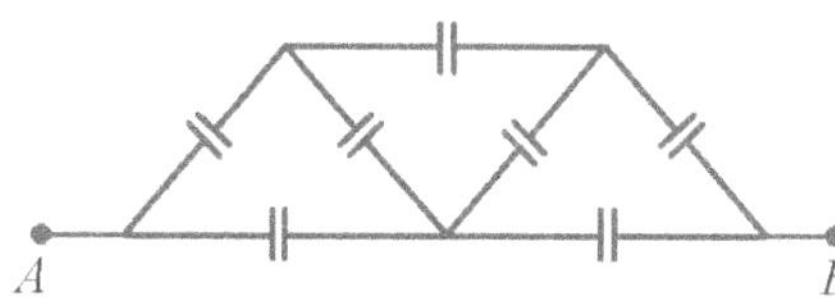


(a) $\frac{7}{8}\mu F$ (b) $\frac{8}{7}\mu F$

(c) 7 μF (d) $\frac{14}{7}\mu F$

30. Plates of area $A$ are arranged as shown. The distance between each plate is $d$, the net capacitance is

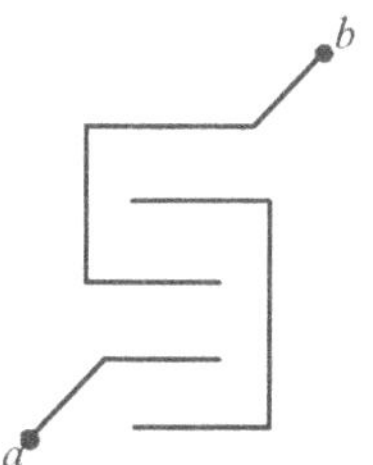


(a) $\frac{\varepsilon_0 A}{d}$ (b) $\frac{7\varepsilon_0 A}{d}$

(c) $\frac{6\varepsilon_0 A}{d}$ (d) $\frac{5\varepsilon_0 A}{d}$

| Answer Key | 21 | (d) | 22 | (b) | 23 | (a) | 24 | (c) | 25 | (b) |
|---|---|---|---|---|---|---|---|---|---|---|
| Sol. from page 203 | 26 | (b) | 27 | (c) | 28 | (b) | 29 | (a) | 30 | (a) |

**31.** Six capacitors each of capacitance of $2\mu F$ are connected as shown in the figure. The effective capacitance between $A$ and $B$ is

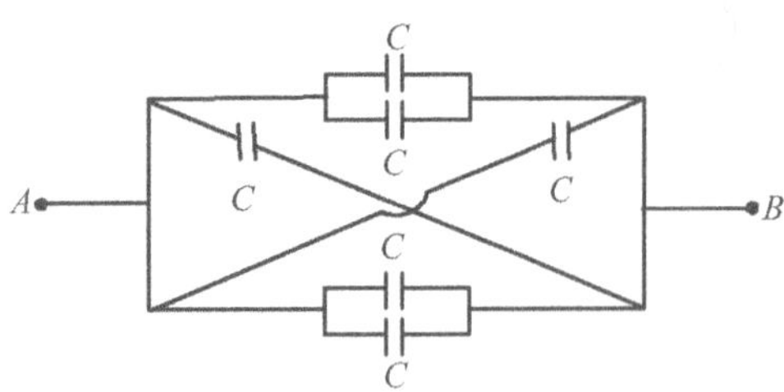


(a) $12\ \mu F$ (b) $8/3\ \mu F$
(c) $3\ \mu F$ (d) $6\ \mu F$

**32.** The combination of capacitors with $C_1 = 3\mu F$, $C_2 = 4\mu F$ and $C_3 = 2\mu F$ is charged by connecting $AB$ to a battery. Consider the following statements.

I. Energy stored in $C_1$ = energy stored in $C_2$ + energy stored in $C_3$
II. Charge on $C_1$ = charge on $C_2$ + charge on $C_3$
III. Potential drop across $C_1$ = potential drop across $C_2$ = potential drop across $C_3$

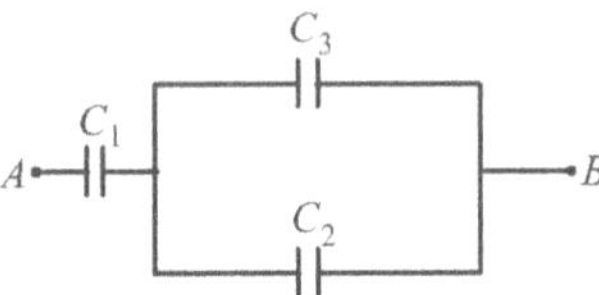


Which of the following is/are correct
(a) I and II (b) II only
(c) I and III (d) III only

**33.** In figure, there is a four way key at the middle. If key is shown from situation $BD$ to $AD$, then how much charge will flow through point $O$ ?

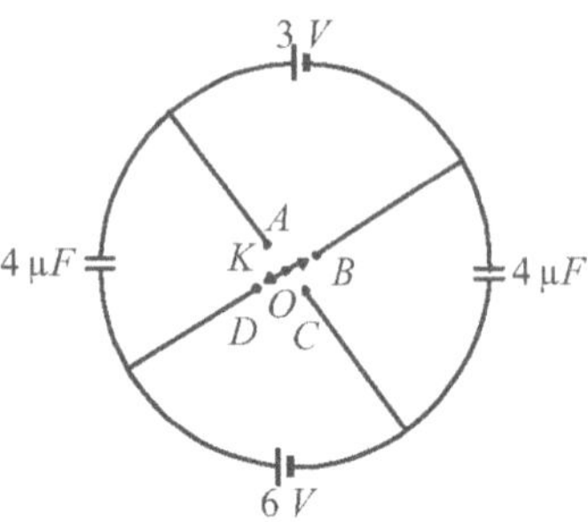


(a) $24\ \mu C$ (b) $36\ \mu C$
(c) $72\ \mu C$ (d) $12\ \mu C$

**34.** A circuit is connected as shown in the figure with the switch $S$ open. When the switch is closed, the total amount of charge that flows from $y$ to $x$

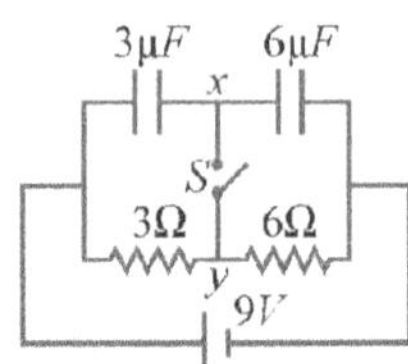


(a) 0 (b) $54\ \mu C$
(c) $27\ \mu C$ (d) $81\ \mu C$

**35.** What is equivalent capacitance of circuit between points $A$ and $B$?

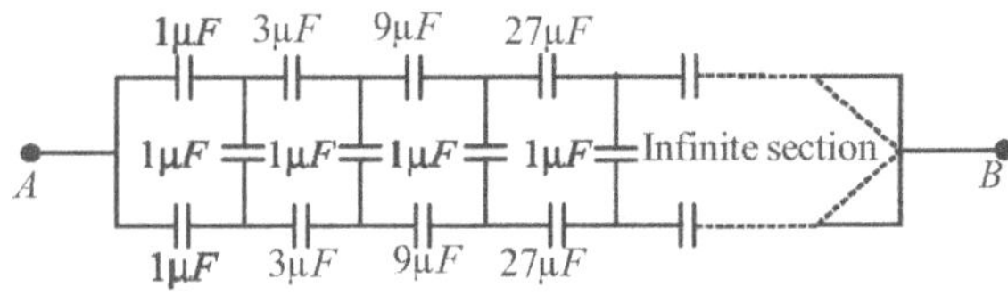


(a) $\frac{2}{3}\mu F$ (b) $\frac{4}{3}\mu F$

(c) Infinite (d) $(1+\sqrt{3})\mu F$

**36.** A parallel plate capacitor $C$ with plates of unit area and separation $d$ is filled with a liquid of dielectric constant $\kappa = 2$. The level of liquid is $\frac{d}{3}$ initially. Suppose the liquid level decreases at a constant speed $v$, the time constant as a function of time $t$ is

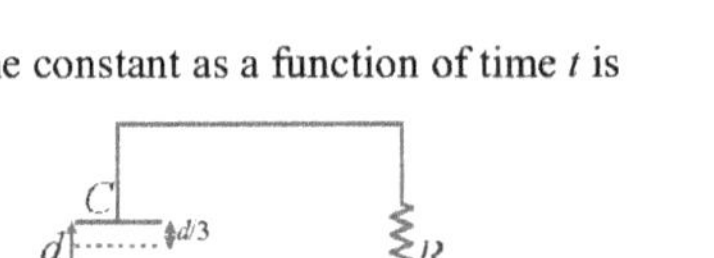


(a) $\frac{6\ \epsilon_0\ R}{5d+3vt}$ (b) $\frac{(15d+9vt)\ \epsilon_0\ R}{2d^2-3dvt-9v^2t^2}$

(c) $\frac{6\ \epsilon_0\ R}{5d-3vt}$ (d) $\frac{(15d-9vt)\ \epsilon_0\ R}{2d^2+3dvt-9v^2t^2}$

**37.** Equivalent capacitance between $A$ and $B$

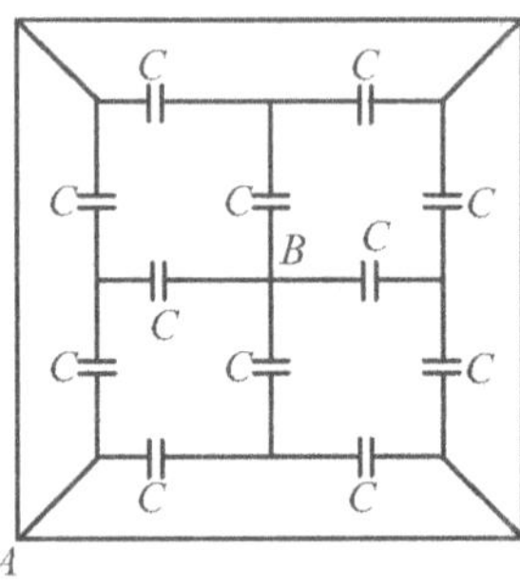


(a) $\frac{4C}{3}$ (b) $\frac{8C}{3}$

(c) 12 C (d) $\frac{5C}{12}$

| Answer Key | 31 | (a) | 32 | (b) | 33 | (c) | 34 | (c) |
|---|---|---|---|---|---|---|---|---|
| Sol. from page 203 | 35 | (b) | 36 | (a) | 37 | (b) | | |

**38.** A parallel plate capacitor $C$ carries a charge $Q$. The distance between the plates is doubled by application of force. The work done by force is

(a) zero (b) $\frac{Q^2}{2C}$

(c) $\frac{Q^2}{C}$ (d) $\frac{Q^2}{4C}$

**39.** Diagram shows three capacitors with capacitance and breakdown voltage mentioned. What should be maximum value of the external emf of source such that no capacitor breaks down?

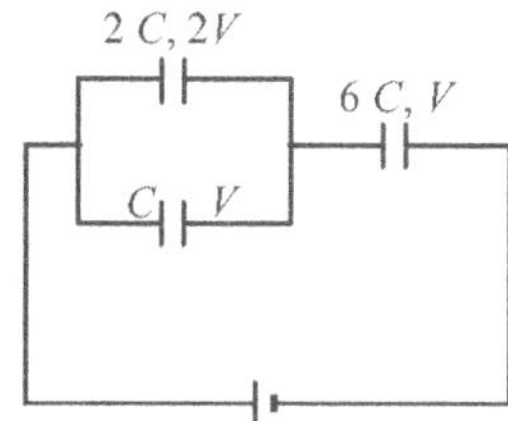


(a) 1 $V$ (b) 2 $V$
(c) 1.5 $V$ (d) 4 $V$

**40.** What is equivalent time constant of following $RC$ circuit?

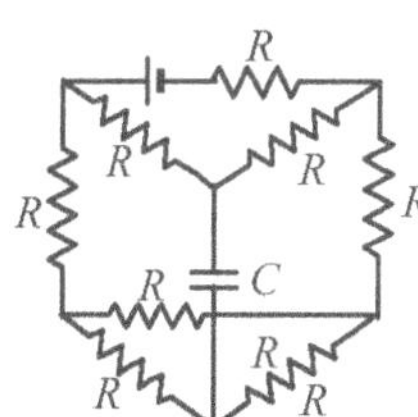


(a) 1.5 $RC$ (b) 3 $RC$

(c) 2 $RC$ (d) $\frac{RC}{2}$

**41.** In the circuit shown in figure, find the steady state charge on capacitor $C_1$.

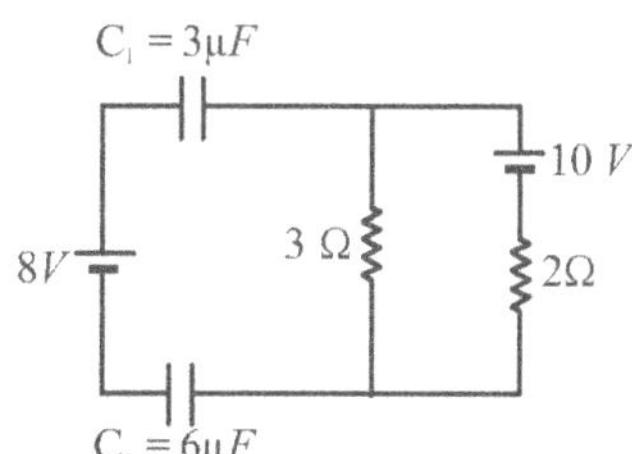


(a) 2 $\mu C$ (b) 3 $\mu C$
(c) 4 $\mu C$ (d) zero

**42.** If key $K_1$ is closed in circuit shown in figure and galvanometer doesn't give deflection at any time, then value of $C$ is

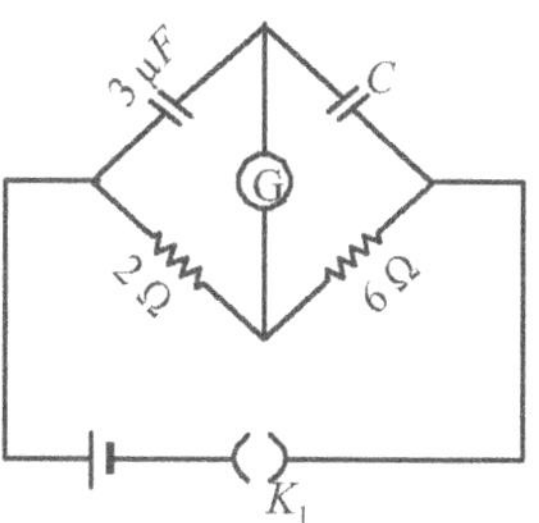


(a) 3 $\mu F$ (b) 9 $\mu F$
(c) 4 $\mu F$ (d) 1 $\mu F$

**43.** The circuit shown in figure is closed at $t = 0$. Calculate the total amount of heat generated in $R_2$ during the time capacitor gets fully charged

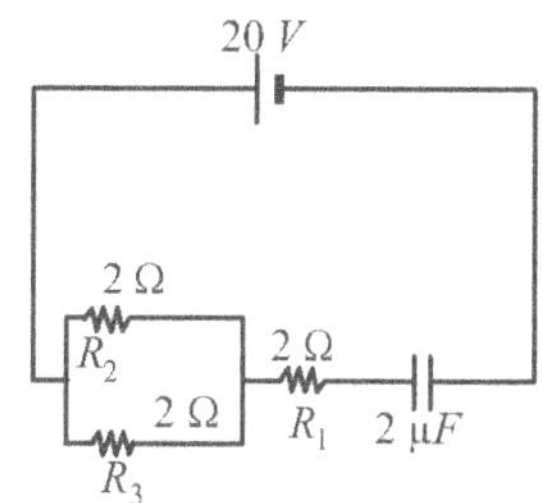


(a) $\frac{200}{3}$ μ J (b) $\frac{400}{3}$ μ J

(c) $\frac{800}{3}$ μ J (d) 400 μJ

**44.** In the circuit shown in figure if battery is ideal, then time after which current in $R_3$ becomes $\frac{1}{e}$ time of maximum current through it is

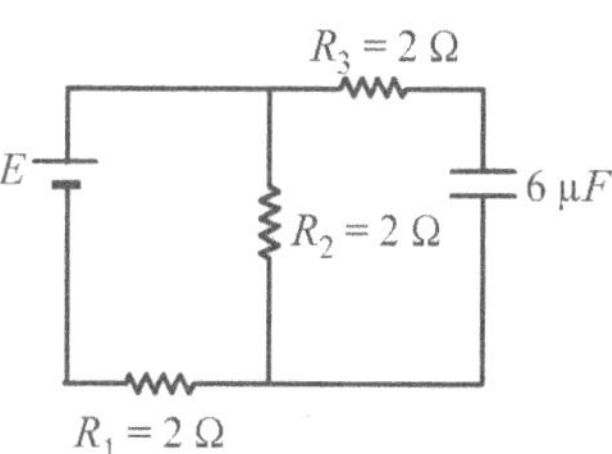


(a) 18 μs (b) 12 μs
(c) 6 μs (d) 2 μs

| Answer Key | 38 | (b) | 39 | (c) | 40 | (a) | 41 | (c) |
|---|---|---|---|---|---|---|---|---|
| Sol. from page 203 | 42 | (d) | 43 | (a) | 44 | (a) | | |

**45.** In the circuit show the capacitor of capacitance $C$ charged to a potential $V$. The current in the circuit just after the closing of switch $S$ is:

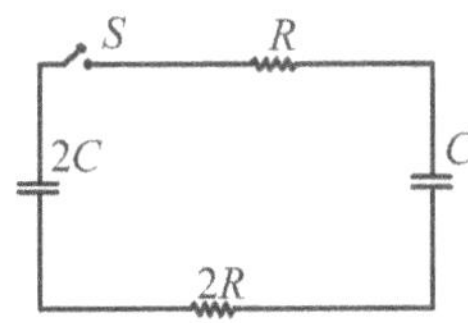


(a) $\frac{V}{3R}$ (b) $\frac{3V}{R}$

(c) $\frac{V}{2R}$ (d) zero

**46.** A capacitor of capacity 6μF and initial charge 160 μC is connected with a switch $S$ and resistors as shown in figure. If switch is closed at $t = 0$, then the current through resistor of 4 Ω at $t = 16$ μs is :

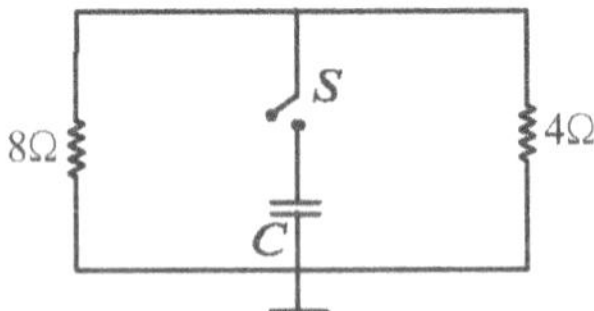


(a) $\frac{10}{e}A$ (b) $\frac{20}{3e}A$

(c) $\frac{10}{3e}A$ (d) zero

**47.** In the given circuit the quantity of charge that flows to ground long time after closing the switch is:

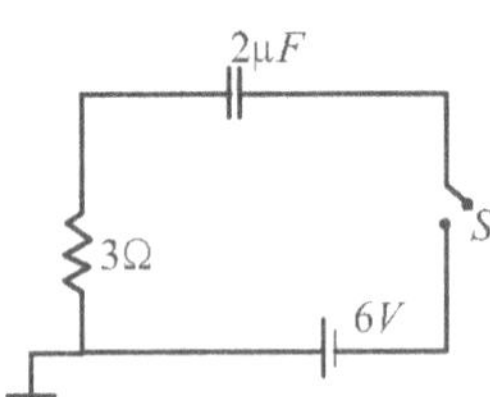


(a) 9 μC (b) 12 μC
(c) 15 μC (d) zero

**48.** A capacitor of capacitance of 1 μF is to a potential 12 V with a battery. After charging the battery is disconnected and an additional charge 10 μC is given to the positive plate of the capacitor. The final potential difference across the capacitor is:

(a) 12 $V$ (b) 17 $V$
(c) 22 $V$ (d) 27 $V$

**49.** A capacitor is filled with an insulator and a certain potential difference is applied to its plates. The energy stored in the capacitor is U. Now the capacitor is disconnected from the source and the insulator is pulled out of the capacitor. The work performed against the forces of electric field in pulling out the insulator is 4 U. The dielectric constant of the insulator is

(a) 3 (b) 4
(c) 5 (d) 7

**50.** Five metal plates are placed parallel to each other. The separation between neighbouring plates is d and area of each plate is A. The plated are connected as shown in figure. The charge on plate 1 is :

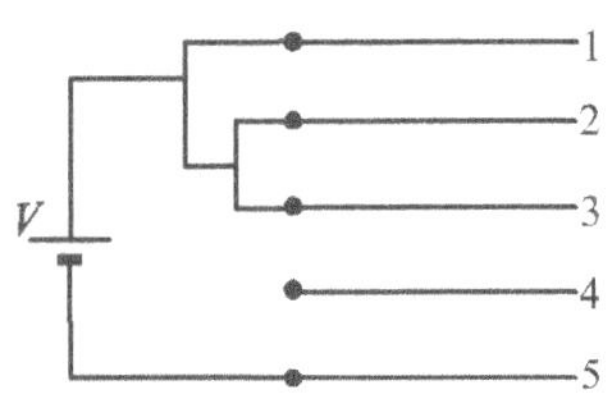


(a) $\frac{\varepsilon_0 AV}{d}$ (b) $2\frac{\varepsilon_0 AV}{d}$

(c) $\frac{\varepsilon_0 AV}{2d}$ (d) zero

**51.** In the infinite grid consisting of capacitors each of capacitance $C$, the equivalent capacitance between terminals $A$ and $B$ is :

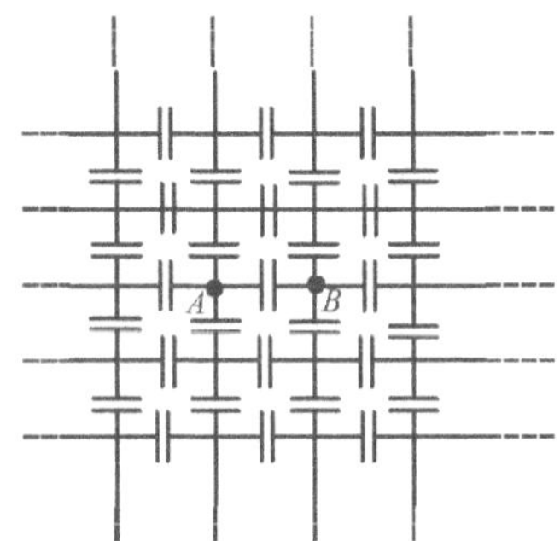


(a) $\frac{C}{2}$ (b) $C$

(c) $\frac{3C}{2}$ (d) 2 $C$

**52.** A 2μ$F$ capacitor is charged as shown in the figure. The percentage of its stored energy dissipated after the switch $S$ is turned to position 2 is

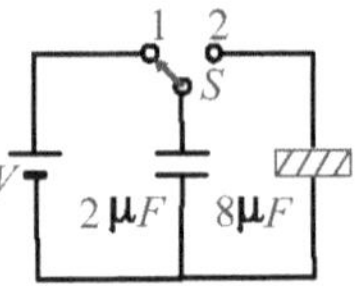


(a) 0% (b) 20%
(c) 75% (d) 80%

**53.** For the arrangement shown in figure, identify the correct statement:

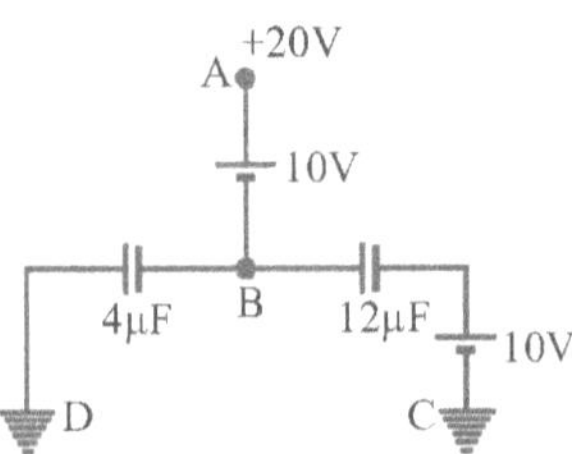


(a) the charge on the 12μF capacitor is zero
(b) the charge on the 12μF capacitor is 30μC
(c) the charge on the 4μF capacitor is 30μC
(d) none of these

| Answer Key | 45 | (a) | 46 | (b) | 47 | (d) | 48 | (b) | 49 | (c) |
|---|---|---|---|---|---|---|---|---|---|---|
| Sol. from page 203 | 50 | (d) | 51 | (c) | 52 | (d) | 53 | (a) | | |

ELECTRICITY

# MCQ Type 2

*Exercise 2.2*

**Multiple correct options**

**1.** A capacitor with no dielectric is connected to a battery at $t = 0$. Consider a point $A$ in the connecting wires and a point $B$ in between the plates.
(a) There is no current through $A$.
(b) There is displacement current through $B$ till electric field changes between the plates.
(c) There is a current through $A$ as long as the charging is not complete.
(d) The current always flows between the plates of capacitor.

**2.** A capacitor $C_1$ of capacitance $1\mu F$ and a capacitor $C_2$ of capacitance $2\mu F$ are separately charged by a common battery for a long time. The two capacitors are then separately discharged through equal resistors. Both the discharge circuits are connected at $t=0$.
(a) The current in each of the two discharging circuits is zero at $t=0$.
(b) The currents in the two discharging circuits at $t=0$ are equal but not zero.
(c) The currents in the two discharging circuits at $t=0$ are unequal.
(d) $C_1$ losses 50% of its initial charge sooner than $C_2$ loses 50% of its initial charge.

**3.** Each plate of a parallel plate capacitor has a charge $q$ on it. The capacitor is now connected to a battery. Now
(a) the facing surfaces of the capacitor have equal and opposite charges.
(b) the two plates of the capacitor have equal and opposite charges.
(c) the battery supplies equal and opposite charges to the two plates.
(d) The outer surfaces of the plates have equal charges.

**4.** The separation between the plates of a charged parallel plate capacitor is increased. Which of the following quantities will change ?
(a) charge on the capacitor
(b) potential difference across the capacitor
(c) energy of the capacitor
(d) energy density between the plates of the capacitor.

**5.** Which one statement is correct ? A parallel plate air condenser is connected with a battery. Its charge, potential, electric field and energy are $Q_0$, $V_0$, $E_0$ and $U_0$ respectively. In order to fill the complete space between the plates a dielectric slab is inserted, the battery is still connected. Now the corresponding values $Q$, $V$, $E$ and $U$ are in relation with the initially stated as
(a) $Q > Q_0$ (b) $V > V_0$
(c) $E > E_0$ (d) $U > U_0$

**6.** Figure shows three circuits, each consisting of a switch and two capacitors, initially charged as indicated. In which circuit the charge on the left hand capacitor will change after the closing of the switch is :

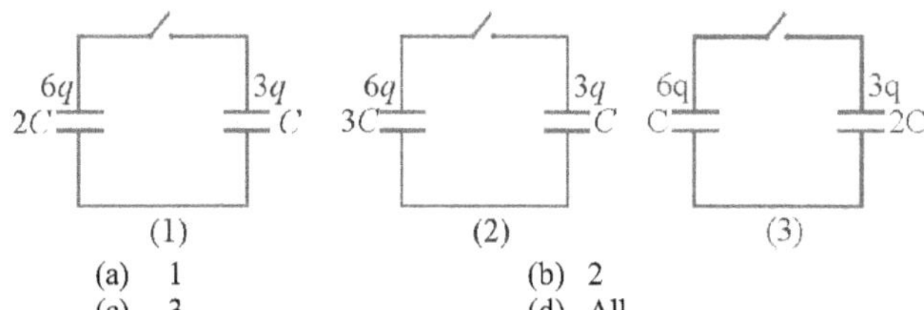


(a) 1 (b) 2
(c) 3 (d) All

**7.** A dielectric slab of thickness $d$ is inserted in a parallel plate capacitor whose negative plate is at $x = 0$ and positive plate is at $x = 3d$. The slab is equidistant from the plates. The capacitor is given some charge. As one goes from 0 to $3d$
(a) The magnitude of the electric field remains the same
(b) The direction of the electric field remains the same
(c) The electric potential increases continuously
(d) The electric potential increases at first, then decreases and again increases

**8.** A leaky parallel plate capacitor is filled completely with a material having dielectric constant $k$, electrical conductivity $\sigma$. The charge on the plate initially is $q_0$ and the leakage current at time $t$ is $i$. The time constant of the circuit is $\tau$. Then

(a) $\tau = \dfrac{\varepsilon_0 k}{\sigma}$ (b) $i = \dfrac{q_0 \sigma}{\varepsilon_0 k}$

(c) $i = i_0 e^{\left(\frac{t\sigma}{\varepsilon_0 k}\right)}$ (d) $i_0 = -\dfrac{q_0 \sigma}{\varepsilon_0 k}$

**9.** In the circuit shown, the potential difference across the $3\mu F$ capacitor is $V_1$ and the equivalent capacitance between $A$ and $B$ is $C$. Then

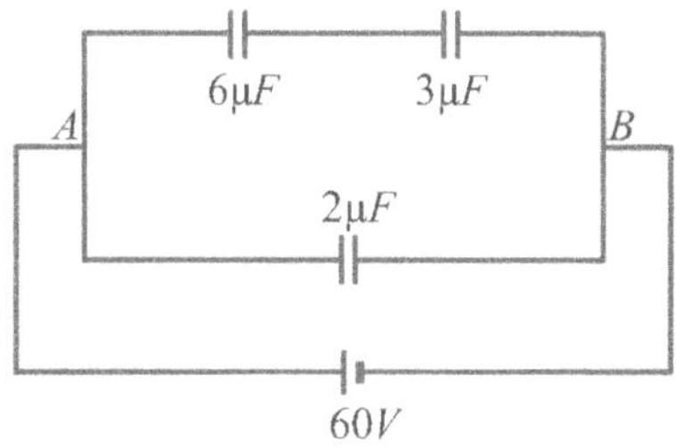


(a) $C = 4\mu F$ (b) $C = 11\mu F$
(c) $V = 20V$ (d) $V = 40\ V$

| Answer Key | 1 | (b, c) | 2 | (b, d) | 3 | (a, c, d) | 4 | (b, c) | 5 | (a, d) |
|---|---|---|---|---|---|---|---|---|---|---|
| Sol. from page 208 | 6 | (b, c) | 7 | (b, c) | 8 | (a, b) | 9 | (a, d) | | |

ELECTRICITY

# Statement Questions

Exercise 2.3

Read the two statements carefully to mark the correct option out of the options given below. Select the right choice.

(a) If both the statements are true and the ***Statement* - 2** is the correct explanation of ***Statement* - 1**.

(b) If both the statements are true but ***Statement* - 2** is not the correct explanation of the ***Statement* - 1**.

(c) If ***Statement* - 1** true but ***Statement* - 2** is false.

(d) If ***Statement* - 1** is false but ***Statement* - 2** is true.

**1.** ***Statement* 1**

Second conductor in the capacitor increases its capacitance.

***Statement* - 2**

Second conductor decreases the potential difference between the conductors.

**2.** ***Statement* - 1**

The capacitance of a capacitor with charge $Q$ on its one plate is $C$

***Statement* - 2**

The capacitance of a capacitor with charge $2Q$ on its one plate will be $2C$.

**3.** ***Statement* - 1**

Capacitance $C = \frac{Q}{V}$; it means $C$ is proportional to $Q$.

***Statement* - 2**

Charge $Q = CV$; it means charge on the capacitor is proportional to $V$.

**4.** ***Statement* - 1**

Electric energy resides out of the spherical isolated conductor.

***Statement* - 2**

The electric field at any point inside the conductor is zero.

**5.** ***Statement* - 1**

The electric energy resides between the plates of a capacitor.

***Statement* - 2**

The electric field at any point outside the plates is zero.

**6.** ***Statement* - 1**

A parallel plate capacitor is connected across battery through a key. A dielectric slab of dielectric constant k is introduced between the plates. The energy stored becomes k times.

***Statement* - 2**

The surface density of charge on the plate remains constant.

**7.** ***Statement* - 1**

Two metal plates having charges $Q$, $-Q$ face each other at some separation and are dipped into an oil tank. If the oil is pumped out, the electric field between the plates increases.

***Statement* - 2**

Electric field between the plates,

$$E_{\text{med}} = \frac{E_{\text{air}}}{\kappa}.$$

**8.** ***Statement* - 1**

A charge $Q_1$ is given to the one plate and a charge $-Q_2$ to the other plate of a capacitor. The charge on the capacitor is $Q_1 - Q_2$.

***Statement* - 2**

The charge on the capacitor is $\frac{Q_1 + Q_2}{2}$.

**9.** ***Statement* - 1**

The plates of a parallel plate capacitor are given equal positive charges. The charge on the facing surfaces of the plates are zero.

***Statement* - 2**

The potential difference between the plates is zero.

**10.** ***Statement* - 1**

When a dielectric slab is gradually inserted between the plates of an isolated parallel-plate capacitor, the energy of the system decreases.

***Statement* - 2**

The force between the plates decreases.

**11.** ***Statement* - 1**

A dielectric is inserted between the plates of a battery connected capacitor. The energy of the capacitor increases.

***Statement* - 2**

$$U = \frac{1}{2}CV^2.$$

| Answer Key | 1 | (a) | 2 | (c) | 3 | (d) | 4 | (a) | 5 | (a) | 6 | (c) |
|---|---|---|---|---|---|---|---|---|---|---|---|---|
| Sol. from page 208 | 7 | (a) | 8 | (d) | 9 | (d) | 10 | (c) | 11 | (a) | | |

ELECTRICITY

# Passage & Matrix

Exercise 2.4

## PASSAGES

**Passage for Q. No. 1 to Q. No. 3**

A system consists of two concentric thin spherical shells of radii $a$ and $b$ ($b > a$).

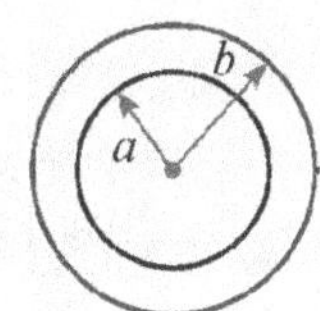


1. Outer shell is earthed and inner shell is given charge $Q$, then charge on the outer shell is :

(a) zero (b) $-\frac{Q}{2}$

(c) $\frac{Qb}{a}$ (d) $-Q$

2. If inner shell is earthed and charge $Q$ is given to the outer shell, then charge on the inner shell is :

(a) zero (b) $-\frac{Qa}{b}$

(c) $\frac{Qb}{a}$ (d) none of these

3. The capacitance of the system in second case :

(a) $4\pi \epsilon_0 \left(\frac{ab}{b-a}\right)$ (b) $4\pi \epsilon_0 (a+b)$

(c) $4\pi \epsilon_0 b$ (d) $4\pi \epsilon_0 \left(\frac{b^2}{b-a}\right)$

**Passage for Q. 4 to Q. 6**

In the circuit shown in the figure the emf of each battery is $\xi$ and capacitors of capacitances $C_1$ and $C_2$ are connected as shown.

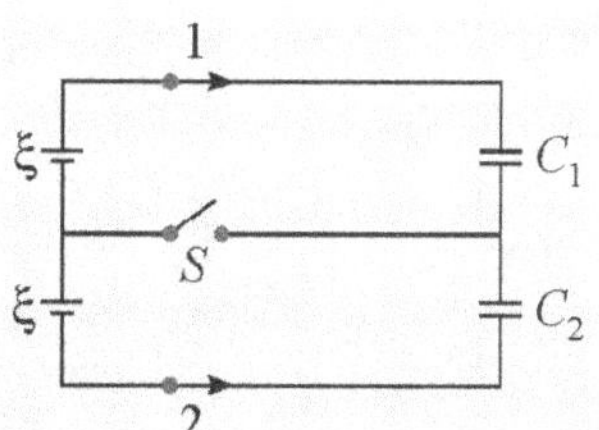


4. The charge on the each capacitor before closing the switch is :

(a) $(C_1 + C_2)\xi$ (b) $\frac{3C_2}{C_1}\xi$

(c) $\frac{\xi C_1C_2}{C_1+C_2}$ (d) $\frac{2\xi C_1C_2}{C_1+C_2}$

5. The switch $S$ is now closed, the amount of charge flows through the section 1:

(a) $\frac{\xi C_1(C_1-C_2)}{(C_1+C_2)}$ (b) $\frac{\xi C_1C_2}{C_1+C_2}$

(c) $\frac{\xi C_1(C_1-2C_2)}{C_1+C_2}$ (d) zero

6. The amount of charge flows through section 2 :

(a) $\frac{\xi C_1(C_1-C_2)}{C_1+C_2}$ (b) $\frac{\xi C_2(C_1-C_2)}{(C_1+C_2)}$

(c) zero (d) none of these

**Passage for Q. 7 to Q. 9**

A capacitor having a capacitance of $100\mu F$ is charged to a potential difference of 24V. The charging battery is disconnected and the capacitor is connected to another battery of 12 V with the positive plate of the capacitor joined with the positive terminal of the battery.

7. The charge flown through the 12 V battery.

(a) – 600 μC (b) – 1200 μC

(c) 600 μC (d) 1800 μC

8. The decrease in electrostatic field energy is.

(a) 21.6 mJ (b) 27.6 mJ

(c) 30 mJ (d) none of these

9. The heat developed during the flow of charge after reconnection.

(a) 21.6 mJ (b) 27.6 mJ

(c) 7.2 mJ (d) zero

| Answer Key | 1 | (d) | 2 | (b) | 3 | (d) | 4 | (d) |
|---|---|---|---|---|---|---|---|---|
| Sol. from page 209 | 5 | (a) | 6 | (b) | 7 | (b) | 8 | (a) |

**Passage for Q. 10 to Q. 12**

In fig. the battery has a potential difference of 20V. :

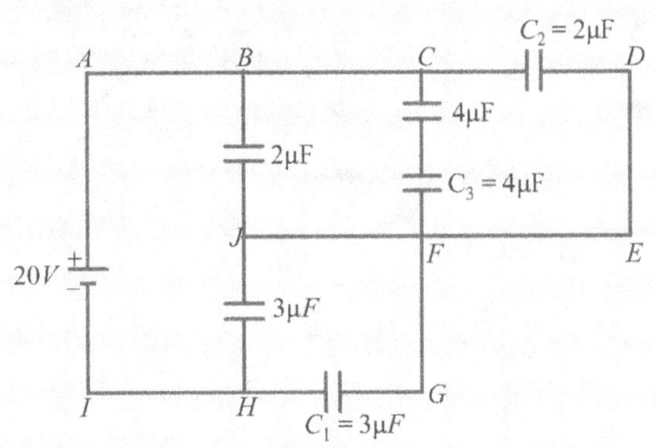


10. The equivalent capacitance of all the capacitors is
    (a) 1 μ F (b) 2μF
    (c) 3μF (d) 4μF

11. The charge stored on that equivalent capacitance is
    (a) 30 μC (b) 40μC
    (c) 90μC (d) 60μC

12. The potential difference across $C_1$ is
    (a) 10 V (b) 20 V
    (c) 30 V (d) 40 C

**Passage for Q. 13 to Q. 15**

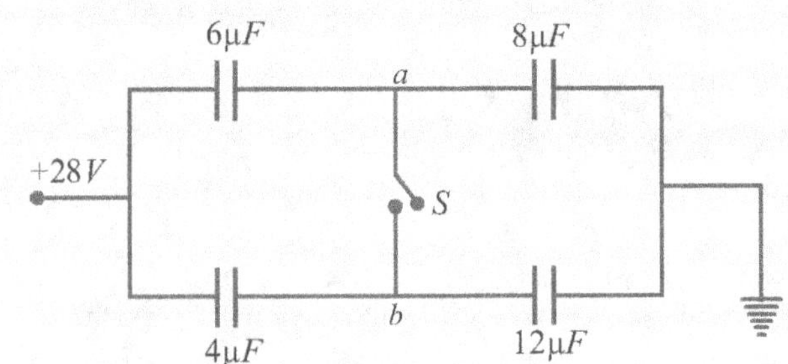


13. What is the potential difference $V_{ab}$?
    (a) 5 V (b) 6 V
    (c) 4 V (d) 8 V

14. Now the key S is closed. What is the potential of point $a$?
    (a) 9.2 V (b) 9.4 V
    (c) 9.3 V (d) 7.8 V

15. How much charge flowed through the switch when it was closed?
    (a) 3.70 μ C (b) 37.8 μ C
    (c) 3.78 μ C (d) none of these

## MATRIX MATCHING

16. When a dielectric slab is inserted between the plates of one of the two identical capacitors shown in the figure then match the following:

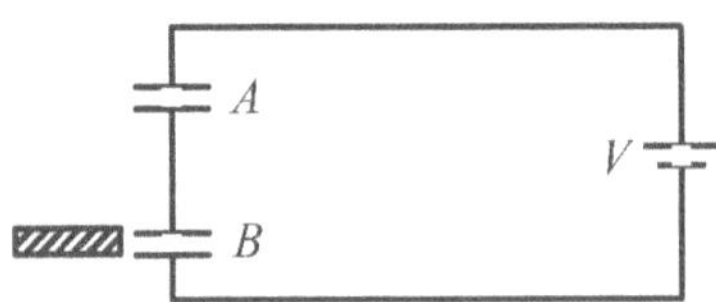


| Column-I | Column -II |
|---|---|
| A. Charge on A | (p) increases |
| B. Potential difference across A | (q) decreases |
| C. Potential difference across B | (r) remains constant |
| D. Charge on B | (s) will change |

| Answer Key | 9 | (c) | 10 | (d) | 11 | (c) | 12 | (a) | 13 | (a) | 14 | (c) |
|---|---|---|---|---|---|---|---|---|---|---|---|---|
| Sol. from page 209 | 15 | (b) | | | | | 16 | A-p, s ; B-p, s ; C-q, s ; D-q, s | | | | |

**17.** **Column II** gives certain systems undergoing a process. **Column I** suggests changes in some of the parameters related to the system.

| **Column-I** | **Column-II** |
|---|---|
| (A) The energy of the system is increased | (p) System: A capacitor, initially uncharged<br>Process: It is connected to a battery |
| (B) Mechanical energy is provided to the system, which is converted into energy of random motion of its parts | (q) System: A gas in an adiabatic container fitted with an adiabatic piston<br>Process: The gas is compressed by pushing the piston |
| (C) Internal energy of the system is converted into its mechanical energy | (r) System: A gas in a rigid container<br>Process: The gas gets cooled due to colder atmosphere surrounding it |
| (D) Mass of the (s) system is decreased | (s) System: A heavy nucleus, initially at rest<br>Process: The nucleus fissions into two fragments of nearly equal masses and some neutrons are emitted |
| | (t) System: A resistive wire loop<br>Process: The loop is placed in a time varying magnetic field perpendicular to its plane |

**18.** In the given circuit diagram, both capacitors are initially uncharged. The capacitance $C_1 = 2\mu F$ and $C_2 = 4F$ emf of battery $A$ and $B$ are 2V and 4V respectively.

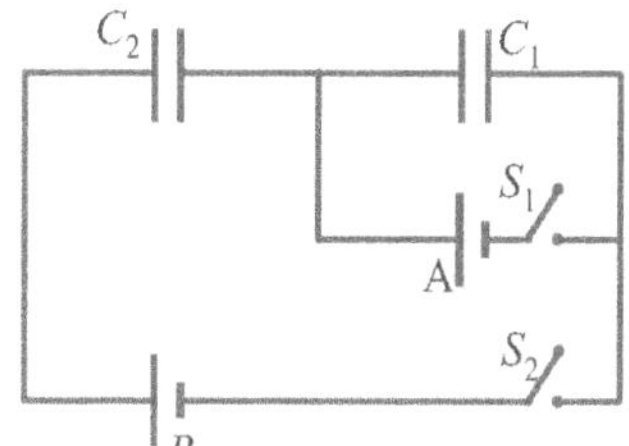


| **Column - I** | | **Column - II (Magnitude only)** |
|---|---|---|
| A. On closing switch $S_1$ with $S_2$ open work done by battery $A$ is | (p) | $\frac{64}{3}$ |
| B. Switch $S_1$ is open and $S_2$ is closed, work done by battery $B$ is | (q) | 4 |
| C. Charge on capacitor $C_2$ is (after $S_1$ open and $S_2$ closed) | (r) | 8 |
| D. Charge on $C_1$ when both are closed | (s) | $\frac{16}{3}$ |
| | (t) | zero |

**19.** A parallel plate capacitor with air between its plates is charged using a battery and then disconnected from the battery.

| **Column - I** | | **Column - II** |
|---|---|---|
| A. Potential difference between the plates will decrease if | (p) | Separation between the plates is increased to K/2 times the initial value and space between the plates after the separation has increased, is completely filled with a dielectric (here K is the dielectric constant) |
| B. Electric field strength between the plates will reduce if | (q) | Separation between the plates is increased |
| C. Electric energy stored in the capacitor will decrease if | (r) | A dielectric with K>1 is filled between the plates of capacitor. |
| D. Electric energy density will decrease if | (s) | Separation between the plates is reduced |
| | (t) | None |

| *Answer Key* | 17 | A. -p, s ; B -p, s ; C-q, s ; D - p, s | 18 | A. -r ; B - p ; C. - s; D.- q |
|---|---|---|---|---|
| Sol. from page 209 | 19 | A.-p, r, s ; B - p, r ; C- p , r, s ; D. - p, r | | |

ELECTRICITY

# Subjective Integer Type

Exercise 2.5

*Solution from page 211*

1. Find the charged supplied by the battery in the arrangement shown in figure.

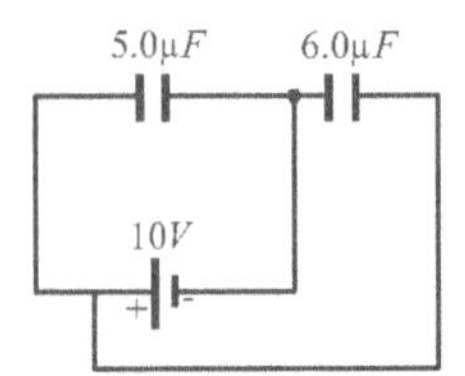


***Ans.*** 110 μC.

2. The particle $P$ shown in figure has a mass of 10 mg and a charge of - 0.01 $\mu C$. Each plate has a surface area 100 cm$^2$ on one side. What potential difference $V$ should be applied to the combination to hold the particle $P$ in equilibrium?

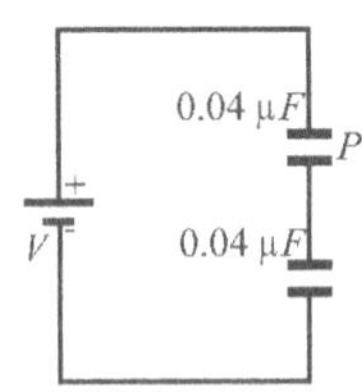


***Ans.*** 43 mV

3. Take $C_1$ = 4.0 $\mu F$ and $C_2$ = 6.0 $\mu F$ in figure. Calculate the equivalent capacitance of the combination between the points indicated.

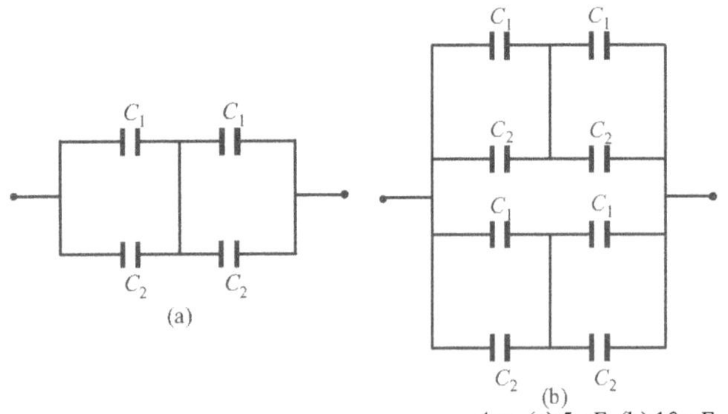


***Ans.*** (a) 5 μF, (b) 10 μF.

4. Four capacitors of equal capacitance are joined in series with a battery of 10 volts. The mid point $B$ of these capacitors is earthed. Calculate the potentials of $A$ and $C$.

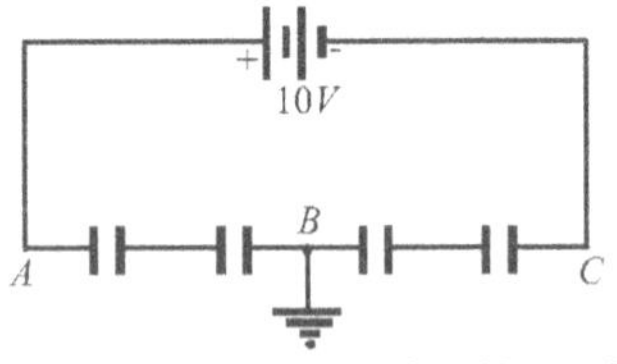


***Ans.*** $V_A = +5V$ and $V_C = -5\ V$.

5. Infinite number of identical capacitors (each of capacity 1μF) are connected as shown in figure. Find the equivalent capacitance of system between the terminals shown in figure.

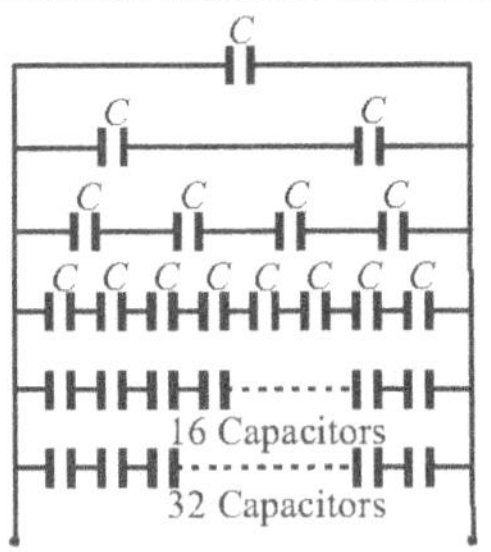


***Ans.*** 2 μF.

6. A finite ladder is constructed by connecting several sections of 2 μF, 4 μF capacitor combinations as shown in figure. It is terminated by a capacitor of capacitance $C$. What value should be chosen for $C$, such that the equivalent capacitance of the ladder between the points A and B becomes independent of the number of sections in between?

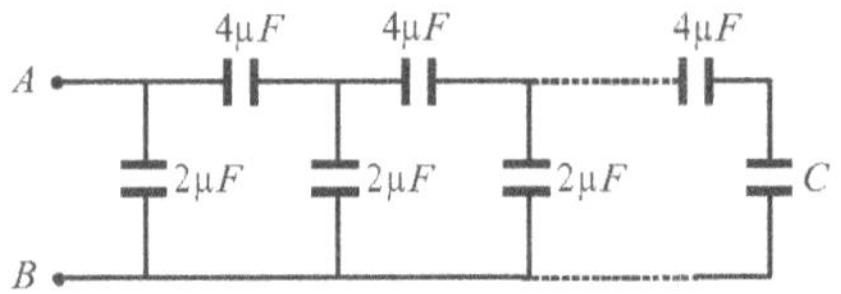


***Ans.*** 4 μF.

7. A capacitor stores 50 μC charge when connected across a battery. When the gap between the plates is filled with a dielectric, a charge of 100 μC flows through the battery. Find the dielectric constant of the material inserted.

***Ans.*** 3.

8. A battery of 10 $V$ is connected to a capacitor of capacity 0.1 $F$. The battery is now removed and this capacitor is connected to a second uncharged capacitor. If the charge distributes equally on these two capacitors, find the total energy stored in the two capacitors. Further compare this energy with the initial energy stored in the capacitors.

***Ans.*** 5J, 1/2.

ELECTRICITY

# Subjective

## Exercise 2.6

*Solution from page 211*

1. Take the potential of the point $B$ in figure to be zero.
 (a) Find the potentials at the points $C$ and $D$.
 (b) If a capacitor is connected between $C$ and $D$, what charge will appear on this capacitor ?

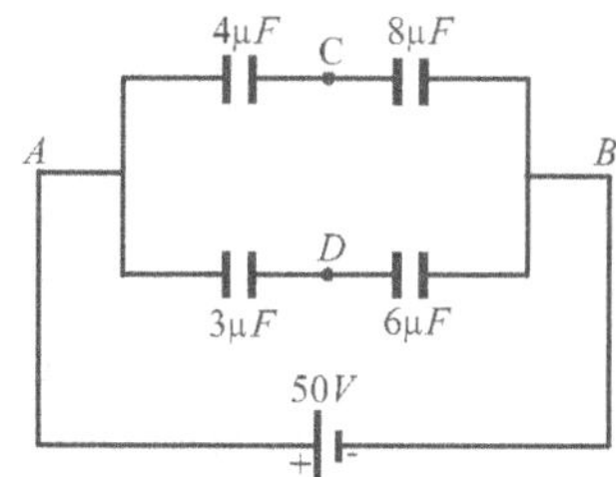


**Ans.** $\frac{50}{3}\mu V$ at each point (b) zero.

2. In figure each capacitance $C_1 = 2\ \mu F$ and $C_2 = 3\ \mu F$.

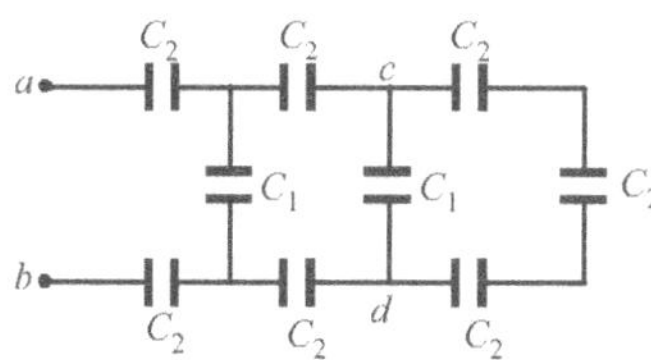


 (a) Calculate equivalent capacitance of the network between points $a$ and $b$.
 (b) Calculate the charge on each of capacitors nearest to a and b when p.d. across $a$ and $b$,
 $V_{ab} = 900$ volt.
 (c) With 900 volts across a and b, calculate the p.d. across $c$ and $d$ [i.e. $V_{cd}$]

**Ans.** (a) 1 $\mu F$ (b) 900 $\mu C$ (c) 100 $V$.

3. Find the equivalent capacitances of the combinations shown in figure between the indicated points.

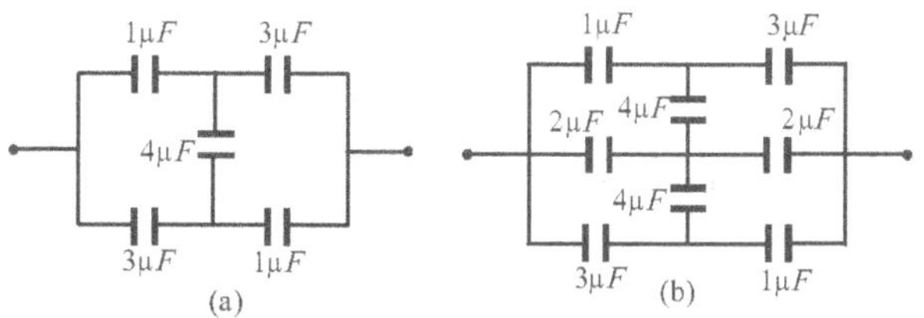


**Ans.** (a) $\frac{11}{6}\ \mu F$, (b) $\frac{11}{4}\ \mu F$.

4. Find the equivalent capacitances of the combinations shown in figure between the indicated points.

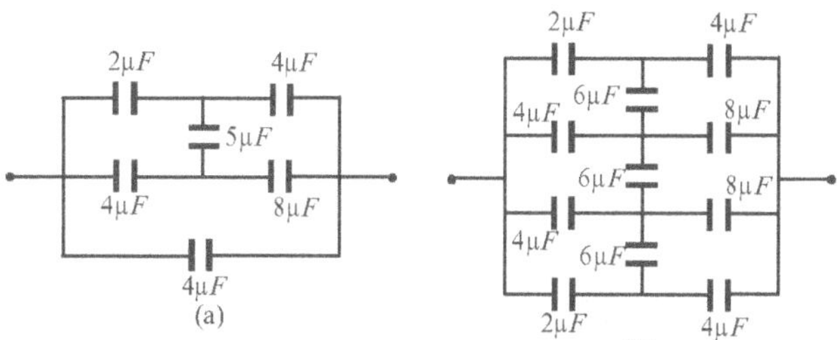


**Ans.** (a) 8 μF, (b) 8 μF.

5. Find the potential difference $V_a - V_b$ between the points $a$ and $b$ shown in each part of the figure.

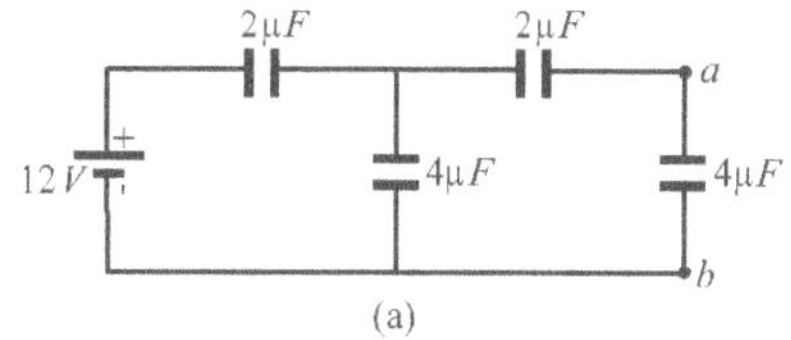


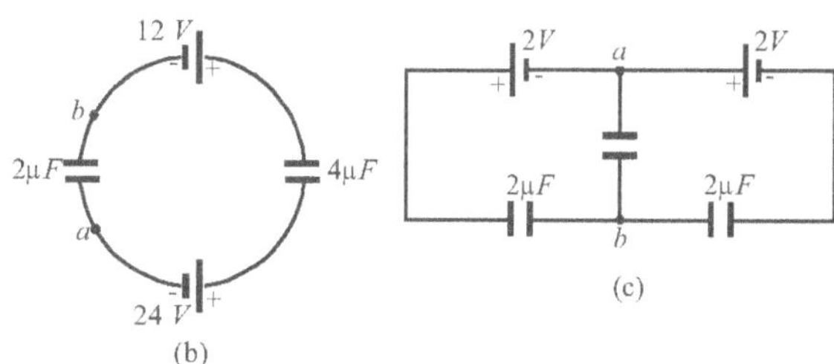


**Ans.** (a) 12 / 11 V, (b) - 8 V, (c) zero .

6. Find the potential difference $V_a - V_b$ between the points $a$ and $b$ shown in each part of the figure.

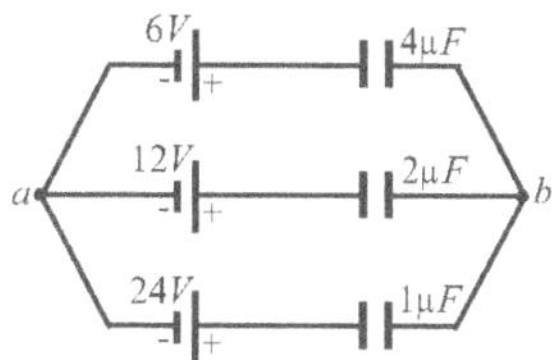


**Ans.** – 10.3 V.

7. An infinite circuit is formed by the repetition of same link consisting of two identical capacitors, each of capacitance $C$. Calculate the effective capacitance between points $x$ and $y$.

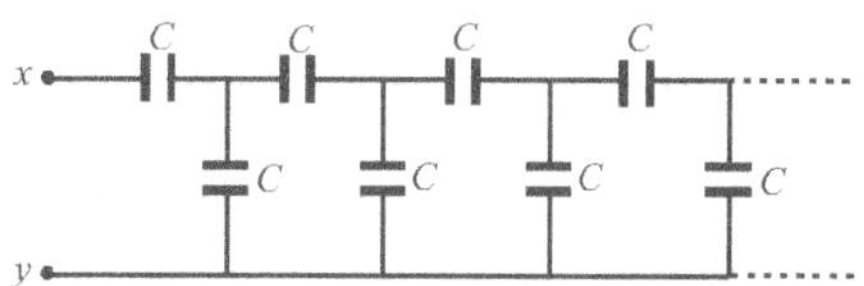


**Ans.** 0.618 $C$.

8. Find the equivalent capacitance of given network of capacitors between $A$ and $B$. Each capacitor has capacitance $C = 1\ \mu F$.

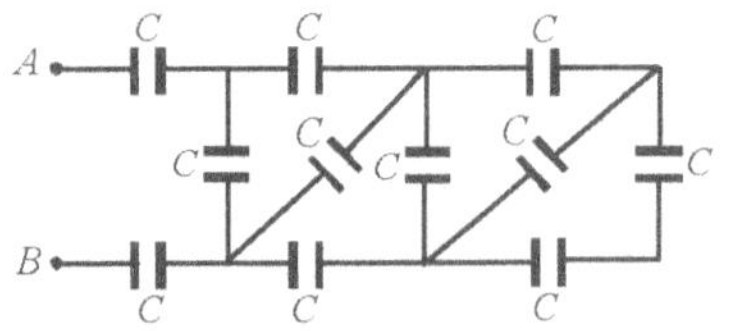

*Ans.* 0.38 μF.

9. A metal sphere of radius $R$ is charged to a potential $V$.
   (a) Find the electrostatic energy stored in the electric field within a concentric sphere of radius 2 $R$.
   (b) Show that the electrostatic field energy stored outside the sphere of radius 2 $R$ equals that stored within it.

*Ans.* (a) $\pi\varepsilon_0 RV^2$.

10. A parallel-plate capacitor having plate area 20 cm$^2$ and separation between the plates 1.00 mm is connected to a battery of 12.0 $V$. The plates are pulled apart to increase the separation to 2.0 mm.
   (a) Calculate the charge flown through the circuit during the process.
   (b) How much energy is absorbed by the battery during the process ?
   (c) Calculate the stored energy in the electric field before and after the process.
   (d) Using the expression for the force between the plates, find the work done by the person pulling the plates apart.
   (e) Show and justify that no heat is produced during this transfer of charge as the separation is increased.

*Ans.* (a) $1.06 \times 10^{-10}$ C (b) $12.7 \times 10^{-10}$ J, (c) $12.7 \times 10^{-10}$ J, $6.35 \times 10^{-10}$ J, (d) $6.35 \times 10^{-10}$ J.

11. Figure shows two parallel plate capacitors with fixed plates and connected to two batteries. The separation between the plates is the same for the two capacitors. The plates are rectangular in shape with width b and lengths $l_1$ and $l_2$. The left half of the dielectric slab has a dielectric constant $k_1$ and the right half $k_2$. Neglecting any friction, find the ratio of the emf of the left battery to that of the right battery for which the dielectric slab may remain in equilibrium.

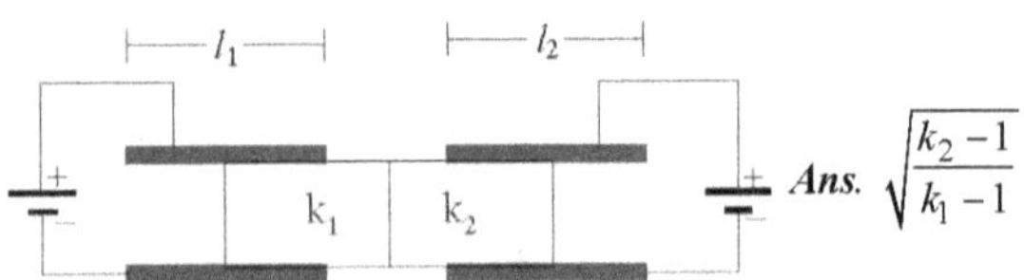

*Ans.* $\sqrt{\dfrac{k_2 - 1}{k_1 - 1}}$

12. A 5.0 μF capacitor is charged to 12 $V$. The positive plate of this capacitor is now connected to the negative terminal of a 12 $V$ battery and vice versa. Calculate the heat developed in the connecting wires.

*Ans.* 1.44 mJ.

13. A radioactive source in the form of a metal sphere of diameter $10^{-3}$ m emits β particles at a constant rate of $6.25 \times 10^{10}$ particles per second. If the source is electrically insulated, how long will it take for its potential to rise by 1.0 volt, assuming that 80% of emitted β particles escape from the surface.

*Ans.* 6.95 μs.

14. The capacitance of a variable radio capacitor can be changed from 50 $pF$ to 950 $pF$ by turning the dial from $0^0$ to $180^0$. With the dial set at $180^0$, the capacitor is connected to a 400 V battery. After charging, the capacitor is disconnected from the battery and the dial is turned at $0^0$.
   (a) What is the potential difference across the capacitor when the dials reads $0^0$ ?
   (b) How much work is required to turn the dial, if friction is neglected ?

*Ans.* (a)7600 $V$ (b) $1.368 \times 10^{-3}$ J.

15. Two square metallic plates of 1 m side are kept 0.01 m apart, like a parallel plate capacitor, in air in such a way that one of their edges is perpendicular to an oil surface in a tank filled with in an insulating oil. The plates are connected to a battery of emf 500 $V$. The plates are then lowered vertically into the oil at a speed of 0.001 m/s. Calculate the current drawn from the battery during the process (dielectric constant of oil = 11, $\varepsilon_0 = 8.85 \times 10^{-12}$ C$^2$/N–m$^2$).

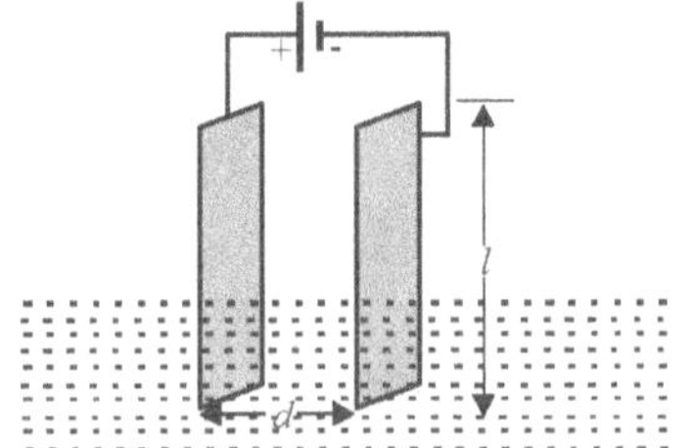

*Ans.* $4.425 \times 10^{-9}$ A.

16. (a) Find the capacitance of a spherical capacitor, if the outer sphere is charged and the inner sphere is earthed. Given radius of inner sphere = $a$, radius of outer sphere = $b$.
   (b) Two conducting spheres are placed concentrically. The inner sphere is earthed and the outer given a charge 30 nC. The radii of sphere are 8 cm and 10 cm. What is the charge on the inner sphere? Will there be any charge on the inner surface of the outer sphere ? Explain.

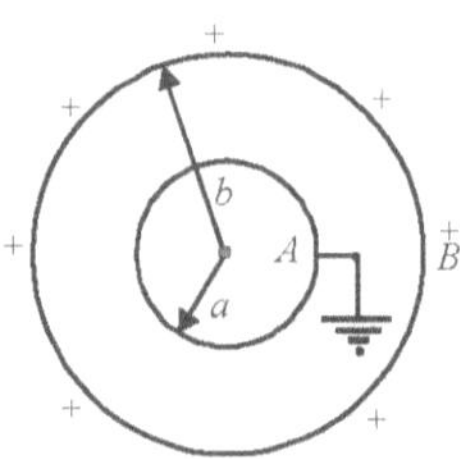

*Ans.* (a) $4\pi\varepsilon_0\left(\dfrac{b^2}{b-a}\right)$, (b) –24 $nC$.

17. The lower plate of a parallel plate capacitor lies on an insulating plane. The upper plate is suspended from one end of a balance. The two plates are joined together by a thin wire and subsequently disconnected. The balance is achieved. A voltage $V = 5000\ V$ is applied between the plates, what additional weight should be placed to maintain the balance? The separation between the plates $d = 5$ mm and the area of each plate, $A = 100\ \text{cm}^2$.

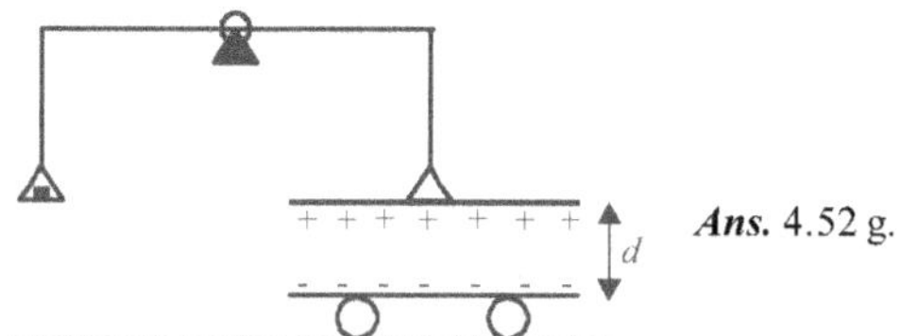


**Ans.** 4.52 g.

18. The two capacitors $C_1$ and $C_2$ are made of square plates of edge $l$. The separation between the plates of capacitors are $d_1$ and $d_2$ as shown in figure. A potential difference V is applied between the points $a$ and $b$. An electron is projected between the plates of the upper capacitor along the central line. With what minimum speed should the electron be projected so that it does not collide with any plate. Consider the effect of only dielectric forces.

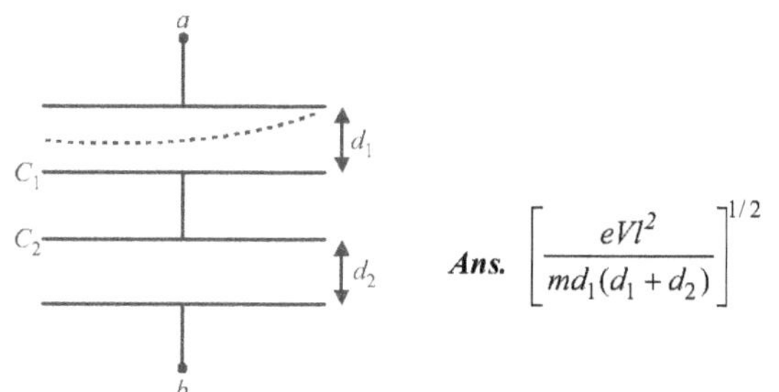


**Ans.** $\left[\dfrac{eVl^2}{md_1(d_1+d_2)}\right]^{1/2}$

19. Find the potential difference between points $A$ and $B$ of the system shown in figure. If emf is equal to $\xi = 110\ V$ and the capacitance ratio $\dfrac{C_2}{C_1} = \eta = 2.0$.

**Ans.** $\dfrac{\xi}{(1+3\eta+\eta^2)} = 10V$.

20. A circuit has a section $AB$ shown in figure. The emf of the source $\xi = 10\ V$, the capacitor capacitances are equal to $C_1 = 1.0\ \mu F$, $C_2 = 2.0\ \mu F$, and the potential difference $V_A - V_B = 5.0$ V. Find the voltage across each capacitor.

**Ans.** $V_1 = \dfrac{q}{C_1} = 10V$, $V_2 = \dfrac{q}{C_2} = 5V$,

where $q = \dfrac{(V_A - V_B + \xi)C_1C_2}{(C_1+C_2)}$.

21. In a circuit shown in figure find the potential difference between the left and right plates of each capacitor.

**Ans.** $V_1 = \dfrac{(\xi_2-\xi_1)}{\left(1+\dfrac{C_1}{C_2}\right)}$, $V_2 = \dfrac{(\xi_1-\xi_2)}{\left(1+\dfrac{C_2}{C_1}\right)}$.

22. Determine the potential difference $V_A - V_B$ between points $A$ and $B$ of the circuit shown in figure. Under what condition is it equal to zero ?

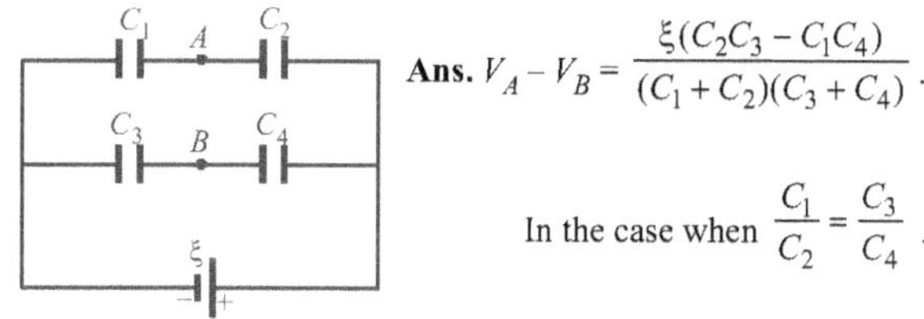


**Ans.** $V_A - V_B = \dfrac{\xi(C_2C_3 - C_1C_4)}{(C_1+C_2)(C_3+C_4)}$.

In the case when $\dfrac{C_1}{C_2} = \dfrac{C_3}{C_4}$.

23. Find the potential difference $V_A - V_B$ between points $A$ and $B$ of the circuit shown in figure.

**Ans.** $V_A - V_B = \dfrac{(C_2\xi_2 - C_1\xi_1)}{(C_1+C_2+C_3)}$

24. Determine the potential at point 1 of the circuit shown in figure assuming the potential at the point $O$ to be equal to zero. Using the symmetry of the formula obtained, write the expressions for the potentials at point 2 and 3.

**Ans.**

$$V_1 = \frac{\xi_2C_2 + \xi_3C_3 - \xi_1(C_2+C_3)}{(C_1+C_2+C_3)}$$

$$V_2 = \frac{\xi_1C_1 + \xi_3C_3 - \xi_2(C_1+C_2)}{C_1+C_2+C_3},$$

$$V_3 = \frac{\xi_1C_1 + \xi_2C_2 - \xi_3(C_1+C_2)}{C_1+C_2+C_3}.$$

25. What charges will flow after the shorting of the switch $S$ in the circuit illustrated as shown in the figure through sections 1 and 2 in the directions indicated by the arrows ?

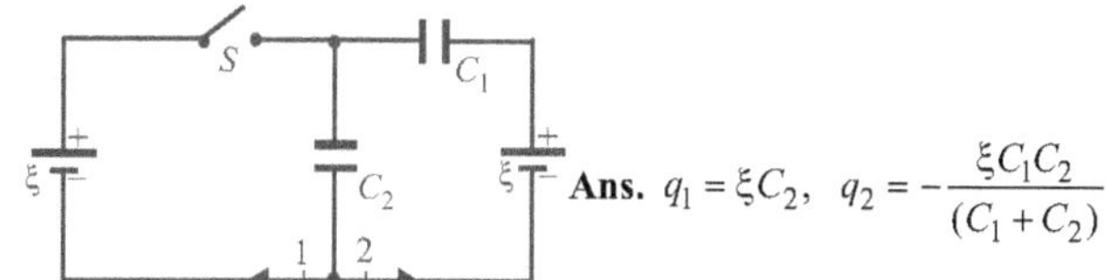


**Ans.** $q_1 = \xi C_2$, $q_2 = -\dfrac{\xi C_1C_2}{(C_1+C_2)}$

**26.** A conducting sphere $S_1$ of radius $r$ is attached to an insulating handle. Another conducting sphere $S_2$ of radius $R$ is mounted as an insulating stand, $S_2$ is initially uncharged. $S_1$ is given a charge $Q$, brought into contact with $S_2$ and removed. $S_1$ is recharged such that the charge on it is again $Q$ and is again brought into contact with $S_2$ and removed. This procedure is repeated n times.

(a) Find the electrostatic energy of $S_2$ after n such contacts with $S_1$.

(b) What is the limiting value of this energy as $n \to \infty$.

***Ans.*** (a) $U_n = \dfrac{q_n^2}{8\pi \in_0 R}, q_n = \dfrac{QR}{r}\left[1-\left(\dfrac{R}{R+r}\right)^n\right]$ (b) $\dfrac{Q^2 R}{8\pi\varepsilon_0 r^2}$ .

**27.** The circular plates $A$ and $B$ of a parallel plate air capacitor have a diameter of 0.1 m and are 2 x $10^{-3}$ m apart. The plates $C$ and $D$, of a similar capacitor have a diameter of 0.12 m and are 3 x $10^{-3}$ m apart. Plate A is earthed. Plates $B$ and $D$ are connected together. Plate $C$ is connected to the positive pole of a 120 $V$ battery whose negative is earthed. Calculate

(a) the combined capacitance of the arrangement and

(b) the energy stored in it.

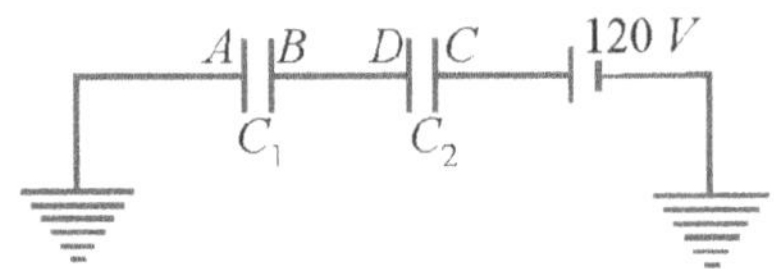


**Ans.** (a) 17 μF, (b) 12.24 × $10^{-8}$ J.

**28.** Two parallel plate capacitors $A$ and $B$ have the same separation $d$ = 8.85 × $10^{-4}$ m between the plates. The plate areas of $A$ and $B$ are 0.04 $m^2$ and 0.02 $m^2$ respectively. A slab of dielectric constant (relative permittivity) $k$ = 9 has dimensions such that it can exactly fill the space between the plates of capacitor $B$.

(i) The same dielectric slab is now placed inside $A$ as shown in figure. $A$ is then charged to a potential difference of 110 $V$. Calculate the capacitance of $A$ and the energy stored in it.

(ii) The battery is disconnected and then the dielectric slab is removed from $A$. Find the work done by the external agancy is removing the slab from $A$.

(iii) The same dielectric slab is now placed inside $B$, filling it completely. The two capacitors $A$ and $B$ are then connected as shown in figure. Calculate the energy stored in the system.

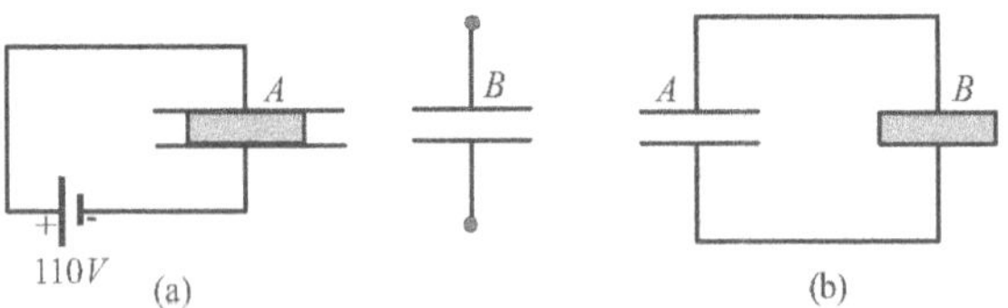


***Ans.*** (i) 2 × $10^{-9}$ $F$, 1.21 × $10^{-5}$ J (ii) 6.05 × $10^{-9}$ J, 4.84 × $10^{-5}$ J (iii) 100 V, 1.1 × $10^{-5}$ J.

# Hints & Solutions

## Solutions EXERCISE 2.1 LEVEL -1

1. (b)
2. (d) The capacitance of each of (a), (b) and (c) is equal to C. The capacitance of (d) is $\frac{7C}{3}$.
3. (d) $q_1 = C_1V, q_2 = C_2V$, and $q_3 = \left(\frac{C_1C_2}{C_1+C_2}\right)V$.
   As $C_1 > C_2$, $\therefore q_1 > q_2 > q_3$.
4. (c) The p.d. across each capacitor, $= \frac{V}{2}$.
   So capacitance, $C = \frac{Q}{V/2} = \frac{2Q}{V}$.
5. (d) $C = \frac{\epsilon_0 A}{d}$; when $d \to \infty$, $C \to 0$
6. (d) If $C'$ is the capacitance of each capacitor, then $\frac{C'}{2} = 2C$,
   $\therefore C' = 4C$.
   Now in parallel, equivalent capacitance $= 8C$.
7. (c) For isolated capacitor, charge on it remains some and so electric bulb between then, $E = \frac{\sigma}{\epsilon_0}$ remains constant.
8. (b) If $V$ is the potential applied across the capacitor, then p.d. across each capacitor will be $V/2$. Energy,
   $U = \frac{1}{2}C\left(\frac{V}{2}\right)^2$. When dielectric is inserted, then
   $$V_1 + V_2 = V \quad ...(i)$$
   and
   $$CV_1 = k\,CV_2 \quad ....(ii)$$
   On solving above equations, we get
   $V_2 = \left(\frac{V}{k+1}\right)$, $V_1 = \left(\frac{kV}{k+1}\right)$
   Now energy of the capacitor, A
   $$U_A = \frac{1}{2}CV_1^2 = \frac{1}{2}CV^2\frac{k^2}{(k+1)^2}$$
   It represents, that energy of capacitor $A$ will increase.
9. (c) $V' = \frac{V}{k} = \frac{V}{8}$, $\therefore k = 8$.
10. (d) For $V_1 = V_2$ or $\frac{kQ_1}{R_1} = k\frac{Q_2}{R_2}$ or $Q_1R_2 = Q_2R_1$, there is no flow of change between the spheres, and so no loss of electrical energy.
11 .(c) The energy resides between the plates of capacitor.
12. (c) The capacitance of smaller drop of radius $r$,
   $$C = 4\pi\epsilon_0 r.$$
   The radius of bigger drop,
   $$\frac{4}{3}\pi R^3 = 8 \times \frac{4}{3}\pi r^3 \Rightarrow R = 2r$$
   Thus
   $$C' = 4\pi\epsilon_0(2r) = 2C.$$
13.(a)
$$V = E_1t_1 + E_2t_2 = \frac{\sigma}{k_1\epsilon_0}t_1 + \frac{\sigma t_2}{k_2\epsilon_0} = \frac{Q}{A\epsilon_0}\left(\frac{t_1}{k_1} + \frac{t_2}{k_2}\right)$$
14. (b) Given, $C = \frac{\epsilon_0 A}{d} = 1\,pF$
   Now $C' = \frac{\epsilon_0 kA}{(2d)} = 2pF$.
   $\therefore$ $k = 4$.
15. (b) Increase in energy of capacitor $= \frac{1}{2}C[V_f^2 - V_i^2]$
16. (c) $= \frac{1}{2} \times 6 \times 10^{-6}[20^2 - 10^2] = 9 \times 10^{-4}J$.
17. (d) When capacitor in removed from the battery its change becomes constant. Its energy $U = \frac{Q^2}{2C}$. As $C$ decreases with increase in separation of plates and so $U$ will increase.
18. (c) Work done = energy stored $= \frac{1}{2}CV^2$.
19. (b) Energy stored $= n \times \frac{1}{2}CV^2$.
20. (a) $W = U = \frac{q^2}{2C} = \frac{(8\times10^{-18})^2}{2\times100\times10^{-6}} = 32\times10^{-32}J$
21. (d) P.d. across the capacitors in series.
   $= V + V = 2V$.
22. (a) The capacity of the capacitors in parallel is $10\,\mu F$, and capacity of two capacitors in series is $1\,\mu F$. Thus equivalent capacitance
   $C = \frac{1\times10}{1+10} = \frac{10}{11}\mu F$.
23. (c) As $C_2$ and $C_3$ are in parallel and so,
   $V_2 = V_3$. Thus $V = V_1 + V_2 = V_1 + V_3$.
   Also $Q_1 = Q_2 + Q_3$.
24. (a) In the given circuit all the capacitors are in parallel, and so $C = 4 \times 8 = 32\,\mu F$.
25. (d) The equivalent circuit is shown in figure. Then

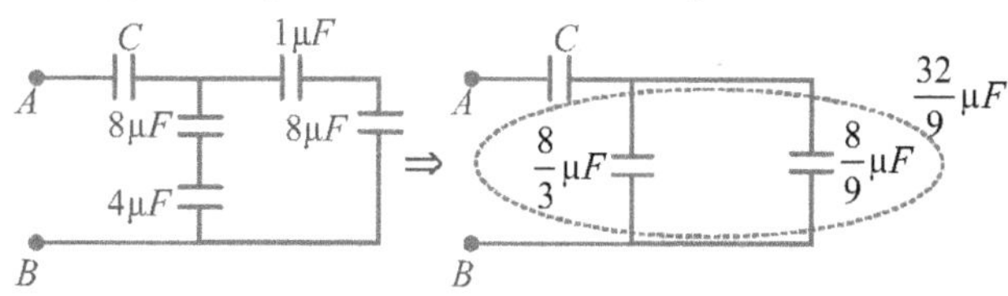

$$\frac{C \times \frac{32}{9}}{C + \frac{32}{9}} = 1, \quad \text{or} \quad C = \frac{32}{23}\mu F$$

$C = 4 \times 8 = 32\ \mu F.$

26. (b) $5\mu F$ capacitor is ineffective, and so equivalent capacitance, will be
$C_{PQ} = 1\mu F.$

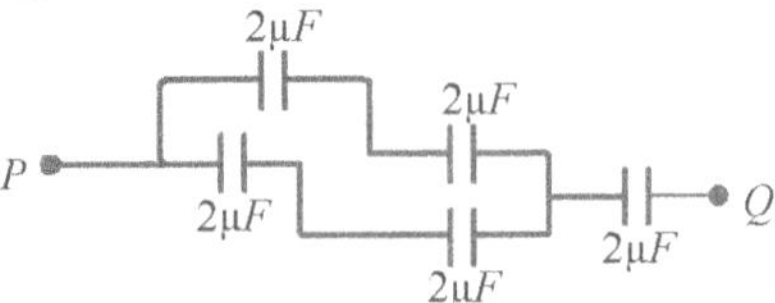


27. (a) $C_{PQ} = 3C.$

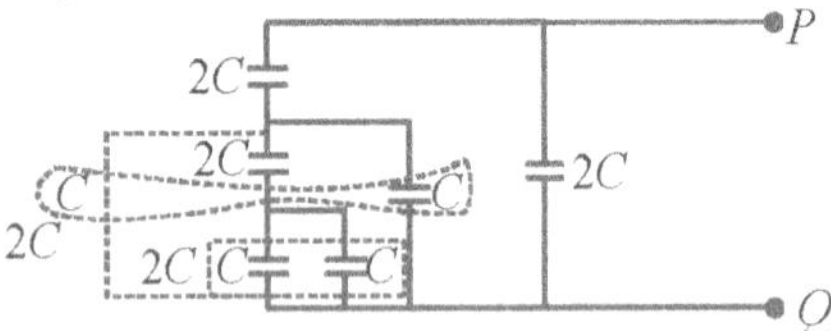


28. (d) $C_{AB} = 5\mu F.$

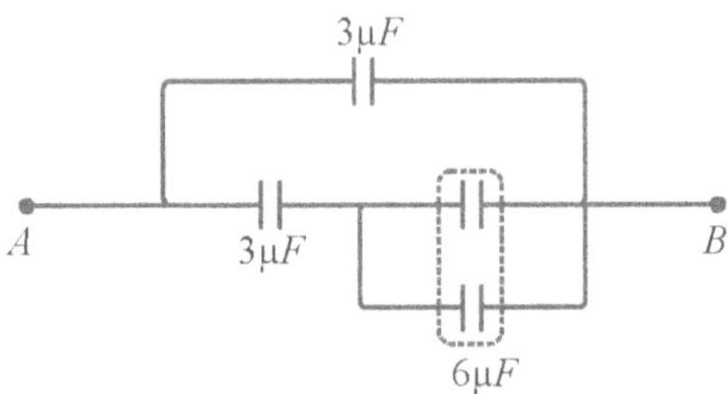


29. (c) Common potential, $V = \left(\frac{CV_1 + CV_2}{C + C}\right) = \left(\frac{V_1 + V_2}{2}\right)$

The decrease in energy of the system

$= U_i - U_f$

$$= \left[\frac{1}{2}CV_1^2 + \frac{1}{2}CV_2^2\right] - \frac{1}{2}(C + C)\left[\frac{V_1 + V_2}{2}\right]^2$$

$$= \left[\frac{1}{2}CV_1^2 + \frac{1}{2}CV_2^2\right] - \frac{1}{2}(C + C)\left[\frac{V_1 + V_2}{2}\right]^2$$

$$= \frac{1}{4}C(V_1 - V_2)^2$$

30. (a) These is no flow of charge between plates $A$ and $B$ because positive plate attracts the negative plate.

31. (c) $V = \frac{1}{4\pi\epsilon_0}\left[\frac{q}{R} - \frac{(-q)}{R}\right] = \frac{q}{2\pi\epsilon_0 R}.$

Now, $C = \frac{q}{V} = 2\pi\ \epsilon_0\ R.$

32. (d) $V = 0$, and so $C = \frac{q}{V} \to \infty.$

33. (c) $R_{eq} = \frac{6 \times 3}{6 + 3} = 2\Omega.$

The time constant, $C = CR_{eq} = \frac{1}{5} \times 2 = 0.4$ s

Now, $V = V_0(1 - e^{-t/\tau})$
$= 10(1 - e^{-1/0.4}) = 8V.$

34. (c) $q = it = 1 \times 4 = 4C$. So, $C = \frac{q}{V} = \frac{4}{4} = 1F.$

35. (a) When dielectric is inserted between the plates, capacitance will increase and so $V = \frac{q}{C}$, will decrease ($q$ constant).

36. (a)

37. (c) The common potential, $V' = \frac{CV - CV}{C + C} = 0.$

Thus loss of energy $= \left(\frac{1}{2}CV^2 + \frac{1}{2}CV^2\right) - \frac{1}{2}(2C)(0)^2$
$= CV^2$

38. (c) $U = \frac{1}{2}CV^2 = \frac{1}{2} \times 2 \times 10^{-6} \times (100)^2 = 0.01J.$

So heat produced, $= 0.01J.$

39. (b) Power delivered,

$$P = \frac{U}{t} = \frac{\frac{1}{2}CV^2}{t} = \frac{\frac{1}{2} \times 40 \times 10^{-3} \times (3000)^2}{2 \times 10^{-3}}.$$

$= 90 \times 10^3\ W.$

40. (b) The equivalent circuit is shown in figure.
$C_{AB} = 3\mu F.$

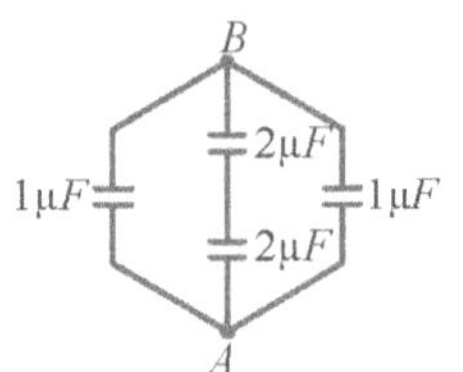


41. (c) $V_1 + V_2 = 1200$
and $3V_1 = 6V_2$

3μF 6μF
A — P — B
$V_1$ $V_2$

On solving above equations, we have
$V_1 = 800$V and $V_2 = 400$V
Now $V_P - V_B = 400$ ;
As $V_B = 0$, $\therefore V_P = 400$ V

42. (b) The current in the circuit, $i = \frac{\varepsilon}{(R + r)}$. The *p.d.* across $R$,

$V = iR = \left[\frac{\varepsilon R}{R + r}\right]$. This potential difference will equally divided across the capacitors, and so potential difference across each capacitor, $V = \frac{\varepsilon R}{2(R + r)}$.

43. (c) The common potential,

$$V' = \frac{CV + 2CV}{kC + 2C} = \left(\frac{3V}{k + 2}\right).$$

## Solutions EXERCISE 2.1 LEVEL -2

1. (a) 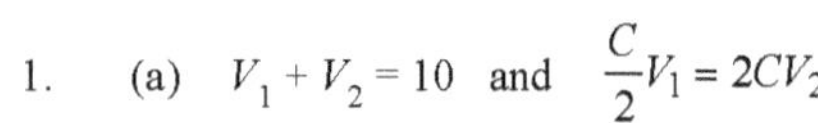
$V_1 + V_2 = 10$ and $\frac{C}{2}V_1 = 2CV_2$

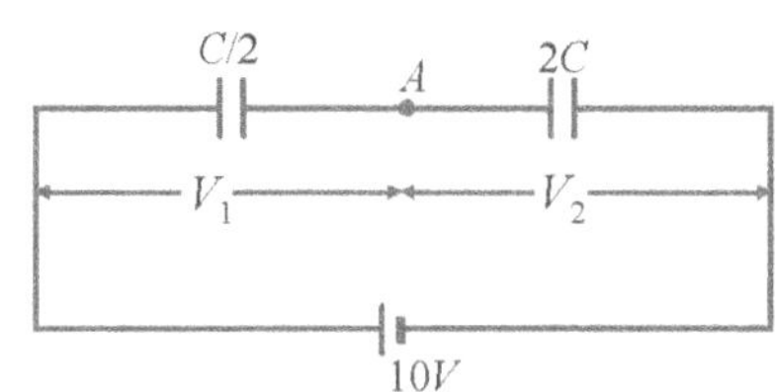


On solving, above equations, we get
$V_1 = 8V$ and $V_2 = 2V$.

2. (c)

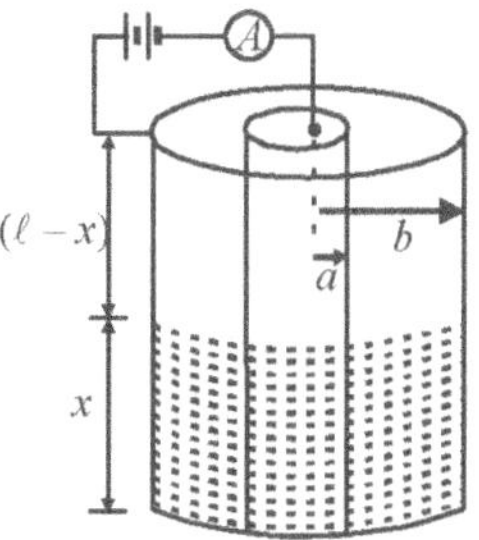


$q = CV$

$$= \left[\frac{\varepsilon_0 (l - x)}{\ell n\left(\frac{b}{a}\right)} + \frac{\varepsilon_0\, x\, k}{\ell n\left(\frac{b}{a}\right)}\right] V$$

Now $i = \frac{dq}{dt}$

$$= \frac{\varepsilon_0}{\ell n\left(\frac{b}{a}\right)}(k - 1)\left(\frac{dx}{dt}\right) V$$

As $\frac{dx}{dt}$ depends on the area of the hole, so $i$ in the circuit depends on area of the hole.

3. (d) Circuit I : $C = \frac{2 \times 4}{2 + 4} = \frac{4}{3}\mu F,\ R = \frac{1 \times 2}{1 + 1} = \frac{2}{3}\Omega.$

$$\tau_1 = CR = \frac{4}{3} \times \frac{2}{3} = \frac{8}{9}\mu s.$$

Circuit II : $C = 2 + 4 = 6,\ R = 1 + 2 = 3\Omega.$
$\tau_2 = CR = 6 \times 3 = 18\ \mu s.$

Circuit III : $C = 2 + 4 = 6\ \mu F,\ R = \frac{1 \times 2}{1 + 2} = \frac{2}{3}\Omega$

$$\tau_3 = CR = 6 \times \frac{2}{3} = 4\mu s.$$

4. (a) $A = 4L^2$, and $C = \frac{\epsilon_0 A}{d} = \frac{\epsilon_0 (4L^2)}{d}$

$$C' = \frac{\epsilon_0 (2L \times L)}{d} = \frac{\epsilon_0 A/2}{d}$$

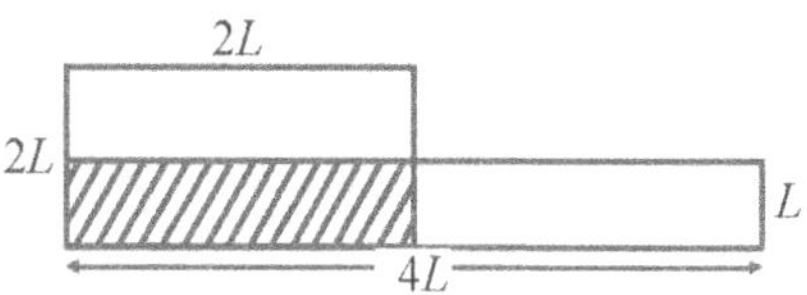


5 .(c) Displacement current, $i_d = \epsilon_0 A\left(\frac{dE}{dt}\right)$

From $t = 0$ to $4\ \mu s$,

$$i_d = 8.85 \times 10^{-12} \times 1 \times \frac{0.4 \times 10^6}{y \times 10^{-6}} = 0.885\ A\ .$$

From $t = 4\mu s$ to $8\mu s$, $i_d = 8.85 \times 10^{-12} \times 1 \times 0 = 0$

6. (b) Initially; $C = \frac{\epsilon_0 A}{d}, Q = CV = \frac{\epsilon_0 AV}{d}$.

After removed from the battery,

$$C' = kC = \frac{\epsilon_0 kA}{d},\quad Q' = \frac{\epsilon_0 AV}{d} = Q$$

$$V' = \frac{V}{k},\ \text{and}\ E' = \frac{E}{k} = \frac{V}{kd}.$$

$$W = U_f - U_i = \frac{\epsilon_0 AV^2}{2d}\left(1 - \frac{1}{k}\right)$$

7. (a) Common potential, $V = \left[\frac{C_1 V_0 + 0}{C_1 + C_2}\right] = \frac{C_1 V_0}{C_1 + C_2}$

Now $$\frac{U_i}{U_f} = \frac{\frac{1}{2}C_1 V_0^2}{\frac{1}{2}(C_1 + C_2)V_0^2} = \left[\frac{C_1 + C_2}{C_1}\right].$$

8. (d) The equivalent circuit is shown in figure.

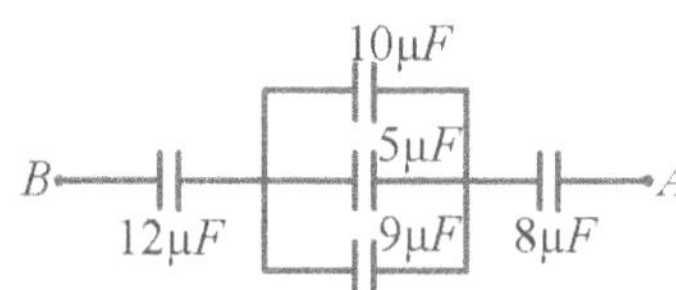


$$\frac{1}{C_{AB}} = \frac{1}{12} + \frac{1}{24} + \frac{1}{8}$$

or $C_{AB} = 4\mu F$
Also $V_1 + V_2 + V_3 = 60$
and $12V_1 = 24V_2 = 8V_3$, $\therefore V_2 = 10V$
Now $q = 5 \times 10 = 50\ \mu C.$

9. (c) Change stored on capacitor $C_1$, $q_1 = C_1 V = 6 \times 20 = 120\ \mu C.$
Common potential when switch $S_2$ is closed and $S_1$ is opened,

$$V = \left[\frac{120 + 0}{6 + 3}\right] = \frac{120}{9}V$$

Now, change on $C_2$, $q_2 = C_2 V = 3 \times \frac{120}{9} = 40\mu C.$

10. (c)

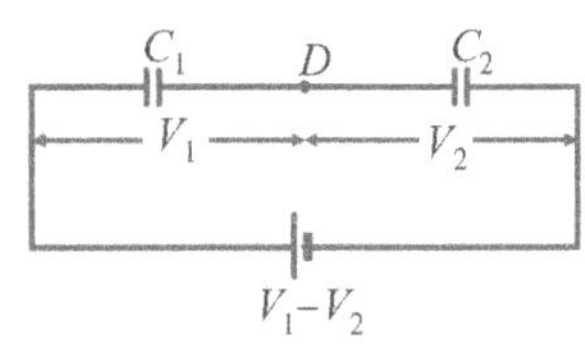


$$V_1' + V_2' = V_1 - V_2$$

and $\quad C_1 V_1' = C_2 V_2'$

On solving above equations, we get

$$V_1' = \left[\frac{(V_1 - V_2)C_2}{C_1 + C_2}\right]$$

Now $V_1 - V_D = \dfrac{(V_1 - V_2)C_2}{C_1 + C_2}$

$$\therefore\ V_D = \left[\frac{C_1 V_1 + C_2 V_2}{C_1 + C_2}\right].$$

11. (a) The current in 2Ω resistor, $i = \dfrac{2}{2} = 1A$

P.d. across 2Ω resistor, $V = 2 \times 1 = 2V$.
Charge on the capacitor, $q = 10 \times 2 = 20\ \mu C$.

12. (b) The equivalent capacitance, $C_{eq} = 2C = 2\ \dfrac{\epsilon_0 A}{d}$

$$= \frac{2 \times 8.85 \times 10^{-12} \times 50 \times 10^{-4}}{3 \times 10^{-3}}$$

$= 2.95 \times 10^{-11} F$

Now energy stored, $U = \dfrac{1}{2} C_{eq} V^2$

$$= \frac{1}{2} \times 2.95 \times 10^{-11} \times 12^2$$

$= 2.1 \times 10^{-9}\ J$.

13. (b) The current in $R_2$,

$$i = \left[\frac{V}{R_1 + R_2}\right]$$

p.d. across capacitor = p.d. across $R_2$

$$iR_2 = \left[\frac{VR_2}{R_1 + R_2}\right].$$

14. (b) Common potential, $V = \dfrac{Q}{C_1 + 2C_1} = \dfrac{Q}{3C_1}$

Now charge, $Q_1 = C_1 V = \dfrac{Q}{3}$,

and $\quad Q_2 = C_2 V = \dfrac{2Q}{3}$

15. (d) To get 1000V from 250V capacitor, we need four capacitors in series. Their capacitance becomes 2μ$F$. To get 16μF, we have to connect 8 series, each of 4 capacitors in parallel. So total number of capacitors is $8 \times 4 = 32$.

16. (c) The charge on the plates are shown in figure. The capacitance between neighbouring two plates, $C = \dfrac{\epsilon_0 A}{d}$ charge on plate 1, $q_1 = +CV = \dfrac{\epsilon_0 AV}{d}$, and $q_2 = -2CV = \dfrac{-2\epsilon_0 AV}{d}$.

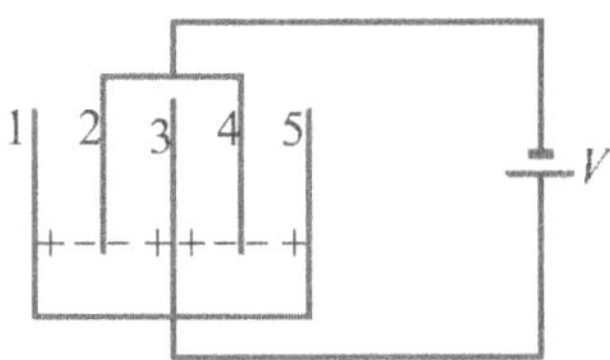


17. (c) The equivalent circuit is shown in figure.
$V_1 + V_2 = 100$
and $2V_1 = 6V_2$

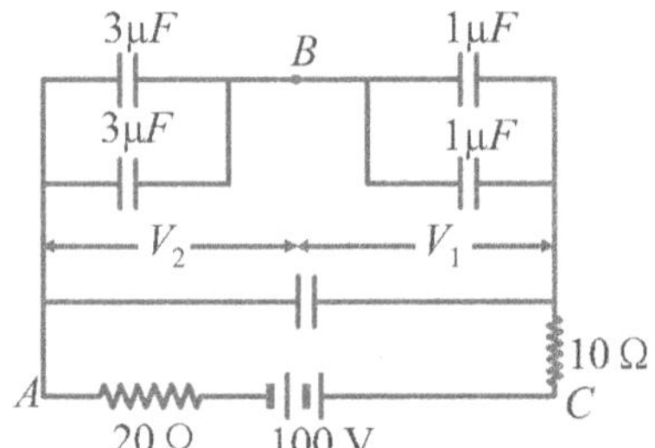


On solving above equations, we get
$V_1 = 75V,\ V_2 = 25V$

18. (c) Common potential, $V' = \dfrac{-CV + 2C \times 2V}{C + 2C} = V$

Final energy of the system of capacitor,

$$U = \frac{1}{2}(C + 2C)V^2$$

$$= \frac{3}{2}CV^2.$$

19. (b) The capacitance of condenser $A$ without dielectric will be,

$$C = \frac{15}{15} = 1\mu F.$$

Common potential, $V = \dfrac{15 \times 100 + 1 \times 100}{1 + 1} = 800\ V$.

20. (c) The charges, $Q_2 = Q_3$.
The potential difference between the plates,

$$V = \frac{Q_2}{C} = \frac{Q_2 + Q_2}{2C} = \left(\frac{Q_2 - Q_3}{2C}\right).$$

21. (d) Charges on the capacitors will redistribute only when all the three switches will be closed.

22. (b) $\dfrac{1}{2}CV^2 = ms\Delta T$

$$\therefore\quad V = \sqrt{\frac{2ms\Delta t}{C}}.$$

23. (a) $\quad 4V_1 = 12$

or $\quad V_1 = 3V$.

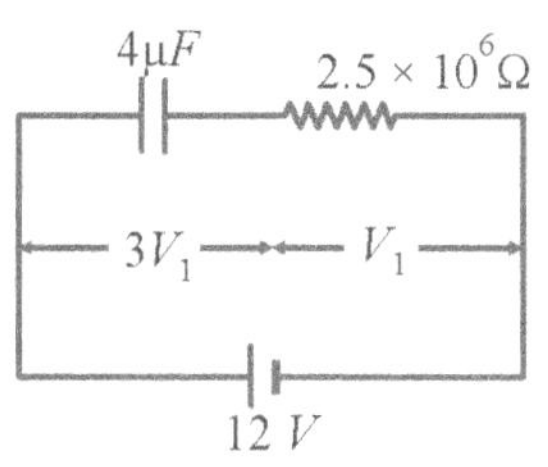


Time constant, $\tau = CR$
$= 4 \times 10^{-6} \times 2.5 \times 10^{6} = 10s$

We have, $V = V_0 (1 - e^{-t/\tau})$

or $9 = 12(1 - e^{-t/10})$

or $e^{t/10} = 4$

or $\frac{t}{10} = \ell n 4$

$\therefore$ $t = 10 \times 2\ell n2$
$= 20 \times 0.693 = 13.86s$

24. (c) From the graph, we have
$V_1 > V_2$, also $q_1 = q_2 = q$

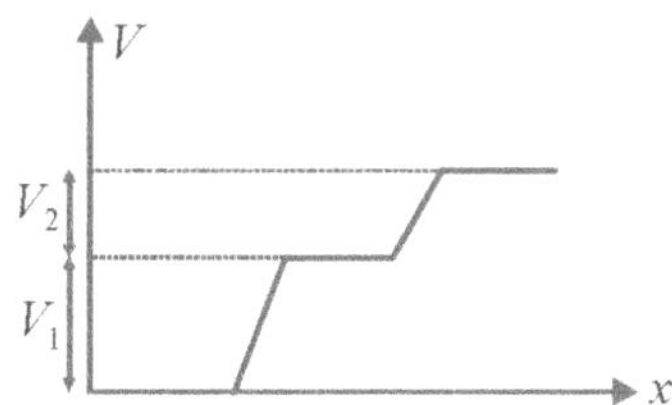


Thus $C_1 = \frac{q}{V_1}$ and $C_2 = \frac{q}{V_2}$

As $V_1 > V_2$, $\therefore C_1 < C_2$.

25. (b) We know that,
$i = i_0 e^{-t/\tau} = i_0 e^{-t/RC}$.

or $\ell n\, i = \ell n\, i_0 - \frac{t}{RC}$

or $\ell n\, i = \ell n\left(\frac{\varepsilon}{R}\right) - \frac{t}{RC}$ ...(i)

when resistance is doubled,

$\ell n\, i' = \ell n \frac{\varepsilon}{2R} - \frac{t}{2RC}$ ...(ii)

Thus $Q$ represents the correct graph.

26. (b) The equivalent resistance, $R_{eq} = \frac{6 \times 12}{6 + 12} + 2 + 2 = 8\Omega$.

Now time constant, $\tau = C_{eq}R_{eq} = \frac{1}{2} \times 8 = 4s$.

27. (c) The change at any time, $q = CV$
$= C \times 150(1 - e^{-20t})$

Current, $i = \frac{dq}{dt} = 150C[0 - \times(-20)e^{-20t}]$

or $i = 3000\, Ce^{-2t}$

or $1.14 \times 10^{-3} = 3000\, C\, e^{-20 \times 0.05}$

or $C = \frac{1.14 \times 10^{-3} \times e^{20}}{3000} = 1.03 \times 10^{-6} F$

28. (b) Given, $\frac{\epsilon_0 A}{d} = 9pF$

$C_1 = \frac{\epsilon_0 k_1 A}{d/3} = (3 \times 3)\frac{\epsilon_0 A}{d} = 9 \times 9 = 81pF$

and $C_2 = \frac{\epsilon_0 k_2 A}{2d/3} = \frac{3 \times 6}{2}\frac{\epsilon_0 A}{d} = 9 \times 9 = 81pF$

Now $C = \frac{C_1 C_2}{C_1 + C_2} = \frac{81}{2} = 40.5\ pF$.

29. (a) The effective circuit is shown in figure.

$C_{AB} = \frac{7}{8}\mu F$.

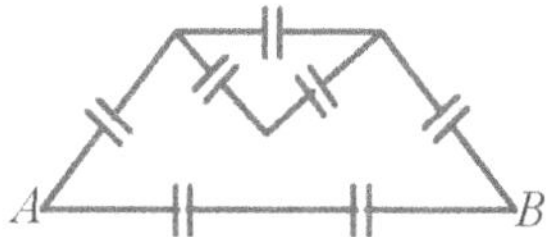


30. (a) The equivalent circuit is shown in figure

Thus $C_{ab} = C = \frac{\epsilon_0 A}{d}$.

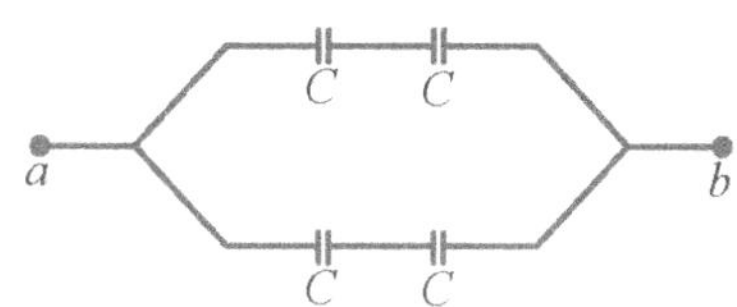


31. (a) The equivalent circuit is shown in figure
$C_{AB} = 6C = 6 \times 2 = 12\ \mu F$

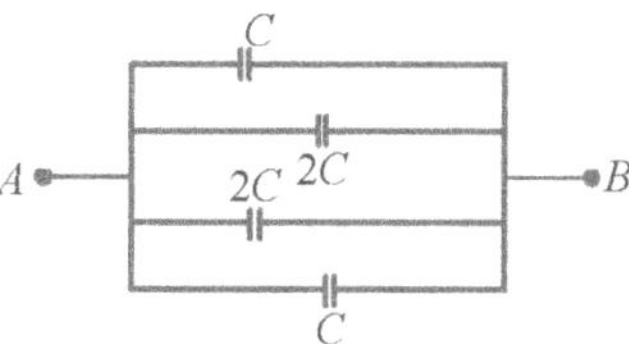


32. (b) $C_1 = 3\mu F$, $C_2 = 4\mu F$ and $C_3 = 2\mu F$.
$V_1 + V_2 = V$
and $3V_1 = 6V_2$

3μF 6μF
V₁ V₂

$\therefore$ $V_2 = V/3$ and $V_1 = \frac{2V}{3}$.

Energy stored, $V_1 = \frac{1}{2}C_1V_1^2 = \frac{1}{2} \times 3 \times \left(\frac{V}{3}\right)^2 = \frac{V^2}{6}$

and $V_2 = \frac{1}{2}(C_1 + C_2)V_2^2 = \frac{1}{2} \times 6 \times \left(\frac{2V}{3}\right)^2 = \frac{4V^2}{3}$.

33. (c) When key is on the position $BD$, the situation is shown in the figure.

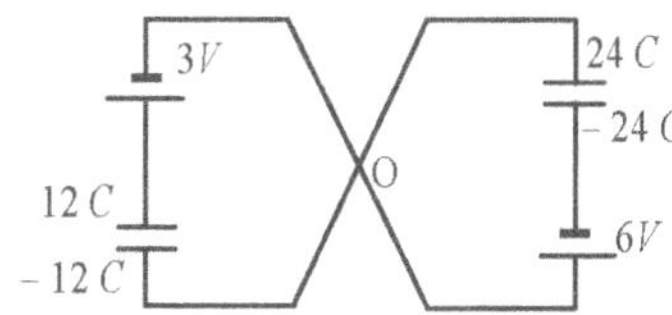

When key is on the position $AD$, the situation is shown in the figure.

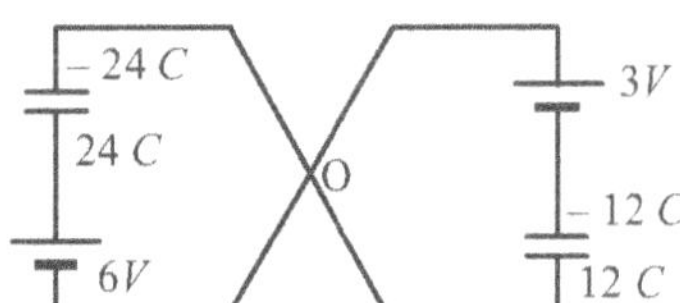


The charge flows to each capacitor is 36 $\mu C$, and so total charge flows through point O is 72 $\mu C$.

34. (c) Before closing of the switch, $i = \frac{9}{9}\ 1A$,

$V_1 + V_2 = 9$ and $3V_1 = 6V_2$,
$\therefore\ V_1 = 6V,\ V_2 = 3V$.
Charge $q_1 = 3 \times 6 = 18\ \mu C$, and $q_2 = 6 \times 3 = 18 \mu C$
The charge at the junction $x$, $q_i = 18 - 18 = 0$.
After closing the switch,

$$i = \frac{9}{9} = 1A,\ V_1 = 3 \times 1 = 3V \text{ and } V_2 = 6 \times 1 = 6V,$$

$q_1 = 3 \times 3 = 9\ \mu C$ and $q_2 = 6 \times 6 = 36\ \mu C$.
Now final charge at junction $x$,
$q_f = -9 + 36 = 27\ \mu C$.
The flow of charge from $y$ to $x$,
$\Delta q = q_f - q_i = 27 - 0 = 27 \mu C$.

35. (b) The effective circuit is shown in figure.

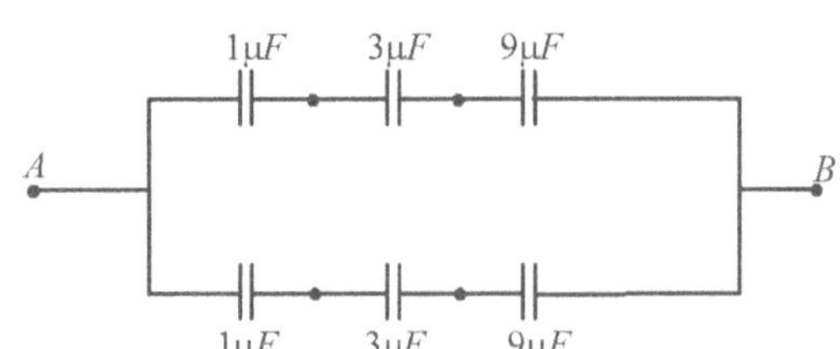


The capacitance of upper series,

$$\frac{1}{C} = \frac{1}{1} + \frac{1}{3} + \frac{1}{9} + \frac{1}{27} + - - - - \infty$$

$$\therefore\ C = \frac{2}{3} \mu C$$

$$\text{Now } C_{AB} = 2C = \frac{4}{3} \mu F$$

36. (a) At any time, the level of liquid

$x_1 = \left(\frac{d}{3} - vt\right)$, and the thickness of the air

$$x_2 = d - \left(\frac{d}{3} - vt\right) = \left(\frac{2d}{3} + vt\right).$$

Now $C = \frac{C_1 C_2}{C_1 + C_2}$; where $C_1 = \frac{\epsilon_0 kA}{x_1}$, and $C_2 = \frac{\epsilon_0 A}{x_2}$.

Time constant $\tau = CR = \left[\frac{6\epsilon_0 R}{5d + 3vt}\right]$

37. (b) The effective circuit is shown in the figure

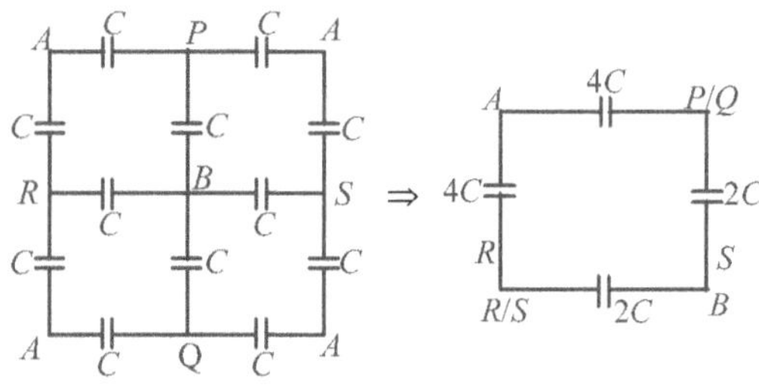


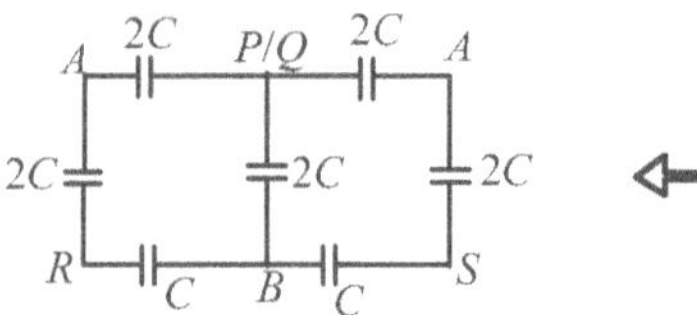


$$\text{Now } C_{AB} = 2 \times \frac{4C \times 2C}{4C + 2C} = \frac{8C}{3}.$$

38. (b) $C' = \frac{C}{2}$

$$\therefore\ W = U_f - U_i = \frac{Q^2}{2(C/2)} - \frac{Q^2}{2C} = \frac{Q^2}{2C}$$

39. (c) The maximum charge delivered to the circuit
$q = CV + 2CV = 3CV$

The equivalent capacitance, $C' = \left[\frac{3C \times 6C}{3C + 6C}\right] = 2C$

The external emf, $\xi = \frac{q}{C'} = \frac{3CV}{2C} = 1.5V$

40. (a) The effective circuit is shown in figure.
The effective resistance across $C$ is

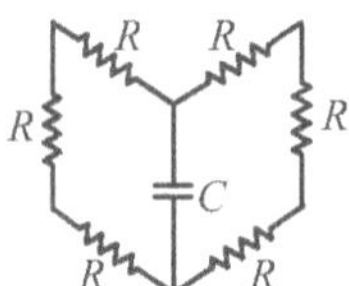


$$R_{eq} = \frac{3R}{2} = 1.5\ R$$

$$\therefore\ \tau = C_{eq} R_{eq} = 1.5\ CR$$

41. (c) At steady state, the current in the resistors are shown in figure.

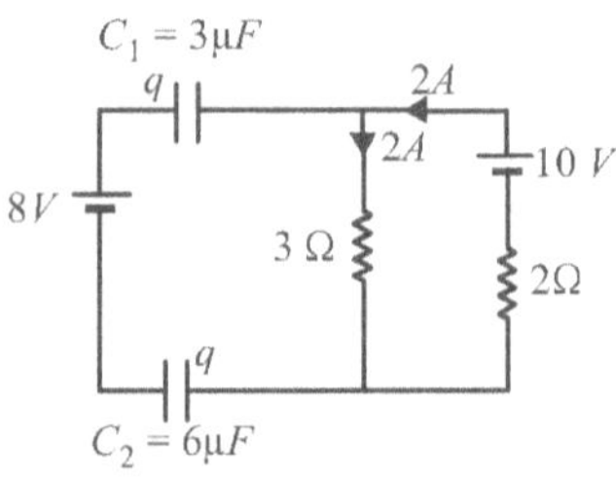


If $q$ be the charge on each of the capacitor, then

$$8 - \frac{q}{3} - 2 \times 3 - \frac{q}{6} = 0$$

$\therefore q = 4\ \mu C$

42. (d) For no current in galvanometer at any time, then

$$\frac{2}{6} = \frac{\frac{1}{3}}{\frac{1}{C}}$$

$\therefore C = 1\ \mu F$

43. (a) Current in $R_2$, $i = \frac{1}{2} \times \frac{20}{3} e^{-\frac{t}{2\times3}} = \frac{10}{3} e^{-\frac{t}{6}}$

$$H = \int_0^{\infty} i^2 R dt$$

$$= \frac{100}{9} \int_0^{\infty} e^{-\frac{t}{3}} \times 2dt$$

$$= \frac{200}{9} \left| \frac{e^{-\frac{t}{3}}}{\left(-\frac{1}{3}\right)} \right|_0^{\infty}$$

$$= \frac{200}{3} \mu J$$

44. (a) After making a short in place of cell, the circuit is shown in figure.

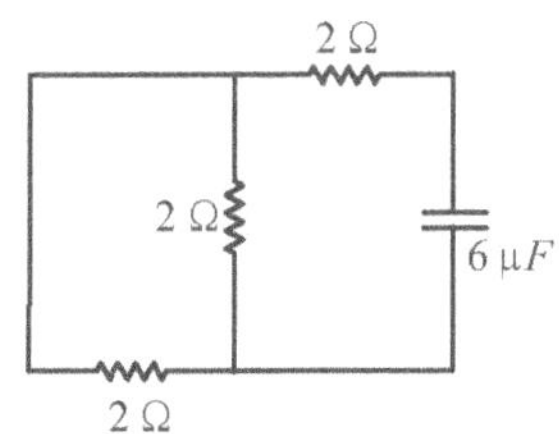


$R_{eq} = 3\Omega$, $C_e = 6\mu F$
$\therefore \tau = C_{eq} R_{eq}$
$= 6 \times 3 = 18\ \mu s$
The current in $R_3$,

$$i = i_0 e^{-t/\tau}$$

or $\frac{i_0}{e} = i_0 e^{-t/\tau}$

or $t = \tau = 18\ \mu s$

45. (a) Just after closing of switch, capacitors offers zero resistance and , so current

$$i = \frac{V}{3R}.$$

46. (b) $\tau = CR = 6 \times 10^{-6} \times \left(\frac{8 \times 4}{8+4}\right) = 16 \times 10^{-6} s$

If $i$ is the current in capacitor arm, then

$$i = i_0 e^{-t/\tau}$$

$$= \frac{\varepsilon}{R} e^{-t/\tau}$$

$$= \frac{160/6}{32/12} e^{-\left(\frac{16\times10^{-6}}{16\times10^{-6}}\right)} = \frac{10}{e} A$$

If $i_1$ and $i_2$ are the currents in $4\Omega$ and $8\Omega$ respectively, then

$$i_1 + i_2 = \frac{10}{e} \quad \ldots \text{(i)}$$

and $\quad 4i_1 = 8\, i_2 \quad \ldots \text{(ii)}$

After solving above equations, we get

$$i_1 = \frac{20}{3e} \text{ and } i_2 = \frac{10}{3e} A.$$

47. (d) Charge will flow from higher to lower potential and so it flows from positive terminal of battery towards negative terminal of the battery.

48. (b) The potential difference

$$V = V_0 + \frac{Q/2}{C}$$

$$= 12 + \frac{10}{2 \times 1} = 17\ V.$$

49. (c) $U_i = U = \frac{1}{2} kCV^2 \quad \ldots \text{(i)}$

After disconnected from the battery and pulling the insulator.

$$U_f = \frac{k^2 CV^2}{2}$$

Now $\quad W = U_f - U_i$

or $\quad 4U = \frac{k^2 CV^2}{2} - U$

or $\quad \frac{k^2 CV^2}{2} = 5U \quad \ldots \text{(ii)}$

Solving equation (i) and (ii), we get

$$k = 5.$$

50. (d) The charge on the plates are shown in figure. The charge on plate 1V will be zero.

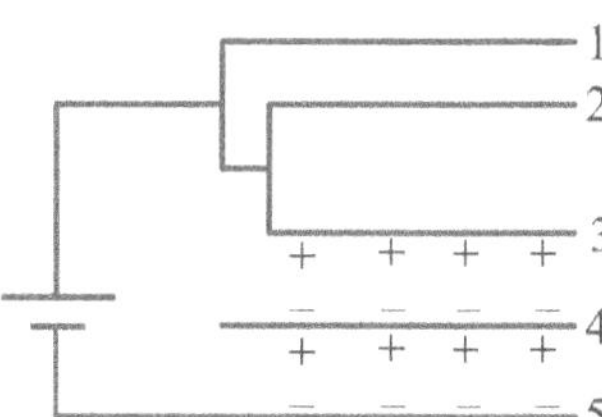


51. (c) The net charge on the capacitor in between $A$ and $B$ is $= \frac{Q}{2}$

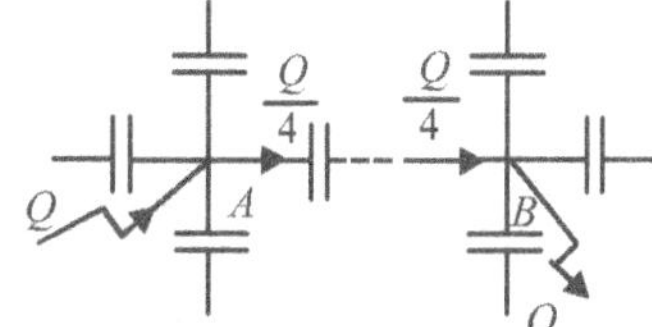

Now $\frac{Q}{C_{AB}} = \frac{\frac{Q}{2}}{C}$

$\therefore \quad C_{AB} = 2C.$

52. (d) **When $S$ and 1 are connected**

The $2\mu F$ capacitor gets charged. The potential difference across its plates will be $V$.

The potential energy stored in $2\ \mu F$ capacitor

$$U_i = \frac{1}{2}CV^2 = \frac{1}{2} \times 2 \times V^2 = V^2$$

**When S and 2 are connected**

The $8\mu F$ capacitor also gets charged. During this charging process current flows in the wire and some amount of energy is dissipated as heat. The energy loss is

$$\Delta U = \frac{1}{2}\frac{C_1 C_2}{C_1 + C_2}(V_1 - V_2)^2$$

Here, $C_1 = 2\mu F$, $C_2 = 8\ \mu F$, $V_1 = V$, $V_2 = 0$

$$\therefore\ \Delta U = \frac{1}{2} \times \frac{2 \times 8}{2+8}(V-0)^2 = \frac{4}{5}V^2$$

The percentage of the energy dissipated $= \frac{\Delta U}{U_i} \times 100$

$$= \frac{\frac{4}{5}V^2}{V^2} \times 100 = 80\%$$

53. (a) The p.d. across capacitor of $12\mu F$ will be,

$V = 10 + 10 - 20 = 0.$

So change on this capacitor, $q = 0$.

## Solutions EXERCISE 2.2

1. (b, c) There is a current between the plates of capacitor due to change in electric field between them, $i_d = \epsilon_0 A \frac{dE}{dt}$.

2. (b, d) The initial currents,

$i_{o1} = \frac{\varepsilon}{R}$, and $i_{o2} = \frac{\varepsilon}{R}$, and so $i_{01} = i_{02}$.

$\tau_1 = C_1 R = 1 \times R = R$ and $\tau_2 = C_2 \times R = 2R$.

As $t_2 > t_1$ and so second capacitor will take more time to discharge for same amount.

3. (a, c)

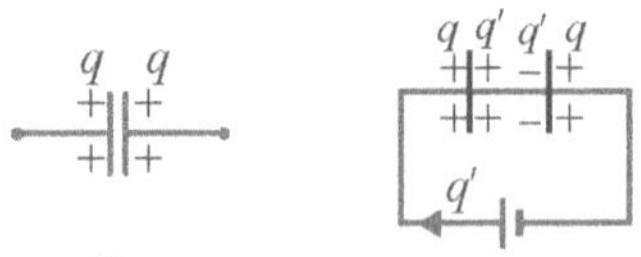

(i)

(ii)

4. (b, c) In case of isolated capacitor, charge on it remains same, while capacitance decreases with increase in separation between the plates, As $V = \frac{q}{C}$, and so $V$ will increase.

The electric field between the plates will not charge and so energy density, $\frac{1}{2}\epsilon_0 E^2$ remains the change.

5. (a, d) When battery remains connected, the potential difference, $V$ remains the same, while charge and energy on it will charge.

6. (b, c) In (1), the potential of the capacitors are : $V_L = \frac{6q}{2C} = \frac{3q}{C}$ and

$V_e = \frac{3q}{C}$. As $V_L = V_R$, and so there is no blow of charge in between the capacitors.

In (2), $V_L = \frac{6q}{3C} = \frac{2q}{C}$, and $V_R = \frac{3q}{C}$. As $V_R > V_L$, and so charge will below towards left capacitor.

7. (b, c)

8. (a, b) $\tau = CR$

$$= \frac{\epsilon_0 Ak}{d} \times \frac{\rho d}{A}$$

$$= \frac{\epsilon_0 k}{\sigma}.$$

$$i = \frac{V}{R} = \frac{q_0}{CR} = \frac{q_0}{k\frac{\epsilon_0 A}{d} \times \frac{\rho d}{A}} = \frac{q_0}{k\epsilon_0\rho} = \frac{\sigma q_0}{k\epsilon_0}.$$

9. (a, d) $C = \frac{6 \times 3}{6+3} + 2 = 4\mu F$

$V_1 + V_2 = 60$

and $\quad 6V_1 = 3V_2$

On solving above equations, we get, $V_1 = 20V$ and $V_2 = 40V$.

## Solutions EXERCISE-2.3

1. (a) On being negative, second conductor decreases the potential difference between the conductors. As $C = \frac{q}{V}$, and so $C$ increases.

2. (c) The capacitance of a capacitor does not depend on its charge given.

3. (d) Capacitance does not depend on charge only, while charge $Q$ is proportional to $V$.

4. (a) As these is no electric field inside the conductor, and so no energy inside it.

5. (a) Statement-2 is the correct explanation of statement-1.

6. (c) $C' = kC$, and so, $U' = \frac{1}{2}(kC)V^2 = kU$. Also $q' = C'V = kCV = kq$, and so charge density increases.

7. (c) Statement-2 is the correct explanation of statement-1.

8. (d) The charge on positive conductor is $q = \frac{Q_1 + Q_2}{2}$.

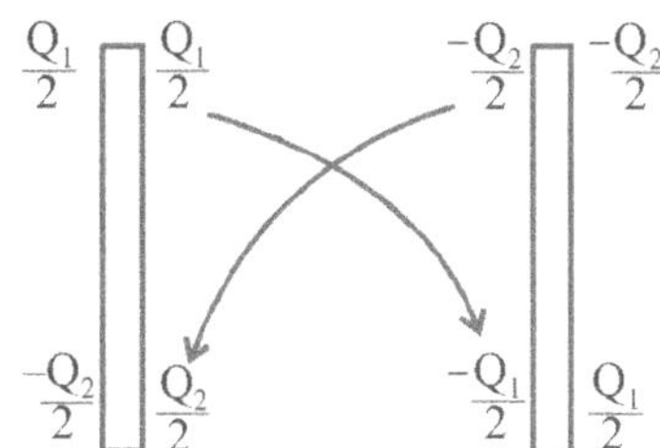


9. (d) Similar charge will reside on outer faces of the plates.

10. (c) $C' = kC$, and $U' = \frac{q^2}{2C'} = \frac{q^2}{2kC}$. With the introduction of dielectric, energy of the system decreases. As charge on the capacitor remains same, and so force between them remains same.

11. (a) $U = \frac{1}{2}CV^2$. In the battery connected capacitor $V$ remains constant while $C$ increases with the introduction of dielectric and so $U$ will increase.

## Solutions EXERCISE-2.4

**Passage for Q.1 to Q.3**

1. (d) When charge is given to inner shell and outer shell is earthed, the charge on inner face of outer shell will be $-Q$.
2. (b) If ($q$) is the charge on the inner shell, then

$$V = 0 = \frac{1}{4\pi \epsilon_0}\left[\frac{Q}{b} + \frac{q}{a}\right]$$

or $$q = -\frac{aQ}{b}.$$

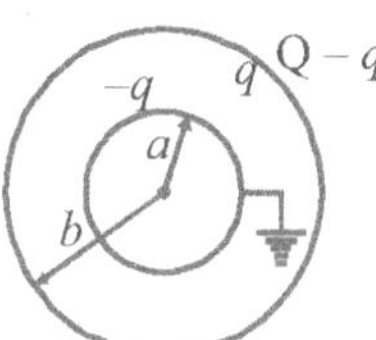


3. (d) $C = C_1 + C_2 = 4\pi \epsilon_0 \left(\frac{ab}{b-a}\right) + 4\pi \epsilon_0 b = 4\pi \epsilon_0 b^2$.

**Passage for Q.4 to Q. 6**

4. (d) Before closing the switch, the charge on each capacitor is same and equal to $q$, where

$$q = C \times 2\varepsilon$$

$$= \frac{2C_1C_2}{C_1 + C_2}\varepsilon.$$

5. (a) When switch is closed, the charge on capacitor $C_1$,

$$q_1 = C_1\varepsilon.$$

Now flow of charge through section 1.

$$\Delta q_1 = q_1 - q$$

$$= C_1\varepsilon - \left(\frac{2C_1C_2\varepsilon}{C_1 + C_2}\right)$$

$$= \frac{\varepsilon(C_1 - C_2)}{C_1 + C_2}$$

6. (b) Similarly flow of charge through section 2,

$$\Delta q_2 = C_2\varepsilon - \left(\frac{2C_1C_2\varepsilon}{C_1 + C_2}\right)$$

$$= \frac{\varepsilon C_2(C_1 - C_2)}{C_1 + C_2}.$$

**Passage for Q.7 to Q. 9**

7. (b) The initial charge on the capacitor,
$q_i = CV = 100 \times 24 = 2400\ \mu C$.
The final charge on the capacitor,
$q_f = CV = 100 \times 12 = 1200 \mu C$.
The flow of charge in the process
$\Delta q = q_f - q_i = 1200 - 2400 = -1200\ \mu C$.

8. (a) The decrease in electrostatic energy

$= U_i - U_f$

$= \frac{1}{2} \times 100 \times 10^{-6} \times 24^2 - \frac{1}{2} \times 100 \times 10^{-6} \times 12^2$

$= 21.6 \times 10^{-3}$ J.

9. (c) Work done by battery, $W = V(\Delta q)$

$= 12\ (-1200)$

$= -14.4$ mJ

Now $U_i + W = U_f +$ heat generated

or $28.8 - 14.4 = 7.2 + 4$

$\therefore$ H = 7.2mJ.

**Passage for Q.10 to Q. 12**

The simplified connections of the capacitors are shown in *fig*.

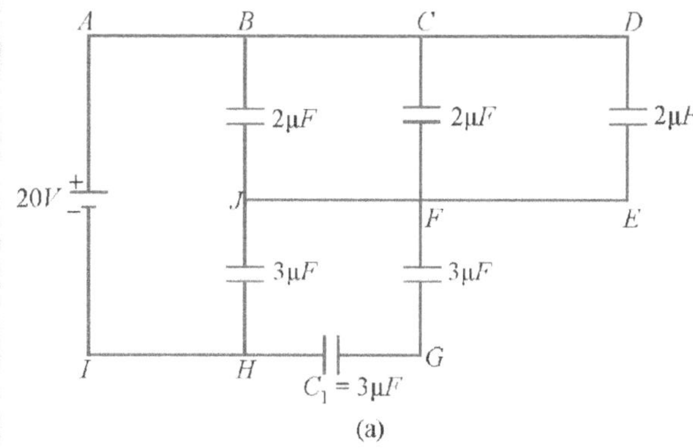


(a)

10 (d) The equivalent capacitance between $C$ and $F$ is 2μF.

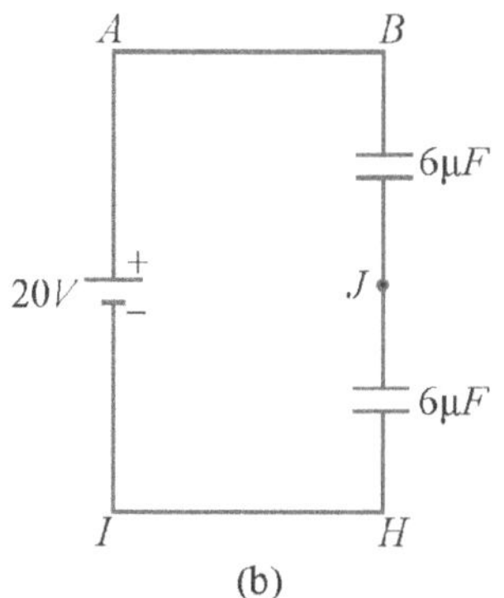


(b)

Capacitors across the arms *BJ*, *CF* and *DE* are in parallel, and so their equivalent capacitance is 6 μF. Similarly capacitors across *JH*, and *FG* are in parallel and so, their equivalent is 6 μF. Now 6 μF and 6 μF are in series across the battery, so their equivalent is capacitance 3 μF.

The charge stored on equivalent capacitor

$$Q = C_{eq} V = 3 \times 20 = 60\ \mu C \quad \textbf{Ans.}$$

11. (c) The potential of the battery is equally divided between the capacitors connected between *B* and *H*. Thus potential difference

$$V_{BJ} = V_{JH} = 10\ V.$$

The potential difference across capacitor 1

$$V_1 = 10\ V$$

and charge $Q_1 = C_1V_1 = 3 \times 10 = 30\ \mu C$ **Ans.**

12. (b) The potential difference across $C_2$ is also 10 V. Thus charge

$$Q_2 = C_2V_2 = 2 \times 10 = 20\ \mu C \quad \textbf{Ans.}$$

The potential difference across $C_3$ will be 5 *V* and so charge

$$Q_3 = C_3V_3 = 4 \times 5 = 20\ \mu C. \quad \textbf{Ans.}$$

**Passage for Q.13 to Q. 15**

13. (a) $V_1 + V_2 = 28$

and $6V_1 = 8V_2$

On solving above equations, we get

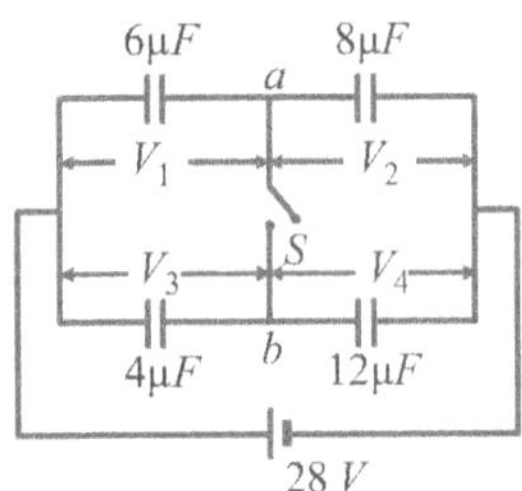


$V_1 = 16V,\ V_2 = 12V$

Also, $V_3 + V_4 = 28$

and $4V_3 = 12V_4$

On solving above equations, we get

$V_3 = 21\ V,\ V_4 = 7V.$

Thus $V_{ab} = V_2 - V_4 = 12 - 7 = 5V.$

14. (c) After closing of the switch,

$V_1 + V_2 = 28$

and $2.4\ V_1 = 4.8\ V_2$

$\therefore\ V_1 = 18.7V$

and $V_2 = 19.3V$

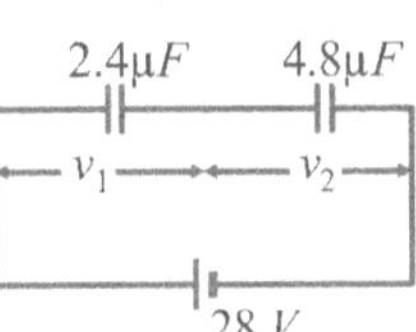


Thus potential of point *a*, $V_a = 9.3V.$

15. (b) Initial charge on the junction *a*,

$q_i = 6 \times 16 - 8 \times 12 = 0.$

Final charge at the junction *a*,

$q_f = 6 \times 18.7 - 8 \times 9.3$

$= 37.8\ \mu C.$

16. If V is the potential applied across the capacitor then p.d. across each capacitor will be $\frac{V}{2}$. When

A- p, s : dielectric is inserted in capacitor B, then

B- q, s : $V_1 + V_2 = V$

C- q, s : and $CV_1 = kCV_2$

D-p, s : On solving above equations, we get

$$V_1 = \left(\frac{kV}{k+1}\right) \text{ and } V_2 = \left(\frac{V}{k+1}\right).$$

Clearly potential of A increases and that of B decreases.

Initial charges on the capacitors are :

$$q_1 = \frac{CV}{2},\quad q_2 = \frac{CV}{2}$$

Find changes :

$$q_1' = CV_1 = \frac{kCV}{k+1}$$

and $$q_2' = \frac{CV}{k+1}.$$

Charge on capacitor A will increase, and on B will decrease.

17. See theory of the chapter.

18. A -r : W.d. by battery A, $= 2\left(\frac{1}{2}C_1V_1^2\right) = 2 \times 2^2 = 8J$

B-p : W.d. by battery B, $= 2\left[\frac{1}{2}CV_2^2\right]$

$$= 2\left[\frac{1}{2} \times \frac{4 \times 2}{4+2} \times 4^2\right]$$

$$= \frac{64}{3}J$$

C-s : $q_2 = CV = \left(\frac{4 \times 2}{4+2}\right) \times 4 = \frac{16}{3}$

D-q : $q_1 = C_1V_1 = 2 \times 2 = 4$

19. See theory of the chapter.

## Solutions EXERCISE-2.5

1. The equivalent capacitance,

$$C = 5+6 = 11\mu F.$$

The charge supplied by the battery,

$$q = CV$$
$$= 11\times10 = 110\ \mu C. \quad \textbf{Ans.}$$

2. For the equilibrium of the particle, we have

$$mg = Eq$$

$$\therefore \quad E = \frac{mg}{q}.$$

The potential difference across each capacitor is $\frac{V}{2}$,

$$\therefore \quad E = \frac{V}{2d}$$

So, $$\frac{V}{2d} = \frac{mg}{q}$$

Given, $$C = \frac{\epsilon_0 A}{d}, \quad \therefore d = \frac{\epsilon_0 A}{C}$$

Now $$\frac{V}{2\left(\frac{\epsilon_0 A}{C}\right)} = \frac{mg}{q}$$

or $$V = \frac{2\epsilon_0 A\ mg}{Cq}.$$

After substituting the values, we get

$$V = 43\ mV. \quad \textbf{Ans.}$$

3. The given circuit is:

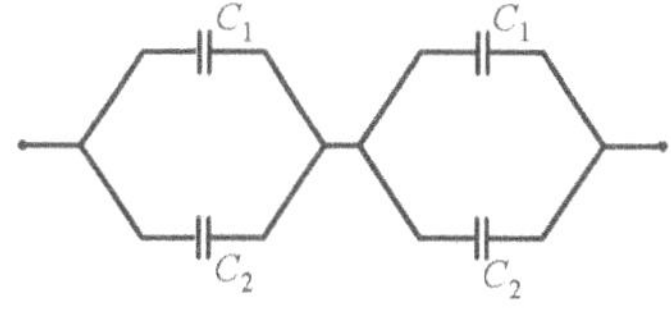


(a) The equivalent capacitance, $C$ is

$$\frac{1}{C} = \frac{1}{C_1+C_2} + \frac{1}{C_1+C_2}$$

$$\therefore \quad C = 5\mu F.$$

(b) Do this part similarly.

4. The equivalent circuit is shown in figure :

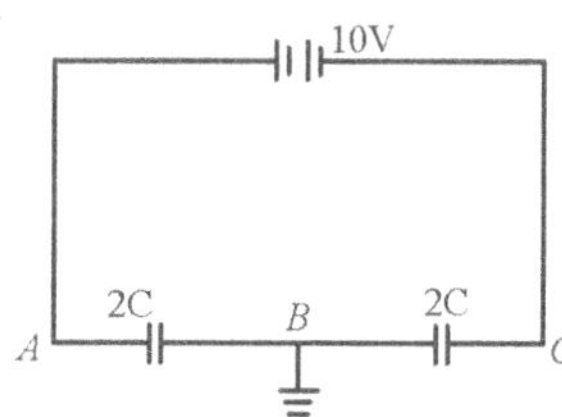


Let $$V_1 = V_A - V_B$$

and $$V_2 = V_B - V_C$$

$$V_1 + V_2 = 10\text{ V} \quad ...(i)$$

and $$(2C)V_1 = (2C)V_2 \quad ...(ii)$$

From equations (i) and (ii), we have

$$V_1 = 5V \text{ and } V_2 = 5V.$$

As $$V_B = 0, \quad \therefore V_A = 5V \text{ and } V_C = -5V.$$

5. The equivalent system of capacitors is shown in figure.

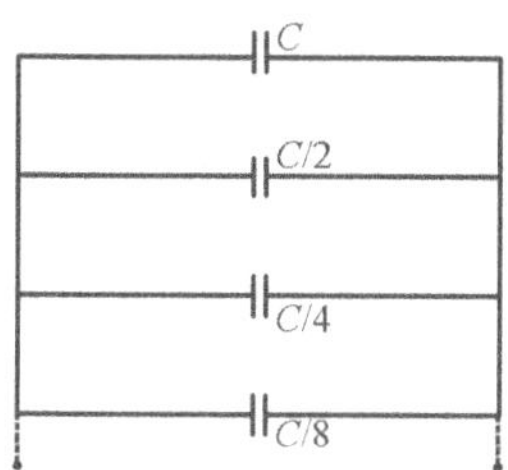


If $C'$ is the equivalent capacitance, then

$$C' = C + \frac{C}{2} + \frac{C}{4} + \frac{C}{8} + .......$$

$$= C\left[\frac{1}{1-\frac{1}{2}}\right] = 2C = 2\mu F \quad \textbf{Ans.}$$

6. If the equivalent capacitance between $A$ and $B$ is independent of the number of sections, then

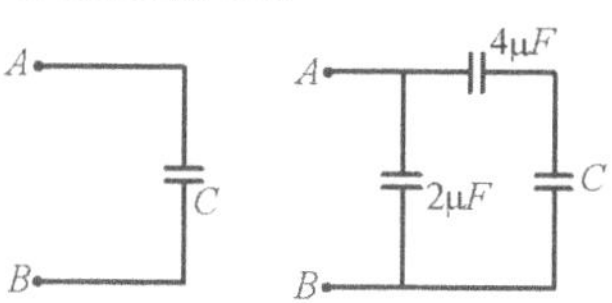


or $$C = 2 + \left[\frac{4C}{4+C}\right]$$

$$\therefore \quad C = 4\ \mu F. \quad \textbf{Ans.}$$

7. For the constant potential,

$$K = \frac{q'}{q} = \frac{50+100}{50} = 3. \quad \textbf{Ans.}$$

8. Initial energy stored in the capacitors

$$U_i = \frac{1}{2}C_1V_1^2 + \frac{1}{2}C_2V_2^2$$

$$= \frac{1}{2}\times0.1\times10^2 + \frac{1}{2}\times C_2\times0 = 5\text{ J}$$

After connection with identical capacitor, the common potential,

$$V' = \frac{C_1V_1+0}{C+C} = \frac{V_1}{2} = 5V.$$

The final energy stored, $$U_f = \frac{1}{2}(C+C)V^2$$

$$= CV^2 = 0.1^2\times5^2$$
$$= 2.5\text{ J}.$$

$$\therefore \quad \frac{U_f}{U_i} = \frac{2.5}{5} = \frac{1}{2}. \quad \textbf{Ans.}$$

## Solutions EXERCISE-2.6

1. (a) Let, $V_A - V_C = V_1$ and $V_C - V_B = V_2$

$\therefore \quad V_1 + V_2 = 50 \quad$ ...(i)

and $\quad 4V_1 = 8V_2$

or $\quad V_1 = 2V_2 \quad$ ...(ii)

From equations (i) and (ii), we have

$$V_1 = \frac{100}{3}V \text{ and } V_2 = \frac{50}{3}V.$$

As $V_B = 0$, $\therefore V_C = \frac{50}{3}V.$

Similarly $\quad V_D = \frac{50}{3}V.$

(b) The potential difference,

$$V_C - V_D = 0$$

2. The effective circuit is shown in figure

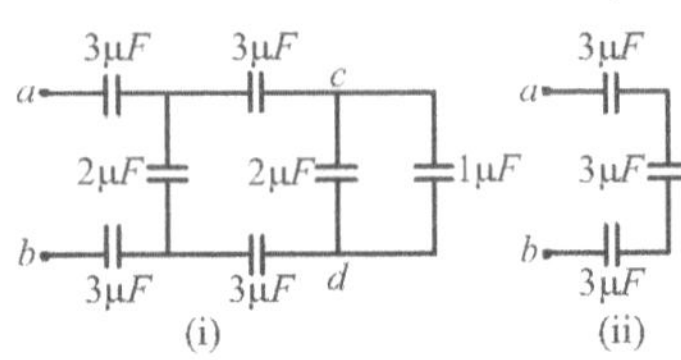


(a) Clearly the equivalent capacitance

$$C = 1\mu F.$$

(b) The p.d. across each of the capacitors nearest to $a$ and $b$ will be 300 V. So charge on each one, $q = 3 \times 300 = 900\ \mu C$.

(c) The p.d., $\quad V_{cd} = \frac{300}{3} = 100$ V. ***Ans.***

3. (a) The equivalent capacitance is given by

$$C = \left[\frac{2C_1C_2 + C_1C_3 + C_2C_3}{C_1 + C_2 + 2C_3}\right]$$

Here, $\quad C_1 = 1\mu F, C_2 = 3\mu F$ and $C_3 = 4\mu F.$

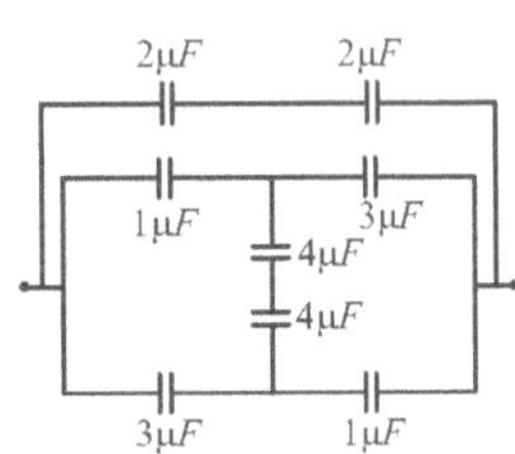


After substituting these values in above equation, we get

$$C = \frac{11}{6}\mu F.$$

(b) The effective circuit is : $C = \frac{11}{4}\mu F.$

4. (a) The given circuit can be redrawn as :

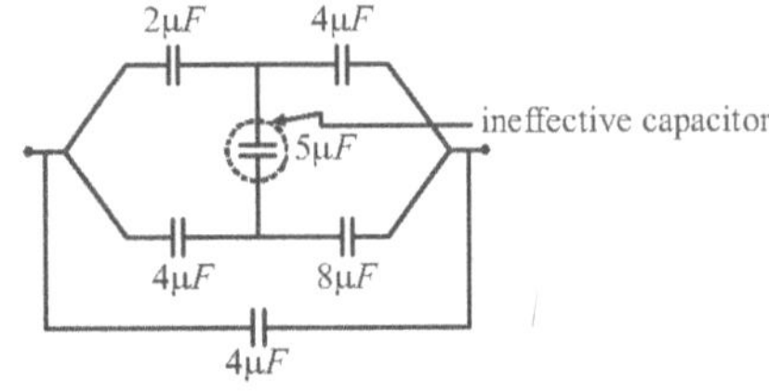


The equivalent capacitance of upper part of the circuit is

$$C_1 = \frac{4}{3} + \frac{8}{3} = 4\mu F.$$

The total capacitance, $C = 4 + 4 = 8\mu F.$

(b) The effective circuit is :

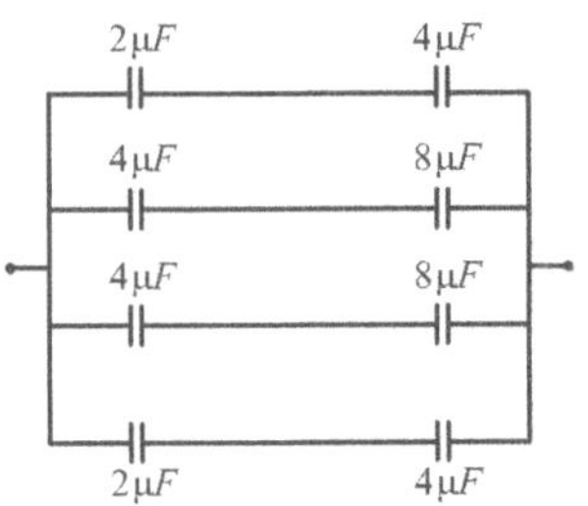


$$C = \frac{4}{3} + \frac{8}{3} + \frac{8}{3} + \frac{4}{3}$$

$$= 8\ \mu F.$$

5. (a) The given circuit can be drawn as :

If $V_1$ and $V_2$ be the p.d. across $2\mu F$ and $4\mu F$ respectively then

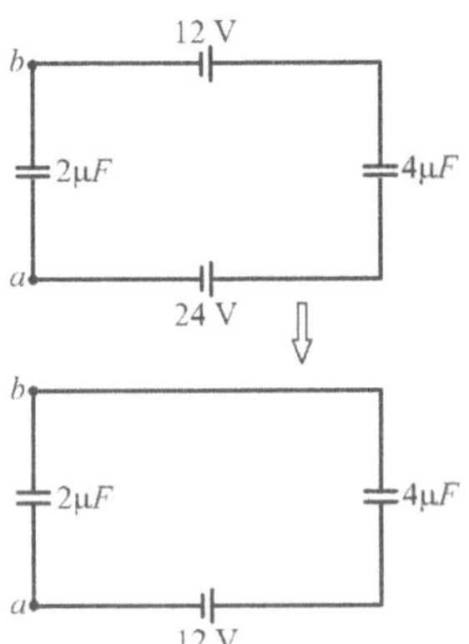


$V_1 + V_2 = 12$

and $\quad 2V_1 = 4V_2$

$\therefore \quad V_1 = 8V, V_2 = 4V.$

As $\quad V_1 = V_b - V_a \quad \therefore \quad V_a - V_b = -8V.$

(b) As both parts of the circuit are symmetrical, so the charges on then may be :

As the charge on the capacitor connected between $a$ and $b$ is zero, so $V_a - V_b = 0.$

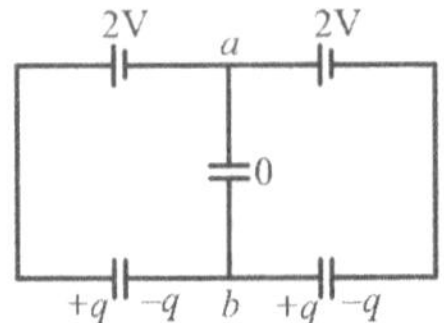

6. In close loop, $abcda$,

$$12+\frac{q_2}{2}-\frac{q_1}{4}-6 = 0$$

or $$q_1-2q_2 = 24 \quad ...(i)$$

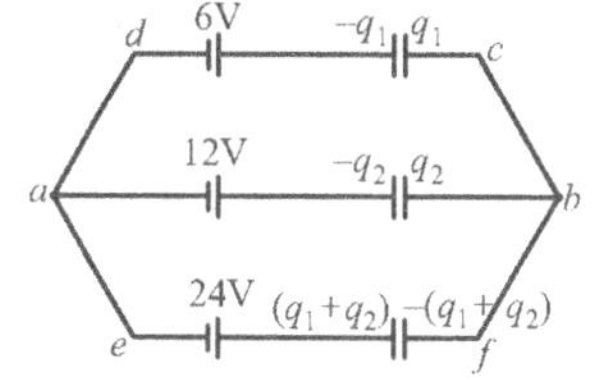


Now in close loop, $abfea$,

$$12+\frac{q_2}{2}+\frac{(q_1+q_2)}{1}-24 = 0$$

or $$2q_1+3q_2 = 24 \quad ...(ii)$$

From equations (i) and (ii), we get

$$q_2 = \frac{-24}{7}\mu C.$$

If $V_{ab}$ is the p.d. then $V_{ab} = -12+\frac{q_2}{2}=-10.3V.$ **Ans.**

7. If $C'$ is the equivalent capacitance, then

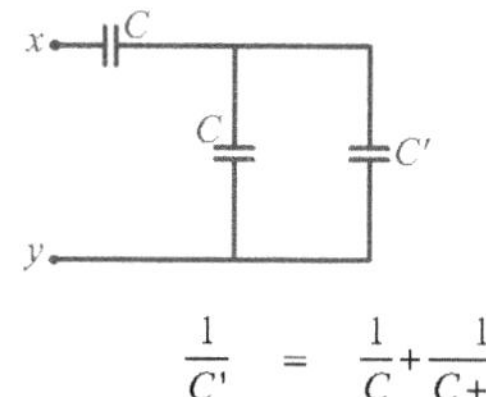


$$\frac{1}{C'} = \frac{1}{C}+\frac{1}{C+C'}$$

$\therefore$ $$C' = 0.618C.$$

8. The successive solution is shown in figure.

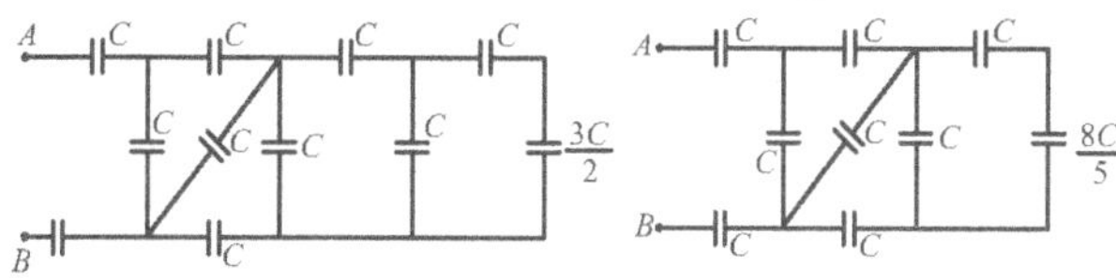


After simplifying, we get $C'=0.38\,\mu F.$ **Ans.**

9. (a) Given, $$V = \frac{1}{4\pi\epsilon_0}\frac{q}{R}.$$

The electric field due to sphere, at a distance $r$ from the centre of the sphere, $(r>R)$

$$E = \frac{1}{4\pi\epsilon_0}\frac{q}{r^2} = V\frac{R}{r^2}.$$

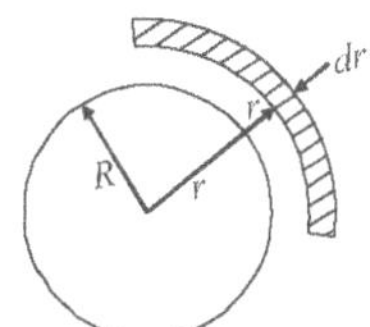


The electrical energy stored is given by

$$U = \int_R^{2R}\frac{1}{2}\epsilon_0 E^2\,dV$$

or $$U = \int_R^{2R}\frac{1}{2}\epsilon_0\left[\frac{VR}{r^2}\right]^2\times 4\pi r^2\,dr$$

$$= \pi\epsilon_0 V^2 R.$$ **Ans.**

(b) Energy stored in electric field of sphere beyond 2R,

$$U' = \int_{2R}^{\infty}\frac{1}{2}\epsilon_0\left[\frac{VR}{r^2}\right]^2\times 4\pi r^2\,dr$$

$$= \pi\epsilon_0 V^2 R.$$

Thus $U = U'$.

10. (a) Initial capacitance, $C = \frac{\epsilon_0 A}{d}$, and final capacitance

$$C' = \frac{\epsilon_0 A}{d'}$$

The charge flown, $$\Delta q = q'-q=C'V-CV$$

$$= \epsilon_0 AV\left[\frac{1}{d'}-\frac{1}{d}\right]$$

$$= (8.86\times10^{-12})\times20\times10^{-4}\times12\times\left[\frac{1}{2\times10^{-3}}-\frac{1}{1\times10^{3}}\right]$$

$$= -1.06\times10^{-10}\text{C}.$$

(b) Energy absorbed by the battery

$$= W-W'$$

$$= CV^2-C'V^2$$

$$= \epsilon_0 AV^2\left[\frac{1}{d}-\frac{1}{d'}\right]$$

$$= 8.86\times10^{-12}\times20\times10^{-4}\times12^2\left[\frac{1}{1\times10^{-3}}-\frac{1}{2\times10^{-3}}\right]$$

$$= 12.7\times10^{-10}\text{ J}$$

(c) The energy stored

$$U = \frac{1}{2}CV^2=\frac{1}{2}\frac{\epsilon_0 A}{d}V^2$$

$$= \frac{1}{2}\times8.86\times10^{-12}\times\frac{20\times10^{-4}}{(1\times10^{-3})}\times12^2$$

$$= 12.7\times10^{-10}\text{ J}$$

and $$U' = \frac{1}{2}C'V^2$$

$$= 6.35\times10^{-10}\text{ J}$$ **Ans.**

(d) If $x$ is the separation between the plates, then force between them

$$F = \frac{\epsilon_0 V^2 A}{2x^2}$$

The work done, $$W = \int_d^{d'}Fdx=\frac{\epsilon_0 AV^2}{2}\int_d^{d'}x^{-2}dx$$

$$= \frac{\epsilon_0 AV^2}{2}\left[\frac{1}{d}-\frac{1}{d'}\right]$$

$$= 6.35\times10^{-10}\text{ J.}$$

11. The force on a dielectric for constant potential is given by,

$$F = \frac{\epsilon_0 bV^2}{2d}(k-1).$$

For equilibrium of the slab,

$$F_1 = F_2$$

or
$$\frac{\epsilon_0 bV_1^2(k_1-1)}{2d} = \frac{\epsilon_0 bV_2^2(k_2-1)}{2d}$$

$$\therefore \quad \frac{V_1}{V_2} = \sqrt{\frac{k_2-1}{k_1-1}}.$$ **Ans.**

12. The initial charge, $q_i' = CV$,

and final charge, $q_f = -CV$.

The charge flows, $|\Delta q| = 2CV$.

The heat developed in connecting wire

$$= V(\Delta q) = 2CV^2$$

$$= 2\times(5\times10^{-6})\times12^2$$

$$= 1.44 \text{ mJ}$$ **Ans.**

13. If $q$ be the charge of the metal sphere corresponding to the potential $V$, then

$$V = \frac{1}{4\pi\epsilon_0}\frac{q}{R}$$

or
$$q = (4\pi\epsilon_0 R)V$$

$$= \left(\frac{1}{9\times10^9}\right)\times\frac{10^{-3}}{2}\times1 = 5.5\times10^{-10}\text{ C}$$

$$t = \frac{q}{0.80\times6.25\times10^{10}\times1.6\times10^{-19}}$$

$$= 6.95\ \mu s$$ **Ans.**

14. With the dial at 180°, the capacitance $C = 950\ PF$

The corresponding charge,

$$q = CV$$

$$= 950\times10^{-12}\times400$$

$$= 0.38\times10^{-6}\text{C}$$

(a) For the dial at 0°, capacitance

$$C' = 50\times10^{-12}F$$

The corresponding potential

$$V' = \frac{q}{C'} = \frac{0.38\times10^{-6}}{50\times10^{-12}}$$

$$= 7600\text{ V}$$ **Ans.**

(b) Work needed,

$$W = \frac{1}{2}C'V'^2 - \frac{1}{2}CV^2$$

$$= \frac{1}{2}\times50\times10^{-12}\times7600^2 - \frac{1}{2}\times950\times10^{-12}\times400^2$$

$$= 1.368\times10^{-3}\text{ J}$$ **Ans.**

15. Suppose at some instant, $y$ is the depth of plate inside oil, then

$$C = C_{\text{air}} + C_{\text{oil}}$$

$$= \frac{\epsilon_0 \ell(\ell-y)}{d} + \frac{k\epsilon_0 \ell y}{d}$$

$$= \frac{\epsilon_0 \ell}{d}[\ell + (k-1)y]$$

Charge on the capacitor $q = CV = \frac{\epsilon_0 \ell V}{d}[\ell + (k-1)y]$

The current, $i = \frac{dq}{dt} = \frac{\epsilon_0 \ell V}{d}\left[0 + (k-1)\frac{dy}{dt}\right]$

or
$$i = \frac{8.86\times10^{-12}\times1\times500}{0.01}[(11-1)\times0.001]$$

$$= 4.425\times10^{-9}\ A.$$ **Ans.**

16. (b) When inner sphere is earthed, its potential becomes zero. To make the potential of inner sphere to be zero, some negative charge must be appear on the inner sphere to cancel the positive potential of outer sphere. If $q_2$ be the charge on the inner sphere, then

$$V_A = 0 = \frac{1}{4\pi\epsilon_0}\left(\frac{q}{b} - \frac{q_2}{a}\right)$$

$$\therefore \quad q_2 = \frac{q}{b}a = \frac{8}{10}\times30 = 24\ nC(-)$$

(a) Capacitance, $C = C_{AB} + C_B$

$$= 4\pi\epsilon_0\left(\frac{ab}{b-a}\right) + 4\pi\epsilon_0 b$$

$$= 4\pi\epsilon_0\left(\frac{b^2}{b-a}\right).$$ **Ans.**

17. The force between the plates of capacitor

$$F = \frac{1}{2}\epsilon_0 A\frac{V^2}{d^2}.$$

For the balance,

$$mg = F$$

$$= \frac{1}{2}\epsilon_0 A\frac{V^2}{d^2}$$

$$\therefore \quad m = \frac{1}{2}\frac{\epsilon_0 AV^2}{md^2}.$$ **Ans.**

18. The capacitances of capacitors are :

$$C_1 = \frac{\epsilon_0 A}{d_1}, \text{ and } C_2 = \frac{\epsilon_0 A}{d_2}$$

If $V_1$ and $V_2$ be the potential drop across $C_1$ and $C_2$, then

$$V_1 + V_2 = V \qquad \text{...(i)}$$

and
$$C_1V_1 = C_2V_2 \qquad \text{...(ii)}$$

$$\therefore \quad V_1 = \frac{C_2V}{C_1+C_2} = \frac{\epsilon_0 A}{d^2}V\left[\frac{1}{\frac{\epsilon_0 A}{d_1} + \frac{\epsilon_0 A}{d_2}}\right]$$

$$= V\left[\frac{d_1}{d_1+d_2}\right]$$

The electric field between the plates of capacitor 1,

$$E = \frac{V_1}{d_1} = \left[\frac{V}{d_1+d_2}\right].$$

If $u$ is the speed of projection, then

$$t = \frac{\ell}{u}, \text{ and}$$

$$\frac{d_1}{2} = \frac{1}{2}at^2$$

$$= \frac{1}{2}\left(\frac{Ee}{m}\right)t^2$$

From above equations, we get

$$\frac{d_1}{2} = \frac{1}{2}\left(\frac{Ee}{m}\right)\left(\frac{\ell}{u}\right)^2$$

$$\therefore \quad u = \left[\frac{E e \ell^2}{m d_1}\right]^{1/2}$$

$$= \left[\frac{V e l^2}{m d_1 (d_1 + d_2)}\right]^{1/2}. \quad \textbf{Ans.}$$

19. In close loop 1-2-5-6-1

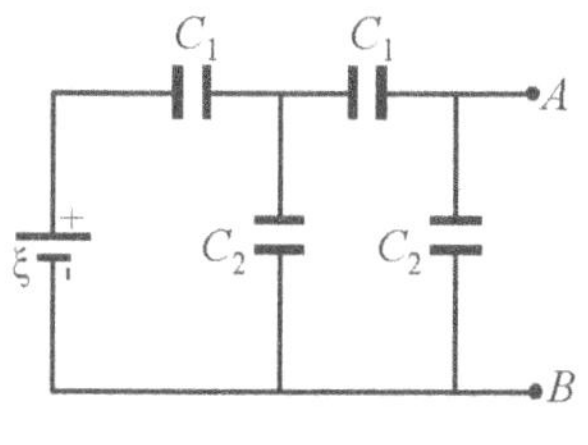


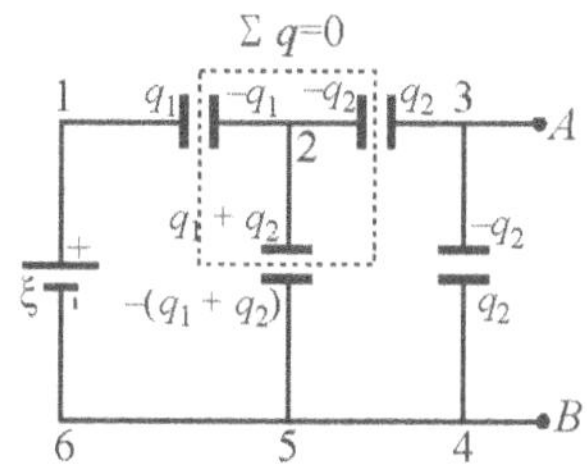


$$-\frac{q_1}{C_1} - \frac{(q_1 + q_2)}{C_2} + \xi = 0$$

and in close loop 1-2-3-4-5-6

$$-\frac{q_1}{C_1} + \frac{q_2}{C_1} + \frac{q_2}{C_2} = 0$$

Solving above equations for $q_2$. $V_{AB} = -\dfrac{q_2}{C_2}$

20. $\dfrac{q}{C_1} + \xi - \dfrac{q}{C_2} = 5.0$ ; $V_1 = \dfrac{q}{C_1}$ & $V_2 = \dfrac{q}{C_2}$

21. Charge on each capacitor will be same, let it is $q$,

$$-\frac{q}{C_1} + \xi_1 - \frac{q}{C_2} - \xi_2 = 0$$

$$\Rightarrow \quad q = \frac{[\xi_1 - \xi_2]C_1C_2}{C_1 + C_2}$$

$$V_1 = \frac{q}{C_1} \ \& \ V_2 = -\frac{q}{C_2}$$

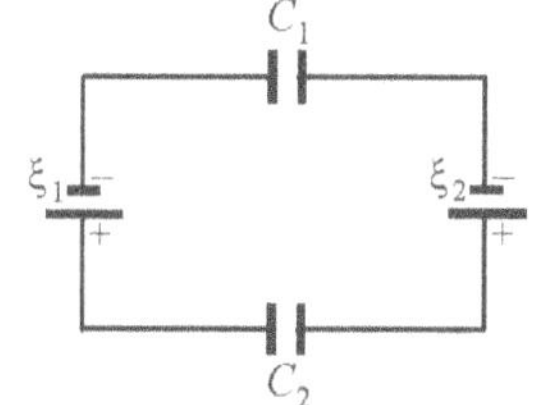


22. If $V_1$ and $V_2$ be the p.d. across capacitors $C_1$ and $C_2$, then

$$V_1 + V_2 = -\xi$$

and $$C_1V_1 = C_2V_2$$

$$\therefore \quad V_1 = -\frac{\xi C_2}{C_1 + C_2}, \ V_2 = -\frac{\xi C_1}{C_1 + C_2}$$

Similarly if $V_3$ and $V_4$ be the p.d. across the capacitors $C_3$ and $C_4$ respectively, then

$$V_3 = \frac{-\xi C_4}{C_3 + C_4}, \ V_4 = \frac{-\xi C_3}{C_3 + C_4}$$

The potential difference $V_A - V_B = V_1 - V_3$

$$= \frac{-\xi C_2}{C_1 + C_2} + \frac{\xi C_4}{C_3 + C_4}$$

$$= \frac{\xi(C_2C_3 - C_1C_4)}{(C_1 + C_2)(C_3 + C_4)}$$

23. In close loop,

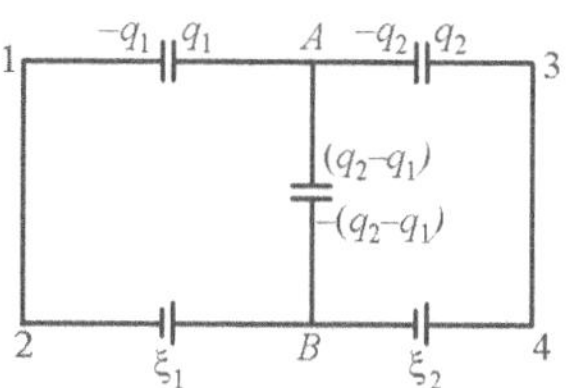


$$1 - A - B - 2 - 1, \ +\frac{q_1}{C_1} - \frac{(q_2 - q_1)}{C_3} - \xi_1 = 0 \quad \text{...(i)}$$

and in close loop, $A - 3 - 4 - B - A$

$$+\frac{q_2}{C_2} - \xi_2 + \frac{(q_2 - q_1)}{C_3} = 0 \quad \text{...(ii)}$$

From above equations, we get $q_2 - q_1 = \dfrac{\xi_2 C_2 - \xi_1 C_1}{\left[\dfrac{C_2}{C_3} + \dfrac{C_1}{C_3} + 1\right]}$

The potential difference, $V_A - V_B = \dfrac{q_2 - q_1}{C_3} = \left[\dfrac{\xi_2 C_2 - \xi_1 C_1}{C_1 + C_2 + C_3}\right]$

**Ans.**

24. In close loop $ABDEA$–

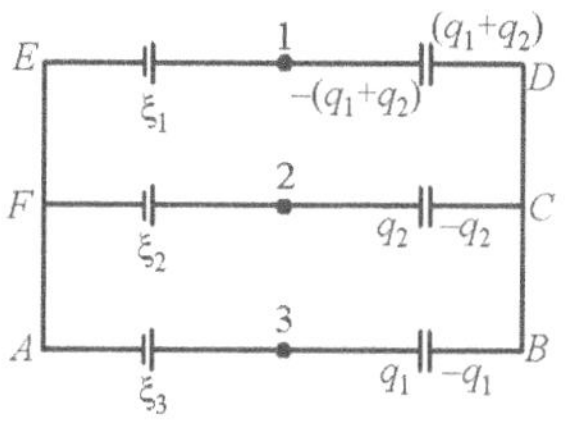


$$\xi_3 + \frac{q_1}{C_3} + \frac{q_1 + q_2}{C_1} + \xi_1 = 0 \quad \text{...(i)}$$

In close loop $CDEFC$

$$\frac{q_1 + q_2}{C_1} + \xi_1 - \xi_2 + \frac{q_2}{C_2} = 0 \quad \text{...(ii)}$$

From equations (i) and (ii), we get

$$q_1 + q_2 = \frac{\xi_2 C_2 - \xi_1 C_2 - \xi_1 C_3 + \xi_3 C_3}{\left(1 + \dfrac{C_3}{C_1} + \dfrac{C_2}{C_1}\right)}$$

Given, $$V_0 = V_C = 0$$

$$\therefore \quad V_1 = -\left(\frac{q_1 + q_2}{C_1}\right) = \frac{\xi_1(C_2 + C_3) - \xi_2 C_2 - \xi_3 C_3}{C_1 + C_2 + C_3}$$

Similarly $V_2$ and $V_3$ can be obtained.

25. When switch $S_w$ is opened, the capacitors are in series. Thus, the charge on each of the capacitor is

$$q = \frac{\xi C_1 C_2}{C_1 + C_2} \quad \text{...(i)}$$

After closing of the switch $S_w$, the charges on the capacitors are shown in figure.

Initially charge of capacitors joining at $B = q - q = 0$.
After shortening of switch the charge on then are

$$= q_1 + q_2 - 0 + C\xi_2$$

$$= C\xi_2.$$

Therefore flow of charge through section 1.

$$= (q_1 + q_2) - (q - q)$$

$$= C\xi_2. \qquad \textbf{Ans.}$$

The flow of charge through section 2,

$$= -q_1 - q$$

$$= -\left(\frac{C_1 C_2 \xi}{C_1 + C_2}\right). \qquad \textbf{Ans.}$$

26. If $C_1$ and $C_2$ be the capacities of $S_1$ and $S_2$, then

$$\frac{C_1}{C_2} = \frac{r}{R}$$

(a) If $q_1$ is the charge acquired by $S_2$ in first contact, then

$$\frac{q_1}{Q - q_1} = \frac{C_2}{C_1} = \frac{R}{r}$$

or

$$q_1 = Q\left(\frac{R}{R+r}\right)$$

Before second contact the charge of $S_1$ becomes $Q$ and so in second contact, the total charge on $S_1$ and $S_2$ together

$$= Q + q_1 = Q\left(1 + \frac{R}{R+r}\right)$$

The charge again distributed in the ratio of their capacitances, and so

$$q_2 = Q\left(1 + \frac{R}{R+r}\right)\left(\frac{R}{R+r}\right)$$

$$= Q\left[\frac{R}{R+r} + \left(\frac{R}{R+r}\right)^2\right]$$

$$\therefore \quad q_n = Q\left[\frac{R}{R+r} + \left(\frac{R}{R+r}\right)^2 + \dots + \left(\frac{R}{R+r}\right)^n\right]$$

$$= Q\frac{R}{r}\left[1 - \left(\frac{R}{R+r}\right)^n\right]$$

The electrostatic energy stored in $S_2$,

$$U_n = \frac{q_n^2}{2C_2} = \frac{q_n^2}{2(4\pi \epsilon_0 R)} = \frac{q_n^2}{8\pi \epsilon_0 R}.$$

(b)

$$q_\infty = \frac{QR}{r}.$$

$$\therefore \quad U_\infty = \frac{Q^2 R}{8\pi \epsilon_0 r^2} \qquad \textbf{Ans.}$$

27. The given circuit may be redrawn as :

$C_1$ $C_2$

120 V

$$C_1 = \frac{\epsilon_0 A_1}{d_1} = \frac{1}{288} \times 10^8 F$$

and

$$C_2 = \frac{\epsilon_0 A_2}{d_2} = \frac{1}{300 \times 10^8} F$$

(i) The equivalent capacitance

$$C = \frac{C_1 C_2}{C_1 + C_2} = 17\ PF$$

(ii) The energy stored in capacitors

$$U = \frac{1}{2}CV^2 = \frac{1}{2} \times (17 \times 10^{-12}) \times 120^2$$

$$= 1.224 \times 10^{-7}\ \text{J}. \qquad \textbf{Ans.}$$

28. (i) The capacitance of capacitor $A$,

$$C_A = \frac{\epsilon_0 A_1}{d} + \frac{\epsilon_0 K\left(\frac{A_1}{2}\right)}{d}$$

$$= \frac{\epsilon_0 A_1}{2d}(1 + K)$$

$$= \frac{8.85 \times 10^{-12} \times 0.04}{2 \times 8.85 \times 10^{-4}}(1 + 9)$$

$$= 2 \times 10^{-9} F$$

Energy stored in $A$, $U_A = \frac{1}{2}C_A V^2$

$$= \frac{1}{2} \times (2 \times 10^{-9})(110)^2$$

$$= 1.21 \times 10^{-5}\ \text{J}$$

(ii) The charge stored in capacitor $A$,

$$q_A = C_A V = (2 \times 10^{-9}) \times 110$$

$$= 2.2 \times 10^{-7}\ \text{C}.$$

When battery is disconnected, the charge on the capacitor remains same. When dielectric is removed, the new capacitance of $A$,

$$C_A' = \frac{\epsilon_0 A}{d} = \frac{C}{K}$$

$$= 0.4 \times 10^{-9} F.$$

Final energy stored, $U_A' = \frac{q_A^2}{2C_A'}$

$$= \frac{(2.2 \times 10^{-7})^2}{2 \times 0.4 \times 10^{-9}}$$

$$= 6.05 \times 10^{-9}\ \text{J}$$

Work done by external agency

$$W = U_A' - U_A$$

$$= 4.84 \times 10^{-5}\ \text{J}$$

(iii) The capacitance of $B$,

$$C_B = \frac{\epsilon_0 K A_2}{d} = \frac{9 \times 8.85 \times 10^{-12} \times 0.02}{8.85 \times 10^{-4}}$$

$$= 1.8 \times 10^{-9} F.$$

Common potential, $V = \frac{q_A + 0}{C_A' + C_B}$

$$= 100\ \text{V}$$

Net energy stored, $U = \frac{1}{2}(C_A' + C_B)V^2$

$$= 1.1 \times 10^{-5}\ \text{J} \qquad \textbf{Ans.}$$

☆☆☆

www.ingramcontent.com/pod-product-compliance
Lightning Source LLC
LaVergne TN
LVHW080055160726
843469LV00047B/1822

* 9 7 8 9 3 8 6 3 2 0 0 8 7 *